SECOND EDITION

BASIC
For Students Using the IBM PC

MICHAEL TROMBETTA

Queensborough Community College

The Benjamin/Cummings Publishing Company, Inc.

Redwood City, California • Menlo Park, California
Reading, Massachusetts • New York • Don Mills, Ontario
Wokingham, U.K. • Amsterdam • Bonn • Sydney
Singapore • Tokyo • Madrid • San Juan

The procedures and applications in this book have been included for their instructional value. They have been tested with care but are not guaranteed for any particular purpose. The publisher does not offer any warranties, nor does it accept any liabilities with respect to the programs or applications.

Keith Wollman, *Sponsoring Editor*
Linda J. Bedell, *Developmental Editor*
Helen M. Wythe, *Production Supervisor*
Nancy Campbell Wirtes, *Copy Editor*
The Book Company, *Text Designer*
Scot Graphics, *Illustrator*
Dick Morton, *Art Consultant*
Amy Willcutt, *Production Coordinator*
Roy Logan, *Manufacturing Manager*
Nancy Marx, *Cover Designer*

IBM is a registered trademark of International Business Machines Corporation.

Library of Congress Cataloging-in-Publication Data

Trombetta, Michael.
  BASIC for students using the IBM/PC/Michael Trombetta. –2nd ed.
        p.   cm.
  ISBN 0-201-50416-2
  1. IBM Personal Computer–Programming. 2. BASIC (Computer program language)
I. Title.
QA76.8.I2594T74   1991
005.265–dc20
                                                              90-243
                                                              CIP

Reprinted with corrections June, 1991

3 4 5 6 7 8 9 10-MU-95 94 93 92

To my mother, Rose Trombetta,
and the memory of my father, Louis Trombetta

Preface

This book is the second edition of *BASIC for Students Using the IBM PC*. As I taught from the book over the last five years, I discovered a number of improvements that could be made to help students learn BASIC on IBM PCs and PC-compatibles. In addition, teachers using the book provided me with feedback on how the book worked in their courses. My goal when incorporating the many suggested improvements was to retain the outstanding feature of the first edition: its gentle approach to learning computer programming.

This Book is for Students

Many people who have been programming for years forget how enormously difficult programming can be for beginners. Often students are apprehensive about programming, and texts may add to their concern by plunging into BASIC syntax statements and lengthy programs with little overture. To help ease students' fears, I have used puns and humorous names for the subjects of problems in this text. Chapter 1 introduces the PC itself, explaining the operation of the major parts, with special focus on both the standard and enhanced keyboards. To help make BASIC programming understandable, this text uses several techniques described below.

A Structured Approach to Programming Students frequently have as much difficulty developing an algorithm for a problem as they have understanding BASIC syntax. Chapter 2 introduces a formalized eight-point procedure for problem-solving. This procedure is used consistently in developing programs in this text and serves as a guide for students when they solve problems on their own. The focus of this approach is to develop an algorithm, translate it into a program, check the program for accuracy, and debug the program as needed.

Flowcharts are the primary tool used to help translate algorithms into programs. Pseudocode, introduced in Chapter 4, is used to develop programs that do not involve complex logic. In later chapters, hierarchy diagrams illustrate the structure of complicated programs.

The syntax of BASIC statements is always introduced in the context of the program in which it is first used. In this way, students learn not only the syntax of the statement, but also how the statement works in a program.

New to this edition, each time a new statement is introduced several examples of the use of the statement are presented and explained. These additional examples will give students a stronger grasp of a statement's syntax. In addition, at the end of the section a "Syntax Summary" presents the statement's syntax, an example of the use of the statement, and an explanation of how the statement works. These syntax summaries provide a convenient place for students to refer to when they need help coding a statement.

New to this edition

v

The text emphasizes good programming practices—in the use of meaningful data names, documentation, indentation of loops and IF statements, and subroutines.

The clearest way to show students exactly what a program does is by tracing it. Therefore, programs are traced not only in the early chapters, but whenever a new concept—IF statements, accumulators, FOR-NEXT loops, arrays etc.—is introduced. The tracing figures in this edition have been redesigned to be easier to understand and follow.

Every instructor has had a student, overjoyed at finally getting the computer to produce some output, submit a program that is totally wrong. Therefore, I have emphasized the crucial need to check computer-produced answers against hand-calculated answers to ensure that a program is free of logic errors. Since students can make errors the first time they enter a program, debugging is stressed from the beginning.

New in this edition are "Getting the Bugs Out" sections that follow the introduction of each new statement. When students start using a new statement, they will make new errors. Students are puzzled by BASIC's cryptic error messages: Redo from start? or Bad file number. "Getting the Bugs Out" explains what causes the errors and how to correct the program.

Programming Practice   The only way to learn to program is actually to do it. Thus, at the end of major sections in each chapter, beginning with Chapter 2, there are programming assignments that draw on the material introduced in the section. The assignments start with a problem that is virtually a restatement of the example problem in the section (which every student should be able to program) and progress through problems of increasing difficulty. The variety of problems available means that weaker students need not be overwhelmed by problems they can't solve, nor stronger students bored by problems they find too simple.

Almost all the programming assignments involve simple applications that students can immediately understand. Examples include calculating gross pay and average gas mileage, writing a form letter, and translating English into Pig Latin. When more complicated applications are discussed, such as calculating a mortgage payout table, the application is thoroughly explained. This text includes some problems involving recreational mathematics, but the only mathematics required to understand the examples and solve the assignments is a knowledge of elementary algebraic notation.

As further practice, additional programming assignments at the end of each chapter draw on all the material in the chapter. And beginning in Chapter 4, a series of problems called "Beyond the BASICs" provides greater challenges for the more advanced/curious student. The answers to selected programming assignments are given in Appendix B. Solutions to the remaining programming assignments are given in the Instructor's Manual available to adopters from the publishers.

Strong Pedagogy   To help students learn how to program in BASIC, I have incorporated a number of pedagogical features in this text:

New features in this edition

■ **BASIC Objectives of this Chapter.** Chapters begin with a list of learning objectives and a brief overview of the chapter.

■ **Syntax Summary.** This box presents a new statement's syntax, provides an example of how to use the statement, and explains how the statement works.

■ **Getting the Bugs Out.** This section shows how to interpret cryptic error messages, explains what causes the errors, and shows how to correct the program.

■ **Annotated programs.** Annotations to programs point out clearly important parts of the code.

■ **Key Terms/Glossary.** Important terms introduced in the chapter are printed in bold type the first time they appear and are defined in the margin. A list of these terms with page references appears at the end of the chapter. A glossary at the end of the book repeats these definitions.

■ **Exercises and Questions for Review.** At the end of each major section, a set of exercises asks students to demonstrate their understanding of the material just covered by writing BASIC statements and predicting the outcome of program segments. At the end of each chapter, Questions for Review test students' knowledge of BASIC statements and commands and their understanding of key terms. Answers to selected Exercises are included in Appendix B. Answers to the remaining Exercises and all the Questions for Review are included in the Instructor's Manual.

■ **Color Coding.** Two colors in program listings distinguish output generated by the computer from values entered by the user.

■ **Summaries.** A summary at the end of each chapter highlights major points and recaps the use of new BASIC statements.

■ **Appendixes.** At the end of the text, five appendixes form a reference for students. Appendix A provides a list of reserved words in BASIC. Appendix B gives answers to selected problems in the text. Appendix C recaps important tables. Appendix D lists the syntaxes of BASIC commands and statements. New to this edition, Appendix E discusses several important DOS commands.

What this Book Is and Isn't

Although this book moves carefully and slowly, it also travels far. In addition to the standard "core" topics, this text includes such "advanced" topics as compound conditions, a report with subtotals, and a binary search. In addition, Chapters 11 and 12 contain an extensive discussion of sequential and random file processing and Chapters 13 and 14 discuss graphics.

I have deliberately included more material than can be covered in a one-semester course, but no text can explore all the options of PC BASIC. In some cases, I have indicated other sources—such as the BASIC manual—where additional information can be found. Some esoteric topics have been omitted altogether.

The existing coverage is both thorough and flexible. While the first ten chapters must be covered in order, the remaining chapters are independent and may be covered in any order. In fact, Chapter 13 on graphics can be covered any time after Chapter 6. Some instructors may choose to emphasize file processing, while others may wish to emphasize graphics.

Like any book, this text reflects its author's views. As a programmer and teacher, I want my students to learn good programming techniques. To help students understand the use of variables, I divide variables into three types: input, internal, and output.

I am also concerned that my students get a feel for real-world programming. To allow them to process multiple sets of data almost from the start, I introduce loops early. In this edition the use of trailer data to stop execution has been moved from Chapter 7 to Chapter 3. Menus are introduced earlier (Chapter 6) and used more extensively than in the first edition.

Some readers may be surprised by the early treatment (Chapter 5) of subroutines. I have chosen this placement because modularizing programs not only is a good programming practice, but also reflects programming in the real world. I urge those instructors who are unaccustomed to extensive use of subroutines in BASIC to try this style; they will find it helps their students develop algorithms and write correct programs. Moreover, reusing subroutines and building on existing programs—also features of this text— let students write more complex programs.

Supplements

Instructor's Manual   Contains twenty-five multiple-choice test questions for each chapter; additional programming assignments; teaching tips for each chapter; sample syllabus; and answers to Programming Assignments, Exercises, and Questions for Review and 86 transparency masters from the text.

Disk Package   A series of disks contains every example program in the text as well as the answers to all Programming Assignments. The disks also contain several .DAT files that students can merge into their programs to supply data, and .SEQ and .RND files they can use with their programs for Chapters 13 and 14.

Computerized Test Bank   The test items in the Instructor's Guide are also available in electronic form to allow professors to create and run a variety of tests.

Acknowledgments

Many of my colleagues at Queensborough Community College taught from my earlier books and have given me the benefit of their experience. I would like to thank: Barry Appel, Edward Berlin, Stephen Berlin, Layne Bonaparte, Charles Fromme, Melchiore LaSala, Emil Parinello, Arlene Podos, Daniel Tsang, and John Zipfel.

A number of people at Addison-Wesley lent their efforts to this project. My editor Keith Wollman encouraged this second edition. Linda Bedell was once again a superlative developmental editor. As production supervisor, Helen Wythe was always ready to solve problems and smooth the way. My art editor, Dick Morton, took great pains to make sure the art was always exactly what I wanted.

Finally, I would like to thank the following reviewers for their thoughtful, helpful comments: Bruce Eure, Southern College of Technology; Jeffrey Mock, Diablo Valley College; Dennis Wolf, Indiana University of South Bend; Leonard Presby, William Paterson State College; Deborah Hammonds, Rutledge College; and Thomas F. Critzer, Southern Ohio College.

Manhassett, N.Y.   M.T.

Contents

CHAPTER 13   DRAWING POINTS, LINES, AND CIRCLES   **395**

CHAPTER 14   GRAPHS, CHARTS, AND ANIMATION   **429**

1

Introducing BASIC and Personal Computers

BASIC OBJECTIVES OF THIS CHAPTER

☐ To name the components and functions of a computer system

☐ To use the personal computer's keyboard

☐ To explain the concept of computer languages

☐ To start BASIC

INTRODUCTION TO COMPUTERS

Computer
An electronic device that can accept data, process the data according to your instructions, and display results.

Data
Values in the form of numbers or words that are to be processed by a computer.

Program
A set of instructions to be followed by a computer to solve a problem.

Everyone knows that these days computers are widely used. They prepare our pay checks and our bills, they serve as word processors, and they are used to play games. But what is a computer? A **computer** is an electronic device that can follow our instructions and process data. **Data** are the values we give the computer to work with. For example, in a student grading system, the data consist of each student's name and test scores, and the processing consists of calculating the average test score for each student.

The processing a computer does depends on the instructions we give it. Thus, before a computer can be used to solve a problem, a person must tell it exactly what to do by giving it a set of instructions. This set of instructions is called a **program**. The objective of this book is to teach you how to write programs in the BASIC language.

We begin this chapter by discussing the components of computer systems. Since you will be using the keyboard to enter your programs and data, we explain how to use it in some detail. We then discuss the concept of a computer language and how to start BASIC.

Components of Computer Systems

PC
Personal computer.

The best way to learn how to write programs is actually to write and execute them, and for that you will need a personal computer (**PC**). In this book, you will learn how to write programs for the IBM Personal Computer, which comes in several models, and for computers manufactured by other companies that work like IBM computers (compatibles). Programs are writ-

FIGURE 1.1   **A Personal Computer.**
Courtesy of International Business Machines Corporation.

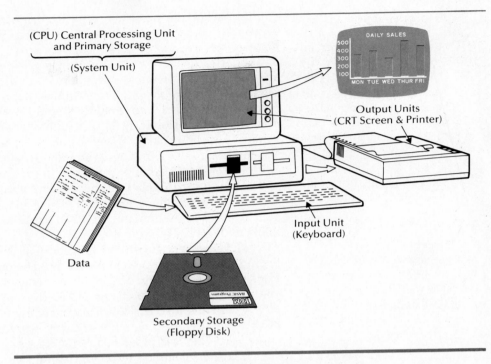

(CPU) Central Processing Unit
and Primary Storage

(System Unit)

Output Units
(CRT Screen & Printer)

Input Unit
(Keyboard)

Data

Secondary Storage
(Floppy Disk)

FIGURE 1.2   **The major components of a personal computer system.**

ten the same way for all these computers, so we can refer to each of them as a PC. Figure 1.1 shows a typical PC.

To use a PC—or any computer—effectively, it is important to know a little about the parts of a computer and what they do. Figure 1.2 shows the five basic components common to all personal computers.

1) The **input unit** allows us to enter data and instructions into the computer. On a PC, the keyboard is the input unit. We will discuss the keyboard in more detail later in this chapter.

2) The **output unit** displays the computer's results. On a PC, the output unit is a **monitor**, a display device that looks like a television set. The monitor displays 25 lines on a screen and 80 characters—letters, digits, special characters like commas and dollar signs, and spaces—on a line.

What a PC's output unit displays depends on an electronic component, called the adaptor, that is installed inside. Some PCs use a monochrome adaptor and display, which produce extremely sharp characters, but which cannot display graphics, such as pie charts, or color. Other PCs use one of several available color/graphics adaptors and displays that can display both color and graphics. The first color/graphics adaptor was called simply the color graphics adaptor, or CGA. Later the enhanced graphics adaptor, or EGA, and the video graphics array, or VGA, were introduced. Although there are differences between the various graphic adaptors, in this book they are treated alike. In fact, for most of this book, the BASIC programs described can be run on either monochrome or color/graphics displays. Only Chapters 13 and 14, which deal with graphics, require a color/graphics display.

When the computer is turned off, the information on the screen disappears. But you will often want a permanent copy of your output, and for this you will use a printer. Printed output is called **hard copy output**, in contrast to output on the monitor, which is called **soft copy output**.

Input unit
The component of a computer system that allows you to enter data and instructions into the computer.

Output unit
The component of a computer system that displays the computer's results.

Monitor
A television-like display device.

Hard copy output
Printed output.

Soft copy output
Output displayed on the monitor's screen.

CPU (central processing unit)
The computer component in which arithmetic and logical operations are performed.

Primary storage unit
The computer component in which data and instructions that are being processed are stored.

ROM (read only memory)
The part of primary storage whose contents cannot be changed by a program.

RAM (random access memory)
The part of primary storage whose contents can be changed by a program.

Byte
A unit of storage that can hold one character.

K
1024 bytes.

Secondary storage device
A computer component that supplements primary storage, allowing data and programs to be stored permanently.

Diskette drive
A secondary storage device that can read and write data on diskettes.

Hard disk
A high-capacity, fast-access, secondary storage device.

Diskette or floppy disk
A magnetic-coated plastic disk that is used to store programs and data.

M
Approximately 1 million bytes (exactly 1,048,576 bytes).

3) Inside the system unit is the **central processing unit**, which is usually abbreviated **CPU**. The CPU is where the computer executes instructions.

4) Also inside the system unit is the **primary storage unit**. There are two kinds of primary storage: ROM and RAM. **ROM**, which stands for read only memory, is where critical instructions that the computer requires for its operation are permanently stored. As the name implies, you can only read the information in ROM; you cannot change it. **RAM**, which stands for random access memory, is where your programs and data are stored while the computer is working on them. You can change information in RAM.

The size of primary storage is measured in bytes. A **byte** is a unit of storage that can hold one character, for example, a single letter or digit. PCs come with about 40K of ROM. (One **K** is 1024 bytes, so 40K is 40,960 bytes.) The amount of RAM installed varies, but values between 256K and 640K are typical.

5) When you finish working on a problem and tell the computer to begin a new one, or when you turn the computer off, the data and instructions you entered up to that point are erased from RAM. But what if later you want to work again on the same problem? It would be tedious to retype all the data and instructions. To avoid doing so, you need the last component of the computer system, a **secondary storage device**. Secondary storage saves your data and programs for as long as you like.

The most common secondary storage devices are **diskette drives** and **hard disks**. A typical configuration is two diskette drives or one diskette drive and a hard disk. If a PC has two diskette drives, the one on the left (or sometimes on the top) is called the A drive, while the drive on the right (or on the bottom) is called the B drive. If a PC has only one diskette drive, it is called the A drive. The hard disk is usually called drive C.

A **diskette**, often called a **floppy disk**, is used with a diskette drive. A diskette consists of a thin layer of magnetic material on a plastic support. Programs and data are stored in the form of tiny magnetized spots. Diskettes come in two sizes. The older style is 5¼ inches in diameter, is easily bent, and can store either 360K or 1.2M of data (one **M** is approximately 1 million bytes). The newer style is 3½ inches, is rigid, and can store either 720K or 1.44M. Unless you use special techniques, either type of diskette can store only a maximum of 112 programs, which should be sufficient for a term's work.

As Figure 1.3 shows, the proper way to insert a diskette into a disk drive is to hold it with the label up. Diskettes are delicate and should be handled with care. Never touch the recording surface that can be seen through the oblong slot. Protect the diskette from dust by putting it back into its protective envelope as soon as you remove it from the drive. Also keep the diskette away from extremes of hot and cold and from strong magnets. Use only a felt-tip pen to write on the label.

A hard disk typically can store between 20M and 100M. One advantage of a hard disk is that reading and writing to a hard disk are much faster than with a floppy diskette. Another advantage of a hard disk is that you can store on it all the programs you routinely use, for example, BASIC, word processors, spreadsheets, and databases. In contrast, if your PC has only diskette drives, you have to search through a box of diskettes looking for the one with the program you want to execute.

The PC's Keyboard

Because you will be using it to type programs and data into the computer, you will need to be particularly familiar with your PC's keyboard. Different

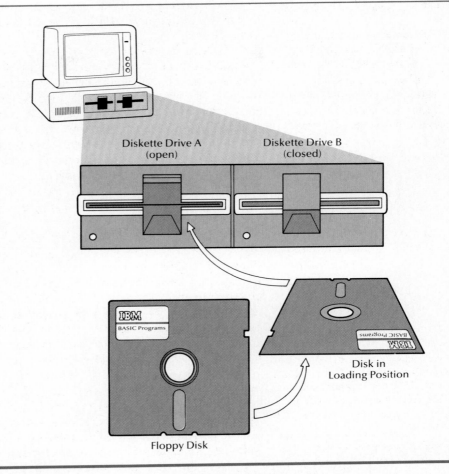

Diskette Drive A (open)   Diskette Drive B (closed)

IBM
BASIC Programs

Disk in
Loading Position

Floppy Disk

FIGURE 1.3   **Inserting a floppy disk into a diskette drive.**

computers use slightly different keyboards, but two are typical: the standard keyboard, shown in Figure 1.4(a), and the newer, enhanced keyboard, shown in Figure 1.4(b). On both keyboards, all the keys, including the Space Bar, repeat automatically if they are held down. This means that when you type, you must be careful not to hold down a key, or you may find the key repeated. At the times when you want to repeat a key, you will find the automatic repeat feature convenient.

Function keys
Any of the keys labeled F1 through F12.

All keyboards have **function keys** labeled F1, F2, etc. As you will learn in Chapter 2, these keys perform special tasks. Depending on the make and model of your keyboard, you may have 10 or 12 function keys located at the far left of the keyboard or across its top.

THE TYPEWRITER KEYBOARD

In the center of both keyboards are letter and number keys similar to those found on a typewriter. As on a typewriter, you can use these keys together with one of the two Shift keys (marked with large upward pointing arrows) to type capital letters and symbols like @, #, and %. There are, however, some important differences between a typewriter keyboard and a PC keyboard. For example, to type zero, you must use the number 0 key, and not the letter O key. Similarly, to type the number one, you must use the number 1 key, not the letter l. PC keyboards also include keys not found on most typewriters:

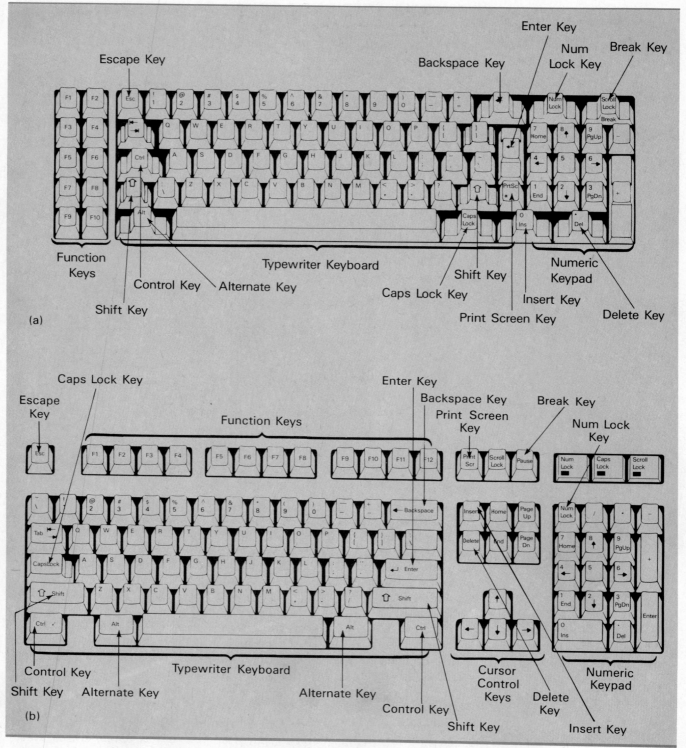

FIGURE 1.4   **(a) The standard keyboard. (b) The enhanced keyboard.**
Courtesy of International Business Machines Corporation.

Reserved words
Words that have special meanings in BASIC.

1) *Alternate key.* Like the Shift keys on a typewriter, you use the Alternate key (Alt) by holding it down while you press another key. You use the Alt key to enter BASIC **reserved words**, words that have meanings special to BASIC, with only one keystroke. In this book, the Alt form (if there is one) will be given whenever a reserved word is introduced. See Appendix C for a complete table of the Alt forms. (Note: In this text, a + between two keys indicates that you should press the two keys together. For example, Alt + C means press and hold the Alt key while you press the C key. Do *not* type the +.)

2) *Backspace key.* The Backspace key erases characters as it goes over them, allowing you to correct typing errors.

3) *Caps Lock key.* The Caps Lock key does not stay down when you press it (as it does on a typewriter). Rather, the Caps Lock key acts as a **toggle** switch; one push turns it on, and a second push turns it off. When a PC is first turned on, the letter keys are set for lower case. After you press the Caps Lock key, the letter keys type capital letters. The Caps Lock key affects only the letter keys; it does not give you the special symbols printed on the tops of keys. For those you must use one of the two Shift keys. To get a $, for example, you must hold down a Shift key and press the number 4 key.

Toggle
A key that is alternately turned on and off with the same keystroke.

When you press a Shift key, you reverse the condition set by the Caps Lock key. If the Caps Lock key is on (that is, typing capital letters), holding down the Shift key will give lower case letters, and vice versa. On the enhanced keyboard, a green light indicates that the Caps Lock key is on.

4) *Control key.* Like Alt, the Control key (Ctrl) is a shift-type key.

5) *Enter key.* When you finish typing a line, you must press the Enter key to signal your PC that the line is finished. In general, a PC does not act on anything you type until you press the Enter key. In this chapter and in Chapter 2, the symbol ⏎ is drawn on the figures to remind you to press the Enter key (although no symbol will appear on the screen). After that, you will have to remember to press it on your own.

6) *Escape key.* When you press the Escape key (Esc), the line you are currently typing is erased from the screen and is not processed.

7) *Print Screen key.* The Print Screen key (PrtSc) is used to print whatever is on the screen. The enhanced keyboard has a separate Print Screen key located on the top row, to the right of the function keys. To get the Print Screen function on a standard keyboard, hold down a Shift key while you press the PrtSc key. Of course, the printer must be turned on and have paper in it. (On a standard keyboard, if you press the PrtSc key while not holding down a Shift key, you will get an asterisk, *. This is more convenient than using a Shift key and the number 8 key.) On the enhanced keyboard, you do not have to use the Shift key when you press the Print Screen key.

On both keyboards, if you hold down the Ctrl key and press the Print Screen key, everything that appears on the screen will also be sent to the printer. The result is a hard copy log of a computer session. Pressing Ctrl and Print Screen again turns off the print function.

Notice that Ctrl + Print Screen is different from Shift + Print Screen. Shift + Print Screen print only what is currently on the screen, while Ctrl + Print Screen print everything that appears on the screen from the time those keys are pressed until they are pressed again.

THE NUMERIC KEYPAD

On the far right of the keyboard is the numeric keypad. These keys can be used either to type numbers or to move around the screen to correct errors.

The Num Lock key toggles between these two modes. When you start a computer that has a standard keyboard, these keys are set in the error-correcting mode—you must press Num Lock if you want to use them to type numbers. In contrast, when you start a computer that has an enhanced keyboard, these keys are set in number mode—you must press Num Lock if you want to use them to correct errors. On enhanced keyboards, a green light goes on when these keys are in number mode. The enhanced keyboard has a separate group of keys for moving around to correct errors.

We will discuss the use of these error-correcting keys and the Insert (Ins) and Delete (Del) keys at the base of the numeric pad in Chapter 2. One key you should understand now is the 7/Home key—the combination Ctrl + Home clears the screen.

RESETTING THE SYSTEM

System reset
An action equivalent to turning the computer off and then on. Accomplished by pressing the Ctrl + Alt + Del keys.

The combination Ctrl + Alt + Del causes a **system reset**. A system reset produces the same effect as turning the PC off and then on; the PC restarts itself from scratch. A system reset takes less time than turning the PC off and then on, and it causes less wear and tear on the computer.

When you perform a system reset, the program in RAM is erased. That can be an advantage, particularly when you are first learning, because sometimes a PC may get into a state where it doesn't seem to respond to any of the instructions you give it. Under those circumstances, you can show it that you are still in charge by performing a system reset. Notice, however, how awkward it is to perform a system reset—it is the only function that requires three keys. The reason is so you will not reset the system accidentally. (You wouldn't want to erase by mistake a program that you had just laboriously typed!)

On rare occasions, a PC will not respond to the Ctrl + Alt + Del keys; in those cases, you must turn the PC off, wait a few seconds, and turn it on again. Even then, you see, you are still in charge!

COMPUTER LANGUAGES AND BASIC

If you want to use a computer to solve a problem, you must write a program. For the computer to follow the program, the program must be written in a language the computer understands. The PC understands many languages, among them Pascal, COBOL, and FORTRAN. In this book, you will learn BASIC (the name stands for Beginner's All-purpose Symbolic Instruction Code).

Actually it's cutting corners to say that a PC understands BASIC or the other languages mentioned. The only language a PC really understands is **machine language**. Machine language is fine for computers, but it is very difficult for people. Programs written in BASIC are translated into machine language by a special program called an **interpreter**.*

Machine language
The only language that does not have to be translated for the computer to understand it.

Interpreter
A program that translates a program written in BASIC into machine language.

On IBM PCs, the BASIC interpreter is named BASICA; on non-IBM PCs, it is called GWBASIC. (There are other, less powerful versions of BASIC available, which were designed to be used on computers with very little

---

*Most other languages use a compiler instead of an interpreter. Although a compiler and an interpreter are not the same, for our purposes we can consider an interpreter and a compiler to be equivalent.

RAM. Since today's computers have enough RAM to run the more powerful versions of BASIC, we will not discuss these other versions.) The BASIC interpreter is supplied with the DOS diskettes provided by the manufacturer. **DOS**, which stands for disk operating system, is a collection of programs that control the PC and that make it easier for you to run it. DOS is discussed in Appendix E.

DOS (disk operating system)
A collection of programs that control the PC and make it easier for you to use it.

From time to time new versions of DOS and BASIC appear on the market. These new versions usually incorporate improvements in the form of either new instructions or enhancements to existing instructions. The programs in this book were executed using the BASIC supplied with Version 4 of DOS. (Sometimes, for short, that version is called DOS 4, and the BASIC supplied with it is called BASIC 4.) The programs will execute identically on any version of BASIC labeled 2.1 or higher.

Starting BASIC

The supplies you need to start and run BASIC depend on whether you are using a PC with only diskette drives or one with a hard disk. If you are using a diskette-based PC, you will need a diskette that contains DOS and BASIC. (This diskette will have enough free space to store your programs, too.) If you are using a PC with a hard disk, you will need a formatted diskette on which to store your programs. Instructions for making a DOS/BASIC diskette and for formatting a diskette are given in Appendix E.

The way you start BASIC also depends on whether you are using a PC with diskette drives or one with a hard disk. If you are using a diskette-based PC, then before you turn the computer on you should insert the DOS/BASIC diskette into diskette drive A (the one on the left). Close the drive door and turn the PC on. You may also have to turn on the monitor if it has a separate switch. If the computer is already on, insert your disk and perform a system reset (press Ctrl + Alt + Del).

You will hear the fan start and then a beep, which indicates that the PC is performing self-checking tests. On some PCs, you will see numbers flash on the screen. These numbers indicate that the memory is being checked. You will see the light on the drive go on. This light indicates that the drive is in use.* You may hear some strange noises. These noises indicate that the PC is reading DOS into RAM. Reading a program from a diskette into RAM is known as **loading** the program.

Loading
Reading a program from secondary storage into RAM.

If you are using a PC with a hard disk, you must turn the PC on *before* you insert a diskette into the drive.

ENTERING THE TIME AND DATE

Regardless of your drive system, after a few seconds your monitor screen will display a message, as shown in the first two lines in Figure 1.5, asking you to enter the date. (In this and all subsequent figures and programs, characters typed by the computer are printed in blue; those you must type are printed in black.) Some PCs have a built-in clock calendar, so you don't have to enter the date and the time. If your machine does not, you must enter the date to proceed. Despite the example the machine provides, do *not* type the day of the week. Instead, enter a number between 1 and 12 indicating the month, then type a hyphen, a number between 1 and 31 indicating

---

*Never insert or remove a diskette while the light is on, or you may damage the diskette or drive.

```
Current date is Tue 1-01-1980
Enter new date (mm-dd-yy): 10-5-91⏎
Current time is 0:01:58.57
Enter new time: 15:25⏎

IBM DOS Version 4.00
     (C)Copyright International Business Machines Corp 1981, 1988
     (C)Copyright Microsoft Corp 1981-1986

A>BASICA⏎
   ⟵ (DOS prompt)
```

FIGURE 1.5   **Starting Advanced BASIC.**

the day, a hyphen, and a number between 80 and 99 indicating the year. Instead of hyphens, you may use slashes (/) to separate the parts of the date. Then press the Enter key.

After you press the Enter key, the computer asks for the time of day. You must use a 24-hour clock and type a colon to separate the hours and minutes. After you have typed in the time, press the Enter key again.

It is not really necessary to enter the date and time. You can simply press the Enter key in response to one or both requests. It's a good idea to enter the date, however, because if you save a program (saving is explained in Chapter 2) the date is also saved. Knowing the date a program was saved can be helpful if you later need to determine which version of a program is the most recent. But when you do not intend to save any programs, pressing the Enter key instead of typing the date and time is convenient.

LOADING BASIC

After you enter the time, the PC will display two lines similar to those shown in Figure 1.5. If you are using a different version of DOS, the version number and copyright dates will be different.

> **Prompt**
> A message indicating that the computer is waiting for you to enter instructions or data.

On diskette PCs, the last line will be A>. On hard disk PCs it will be C>. A> or C> is the DOS prompt. A **prompt** is a message that indicates the computer is waiting for you to enter an instruction or data. Although you can't see it in the figure, next to the prompt is a short flashing line. The flashing line is called the **cursor**, which indicates where you are on the screen. The next character you type will appear on the screen at the cursor's position.

> **Cursor**
> A flashing line that indicates where the next character you type will appear on the screen.

The letter A or C indicates which drive is the **DOS default drive**. Unless you specify otherwise, the default drive is the drive that is used when you save your programs to a disk. (How you save your programs to a disk will be explained in Chapter 2.) You will want to save your programs on your own diskette, so on hard disk PCs you must change the default drive from C to A. First insert your formatted diskette into drive A. Then type the command A: (notice that there is no space between the A and the :) and press the Enter key. If you enter this command correctly, the prompt should change to A>, indicating that A is now the default drive.

> **DOS default drive**
> The drive that is used when you read from and write to a disk, unless you specify otherwise.

To start BASIC on an IBM PC, type BASICA (notice the final A). To start BASIC on a non-IBM PC, type GWBASIC and press the Enter key. These commands cause the PC to load BASIC from the DOS diskette or hard drive into RAM. The screen will clear momentarily and then appear looking similar to

```
The IBM Basic
Version A4.00 Copyright IBM Corp. 1981, 1988
60225 Bytes free

Ok ◄─────( BASIC prompt )




1LIST   2RUN ◄ 3LOAD"  4SAVE"  5CONT ◄ 6,"LPT1 7TRON ◄ 8TROFF ◄ 9KEY 0SCREEN
```

FIGURE 1.6   **The initial BASIC screen.**

Figure 1.6. If you are using a different version of BASIC, the numbers and the copyright dates displayed will be different. The OK is BASIC's prompt and indicates that you may now type BASIC instructions. We will explain the bottom line in the next chapter.

Warning: On diskette PCs, if you turn on the computer before you insert your DOS/BASIC disk into drive A, you will see a screen similar to Figure 1.6, but you will be running a simple version of BASIC, one in which it is not possible to save programs. You won't know that until after you have typed a program and tried to save it. At that point, it will be necessary to start over again from the beginning and retype your program. You don't want to do that, so make sure you follow the instructions for starting BASIC carefully.

The procedure is somewhat complicated, so let's summarize it. If you are using a diskette PC, follow these steps:

1. Insert a diskette that contains DOS and BASIC into drive A and close the door.
2. Turn on the computer, and, if necessary, the monitor.
3. If necessary, enter the date and the time.
4. Start BASIC by typing BASICA on IBM PCs and GWBASIC on non-IBM PCs.

If you are using a hard disk PC, follow these steps:

1. Turn on the computer, and, if necessary, the monitor.
2. If necessary, enter the date and the time.
3. Insert a formatted diskette into drive A.
4. Type A: to make drive A the default drive.
5. Start BASIC by typing BASICA on IBM PCs and GWBASIC on non-IBM PCs.

At some schools, a different procedure may be followed. If you will be using a different procedure, your instructor will tell you what it is.

Getting the **Problem:** When you try to start the computer, the screen displays the
Bugs Out   error message

> Non-System disk or disk error
> Replace and strike any key when ready

Reason: The disk in drive A does not contain DOS.

Solution: Remove the disk and replace it with a disk that contains DOS.

Problem: When you try to start BASIC, the screen displays the error
              message

> Bad command or file name

Reason: You typed BASICA incorrectly, or your diskette does not contain BASICA, or the system cannot find BASICA on the hard disk.

Solution: Make sure you typed BASICA correctly. If you typed it correctly, make sure your DOS/BASIC disk is in drive A.

SUMMARY

In this chapter you have learned that

- [ ] All computer systems contain five components: an input unit, output units, a central processing unit (CPU), and primary and secondary storage units.

- [ ] The input unit sends data and instructions from the outside world to the computer. On a PC, the input unit is the keyboard.

- [ ] The output unit sends the computer's answers to the outside world. A PC uses a monitor and a printer as output units.

- [ ] The CPU executes instructions.

- [ ] The primary storage unit stores programs that are being executed and data that are being processed.

- [ ] Secondary storage devices enable you to store programs and data when they are not being worked on and when the computer is turned off. On a PC, the most common secondary storage devices are diskette drives and hard drives. A PC can have one or two diskette drives.

- [ ] A PC's keyboard is similar to that of a typewriter, but it is divided into three sections: the function keys, the typewriter keys, and the numeric keypad. The enhanced keyboard has a separate cursor control keypad.

- [ ] Pressing the Ctrl + Alt + Del keys causes a system reset. A system reset is equivalent to turning the computer off and then on, but it causes less wear and tear on the computer.

- [ ] To start BASIC on a PC with diskette drives only: 1) insert a DOS/BASIC diskette into drive A, 2) turn on the computer, 3) enter the date and time, 4) type BASICA or GWBASIC. To start BASIC on a PC with a hard drive: 1) turn on the computer, 2) enter the data and time, 3) insert a diskette into drive A, 4) type A:, 5) type BASICA or GWBASIC.

KEY TERMS IN THIS CHAPTER

....

byte 4

central processing unit (CPU) 4

computer 2

cursor 10

data 2

disk operating system (DOS) 9

diskette (floppy disk) 4

diskette (floppy disk) drive 4

DOS default drive 10

function keys 5

hard copy output 3

hard disk 4

input unit 3

interpreter 8

K 4

loading 9

M 4

machine language 8

monitor 3

output unit 3

PC 2

primary storage unit 4

program 2

prompt 10

random access memory (RAM) 4

reserved words 7

read only memory (ROM) 4

secondary storage device 4

soft copy output 3

system reset 8

toggle 7

QUESTIONS FOR REVIEW

....

1.1 Complete the following sentences:

   a) Pressing the Ctrl, Alt, and Del keys at the same time causes a _____ .

   b) The unit of storage that can hold one character is a _____ .

   c) A message that indicates the computer is waiting for you to enter instructions or data is a _____ .

   d) The _____ shows where on the screen the next character you type will appear.

   e) The _____ translates your BASIC program into machine language.

1.2 What is the difference between RAM and ROM?

1.3 Which keys are used to clear the screen?

1.4 Output on the screen is called _____, while output on the printer is called _____ .

1.5 Name the five basic components of a computer.

1.6 You must end every line you type by pressing the _____ key.

1.7 What does the abbreviation CPU stand for?

1.8 Would a computer whose primary storage contains 500 bytes be useful? What about one with 500K bytes?

1.9 The BASIC prompt is _____ .

1.10 What does an interpreter do?

1.11 What devices are most frequently used as output units?

2

Programming
in BASIC

- ☐ To construct a structured procedure for solving problems using a computer
- ☐ To draw a simple flowchart
- ☐ To write, enter, and execute a BASIC program
- ☐ To trace a program
- ☐ To debug a program
- ☐ To use the BASIC statements LET, PRINT, END, and REM
- ☐ To use the BASIC commands RUN, LIST, SAVE, LOAD, and NEW

Now that you are familiar with the workings of a PC, you are ready to learn to use it to program in BASIC. To help you write correct programs, you will learn an eight-step procedure that you should follow when you develop a program. As part of this procedure, you will learn how to enter and execute a program and how to find and eliminate errors. You will also learn your first BASIC instructions and how to save and later retrieve your programs.

A STRUCTURED APPROACH TO PROGRAMMING

Consider the following problem: You make $6.25 an hour working part time for the Merchant of Venison Butcher Shop. Last week you put in 25 hours. To collect your pay, you must bill the store. How would you go about it? You could, of course, find the answer by hand (or with a calculator) and type a bill. But since the purpose of this course is for you to learn BASIC, we will write a BASIC program to calculate your pay.

To write BASIC programs, you must learn two skills. To give the computer instructions, you must learn the BASIC instructions to do things like add numbers and print answers. This part is relatively easy. Somewhat harder is learning how to put the BASIC instructions together to solve a problem.

To help you learn how to put the BASIC instructions together, this text uses an eight-step procedure:

1. Choose names for the variables in the problem.
2. Develop an algorithm for solving the problem.
3. Calculate an answer to the problem by hand.
4. Write a BASIC program.
5. Enter the program and execute it.
6. Correct syntax errors.
7. Check the computer's answer against the answer you calculated in step 3.
8. Correct logic errors.

You should follow this procedure when you write BASIC programs. Don't be intimidated by the thought of having to follow eight steps every time you want to solve a problem. Some of the steps are easy, and all contribute to a successful program.

Naming Variables

Variable
A quantity that is given a name and whose value may change when a program is executed.

Numeric or **ordinary variable**
A variable whose value is a number.

String variable
A variable whose value is one or more letters, or a combination of letters and numbers.

The first step is to choose names for the variables in the problem. A **variable** is any quantity in a problem that is referred to by name and whose value may change. Although it is true that in this problem the pay rate and the hours worked are fixed at $6.25 an hour and 25 hours, next week you might work 30 hours, or you might get a raise to $7 an hour. If either your pay rate or the number of hours worked were to change, your gross pay would also change. Therefore, in this problem the variables are pay rate, hours worked, and gross pay.

BASIC has two kinds of variables. The value of a **numeric** or **ordinary variable** is a number. The value of a **string variable** is a **string**—a group of letters or a combination of letters and numbers. In this chapter,

String
A group of letters, numbers, or special characters.

we will use only numeric variables. You will learn about string variables in Chapter 3.

In choosing names for the variables, you must follow the first BASIC rule:

....

BASIC Rule 1

A variable name may consist of capital letters,* digits, and the period. A name may not contain a blank space. A name must start with a letter and may contain up to 40 characters. You may not use a BASIC reserved word as a name (a complete list of BASIC reserved words is given in Appendix A). Here is a list of some valid and invalid variable names. For the invalid names, the reason they are invalid is given.

Proposed variable name	Status
A	Valid.
4SALE	Invalid—a name must start with a letter.
RUMPELSTILTSKIN	Valid.
%INTEREST	Invalid—a name must start with a letter.
GROSS PAY	Invalid—a name may not contain a blank space.
GROSSPAY	Valid.
GROSS.PAY	Valid—using a period where in English there would be a space makes this easier to read than GROSSPAY.
BEEP	Invalid—BEEP is a reserved word, which may not be used as a name.
BEEPER	Valid—you cannot use a reserved word as a variable name, but a reserved word may be *part* of a variable name.

Now that you know how to choose names for variables, let's choose names for the three variables in our problem: pay rate, hours worked, and gross pay. You could choose A, B, and C, but it is better to use names that will help you remember what they stand for. So we will use:

Pay rate	PAY.RATE
Hours worked	HOURS
Gross pay	GROSS.PAY

When you choose names, you have to strike a balance between names that are too short to help you remember what they stand for and names that are so long that they increase the chance that you'll make a mistake when you type them. In this case, P, H, and G are too short, but HOURLY.PAY.RATE and TOTAL.WEEKLY.GROSS.PAY are too long.

Developing an Algorithm

The second step of our systematic procedure is to develop a plan to solve the problem. In computer terminology, the plan to solve a problem is called an

---

*Although the rule says you must use capital letters, you may in fact type variable names in lower case. If you do, BASIC simply converts the letters to capital letters.

Algorithm
A series of steps that a computer can follow to solve a problem.

algorithm. An algorithm is a series of steps that a computer can follow to solve a problem. Some people are surprised that we have to have a plan to solve the problem. They thought the computer was going to solve the problem. But remember, the computer does not know anything about your problem. It will just follow the instructions you give it. If you do not know how to solve a problem by hand, you won't be able to solve it using a computer. (This idea may come as a shock if you enrolled in this course with the idea of asking a PC to print a list of stocks that will double in price next year. You have to know how to pick a stock that will double in price next year and explain your method to the PC. Then the PC will print the list.)

For our relatively simple problem, the algorithm is straightforward:

1. Assign 6.25 to the variable PAY.RATE.
2. Assign 25 to the variable HOURS.
3. Multiply the variables PAY.RATE and HOURS and assign the product to the variable GROSS.PAY.
4. Print the value of the variable GROSS.PAY.

The order of the steps in the algorithm is important. We first assign values to some variables (PAY.RATE and HOURS), then we use those values to calculate a new variable (GROSS.PAY), and finally we print the new variable. That the order of the steps is important should not surprise you, since in everyday life the order is often crucial. For example, in the algorithm to determine whether it is raining, there is a big difference between

1. Open the window.
2. Put your head out the window.

and

1. Put your head out the window.
2. Open the window.

FLOWCHARTS

Flowchart
A picture of an algorithm that shows the logical structure of the algorithm clearly.

There are several techniques that you can use to help develop an algorithm. One technique is to draw a flowchart. A **flowchart** is a picture of an algorithm that shows its logical structure clearly. It is often easier to develop and understand an algorithm when it is given in the form of a flowchart than when it is given in the form of a series of English sentences. A flowchart for the butcher shop algorithm is shown in Figure 2.1.

Flowline
A line on a flowchart that connects boxes.

Terminal symbol
A flowchart symbol in the shape of an oval that is used to show the start and the end of a flowchart.

Arithmetic step
A step in which a value is assigned to a variable.

As Figure 2.1 illustrates, a flowchart consists of boxes connected by lines. These lines are called **flowlines**. Flowlines end in arrows, which show their direction. You may notice that three differently shaped boxes appear in this flowchart. An oval is used to show the beginning and the end of a flowchart. It is called a **terminal symbol**. As Figure 2.1 shows, the beginning of the flowchart is indicated by an oval with the word START in it, and the end of the flowchart is shown by an oval with the word END in it. The purpose of the terminal symbols is to make it easy for a reader to locate quickly the beginning and the end of a complicated flowchart.

A rectangle is used to show an **arithmetic step**—a step in which a value is assigned to a variable. The rectangle is called a **process symbol**. A step like PAY.RATE = 6.25 is considered a very simple form of arithmetic

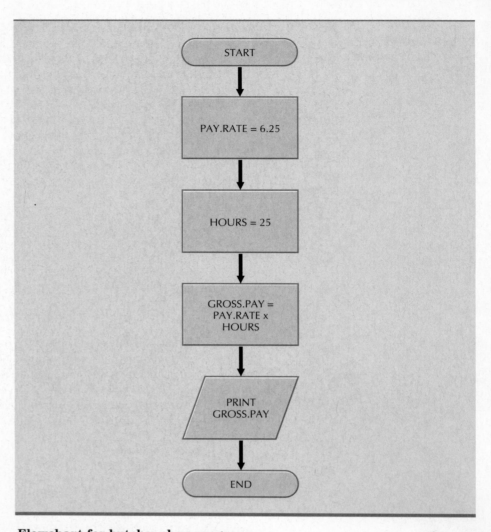

FIGURE 2.1

Flowchart for butcher shop program.

Process symbol
A flowchart symbol in the shape of a rectangle that is used to show an arithmetic step.

Input/output symbol
A flowchart symbol in the shape of a parallelogram that is used to show both input and output operations.

step. Finally, a parallelogram is used to show the step in which the computer will print an answer. Because a parallelogram is also used for the step in which the computer reads in data (as you will learn in Chapter 3), this box is called an **input/output symbol**. Other symbols used in drawing flowcharts will be introduced as you need them.

Notice that, with the exception of the terminal symbols, the symbols in the flowchart correspond to the steps in the algorithm. The three process symbols correspond to the first three steps of the algorithm, and the input/output symbol corresponds to the fourth step of the algorithm.

Calculating an Answer

The third step in our systematic procedure is to calculate an answer to the problem by hand. For the butcher shop problem we can easily calculate that the gross pay should be $6.25 per hour times 25 hours, which is $156.25. We have to calculate an answer by hand because only by comparing the computer's solution to the solution you calculate using paper and pencil (or a hand calculator) can you be sure that your program is correct. You might argue that if we calculate the answer to a problem by hand you do not need a computer. At this point in your study of BASIC that is a good argument, but in later chapters we will discuss more complex programs, where you will see why computers are very useful, even though you must calculate an initial answer by hand.

Writing a BASIC Program

The fourth step in developing a program is to translate the algorithm (and the flowchart) for a problem into a BASIC program. A BASIC program consists of a set of BASIC statements that the computer follows to solve a problem. A BASIC program for the butcher shop problem is shown in Program 2.1.

Although this is the first BASIC program you have seen, BASIC is so straightforward that you can probably "read" it enough to see that lines 10, 20, and 30 correspond to the first three steps of the algorithm and the three process symbols in the flowchart and that line 40 corresponds to the fourth step of the algorithm and the input/output symbol in the flowchart. In fact, this particular program is so simple that it could have been written directly from the algorithm, without the help of the flowchart. But as we get into more complicated problems, the flowchart will be essential, so you should begin now by drawing simple flowcharts.

```
10 LET PAY. RATE = 6.25
20 LET HOURS = 25
30 LET GROSS. PAY = PAY. RATE * HOURS
40 PRINT GROSS. PAY
50 END
```

PROGRAM 2.1   **The butcher shop program.**

LINE NUMBERS

Let's examine this program in detail. You will notice that every line begins with a line number. This is another BASIC rule:

....

BASIC Rule 2   Every line in a BASIC program begins with a line number.

Line numbers can be any whole number from 0 to 65529. Although the statements in the example could have had the line numbers 1, 2, 3, 4, and 5, the advantage to numbering by tens is that if you later find you left out a line, you can go back and insert it, using a number between the tens.

Line numbers correspond to the symbols in the flowchart. In fact, when you have completed a flowchart, you should number it as in Figure 2.2 to help you write the program.

SHOWING NUMBERS AND ARITHMETIC OPERATIONS

Besides line numbers, Program 2.1 uses two other numbers (or as they are called in BASIC, two constants): a 6.25 in line 10 and a 25 in line 20. Notice that although the 6.25 stands for $6.25 an hour, we write it as the number 6.25, without the dollar sign. BASIC always uses pure numbers, without any units. It does not know or care whether the 6.25 stands for $6.25 an hour, 6.25 marks per month, or 6.25 yen per year. Clearly, BASIC does not

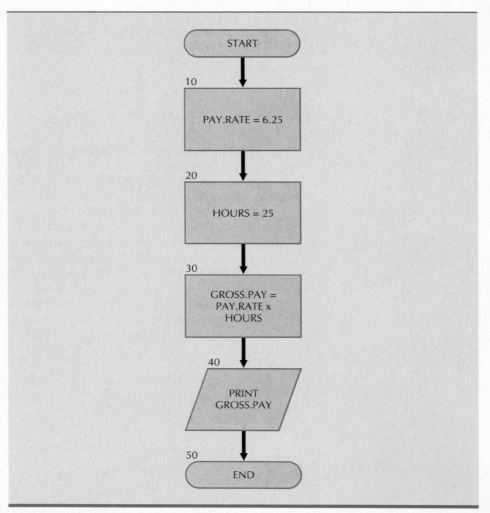

FIGURE 2.2   **Flowchart for butcher shop program with line numbers.**

know anything about the problem. It simply follows instructions. You have to know that the 6.25 stands for dollars per hour to interpret the output.

Whenever you have to use a number in a BASIC program, write it the way you usually would. There are just two exceptions to this rule. First, always use decimals, not fractions, that is, the pay rate is 6.25, not 6¼. Second, never use commas in numbers larger than 999. If a plane flies 4,352 miles, write the number in BASIC as 4352, without the comma between the 4 and the 3. Do not use commas in line numbers either.

Notice the asterisk (*) in line 30 of the program. In BASIC, you use an asterisk when you want BASIC to multiply. Do not use the usual X for multiplication, since BASIC won't know if the X stands for multiplication or a variable named X. You will be happy to know, however, that for the other arithmetic operations the usual symbols are used. So when you want to add, use a +; to subtract, use a -; and to divide, use a /.

BASIC STATEMENTS

Statement
An instruction the computer is to follow.

Finally, Program 2.1 contains BASIC **statements**, which are the instructions the computer is to follow. In this program, we need three different kinds of BASIC statements: the LET statement, the PRINT statement, and the

END statement. The words LET, PRINT, and END, which begin each statement, are BASIC reserved words. Thus, we have a third rule:

....

BASIC Rule 3

Every BASIC statement begins with a reserved word.

Syntax statement
A model that shows the correct way of writing a particular BASIC statement.

The rules that specify the proper way to write each kind of statement are called the statement's syntax. In this book, a **syntax statement**—a model of the correct format—will be given when each new BASIC statement is introduced. A complete list of syntax statements appears in Appendix D of this book. The BASIC manual uses a simple but effective way to describe briefly and clearly the syntax of statements. Because the method is so effective, and because you should learn how to read your manual, this book will use the same method.

One general syntax rule, which applies in every case, is that BASIC reserved words must be separated from other parts of a BASIC statement. Most often a space is used as a separator, but in some cases a comma or parentheses may be used. The syntax of each statement shows which separators may be used. This means that

```
40 PRINTGROSS.PAY
```

is illegal, because there is no separator between the reserved word PRINT and the variable name GROSS.PAY.

Extra spaces are never wrong. You should use extra spaces to help make your program easy to read and understand. For example, in the LET statements given in Program 2.1, you will find a space used around the equal signs and the multiplication symbol, *.

If you don't leave a space between the line number and the first word, BASIC will insert one.

THE LET STATEMENT

The LET statement is used when you want BASIC to calculate a value and assign it to a variable. In Program 2.1, lines 10, 20, and 30 are examples of LET statements.

```
10 LET PAY.RATE = 6.25
20 LET HOURS = 25
30 LET GROSS.PAY = PAY.RATE * HOURS
```

The syntax of the LET statement is

```
[LET] variable = expression
```

In this and all syntax statements, words printed in capital letters are BASIC reserved words and must be typed as shown. Words and letters in lowercase stand for items supplied by you, the programmer. This particular syntax statement contains an equal sign. The equal sign and other punctuation shown in a syntax statement, such as commas, semicolons, and parentheses, must be included when you write the BASIC statement.

Square brackets, [ ], are not part of the statement. They are never typed. Square brackets mean that part of the statement, in this case the word LET, is optional. BASIC is smart enough to analyze the form

```
variable = expression
```

and figure out that you mean a LET statement. Since the word LET is not required, it will not be used in any future programs in this book. The LET statement is the only exception to the rule that every BASIC statement must begin with a reserved word.

Note that the right side of the LET statement is an expression. For the moment, let's simply say that an expression is the part of a LET statement where we ask BASIC to calculate a value.

When BASIC executes a program, it assigns locations in the PC's RAM where it will remember the value of each variable used in the program. For the butcher shop program, BASIC sets up locations for PAY.RATE, HOURS, and GROSS.PAY. It may help to think of these storage locations as separate boxes, each of which contains the value of a variable. An important fact to remember about these boxes is that they can hold only one number at a time. When a BASIC statement causes a new number to be put in a box, the old number in that box is erased.

To execute a LET statement, BASIC first does the arithmetic it is asked to do in the expression. When the arithmetic is done, BASIC is left with a number. It then puts that number in the storage location (that is, the box) for the variable given on the left side of the equal sign.

Let's see how this procedure applies to the three LET statements in Program 2.1. In line 10, the expression is particularly simple: it is just the number 6.25. Since BASIC does not have to do any arithmetic to convert the expression into a number (it already is a number), it simply puts the number 6.25 into the PAY.RATE box. Line 20 is equally simple, and BASIC puts the number 25 into the HOURS box.

The expression in line 30 is more complicated. BASIC must first take the number in the PAY.RATE box (which is 6.25) and multiply it by the number in the HOURS box (which is 25). When it gets the answer, 156.25, it will put that answer into the GROSS.PAY box.

When BASIC uses a number from a box to evaluate an expression, it does not change the number. So after line 30 is executed, the PAY.RATE box still contains the number 6.25, and the HOURS box still contains the number 25.

Now that we have examined several LET statements, we can define an expression more precisely. An **expression** is a combination of variables, numbers, and arithmetic operation symbols that can be evaluated to produce a number. (When you study string variables in Chapter 3, you will learn that some expressions produce a string when they are evaluated.) The number calculated is assigned to the variable on the left side of the equal sign.

Expressions can be much more complicated than those we have used so far. We will discuss the rules for more complicated expressions when you need them, but for now you need to know only that expressions can mix variables and numbers, as in the following examples:

Expression
A combination of variables, numbers, and arithmetic operation symbols that can be evaluated to produce a number or a string.

LET Statement

H = N/80

Effect

Divides the number in the N box by 80 and puts the answer in the H box.

LET Statement

TOTAL = N1 + N2 + N3

Effect

Adds the numbers in the N1, N2, and N3 boxes and puts the answer in the TOTAL box.

LET Statement

```
GRADE = NUMBER.RIGHT/TOTAL.QUESTIONS
```

Effect

Divides the number in the NUMBER.RIGHT box by the number in the TOTAL.QUESTIONS box and puts the answer in the GRADE box.

LET Statement

```
CHANGE = PAID - PRICE
```

Effect

Subtracts the number in the PRICE box from the number in the PAID box and puts the answer in the CHANGE box.

The syntax of the LET statement says that the variable must be on the left side of the equal sign and the expression must be on the right side. To see why, consider the following two *incorrect* LET statements:

```
6.25 = PAY.RATE
PAY.RATE * HOURS = GROSS.PAY
```

Both these statements are wrong. The first says to take the number in the PAY.RATE box and put it in the 6.25 box. But there is no 6.25 box! Boxes are set up just for variables, not for a constant like 6.25. Similarly, the second example says to take the number in the GROSS.PAY box and put it in the PAY.RATE * HOURS box. But while there is a PAY.RATE box and there is an HOURS box, there is no PAY.RATE * HOURS box.

Being aware of the two sides of the equal sign is especially important in cases like the following:

```
A = B
B = A
```

Both of these are legal LET statements, but they have very different effects. Suppose that initially there is a 1 in the A box and a 2 in the B box. To understand what BASIC will do when it executes a statement, it is helpful to set up on paper a box for each variable, corresponding to the boxes BASIC sets up in the computer's RAM. In this case, we start with

```
A   B
1   2
```

The first LET statement says to take the number in the B box and put it in the A box. After that statement is executed, we have the following situation:

```
A   B
1   2
2
```

Since location boxes can hold only one number at a time, the 1 that was in the A box is erased and replaced by a 2, so that there is a 2 in both boxes. Notice that nothing happens to the 2 that is in the B box.

Suppose we return to the original situation, with a 1 in the A box and a 2 in the B box. What will be in the A and B boxes after the second LET statement, B = A, is executed?*

---

*There will be a 1 in both boxes.

THE PRINT STATEMENT

A PRINT statement is shown in line 40. This statement simply tells BASIC to print the number in the GROSS.PAY box. Nothing is actually printed; the number in the GROSS.PAY box is displayed on the screen. Nevertheless, in "computerese" we say the answers are printed. Using the Alt + P keys is equivalent to typing the word PRINT. BASIC will also interpret a question mark, ?, typed as the first character on a line as the word PRINT.

The syntax of the PRINT statement is

PRINT expression, . . .

Notice that the syntax statement shows that an expression may be printed. In Program 2.1, we printed the variable GROSS.PAY. Of course, a variable is just a simple expression, so our coding follows the syntax. An ellipsis (. . .) in a syntax statement means that the previous item may be repeated as often as you want. In this case, it means that you can list as many expressions as you want. For example, line 40 could have been

40 PRINT PAY.RATE, HOURS, GROSS.PAY

This statement tells BASIC to print the numbers in the PAY.RATE box, the HOURS box, and the GROSS.PAY box, in that order. Be careful to follow the form shown *exactly,* putting a comma between PAY.RATE and HOURS and between HOURS and GROSS.PAY, but not after PRINT or GROSS.PAY.

Since it is legal to print expressions, line 40 could have been written as

40 PRINT PAY.RATE * HOURS

or

40 PRINT PAY.RATE, HOURS, PAY.RATE * HOURS

For clarity's sake, however, in this text we will usually assign separate variable names to calculated answers, as we did in line 30, and then tell BASIC to print those variables.

THE END STATEMENT

An END statement is shown in line 50. Its syntax is

END

The END statement is the simplest statement of all. It simply tells BASIC to stop executing a program. The END statement is not required at the end of your program. BASIC is smart enough to stop executing when it comes to the end of a program. But the END statement helps you see the end of the program, so it appears in all examples in this book.

Syntax Summary

LET Statement
Form: [LET] variable = expression
Example: AREA = HEIGHT * BASE
Function: Evaluates the expression on the right of the equal sign and assigns the resulting value to the variable on the left of the equal sign.

PRINT Statement
Form: PRINT expression, . . .
Example: PRINT HEIGHT, BASE, AREA
Function: Displays the values of the variables and/or expressions on the screen

END Statement
Form: END
Example: END
Function: Indicates the end of the program and causes the program to stop executing.

EXERCISES

(Answers to questions marked with an asterisk are given in Appendix B.)

2.1 Which of the following variable names are legal and which are illegal?

   a) NUMBERTALLERTHANTENFEET
   b) 1ST.CLASS
   c) FOUR.SALE
*d) OVERTIME-PAY
*e) AUTO
   f) END.OF.DATA

2.2 Which of the following numeric constants are legal and which are illegal?

*a) $81
*b) 16.4
   c) 21,643
   d) 46.25
   e) 90 ozs

2.3 Which of the following LET statements contain errors? Rewrite the incorrect statements correctly.

*a) B = 6,500
   b) T = S / V
*c) P3 = −12
   d) M * C * C = E
   e) LENGTH = 30 FEET
   f) A = A + 5

2.4 If A = 7, B = 8, and C = 12, what values are assigned by the following LET statements?

   a) G = A + B + C
   b) H = C/3
*c) B = B + 1

2.5 Let BALANCE stand for the amount of money in a savings account for one year and INTEREST stand for the interest earned. Write a LET statement to calculate INTEREST if the interest rate is 8%. (Hint: The interest rate must be expressed as a decimal, .08, not a percent.)

2.6 Which of the following PRINT statements contain errors? Rewrite the incorrect statement(s) correctly.

   a) PRINT PHI, BETA, KAPPA
   b) PRINT REGULAR.PAY, OVERTIME.PAY, AND TOTAL.PAY

*2.7 Let SPEED stand for speed in miles per hour, TIME for time in hours, and DISTANCE for total distance in miles. Does the following program calculate and print the distance traveled by a car going 40 miles per hour for 3 hours? If not, correct the program.

```
10 SPEED = 40
20 TIME = 3
30 PRINT DISTANCE
40 DISTANCE = SPEED * TIME
50 END
```

2.8 In the butcher shop program, suppose we used PR to stand for pay rate and wrote line 10 as

```
10 PR = 6.25
```

What other changes in the program, if any, would be required?

2.9 We said that when you write a numeric value, you should write just the number, without any units. Yet in line 20 in Program 2.1, we used the word HOURS. Explain.

PROGRAMMING ASSIGNMENTS

In these and other programming assignments, you should develop your programs by following the eight steps described in the text. Start by inventing variable names to stand for the variables and assigning values to the variables, just as we did for the butcher shop problem. (Answers to questions marked with an asterisk are given in Appendix B.)

2.1 Suppose you traveled 335 miles and your car used 9.8 gallons of gasoline. Write a program to calculate and print average gas mileage by dividing miles traveled by gasoline used.

*2.2 Twice Sold Tales, a used-book store, is having a sale, where everything is reduced 20 percent. An unabridged dictionary regularly costs $19.98. Write a program to calculate and print the sale price of that dictionary.

2.3 You got 18 questions correct on a 25-question multiple-choice test. Write a program to calculate and print your percentage grade.

2.4 Write a program to calculate and print the number of grams in 13 ounces. You can convert from ounces to grams using the formula grams = 28.4 * ounces.

*2.5 Mark O. Polo is traveling in Japan and wants to buy a VCR that costs 30,000 yen. You get 131.46 yen for a dollar. Write a program to calculate and print the cost of the VCR in dollars.

2.6 Casey Batt made 42 hits in 228 times at bat. Write a program to calculate and print her batting average. To calculate batting average, divide hits by at bats and multiply the quotient by 1000.

2.7 Each chocolate bar uses three quarters of an ounce of nuts, and nuts cost $.12 per ounce. A candy manufacturer produces 600 chocolate bars. Write a program to calculate and print the cost of the nuts.

*2.8 A room that is 4 yards wide and 5.3 yards long is to be covered with a rug that costs $18 a square yard. Write a program to calculate and print the cost of the rug.

2.9 Tom is painting a picket fence that contains 82 pickets. He paints 8 pickets an hour and has been painting for 2¾ hours. Write a program to calculate and print the percentage of the fence that has been painted.

*2.10 Scientists estimate that each hour spent watching the TV program *Loving Hospitals* causes ¼ cubic centimeter of the human brain to turn to oatmeal. The average human brain contains 1456 cubic centimeters. Suppose you have watched *Loving Hospitals* for 250 hours. Write a program to calculate and print the percent of your brain that has turned to oatmeal.

2.11 Suppose that each cigarette you smoke reduces your life span by 14 minutes. Suppose also that you smoke two packs a day for 12 years. Write a program to calculate and print the number of days your life span has been reduced. You should use a variable to represent the number of years you have smoked, but you can use the other numbers, 14 minutes, 2 packs a day, and 20 cigarettes in a pack, as constants.

ENTERING AND EXECUTING THE PROGRAM

The fifth step in our structured procedure is to enter the program into the computer. (To start BASIC, see Chapter 1.) When your PC displays the word 0k (the BASIC prompt), you may begin typing.

Type the program just as we wrote it, one statement on a line. You can type in either uppercase or lowercase letters. You must press the Enter key at the end of each line. This is the fourth rule:

BASIC Rule 4   Every line in a BASIC program is ended by pressing the Enter key.

Most statements are relatively short, like the ones in this program, and easily fit on one line. But occasionally, long statements may extend beyond the right edge of the screen. Don't let that bother you. Just keep typing—the statement will continue onto the next line. In fact,

BASIC Rule 5   BASIC statements can be 255 characters long, which is equivalent to three full lines of 80 characters each and 15 characters on the fourth line. Even though such a statement occupies more than one line on the screen, BASIC considers it a single statement.

```
10 PAY.RATE = 6.25 ↵
20 HOURS = 25 ↵
30 GROSS.PAY = PAY.RATE * HOURS ↵
40 PRINT GROSS.PAY ↵
50 END ↵

RUN ↵ ◄── ( RUN, causes program to be executed )
  156.25 ◄── ( Answer, displayed by line 40 )
Ok
```

PROGRAM 2.2   **The butcher shop program as it appears on the computer.**

Program 2.2 shows how the butcher shop program should look on the screen. In addition to the program, you can see the word RUN. Merely typing the program does not cause anything to happen: You must type RUN if you want BASIC to execute the program. RUN is a BASIC **command**, not a BASIC statement. One difference between commands and statements is that commands never have line numbers. Another difference is that when you type a command you are giving BASIC an order to do something immediately. In contrast, when you type a statement you are just adding another line to the program, and BASIC does not execute the statement until later. As you study BASIC you will learn additional commands.

Command
An order to the computer to perform some function immediately.

When you type RUN, BASIC translates and executes the statements one at a time. When it executes lines 10, 20, and 30, nothing is displayed on the screen, so you cannot see what is happening. But when line 40 is executed, the answer, 156.25, is displayed. When line 50 is executed, execution stops, and the Ok prompt is displayed again.

Tracing the Program

Let's pause for a moment from developing the program to consider exactly what happens when BASIC executes a program. The best way of doing that is to execute the program, line by line, just the way BASIC does. We call this **tracing** the program. To begin, set up on paper a box for each variable, as we did earlier when we were following the execution of LET statements.

Tracing
Executing a program by hand, line by line, and keeping track of the changing values of the variables.

When BASIC executes a program, it always starts with the lowest line number. For Program 2.2, it starts with line 10. when BASIC executes line 10, it puts a 6.25 in the PAY.RATE box and so should you (see Figure 2.3a). BASIC then moves to the next line, which in this case is line 20. It executes

Statement	PAY.RATE	HOURS	GROSS.PAY
a) 10 PAY.RATE = 6.25	6.25		
b) 20 HOURS = 25	6.25	25	
c) 30 GROSS.PAY = PAY.RATE * HOURS	6.25	25	156.25

FIGURE 2.3   **Tracing Program 2.2.**

line 20 by putting a 25 in the HOURS box (see Figure 2.3b). BASIC next executes line 30. Line 30 tells BASIC to take the number in the PAY.RATE box, which is 6.25, and multiply it by the number in the HOURS box, which is 25. The answer, which is 156.25, is put in the GROSS.PAY box. You should also put a 156.25 in the GROSS.PAY box (Figure 2.3c). Line 40 tells BASIC to display the number that is in the GROSS.PAY box. Recall that in Program 2.2, when the program was executed the answer displayed was 156.25. Finally, the END statement in line 50 is executed. This causes execution to stop and the Ok prompt to be displayed.

Tracing is valuable because it helps you understand how a BASIC program is executed. Later in this chapter, you will see another use of tracing.

Additional Commands

Besides the RUN command you learned earlier, to use a PC effectively you will have to use several other BASIC commands.

THE LIST COMMAND

Typing the command LIST causes the current version of your program to be displayed. You can type LIST whenever you see the Ok prompt.

If your program is large, you may want to list only part of it. To do so, include the line numbers of the first and last lines you want listed. For example,

LIST 30–120

lists lines 30 to 120. To list from the beginning of the program, include a hyphen before the ending line number. For example,

LIST –120

lists the lines from the beginning of the program to line 120. To list to the end of the program, include a hyphen after the starting line number. For example, the command

LIST 30–

lists the lines from line 30 to the end of the program. To list one line, include just the number of the desired line. For example,

LIST 70

lists line 70.

When you list the program, you will see that BASIC converts reserved words and variable names to uppercase. You will also see that lines are listed in their numerical order. BASIC always puts lines in their numerical order, not in the order in which they are typed.

THE SAVE COMMAND

Suppose you have a program that you would like to use in the future. You know that when you turn off the computer the program in RAM will be erased. You can have BASIC save a copy of your program on a diskette or on a fixed disk by using the command SAVE.

File
A program (or other data) that is given a filename and is stored on a diskette or fixed disk.

When a program is saved, it is known as a **file**; when you use the SAVE command, you must specify the **filename** that you want to have associated with the file. You will use the same name when you want to retrieve the file. The name you choose for the file may consist of from one to eight symbols,

Filename
The name of a file.

which may include letters, digits, and the characters ( ) { } @ # $ % & ! — _ ' / and ~. The first symbol must be a letter. A name may not contain a blank space or a period. But it *must* be enclosed in quotation marks.

The command

SAVE "BUTCHER"

writes the program in RAM to the disk and names it BUTCHER.BAS. The three letters BAS, in the filename BUTCHER.BAS, are called the **filename extension**. They and the period are automatically added by BASIC.

Filename extension
Up to three characters that may be added to the end of a filename. BASIC automatically uses BAS as the filename extension.

Of course, to save a program you must have a diskette in the diskette drive. You can save programs on the disk you used to start BASIC or on a separate diskette, provided the diskette was formatted. Your instructor will tell you the procedure followed at your school. If you will be using a separate diskette, you can refer to Appendix E to learn how to format it.

If you save a program with the same name you used previously, the new version of the program replaces the old version. For example, suppose you save a program with the name BUTCHER. Then you discover and correct errors in that program. When you execute the command SAVE "BUTCHER" again, the new, corrected version of BUTCHER replaces the old, erroneous version.

A program is saved on the DOS default drive, which, as you learned in Chapter 1, is usually drive A. You can specify an alternative drive by including the drive letter followed by a colon, for example,

SAVE "B:TAX"

Device name
The name of the device that is to be used with a command. The name always ends in a colon (:). In this book, the device names used are A: and B:, which refer to the A and B diskette drives.

This command writes the program in RAM to the diskette in drive B and names it TAX.BAS. B: is called the **device name**. Notice that there are no spaces between the drive letter and the colon or between the colon and the filename.

There is a trick you can use to save a little typing. The closing quotation marks are not required on a command. Thus, the command

SAVE "PAYROLL

is valid.

THE LOAD COMMAND

You can retrieve a previously saved program by using the command LOAD. For example, to retrieve the BUTCHER program we saved earlier, we could use the command

LOAD "BUTCHER"

If the file is not on the DOS default drive, you can specify the drive, just as we did in the SAVE command:

LOAD "B:TAX"

Loading a program does not alter the disk; the program is still stored on the disk and can be loaded as many times as you wish. When you load a program, the program is retrieved from secondary storage and placed into RAM, erasing the program that was there. The program is not listed or executed. When you see BASIC's Ok prompt, it is as though you had just typed the program. You can then correct the program, list it, or execute it.

THE NEW COMMAND

The NEW command is used to erase the current program from RAM. It must be used when you want to start working on a new program. If you forget to use NEW, the program in RAM will be a combination of lines left over from the old program and lines you have typed for the new program—in other words, a complete mess. To use this command, you simply type

NEW

NEW does not clear the screen; to do that, you use the Ctrl + Home keys.

Usually before you erase the program in RAM, you would save it. A typical sequence is to develop a program, type SAVE and the filename to save it, type NEW to clear RAM, and then work on a new program.

Using the Function Keys

You can use the function keys (see Figures 1.4(a) and (b)) to type BASIC commands with just one or two keystrokes. You may have noticed numbers and commands at the bottom of the BASIC screen. These refer to the function key numbers and how they may be used. For example, the first part of the line says

1LIST

This means that pressing the F1 function key is the same as typing the word LIST. So if you want to list your program, you only have to press the F1 key and then press the Enter key. If you want to list only part of your program, press the F1 key, type the line numbers you want to list, and then press the Enter key.

Similarly, the F2 key means RUN←. The ← stands for the Enter key and means that pressing the F2 key is the same as typing RUN and pressing the Enter key. So if you want to execute your program, all you have to do is press the F2 key; you need not press the Enter key.

Pressing function key F4 is the same as typing SAVE", so when you want to save a program, using F4 can save a little typing. Pressing the F3 function key is equivalent to typing LOAD".

You will learn how to use the other function keys when you need them.

Correcting Syntax Errors

Bugs
Errors in a program.

Debugging
Eliminating errors (bugs) in a program.

So far we have been discussing an ideal situation, one in which no errors were made. Unfortunately, when you write BASIC programs, you will frequently make errors, so it is important to know how to correct them. Errors are often called **bugs**, and the process of correcting errors is called **debugging**. The last three steps of our structured procedure are designed to help you debug your programs.

The simplest errors are typing errors. If you hit the wrong key, you can use the Backspace key to backspace, type the correct character, and continue.

Sometimes, however, you will not notice a mistake until after you have pressed the Enter key. At that point, it is too late to use the Backspace key. In Chapter 4, you will learn how to use the BASIC Program Editor to correct such errors, but for now you can simply retype the line, number and all, correctly. Whenever you retype a line, the new version of that line replaces the old version. You do not have to retype the line immediately. For example, suppose you type lines 10, 20, and 30 and then notice that you made a mistake in line 10. At that point, after you have typed line 30, if you retype line 10, the new version of line 10 will replace the old version.

You might also make a typing error, but not notice it. For example, let's assume you make a mistake and type line 40 as

```
40 PRITN GROSS.PAY
```

If you do not notice this mistake and go on to type RUN, BASIC will display an error message like that in Program 2.3. You get this message because when you type RUN, BASIC translates your statements into machine language. PRITN GROSS.PAY is not a legal BASIC statement and therefore cannot be translated into machine language. BASIC will always tell you when your program contains a **syntax error**, a mistake that produces a statement that is not legal in BASIC.

Syntax error
A violation of the rules for writing BASIC statements.

The sixth step in developing a program, then, is to correct syntax errors. To help you find and correct them, BASIC displays not only an error message with the line number of the illegal statement, but also the illegal statement. Later we will discuss faster ways to correct illegal statements; for now, you can just press the Enter key and replace the line by retyping it correctly, as shown in Program 2.3. (Notice that you can replace a line by retyping it even after you have typed RUN.)

In Program 2.3, after line 40 was corrected, the LIST command was used to list the program. You can see that the corrected line 40 replaced the original version. It is not necessary to list a program after correcting a syntax error, but it helps you make sure that the correction was made as you intended.

After you correct syntax errors, you must type RUN again to have a program executed. If your corrections were right, your program should execute properly. Program 2.3 shows that the program executed properly after line 40 was corrected.

Most of the time, your syntax errors will be the result of simple typing errors, and you will spot the mistake as soon as you look at the statement, as

```
10 PAY.RATE = 6.25
20 HOURS = 25
30 GROSS.PAY = PAY.RATE * HOURS
40 PRITN GROSS.PAY          ← ( Line 40 typed incorrectly )
50 END


RUN
Syntax error in 40          ← ( Error message )
Ok
40 PRITN GROSS.PAY          ← ( BASIC displays illegal statement. Press Enter key. )

40 PRINT GROSS.PAY          ← ( Retype line correctly )
LIST  ←                        ( List program )
10 PAY.RATE = 6.25
20 HOURS = 25
30 GROSS.PAY = PAY.RATE * HOURS
40 PRINT GROSS.PAY          ← ( Correct line 40 replaces incorrect version )
50 END
Ok
RUN  ←  ( Run again )
 156.25 ←                   ( Correct answer )
Ok
```

PROGRAM 2.3   **Correcting a syntax error—misspelling a reserved word.**

```
10 WIDTH = 5
20 LENGTH = 15
30 AREA = WIDTH * LENGTH
40 PRINT AREA
50 END

RUN  ◄──( Run program )
Syntax error in 10  ◄──( Error message )
Ok
10 WIDTH = 5  ◄──( Computer displays illegal statement. Press Enter key. )

10 WDTH = 5  ◄──( Return line correctly )

RUN  ◄──( Run again )
Syntax error in 30
Ok
30 AREA = WIDTH * LENGTH  ◄──( Line 30 still contains an error )
```

PROGRAM 2.4   **Correcting a syntax error—using a reserved word as a variable name.**

we did in Program 2.3. Sometimes, however, the error will be the result of a more subtle mistake and won't be immediately obvious. In that case, you should compare your statement with the correct syntax of the statement given in the Syntax Summary or in Appendix D. If after that comparison you still can't locate the error, you should suspect that you used a reserved word as a variable name. Program 2.4 illustrates this kind of error. As you can see, the statement that BASIC is complaining about, line 10, looks perfectly correct. But if you check the list of reserved words in Appendix A, you'll find that WIDTH is a reserved word. Program 2.4 shows that after changing the variable name in line 10 to WDTH and running the program again, we got a syntax error for line 30. Determining what is wrong with line 30 and how to fix it will be left as an exercise.

Another easy error to make is including a space in a variable name. For example, if you use the variable named SALE PRICE in the LET statement

SALE PRICE = .80 * REGULAR.PRICE

BASIC will display the Syntax error message. Sometimes in a case like this, you might get so involved looking for a subtle error that you overlook the space in SALE PRICE.

■ *Checking the Answers*

Once you have gotten BASIC to execute a program and print an answer, you must check to make sure the answer is correct. To do this you must compare the answer you hand-calculated in step 3 with the figures displayed by the computer. This check is the seventh step of our structured procedure. If the figures agree, your program is free of logic errors and you are finished.

LOGIC ERRORS

Logic error
An error in a program that causes the program to produce the wrong answer.

You may find, however, that the figures do not agree. If so, your program has given the wrong answer. A program that executes but gives the wrong answer is said to contain a **logic error**.

How can a program give the wrong answer? Easily enough. Suppose, for example, that you incorrectly typed line 30 as

```
30 GROSS.PAY = PAY.RATE + HOURS
```

Program 2.5 contains this incorrect line 30. Notice that BASIC does not print any messages about this line containing a syntax error. Why not? Because the expression PAY.RATE + HOURS is perfectly legal in BASIC! Of course, adding PAY.RATE and HOURS does not make any sense if you are trying to calculate GROSS.PAY, but BASIC does not know that. If you tell it to add PAY.RATE and HOURS, that is what it will do. We know, though, that the program has a logic error because its answer, 31.25, does not agree with the 156.25 we calculated by hand.

Correcting logic errors is the eighth and final step of our systematic procedure. Since BASIC does not indicate that a particular line is wrong, logic errors are more difficult to find and correct than syntax errors. BASIC does offer some sophisticated debugging aids that you will learn about in later chapters. But for now, the best way of discovering logic errors is to trace the program as we did earlier.

In order to trace the program, you must first make sure that you and BASIC are executing the same program. After you have run your program, made some corrections, and rerun the program, the screen will be a confused assemblage of your original typing, the computer's output, and your corrections. Nowhere on the screen will there appear the current version of the program. By typing LIST, you will get to see the current version of the program. Therefore, as a general rule, you should always LIST your program before you start to correct logic errors. In fact, it is a good idea to list your program whenever BASIC gives you unexpected output.

Program 2.5 also shows that, after the incorrect answer was printed, the program was listed and line 30 was corrected. To have BASIC execute

```
10 PAY.RATE = 6.25
20 HOURS = 25
30 GROSS.PAY = PAY.RATE + HOURS          + typed instead of *
40 PRINT GROSS.PAY
50 END

RUN          Run program
 31.25       Incorrect answer
Ok
LIST         List program
10 PAY.RATE = 6.25
20 HOURS = 25
30 GROSS.PAY = PAY.RATE + HOURS          Incorrect operation
40 PRINT GROSS.PAY
50 END
Ok
30 GROSS.PAY = PAY.RATE * HOURS          Retype line correctly

RUN          Run again
 156.25      Correct answer
Ok
```

PROGRAM 2.5   **Correcting a logic error—using an incorrect mathematical operation.**

```
10 PAY.RATE = 6.25
20 HOURS = 25
30 GROSS.PAY = PAYRATE * HOURS
40 PRINT GROSS.PAY
50 END

RUN  ←——( Run program )
  0  ←——( Gross pay is zero )
Ok
```

PROGRAM 2.6   **A program with a logic error—using an uninitialized variable.**

your program again, you must type the command RUN. As you can see, the program finally produced the correct answer, 156.25.

Another kind of logic error is shown in Program 2.6. We know the program has a logic error because it printed 0 as the value of GROSS.PAY. The source of the error is the misspelling of PAY.RATE as PAYRATE in line 30. When BASIC evaluated the expression in line 30, it needed the number in the PAYRATE box but found no number there (when line 10 was executed, 6.25 was put in the PAY.RATE box). BASIC's response was to use zero for PAYRATE. Anytime you use a variable without first assigning a value to the variable, BASIC assumes that you wanted that variable to be zero!

Uninitialized variable
A variable to which a value has not been assigned.

This kind of error is called using an **uninitialized variable**, because a variable is used before it is assigned a value. Unfortunately, BASIC does not stop and print an error message warning you that you are using an uninitialized variable.

In a long, complicated program, finding uninitialized variables can be particularly difficult. That is why the first step of our procedure, choosing names for variables, is so important. If you write down the variable names you have chosen and keep the list handy when you write the program, you will be less likely to use two different names for a variable.

The REM Statement

It is a good idea to use REM statements like those in Program 2.7 to include the title of the program, your name, the date, the list of variable names, and any other information you think someone reading your program would find helpful. Every program you write should contain such REM statements. Including comments in your program that will be helpful to someone who reads it is called **documenting** a program. The syntax of the REM statement is

Documenting
Adding comments to a program to explain what the program does and how it does it.

```
REM any comment you like
```

You can use an apostrophe instead of the word REM, as in

```
'any comment you like
```

Apostrophes are also used in Program 2.7 to insert blank lines, thus improving the readability.

When BASIC encounters a REM statement, it knows that that line contains a comment that is not supposed to be translated into machine language, and BASIC completely ignores it. Thus, REM statements have *no effect* on the answers produced by the program. You can use as many REM state-

```
10 REM *** BUTCHER SHOP PROBLEM ***
20 REM Programmer: Michael Trombetta        Date: April 6, 1990
30 '
40 REM This program calculates gross pay by multiplying
50 REM pay rate by hours worked.
60 '
70 REM       Variables Used in the Program
80 REM       GROSS.PAY      Gross pay
90 REM       HOURS          Hours worked
100 REM      PAY.RATE       Pay rate
110 '
120 PAY.RATE = 6.25
130 HOURS = 25
140 GROSS.PAY = PAY.RATE * HOURS
150 PRINT GROSS.PAY
160 END

RUN
 156.25
Ok
```

PROGRAM 2.7   **Using REM statements to document a program.**

ments as you like and place them anywhere in the program. Since REM statements are not part of the logic of the program, they are not shown on the flowchart.

Beginners often underestimate the importance of documenting programs. Experience shows that programs are almost always modified. Nothing is more frustrating than trying to modify a program you wrote only a short time ago and discovering that you cannot because you don't understand it. You could wind up spending as much time trying to understand the program as you did developing it.

Notice that the comments in the REM statements contain both capital letters and lowercase letters. BASIC converts only reserved words and variable names to capital letters.

Reviewing the Eight-Step Procedure

Now that we have completely solved a problem using our eight-step procedure, let's review it. When solving a problem on a computer, most people are tempted to jump immediately to Step 5, "Enter the program and execute it." *Resist this temptation!* Step 2, "Develop an algorithm for solving the problem," is the hardest and most important step. If you don't have a correct algorithm, then everything else you do will be a waste of time. Typically, Step 2 requires up to 75 percent of the total time spent solving the problem.

The second most important step is Step 4, "Write the BASIC program." When you write a program, you should carefully check the syntax of the statements you use. It is far better to avoid syntax errors from the start than to have to correct them later. The first four steps do *not* require a computer. They require human thought. If you have thoroughly and carefully completed Steps 1 through 4, then Step 6, "Correct syntax errors," and Step 8, "Correct logic errors," will require no time.

Although the procedure is presented here as eight sequential steps, in practice you may have to backtrack. For example, you may develop an algorithm (Step 2), but when you calculate an answer by hand (Step 3), you may discover that the algorithm is incorrect. You would then have to return to Step 2. Similarly, when you write the program (Step 4), you may discover that you omitted a variable. In that case, you would return to Step 1 and add that variable to your list of variable names.

Executing Statements in Direct Mode

Earlier we said that one difference between commands and statements is that commands never have line numbers. Actually the difference between statements and commands is mainly a matter of tradition, because it is possible to enter most statements without line numbers. When you enter a statement without a line number, BASIC executes it immediately. When a statement is entered without a line number, we say it is entered in **direct mode**. In **indirect mode**, a statement is entered with a line number and stored in the computer's memory until the program is run.

Entering statements in direct mode allows you to use the computer as a calculator. For example, the statement

                        PRINT 6.25 * 25

will cause 156.25 to be displayed on the screen. You can even enter a series of statements, such as

                    PAY.RATE = 6.25
                    HOURS = 25
                    GROSS.PAY = PAY.RATE * HOURS
                    PRINT GROSS.PAY

These statements also cause 156.25 to be displayed on the screen.

If direct mode is so effective and easy, why do we use indirect mode most of the time? Simply because it is faster in the long run. Direct mode provides one answer for one set of data. If you want to change any of those data, you must retype *all* the statements in direct mode. Certainly, you would not want to retype a long program over and over. Nevertheless, entering statements in direct mode is helpful when you are calculating answers by hand. And as you will see in Chapter 7, it is even more helpful when you are trying to debug a complicated program.

Direct mode
The operating style in which a statement is entered without a line number.

Indirect mode
The operating style in which a statement is entered with a line number.

Getting the Bugs Out

Problem: When you try to save a file, BASIC displays the error message.

                        Disk not Ready

Reason: Either there is no disk in the drive or the drive door is open.

Solution: Insert a disk into the drive or close the door and retype the command.

Problem: When you try to save a file, BASIC displays the error message

                        Type mismatch

Reason: You forgot to put the filename inside the quotation marks.

Solution: Retype the SAVE command correctly.

Problem: When you try to load a file, BASIC displays the error message

File not found

Reason: You typed the filename incorrectly.

Solution: Check the name you used when you saved the file and retype the command.

EXERCISES

2.10 Explain why BASIC found a syntax error on line 30 in Program 2.4. How would you fix it?

2.11 Several students are trying to correct the syntax error in Program 2.6. Moe says you must change PAYRATE in line 30 to PAY.RATE. Larry says you must change PAY.RATE in line 10 to PAYRATE. Curly says it doesn't matter as long as you spell the variable the same in lines 10 and 30. Who is correct?

*2.12 In Program 2.2, interchange the order of lines 10 and 20. Trace the program to determine what the output will be.

2.13 In Program 2.2, interchange the order of lines 40 and 50. Trace the program to determine what the output will be.

*2.14 Trace the following program to determine what the output will be:

```
10 A = 6
20 B = 8
30 C = A + B
40 D = A - B
50 PRINT A, B, C, D
60 END
```

2.15 Trace the following program to determine what the output will be:

```
10 P = 24
20 M = P / 4
30 R = 2 * M
40 PRINT P, M, R
50 END
```

2.16 How do you know if a program contains a syntax error? A logic error?

*2.17 How do you correct a syntax error? A logic error?

2.18 Program 2.8 shows a solution to Programming Assignment 2.4 that contains a logic error. How would you fix the error?

2.19 What would be printed by this one-line program?

```
10 PRINT A, B, C, D
```

2.20 Write the statement to add the comment

Programmer: Roy G. Biv

to a program.

2.21 Write the statement to display the values of the variables WEIGHT, VOLUME, and DENSITY.

2.22 Write the command to list lines 30 through 60 on the screen.

2.23 Write the command to store a program that is currently in RAM on the diskette in the DOS default drive, using the filename PGM1.

2.24 Write the command to retrieve a program called FIRSTPGM, which is stored on the diskette in drive B.

2.25 Write the command to erase the current program from RAM.

```
10 REM *** CONVERTING OUNCES TO GRAMS ***
20 REM Programmer: Michael Trombetta      Date: April 8, 1990
30 REM This program converts a weight given in ounces to grams
40 REM      Variables Used in the Program
50 REM         OUNCES        Weight in ounces
60 REM         GRAMS         Weight in grams
70 OUNCES = 13
80 PRINT GRAMS
90 END

RUN
 0
Ok
```

PROGRAM 2.8   An incorrect solution to Programming Assignment 2.4.

PROGRAMMING ASSIGNMENTS

In these and other programming assignments, to get printed copies of each program and its answers you should (1) make sure the program is running perfectly; (2) use Ctrl + Home *keys to clear the screen; (3)* LIST *the program; (4)* RUN *the program; and (5) use the Print Screen key to print the screen. You should then* SAVE *the program so you can refer to it later. Use a filename that will help you remember which assignment the program goes with. For example, the solution to the first programming assignment in this chapter should be saved with the filename* P2–1. *(You should not try to use the filename* P2.1—*why?)*

2.12 Enter the program given in Program 2.2 into your computer. Try to make syntax errors so you will get experience correcting them. After the program is working, give yourself a raise to $7 an hour.

2.13 Enter and execute the programs you wrote as answers to the programming assignments earlier in this chapter. Correct syntax and logic errors. Remember to use the NEW command to clear RAM before you start a new program.

SUMMARY

In this chapter you have learned that

☐ A structured procedure for solving problems using a computer involves
1. Choosing names for the variables in the problem.
2. Developing an algorithm for solving the problem.
3. Calculating an answer to the problem by hand.
4. Writing a BASIC program.
5. Entering the program and executing it.
6. Correcting syntax errors.
7. Checking the computer's answer against the answer you calculated by hand in Step 3.
8. Correcting logic errors.

☐ Variable names may consist of capital letters, digits, and the period. A variable name must start with a letter and may contain up to 40 characters. A reserved word may not be used as a variable name.

☐ Flowcharts are helpful when you are developing an algorithm and when you are trying to understand someone else's algorithm.

☐ Every line in a BASIC program begins with a line number, and every BASIC statement begins with a reserved word.

☐ To add, use +; to subtract, use −; to multiply, use *; to divide, use /.

☐ In a syntax statement, words in capital letters represent BASIC reserved words and must be typed as shown; words in lowercase letters represent values supplied by the programmer. Square brackets ([ ]) enclose optional parts of the statement, and ellipses (...) indicate that the previous item may be repeated as often as you want.

☐ A LET statement is used to compute a value.

☐ A PRINT statement is used to display answers.

☐ An END statement is used to mark the end of a BASIC program.

☐ A BASIC statement may contain up to 255 characters.

☐ If you use a variable without assigning it a value, BASIC gives it the value zero.

□ To trace a program, set up on paper boxes that correspond to the storage locations that BASIC assigns to each variable. Then execute each line in the program, putting values in the boxes, just as BASIC puts values in the storage locations. Tracing is helpful in understanding how a program works and in correcting logic errors.

□ The RUN command is used to execute a program.

□ The LIST command is used to list a program on the screen.

□ The SAVE command is used to save a program on a diskette.

□ The LOAD command is used to retrieve a program from a diskette.

□ The NEW command is used to clear RAM to start a new program.

□ You can correct syntax errors by retyping the incorrect statements.

□ A REM statement is used to add comments to a program.

□ A PC may be used as a calculator by entering statements in direct mode.

KEY TERMS IN THIS CHAPTER

algorithm 17
arithmetic step 17
bugs 30
command 27
debugging 30
device name 29
direct mode 36
documenting 34
expression 22
file 28

filename 29
filename extension 29
flowchart 17
flowline 17
indirect mode 36
input/output symbol 18
logic error 32
numeric (ordinary) variable 15
process symbol 18

statement 20
string 16
string variable 15
syntax error 31
syntax statement 21
terminal symbol 17
tracing 27
uninitialized variable 34
variable 15

QUESTIONS FOR REVIEW

2.1 Which statement is used to display answers on the screen?

2.2 What is the name of the flowchart symbol

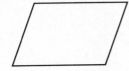

2.3 Indicate which of the following LET statements contain errors. Rewrite the incorrect statements correctly.
   a) B4 = C + E
   b) N = $625.00
   c) A = Y MINUS Q
   d) KEY = 415 / DOOR

2.4 Which statement is used to store the program that is in RAM on a diskette?

2.5 When BASIC puts a new value into a storage location, what happens to the value that was there?

2.6 In a syntax statement, what do brackets mean? What do words printed in capital letters represent?

2.7 Which command is used to execute a program?

2.8 Which characters may be used in a variable name?

2.9 Which command is used to list a program?

2.10 What is debugging?

2.11 What does the NEW command do? When do you use it?

2.12 What is a logic error?

2.13 Which statement is used to retrieve a program from a diskette?

2.14 Which statement is used to include documentation in a program?

2.15 When you type a BASIC program, you must end each line by pressing which key?

2.16 What happens if you use a reserved word as a variable name?

2.17 What is a syntax error?

2.18 What happens when a statement is entered in direct mode?

2.19 How many characters may a filename contain?

2.20 What does it mean if you execute a LOAD command and, instead of retrieving a program, BASIC displays the error message File not found?

Writing Complete Programs

BASIC OBJECTIVES OF THIS CHAPTER

☐ To write programs that process many cases

☐ To use trailer data to end program execution

☐ To use string variables

☐ To supply rules for the BASIC statements GOTO, INPUT, LPRINT, and IF

☐ To supply rules for the BASIC commands LLIST, AUTO, FILES, NAME, KILL, and SYSTEM

In Chapter 2, we calculated gross pay for one person—you. To use that program to calculate gross pay for a different employee, we would have to retype lines 120 and 130 in Program 2.7 using the new employee's pay rate and hours worked. This procedure is obviously inconvenient. In this chapter, you will learn an easy way to have a computer calculate gross pay for any number of employees. You will also learn how BASIC programs process data that consist of letters, such as a name. Finally you will learn some additional commands that help in writing BASIC programs.

A PAYROLL PROBLEM WITH MANY EMPLOYEES

Let's develop a program to solve the following problem. Suppose you get a job in the data processing department of the Bat-O Boat Company. Bat-O is a small firm with only three hourly employees. Their pay rates and hours worked last week are

Employee Number	Pay Rate	Hours Worked
1	6.75	40
2	6.00	30
3	5.75	25

Your first assignment is to write a program to calculate and print the gross pay for these three employees.

Variable Names

Following our structured procedure, you should begin by choosing variable names. The names used in Chapter 2 will do quite well here:

Pay rate   PAY.RATE
Hours worked   HOURS
Gross pay   GROSS.PAY

Notice that although there are three employees, each with a different pay rate, you should define only one pay rate variable, PAY.RATE. This one PAY.RATE will be used for all the employees. Similarly, define only one HOURS and one GROSS.PAY.

Algorithm

The second step is to develop an algorithm. The algorithm for this problem is similar to that used in Chapter 2.

1. Accept values for PAY.RATE and HOURS for an employee.
2. Calculate GROSS.PAY by multiplying PAY.RATE by HOURS.
3. Print PAY.RATE, HOURS, and GROSS.PAY.
4. Repeat steps 1 through 3 until all employees have been processed.

To expand on the algorithm in preparation for writing a BASIC program, you should draw a flowchart. A flowchart illustrating this algorithm is shown in Figure 3.1. Several aspects of this flowchart differ from the one we discussed in Chapter 2. First, because we anticipate that the program will contain a REM statement in line 10, the first box number used is 20. Second, box 20 is an input/output symbol containing the word INPUT. Third, box 30 shows the multiplication of PAY.RATE by HOURS with an asterisk. Since the reason for drawing a flowchart is to help in writing the BASIC program, it makes sense to use the same multiplication symbol in the flowchart as in the program. Finally, box 40 shows an LPRINT statement.

Notice that step 3 of the algorithm and box 40 in the flowchart call for BASIC to print PAY.RATE and HOURS as well as GROSS.PAY. Since this program will calculate GROSS.PAY for three employees, it is helpful to print PAY.RATE and HOURS as well as GROSS.PAY, so we can tell which GROSS.PAY goes with which PAY.RATE and HOURS.

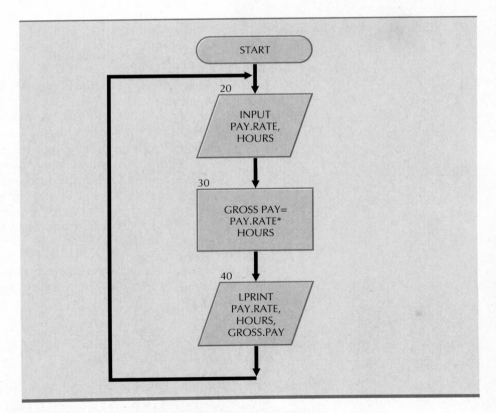

FIGURE 3.1   **Flowchart for payroll with more than one employee.**

Printing PAY.RATE and HOURS also can help you locate and eliminate logic errors. Suppose BASIC prints an incorrect value for GROSS.PAY. We know we have a logic error, but we do not know where it is. You can easily check the printed values of PAY.RATE and HOURS against their proper values. If they are correct, you know that the logic error must be in the calculation of GROSS.PAY. If they are not correct, the error must be in the statements that assign values to PAY.RATE and HOURS.

The most important new feature of the flowchart shown in Figure 3.1 is the flowline that goes from box 40 to box 20. The flowline indicates that after BASIC executes line 40 it should execute line 20. Thus, the flowline establishes a **loop**. Loops are important in computer programming because the typical computer programming problem has the following structure:

Loop
A series of instructions that are executed repeatedly.

1. Get the data for a case. (A case might be an employee, an inventory item, etc.) This is the input step.
2. Calculate the answer for the case. This is the process step.
3. Print the answer for the case. This is the output step.
4. Repeat steps 1, 2, and 3 until all the cases have been processed. This is the repeat step.

Notice that the algorithm for this problem involves exactly these four steps. You will meet this basic sequence (input, process, output, repeat) many times as you study this book.

Because of the loop, the flowchart in Figure 3.1 does not have a logical endpoint, so it does not contain an end terminal symbol. As you will see, however, the program will contain an END statement.

Hand-Calculated Answer

In the third step of our structured procedure, you must calculate an answer by hand. For employee number 1, GROSS.PAY is $6.75 \times 40 = 270$. That's all you have to do! You do not need to calculate GROSS.PAY for the other two employees. If the computer's answer agrees with your hand-calculated answer for one employee, you can assume that the program is correct and need not check the answers for the other employees.

Now you can see why computers are useful, even though it is necessary to calculate an answer by hand. If you can prove that a program is correct for one case, you can then use that program to calculate two, two thousand, or even two million additional cases and be sure the answers for these additional cases are correct. (In Chapter 5, you will learn that in more complicated problems it is necessary to check more than one case. But the basic idea remains the same: You prove that a program is correct by checking a limited number of cases and then use that program to calculate many additional cases.)

The BASIC Program

The fourth step of our structured procedure is to write a BASIC program. Program 3.1 shows a program based on the flowchart in Figure 3.1. Notice that there are three new statements in this program: the INPUT statement in line 20, the LPRINT statement in line 40, and the GOTO statement in line 50.

```
10 REM  *** BAT-O PROGRAM ***
20 INPUT "Enter Pay Rate and Hours Worked"; PAY.RATE, HOURS
30   GROSS.PAY = PAY.RATE * HOURS
40   LPRINT PAY.RATE, HOURS, GROSS.PAY
50 GOTO 20
60 END
```

PROGRAM 3.1　　**A program for payroll with more than one employee.**

We'll discuss the INPUT statement later in this chapter. For now, let's explore the LPRINT and GOTO statements.*

THE LPRINT STATEMENT AND THE LLIST COMMAND

So far, our programs have displayed answers on the screen. Unfortunately, when the computer is turned off, the answers disappear. You can get a hard copy of your answers by using the LPRINT statement instead of the PRINT statement. The syntax of the LPRINT statement is

```
LPRINT expression, ...
```

Notice that the syntax of the LPRINT statement is just like that of a PRINT statement. It functions just like a PRINT statement, except that it sends the output to the printer instead of the screen.

In much the same way, you can instruct the computer to LIST a program on the printer, not the screen, by using the LLIST command, which differs in syntax from the LIST command only by having an extra L.

Line 40 in Program 3.2 shows an LPRINT statement for our payroll problem. In this and all future programs, a horizontal line is used to separate the output that appears on the screen (above the line) and the output that appears on the printer (below the line).

When you develop your programs, initially you should use PRINT statements instead of LPRINT statements. While you are debugging, it is more convenient to have your answers displayed on the screen rather than on the printer. When your program is completely debugged, you can change the PRINT statements to LPRINT statements to get a permanent copy of your answers.

THE GOTO STATEMENT

The GOTO statement shown on line 50 creates the loop that corresponds, in Figure 3.1, to the flowline that goes from box 40 to box 20. Remember from Chapter 2 that, after BASIC executes a particular line, it automatically goes to the next line. In this problem, however, after BASIC executes line 40, you want it to execute line 20. The GOTO statement allows you to change the order in which the lines are executed. After BASIC executes the statement GOTO 20, it will next execute the INPUT statement in line 20.

---

*Note that this program contains only one REM statement, which contains the program name. Unlike Program 2.7, it does not include REM statements with the programmer's name or with the definitions of the variable names used in the program. Since I wrote all the programs in this book, including a REM statement with my name in each program would just waste space. Similarly, since a list of variable name definitions is presented as part of the development of each program, including such a list in the program would waste space. Your programs, however, must stand on their own, so they *must* include REM statements with your name and the definitions of the variable names used in the program.

```
10 REM  *** BAT-O PROGRAM ***
20 INPUT "Enter Pay Rate and Hours Worked"; PAY.RATE, HOURS
30   GROSS.PAY = PAY.RATE * HOURS
40   LPRINT PAY.RATE, HOURS, GROSS.PAY
50 GOTO 20
60 END


RUN
Enter Pay Rate and Hours Worked? 6.75,40          ( BASIC prints prompt when it executes line 20 )
Enter Pay Rate and Hours Worked? 6,30      }  ( Enter Pay Rate and Hours for each employee )
Enter Pay Rate and Hours Worked? 5.75,25
Enter Pay Rate and Hours Worked?    ◄──      ( Use Ctrl and Break to break execution )
Break in 20
Ok
_____

6.75          40          270
6             30          180     }  ( Answers printed by line 40 )
5.75          25          143.75
```

PROGRAM 3.2   **Executing Program 3.1.**

The syntax of the GOTO statement is

GOTO line number

Using the Alt + G keys is equivalent to typing GOTO. The line number specified can be either higher or lower than the line number of the GOTO itself. For example, both of the following statements are correct:

70 GOTO 40
70 GOTO 110

You might wonder how you can know the line number to use when you want to go to a higher numbered line—a line you haven't written yet. (You can't use the line numbers on the flowchart, since those numbers are added to the flowchart after the program is written to show the connection between the flowchart and the program.) In simple programs, you can look ahead, but sometimes you will find you have to code a GOTO when you do not know the line number of the statement you want to go to. In that case, write the statement as GOTO? After the rest of the program has been written, *and before you enter it into the computer*, you can go back and change all the ?s to line numbers.

Branching statement
A statement that causes a change in the normal sequence of execution, so that BASIC executes some line other than the line with the next higher line number.

GOTO and other statements that cause a change in the order in which lines are executed are called **branching statements** because they cause BASIC to split off from the straight line sequence and go to a specified line number. For example, in Program 3.1, the GOTO in line 50 causes BASIC to go to line 20 instead of line 60. Because a branch occurs every time a GOTO statement is executed, it is called an **unconditional branching statement**.

■ *Entering and Executing the Program*

Unconditional branching statement
A statement that causes the same branch to be taken every time the statement is executed.

At this point, you should follow step 5 of our structured procedure and enter Program 3.1 into your PC. Notice that in Program 3.1 lines 30 and 40 are indented two spaces. BASIC does not require that these lines be indented, but the indentation helps show the loop more clearly and makes the program easier to read. You will find this convention used in all the programs in this book. You should follow the same convention in your programs.

After you have entered the program, type RUN to execute it. At this time you can correct any syntax errors, as called for in step 6 of our procedure. When the syntax errors have been corrected, and you then execute the program, BASIC will display the prompt Enter Pay Rate and Hours Worked?, as shown in Program 3.2. This prompt is produced by the INPUT statement in line 20.

THE INPUT STATEMENT

When you use an INPUT statement in a program, you are saying to BASIC, "Later I'll tell you the values I want to use for these variables." Then, when the program is executed and BASIC encounters the INPUT statement, it prints a prompt and waits for you to type the values you want to use, as if to say, "Now is the time to specify the values you want to use for these variables."

When you see the prompt, you must enter one value for each variable in the INPUT list, separating those values by commas. For example, if, as in Program 3.2, you type 6.75, 40 (and then press the Enter key), BASIC will assign 6.75 to PAY.RATE and 40 to HOURS and then continue executing the program.

The syntax of the INPUT statement is

```
INPUT[;] ["prompt";] variable, . . .
```

As noted in Chapter 2, the square brackets in a syntax statement indicate that the prompt is optional. If you do omit the prompt, BASIC prints only the question mark when the INPUT statement is executed. The ellipses indicate that the variable may be repeated as many times as you wish. The function of the optional semicolon directly after the word INPUT will be explained in Chapter 6. Using the Alt + I keys is equivalent to typing INPUT.

To cause the INPUT statement to print a prompt, you *must* enclose the prompt in quotation marks and separate it from the input variables by a semicolon. A prompt may contain any characters other than quotation marks.

Although the prompt is optional, you should always include one when you code an INPUT statement. If you don't, a user of the program (or even you several weeks after you have written the program) will not know what data are supposed to be entered or in what order. Imagine being confronted with just a question mark instead of the following "Enter" prompts:

INPUT Statement
```
INPUT "Enter shipping weight"; WEIGHT
```

Effect
Assigns the value entered to WEIGHT.

INPUT Statement

```
INPUT "Enter gallons and price"; GALLONS, PRICE
```

Effect

Assigns the first value entered to GALLONS and the second value entered to PRICE.

INPUT Statement

```
INPUT "Enter length, width, and depth"; LENGTH, WDTH, DEPTH
```

Effect

Assigns the first value entered to LENGTH, the second to WDTH, and the third to DEPTH. Notice that WIDTH is a reserved word and may not be used as a variable name.

Endless Loop

Endless loop
A loop that executes continuously.

After you have entered the data for the first employee, BASIC will print the pay rate, hours, and gross pay for that employee. It will then prompt you to input more data and will repeat this process as long as you enter new data, because this program contains an **endless input loop.** To tell BASIC that you are finished, hold down the Ctrl key and press the Scroll Lock/Break key on the upper right side of the keyboard. BASIC will then print the message Break in 20 that you see in Program 3.2.

You can use the Ctrl + Break keys *any time* to break execution of a BASIC program. It is particularly handy in dealing with endless loops, both input loops (like the one we have just discussed) and output loops. You might, for example, create an endless loop in which BASIC keeps printing the same answers over and over again. Using the Ctrl + Break keys will break execution of that loop.

Checking and Debugging the Program

The final two steps in our structured procedure are to check the computer's answer against a hand-calculated answer and, if the two answers do not agree, to correct logic errors. For the first employee in Program 3.2, BASIC printed a gross pay of 270. Since that was the value we calculated by hand, we can be sure our program is free of logic errors.

Tracing the Program

Now that you know the program works, let's trace it and see *how* it works. We begin by setting up boxes to hold the values of the variables PAY.RATE, HOURS, and GROSS.PAY. When you type RUN, BASIC starts by executing line 10, but since that is a REM statement, nothing happens, so BASIC goes on to line 20. When BASIC executes line 20, it prints a question mark and waits for you to enter the data. For the first employee, the data were 6.75, 40. BASIC puts the 6.75 into the PAY.RATE box and the 40 into the HOURS box, as shown in Figure 3.2(a). BASIC next executes line 30, which causes it to multiply the number in the PAY.RATE box by the number in the HOURS box and put the answer in the GROSS.PAY box. So, on paper, multiply 6.75 by 40 and put the answer, 270, in the GROSS.PAY box (see Figure 3.2b). Then BASIC executes

```
Statement                                   PAY.RATE   HOURS   GROSS.PAY
a)  20 INPUT PAY.RATE, HOURS                   6.75      40

b)  30 GROSS.PAY = PAY.RATE * HOURS            6.75      40        270

c)  20 INPUT PAY.RATE, HOURS                   6         30        270

d)  30 GROSS.PAY = PAY.RATE * HOURS            6         30        180
```

FIGURE 3.2   **Tracing Program 3.2.**

line 40 and prints the numbers in the PAY.RATE, HOURS, and GROSS.PAY boxes. Since Figure 3.2b shows that the numbers in the PAY.RATE, HOURS, and GROSS.PAY boxes are 6.75, 40, and 270, we expect a line of output containing these three numbers. Referring to Program 3.2 we see that 6.75, 40, and 270 are exactly what BASIC printed for its first line of output. So far, so good, but let us continue tracing.

When BASIC executes line 50, it branches to line 20 and requests a second set of data (6, 30). BASIC puts the 6 into the PAY.RATE box and the 30 into the HOURS box, as shown in Figure 3.2c. But because location boxes can hold only one number at a time, when a new number is put into a box, the old number is erased.

Now when BASIC executes line 30, it will multiply the 6 in the PAY.RATE box by the 30 in the HOURS box and put the answer, 180, in the GROSS.PAY box. As shown in Figure 3.2d, when BASIC puts the 180 in the GROSS.PAY box, the 270 that was there is erased. When BASIC executes line 40, it prints the numbers in the PAY.RATE, HOURS, and GROSS.PAY boxes, the numbers being in this case 6, 30, and 180. Referring to Program 3.2, we see that this is exactly what BASIC printed for its second line of output.

We developed the Bat-O program to calculate and print gross pay for three employees. It should be clear by now, however, that the same program could be used for any number of employees. You only need to keep entering a pay rate and a number of hours worked for each employee. BASIC will keep calculating and printing gross pay as long as you enter data.

Syntax Summary

LPRINT Statement
Form: LPRINT expression, . . .
Example: LPRINT HEIGHT, BASE, AREA
Interpretation: The values of the variables and/or expressions are printed on the printer.

GOTO Statement
Form: GOTO line number
Example: GOTO 20
Interpretation: BASIC branches to the specified line number and continues execution there.

INPUT Statement
Form: INPUT [;] ["prompt";] variable, . . .
Example: INPUT "Enter height and weight"; HEIGHT, WEIGHT
Interpretation: The prompt is displayed and the program waits for values to be entered from the keyboard. The values entered are assigned to the variables listed.

Getting the Bugs Out

Problem: You run a program that contains an LPRINT statement, but instead of giving you printed output, the computer seems to freeze. After some time the screen displays the message

```
Device Timeout in nn
```

or

```
Device Fault in nn
```

where nn is the line number of an LPRINT statement.

Reason: The printer is not ready.

Solution: Make sure the printer is turned on, that the On Line indicator is lit, and, if you share a printer, that the printer is switched to your computer. The same error occurs if you execute an LLIST command when the printer is not ready.

Problem: You enter data in response to an INPUT prompt and get the message

```
?Redo from start
```

Reason: You typed too many or too few values or you typed nonnumeric data (like typing a $ or a comma as part of a number).

Solution: Remember that you must enter one value for each variable in the INPUT list, that the values must be separated by commas, and that numeric data are entered as pure numbers. Reenter the data correctly.

Problem: During execution, BASIC displays the error message

```
Undefined line number nn
```

where nn is the line number of a GOTO statement.

Reason: The line number coded in the GOTO statement does not exist.

Solution: Correct the line number or add the missing line.

EXERCISES

3.1 Trace Program 3.2 for the third employee.

*3.2 Write an INPUT statement to accept three test scores. Invent any legal data names you like. Print a prompt.

3.3 Trace Program 3.2 to determine what output will be produced if the following changes are made. Before making each new change, assume that the program is restored to its original form.

*a) The LPRINT statement in line 40 is eliminated.

b) The LPRINT statement in line 40 is written as

```
40 LPRINT GROSS.PAY, HOURS, PAY.RATE
```

*c) The GOTO statement in line 50 is eliminated.

d) The GOTO statement in line 50 is changed to

```
50 GOTO 30
```

*e) The GOTO statement in line 50 is changed to

```
50 GOTO 40
```

f) The GOTO statement in line 50 is eliminated, and the following new statement is inserted:

```
35 GOTO 20
```

PROGRAMMING ASSIGNMENTS

. . . .

In each of the following programming assignments, you should develop your program by following our structured procedure. Be sure to use REM *statements to document your program, including your name and a list of variable names. Use a loop so your program is able to process multiple cases. Be sure to include a prompt for requesting input and to print the input data as well as the calculated answers. Save your program so you can use it in later assignments. These are the standard instructions that should be followed in all future programming assignments. To obtain output, follow these four steps: (1) Make sure the program is running perfectly; (2) change the* PRINT *statement to an* LPRINT *statement; (3)* LLIST *the program; and (4)* RUN *the program. Most of these assignments are modifications of assignments in Chapter 2. The earlier assignment number is given in parentheses at the end of the assignment, as in (PA 2.2).*

*3.1 All the used books at Twice Sold Tales are reduced 20 percent. Accept as input the usual price of an item. Write a program to calculate and print the sale price of the item. (PA 2.2)

3.2 Write a program that will accept any three numbers as input and print them in reverse order.

3.3 Accept as input the number of times different baseball players were at bat and the number of hits made. Write a program to calculate and print their batting averages. Hint: To calculate batting average, divide hits by at bats and multiply the quotient by 1000. (PA 2.6)

3.4 Accept as input the length and width of a room (in yards). Write a program to calculate and print the cost of a rug for the room. Assume the rug costs $18 a square yard. (PA 2.8)

*3.5 Scientists estimate that each hour spent watching *Loving Hospitals* causes ¼ cubic centimeter of the human brain to turn to oatmeal. The average human brain contains 1456 cubic centimeters. Write a program to accept as input the number of hours you have watched this soap and to calculate and print the percent of your brain that has turned to oatmeal. Do the same for several of your friends. (PA 2.10)

TRAILER DATA AND DECISIONS

. . . .

Although you might think that Program 3.2 works well, it in fact contains an error: an endless loop, which can be stopped only by using the Ctrl + Break keys. To eliminate endless loops, we have to be able to tell the program that we are finished entering data and that the program should stop executing.

One way to indicate that we have finished entering data in a problem like this one is to enter data for an imaginary employee after the data for the real employees have been entered. Because these data are entered after all the real data, they are called **trailer data.**

Trailer data
Extra data entered after all the real data to indicate that all the real data have been entered.

Trailer data must be so peculiar—so wildly outside of possibility—that the program cannot mistake them for real data. For instance, the pay rate for a real employee could never be negative, so a negative number is a good choice for the imaginary employee's pay rate.

The algorithm that uses trailer data to stop executing is

1. Accept PAY.RATE and HOURS for an employee.
2. If these are the trailer data, go to step 6.

3. Calculate GROSS.PAY by multiplying PAY.RATE by HOURS.
4. Print PAY.RATE, HOURS, and GROSS.PAY.
5. Repeat steps 1 through 4 for all employees.
6. Stop execution.

To implement step 2, we have to provide some way for the program to recognize the trailer data. We do that by using a decision. Figure 3.3 shows a revised flowchart for the Bat-O problem that includes a decision. The new feature of this flowchart is the **decision symbol**, which is in the shape of a diamond.

Inside the decision symbol we write a **condition.** In Figure 3.3, the condition is PAY.RATE = -1. We will discuss conditions in greater detail in Chapter 5, but for now in our conditions we will compare a variable with a constant. A condition is read as a question. The condition PAY.RATE = -1 is read, "Is PAY.RATE equal to -1?" Only when PAY.RATE really is equal to -1 is the condition true; otherwise, the condition is false. Notice that the condition PAY.RATE = -1 is very different from the LET statement PAY.RATE = -1. In

Decision symbol
A flowchart symbol in the shape of a diamond, used to show a decision.

Condition
An expression in which a variable is compared with another variable or with a constant. A condition is either true or false.

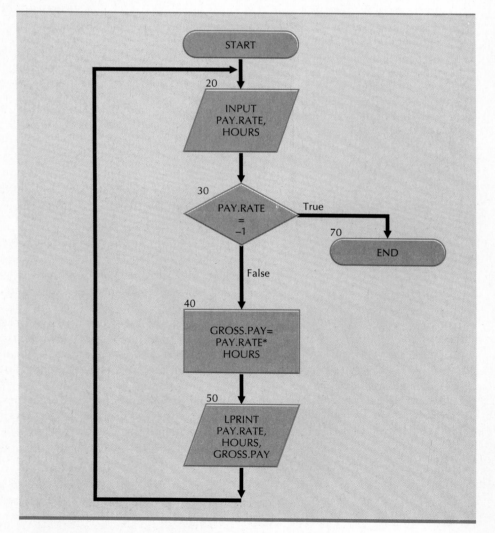

FIGURE 3.3   **Using trailer data to stop execution.**

a LET statement, you tell the computer to put the value of -1 in the PAY.RATE box. In a condition, you ask the computer to decide if PAY.RATE is equal to - 1. Similarly, in a flowchart PAY.RATE = -1 in a process (rectangular) box represents a LET statement, while the same statement in a diamond represents a condition.

Notice that Figure 3.3 shows two flowlines, or branches, leaving the decision symbol. One of the branches is labeled "True," the other "False." If the condition is true, we leave the decision symbol along the true branch. If the condition is false, we leave the decision symbol along the false branch. Because the branch that is taken depends on whether the condition is true or false, an IF statement is called a **conditional branching statement.**

Conditional branching statement
A statement that causes one branch to be taken if a condition is true and a different branch if the condition is false.

In this case, if PAY.RATE is equal to -1, the condition is true. The "True" branch leads to the END terminal symbol, and the program stops executing. So when we enter -1 for PAY.RATE, the program stops executing without the use of the Ctrl + Break keys.

If PAY.RATE is not equal to -1, the condition is false. The "False" branch leads to the process symbol in which GROSS.PAY is calculated. So when we enter real values for PAY.RATE, the program calculates GROSS.PAY, just as we want. In this way, adding trailer data and a decision step allows us to calculate the pay for as many employees as we wish and then to end the program by entering the trailer data.

A significant feature of Figure 3.3 is the placement of the decision. Whenever you use trailer data, the decision that tests for trailer data must immediately follow the INPUT step. Clearly it cannot be placed before the INPUT step, because at that point we don't have any data to test. Neither can it be placed after any process or printing steps, because then BASIC would be processing or printing the trailer data.

The IF Statement

Program 3.3 shows an improved payroll program based on the flowchart in Figure 3.3. In the program, the decision symbol is written as an IF statement:

```
30 IF PAY.RATE = -1
   THEN GOTO 70
```

THEN can be typed as Alt + T.

When BASIC executes line 30, it evaluates the condition PAY.RATE = -1. If the condition is true, the statement following the reserved word THEN is executed. In this case, BASIC will execute the statement GOTO 70 and branch to line 70. Line 70 contains the END statement, so the program will stop. If the condition is false, BASIC ignores the statement following THEN and executes the next line, a process sometimes called "falling through" the IF statement. In this case, if PAY.RATE has any value other than -1, BASIC will fall through the IF statement and execute line 40, where it will calculate GROSS.PAY. Thus, Program 3.3 produces the same output as Program 3.2, but by using trailer data we can end the program "gracefully."

A PAY.RATE of -1 is not the only possible trailer data for this problem. We might have used HOURS of -1 instead. In that case, the IF statement would have been

```
30 IF HOURS = -1
   THEN GOTO 70
```

The important point is to be sure that trailer data are *obvious* as such. For example, in Programming Assignment 2.5, which asks you to convert a price

```
10  REM   *** BAT-O PROGRAM ***
20  INPUT "Enter Pay Rate and Hours Worked, -1 to stop"; PAY.RATE, HOURS
30    IF PAY.RATE = -1
        THEN GOTO 70          } Test for trailer data
40    GROSS.PAY = PAY.RATE * HOURS
50    LPRINT PAY.RATE, HOURS, GROSS.PAY
60  GOTO 20
70  END

RUN
Enter Pay Rate and Hours Worked, -1 to stop? 6.75,40
Enter Pay Rate and Hours Worked, -1 to stop? 6,30      } Enter Pay Rate and Hours for each employee
Enter Pay Rate and Hours Worked, -1 to stop? 5.75,25
Enter Pay Rate and Hours Worked, -1 to stop? -1,0   <- Enter trailer data
Ok
```

```
6.75          40          270
6             30          180      } Answer printed by line 50
5.75          25          143.75
```

PROGRAM 3.3   **Using trailer data to stop execution.**

in yen to a price in dollars, a price of 0 yen is meaningless, so it makes good trailer data. If PRICE.YEN stands for the price in yen, then the IF statement could be

```
IF PRICE.YEN = 0
THEN GOTO nn
```

where nn is the line number of the END statement.

In Program 3.3, the INPUT prompt tells the user not only what data to enter, but also how to stop execution. Notice also how the trailer data are entered. The only function of these data is to set PAY.RATE equal to -1. However, since the INPUT statement expects data for the pay rate and hours, we must enter data for both variables. It doesn't matter what value is entered for the hours since it is never used, so here HOURS are set at 0.

In this chapter, you have learned a simplified version of the IF statement, whose syntax is

```
IF condition THEN GOTO line number
```

The syntax of the full IF statement is much more complex, and IF statements are used for more purposes than just determining whether trailer data have been entered. Until we get to Chapter 5, however, this simple version of the IF statement is all you will need.

The IF statement does not have to be written on two lines. But doing so makes the statement easier to read, just as indenting loops makes them stand out. For this reason, you should also indent your IF statements. However, indenting IF statements takes a little care. You cannot simply press the Enter key after you have typed the condition and continue the statement on the next line, because pressing the Enter key ends the statement. You could just hold down the Space Bar and allow the cursor to travel to the right edge of the screen and wrap around to the next line. But it is easier and faster to press Ctrl + Enter to move the cursor to the next line.

Syntax Summary   IF Statement (simplified version)
Form: `IF condition THEN GOTO line number`
Example: `IF AGE = 0`
                  `    THEN GOTO 90`
Interpretation: If the condition is true, the program
                  branches to the statement whose line number
                  is specified. If the condition is false, the
                  next statement is executed.

    Getting the   **Problem:**   You enter an IF statement and get the message
                        Bugs Out

                                                         `Syntax error`

                        Reason: After you typed the condition, you pressed the Enter key in-
                                        stead of using Ctrl + Enter to move to the next line.
                        Solution: Retype the IF statement correctly.

EXERCISES

. . . .

3.4 Which of the following could be used as the trailer
data for Program 3.3?

 a) −1, 40
 b) −1, −1
 c) 0, −1
 d) 0, 0

3.5 What output will be produced if the following
changes are made to Program 3.3? Trace the program. Before making each new change, assume the
program is restored back to its original form.

a) The IF statement in line 30 is changed to

        `30 IF PAY.RATE = -1`
        `      THEN GOTO 50`

b) The IF statement in line 30 is moved to line 55

3.6 What changes, if any, would have to be made to
Program 3.3 to process six employees?

PROGRAMMING ASSIGNMENTS

. . . .

*Re-solve the following programming assignments, which you solved earlier on
page 51 in this chapter, but this time include a test for trailer data to end the
program.*

*3.6 Re-solve Programming Assignment 3.1.

3.7 Re-solve Programming Assignment 3.2.

3.8 Re-solve Programming Assignment 3.3.

3.9 Re-solve Programming Assignment 3.4.

*3.10 Re-solve Programming Assignment 3.5.

STRING VARIABLES

. . . .

So far, all of our programs have accepted only numbers as input and
produced only numbers as output. But no doubt, you have received
computer-prepared checks and bills with your name and address on them.

These labels are possible because, as noted in Chapter 2, computers can process data that consist of letters (*string data* or simply *strings*) as well as numbers. Strings can take many shapes. Some consist solely of letters, as in the case of the prompt we used in Programs 3.2 and 3.3–Enter Pay Rate and Hours Worked. Some strings contain both numbers and letters, as in the address 14 Elm Street. Some strings even contain special symbols like !, #, @, >, and %.

When using variables to store strings, you must follow a special rule:

....

BASIC Rule 5   A legal name for a string variable is created by adding a $ to the end of a legal name for a numeric variable.

When we talk about string variables, we pronounce the $ as the word "string," that is, N$ is pronounced "N-string." Here is a list of valid and invalid string variable names. For the invalid names, the reason they are invalid is given.

Proposed variable name	Status
A$	Valid.
$A	Invalid—a string variable name must end with a dollar sign, not begin with one.
CITY$	Valid.
NAME$	Invalid—NAME is a reserved word and may not be used as a variable name.
STUDENT.NAME$	Valid.

The last two examples illustrate that although you may not use a reserved word as a variable name, a reserved word may be *part* of a variable name.

When BASIC encounters a string variable, it sets up a storage location (box) for that variable just as it does for numeric variables. A maximum of 255 characters can fit in one of these boxes. Each letter, number, special symbol, and blank space counts as one character.

Using String Variables

String variables may be used just like ordinary variables, although, of course, you cannot do arithmetic with them. So if ADDRESS$ stands for an address, and we want to assign the string 14 Elm Street to ADDRESS$, we could use the LET statement

ADDRESS$ = "14 Elm Street"

After this LET statement is executed, ADDRESS$ will contain 14 Elm Street. Notice that within strings, blank spaces are significant and that BASIC does not change lowercase letters to uppercase. This LET statement also illustrates another rule:

....

BASIC Rule 6   String data must be enclosed in quotation marks.

BASIC uses quotation marks to determine the beginning and the end of a string, but the quotation marks are not part of the string. In fact, the one character you cannot include in a string is a quotation mark. The reason strings may not contain quotation marks is that BASIC cannot tell which quotation marks indicate the beginning and the end of the string and which are parts of the string. In Chapter 7, you will learn a special technique to include quotation marks in a string.

A string variable may be set equal to another string variable, as in the LET statement

$$Q\$ = P\$$$

When BASIC executes this statement, it takes the string in the P\$ box and puts it in the Q\$ box.

String variables may be equated only to other string variables, to strings, or to string expressions. (You will learn about string expressions later.) The following LET statements are therefore illegal:

$$A\$ = P$$
$$A\$ = 46$$

The first LET statement is illegal because it sets a string variable equal to a numeric variable, and the second LET statement is illegal because it sets a string variable equal to a number. Similarly, numeric variables may be equated only to other numeric variables, to numbers, or to numeric expressions. The following LET statements are therefore illegal:

$$F = L\$$$
$$DAY = "July\ 4"$$
$$C\$ = A\$ * B\$$$

The first LET statement is illegal because it sets a numeric variable equal to a string variable. The second LET statement is illegal because it sets a numeric variable equal to a string. The third LET statement is illegal because you cannot multiply strings.

Concatenation

Concatenation
The operation of adding together strings or string variables.

Unlike numeric variables or constants, string variables cannot be multiplied or divided. You can, however, "add" (put together) strings. The technical word for putting strings together is **concatenation**.

As an example of concatenation, consider the following BASIC statements

```
10 A$ = "WATER"
20 B$ = "MELON"
30 F$ = A$ + B$
```

In line 30 the plus sign, +, indicates that A\$ and B\$ are to be concatenated, or put together, and the result assigned to F\$. After line 30 is executed, F\$ will contain WATERMELON. Notice that the two strings are put together end to end; no blank space is inserted between them.

Strings, as well as string variables, may be concatenated, and as many strings and string variables as you like may be concatenated in a single expression. So we can expand our example to the following statements:

```
10 A$ = "WATER"
20 B$ = "MELON"
30 C$ = "SWEET"
40 F$ = "RIPE " + C$ + " " + A$ + B$
```

After line 40 is executed, F$ will contain RIPE SWEET WATERMELON. Notice that to get a space between RIPE and SWEET you must include a space at the end of RIPE, and to get a space between SWEET and WATERMELON you must concatenate a string that consists of a single space.

Inputting String Variables

You can assign values to string variables by using an INPUT statement. An especially nice feature of the INPUT statement is that the string value you enter does not have to be enclosed in quotation marks, *as long as it does not contain a comma.* (However, the INPUT statement ignores blanks that come before or after a string, so if you want such blanks to be included as part of the string data, you must enclose the whole string in quotation marks.) For example, you could enter an employee's name and age by using the following INPUT statement:

```
INPUT "Enter name and age"; EMP.NAME$, AGE
```

Then, when BASIC prints the prompt, you could type

```
Mary Jones, 24
```

Mary Jones would be put in the EMP.NAME$ box, and 24 would be put in the AGE box. To type the name as Jones, Mary, however, you must use quotation marks, as in

```
"Jones, Mary", 24
```

If you do not use quotation marks in this case, BASIC will assume that both commas are separators and that you have typed three values: Jones, Mary, and 24. Since the INPUT statement contains only two variables, BASIC will print the error message ?Redo from start.

Note that the data you enter in response to an INPUT statement must agree with the types of variables listed in the INPUT statement. For example, if in response to the INPUT statement

```
INPUT "Enter employee name, age"; EMP.NAME$, AGE
```

you type

```
24, Mary Jones
```

BASIC will print the by now familiar error message ?Redo from start because, although it can convert the number 24 to a string and store that in the EMP.NAME$ box (that may not make sense, but it is not illegal), it cannot convert Mary Jones to a number and store it in the AGE box.

Program 3.4 shows a modification of the Bat-O program that accepts and prints the employee's name as a new variable, EMP.NAME$. To make this change, we modify line 20 to include Name in the prompt and EMP.NAME$ as a variable. Then in line 40, we add EMP.NAME$ to the print list along with PAY.RATE.HOURS and GROSS.PAY.

Since any of the input variables could be used for the trailer data, Program 3.4 uses an employee's name of Stop for trailer data. (We assume that no employee would ever have the name Stop.) Notice, however, that because in strings capital and lowercase letters are different, you must enter Stop for the trailer data. If you enter STOP instead, the test for trailer data will fail.

```
10 REM   *** BAT-O PROGRAM WITH NAMES ***
20 INPUT "Enter Name, Rate, Hours, Stop to end "; EMP.NAME$, PAY.RATE, HOURS
30   IF EMP.NAME$ = "Stop"
       THEN GOTO 70
40   GROSS.PAY = PAY.RATE * HOURS
50   LPRINT EMP.NAME$, PAY.RATE, HOURS, GROSS.PAY
60 GOTO 20
70 END

RUN
Enter Name, Rate, Hours, Stop to end ? Joe Tinker,6.75,40
Enter Name, Rate, Hours, Stop to end ? John Evers,6,30
Enter Name, Rate, Hours, Stop to end ? Frank Chance,5.75,25
Enter Name, Rate, Hours, Stop to end ? Stop,0,0
Ok
```

```
Joe Tinker      6.75        40          270
John Evers      6           30          180
Frank Chance    5.75        25          143.75
```

PROGRAM 3.4   **Payroll program with names.**

Getting the Bugs Out

Problem: During executing, BASIC displays the error message

Type mismatch in nn

where nn is the line number of a LET statement.

Reason: In the LET statement you assigned a number to a string variable or a string to a numeric variable.

Solution: Rewrite the LET statement correctly.

Problem: When you enter data in response to an INPUT prompt, you get the message

?Redo from start

Reason: When you entered the data, you typed a string where you should have typed a number.

Solution: Enter the data correctly.

EXERCISES

....

3.7 Which of the following are legal and which are illegal variable names for string variables?

   a) $ADDRESS
 *b) ANSWER$
   c) 1ST.NAME$
   d) LAST.NAME$
 *e) COLOR$

*3.8 Write the LET statement to assign the string Button Gwinnett to the string variable SIGNER$.

3.9 Which of the following LET statements contain errors? Rewrite the incorrect statements correctly.

   a) NUMBER$ = "123"
 *b) ZIP.CODE = "10050"
   c) MONTH = "APRIL"
 *d) FLOWER$ = ROSE
   e) SOUND$ = "LOUD"
   f) FRUIT.SALAD = APPLES * ORANGES

3.10 In Program 3.4, what values were entered for the pay rate and the hours for the trailer data employee?

3.11 How would the output of Program 3.4 change if you entered STOP, 0, 0 for the trailer data?

3.12 George says that to use End as the name for the trailer data employee in Program 3.4, he would just

have to change line 30 to:

```
30 IF EMP.NAME$ = "End"
   THEN GOTO 70
```

Gracie says that you can't use End this way because End is a BASIC reserved word. Who is correct?

PROGRAMMING ASSIGNMENTS

· ·

In the following programming assignments, follow the standard instructions given on page 51.

*3.11 All the items at the Twice Sold Tales bookstore are reduced 20 percent. Accept as input the name and the usual price of an item. Write a program to calculate and print the sale price of the item. (PA 3.1)

3.12 Accept as input a student's name, the number of questions on the test, and the number he or she got right. Write a program to calculate and print the student's percentage grade. (PA 2.3)

*3.13 Mark O. Polo is traveling in Japan and wants to buy different gifts. Write a program that accepts the names and prices (in yen) of different gifts and prints the names and prices in dollars. You get 131.46 yen for a dollar. (PA 2.5)

3.14 Each chocolate bar uses three quarters of an ounce of nuts, and nuts cost $.12 per ounce. Write a program that accepts the number of chocolate bars manufactured and calculates and prints the cost of the nuts. (PA 2.7)

3.15 A number of people are painting picket fences. For each painter, accept as input the painter's name, the number of pickets in the fence, the number of pickets painted per hour, and the number of hours spent painting. Write a program to calculate and print the percentage of the fence that has been painted. (PA 2.9)

ADDITIONAL COMMANDS

· ·

In Chapter 2 you learned the "essential" commands: RUN, LIST, etc. Now you will learn some additional commands that make using BASIC more convenient.

 ### *The AUTO Command*

The AUTO command automatically generates line numbers. When you are entering a new program or adding lines to an existing program, you can use the AUTO command to save yourself the trouble of typing line numbers. The simplest form of the AUTO command is

```
AUTO
```

This command causes BASIC to display line number 10 on the screen and then to wait for you to type the BASIC statement that belongs on line 10. After you type the statement and press the Enter key, line number 20 is displayed. After you have typed the statement that belongs on line 20, line number 30 is displayed, and then 40, 50, etc. Instead of typing AUTO, you can press the Alt + A keys.

The syntax of the AUTO command is

```
AUTO [number] [,increment]
```

Default value
A value assigned automatically.
This value is used if you don't
specify a value.

where number is the initial line number used, and increment is the number added to each line number to get the next line number. The default value for number and increment is 10. A **default value** is a value assigned if you don't specify a value. Since the default value for number and increment is 10, typing

                    AUTO

is equivalent to typing

                AUTO 10, 10

In the command

                AUTO ,20

the initial line number is omitted, so the default value of 10 is used for the first line, and 20 is used for the increment. This command generates the line numbers 10, 30, 50, etc. Notice that it is necessary to put in the comma to indicate that number is being omitted. If we wrote

                AUTO 20

BASIC would assume that number was 20, and that increment was omitted. It would therefore use the default value of 10 for increment and generate the line numbers 20, 30, 40, etc. As you can see, a little comma makes a big difference.

If your choice of values for number and increment causes AUTO to generate a line number that already exists in the program, an asterisk is printed after the line number. If you then type a line, the new line will replace the old line. If you did not intend to replace the line, pressing the Enter key after the asterisk appears will cause AUTO to generate the next line number without replacing the existing line.

To escape from the auto mode, use the Ctrl + Break keys. The line on which you type Ctrl + Break is not saved, so you must type Ctrl + Break in response to the line number *after* the last one you want.

The FILES Command

When you save a new program, you invent a new filename for it. Sometimes, however, you may think you are inventing a new name for a program, forgetting that there is already a program with that name stored on the diskette or hard disk. Saving with the same name under these circumstances would be a disaster, since the old program would be destroyed without warning. What you want is a way of listing the names of the files on a diskette or hard disk. The FILES command gives you that list.

In its simplest version, the command

                FILES

displays the names of all the files on the diskette or hard disk in the DOS default drive. Notice that this command displays the names of all the files, not only the names of BASIC programs, which have the extension BAS. To list only the files with the extension BAS, use the command

                FILES "*.BAS"

In this command, the asterisk stands for any number of characters. This command will list the names of all the files with the extension BAS.

The question mark may also be used in the filename. Suppose you have saved a number of versions of a stock market program, and you have named these versions MARKET1, MARKET2, etc. You can list the names of all these programs using the command

FILES "MARKET?.BAS"

Each question mark stands for any one or no character; that is, this command will list MARKET, MARKET1, etc., but not MARKET10. To list all the files that start with the letters MARKET, you could use either FILES "MARKET??.BAS" or FILES "MARKET*.BAS".

An asterisk or question marks may also be used in the filename extension. The command FILES "BAT-0.*" will list all files that have a filename of BAT-0 no matter what their extension is.

As in the SAVE command, a different drive may be specified. For example, the command

FILES "B:*.BAS"

lists the files with the extension BAS on the diskette in drive B.

The NAME Command

The NAME command is used to rename a file. For example,

NAME "TEMP.BAS" AS "SALES.BAS"

changes the name of a file from TEMP.BAS to SALES.BAS. All the NAME command does is change the name of the file; it does not make a new copy of the file. Notice that it is necessary to include the filename extension. Also, there cannot already be a file with the new name on the disk.

If the file is not on the default drive, the device name must be included as part of the filenames:

NAME "B:DEMO.BAS" AS "B:GAME.BAS"

Notice that the device name must be included with *both* names.

The KILL Command

When you no longer need a program, you can erase it from a diskette or fixed disk by using the command KILL. To help prevent accidental erasures, the KILL command requires that you include the extension as part of the filename. For example, to erase a program you saved using the command SAVE "BAT-0", you must use the command

KILL "BAT-0.BAS"

If the file is not on the DOS default drive, you must specify the drive, just as for other commands:

KILL "B:INVENTRY.BAS"

The SYSTEM Command

You can use the SYSTEM command to return to DOS from BASIC. The format of the command is simply the word SYSTEM. When you return to DOS, the program in RAM that you were working on is erased, so be sure to save it before you type SYSTEM.

EXERCISES

*3.13 Write the command that will automatically generate the line numbers 100, 120, 140, ...

3.14 Write the command that will change the name of a file from SCORES.BAS to GRADES.BAS.

3.15 Suppose you have saved a file using the command SAVE "BALANCE". Write the command to erase that file.

3.16 Program 3.5 shows an attempt to execute a solution to Programming Assignment 3.13. As you can see, BASIC displayed the ?Redo from start error message. What is wrong?

```
10 REM *** PROGRAMMING ASSIGNMENT 3.13 ***
20 INPUT "Enter name and price, 0 to stop"; ITEM.NAME$, PRICE.YEN
30   IF PRICE.YEN = 0
        THEN GOTO 70
40   PRICE.DOLLARS = PRICE.YEN / 131.46
50   PRINT ITEM.NAME$, PRICE.YEN, PRICE.DOLLARS
60 GOTO 20
70 END

RUN
Enter name and price, 0 to stop? Camera, 30,000
?Redo from start
Enter name and price, 0 to stop?
```

PROGRAM 3.5   **Trying to execute a solution to Programming Assignment 3.13.**

SUMMARY

In this chapter you have learned that

☐ An LPRINT statement is used to print answers on the printer.

☐ The LLIST command is used to list a program on the printer.

☐ The GOTO statement creates an unconditional branch and may be used to create a loop so that a program can process multiple cases.

☐ The INPUT statement is used to prompt the user and to accept data entered from the keyboard.

☐ Prompts are used to tell the user what data must be entered.

☐ The Ctrl + Break keys may be used to stop execution.

☐ Trailer data are used to control the number of times a loop is executed.

☐ The flowchart symbol for a decision is a diamond.

☐ An IF statement is used to test a condition and make a decision.

☐ Strings must be enclosed in quotation marks and may contain a maximum of 255 characters.

☐ String variable names are formed by adding a $ to the end of a legal numeric variable name.

☐ The + operator concatenates strings.

☐ The AUTO command is used to automatically generate line numbers.

☐   The FILES command is used to list the names of the files on a diskette.

☐   The NAME command is used to rename a file.

☐   The KILL command is used to erase a file.

☐   The SYSTEM command is used to return to DOS.

KEY TERMS IN THIS CHAPTER

branching statement 46
concatenation 57
condition 52
**conditional branching
statement** 53

decision symbol 52
default value 61
endless loop 48
loop 44

trailer data 51
**unconditional branching
statement** 47

QUESTIONS FOR REVIEW

3.1   Name two statements that may be used to assign a value to a variable.

3.2   Suppose Program 3.2 were used to calculate gross pay for 17 employees. For how many cases would you have to calculate the answers by hand?

3.3   How do you stop an endless loop?

3.4   True or False: A GOTO statement may branch only to a line number lower than its own line number.

3.5   Give two reasons why it is useful to print the input data along with the answer to a problem.

3.6   When a variable is assigned a new value, what happens to the value it was previously assigned?

3.7   When do you have to enclose in quotation marks a string that is entered in response to an INPUT statement?

3.8   What is the purpose of printing a prompt with an INPUT statement?

3.9   What is the purpose of indenting the statements in a loop?

3.10 The GOTO statement is an example of a(n) _____ branching statement.

3.11 What is the least number of variables that may be listed in an INPUT statement?

3.12 Explain the difference between the equal sign used in a condition and the one used in a LET statement.

3.13 What shape is the flowchart symbol for a decision?

3.14 Trailer data are entered (before/after) the data for the other cases.

3.15 What command is used to do each of the following?
  a) Rename a file.
  b) Erase a file.
  c) Return to DOS.
  d) Generate line numbers automatically.
  e) List the names of the files on a diskette or hard disk.

3.16 True or False: A string may contain both capital and lowercase letters.

3.17 How is a loop shown on a flowchart?

3.18 What is the maximum number of characters a string variable can hold?

ADDITIONAL PROGRAMMING ASSIGNMENTS

In the following programming assignments, follow the standard instructions given with Programming Assignments 3.1 through 3.5.

3.16 Accept as input drivers' names, distances driven, and gas used. Write a program to calculate and print average gas mileage, in miles per gallon. (PA 2.1)

*3.17 Suppose that each cigarette smoked reduces a person's life span by 14 minutes. Accept different people's names, the number of packs per day each smokes, and the number of years that each has been smoking. Write a program to calculate and print the number of days each person's life span has been reduced. (A pack contains 20 cigarettes.) (PA 2.11)

3.18 Accept as input different salespersons' names and sales. Write a program to calculate and print each salesperson's commission. Commission is calculated as 12% of sales. (Hint: 12% of a number is calculated by multiplying the number by .12.)

4

Writing More Complicated Programs

BASIC OBJECTIVES OF THIS CHAPTER

☐ To write complex expressions
☐ To further explore the PRINT and LPRINT statements
☐ To explain more about correcting errors
☐ To use the BASIC commands EDIT and DELETE

All the expressions we have used so far have been relatively simple; typically, we added two values or multiplied two values. Obviously, we sometimes must do more complicated arithmetic. In this chapter, you will learn the rules for writing complicated expressions. You will also learn more about the PRINT and LPRINT statements, including how to print titles and headings to improve the appearance of your output. Finally, since you will probably be making more complicated errors, you will learn more about correcting these errors, including how to use the BASIC Program Editor.

MORE COMPLICATED EXPRESSIONS

Before we can discuss complicated expressions, you must learn about several additional arithmetic operations that BASIC provides.

■ *Additional Arithmetic Operations*

Exponentiation
Raising to a power.

Integer division
Division that yields as its answer only the integer part of the quotient. Specified by the backslash, \.

Modulo arithmetic
Arithmetic in which the answer is the integer that is the remainder of an integer division. Specified by the operator MOD.

Besides adding, subtracting, multiplying, and dividing, which we discussed earlier, three other arithmetic operations are also possible in BASIC. Raising to a power, or **exponentiation**, is indicated by the symbol $^\wedge$, which is typed as Shift + 6. Thus, A^4, the algebraic notation raising A to the fourth power, is written as A $^\wedge$ 4 in BASIC.

Two other arithmetic operations are sometimes useful. The backslash, \, specifies **integer division**. Don't confuse the backslash, \, with the ordinary slash, /, which is used for usual division. Integer division gives the integer (whole number) part of a quotient. For example, the statement

```
A = 14 \ 4
```

assigns the whole number 3 (rather than 3.5) to A. If the values to be divided are not themselves integers, they are rounded to the nearest integer before they are divided. Hence,

```
B = 11.3 \ 5.7
```

assigns the value 1 to B. The 11.3 is rounded down to 11, the 5.7 is rounded up to 6, and then the answer, 1.8333, is converted to 1.

The word MOD specifies modulo arithmetic. **Modulo arithmetic** gives the integer value that is the remainder of an integer division. That is, the statement

```
C = 14 MOD 4
```

assigns the value 2 to C because when 14 is divided by 4, the remainder is 2. Again, if the values involved are not integers, they are rounded to the nearest integer before they are divided. Therefore,

```
D = 11.3 MOD 5.7
```

assigns the value 5 to D because when 11 is divided by 6, the remainder is 5.

You might wonder when integer division and the MOD operator would be useful. It turns out that there are many such occasions, especially in problems where only an integer makes sense as an answer. For example, suppose the number of eggs a farmer has is EGGS, and she can sell only by the dozen. The number of dozens she can sell is

```
DOZENS = EGGS \ 12
```

and the number of eggs left over is

REMAINING = EGGS MOD 12

Another situation in which MOD is useful is when you want to know if one variable divides into another variable exactly. Since the MOD operator gives the remainder, if the second variable divides into the first variable exactly, the MOD operator gives a value of zero. For example, 6 MOD 2 = 0, because 2 divides into 6 exactly. Therefore, if A MOD B = 0 you know that B divides into A exactly.

■ *Rules of Precedence*

Rules of precedence
The order in which the computer evaluates expressions.

You now have the tools to write complicated expressions, but you still do not know how BASIC evaluates them. For example, suppose that A equals 2 and B equals 3. What value will be assigned to C when the following LET statement is executed?

C = 4 * A + B

Some students assume that BASIC will multiply 4 by A to get 8, and then add B to get 11, so that C will equal 11. Others assume that BASIC will add A and B to get 5, then multiply by 4, so that C will equal 20. In truth, both answers are "reasonable," but one is right and the other is wrong. To know which value C will have, you must understand the rules used in BASIC to evaluate expressions.

When BASIC evaluates an expression, it follows certain **rules of precedence**, which are pretty much the same rules you learned when you studied algebra. That is, it scans the expression from left to right several times and does the arthmetic operations in the following order:

1. Exponentiations
2. Multiplications and divisions
3. Additions and subtractions*

Let's see how these rules affect the evaluation of the expression 4 * A + B. In step 1, BASIC scans the expression looking for exponentiations to perform. This expression does not contain any exponentiations, so BASIC goes to step 2. In step 2, BASIC performs multiplications and divisions. It performs the multiplication 4 * A and gets the answer 8. So by the start of step 3, the expression has been reduced to 8 + B. In step 3, BASIC performs the addition, gets the answer 11, and assigns this value to C.

Note that when BASIC performs step 2, it does not do all the multiplications first and then all the divisions. It does multiplications and divisions as it encounters them while scanning the expression from left to right. Suppose A equals 12 and B equals 2. What is the value of the expression A / 3 * B? Since there is no exponentiation, nothing happens when BASIC performs step 1. During step 2, as BASIC scans the expression from left to right, it first encounters the division. It divides 3 into A and gets 4. At this point, the expression is 4 * B. BASIC then multiplies 4 by B and gets 8 as the value of the expression.

Similarly, when BASIC performs step 3, it does additions and subtractions as it encounters them. So if A equals 20, B equals 5, and C equals 3, the expression A - B + C equals 18.

It is particularly easy to make mistakes with expressions in which an arithmetic step follows division. For example, consider the expression

---

*Integer division and modulo arithmetic are done between steps 2 and 3.

A / B + 1, with A equal to 12 and B equal to 2. When it evaluates this expression, BASIC will first divide A by B to get 6 and then add 6 and 1 to get 7. Many students would mistakenly add the B and 1 to get 3, and then divide A by 3 to get the wrong answer, 4.

Use of Parentheses

While the rules of precedence permit us to predict how BASIC will evaluate expressions, they also pose some problems. Returning to the statement C = 4 * A + B, suppose the logic of the problem required that A and B be added *before* the multiplication. How can you get BASIC to do what you want instead of what it does automatically by following the rules of precedence? The answer is to use parentheses. In fact, the rules of precedence really include a zero step:

   0. Evaluate expressions inside parentheses.

That is, BASIC evaluates expressions inside parentheses first. Inside parentheses, the operations are performed following the rules of precedence on page 68.

Therefore, if you want A and B to be added before the multiplication, you must write the expression as 4 * (A + B). In this last expression, notice that the asterisk indicating multiplication must be present. In algebra, multiplication is often implied by simply writing two terms together, for example, 4(A + B). In BASIC, this is wrong; if you want to indicate multiplication, you must use an asterisk. Parentheses are also used to separate two consecutive operators. For example, write A * (−B), not A * −B.

Whenever you use parentheses, remember that there must be the same number of right parentheses as left parentheses. You must also be careful to use the correct keys when you are typing; (is the upper shift character on the 9 key, and) is the upper shift character on the 0 (zero) key. Do not use square brackets, [ ], or curly braces, { }; they are illegal in BASIC.

You may use as many parentheses as you want. Unnecessary parentheses are simply ignored. The following expressions are all legal and equivalent:

```
A / (B + 1)
(A) / (B + 1)
(A / ((B) + 1))
```

Study the following examples to be sure you understand how BASIC, evaluates these expressions.

Expression	Evaluation
4 + 6 / 2 = 7	Divide 6 by 2 to give 3, then add 4 and 3 to give 7.
(4 + 6) / 2 = 5	Add 4 and 6 to give 10, then divide 10 by 2 to give 5.
6 + 15 / 3 + 2 = 13	Divide 15 by 3 to give 5, then add 6, 5, and 2 to give 13.
6 + 15 / (3 + 2) = 9	Add 3 and 2 to give 5, then divide 15 by 5 to give 3, then add 6 and 3 to give 9.
2 ^ 3 + 5 = 13	Raise 2 to the third power to give 8, then add 8 and 5 to give 13.
2 ^ (3 + 1) = 16	Add 3 and 1 to give 4, then raise 2 to the fourth power to give 16.

A Savings Account Problem

Now that you know how to write complicated expressions, let's solve a problem. Suppose you make a DEPOSIT into a savings account at the Loansome Bank at a certain interest RATE. You can calculate what your BALANCE will be if your money stays in the bank for a given number of years (NO.YEARS) by using the compound interest formula

$$\text{BALANCE} = \text{DEPOSIT} * (1 + \text{RATE}) \char`^ \text{NO.YEARS}$$

Now, how would you go about writing a program that will accept DEPOSIT, RATE, and NO.YEARS and calculate and print BALANCE?

NAMING VARIABLES

The first step in our structured procedure is to choose names for the variables. In this problem, the names have already been assigned in the statement of the problem. But in this and more complicated problems, it is useful to indicate which variables are input variables and which are output variables. The input variables are those variables whose values we know and that are given to the computer in, for example, INPUT statements. In this problem, the input variables are DEPOSIT, RATE, and NO.YEARS. The output variables are those variables whose values we do not know and that the computer is supposed to calculate. In this problem, the output variable is BALANCE.

Two circumstances sometimes cause students to get confused about which are the input and which are the output variables. First, even though DEPOSIT, RATE, and NO.YEARS are input variables, we will print them. Printing these variables helps in debugging the program. It also lets us see which BALANCE goes with which set of DEPOSIT, RATE, and NO.YEARS. But we know the values of DEPOSIT, RATE, and NO.YEARS *before* we run the program. That knowledge is what makes them input variables.

Our procedure, however, also leads to knowing one value of an *output* variable, and that can be a second cause of confusion for students. Because we will calculate an answer by hand to check our program, we will know a value of BALANCE before running the program. But remember, we will know only *one* value of BALANCE before we run the program. Once the program is written, we expect to use it to calculate many values of BALANCE.

From now on we will specify the variable names as follows:

Input variables	Amount deposited	DEPOSIT
	Interest rate	RATE
	Number of years	NO.YEARS
Output variable	Balance in account	BALANCE

DEVELOPING AN ALGORITHM

The second step in our structured approach is to develop an algorithm for the problem. In this case, the algorithm we will use is

1. Input values for DEPOSIT, RATE, and NO.YEARS.
2. If these are the trailer data, go to step 6.
3. Calculate BALANCE using the compound interest formula.
4. Print DEPOSIT, RATE, NO.YEARS, and BALANCE.

5. Repeat steps 1 through 4 for all sets of DEPOSIT, RATE, and NO.YEARS.
6. Stop execution.

Figure 4.1 shows a flowchart for this problem. Notice that the structure of this flowchart is identical to the structure of the flowchart in Figure 3.3. They both involve input, processing, output, and a loop to repeat, and a test for trailer data.

PSEUDOCODE

Pseudocode
A language somewhere between English and BASIC, used in developing the algorithm for a program.

In addition to flowcharts, which we have used so far, programmers use several other techniques to help develop algorithms. One such technique is to write the program first in pseudocode. **Pseudocode** refers to a way of writing program steps using a language somewhere between English and BASIC. You might wonder why you should use pseudocode at all; why not simply write the program statements in BASIC, since that is what you will have to

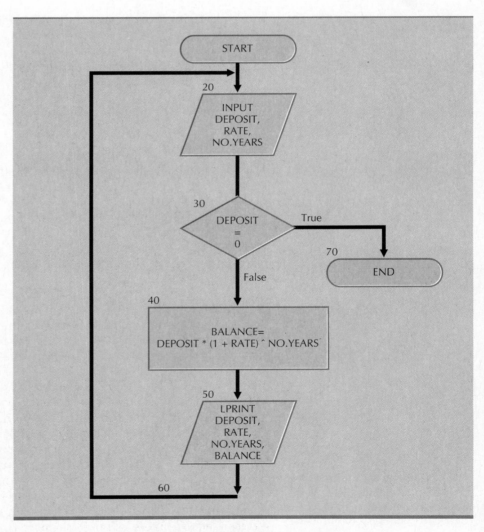

FIGURE 4.1   **Flowchart to calculate balance in a savings account.**

do eventually? The answer is that by using pseudocode you postpone having to think about the details of how to code BASIC instructions and can concentrate on developing the algorithm. Once the algorithm is fully developed, you can translate it easily into BASIC statements. Often, individual pseudocode statements are translated into individual BASIC statements.

There are no specific rules for pseudocode; anything that helps make it easy to write and understand is helpful. So when writing pseudocode for a problem, we will write the problem name on the first line. We will also use the variable names we have chosen for the problem, and we will indent loops so they stand out clearly. The pseudocode description for the savings account problem is:

> Calculate Balance in Savings Account
> INPUT DEPOSIT, RATE, NO.YEARS
>   IF trailer data THEN stop
>   BALANCE = DEPOSIT * (1 + RATE) ^ NO.YEARS
>   PRINT DEPOSIT, RATE, NO.YEARS, BALANCE
> Repeat for all sets of DEPOSIT, RATE, and NO.YEARS

You know that "Repeat" is not a BASIC statement; in the program, we will use a GOTO statement to create a loop. We use the word "Repeat" in the pseudocode because if we used GOTO, we would have to know the line number to code with the GOTO statement. At this point, we want to concentrate on how to solve the problem and not get bogged down in details like line numbers.

In this case, the pseudocode outline is very similar to the algorithm; in more complicated programs, the two will not be so similar.

CALCULATING AN ANSWER

Next, we must calculate an answer by hand. Let's use the following values: DEPOSIT = 1000, RATE = .05 (notice that RATE must be expressed as a decimal, not a percent), and NO.YEARS = 20. Calculating an answer to this problem by hand presents some problems. One calculator gave an answer of 2653.2964, and another gave 2653.2977. An exact calculation gave the correct BALANCE to eight digits as 2653.2977. The two calculators gave different answers because of round-off errors, which we will discuss next.

ROUND-OFF ERRORS

At this point, you should follow steps 4 through 6 of our structured procedure and write, enter, and execute a program to solve this problem, correcting any syntax errors. When you are done, your program should produce output that looks like the first line of output in Program 4.1. (The second line of output will be discussed shortly.) But if you then proceed to step 7 and check the computer's output (2653.293) against the exact answer 2653.2977), you will find that the two do not exactly agree. This small difference does not reflect a logic error in the program. There is no need to follow step 8 of our procedure and debug the program. Rather, the difference is due to a round off error. **Round-off errors** are small numeric errors that sometimes occur in computer-calculated answers.

Round-off errors occur for two reasons. First, the boxes that BASIC sets up to store the values of variables can hold only seven digits. But some values require more digits to represent them. For instance, $1/3 =$

Round-off error
A small numerical error that occurs in a computer-calculated answer because of the way computers store numbers.

```
10 REM *** LOANSOME BANK PROBLEM ***
20 INPUT "Enter Deposit, Rate, Years, 0 to stop "; DEPOSIT, RATE, NO.YEARS
30    IF DEPOSIT = 0
         THEN GOTO 70
40    BALANCE = DEPOSIT * (1 + RATE) ^ NO.YEARS
50    LPRINT DEPOSIT, RATE, NO.YEARS, BALANCE
60 GOTO 20
70 END

RUN
Enter Deposit, Rate, Years, 0 to stop ? 1000,.05,20
Enter Deposit, Rate, Years, 0 to stop ? 100000,.20,50
Enter Deposit, Rate, Years, 0 to stop ? 0,0,0
Ok
```

1000	.05	20	2653.293
100000	.2	50	9.100439E+08

Answer with round off error

Value printed using scientific notation

PROGRAM 4.1   **Program to print balance at Loansome Bank.**

.333333333 . . . , and the 3s keep going forever. So there is no way to store 1/3 exactly.*

Round-off errors also arise because BASIC does not store numbers the same way as human beings do. We do not have to be concerned with the complexities of how BASIC stores numbers, except to note that when it stores numbers containing a fractional part, like .05, small errors sometimes occur.

Often round-off errors have no detectable effect on the final answers, but sometimes, as in this case, they result in a small error. Notice that the error in this case is less than half of one cent in more than $2000.

VALUES PRINTED IN SCIENTIFIC NOTATION

Scientific notation
A method of printing very small and very large values.

The second line of output in Program 4.1 shows the answers calculated when the input data are changed to DEPOSIT = 100000, INTEREST = .2 (20 percent), and NO.YEARS = 50. As you can see, the value of BALANCE is printed as 9.100439E+08. This form of output, which is known as **scientific notation**, is used when a variable has a value that is too large to be represented in seven digits. The portion after the E tells us how many places to move the decimal point and whether to move it to the left (because there is a minus sign) or to the right (because there is a plus sign). In this case, the E+08 tells us that to get the value represented by this number we must shift the decimal point eight places to the right. If you shift the decimal point eight places to the right, you will get 910,043,900, which is the value of BALANCE.

Scientific notation is also used for very small numbers. Suppose a variable has the value 0.000013596426. This value would be printed as 1.359643E-05. The E-05 tells us that, to get the value represented by this

*BASIC can also store values in "double precision" form, in which 17 digits are stored. This method of storage reduces the size of the round-off error but slows execution. For a complete discussion of double precision, see *Using BASIC on the IBM PC*, by Angela and Michael Trombetta, Addison-Wesley, 1984.

number, we must shift the decimal point five places to the left. If you shift the decimal point five places to the left you will get 0.00001359643, which is the original value rounded to seven digits.

It is also possible to use scientific notation to define constants. For example, if you want A to equal one million, you could code

$$A = 1.0E + 06$$

Getting the Bugs Out

Problem: When a program is run, BASIC stops and prints the message

```
Overflow in nn
```

where nn is the line number of a statement that performs integer division or modulo arithmetic.

Reason: The numbers being used were outside the acceptable range. Integer division and modulo arithmetic can operate only on numbers in the range $-32{,}768$ to $32{,}767$.

Solution: Rerun the program using numbers in the acceptable range.

EXERCISES

4.1 Identify the syntax errors, if any, in the following LET statements:

  a) A = B TIMES C
  b) 2 * P = Q
  *c) M = 5 (N - S)
  *d) W = R * ((S + T) * V - P / N
  e) A = B * ((1 + C) ^ (E - F) + G) / (H + 1)

4.2 Calculate the value assigned to A by the following LET statements if B = 2, C = 12, D = 3, and E = 1.

  a) A = B + C / D + E
  b) A = (B + C) / D + E
  *c) A = (B + C) / (D + E)
  *d) A = B + 3 * C / D ^ 2 + E
  e) A = (B + 3 * C) / (D ^ 2 + E)

4.3 Calculate the value assigned to A by the following LET statements if B = 28, C = 8, D = 37, and E = 9.

  *a) A = B \ C
  b) A = D \ E

  *c) A = B MOD C
  d) A = D MOD E

4.4 Translate the following algebraic equations into LET statements.

  a) $a = \dfrac{b + c + d}{3}$

  b) $g = \dfrac{b + 2c + 3d}{6e}$

  *c) $t = \dfrac{d((1 + r)^n - 1)}{r}$

  d) $p = \dfrac{m \cdot r}{1 + (1 + r)^{-n}}$

4.5 What is the value of a number that is printed as $1.43826E + 08$? Of one that is printed as $6.03498E - 04$?

PROGRAMMING ASSIGNMENTS

Although making up test data and calculating answers by hand are important skills, some students may have trouble doing that. Therefore, from now on several problems in each set will give sample test data and hand-calculated answers.

4.1 The equation used in Program 4.1 assumes that the interest is compounded once a year. If the interest is compounded M times a year, the correct equation is

```
BALANCE = DEPOSIT * (1 + RATE / M)
            ^ (NO.YEARS * M)
```

Modify Program 4.1 so that it will use this equation and accept M as an additional input value. Run the program with M = 1, which should give the same answers as the unmodified program; with M = 2, which is semiannual compounding; with M = 4, which is quarterly compounding; with M = 12, which is monthly compounding; and with M = 365, which is daily compounding. When M = 4, BALANCE should be 2701.50 for the first set of data.

*4.2 Scientists estimate that the greenhouse effect causes the Earth's average temperature to increase .08 degree each year. If the average temperature in 1990 were 72 degrees, the temperature in YEAR would be given by the equation

TEMP = 72 + .08 * (YEAR − 1990)

Write a program that accepts a year and calculates and prints the average temperature in that year.

4.3 You are given each student's name and test scores on three tests. Write a program to calculate the student's average score by adding the three test scores and dividing by three. For each student, print the name, three test scores, and the average test score.

4.4 Renting a car costs $40 plus a mileage charge. The first 25 miles are free, but above that the charge is 18 cents a mile. Write a program that accepts a mileage and calculates and prints the bill. (Assume that all customers drive at least 25 miles.)

4.5 Write a program for the Vanity Flair Gym that accepts a person's name, the number of push-ups she was able to do last week, and the number of push-ups she was able to do this week. Calculate and print the percent change in her performance.

*4.6 Write a program that will accept an item's price today and a year ago and will calculate and print the percent change in the price. Then assume the price will change by the same percent next year and calculate and print the price a year from now. For example, if the price a year ago was $10 and the price today is $11, the percent change will be 10, and the price next year will be 12.1.

4.7 Write a program that accepts a radius and calculates and prints the area of a circle of that radius and the volume of a sphere of that radius. The area of a circle is πR^2, and the volume of a sphere is $\frac{4}{3}\pi R^3$, where π is the numeric constant 3.14159.

4.8 If you are standing HEIGHT feet above sea level, the distance to the horizon, in miles, is given by

HORIZON = 1.23 * HEIGHT ^ .5

Write a program that accepts the height above sea level and calculates and prints the distance to the horizon.

*4.9 A video cassette contains 275 feet of tape. Write a program that accepts the number of feet of tape a company has on hand, and calculates and prints the number of cassettes it can manufacture. Also calculate the number of feet left over after all the cassettes have been made.

MORE ABOUT THE PRINT AND LPRINT STATEMENTS

We have used PRINT and LPRINT statements in our programs to display answers, but we have not yet explained exactly how these statements work.

Printing Numeric Variables

Your monitor screen and printer paper are divided into zones that are 14 characters wide, with any remaining characters forming a short zone. Screens and printers that print 80 characters on a line have five full zones and one short zone that is only ten characters wide.*

The PRINT and LPRINT statements we have used so far print one value in each zone. However, some versions of BASIC are inconsistent. In these versions, the PRINT statement uses only full zones, so only five values are printed on a line, but the LPRINT statement uses all the zones and therefore prints six values on a line.

If you are using the PRINT statement and specify more than five variables to be printed, BASIC prints the values of five variables on a line and uses as many lines as necessary to print the values of all the variables. So if the PRINT statement were

PRINT A, B, C, D, E, F, G, H

*If SIZE represents the number of characters on a line, the number of full print zones is SIZE\14, and the number of characters in the short zone at the end of the line is SIZE MOD 14.

the values of A, B, C, D, and E would be printed on the first line, and the values of F, G, and H on the second. But if you used an LPRINT statement, then values A through F would be printed on the first line and only values G and H would be printed on the second line.

USE OF SEMICOLONS

It often happens that we want to print more than five (or six) values on a line. BASIC makes that very easy; just separate the variables with semicolons instead of commas. A legal PRINT (or LPRINT) statement would be

```
PRINT A; B; C; D; E; F; G; H
```

This PRINT statement would cause all eight values to be printed on one line. Leaving one or more spaces between variables has the same effect as typing semicolons, so the following statement would give the same output:

```
PRINT A B C D E F G H
```

When semicolons or spaces are used to separate the variables in a print list, the values are printed next to each other. Numbers are printed with a space before and after. The space before the number is used to show the sign of the number. If the number is positive, the space is left blank; if the number is negative, a minus sign is printed. The space after the number is always left blank, so there will be at least one blank space between numbers.

You might wonder how many values will be printed on a line when semicolons are used. Unfortunately, there is no simple answer because different values take different numbers of columns to print. For example, the number 1 requires only three columns to print (including the spaces before and after), while the number 16976 requires seven columns.

HANGING PUNCTUATION

In the examples we have seen so far, whenever a PRINT or LPRINT statement has been executed, it has started printing on a new line. That's fine, since usually you want to keep the output for each case on its own line. But if you put a comma or a semicolon after the *last* variable in a PRINT or LPRINT statement (**hanging punctuation**), the next PRINT or LPRINT statement executed will not start on a new line. Instead, it will begin printing where the previous printing stopped. Program 8.7 shows that sometimes that may be desirable. But most of the time, hanging punctuation is not desirable because the output for different cases becomes mixed on the same line.

Hanging punctuation
A comma or a semicolon that appears after the last variable in a print list.

Printing String Variables and Strings

Besides printing values of numeric variables, the PRINT and LPRINT statements can be used to print string variables. Like numeric variables, string variables are printed one to a zone. If you print a string variable that contains 14 or more characters, it will occupy more than one print zone, and the next variable will be printed at the start of the next zone. For example, if N$ contains 18 characters, the statement

```
PRINT N$, A
```

will cause the value of N$ to fill all of print zone 1 and the first four columns of print zone 2. The value of A will be printed in print zone 3.

Using LPRINT and PRINT statements with strings can also make your output clearer. For example, to print a heading for the output in Program 3.4, simply add the statement

```
12 LPRINT "PAYROLL REPORT"
```

(Remember that strings must be enclosed in quotation marks.) This LPRINT statement will cause the printing of PAYROLL REPORT to start in the first print zone. If you want to approximately center the heading, you can have BASIC skip print zones by inserting commas before the string:

```
12 LPRINT , , "PAYROLL REPORT"
```

The two commas tell BASIC to skip the first two print zones and to begin printing the heading in zone 3.

Similarly, you can make BASIC print headings for columns by adding a statement like the following:

```
16 LPRINT "Employee Name", "Rate", "Hours", "Gross Pay"
```

Employee Name will be printed in zone 1, Rate in zone 2, Hours in zone 3, and Gross Pay in zone 4. However, if a column heading is 14 characters or longer, it will spill into the next zone and force subsequent headings into later zones.

To improve the appearance of output, you may want to add some blank lines. To do so, add a blank LPRINT statement as follows:

```
14 LPRINT
```

Program 4.2 shows the simple gross pay program from Program 3.4 modified by the addition of three LPRINT statements to print a report heading (line 12), a blank line (line 14), and column headings (line 16). Since you want to print the headings only once, the three new LPRINT statements must be inserted before the INPUT statement. If these LPRINT statements were inserted after the INPUT statement, they would be inside the loop and would be executed every time the INPUT statement was executed.

You can also mix strings and variables in the same PRINT statement, for example,

```
PRINT EMP.NAME$, "earned", GROSS.PAY, "dollars last week."
```

A comma or a semicolon that appears after the last variable in a print list.

For the first values in Program 4.2, this statement would print

```
Joe Tinker      earned          270         dollars last week.
```

To make this statement "read" better, you may want to use semicolons so the values will be printed closer together. The statement

```
PRINT EMP.NAME$; "earned"; GROSS.PAY; "dollars last week."
```

would print

```
Joe Tinkerearned 270 dollars last week.
```

Obviously, Tinkerearned should not be one word. This problem would occur because when strings or string variables are printed with semicolons, they are printed right next to each other. To correct it, you must add a space at the beginning of the earned string, as in the following statement:

```
PRINT EMP.NAME$; " earned"; GROSS.PAY; "dollars last week"
```

One further comment: You should be able to see now why the quotation marks are important—they make the difference between printing a numerical variable and printing a string. The statement

```
PRINT RATE
```

```
10 REM *** BAT-O PROGRAM WITH HEADINGS ***
12 LPRINT ,,"PAYROLL REPORT"                        ⎫ Statements that
14 LPRINT                                           ⎬ print headings
16 LPRINT "Employee Name","Pay Rate","Hours","Gross Pay" ⎭
20 INPUT "Enter Name, Rate, Hours, Stop to end "; EMP.NAME$, PAY.RATE, HOURS
30   IF EMP.NAME$ = "Stop"
        THEN GOTO 70
40   GROSS.PAY = PAY.RATE * HOURS
50   LPRINT EMP.NAME$, PAY.RATE, HOURS, GROSS.PAY
60 GOTO 20
70 END

RUN
Enter Name, Rate, Hours, Stop to end ? Joe Tinker,6.75,40
Enter Name, Rate, Hours, Stop to end ? John Evers,6,30
Enter Name, Rate, Hours, Stop to end ? Frank Chance,5.75,25
Enter Name, Rate, Hours, Stop to end ? Stop,0,0
Ok
```

```
                    PAYROLL REPORT   ← Printed by line 12
                                     ⎬ Blank line printed by line 14
Employee Name   Pay Rate    Hours          Gross Pay  ← Printed by line 16
Joe Tinker        6.75       40              270
John Evers        6          30              180
Frank Chance      5.75       25              143.75
```

PROGRAM 4.2   Bat-O program with headings.

prints the value of the variable RATE, which could be any number and which might be a different number each time the statement is executed. In contrast, the statement

```
PRINT "RATE"
```

always prints the word RATE.

PERSONAL FORM LETTERS

Manipulating strings is the essence of those "personalized" letters so dear to the hearts of advertisers. "Dear Mr. Swell," they begin. "We are delighted to be able to offer our incredible six-passenger hot air balloon to you and your neighbors in Blimpton at the unbelievably low price of only $19.95." Of course, few Americans these days believe they are really being singled out. Most realize that computers are used to generate such "personal" form letters. Program 4.3 shows a BASIC program that writes personalized form letters.

```
100 REM *** PERSONAL FORM LETTERS ***
110 INPUT "Enter name, town and item, XXX to stop"; LNAME$, TOWN$, ITEM$
120   IF LNAME$ = "XXX"
          THEN GOTO 250
130   LPRINT "Dear Mr. and Mrs. "; LNAME$; ":"
140   LPRINT
150   LPRINT "     Because the "; LNAME$; "s are leaders in "; TOWN$
160   LPRINT "we have decided to let the ";LNAME$; "s be the first"
170   LPRINT "family in "; TOWN$; " to have the opportunity to buy"
180   LPRINT "the amazing new "; ITEM$; ".  I'm sure you will enjoy"
190   LPRINT "your "; ITEM$; "; you will be the envy of all your"
200   LPRINT "neighbors in ";TOWN$; ".  So send your check today!"
210   LPRINT
220   LPRINT "                              Yours truly,"
230   LPRINT "                              Robemblind Corp."
240 GOTO 110
250 END

RUN
Enter name, town and item, XXX to stop? Jackson,Williamsport,Abacus Computer
Enter name, town and item, XXX to stop? XXX,X,X
Ok
```

```
Dear Mr. and Mrs. Jackson:

     Because the Jacksons are leaders in Williamsport
we have decided to let the Jacksons be the first
family in Williamsport to have the opportunity to buy
the amazing new Abacus Computer.  I'm sure you will enjoy
your Abacus Computer; you will be the envy of all your
neighbors in Williamsport.  So send your check today!

                              Yours truly,
                              Robemblind Corp.
```

PROGRAM 4.3   A program that prints a "personalized" form letter.

EXERCISES

4.6 Write a PRINT statement to print a blank line.

4.7 You want to print the values of the variables R, M, L, W, Z, P, and G. Write the statement(s) that will print them all on one line. Write the statement(s) that will print one on each line.

***4.8** Write PRINT statements to print the title and two column headings shown below, where the B in BOOKS is in column 4.

```
   BOOKS BORROWED
Author        Title
```

4.9 What output is produced by the following program?

```
10 A = 6
20 PRINT "A"
30 END
```

PROGRAMMING ASSIGNMENTS

. . . .

Follow the general directions on page 51 to construct programs that solve the following problems. Wherever appropriate, be sure to print headings.

4.10 a) Write a program that accepts the names of foods and the amount of cholesterol they contain and produces a report like the following:

```
CHOLESTEROL CONTENT OF FOODS
Food            Cholesterol
Hamburger       375
Chicken         60
Broccoli        0
```

   b) Modify the program to print the output in the following format:

```
Hamburger contains 375 milligrams
of cholesterol.
```

   (The output should be on one line).

*4.11 Write a program that accepts a name and prints a message like

```
Good Morning, George
Have a good day
```

*4.12 Make Program 4.2 more realistic by deducting income tax, social security tax, and medical in-surance premiums from gross pay to get net pay. Assume the withholding tax rate is 18%, the social security tax rate is 8%, and the medical insurance is $15. Print name, pay rate, hours worked, gross pay, income tax withholding, social security tax, and net pay. Use semicolons in the print list so that all the output for a case will be printed on one line. If you use the data in Program 4.2 you should find that Joe Tinker's withholding is $48.60, his social security tax is $21.60, and his net pay is $184.80.

4.13 Modify your solution to Programming Assignment 4.2 so that the output is like

```
In 2030 the average temperature will be
75.2 degrees.
```

   (The output should be on one line).

4.14 Write a program that will print a personalized form letter. The program can print any letter you like; some suggestions are a love letter, a politician's reelection letter, a real estate agent's letter.

MORE ON ERRORS

. . . .

Now that you can write more sophisticated programs, you will make more sophisticated errors. It is important to know how to detect and correct these more sophisticated errors. BASIC's powerful Program Editor facilitates the process. Using the Editor, you can add, delete, and change characters in a line.

   In Chapter 2, we noted that BASIC identifies the line number of syntax errors and prints the line. At that time, you were told to press the Enter key and retype the line. In fact, what BASIC does when it detects a syntax error is to automatically turn on the Program Editor. Rather than use the Enter key and retype, you can use the Editor to correct the line. In the case of logic errors, however, BASIC does not automatically turn control over to the Editor. You must call for the Editor yourself by using the EDIT command, as you will see shortly.

Using the BASIC Program Editor

The Program Editor is easier to use than to illustrate or describe, so it will be helpful if you edit a line on your PC as you read this discussion. To begin, type line 40 in Program 4.2 incorrectly as

```
40 GROSS.SALARY = RATE * HOURS.WORKED
```

This line has three errors: GROSS.SALARY should be GROSS.PAY, RATE should be PAY.RATE, and HOURS.WORKED should be HOURS. To edit a line, type the command EDIT and the line number. To edit this line, you would use the command

EDIT 40

In response to this command, line 40 is displayed, and the cursor is positioned under the first digit of the line number.

To use the Editor, you must move the cursor to the position on the line where the correction is to be made. The cursor is moved by using the keys in the numeric keypad as shown in Figure 4.2(a) or, if you have an enhanced keyboard, the separate cursor control keys shown in Figure 4.2(b). Every time you press an arrow key, the cursor moves one space in the direction of the arrow. Like all the keys, the cursor control keys repeat when they are held down, so it is easy to move the cursor large distances. (If when you press one of these keys, you see a number printed on the screen, it means that sometime earlier you pressed the Num Lock key. Num Lock is a toggle key that changes the numeric keypad from cursor control keys to numeric keys and vice versa each time it is pressed. Press the Num Lock key to change back to cursor control mode.)

You can use the Ctrl key with the → and ← keys to make the cursor move faster. The combination Ctrl + → causes the cursor to move forward to the beginning of the next word. (A "word" is any group of characters that begins with a letter or a digit.) Similarly, the combination Ctrl + ← causes the cursor to move back to the beginning of the previous word. The End key moves the cursor to the end of the line, which is convenient if you want to add characters to the end of a line.

You can use the cursor control keys any time, not only when you are using the Editor. For example, suppose you are typing a line and you notice a mistake. You could use the Backspace key to correct the error, but the Backspace key erases as it backspaces. If you are near the end of the line and the error is near the start, backspacing to the error would force you to retype almost the whole line. However, if you use the cursor control keys to move the cursor, the characters you move over are not erased.

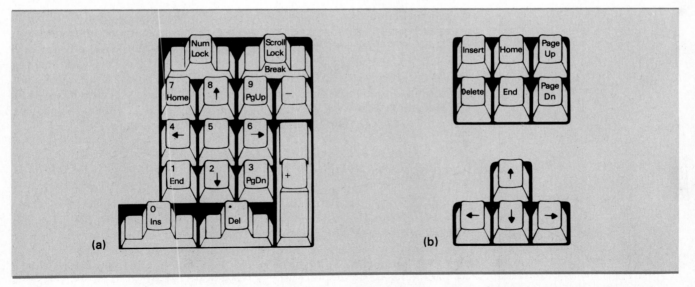

FIGURE 4.2 **(a) The numeric keypad. (b) The cursor keypad on the enhanced keyboard.**
Courtesy of International Business Machines Corporation.

To change GROSS.SALARY to GROSS.PAY, then, use the → key to move the cursor until it is under the S of SALARY and type PAY. These three letters replace the three letters SAL. In general, the contents of any column may be changed by moving the cursor to that column and overtyping.

At this point, line 40 is

```
40 GROSS.PAYARY = RATE * HOURS.WORKED
```

and the cursor is under the second A in PAYARY. You must now delete the three letters ARY. To do so, press the Del (Delete) key three times. Be careful when you press the Del key, since, like all keys, it repeats, and if you hold it down too long you may delete more than you wanted to.

The next step is to change RATE to PAY.RATE. This correction requires you to insert the four characters PAY. before RATE. Use the → key to move the cursor under the R of RATE and press the Ins (Insert) key, another toggle switch, to change to insert mode. When the Ins key is pressed, the cursor becomes larger, to remind you that you are in insert mode. When you are in insert mode, characters you type are inserted to the left of the cursor; that is why you had to place the cursor under the R of RATE instead of under the blank just to the left of the R. Type the characters PAY. and press the Ins key to leave the insert mode.

There are other ways to leave the insert mode besides pressing the Ins key. Pressing any cursor control key or the Enter key also causes you to leave the insert mode. Whichever way you do it, you can tell that you have left the insert mode because the cursor returns to its normal size.

At this point, the line reads

```
40 GROSS.PAY = PAY.RATE * HOURS.WORKED
```

The final correction is to change HOURS.WORKED to HOURS. Again use the → key to move the cursor under the period in HOURS.WORKED. Then use the Ctrl + End keys. .WORKED will disappear. The combination Ctrl + End erases everything from the cursor position to the end of the line.

Although you have made all the corrections needed, you are not finished yet. When the line is correct, you must press the Enter key to enter your changes and leave the Program Editor. (The cursor doesn't have to be at the end of the line when you press the Enter key; the changes are made as long as the cursor is anywhere on the line.) This is an important step that is often forgotten. Although you can see the changes you made on the screen, no changes are made to the program in RAM until you press the Enter key.

Until you press the Enter key, you also have the option of cancelling your changes. This feature can be very useful. Suppose, for example, that you intended to use the End key to move to the end of a line, and by mistake you pressed Ctrl + End, erasing to the end of the line. To cancel the change, you can use either the Ctrl + Break keys or the Esc key.

Full-Screen Editing

Typing EDIT is not the only way to edit lines. You can use the cursor at any time to edit whatever lines appear on the screen, no matter how they got there. This form of editing is called **full-screen editing**.

If you have to correct many lines, it is convenient to LIST either all or part of the program. You can then use the cursor control keys to move the cursor anywhere on the screen to a position where a correction is to be made. Remember, however, that after the corrections have been made on a

Full-screen editing
The technique of changing any line on the screen simply by moving the cursor to the line and making the change.

line, you must press the Enter key to transfer the corrections from the screen to the program in RAM. You can then move the cursor to the next line that needs corrections.

After you have made the last correction and pressed the Enter key, it is likely that the cursor will be on a line that contains displayed characters—for example, a BASIC statement. Before you can enter a command or a new BASIC statement, the cursor must be on a clean line. One way to get a clean line is to clear the whole screen using the Ctrl + Home keys, as you learned in Chapter 1. Another way is to press the Esc key. Pressing the Esc key clears the line the cursor is on but has no effect on the program in the computer. You may then type anything you want.

Full-screen editing is a convenient way to change `PRINT` statements to `LPRINT` statements. You can initially write your programs using `PRINT` statements, putting all the output on the screen, which makes debugging easier. After the program is completely debugged, you can `LIST` the program and use the full-screen editing technique to change all the `PRINT` statements to `LPRINT` statements, thus obtaining hard copy output.

Although full-screen editing is helpful, there is one danger you must be aware of. Imagine you are running a program to debug it, and you enter a set of data that gives incorrect answers. You might examine the lines of the program that are visible on the screen and discover the error. At that point, you may be tempted to move the cursor to the incorrect statement and correct the error. If you do, BASIC will respond with the error message `?Redo from start`. The problem is that because of the loop in the program, BASIC has executed the `INPUT` statement and is waiting for you to enter the second set of data. You must remember to use the Ctrl + Break keys to stop execution of your program before you can correct the error.

Invalid Line Numbers

A special kind of editing problem involves invalid line numbers. This kind of syntax error occurs when you accidentally type the letter O instead of the number 0, or the letter I or l instead of the number 1. Program 4.4 shows what happens in such a case. Here, when typing Program 3.4, someone typed line 40 incorrectly as

```
40 GROSS.PAY = PAY.RATE * HOURS
```

where the character following the number 4 is the letter O, not the number 0. As Program 4.4 shows, BASIC will print the error message

```
Syntax error in 4
4 O GROSS.PAY = PAY.RATE * HOURS
```

BASIC has interpreted this statement as line 4, which starts as 0 `GROSS.PAY`. Since the statement contains an "obvious" syntax error, BASIC turns control over to the Program Editor.

The first step in correcting this error is to type a 0 in column 2 and delete the O in column 3. This will yield a correctly typed line 40. Although you cannot see it very clearly in Program 4.4, that is what was done. But if you simply type `RUN` again, Program 4.4 shows you will get the same error message, `Syntax error in line 4`! Whenever BASIC gives a response you do not understand, you should `LIST` or `LLIST` the program (in this case, first press the Enter key to exit from the Editor). The listing clearly shows the problem: Line 40 is now correct, but the original line 4 is still in the program. As a second step, then, line 4 must be deleted.

```
10 REM  *** BAT-O PROGRAM WITH NAMES ***
20 INPUT "Enter Name, Rate, Hours, Stop to end "; EMP.NAME$, PAY.RATE, HOURS
30    IF EMP.NAME$ = "Stop"
         THEN GOTO 70              ("O" typed intead of zero)
40 ◄     GROSS.PAY = PAY.RATE * HOURS
50    LPRINT EMP.NAME$, PAY.RATE, HOURS, GROSS.PAY
60 GOTO 20
70 END

RUN ◄──(Execute program)
Syntax error in 4 ◄──(Error message)
Ok
4 O    GROSS.PAY = PAY.RATE * HOURS ◄──(Use the Editor to correct statement)

RUN ◄──(Execute again)
Syntax error in 4 ◄──(Same error message)
Ok
4 O    GROSS.PAY = PAY.RATE * HOURS ◄──(Press Enter Key to exit from Editor)

LIST ◄──(List the program)
4 O    GROSS.PAY = PAY.RATE * HOURS ◄──(Line 4 in its proper numerical position)
10 REM  *** BAT-O PROGRAM WITH NAMES ***
20 INPUT "Enter Name, Rate, Hours, Stop to end "; EMP.NAME$, PAY.RATE, HOURS
30    IF EMP.NAME$ = "Stop"
         THEN GOTO 70
40    GROSS.PAY = PAY.RATE * HOURS
50    LPRINT EMP.NAME$, PAY.RATE, HOURS, GROSS.PAY
60 GOTO 20
70 END
Ok
4 ◄──(Delete line 4)
RUN ◄──(Execute again)
Enter Name, Rate, Hours, Stop to end ? Joe Tinker,6.75,40
Enter Name, Rate, Hours, Stop to end ?
──────────────────────────────────────────────────────
Joe Tinker       6.75          40            270 ◄──(Correct answer)
```

PROGRAM 4.4   **Correcting a line number error using the BASIC Program Editor.**

You can delete line 4 simply by typing a 4 and then pressing the Enter key. Program 4.4 shows that after line 4 is deleted, the program runs correctly.

Deleting Lines

Typing a line number by itself and then pressing the Enter key is the easiest way to delete a single line. But when you have many lines to delete, the DELETE command is faster. The command

                      DELETE 40-120

deletes all the lines from 40 to 120, including lines 40 and 120. Using the Alt + D keys is equivalent to typing the word DELETE.

The DELETE command may also be written in the form

DELETE -90

This command deletes all the lines from the beginning up to and including line 90. Or you can type

DELETE 90-

to delete from line 90 to the end of the program.

Remember that no statement is processed until you press the Enter key. Suppose you want to delete all the lines from line 100 to the end of the program, but you accidentally type

DELETE 10-

All is not lost as long as you notice the error before you press the Enter key. You can still edit this line (using full-screen editing) or you can simply use the Esc key to cancel the command and at the same time to clear the line on the screen so you can retype the command correctly.

Inserting a Line

You sometimes may find that the source of a logic error in your program is a line that was left out. Program 4.5 shows a version of Program 4.1 that produces no output at all. If you examine the listing, you will notice the LPRINT statement is missing.

How can you add an LPRINT (or any other) statement to a program? You can always insert new statements simply by using a previously unused statement number. In this case, the LPRINT statement logically belongs between lines 40 and 50. You can insert an LPRINT statement there by typing

45 LPRINT DEPOSIT, RATE, NO.YEARS, BALANCE

The computer will insert line 45 in its proper numeric position between lines 40 and 50. Program 4.5 shows line 45 being added to the program. To execute the program after the new statements have been inserted, you must type RUN again. The program is then executed, and this time we see the correct answers printed.

Clearly, numbering statements by tens has advantages. It leaves us nine slots between every pair of statements in the program in which to insert additional statements.

Scrolling

We have mentioned before how useful it is in debugging a program to list the program. But as you begin to write larger programs, you may encounter a new problem. As you may have noticed, whenever a new line is displayed on the twenty-fourth line (the line above the function key definitions), all the preceding lines move up one line, and the top line moves off the screen. This process is called **scrolling**. Scrolling can be a nuisance when you are listing a program, since it can make lines disappear off the top of the screen so fast you don't have a chance to read them. To solve the problem, you can suspend the listing (and the scrolling) by pressing Ctrl + Num Lock, or, on the enhanced keyboard, the Pause key. When you are ready to move on, you can resume the listing (and the scrolling) by pressing any key.

Scrolling
The process in which lines move off the top of the screen as new lines are displayed on the bottom of the screen.

```
10 REM *** LOANSOME BANK PROBLEM ***
20 INPUT "Enter Deposit, Rate, Years, 0 to stop "; DEPOSIT, RATE, NO.YEARS
30    IF DEPOSIT = 0
         THEN GOTO 70
40    BALANCE = DEPOSIT * (1 + RATE) ^ NO.YEARS
60 GOTO 20
70 END


RUN
Enter Deposit, Rate, Years, 0 to stop ? 1000,.05,20    ⎫
Enter Deposit, Rate, Years, 0 to stop ? 100000,.20,50  ⎬ ( No output produced )
Enter Deposit, Rate, Years, 0 to stop ? 0,0,0          ⎭
Ok
45    LPRINT DEPOSIT, RATE, NO.YEARS, BALANCE ◄── ( Inserting line 45 )
LIST
10 REM *** LOANSOME BANK PROBLEM ***
20 INPUT "Enter Deposit, Rate, Years, 0 to stop "; DEPOSIT, RATE, NO.YEARS
30    IF DEPOSIT = 0
         THEN GOTO 70
40    BALANCE = DEPOSIT * (1 + RATE) ^ NO.YEARS
45    LPRINT DEPOSIT, RATE, NO.YEARS, BALANCE ◄── ( Line 45 was inserted in its proper place )
60 GOTO 20
70 END
Ok
RUN ◄── ( Execute again )
Enter Deposit, Rate, Years, 0 to stop ? 1000,.05,20
Enter Deposit, Rate, Years, 0 to stop ? 100000,.20,50
Enter Deposit, Rate, Years, 0 to stop ? 0,0,0
Ok
─────────────────────────────────────────────────────────────
1000              .05           20          2653.293
100000            .2            50          9.100439E+08
```

PROGRAM 4.5   **Inserting a statement in a program.**

Scrolling may also occur during program execution—for example, when the output produced by PRINT statements fills more than one screen. In this situation, by using the Ctrl + Num Lock combination or the Pause key, you can suspend the PRINT statement output.

Notice the difference between Ctrl + Break and Ctrl + Num Lock. Ctrl + Num Lock stops an operation temporarily; the operation may be resumed by pressing any key. Ctrl + Break, in contrast, causes the operation to be canceled. Then, to resume listing, for example, you would have to reenter the LIST command.

You might have thought that the Scroll Lock key would be used to stop and start scrolling, but unfortunately it doesn't. In BASIC, the Scroll Lock key doesn't do anything.

 Getting the Bugs Out

Problem: You use full-screen editing to correct an error, but when you run the program, you find the error is still there.

Reason: You forgot to press the Enter key after you made the correction.

Solution: Correct the error again and remember to press the Enter key while the cursor is on the corrected line. If the corrected line is still on the screen, you can simply move the cursor to it and press the Enter key.

EXERCISES

4.10 Write the command to edit a line 60.

4.11 Write the command to delete lines 50 through 80.

*4.12 What will the following command do?

         DELETE 70-

4.13 Program 4.6 shows a solution to Programming Assignment 4.11 that contains a logic error. How would you fix the error?

```
10 REM *** PROGRAMMING ASSIGNMENT 4.11 ***
20 INPUT "Enter first name, XXX to stop "; FIRST.NAME$
30   IF FIRST.NAME$ = "xxx"
        THEN GOTO 70
40   PRINT "Good Morning, "; FIRST.NAME$
50   PRINT "Have a good day"
60 GOTO 20
70 END

RUN
Enter first name, XXX to stop ? George
Good Morning, George
Have a good day
Enter first name, XXX to stop ? XXX
Good Morning, XXX
Have a good day
Enter first name, XXX to stop ?
```

PROGRAM 4.6   **An incorrect solution to Programming Assignment 4.11.**

SUMMARY

In this chapter, you have learned that

- Exponentiation is performed using the symbol $^\wedge$, integer division using the symbol \, and modulo arithmetic using the word MOD.

- In BASIC, complicated expressions are evaluated by following these rules of precedence:

  0. Evaluate expressions inside parentheses.
  1. Perform exponentiations.
  2. Perform multiplications and divisions.
  3. Perform additions and subtractions.

- Using pseudocode will help you develop an algorithm, because it allows you to concentrate on the problem rather than on the syntax rules of BASIC.

- If a variable has a value that is too large or too small to be printed in seven digits, it is printed in scientific notation.

- [ ] When semicolons are used in a print list, the values are printed close together. Each numeric value is printed with a space before it, which will contain a minus sign if the value is negative and a blank space after it. Strings and string variables are printed with no spaces between them.

- [ ] A comma or a semicolon that appears at the end of a print list is called hanging punctuation. Hanging commas and semicolons cause the next PRINT statement to begin printing where the last PRINT statement stopped.

- [ ] Strings may be printed by surrounding them by quotation marks and including them in a print list.

- [ ] To use the Program Editor to edit a line, type the command EDIT followed by the desired line number. The Insert (Ins), Delete (Del), and cursor control keys are used to edit characters within a line.

- [ ] You can edit a statement that appears anywhere on the screen. This technique is called full-screen editing.

- [ ] You delete a line by typing the line number and pressing the Enter key; you delete a range of lines by using the DELETE command.

- [ ] You can insert a statement into a program by using a previously unused line number.

KEY TERMS IN THIS CHAPTER

· ·

exponentiation 67   **modulo arithmetic** 67   **rules of precedence** 68
full-screen editing 82   **pseudocode** 71   **scientific notation** 73
hanging punctuation 76   **round-off error** 72   **scrolling** 85
integer division 67

QUESTIONS FOR REVIEW

· ·

4.1 What is the difference between ordinary division and integer division?

4.2 If A and B are integers, what is the value of

$$B * (A \setminus B) + A \text{ MOD } B$$

4.3 When BASIC evaluates an expression, which does it do first, multiplication or division?

4.4 True or false: When writing a program in pseudocode, it is essential to follow BASIC syntax rules exactly.

4.5 Why do round-off errors occur?

4.6 If an answer is printed as 1.0E + 09, what is its value?

4.7 True or false: When semicolons are used in a print list, exactly eight values are printed on a line.

4.8 A comma at the end of a print list causes the next output to be printed _____ .

4.9 True or false: The following two statements produce the same output:

```
PRINT "NAME ";N$
PRINT "NAME"; N$
```

4.10 What should you do if, when you use the cursor control keys to move the cursor, you see a number displayed on the screen?

4.11 When you are editing a line, what tells you that you are in the insert mode?

4.12 When you are editing a line, how do you delete a character?

4.13 When you are editing a line, how do you move the cursor to the end of the line?

4.14 What is the effect of holding down the Ctrl key when you press a cursor control key?

ADDITIONAL PROGRAMMING ASSIGNMENTS

In the following programming assignments, in addition to following the standard instructions, print headings for all the assignments except 4.17 and 4.19.

4.15 Write a program that accepts a person's age, in years, and prints the number of seconds the person has lived. Assume there are 365 days in a year.

*4.16 If the face value of a bond is FACE, its coupon is COUPON, and the number of years to maturity is NO.YEARS, then for the yield to maturity to be YIELD, the current price, PRICE, is given by the equation

$$PRICE = FACE * V + COUPON * A$$

where V and A are given by

$$V = (1 + YIELD) \, ^\wedge \, (- \, NO.YEARS)$$
$$A = (1 - V) \, / \, YIELD$$

For example, if FACE = 1000, COUPON = 40, NO.YEARS = 10, and YIELD = .08, then V = .4631933, A = 6.710084, and PRICE = 731.5967. Write a program that accepts FACE, COUPON, NO.YEARS, and YIELD and calculates and prints PRICE.

4.17 Write a program to convert inches to yards, feet, and inches. For example, if the input is 94, the output should be

```
94 inches is 2 yards 1 feet and 10 inches
```

*4.18 If the three sides of a triangle are represented by A, B, and C, the area of the triangle is given by the equation:

$$Area = (S * (S - A) * (S - B) * (S - C)) \, ^\wedge \, .5$$

where S is defined as

$$S = (A + B + C) \, / \, 2$$

Write a program that accepts the three sides of a triangle and calculates and prints the area. Make sure that the values you invent for A, B, and C can represent a real triangle. That is, it is necessary that the sum of any two sides be longer than the third side. If you use sides of 3, 4, and 5, the area will be 6.

4.19 Modify Program 3.4 to print the information for each employee in the following format:

```
Name            Joe Tinker
Pay Rate        6.75
Hours Worked    40
Gross Pay       270
```

4.20 If an object is dropped from a height HEIGHT, the time it takes to reach the ground is given by

$$TIME = (HEIGHT \, / \, 16.1) \, ^\wedge \, .5$$

and its final velocity (speed of travel) is

$$VELOCITY = (64.4 * HEIGHT) \, ^\wedge \, .5$$

(These equations ignore air resistance.) In these equations, HEIGHT is in feet, TIME is in seconds, and VELOCITY is in feet per second. Write a program that accepts HEIGHT and calculates and prints TIME and VELOCITY. You might like to know that the World Trade Center towers are 1350 feet tall.

*4.21 a) Given an arithmetic progression,

$$a, a + d, a + 2d, \ldots$$

where a is the first term and d is the common difference, the sum of the first n terms is

$$S = \frac{n}{2}[2a + (n - 1)d]$$

Write a program that accepts a, d, and n and calculates and prints the sum of the arithmetic progression.

b) Given a geometric progression,

$$a, ar, ar^2, \ldots$$

where a is the first term and r is the common ratio, the sum of the first n terms is

$$S = a\left(\frac{r^n - 1}{r - 1}\right)$$

Write a program that accepts a, r, and n and calculates and prints the sum of the geometric progression.

4.22 A bakery packs 12 cookies in a box and 20 boxes in a carton. Write a program that accepts the number of cookies baked and calculates and prints the number of cartons produced, the number of boxes left over, and the number of cookies left over.

BEYOND THE BASICS

....

4.1 If your house has a mortgage of M dollars that must be paid off in Y years, and the bank charges R annual interest rate, then the monthly payment, P, is given by

$$P = \frac{M \cdot i}{1 - (1 + i)^{-n}}$$

where n is the number of monthly payments which is equal to $12Y$, and i is the monthly interest rate, which is equal to $R/12$. Write a program to calculate your monthly payment, the total amount to be paid to the bank, and the total amount of interest to be paid. What is the fraction of the total paid to the bank that repaid the loan? What is the fraction that paid the interest on the loan?

4.2 Drew Draper, interior decorator, wants to order carpet for a room. The amount of carpet must be specified in square yards, but the length and width of the room are given in terms of yards, feet, and inches. For example, the length might be 3 yards, 2 feet, 7 inches. Write a program that accepts the length and width in this form and calculates and prints the area in square yards.

4.3 Help Yourself vending machines sell items that cost less than one dollar, and they accept a dollar as payment, giving correct change as needed. Write a program to calculate the number of half-dollars, quarters, dimes, nickels, and pennies required to make change.

4.4 Write a program that accepts two durations in terms of hours, minutes, and seconds and that calculates and prints their sum, also in terms of hours, minutes, and seconds.

4.5 Every time Frank buys gas, he fills the tank and writes down the odometer reading and the number of gallons of gas he bought. His data looks like this:

Odometer Reading	Gallons of Gas
394	15.1
681	11.4
1018	12.8
1308	11.1

Assume his car was delivered with an odometer reading of 0 and a full tank. Write a program that will process this data to calculate and print the miles per gallon he got for each fill-up. Also calculate and print the average miles per gallon for all the fill-ups. Your output should look like this:

```
Fill-up     Miles     Gallons      MPG
   1         394        15.1     26.09272
   2         287        11.4     25.17544
   3         337        12.8     26.32813
   4         290        11.1     26.12613
Average MPG         25.95238
```

These data are just examples; your program must be able to handle any number of fill-ups. Hint: You may find it helpful to use LET statements of the form

```
TOTAL.MILES = TOTAL.MILES + MILES
```

5

Decisions and Subroutines

In the problems we have considered so far, we treated all cases identically. For example, in the savings account problem in Chapter 4, we compounded interest the same way for every customer. In many problems, however, we would like to treat different accounts differently. For instance, accounts with balances greater than $500 might have an interest rate of 10 percent, while all other accounts have an interest rate of 8 percent. As another example, a store might sell doughnuts for 50 cents each if a customer buys fewer than 12, but only 35 cents each if the customer buys 12 or more.

To solve these kinds of problems, a program must decide in each case which instructions to execute. For example, if the balance is greater than $500, the program must execute the statement in which the interest rate is 10 percent. But if the balance is $500 or less, the program must execute the statement in which the interest rate is 8 percent. In effect, the program must decide which statement to use in each case. You have already done that in a simple way by testing for trailer data and stopping execution when the test is true. In this chapter, you will learn how to write programs with more complicated conditions. Finally, as you will see, when writing more complex programs, it is helpful to divide the programs into sections, where each section solves one part of the problem.

A SALES PROBLEM WITH A DECISION

Consider the problem of Mrs. Crueller, proud owner of the Hole-in-One Doughnut Shop. Her usual price for doughnuts is 50 cents each, but to increase sales she has reduced the price to 35 cents each if a customer buys 12 or more. Mrs. Crueller needs a program that will calculate and print bills for her customers.

As always, our first step is to select names for the variables. Let's use the following:

Input variable	Number of doughnuts purchased	NO.DOUGHNUTS
Output variable	Customer's bill	BILL

The second step in our structured approach is to develop an algorithm. For this problem we can use

1. Accept NO.DOUGHNUTS for a customer.
2. If this is the trailer data, go to step 7.
3. Determine whether this customer bought 12 or more doughnuts.
4. Calculate BILL using the appropriate cost.
5. Print NO.DOUGHNUTS and BILL.
6. Repeat steps 1 through 5 until all the customers have been processed.
7. Stop execution.

The only new step in the procedure is step 3, where we must determine if the customer bought more than 12 doughnuts.

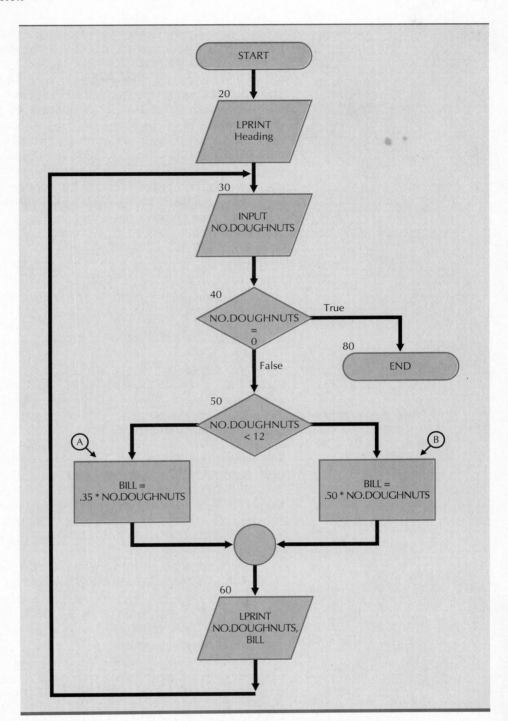

FIGURE 5.1 **Flowchart for the Hole-in-One Doughnut Shop problem.**

The flowchart for this algorithm is shown in Figure 5.1. Notice that in box 20 we print a heading, even though the algorithm did not mention headings. Printing headings is a detail that we do not want to be bothered with when we develop the algorithm; when the flowchart is drawn, we can fill in the details. Notice also that box 20 says simply "LPRINT Heading," which, of course, will not print the heading. When we write the program, "LPRINT Heading" must be translated into the appropriate BASIC statement. However, we do not have to show every detail in the flowchart; doing so sometimes makes the flowchart so complicated that it becomes less useful. The purpose of box 20 is just to remind us that at that point in the program we want to print a heading.

The flowchart in Figure 5.1 contains two decision symbols: the usual one that tests for trailer data and a second one that determines whether this customer bought more than 12 doughnuts. As you know, inside the decision symbol we write a condition. In the conditions we have used so far, we tested for trailer data by determining if a variable was equal to a constant, for example, DEPOSIT = 0. Conditions can be more general, and you can compare not only a variable and a constant, but two expressions, although usually you compare one variable with another variable or with a constant. Further, although so far we have tested only for equality, any of the following comparisons (shown with the symbols used to represent them) can be used in BASIC:

Equal	=
Less than	<
Greater than	>
Less than or equal	<=
Greater than or equal	>=
Not equal	<>

Relational operator
One of the six symbols =, <, >, <=, >=, or <>.

(Note that to express the last three comparisons you must type two symbols next to each other.) Because these six symbols indicate a relation (such as "less than" or "greater than"), they are called **relational operators.**

Returning to Figure 5.1, then, you can see that the condition in the second decision symbol is read, "Is NO.DOUGHNUTS less than 12?" If NO.DOUGHNUTS is less than 12, the condition is true; otherwise, the condition is false. (Question: If NO.DOUGHNUTS is exactly 12, is the condition true or false?*

If NO.DOUGHNUTS is less than 12, the condition is true. The "True" branch leads to process symbol Ⓑ, which shows BILL calculated using the equation BILL = 0.50 * NO.DOUGHNUTS. In this equation, the price of each doughnut is 50 cents, which is the correct price when NO.DOUGHNUTS is less than 12.

If NO.DOUGHNUTS is 12 or greater, the condition is false. The "False" branch leads to process symbol Ⓐ, which shows BILL calculated using the equation BILL = 0.35 * NO.DOUGHNUTS. In this equation, the price of each doughnut is 35 cents, which is the correct price when NO.DOUGHNUTS is 12 or greater. Thus, the flowchart shows BILL being calculated by the correct equation whether or not the customer buys less than 12 doughnuts.

Notice how in Figure 5.1 the "True" and "False" branches rejoin. We enter the decision symbol, take either the "True" or "False" branch, and then continue. Because flowcharts with rejoined branches are easier to read, you should try to draw your flowcharts so that the true and false branches rejoin. However, if either branch contains a GOTO statement, as the True branch does in the test for trailer data, then the two branches won't rejoin.

Hand-Calculated Answer

The third step of our structured approach is to calculate an answer by hand. If a customer buys 10 doughnuts, the bill will be 10 times 50 cents, or $5.00.

*False.

If a customer buys 20 doughnuts, the bill will be 20 times 35 cents, or $7.00. Notice that for this problem we must calculate an answer for two cases: customers who buy fewer than 12 doughnuts and customers who buy 12 or more.

We must calculate an answer for both cases because it is possible for a program to calculate the correct answer for one case, but an incorrect answer for the other case. You can't be sure your program is correct unless the answers calculated for both cases agree with the hand-calculated answers. In more complicated problems, it is possible to have more than two cases; in those problems, it is necessary to calculate answers by hand for each case.

The IF Statement

We are now ready for step 4—writing the BASIC program, which is shown in Program 5.1. Lines 10 through 40 are similar to statements you have seen in earlier programs, but line 50 is new. In it, the decision symbol in the flowchart is written as an IF statement with both THEN and ELSE clauses:

```
50 IF NO.DOUGHNUTS < 12
      THEN BILL = .50 * NO.DOUGHNUTS
      ELSE BILL = .35 * NO.DOUGHNUTS
```

When BASIC executes line 50, it evaluates the condition NO.DOUGHNUTS < 12. As you already know, if the condition is true, the statement following the reserved word THEN is executed. What is new is that if the condition is false, the statement following the reserved word ELSE is executed. (ELSE can be typed as Alt + E.) This IF statement does exactly what the flowchart specified; it charges .50 per doughnut if fewer than 12 are bought and .35 per doughnut if 12 or more are bought.

```
10 REM *** THE HOLE-IN-ONE DOUGHNUT PROBLEM ***
20 LPRINT "Doughnuts", "Bill"
30 INPUT "Enter Number of Doughnuts, 0 to stop "; NO.DOUGHNUTS
40    IF NO.DOUGHNUTS = 0
         THEN GOTO 80
50    IF NO.DOUGHNUTS < 12
         THEN BILL = .50 * NO.DOUGHNUTS
         ELSE BILL = .35 * NO.DOUGHNUTS
60    LPRINT NO.DOUGHNUTS,BILL
70 GOTO 30
80 END

RUN
Enter Number of Doughnuts, 0 to stop ? 10
Enter Number of Doughnuts, 0 to stop ? 20
Enter Number of Doughnuts, 0 to stop ? 0
Ok
```

```
Doughnuts      Bill
   10            5
   20            7
```

PROGRAM 5.1   **Program for the Hole-in-One Doughnut Shop problem.**

Just as we write an IF statement with a THEN clause on two lines to make the statement easier to read, so we write an IF statement with both a THEN and an ELSE clause on three lines. To get the ELSE clause on its own line, after you type the THEN clause, press Ctrl + Enter.

The complete syntax of the IF statement, then, is

```
IF condition THEN clause [ELSE clause]
```

The statement begins with the reserved word IF followed by a condition. The condition is written just as it is on a flowchart. If the condition is true, BASIC executes the clause following the word THEN. If the condition is false, BASIC executes the clause following the word ELSE. Both THEN and ELSE clauses may consist of a single BASIC statement, as in Program 5.1, or several BASIC statements, as we will see later in this chapter. Unless one or both clauses contain a GOTO statement, BASIC will continue with the next line after the clause is executed. In Program 5.1, after the BILL is calculated using either the THEN clause or the ELSE clause, BASIC continues with line 60.

The square brackets around the ELSE clause indicate that the ELSE clause is optional. If the ELSE clause is omitted and the condition is false, BASIC simply falls through the IF statement and executes the next line.

IF Statement

```
IF SALES > 1000
   THEN BONUS = 50
   ELSE BONUS = 0
```

Effect

If SALES is greater than 1000, BONUS is set to 50; otherwise, BONUS is set to 0.

IF Statement

```
IF NUMBER MOD 2 = 0
   THEN PRINT "Number is even"
   ELSE PRINT "Number is odd"
```

Effect

If the remainder when NUMBER is divided by 2 is 0, Number is even will print; otherwise, Number is odd will print.

IF Statement

```
IF GPA > 3.0
   THEN PRINT "DEAN'S LIST"
```

Effect

If GPA is greater than 3.0, DEAN'S LIST will print; otherwise, nothing will print.

It is sometimes desirable to execute a BASIC statement or statements only if a condition is false. For example, the last IF statement above could be written as

```
60 IF GPA <= 3.0
      THEN GOTO 70
      ELSE PRINT "DEAN'S LIST"
```

where 70 is the line number of the next line.

More Complicated Price Schedules

Not all conditions are as straightforward as these. For example, suppose the charges at Otto's Parking Lot are

| First 2 hours or less | $5.00 an hour |
| Additional hours | $3.00 an hour |

If HOURS stands for the number of hours parked and BILL stands for the customer's bill, how would you write the LET statements for this problem? The bill for customers who park for 2 hours or less is straightforward; they are charged a flat $5.00 an hour, so the LET statement would be

$$\text{BILL} = 5 * \text{HOURS}$$

The bill for customers who park for more than 2 hours is slightly more complicated. In such cases, it is helpful to calculate a sample bill for a customer and to use the numeric calculation as an aid in developing the LET statement. Imagine a customer who parks for 6 hours and calculate her bill. For the first 2 hours, she is charged $5 per hour; for the next 4 hours, she is charged $3 per hour. Her bill is

$$\text{BILL} = (5 * 2) + (3 * 4) = 22$$

But we went too fast. We got the 4 in this equation by subtracting 2 hours from the total time she was parked, which is 6 hours. Let's show that subtraction explicitly:

$$\text{BILL} = (5 * 2) + (3 * (6 - 2)) = 22$$

With this numeric equation as a guide, it is not too difficult to write the required LET statement:

$$\text{BILL} = (5 * 2) + (3 * (\text{HOURS} - 2))$$

But according to the rules of precedence, BASIC always performs multiplication before addition, so this statement may be written more simply as

$$\text{BILL} = 5 * 2 + 3 * (\text{HOURS} - 2)$$

Whenever you have difficulty writing a LET statement, do a calculation using numbers. Then use the resulting numeric equation to help you write the required LET statement. This process does not involve any additional work, since you have to do a hand calculation anyway to check your program.

Using String Variables in Conditions

As noted earlier, conditions may compare a string variable to a string or to another string variable. For example, in Program 3.4 we used the condition EMP.NAME$ = "Stop", and its meaning is easily grasped. The condition is true if the variable EMP.NAME$ contains the string Stop. But the conditions N$ < M$ and N$ > M$ are also legal, and these are a little more difficult to understand. What does it mean to say one string is "more" or "less" than another?

ASCII code
American Standard Code for Information Interchange. The code used to store data in the computer.

BASIC compares strings according to their **ASCII codes**. ASCII, which stands for American Standard Code for Information Interchange, is the code used by the computer to store data. In ASCII code, each character is associated with a numeric value; when BASIC compares strings, it does so according to numeric value. The numeric values of the ASCII codes are shown in Appendix C. For example, the table there shows that in ASCII code the numeric value of a space is 32, that of the digit 1 is 49, that of the letter A is 65, and that of the letter a is 97. Therefore, a space is less than the digit 1, which in turn is less than the letter A, which in turn is less than the letter a. (In general, digits have lower ASCII values than capital letters, which have lower values than lowercase letters.)

BASIC compares strings from left to right, taking one character at a time from each string and comparing their ASCII values. If the values are unequal, the string containing the character with the lower value is considered to be less than the other string, and the comparison is finished. If the values are equal, the next pair of characters is compared, and so on down the line. If all the characters are equal in value, the strings are considered to be equal. Finally, if the end of one string is reached before the end of the other string, and all values up to that point have been equal, BASIC considers the shorter string to be less than the longer string. For example,

Comparison	Explanation
"ANDERSON" < "BAKER"	A has a lower ASCII code than B.
"789 Oak Street" < "Five Hundred Fifth Avenue"	7 has a lower ASCII code than F.
"no" > "NO"	n has a higher ASCII code than N.
"Zen" < "apples"	Z has a lower ASCII code than a.
"YES " > "YES"	The first three characters of both strings are equal, and "YES " is longer than "YES".

Notice that the number of characters in a string is significant only if the two strings are equal through the length of the smaller string. Even though ANDERSON has more characters than BAKER, ANDERSON is less than BAKER because A has a lower ASCII code than B.

Syntax Summary

IF Statement
Form:
```
IF condition THEN clause [ELSE clause]
```
Example:
```
IF AGE >= 65
    THEN PRINT "Senior Citizen"
    ELSE PRINT "Not a Senior Citizen"
```
Interpretation: Each clause consists of one or more BASIC statements. If the condition is true, the statement or statements in the THEN clause are executed. If the condition is false, the statement or statements in the ELSE clause are executed. Note that to get this statement to run over several lines you must press the Ctrl and Enter keys.

EXERCISES

. . . .

5.1 Assume the following variables have the values indicated: A = 6; B = 19; C = 19. Which of the following conditions are true and which are false?

   a) A < C
  *b) B > C
   c) C <= B
   d) B <> C

*5.2 Write the IF statement to test the variables A and B. If A is greater than B, print the sentence A is

greater; otherwise, print the sentence A is not greater.

5.3 Suppose S is 25. What will be printed when the following statements are executed?

```
40 IF S > 10
    THEN PRINT "BONUS"
50 PRINT "NO BONUS"
```

5.4 Hearing Things, a record store, is having a sale. The first three tapes cost $8.98 each. Additional tapes cost $6.98 each. Write the IF statement to calculate customers' bills.

*5.5 Presidential elections are held in years that are divisible by 4. Write an IF statement that tests the variable YEAR and prints "Election Year" if YEAR is a presidential election year.

5.6 Assume W$ = "NO", X$ = "no", Y$ = "Sixteen Hundred Pennsylvania Avenue", and Z$ = "1600 Pennsylvania Avenue". Which of the following conditions are true and which are false?

*a) W$ = X$
 b) W$ < X$
 c) Y$ <> Z$
*d) Y$ >= Z$

PROGRAMMING ASSIGNMENTS

In the following programming assignments, follow the standard instructions and make sure you invent test data to check all the branches.

5.1 Solve the parking lot problem described on page 97.

5.2 Accept two numbers and print the larger number (assume the numbers are not equal).

*5.3 Write a program that will decide whether students are passing or failing. The program should accept a student's name and three test marks. It should calculate the average of the three test marks and print the student's name, the three test marks, the average, and a message. If the average is less than 60, the message should be Failing; if it is 60 or greater, the message should be Passing.

5.4 Modify your solution to Programming Assignment 4.4 to allow for the possibility that some customers drive fewer than 25 miles a day. Your program should accept the number of days rented and the total miles driven. Calculate the free miles as 25 times the number of days. Charge 18 cents per mile only for miles above the free miles.

*5.5 The Body and Soul exercise spa charges $20 per month if you join for 12 months or less, and $15 per month if you join for more than 12 months. Write a program that accepts a length of membership and calculates and prints bills. Your program should calculate a bill of $200 for a 10-month membership and $300 for a 20-month membership.

5.6 Popcorn Video rents cassettes for $3 a day, but if you rent more than two you get a 20-percent discount. Write a program that accepts the number of cassettes rented and calculates and prints customers' bills.

5.7 The Pie-in-the-Sky Pizzeria sells both 12-inch and 10-inch pizzas. Write a program that accepts the price for both sizes and calculates the price per square inch for both sizes. The program should print either The 12-inch pizza is a better buy or The 10-inch pizza is a better buy. Assume the price per square inch of the two sizes will not be equal. (Hint: Remember that the area of a circle is 3.14159 times the radius squared.)

*5.8 The Snowbound Ski Shop rents skis for $15 per day if you rent for one or two days, and gives a 20-percent discount if you rent for more than two days. Write a program that accepts the number of days the skis are rented and calculates and prints a bill. Sample data and output are:

Number of Days	Bill
2	$30
5	$60

THE CASE STRUCTURE

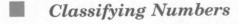

Sometimes decisions involve more than one IF statement, but only one of them can be true.

Classifying Numbers

As an example, suppose we want to write a program that accepts a number and then prints The number is positive, The number is zero, or The number is negative.

The algorithm for this problem is

1. Accept a number.
2. If this is the trailer data, go to step 6.
3. Determine if the number is positive, zero, or negative.
4. Print the appropriate message.
5. Repeat steps 1 through 4 until all numbers have been processed.
6. Stop execution.

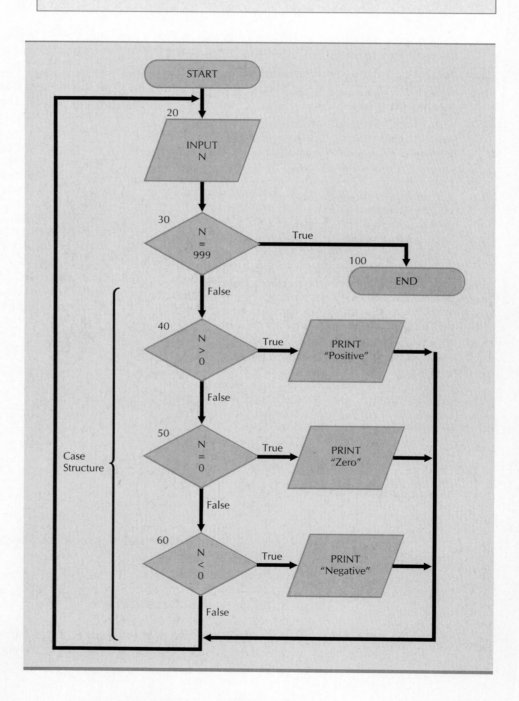

FIGURE 5.2

Flowchart to determine if a number is positive, zero, or negative, using the case structure.

```
10 REM *** DETERMINE IF A NUMBER IS POSITIVE, ZERO, OR NEGATIVE
20 INPUT "Enter a number, 999 to stop"; NUMBER
30   IF NUMBER = 999
       THEN GOTO 100
40   REM Start of case structure to determine number's category
50   IF NUMBER > 0
       THEN PRINT "The number is positive": GOTO 80
60   IF NUMBER = 0
       THEN PRINT "The number is zero": GOTO 80
70   IF NUMBER < 0
       THEN PRINT "The number is negative": GOTO 80
80   REM End of case structure
90 GOTO 20
100 END

RUN
Enter a number, 999 to stop? 16
The number is positive
Enter a number, 999 to stop? -24
The number is negative
Enter a number, 999 to stop? 0
The number is zero
Enter a number, 999 to stop? 999
Ok
```

PROGRAM 5.2 **Determining if a number is positive, zero, or negative.**

Case structure
A structure that tests data against a series of conditions, only one of which can be true.

This algorithm is similar to the one used in the doughnut problem, but step 3, determining if the number is positive, zero, or negative, is more difficult than the corresponding step in the doughnut problem. There are several ways to carry out step 3, but the easiest to understand is shown in the flowchart in Figure 5.2, which includes a group of conditions called a **case structure**. In general, a case structure consists of two or more decision symbols in a row that are joined by their false branches. In all their true branches, one or more statements are executed followed by a branch to the end of the case structure.

The case structure is implemented in lines 40 through 80 in Program 5.2. You might notice that each of the THEN clauses in lines 50, 60, and 70 consists of two statements, for example, in line 50:

```
THEN PRINT "The number is positive": GOTO 80
```

In fact, multiple statements in a line are almost always allowed in BASIC:

BASIC Rule 8 Any line in a program may contain more than one BASIC statement, provided the statements are separated by a colon (:).

Putting more than one statement on a line makes the program harder to read, however, so you should do it only when the statements are closely related, as they are here.

If you study Program 5.2 carefully, you will realize that *in this program* the GOTO 80 statements are not needed. However, this form of the case structure is most easily adapted to a variety of problems, as you will see in later problems.

You may also notice when you examine Program 5.2 the REM statements in lines 40 and 80. This is the first time we have used REM statements other than at the beginning of a program. As your programs get more complicated, it is useful to document various sections of the programs.

A Sales Commission Problem

As another example of a problem that uses the case structure, consider the Re-Bait Fishing Tackle Company, which pays its salespeople according to the following schedule:

Sales	Commission Rate
Sales less than $100	10%
Sales greater than or equal to $100 but less than $500	20%
Sales greater than or equal to $500 but less than $1000	30%
Sales greater than or equal to $1000	40%

How would you write a program to calculate and print commissions?

As step 1 of our structured procedure, we will select the following variable names:

Input variables	Sales	SALES
	Salesperson's name	SALES.NAME$
Output variables	Rate	RATE
	Commission	COMMISSION

DEVELOPING AND CHECKING THE ALGORITHM AND FLOWCHART

The algorithm (step 2) for this problem is

1. Accept SALES.NAME$ and SALES for a salesperson.
2. Determine this salesperson's commission RATE.
3. Calculate COMMISSION using the appropriate commission rate.
4. Print SALES.NAME$, SALES, RATE, and COMMISSION.
5. If there are more salespeople, repeat steps 1 through 4.
6. Stop execution.

Figure 5.3 shows a flowchart for this problem. The case structure in this flowchart is very much like that in Figure 5.2, except that this chart has four decisions, not three. The conditions in the decision symbols numbered 150 and 160, "SALES between 100 and 500" and "SALES between 500 and 1000" are not valid BASIC statements. You will see the correct way to write these conditions when we examine the program.

Instead of using trailer data to know when to stop execution, the INPUT symbol numbered 210 in Figure 5.3 asks the user if there are more salespeo-

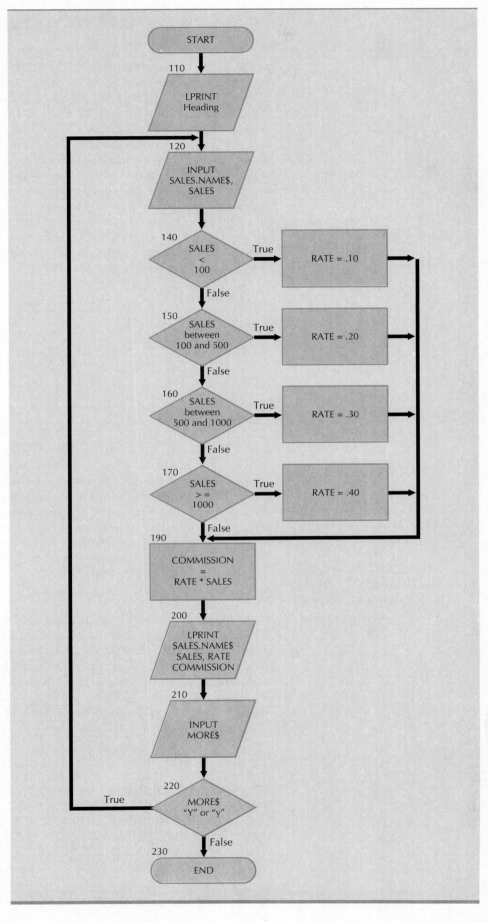

FIGURE 5.3

Flowchart for Re-Bait commission problem.

ple, and the decision symbol numbered 220 branches to the top of the loop if the user enters Y or y and stops if the user enters anything else. This method of controlling execution does not have any particular advantage or disadvantage compared with using trailer data. But it is an effective alternative method of controlling execution.

As your flowcharts get more complicated, you should check them when you finish them. Make sure that every flowchart symbol has a flowline leaving it. Without an exit flowline from a symbol, you haven't specified what you want to do next. The only flowchart symbol that does not require an exit flowline is the terminal symbol.

Once you have checked the flowchart, procede to step 3 of our systematic approach and calculate answers by hand. In this instance, we need four test cases, corresponding to the four categories for commission rate. The four test cases and their answers are

Case Number	Sales	Rate	Commission
1	50	0.1	5
2	200	0.2	40
3	700	0.3	210
4	2,000	0.4	800

THE BASIC PROGRAM—COMPOUND CONDITIONS

Now we are ready for step 4, writing the BASIC program. Program 5.3 shows a listing of the BASIC program based on the flowchart shown in Figure 5.3. Notice how the IF statements in lines 150, 160, and 220 illustrate the use of compound conditions. A **compound condition** is a set of two or more simple conditions, like the ones we have studied so far, that are connected by the reserved words AND or OR. These words, along with the word NOT, are the most common examples of what are known as **logical operators**.

Consider the condition in line 220:

```
MORE$ = "Y" OR MORE$ = "y"
```

This is a compound condition because the two simple conditions, MORE = "Y" and MORE = "y", are connected by the logical operator OR. When two simple conditions are connected by OR, the compound condition is true if *either* of the simple conditions is true. In this case, the compound condition will be true if MORE$ is either Y or y. Although the prompt in the INPUT statement in line 210 suggests that the user enter a Y if there are more salespeople, we want our program to be "user-friendly" and accept either Y or y.

Another example of OR used in a compound condition is

```
IF WEATHER$ = "RAIN" OR WEATHER$ = "SNOW"
THEN PRINT "No swimming today."
```

This statement will print No swimming today if WEATHER$ is equal to either RAIN or SNOW.

The condition in line 150 shows how the condition SALES is greater than or equal to 100 but less than 500 is coded:*

```
SALES >= 100 AND SALES < 500
```

Sidebar definitions:

Compound condition
A set of two or more simple conditions joined by the reserved words AND or OR.

Logical operator
In this book, one of the reserved words AND, OR, and NOT.

---

*A careful examination of Program 5.3 will show that we don't really need the AND operator in lines 150 and 160. However, using AND makes the condition we are testing so clear that we will use it in this and similar cases.

```
100 REM *** RE-BAIT TACKLE PROBLEM ***
110 LPRINT "Name", "Sales", "Rate", "Commission"
120 INPUT "Enter name and sales "; SALES.NAME$, SALES
130   REM Start of case structure to determine commission rate
140   IF SALES < 100
          THEN RATE = .1: GOTO 180
150   IF SALES >= 100 AND SALES < 500
          THEN RATE = .2: GOTO 180
160   IF SALES >= 500 AND SALES < 1000
          THEN RATE = .3: GOTO 180
170   IF SALES >= 1000
          THEN RATE = .4: GOTO 180
180   REM End of case structure
190   COMMISSION = RATE * SALES
200   LPRINT SALES.NAME$, SALES, RATE, COMMISSION
210   INPUT "Are there more salespeople (Y or N)"; MORE$
220 IF MORE$ = "Y" OR MORE$ = "y"
          THEN GOTO 120
230 END

RUN
Enter name and sales ? George, 50
Are there more salespeople (Y or N)? Y
Enter name and sales ? Sue, 200
Are there more salespeople (Y or N)? Y
Enter name and sales ? Paul, 700
Are there more salespeople (Y or N)? Y
Enter name and sales ? Helen, 2000
Are there more salespeople (Y or N)? N
Ok
```

Name	Sales	Rate	Commission
George	50	.1	5
Sue	200	.2	40
Paul	700	.3	210
Helen	2000	.4	800

PROGRAM 5.3   **Re-Bait Fishing Tackle commission problem.**

This is an example of a compound condition that uses the logical operator AND to join two simple conditions. When two simple conditions are connected by AND, the compound condition is true only if *both* simple conditions are true. In this case, the compound condition will be true if SALES is equal to or greater than 100 *and* SALES is less than 500. Since this is the condition for which RATE is 20 percent, in the THEN clause RATE is set equal to .2.

Another example of AND used in a compound condition is

```
IF MONTH$ = "JULY" AND DAY = 4
THEN PRINT "Independence Day"
```

This statement will print Independence Day only if MONTH$ is equal to JULY and DAY is equal to 4.

Sometimes compound conditions can be so complicated that we can't be sure what they mean. For example, the condition

```
YIELD > 10 OR MATURITY < 15 AND TAX.FREE$ = "Y"
```

can be read two ways. The first way is

```
(YIELD > 10 OR MATURITY < 15) AND TAX.FREE = "Y"
```

and the second way is

```
YIELD > 10 OR (MATURITY < 15 AND TAX.FREE = "Y")
```

Just as there are rules of precedence for evaluating arithmetic expressions, so are there rules for evaluating logical expressions. BASIC evaluates the AND operator before the OR operator, so if you don't code parentheses, BASIC will interpret this condition the second way. Rather than take a chance that your interpretation of a complex compound condition will agree with BASIC's, it is safer to use parentheses to force the interpretation you want.

NOT is also a logical operator. NOT negates the condition it operates on. NOT is most useful when it is applied to compound conditions. Suppose we want to print Special Processing if BLOOD.TYPE$ is *not* A, B, or O. There are several correct ways to write this IF statement (and even more wrong ways to write it), but the most straightforward correct way is

```
IF NOT (BLOOD.TYPE$ = "A" OR BLOOD.TYPE = "B" OR BLOOD.TYPE = "O")
   THEN PRINT "Special Processing"
```

Before we leave Program 5.3, there are two additional points that should be called to your attention. The first is that when you list the program some BASICs will display line 140 as

```
RATE = 9.999999E-02
```

even though the correct value of RATE, .10, was typed in. For practical purposes, 9.999999E-02 is .10, so the change has no effect on the answers, even though it may be visually confusing at first.

Also, notice that Program 5.3 starts at line number 100, while the earlier programs started at line number 10. Because this program contains more than nine lines, if the first line number were 10, some lines would have line numbers greater than 100. The shift from two-digit line numbers to three-digit line numbers introduces an unattractive shift in the program listings. For this reason, all the longer programs in this book will start with line number 100 or line number 1000.

EXERCISES

*5.7 A typing instructor grades his students on the basis of how fast they type. Students who type more than 60 words per minute (wpm) are graded "Excellent," those who type between 40 and 60 are "Good," and those who type less than 40 are "Weak." Write the case structure that will test the variable WPM and print the GRADE.

5.8 The class to which a student belongs depends on the number of credits completed, as shown in the following table. Write the case structure that will test the variable CREDITS and print the class.

Credits Completed	Class
0–32	Freshman
33–63	Sophomore
64–95	Junior
96 and above	Senior

5.9 The following table involves two simple conditions, A and B, and two compound conditions, A AND B, and A OR B. For each of the four cases, indicate whether the compound conditions are true or false.

Case	A	B	A AND B	A OR B
1	True	True		
2	True	False		
3	False	True		
4	False	False		

5.10 a) Assuming the input data do not change, what output would be produced by Program 5.3 if lines 150 and 160 were interchanged?

   b) The INPUT statement in line 210 in Program 5.3 suggests that to stop the user should enter N. What will happen if the user mistakenly enters n instead?

5.11 Write the IF statement that will print "Lousy Day" if TEMP and HUMIDITY are *both* over 90.

5.12 For values of A of 1, 2, 3, and 4, determine whether the following compound conditions are true or false:

   a) A <> 2 OR A <> 3
   b) NOT (A = 2 OR A = 3)

PROGRAMMING ASSIGNMENTS

In the following programming assignments, be alert for situations in which the case structure will be helpful, but don't use it where it is not appropriate.

5.9 Write a program that accepts two numbers, A and B, and prints one of three messages: A IS GREATER THAN B, A IS LESS THAN B, or A AND B ARE EQUAL.

*5.10 An electric company measures the amount of electricity its customers use in kwh and charges them according to the following schedule:

First 12 kwh or less	$2.80
Next 78 kwh	$0.08 each kwh
Excess above 90 kwh	$0.10 each kwh

The minimum bill is $2.80. So if a customer uses 5 kwh, the bill for that customer is $2.80. If a customer uses 50 kwh, the charge is $2.80 for the first 12 kwh and $.08 each for the rest. The bill for that customer is therefore

$$Bill = 2.80 + .08 * (50 - 12) = 5.84$$

If a customer uses 120 kwh, the charge is $2.80 for the first 12 kwh, $.08 each for the next 78 kwh, and $.10 each for the rest. The bill for that customer is thus

$$Bill = 2.80 + .08 * 78 + .10 * (120 - 90)$$
$$= 12.04$$

Write a program to calculate and print customer's bills.

5.11 The Flying Start Airline gives discounts to children according to the following schedule:

Age	Discount
Under 2	100%
2 or older, but under 6	50%
6 or older, but under 12	20%
12 or older	None

Write a program that accepts a ticket price and a child's age and prints the discounted ticket price.

5.12 Write a program to assign letter grades to students. The program should accept each student's name and three test marks. It should calculate the average of the three test marks, determine the letter grade, and then print the student's name, the three test marks, the average, and the letter grade. Letter grades are assigned as follows:

Average	Grade
>= 90	A
>= 80, but < 90	B
>= 70, but < 80	C
>= 60, but < 70	D
< 60	F

DETECTING INVALID DATA

Earlier we said that case structures using GOTO statements can be used to solve a variety of problems. They are particularly suitable for detecting when the user has entered invalid data.

■ *Sound Value Record Store*

Consider the problem of writing a billing program for the Sound Value record store. The store has established a coding system to indicate the price of items it sells:

Code	Price
J	9.99
K	10.99
L	12.99
M	14.49

So far, this problem is not very different from the Re-Bait commission problem. What is new, however, is that in this problem we will verify that one of the valid codes, J, K, L, or M, was entered. That is not to say that we can check that the *correct* data have been entered. It is still possible for users to enter a J when they should have entered a K. But we can verify that one of the valid codes has been entered.

Whenever possible, you should check that the data entered are valid. In our earlier programs, we did not make this check, because we had no way of knowing if the data were valid. When a name or a pay rate is entered, just about any value could be valid, so there is no way the program can determine the validity of the data. In this program, we can check that the data are valid because the only valid data are J, K, L, and M.

As step 1 of our structured procedure, we will use the following variable names:

Input variables	Code of item	CODE$
	Number of items	NUMBER
Output variables	Price of item	PRICE
	Bill	BILL

The algorithm (step 2) for this problem is

1. Accept the CODE$ of the item and the NUMBER purchased.
2. If this is the trailer data, go to step 8.
3. Test the CODE$ to determine the PRICE of the item.
4. If an invalid code has been entered, print an error message and return to step 1.

> 5. Calculate the BILL, using the appropriate price.
> 6. Print the NUMBER, CODE$, PRICE, and BILL.
> 7. Repeat steps 1 through 6 for all customers.
> 8. Stop execution.

Figure 5.4 shows a flowchart for this algorithm. In this flowchart, we use a value of Q (for Quit) for CODE$ for trailer data. Consider what would happen if the user entered an invalid value, say B, for CODE$. In that case, all the decisions in the case structure would be false, and we would arrive at process symbol 180 in the flowchart. There we cause the computer to BEEP (more on BEEP in a moment), print an error message, and return to the INPUT statement. In this way, we can detect—"trap"—invalid codes.

In step 3, we calculate answers by hand. The four test cases and their answers are

Case	Code	Number	Price	Bill
1	J	2	9.99	19.98
2	K	3	10.99	32.97
3	L	4	12.99	51.96
4	M	5	14.49	72.45

Program 5.4 shows how easy it is to implement the flowchart logic. Line 180 executes only if *all* the IF statements have been false, which means that an invalid code has been entered. In line 180, BASIC lets the user know that invalid data have been entered through the BEEP statement, which causes the computer's speaker to emit a beep. The syntax of the BEEP statement is simply

```
BEEP
```

Used in conjunction with the printing of an error message, the beep is an effective way of getting the user's attention. Program 5.4 shows this error message when a B is incorrectly entered for CODE$. And although you cannot see it, the speaker would beep, too.

The Sound Statement

Like the BEEP statement, the SOUND statement can be used to generate sounds. The syntax of the SOUND statement is

```
SOUND frequency, duration
```

where frequency is the desired frequency of the sound in hertz (cycles per second) and must be in the range 37 to 32767. To put these frequencies in perspective, the lowest note on a piano has a frequency of 27.5 hertz, and the highest note has a frequency of 4186 hertz. In the SOUND statement, duration is the desired duration of the sound in internal computer clock ticks and must be in the range 0 to 65535. The computer clock ticks 18.2 times a second, so if you code 18.2 for the duration, the sound will last for one second. For example,

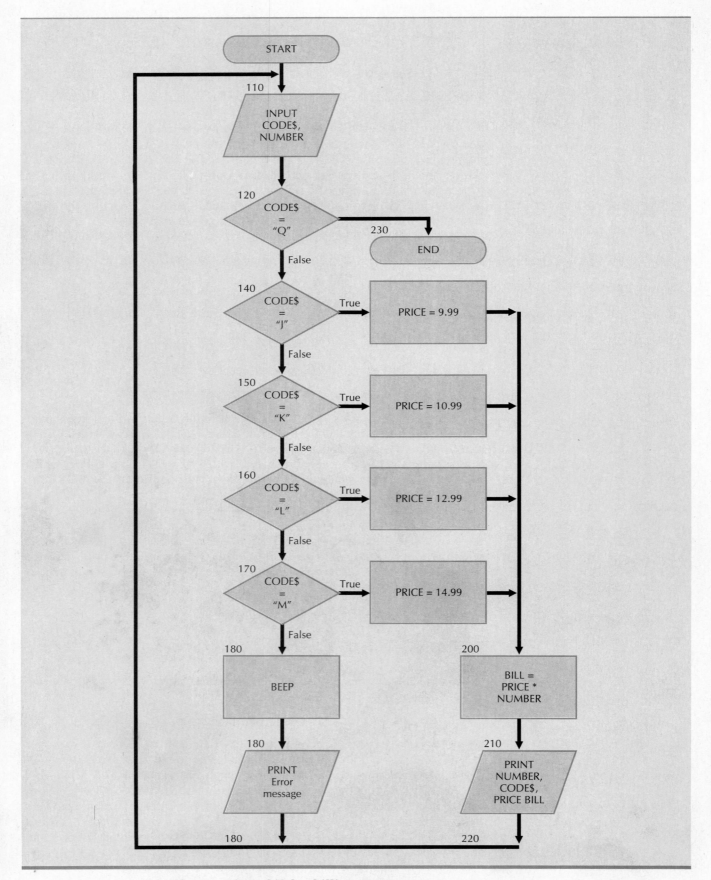

FIGURE 5.4   **Sound Value billing program.**

```
100 REM *** SOUND VALUE BILLING PROGRAM ***
110 INPUT "Enter code, J, K, L or M, and number, Q to quit"; CODE$, NUMBER
120    IF CODE$ = "Q"
          THEN GOTO 230
130    REM Start of case structure
140    IF CODE$ = "J"
          THEN PRICE = 9.99: GOTO 190
150    IF CODE$ = "K"
          THEN PRICE = 10.99: GOTO 190
160    IF CODE$ = "L"
          THEN PRICE = 12.99: GOTO 190
170    IF CODE$ = "M"
          THEN PRICE = 14.49: GOTO 190
180    BEEP: PRINT "Valid codes are J, K, L, or M": GOTO 110
190    REM End of case structure
200    BILL = PRICE * NUMBER
210    PRINT NUMBER; "code "; CODE$; " items at"; PRICE; "each total"; BILL
220 GOTO 110
230 END

RUN
Enter code, J, K, L or M, and number, Q to quit? J,2
 2 code J items at 9.99 each total 19.98
Enter code, J, K, L or M, and number, Q to quit? K,3
 3 code K items at 10.99 each total 32.97
Enter code, J, K, L or M, and number, Q to quit? L,4
 4 code L items at 12.99 each total 51.96
Enter code, J, K, L or M, and number, Q to quit? M,5
 5 code M items at 14.49 each total 72.45
Enter code, J, K, L or M, and munber, Q to quit? B,0      ← Invalid value entered
Valid codes are J, K, L, M, or Q ←                          Error message
Enter code, J, K, L or M, and number, Q to quit? Q,0
Ok
```

PROGRAM 5.4   **Sound Value billing program.**

$$\text{SOUND } 440, 18.2$$

produces a sound with a frequency of 440 hertz (the A above middle C on the piano) that lasts for one second. The statement

$$\text{SOUND } 37,182$$

produces the lowest possible sound and lasts for ten seconds. Experiment with the SOUND statement to see what effects you can achieve.

Syntax Summary

BEEP Statement
Form: BEEP
Example: BEEP
Interpretation: Causes the computer's speaker to beep.

SOUND Statement
Form: SOUND frequency, duration
Example: SOUND 440, 36.4
Interpretation: Causes a sound of the specified frequency, in
                   hertz, to sound for the specified duration,
                   in clock ticks (18.2 per second).

EXERCISES

5.13 How would the output of Program 5.4 change if:

a) The GOTO statements in lines 140 through 170 were changed to GOTO 180?

b) These GOTO statements were changed to GOTO 200?

5.14 If a program accepts the following data, which values could be checked for validity?

a) Name

b) Sex (M/F)

c) Social security number

d) US citizen (Y/N)

*5.15 A program accepts a three-letter abbreviation for the day of the week, SUN, MON, TUE, etc., and prints the day in full. Write the case structure to perform this processing and print an error message if the abbreviation does not represent a day of the week.

5.16 A program accepts a number that represents a college student's year and prints the student's class, according to the following table:

Year	Class
1	Freshman
2	Sophomore
3	Junior
4	Senior

Write the case structure to perform this processing and print an error message if the number is not in the range 1 through 4.

5.17 The frequency of middle C is 261.63 hertz. Write a SOUND statement that will sound middle C for 5 seconds.

PROGRAMMING ASSIGNMENTS

5.13 Write a program that allows the user to enter a vowel in either uppercase or lowercase and checks to make sure the entry is a vowel. Regardless of which case the user chooses, the program should print one of the following messages, using lowercase:

```
A word that uses the vowel a is pat.
A word that uses the vowel e is pet.
A word that uses the vowel i is pit.
A word that uses the vowel o is pot.
A word that uses the vowel u is put.
```

If the user enters any other character, print an error message.

5.14 If you travel to a different planet, your weight will change because of the different gravity on that planet. The factors by which your earth weight must be multiplied to give your weight on the various planets are given below:

Planet	Factor
Mercury	0.38
Venus	0.90
Mars	0.38
Jupiter	2.54
Saturn	1.16
Uranus	0.92
Neptune	1.19
Pluto	0.06

Write a program that accepts a person's earth weight and the name of a planet and calculates and prints the person's weight on that planet. Use a case structure and print an error message if the planet name entered is not valid.

*5.15 The charge for a local telephone call depends on the area to which the call is made and the call's duration. Swell Telephone Company's charges are as follows:

Call Area	Charge for First Minute	Charge for Additional Minutes
A	8.7 cents	0
B	10.6 cents	2.9 cents
C	14.4 cents	4.8 cents
D	18.3 cents	5.8 cents

Write a program that accepts the area to which a call was made and its duration and calculates and prints the charge for that call. Verify that a valid area was entered.

AN OVERTIME PAY PROBLEM

Case structures are, as you have seen, useful in solving some problems. But other problems call for other solutions. For example, returning to the Bat-O payroll program, let's pay overtime. Employees who work more than 40 hours in a week are paid time and a half for the hours over 40. To determine whether an employee is entitled to overtime pay, we will have to test whether the number of hours worked is greater than 40, so you can anticipate that the program will use an IF statement.

As always, the first step is to select names for the variables. Let's use the following:

Input variables	Employee name	EMP.NAME$
	Pay rate	PAY.RATE
	Hours worked	HOURS
Output variables	Regular pay	REGULAR.PAY
	Overtime pay	OVERTIME.PAY
	Gross pay	GROSS.PAY

Our second step is to develop an algorithm:

1. Accept EMP.NAME$, PAY.RATE, and HOURS for an employee.
2. If this is the trailer data, go to step 7.
3. Determine whether this employee is entitled to overtime pay.
4. Calculate pay using the appropriate equations.
5. Print EMP.NAME$, PAY.RATE, HOURS, REGULAR.PAY, OVERTIME.PAY, and GROSS.PAY.
6. Repeat steps 1 through 5 until all employees have been processed.
7. Stop execution.

At this point, step 4—calculating pay using the appropriate equations—is too vague to be the basis of a program, but that's all right. For now we are concentrating on the main logic of the program; once we get that straight, we can fill in the details.

The Flowchart: Subroutines

Figure 5.5(a) shows a flowchart of this algorithm and introduces a new flowchart symbol:

Subroutine
A group of statements that together perform some calculation or function.

A rectangle with two vertical lines drawn as shown is the flowchart symbol for a subroutine. A **subroutine** (or routine) is a group of BASIC statements

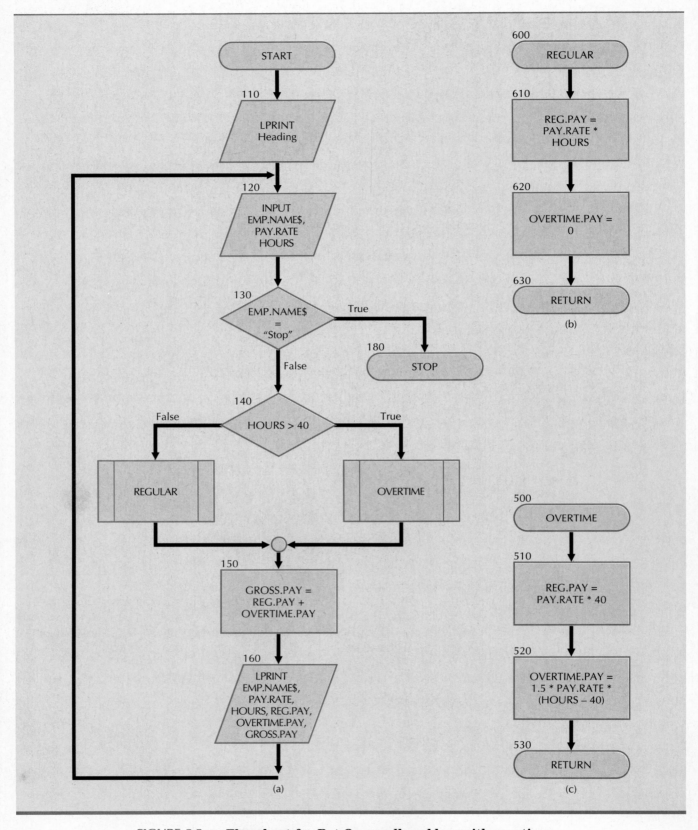

FIGURE 5.5   **Flowchart for Bat-O payroll problem with overtime.**

that together perform some function or calculation. These statements are not included in the main body of the program, where they are needed. Rather, they are inserted somewhere else in the program and called, or executed, from the main program when they are needed.

You might wonder why anyone would use a subroutine instead of simply putting the statements in the main program where they are needed. There are several reasons. As you will see, the statements to calculate regular and overtime pay are so long that they would not fit in one statement if we followed our guidelines and wrote the THEN and ELSE clauses on separate lines.

Another reason for using subroutines is that sometimes we must perform the same function at more than one place in the program. It is easier to group the statements that perform the function as a subroutine. Then you can execute the subroutine from the main program whenever the function is needed, rather than repeat the statements over and over. You will see examples of this use of subroutines in Chapter 11.

The most important reason for using subroutines, however, is that they make the algorithm, the flowchart, and the BASIC program easier to develop and understand.

The algorithm for a problem divides the problem into a number of separate tasks. The simpler tasks are carried out in the main program. More complicated tasks are treated to their own algorithms and are programmed as subroutines in the program. If any tasks in a subroutine are complicated, they are further subdivided and become "sub"-subroutines. This is continued until all the subprograms that must be coded are so simple that they may be coded easily. This method of developing algorithms is called **top-down design** or **stepwise refinement**.

This "divide and conquer" technique is so simple that students often do not appreciate how powerful it is. In fact, it is one of the most powerful tools programmers have. Because our programs up to now have been relatively simple, we have not had occasion to use subroutines. In complicated problems, you will find subroutines very useful. Deciding when to create a subroutine is a matter of judgment and taste, and two experienced programmers might divide a program into subroutines differently. Beginners usually use too few subroutines, so if you are in doubt whether some statements should be a subroutine, you probably should make them a subroutine.

For example, in this problem, when we developed the algorithm, we simply made step 4 "Calculate pay using the appropriate equations." Similarly, when we drew the flowchart, we indicated that if HOURS were greater than 40, the OVERTIME subroutine would be executed, otherwise the REGULAR subroutine would be executed. When we first develop the algorithm, we don't know how to write either of these subroutines, and *we don't have to know*. After we have developed the logic of the main part of the program, we can attack the subroutines.

Once the main program is designed, we can proceed to develop the equations for the OVERTIME and REGULAR subroutines. Here, as in the parking lot problem, we begin with numerical calculations. The equations for the REGULAR subroutine are easier, so let's do those first. Suppose an employee earns $6 per hour and works 30 hours. For that employee, we have

$$\text{REGULAR.PAY} = 6 * 30 = 180$$

and

$$\text{OVERTIME.PAY} = 0$$

Using these two statements as guides, we can write the LET statements required in the REGULAR subroutine:

Top-down design or **stepwise refinement**
A method of developing an algorithm by breaking a complex problem into a set of less complex problems.

$$\text{REGULAR.PAY = PAY.RATE * HOURS}$$

and

$$\text{OVERTIME.PAY = 0}$$

Notice that if we want overtime pay to be 0, we must include a LET statement that sets it equal to 0.

The equations for the OVERTIME subroutine are somewhat more complicated. Given that employees are paid regular time for the first 40 hours, if an employee earns $6.75 per hour and works 50 hours his regular pay is

$$\text{REGULAR.PAY = 6.75 * 40 = 270}$$

and his overtime pay is

$$\text{OVERTIME.PAY = 1.5 * 6.75 * 10 = 101.25}$$

In this equation, 10 represents the number of hours paid at the overtime rate and was calculated as the number of hours worked, 50, minus 40. Let's show that subtraction explicitly:

$$\text{OVERTIME.PAY = 1.5 * 6.75 * (50 - 40) = 101.25}$$

Using these two equations as guides, we can easily write the LET statements required for the OVERTIME subroutine:

$$\text{REGULAR.PAY = PAY.RATE * 40}$$

and

$$\text{OVERTIME.PAY = 1.5 * PAY.RATE * (HOURS - 40)}$$

These equations are used in the OVERTIME and REGULAR subroutines shown in Figure 5.5(b) and (c).

Notice that in the flowcharts for these subroutines the terminal symbols do not contain the words START and END. It is customary to start the flowchart of a subroutine with a terminal symbol that contains the name of the subroutine, in this case, OVERTIME and REGULAR. It is also customary to end the flowchart of a subroutine with a terminal symbol that contains the word RETURN. The RETURN indicates that when we reach the end of a subroutine we want to return to the main program.

The BASIC Program: GOSUB and RETURN Statements

We completed step 3 of our structured procedure—hand-calculating of answers—when we developed the equations for the REGULAR and OVERTIME subroutines. Step 4 is to write a BASIC program for the problem, as shown in Program 5.5.

The only new statements in the program are those that involve the subroutines: the GOSUB statements in line 140 and the RETURN statements in lines 530 and 630.

The GOSUB statement is similar to the GOTO statement. When BASIC executes the statement GOSUB 500, it branches to line 500 just as it would if it executed the statement GOTO 500. When it executes a GOSUB statement, however, BASIC not only branches to the specified line number, it also remembers the statement following the GOSUB. Thus, in Program 5.5, when BASIC executes the GOSUB 500 statement, it remembers the LET statement in line 150. So, after it executes the RETURN statement in line 530, it "returns," or branches back, to line 150.

```
100  REM *** BAT-O PROGRAM WITH OVERTIME ***
110  LPRINT "Name", "Rate", "Hours", "Regular Pay", "Overtime Pay", "Gross Pay"
120  INPUT "Enter Name, Rate, Hours, Stop to end "; EMP.NAME$, PAY.RATE, HOURS
130    IF EMP.NAME$ = "Stop"
          THEN GOTO 180
140    IF HOURS > 40
          THEN GOSUB 500
          ELSE GOSUB 600
150    GROSS.PAY = REGULAR.PAY + OVERTIME.PAY
160    LPRINT EMP.NAME$, PAY.RATE, HOURS, REGULAR.PAY, OVERTIME.PAY, GROSS.PAY
170  GOTO 120
180  STOP
190  '
500  REM *** Overtime pay routine
510    REGULAR.PAY = PAY.RATE * 40
520    OVERTIME.PAY = 1.5 * PAY.RATE * (HOURS - 40)
530  RETURN
540  REM *** End of overtime pay routine
550  '
600  REM *** Regular pay routine
610    REGULAR.PAY = PAY.RATE * HOURS
620    OVERTIME.PAY = 0
630  RETURN
640  REM *** End of regular pay routine
650  END

RUN
Enter Name, Rate, Hours, Stop to end ? Joe Tinker,6.75,50
Enter Name, Rate, Hours, Stop to end ? John Evers,6,30
Enter Name, Rate, Hours, Stop to end ? Frank Chance,5.75,43
Enter Name, Rate, Hours, Stop to end ? Stop,0,0
Break in 180
Ok
```

Name	Rate	Hours	Regular Pay	Overtime Pay	Gross Pay
Joe Tinker	6.75	50	270	101.25	371.25
John Evers	6	30	180	0	180
Frank Chance	5.75	43	230	25.875	255.875

PROGRAM 5.5   **Bat-O payroll program with overtime.**

The syntax of the GOSUB statement is simply

GOSUB line number

The syntax of the RETURN statement is

RETURN [line number]

Notice that line number is optional on the RETURN statement. It is only coded under special circumstances, an example of which you will see in Chapter 6.

It is not necessary to indent the statements in a subroutine, as shown in Program 5.5. However, just as it is a good idea to indent the lines in a loop to show the loop more clearly, it is also a good idea to indent the lines in a subroutine to show the subroutine more clearly. Likewise, you should also use REM statements to mark the beginning and the end of each subroutine (as in lines 500, 540, 600, and 640 of this program) and include blank REM statements consisting of just an apostrophe to create a visual separation between subroutines (lines 190 and 550).

There is nothing special about line numbers 500 and 600, which were used as the first lines in the subroutines. You can use any line number you want for the start of a subroutine, but it should be greater than the highest line number in the main program. By giving a subroutine line numbers higher than those in the main program, you physically separate it from the main program. Since a subroutine is logically self-contained, it's a good idea to make it physically self-contained too.

Another reason for making a subroutine physically separate from the main program is that the separation helps you prevent BASIC from "falling into" a subroutine. Falling into a subroutine means executing the instructions in a subroutine without first having executed a GOSUB statement. You might, for example, incorrectly branch into a subroutine as a result of a GOTO statement. Or, in the normal process of executing statements sequentially, BASIC might arrive at the subroutine statements because there are no instructions to detour around them. Falling into a subroutine is an error because, when the RETURN statement is executed, BASIC won't know where to return. Remember that it is the statement after the GOSUB statement that BASIC remembers and to which the RETURN statement branches. Therefore, BASIC should execute a subroutine *only* as a result of a GOSUB statement. If you do execute a RETURN statement without first executing a GOSUB statement, BASIC will stop executing the program and display the error message RETURN without GOSUB.

Notice that when the trailer data are entered, the IF statement in line 130 branches to line 180. The program would work if instead the branch were to line 650, the last line in the program, but branching to line 180 has the advantage of keeping the main part of the program self-contained. Instead of branching to the last line in the program, which in a complicated program could be a page or two away, we branch to a line just a few lines away. In line 180, you see a new statement: STOP. Like END, STOP causes execution to halt. In fact, we could have used an END statement in line 180, it is clearer to have only one END statement per program, as the last line in the program. So if it is necessary to stop execution anywhere else in the program, we will use a STOP sentence. Program 5.5 shows than when STOP is used to end execution, BASIC displays the message Break in nn, where nn is the line number of the STOP statement.

Tracing the Program

Many students don't really understand the need for line 620 in Program 5.5:

```
620 OVERTIME.PAY = 0
```

To see if you understand why this line is needed, before you read further you should determine the answers that would be printed if this line were omitted. We will trace the program together to check your answers.

Now let's assume that line 620 has been omitted and trace the program. Figure 5.6 shows the boxes set up for EMP.NAME$, PAY.RATE, HOURS, REGULAR.PAY, OVERTIME.PAY, and GROSS.PAY. When we type RUN, BASIC prints the heading and then executes the INPUT statement in line 120. We enter the

Statement	EMP.NAME$	PAY.RATE	HOURS	REGULAR.PAY	OVERTIME.PAY	GROSS.PAY
a) 120 INPUT EMP.NAME$, PAY.RATE, HOURS	Joe Tinker	6.75	50			
b) 510 REGULAR.PAY = PAY.RATE * 40	Joe Tinker	6.75	50	270		
c) 520 OVERTIME.PAY = 1.5 * PAY.RATE * (HOURS – 40)	Joe Tinker	6.75	50	270	101.25	
d) 150 GROSS.PAY = REGULAR.PAY + OVERTIME.PAY	Joe Tinker	6.75	50	270	101.25	371.25
e) 120 INPUT EMP.NAME$, PAY.RATE, HOURS	John Evers	6	30	270	101.25	371.25
f) 610 REGULAR.PAY = PAY.RATE * HOURS	John Evers	6	30	180	101.25	371.25
g) 150 GROSS.PAY = REGULAR.PAY + OVERTIME.PAY	John Evers	6	30	180	101.25	281.25

FIGURE 5.6   Tracing Program 5.5 with line 620 omitted.

first set of data, and BASIC puts Joe Tinker in the EMP.NAME$ box, 6.75 in the PAY.RATE box, and 50 in the HOURS box, as shown in Figure 5.6(a). Since the trailer data were not entered, we fall through line 130. When line 140 is executed, BASIC compares the 50 in the HOURS box with 40. Since 50 is greater than 40, the condition is true, and BASIC executes the THEN clause: GOSUB 500.

BASIC next executes line 500, which is a REM statement that does nothing, and then executes line 510. In line 510, BASIC multiplies the 6.75 in the PAY.RATE box by 40 and puts the answer, 270, in the REGULAR.PAY box, as shown in Figure 5.6(b). When it executes line 520, BASIC must evaluate a complicated expression. It first subtracts 40 from the 50 in the HOURS box and gets 10. It then multiplies 1.5 by the 6.75 in the PAY.RATE box, multiplies this by 10, and puts the answer, 101.25 in the OVERTIME.PAY box, as shown in Figure 5.6(c). BASIC then executes the RETURN statement in line 530 and returns to line 150.

In line 150, BASIC adds the 270 in the REGULAR.PAY box and the 101.25 in the OVERTIME.PAY box and puts the answer, 371.25, in the GROSS.PAY box, as shown in Figure 5.6(d). When BASIC executes the LPRINT statement in line 160, it prints the values in the EMP.NAME$, PAY.RATE, HOURS, REGULAR.PAY, OVERTIME.PAY, and GROSS.PAY boxes. These values are our first line of output and agree with our hand-calculated answers. Of course, this is to be expected, since the change we made, omitting line 620, affects only the regular pay routine, and for this employee we did not execute the regular pay routine. Let's continue.

The GOTO statement in line 170 sends BASIC back to line 120. We enter the second set of data, and BASIC puts John Evers in the EMP.NAME$ box, 6 in the PAY.RATE box, and 30 in the HOURS box, as shown in Figure 5.6(e). This time when line 140 is executed, BASIC compares the 30 in the HOURS box with 40 and determines that the condition is false. Since the condition is false, BASIC executes the ELSE clause: GOSUB 600.

BASIC next executes the REM statement in line 600 and then executes line 610. In line 610, BASIC multiplies the 6 in the PAY.RATE box by the 30 in the HOURS box and puts the answer, 180, in the REGULAR.PAY box, as shown in Figure 5.6(f). Recall that we have removed line 620, so the next statement BASIC executes is the RETURN statement in line 630, which returns it to line 150. In line 150, BASIC adds the 180 in the REGULAR.PAY box and the 101.25 in the OVERTIME.PAY box and puts the answer, 281.25, in the GROSS.PAY box, as shown in Figure 5.6(g). But wait! This employee worked less than 40 hours, and his overtime pay should be 0. That is true, but you must remember that BASIC does not understand anything about our problem. If we tell it to add the number in the OVERTIME.PAY box, it will add whatever number happens to be in the OVERTIME.PAY box. It is our job to make sure that the correct number is in the OVERTIME.PAY box. BASIC next executes the LPRINT statement in line 160 and prints the values shown in Figure 5.6(g), which are, of course, wrong.

Notice that the problem is not line 150, which calculates GROSS.PAY. We could eliminate line 150 and put separate gross pay calculations in both the overtime pay and regular pay routines. For example, we could add the following lines:

```
525 GROSS.PAY = REGULAR.PAY + OVERTIME.PAY
```

and

```
625 GROSS.PAY = REGULAR.PAY
```

This change would mean that GROSS.PAY was calculated correctly, but the LPRINT statement in line 160 would still print 101.25 for OVERTIME.PAY for John Evers.

There are two reasons we just spent so much time tracing this program. One reason is that you must trace your programs to find logic errors, and you should have experience tracing programs. The second reason is that one of the hardest things beginning programmers have to learn is that the computer has no "brains"; it just does what we tell it to do. If you ask it to do something stupid, as we did in this case, it will do it.

The RENUM Command

You learned in Chapter 4 that if you forget a line in a program, you can just insert it. But what can you do if you forget a whole section of the program? If the section omitted is longer than nine lines, it won't fit between two existing lines. The easiest solution is to use the RENUM command to renumber your BASIC program.

The syntax of the RENUM command is

```
RENUM [newnum] [,oldnum] [,increment]
```

where newnum is the first line number to be used in the new sequence, oldnum is the line in the program where renumbering is to begin, and increment is the increment to be used in the new sequence. All three parameters have default values. For newnum and increment, the default value is 10, and for oldnum it is the first line in the program. So the simple command

```
RENUM
```

renumbers the entire program, giving the first line the line number 10 and using an increment of 10. When a program is renumbered, all the line number references (for example, GOSUB 500) are automatically adjusted.

The command

```
RENUM 100, ,50
```

also renumbers the entire program, but gives the first line the line number 100 and uses an increment of 50, permitting you to add up to 49 new lines between existing lines. Notice that we omitted oldnum, because we wanted renumbering to begin with the first line of the program, and we coded two successive commas to indicate that oldnum was omitted. (You may remember using commas to indicate that a parameter is omitted in our discussion of the AUTO command in Chapter 4.)

You may also want to renumber your BASIC program for appearance. For example, suppose a subroutine starts at line 260. Of course, the program works that way, but it doesn't look as nice as it would if the subroutine started at line 300. To make the subroutine start at line 300, we would use the command

RENUM 300, 260

This command gives the old line 260 the new line number 300 and renumbers the following lines using the default increment of 10. The numbers of the lines in the program before 260 are not affected.

Syntax Summary

GOSUB Statement
Form: GOSUB line number
Example: GOSUB 500
Interpretation: BASIC branches to the specified line number and continues execution there. When a RETURN statement is encountered, BASIC branches to the statement following the GOSUB.

RETURN Statement
Form: RETURN
Example: RETURN
Interpretation: BASIC branches to the statement following the last executed GOSUB statement.

STOP Statement
Form: STOP
Example: STOP
Interpretation: The program stops executing, and BASIC displays the line number of the STOP statement.

 Getting the Bugs Out

Problem: During execution, BASIC displays the message

RETURN without GOSUB

Reason: Your program executed a RETURN statement before it executed a GOSUB statement.

Solution: Look for a GOTO statement that should be a GOSUB. Also look for a missing STOP statement, which allowed the program to fall into a subroutine.

Problem: A program terminates unexpectedly, with no error message.

Reason: A missing RETURN statement allowed your program to fall into an END or a STOP statement.

Solution: Insert the missing RETURN statement.

Problem: A program executes the wrong subroutine.

Reason: Either the wrong line number is coded on a GOSUB statement, or a missing RETURN statement allowed your program to fall into the wrong subroutine.

Solution: Either correct the wrong line number or insert the missing RETURN statement.

EXERCISES

5.18 Give the RENUM command needed to make a subroutine that now starts at line 340 start at line 400.

*5.19 Suppose a program contains a subroutine to calculate sales tax. Would the following statement execute that subroutine?

GOSUB SALES.TAX

5.20 Suppose a program contains the following statements:

```
40 INPUT PAY.RATE, HOURS
50 GOSUB 500
60 PRINT GROSS.PAY
```

Upon returning from the subroutine that starts at line 500, which statement will be executed?

*5.21 Which statement belongs in line 520, given that the following statements are part of the program referred to in Exercise 5.20:

```
500 REM *** Calculate Pay ***
510 GROSS.PAY = PAY.RATE * HOURS
```

5.22 What would happen if the IF statement in line 130 in Program 5.5 branched to line 190 instead of to line 180?

5.23 Big Bill's Buying Bonanza classifies its customers into several categories, and two of those categories receive discounts. Category W members receive a 20-percent discount, and category C members receive a 10-percent discount. The other categories receive no discount. Category Q is not used, so you can use that as trailer data. Program 5.6 accepts a membership category and bill and calculates and prints the discount percent and the net bill. As the output shows, the program contains an error. Correct it.

```
100 REM *** BIG BILL'S BUYING BONANZA ***
110 LPRINT "Category", "Bill", "Discount%", "Net Bill"
120 INPUT "Enter category and bill, Q to quit"; CATEGORY$, BILL
130    IF CATEGORY$ = "Q"
          THEN GOTO 210
140    REM Start of case structure
150    IF CATEGORY$ = "W"
          THEN DISCOUNT = .2: GOTO 170
160    IF CATEGORY$ = "C"
          THEN DISCOUNT = .1: GOTO 170
170    REM End of case structure
180    NET.BILL = (1 - DISCOUNT) * BILL
190    LPRINT CATEGORY$, BILL, DISCOUNT * 100, NET.BILL
200 GOTO 120
210 END

RUN
Enter category and bill, Q to quit? A, 300
Enter category and bill, Q to quit? W, 200
Enter category and bill, Q to quit? C, 500
Enter category and bill, Q to quit? A, 300
Enter category and bill, Q to quit? Q, 0
Ok
```

Category	Bill	Discount%	Net Bill
A	300	0	300
W	200	20	160
C	500	10	450
A	300	10	270

PROGRAM 5.6   An incorrect program for Big Bill's Buying Bonanza.

PROGRAMMING ASSIGNMENTS

5.16 Lucy says that a RETURN statement branches to the statement following a GOSUB, but Charlie says that a RETURN statement branches to the next line. Write a program that will settle the argument.

*5.17 Many people think that if a year is divisible by 4 it is a leap year, but the rules are more complicated than that. If a year is divisible by 100, then for it to be a leap year it must be divisible by 400, not merely divisible by 4. This means, for example, that the year 1900 was not a leap year, because 1900 is divisible by 100 but not divisible by 400. (Of course, when we say divisible we mean exactly divisible, with a remainder of zero.) Write a program that accepts a year and determines if that year is a leap year. Use the MOD operator to determine if the year is exactly divisible by 400, 100, and 4.

5.18 Write a program that can calculate the area of a circle or a rectangle. The program should ask the user to enter a C or an R, to indicate the figure whose area is to be calculated. If the user enters a C, the program should request the RADIUS and calculate the AREA.CIRCLE, using the formula AREA.CIRCLE = 3.14159 * RADIUS^2. If the user enters an R, the program should request the LENGTH and HEIGHT of the rectangle and calculate the AREA.RECT, using the formula AREA.RECT = LENGTH * HEIGHT. If neither a C nor an R is entered, the program should print an error message and request the user to enter a correct value. Use separate subroutines for the circle and the rectangle.

5.19 Inna Vestin College (known to its students as Old I.V.) charges tuition depending on whether a student is a resident and on how many credits she takes. If the student is a resident, the charges are

Less than 12 credits	$75 per credit
12 or more credits	$750

If the student is not a resident, the charges are

Less than 12 credits	$95 per credit
12 or more credits	$950

Write a program that will calculate students' tuition bills. Use separate subroutines for residents and nonresidents.

5.20 Write a program that could be used to help people learn about vitamins. Allow the user to enter A, B1, C, or D and have the program print the following information about the vitamin:

```
A  Function: Promotes good eyesight.
   Sources: Liver, carrots, sweet potatoes.
   RDA: 1000 units.
B1 Function: Used by the nervous system, heart,
             and liver.
   Sources: Meat, fish, poultry, whole grains.
   RDA: 1.5 mg.
C  Function: Helps heal wounds and resist
             infections.
   Sources: Citrus fruits, turnips, potatoes,
            cabbage.
   RDA: 60 mg.
D  Function: Important for bone development.
   Sources: Sunlight, fortified milk,
            organ meats.
   RDA: 7.5 units.
```

The information for each vitamin must be printed (as shown for vitamin A), on three lines. If the user does not enter one of these vitamins, print an error message.

SUMMARY

In this chapter you have learned that

☐ The relational operators used in a condition are

=	Equal
<	Less than
>	Greater than
<=	Less than or equal
>=	Greater than or equal
<>	Not equal

- You must make up test data to test all the branches in your program.
- An IF statement is used to make a decision; if the condition is true, the THEN clause is executed; if the condition is false, the ELSE clause is executed. The ELSE clause is optional.
- Strings and string variables may be used in decisions. They are compared according to their ASCII codes.
- The case structure is used when it is necessary to choose from several conditions, only one of which can be true.
- More than one BASIC statement may be written on a line if the statements are separated by a colon.
- The logical operators AND and OR are used to construct compound conditions. The logical operator NOT is used to negate a condition, which may be simple or compound.
- The BEEP statement is used to sound a beep through the computer's speaker.
- The SOUND statement is used to make a sound of a specified frequency for a specified duration.
- The flowchart symbol for a subroutine is a rectangle with two vertical lines.
- The GOSUB statement is used to execute a subroutine. The RETURN statement is used to return from a subroutine.
- Top-down design or stepwise refinement refers to a method of solving complex problems by breaking them into a set of simpler problems.
- The STOP statement is used to stop execution.
- The RENUM command is used to renumber a BASIC program.

KEY TERMS IN THIS CHAPTER

ASCII code 97

case structure 101

compound condition 104

logical operator 104

relational operator 94

stepwise refinement 115

subroutine 113

top-down design 115

QUESTIONS FOR REVIEW

5.1 Which statement is used to make a decision?

5.2 What happens if the condition in an IF statement is false and the statement does not have an ELSE clause?

5.3 What is the relational operator used to mean greater than or equal?

5.4 What is the ASCII code for Z? For a?

5.5 True or false: The case structure is used to choose one of two alternatives.

5.6 How many statements may be coded on one line?

5.7 AND, OR, and NOT are _____ operators.

5.8 What is a compound condition?

5.9 Which two statements can be used to make the computer's speaker sound?

5.10 Why are subroutines used?

5.11 What is the flowchart symbol for a subroutine?

5.12 What statement is used to return to a main program from a subroutine?

5.13 Which two statements can be used to stop execution?

5.14 True or false: The RENUMBER command is used to renumber the lines of a program.

ADDITIONAL PROGRAMMING ASSIGNMENTS

5.21 First class postage is charged according to weight, as follows:

First ounce or less	$0.25
Each additional ounce	$0.20

Write a program that accepts weight and calculates and prints postage.

*5.22 We are given each employee's name, pay rate, and hours worked. Write a program to calculate and print each employee's gross pay, withholding, and net pay. Gross pay is calculated as pay rate times hours worked (no overtime at this company). Withholding is 10 percent of gross pay if gross pay is less than $200, and 20 percent of gross pay otherwise. Net pay is calculated as gross pay minus withholding.

5.23 Write a program that will accept two characters and print them in alphabetical order.

*5.24 To encourage fuel conservation, the government has a gas-guzzler's tax on automobiles. The amount of the tax depends on the gas mileage a car delivers, as follows:

Mileage (mpg)	Tax
21 or higher	0
14 or higher, but less than 21	$500
10 or higher, but less than 14	$1000
Less than 10	$2500

Write a program that accepts the mileage and calculates and prints the tax.

5.25 The Have-A-Byte computer store sells floppy disks according to the following schedule:

9 or fewer	$2.00 each
More than 9	$1.50 each

Write a program that accepts the number of disks purchased and prints the bill. Sample data and output are:

No. of Disks	Bill
5	10.00
10	15.00

5.26 Write a program that accepts three numbers, A, B, and C and prints the largest. (Hint: Compare A and B and assign the larger value to LARGER. Then compare LARGER and C and assign the larger value to LARGEST.)

5.27 Write a program that accepts three numbers and then prints one of three messages: All three numbers are equal, Two of the numbers are equal, or No two of the numbers are equal.

5.28 Write a program that accepts a month number and a year and prints the month number and year six months later.

*5.29 In the New York City area, the major television channels are

Channel Number	Station
2	WCBS
4	WNBC
5	WNYW
7	WABC
9	WWOR
11	WPIX
13	WNET

Write a program that accepts a channel number and prints the station's name. If an invalid channel number is entered, print an error message.

5.30 Great Shapes Health Club has many membership categories, and two of those categories receive discounts. Category G members receive a 20-percent discount, and category S members receive a 10-percent discount. The other membership categories receive no discount. Write a program that accepts a membership category and bill and calculates and prints the discount percent and the net bill. Category Q is not used, so you can use that as trailer data.

5.31 For three numbers to represent the sides of a triangle, it is necessary that the sum of any two of the numbers be greater than the third. For example, 1, 2, and 3 cannot be the sides of a triangle, because 1 + 2 is not greater than 3. Write a program that accepts three numbers and reports either that they do make a triangle or that they do not make a triangle.

BEYOND THE BASICS

5.1 a) A company pays its salespeople a 5-percent commission on their first $10,000 of sales, 10-percent on their second $10,000 of sales, and 20-percent on all their sales above $20,000. Write a program that accepts the salesperson's name and sales and prints the name, sales, and commission.

b) Modify the program from part (a) to print the total sales and total commission. Hint: You may find it helpful to use LET statements of the form

```
TOTAL.SALES = TOTAL.SALES + SALES
```

5.2 Write a program to accept three numbers and print them in sorted order, that is, in the order smallest, middle, and largest.

5.3 Wooden's Lumber Company sells boards in two-foot lengths. This means that if 48 inches are required, 4 feet must be purchased, but if 49 inches are required, 6 feet must be purchased. Write a program that accepts the number of inches required and calculates and prints the number of feet that must be purchased.

5.4 Write a program to solve the quadratic equation

$$ax^2 + bx + c = 0$$

using the quadratic formula

$$x = \frac{-b \pm \sqrt{b^2 - 4ac}}{2a}$$

Your program should handle three cases: (1) the roots are real, (2) the two roots are equal, and (3) the roots are complex, in which case the program should print the real and imaginary parts.

5.5 Write a "Tomorrow" program that accepts three numbers representing the month, day, and year and that determines the month, day, and year of the next day. You may simplify your program by assuming that the three numbers entered represent a valid date and that any year divisible by 4 is a leap year. (Programming Assignment 5.17 explains the real rules for leap year.)

5.6 Write a program that accepts three numbers, A, B, and C, and prints the name of the largest. If two or more variables are tied for largest, print all their names. Your output should be Largest number A or Largest number A and B and C, etc.

6

Advanced Input and Output

BASIC OBJECTIVES OF THIS CHAPTER

☐ To explore a new method of supplying data to a program

☐ To completely control the appearance of output

☐ To control the screen

☐ To use color

☐ To use the BASIC statements READ, DATA, PRINT USING, LPRINT USING, CLS, KEY, LOCATE, SCREEN, and COLOR

☐ To use the BASIC functions SPC, TAB, INPUT$, SPACE$, and INKEY$

☐ To use the BASIC command MERGE

In all the programs we have constructed so far, we have used the INPUT statement to supply data to the program. In this chapter, you will learn how to use the READ and DATA statements and the INPUT$ and INKEY$ functions to supply data to a program. Also, our earlier programs generated output using the PRINT or LPRINT statement. These statements, however, do not give us much control over the appearance of the output, so in this chapter you will learn how to use the PRINT USING and LPRINT USING statements to get complete control over the appearance of the output. Finally, in this chapter you will learn how to control the screen and to use color.

THE OVERTIME PAY PROBLEM REVISITED

In the overtime pay problem in Program 5.5, we entered the name, pay rate, and hours worked for each employee. But if an employee's pay rate does not change from one week to the next (that is, if the only change is in the hours worked), it is a nuisance to enter these data every time you run the program. In this section, we will discuss how you can use the READ and DATA statements to input this information only once and then enter just the hours worked each time the program is run.

We begin by using the same variable names as in Program 5.5. The algorithm is also similar to the algorithm used for Program 5.5. It is

1. Read EMP.NAME$ and PAY.RATE for an employee.
2. If these are the trailer data, go to step 8.
3. Accept the HOURS worked for this employee.
4. Determine whether this employee is entitled to OVERTIME.PAY.
5. Calculate pay using the appropriate equations.
6. Print EMP.NAME$, PAY.RATE, HOURS, REGULAR.PAY, OVERTIME.PAY, and GROSS.PAY.
7. Repeat steps 1 through 6 until all employees have been processed.
8. Stop execution.

Figure 6.1 shows a flowchart for this problem. For hand-calculated answers, you can use the same values as in Chapter 5. Program 6.1 is based on the flowchart in Figure 6.1. Line 120 shows how you can add a comment to the end of a statement by starting the comment with an apostrophe. Note that you do not have to code :REM to add a comment to the end of a statement. You can use an apostrophe to add a comment to the end of any statement, but the comment must be at the *end* of the statement, because BASIC stops examining the statement when it finds a comment. So, for example, in an IF statement that contains both a THEN and an ELSE clause, a comment may be added only at the end of the ELSE clause. It would be useful if line 130 could be written as

```
130 IF HOURS > 40
        THEN GOSUB 500        'Overtime routine
        ELSE GOSUB 600        'Regular pay routine
```

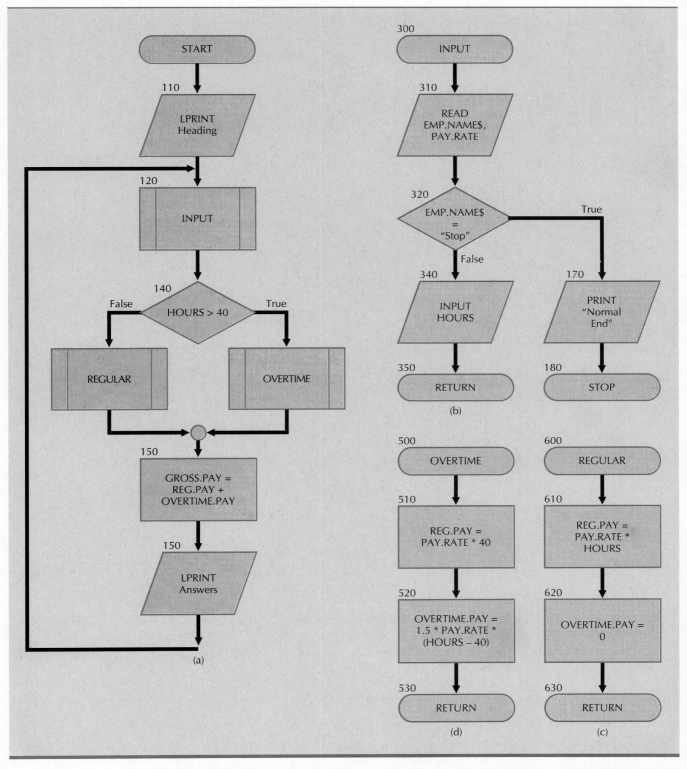

FIGURE 6.1   **Flowchart for Bat-O payroll program with overtime using READ and DATA statements.**

```
100 REM *** IMPROVED BAT-O PROGRAM WITH OVERTIME ***
110 LPRINT "Name", "Rate", "Hours", "Regular Pay", "Overtime Pay", "Gross Pay"
120 GOSUB 300                          'Obtain input ◄──── ( Comment )
130    IF HOURS > 40
          THEN GOSUB 500
          ELSE GOSUB 600
140    GROSS.PAY = REGULAR.PAY + OVERTIME.PAY
150    LPRINT EMP.NAME$, PAY.RATE, HOURS, REGULAR.PAY, OVERTIME.PAY, GROSS.PAY
160 GOTO 120
170 PRINT "Normal end of program"
180 STOP
190 '
300 REM *** Input Routine
310    READ EMP.NAME$, PAY.RATE
320    IF EMP.NAME$ = "Stop"
          THEN RETURN 170
330    PRINT "Enter hours for employee "; EMP.NAME$; ◄── ( Hanging semicolon )
340    INPUT HOURS
350 RETURN
360 REM *** End of input routine
370 '
500 REM *** Overtime pay routine
510    REGULAR.PAY = PAY.RATE * 40
520    OVERTIME.PAY = 1.5 * PAY.RATE * (HOURS - 40)
530 RETURN
540 REM *** End of overtime pay routine
550 '
600 REM *** Regular pay routine
610    REGULAR.PAY = PAY.RATE * HOURS
620    OVERTIME.PAY = 0
630 RETURN
640 REM *** End of regular pay routine
650 '
700 REM *** Data used by input routine
710 DATA Joe Tinker, 6.75
720 DATA John Evers, 6.00
730 DATA Frank Chance, 5.75
740 DATA Stop, 0                          : REM Trailer data ◄── ( Comment at end of
750 END                                                          a DATA statement )

RUN
Enter hours for employee Joe Tinker? 50
Enter hours for employee John Evers? 30
Enter hours for employee Frank Chance? 43
Normal end of program ◄────── ( Normal end message )
Break in 180
Ok
```

Name	Rate	Hours	Regular Pay	Overtime Pay	Gross Pay
Joe Tinker	6.75	50	270	101.25	371.25
John Evers	6	30	180	0	180
Frank Chance	5.75	43	230	25.875	255.875

PROGRAM 6.1   Bat-O program with overtime using READ and DATA statements.

but it *cannot*, because then the comment at the end of the THEN clause would be in the middle of the IF statement.

You can use this apostrophe technique with all BASIC statements, except DATA statements. Line 740 shows the proper way to add a comment to the end of a DATA statement: add :REM, followed by the comment.

The new statements in Program 6.1 are the READ statement in line 310 and the DATA statements in lines 710, 720, 730, and 740. The READ and DATA statements are always used together. Let's trace this program to see how they work.

Tracing the Program

Line 110 prints a heading. Line 120 sends BASIC to line 300. When BASIC executes the READ statement in line 310, it performs two steps. First, it finds a DATA statement. If, as in this case, there is more than one DATA statement, it takes the one with the lowest line number (in this program, the DATA statement in line 710). Second, it takes the first value from the DATA statement and puts it into the box of the first variable listed in the READ statement. Then it takes the second value from the DATA statement and puts it into the box of the second variable listed in the READ statement. In this case, it puts Joe Tinker into the EMP.NAME$ box and 6.75 into the PAY.RATE box. BASIC then marks Joe Tinker and 6.75 as "used," so they will not be used again. If more variables were listed in the READ statement, BASIC would continue this process until all the variables had been assigned values.

Since the value in the EMP.NAME$ box is not STOP, BASIC falls through the IF statement in line 320. When BASIC executes the PRINT statement in line 330, it prints the message Enter hours for employee and, right next to that, the value in the EMP.NAME$ box, Joe Tinker, as shown in the first line following RUN in Program 6.1. You might wonder why we use a PRINT statement to print this line rather than the prompt feature of the INPUT statement. The prompt feature of the INPUT statement permits us to print only a string, not a variable. If we had used an INPUT statement, the computer would have printed only Enter hours for employee instead of Enter hours for employee Joe Tinker (or John Evers or Frank Chance). Thus, we need the PRINT statement in this case. The hanging semicolon in line 330 causes the value input for HOURS to appear next to the employee's name.

When BASIC executes the INPUT statement in line 340, it prints a question mark and pauses. We then enter 50 for the hours Joe Tinker worked. As you can see, we have accomplished our main goal—that of reducing the amount of data that must be entered. Let's continue tracing the program.

The RETURN statement in line 350 returns BASIC to the main routine at line 130 and the pay for Joe Tinker is calculated in the appropriate subroutine and printed. The GOTO statement in line 160 returns BASIC to line 120, which in turn sends it once again to line 300. When BASIC executes the READ statement in line 310, it looks for a DATA statement. It remembers that the values in line 710 have been used, so it goes to the next DATA statement, which is in line 720. It puts John Evers in the EMP.NAME$ box and 6 in the PAY.RATE box. Since these boxes can hold only one value at a time, the old values are erased. The program continues as before, calculating and printing the pay for John Evers and for Frank Chance.

After the pay for Frank Chance is printed, line 160 once again causes a branch back to line 120, which in turn sends BASIC to line 300. This time, however, the trailer data are read. Since the test for trailer data in line 320 is now true, BASIC executes the statement RETURN 170. As you learned in

Chapter 5, when a RETURN statement contains a line number, BASIC returns to the specified line, in this case, the PRINT statement in line 170.

After the trailer data have been read, all we really have to do is stop execution. However, since in this program users do not enter the trailer data (BASIC finds the data in the DATA statements), they might be surprised when the program stops executing. So in line 170, we print a message explaining that the program has ended normally. The STOP statement in line 180 then stops execution. Usually, we code only one RETURN statement in a subroutine, without a line number, but in this case the line number is vital. If we omitted the line number in this RETURN statement, we would return to line 130, the statement following the GOSUB 300. We would then calculate the pay for the imaginary employee, which is clearly wrong.

We could have coded PRINT and STOP statements in the THEN branch of line 320, but it is a much better programming practice to make all subroutines return to the calling routine and for the one STOP statement in a program to be in the main routine.

You have seen how the READ and DATA statements reduce the amount of input users must enter, but they are not without drawbacks. If any employee's pay rate changes, the values in the DATA statement must be changed. That presents no problem to you, since you know how to edit BASIC statements. So in programs you write for yourself, you can use DATA statements wherever they are convenient.

But suppose you are a professional programmer and you have written this program for users who do not know BASIC. You don't want someone who does not know BASIC going into your program and changing things—he or she might destroy the program. Therefore, in programs written for nonprogrammers, DATA statements should be used only for values that never change, for example, the names of months or states. For values that might change, it is better to use the INPUT statement, which you learned about earlier, or to use files, which you will learn about in Chapter 11.

More about the READ and DATA Statements

Now that you have seen how the READ and DATA statements work in a program, let's examine them in more detail. The syntax of the READ statement is

```
READ variable,...
```

and you may list as many variables as you like. The syntax of the DATA statement is

```
DATA value,...
```

Again, you may list as many values as you like. For example,

Statement

```
READ TEMPERATURE, HUMIDITY
DATA 85, 45
```

Effect

Assigns 85 to TEMPERATURE and 45 to HUMIDITY.

Statement

```
READ STUDENT.NAME$, TEST1, TEST2, TEST3
DATA Jose Carlos, 95, 89, 94
```

Effect

Assigns Jose Carlos to STUDENT.NAME$, 95 to TEST1, 89 to TEST2, and 94 to TEST3.

Statement

READ PRESIDENT$, BIRTHDATE$
DATA Abraham Lincoln, "Feb. 12, 1809"

Effect

Assigns Abraham Lincoln to PRESIDENT$ and Feb. 12, 1809 to BIRTHDATE$.

The last example shows that string values in DATA statements, like those in INPUT statements, are enclosed by quotation marks only when a string contains commas or is preceded or followed by blanks that you want to include in the string data. And like INPUT statements, READ and DATA statements require that you enter numeric data for numeric variables and string data for string variables.

Earlier, we said that when BASIC executes a READ statement, it finds a DATA statement. To do so, it searches the whole program. Therefore, you can put the DATA statements anywhere you like without harming the logic of the program. However, if you put the DATA statements at the end of the program, just before the END statement (as in Program 6.1), your programs usually will be less cluttered, easier to read, and easier to follow.

Finally, you should be aware that DATA statements never appear in flowcharts. The reason they don't is that the particular data they represent are not part of the logic of the program. To be useful, the program must work for any values of EMP.NAME$ and PAY.RATE. For example, if Joe Tinker got a raise to $8 an hour, the DATA statement in line 710 would change, but the flowchart—and the rest of the program—would still be perfectly correct.

THE DATA BANK

DATA statements may be coded in more than one way. The DATA statements in Program 6.1 contain two values, which match the two variables in the READ statement. However, it is not necessary that the number of values in the DATA statement and the number of variables in the READ statement be equal. To understand why the numbers do not have to be equal, you must understand more about how the DATA statement works. When BASIC encounters DATA statements in a program, it processes them in numerical order and places the values from all the DATA statement into a single data bank. Figure 6.2 shows the data bank generated from the DATA statements in Program 6.1. Each time a READ statement is executed, BASIC takes the values it

```
Joe Tinker
6.75
John Evers
6
Frank Chance
5.75
Stop
0
```

FIGURE 6.2　　**Data bank formed from DATA statements in Program 6.1.**

```
710 DATA Joe Tinker, 6.75
720 DATA John Evers, 6
730 DATA Frank Chance, 5.75
740 DATA Stop, 0

            (a)


710 DATA Joe Tinker, 6.75, John Evers, 6, Frank Chance, 5.75, Stop, 0



            (b)



710 DATA Joe Tinker, 6.75, John Evers
720 DATA 6, Frank Chance
730 DATA 5.75, Stop
740 DATA 0

            (c)
```

FIGURE 6.3   **Alternative, equivalent DATA statements.**

needs from the next available values in the data bank and marks these values as used so they will not be used again.

The fact that the READ statement really gets its values from the data bank rather than from the DATA statements, as we said originally, has no effect on the answers generated by the program. The fact that BASIC generates a data bank does, however, have one consequence. All the sets of DATA statements shown in Figure 6.3 would give the data bank shown in Figure 6.2. This means that any of these sets of DATA statements could have been used in the program in Program 6.1 and would have given the same answers.

Since all the sets of DATA statements shown in Figure 6.3 give the same answers, which is the best set to use in our program? Consider the set shown in Figure 6.3(a), which is the set we used originally in Program 6.1. When we study the program, we see that line 310 says READ EMP.NAME$, PAY.RATE; when we examine the DATA statements, we see that each DATA statement has a value for EMP.NAME$ and a value for PAY.RATE. This arrangement, where each DATA statement contains exactly the number of values necessary for one execution of a READ statement, is much easier to understand than any of the other sets of DATA statements shown in Figure 6.3. Because we want our programs to be easy to read and understand, we will adopt this rule: Each DATA statement should contain the exact number of values necessary for one execution of the READ statement.

There is only one exception to this rule. In programs with a single variable to be read, a DATA statement may have many values. For example, to read sales for each employee, a program might contain the statement READ SALES. If the sales for three employees were $400, $700, and $200, you could use a DATA statement like DATA 400, 700, 200, instead of a separate DATA statement for each employee, since there is no chance for confusion if you put all the values in one DATA statement. So in this case, we may ignore the rule.

Syntax Summary   READ Statement
                    Form: `READ variable,...`
                    Example: READ STATE$, POPULATION
                    Interpretation: The next available values in the data bank
                                     are assigned to the variables listed.

                    DATA Statement
                    Form: `DATA value,...`
                    Example: DATA Wyoming, 494568
                    Interpretation: The values are stored in a data bank and used
                                     by READ statements.

 Getting the   **Problem:**   During execution, BASIC stops and displays the message
        Bugs Out

                                                     Syntax error in nn

                                     where nn is the line number of a DATA statement.

                      Reason: A READ statement encountered a string value when it expected
                                     a numeric value.

                      Solution: Correct either the READ statement or the DATA statement. This
                                     error is often caused by a missing comma in the DATA state-
                                     ment before the one named in the error message.

                      Problem: During execution, BASIC stops and displays the message

                                                     Out of DATA in nn

                                     where nn is the line number of a READ statement.

                      Reason: A READ statement was executed, but no more values were
                                     available in the data bank.

                      Solution: Most likely, the test for trailer data is incorrect, causing the
                                     READ statement to be executed one extra time.

EXERGISES

EXERCISES

*6.1 a) Write the READ statement to read a runner's
          name and time for the 100-yard dash.
      b) Write three DATA statements to supply the data
          for the READ statement you wrote for part a).

6.2   In Program 6.1, why do we use LPRINT statements in
      lines 110 and 150, but PRINT statements in lines 170
      and 330?

6.3   Consider the following READ statement:

                   READ A, B$, C

      Which of the following DATA statements would cause
      an error when used with this READ statement?

                500 DATA 1, 2, 3
                510 DATA A, B, C
                520 DATA 6, SUNDAY, 24

6.4   Consider the following program.

                10 READ P
                20   IF P > 10

                          THEN R = P − 4
                          ELSE R = P + 4
                30   PRINT R
                40 GOTO 10
                50 DATA 16
                60 DATA 8
                70 END

      a) What is the first value assigned to the variable P?
      b) What is the first number printed?
      c) What is the second number printed?
      d) What output is produced if the following line
          number 9 is added to the program?

                          9 P = 19

      e) Remove line 9 and change line 40 to

                          40 GOTO 20

      What output will be produced?

PROGRAMMING ASSIGNMENTS

....

In the following programming assignments, use READ *and* DATA *statements to supply data to the program.*

6.1 Re-solve Programming Assignment 5.1.

*6.2 Re-solve Programming Assignment 5.3.

*6.3 Re-solve Programming Assignment 5.5.

6.4 Re-solve Programming Assignment 5.11.

6.5 Re-solve Programming Assignment 5.12.

ADVANCED PRINTING

....

Now that you know a little more about obtaining input, let's look at how you can control output. So far, the control we have exercised over the appearance of our output has been crude: To get wide spacing between values, we used commas to separate the variables in the print list; to get narrow spacing, we used semicolons. The functions TAB and SPC, which are used with the PRINT and LPRINT statements, can give you the exact spacing you want on the screen or printer. And two new statements, PRINT USING and LPRINT USING, can give you exact spacing *and* control exactly how each variable is printed.

The TAB Function

The TAB function works like the tab (indent) key on a typewriter. Consider the statement

```
PRINT TAB(5); A; TAB(14); B; TAB(46); C$
```

This statement tells BASIC to tab to column 5 and print the value of A, then tab to column 14 and print the value of B, and finally to tab to column 46 and print the value of C$. As we discussed in Chapter 4, BASIC inserts a space to the left of a number to allow for easier reading and also for a possible minus sign. Therefore, the first digit of A will actually start printing in column 6, and the first digit of B in column 15. However, the first character of C$ will print in column 46 because BASIC does not insert a space before it prints a string.

TAB may be used with the PRINT and LPRINT statements. For example,

```
LPRINT TAB(29); "Payroll Report"
```

will cause Payroll Report to start printing in column 29.

Notice that you must use semicolons, not commas, to separate the items in the LPRINT TAB list. A comma would cause BASIC to space over to the start of the next print zone and would destroy the spacing you were trying to achieve using TAB. If you have already printed beyond the column specified in the TAB function, BASIC advances to the next line and starts printing at the specified column.

The syntax of the TAB function is

```
TAB(column)
```

Function
A part of BASIC, which operates on one or more arguments and returns a value.

Argument
A constant, variable, or expression supplied to a function, and used by the function to determine a result.

TAB is the first function we have studied. **Functions** are a part of BASIC that perform specific operations. In effect, they are very much like the function keys many calculators have. For example, many calculators have a square root function key. If you enter a number into the calculator and press the square root key, the calculator will display the square root of the number you entered. The number you entered is called the **argument**, and we say the square root key "returns" the square root of its argument. In BASIC the argument (sometimes there is more than one) is enclosed in parentheses *immediately* after the function's name, as the column is in the TAB syntax statement. (Do not leave a space between TAB and the left parenthesis.) The argument of the TAB function specifies the column to which you want BASIC to go.

The SPC Function

The SPC function is similar to the TAB function, but it specifies the number of columns to skip, rather than the column number to skip to. For example, if you wanted to print column headings with eight spaces between each heading, you could use

```
PRINT SPC(8); "Name"; SPC(8); "Pay Rate"; SPC(8);
       "Hours"; SPC(8); "Gross Pay"
```

The syntax for the SPC function is

```
SPC(n)
```

As with the TAB function, there must not be a space between SPC and the left parenthesis. And again, semicolons must separate the variables. And like the TAB function, the SPC function may be used with both the PRINT and LPRINT statements.

Students often wonder when to use TAB instead of SPC and vice versa. There are no hard and fast rules. Your choice of TAB or SPC will depend on which is more convenient for the problem at hand.

The PRINT USING and LPRINT USING Statements

The TAB and SPC functions are useful in positioning output on the screen or printer, but sometimes you want to control other aspects of your output. For example, in Program 6.1 John Evers earns $6.00 per hour, but his pay rate is printed as 6. Numerically, 6 and 6.00 are equivalent, so BASIC does not print the two zeros. But since this number represents dollars and cents, we would like it to be printed as 6.00. Also, Frank Chance's gross pay is printed as 255.875. He is going to be paid 255.88, and that is what should be printed. The PRINT USING and LPRINT USING statements give you control over these items. (Note: Except for the fact that PRINT USING sends its output to the screen and LPRINT USING sends its output to the printer, the two statements work identically.)

The syntax of the PRINT USING statement is

```
PRINT USING format string; expression,...
```

(Pressing the Alt + U key is equivalent to typing the word USING.) As with the ordinary PRINT statement, you may list as many variables as you want,

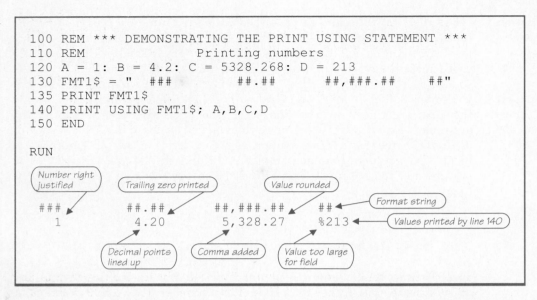

```
100 REM *** DEMONSTRATING THE PRINT USING STATEMENT ***
110 REM                   Printing numbers
120 A = 1: B = 4.2: C = 5328.268: D = 213
130 FMT1$ = "   ###         ##.##       ##,###.##      ##"
135 PRINT FMT1$
140 PRINT USING FMT1$; A,B,C,D
150 END

RUN
```

PROGRAM 6.2   **Printing numbers with the PRINT USING statement.**

and you may print expressions, although you will usually print variables. The PRINT USING statement tells BASIC that you want the variables printed using the format specified in format string. To learn how to use the PRINT USING statement, you must learn how to code format string, which is most easily done by studying the program and the output in Program 6.2.

PRINTING NUMERIC VARIABLES

Line 130 in Program 6.2 shows the coding for FMT1$, which defines four numeric fields: ###, ##.##, ##, ###.## and ##. Each numeric field specifies how and where you want a numeric variable printed. So for each numeric variable in the print list, you must define a numeric field in the format string. As you can see, numeric fields are defined using one or more number signs, #, together with decimal points and commas if needed. Each # corresponds to one digit. Numeric fields may be placed anywhere in a format string; the only rule is that they must be separated from each other by at least one blank. The format string may be either a string that is written as part of the PRINT USING statement or a separately defined string variable. In Program 6.2, we used a separately defined string variable named FMT1$.

When the PRINT USING statement in line 140 is executed, the numeric values of the variables will replace the #s in the format string. The variable A will be printed using the first numeric field, B will be printed using the second numeric field, C using the third, and D using the fourth.

If the numeric field does *not* contain a decimal point, the value will appear **right-justified**. That is, the value will be printed as far to the right in the field as possible. If the numeric field contains more #s than the number of digits in the value being printed, the extra #s are replaced (on the left) by blanks. Let's see how this works in Program 6.2. Line 140 prints A using the numeric field ###. Since A is set equal to 1 in line 120, the first two #s are replaced by blanks. If you examine the output in Program 6.2, you will see that the 1 is printed in the same column as the rightmost #. (To help you clearly see the relationship between the format string and the values printed, line 135 in Program 6.2 prints the format string—of course, normally you would not do so.)

Right-justified
Printed as far to the right in a field as possible.

If the numeric field does contain a decimal point, the decimal point in the value being printed is lined up with the decimal point in the numeric field. This feature allows you to produce columns of output with the decimal points lined up, which makes the output much easier to read. If the numeric field contains more #s to the *left* of the decimal point than the number of digits in the value being printed, the extra #s are replaced by blanks, just as they are when the numeric field does not contain a decimal point. However, if the numeric field contains more #s to the right of the decimal point than are required by the value being printed, the extra #s are replaced by zeros. This feature allows us to force BASIC to print two decimal positions for cents.

In Program 6.2, line 140 prints B using the numeric field ##.##. Since the value of B is 4.2, the first # is replaced by a blank (as we would have expected from our previous discussion of how A was printed), but the last # is replaced by 0. Notice how the decimal point in 4.20 is printed in the same column as the decimal point in ##.##.

The third numeric field in line 130 shows how commas may be inserted when values larger than 999 are printed: just put a comma in the numeric field where the comma should print. Notice also that when line 130 prints C using this numeric field, the comma is inserted and the value of C, 5328.268, is rounded and printed as 5,328.27. The rule is that values are rounded before they are printed. For example, if A has the value 10.674,

PRINT USING Statement

PRINT USING "##"; A

Effect

Rounds to the nearest integer and prints 11.

PRINT USING Statement

PRINT USING "##.#"; A

Effect

Rounds to the nearest tenth and prints 10.7.

PRINT USING Statement

PRINT USING "##.##"; A

Effect

Rounds to the nearest hundredth and prints 10.67.

What happens if you print a value that is too large to fit in a numeric field? BASIC will still print the value, but it cannot align it correctly. Moreover, BASIC will precede such values with a %, which may at first confuse you and which certainly makes the output harder to read. For an example, look again at Program 6.2. There, line 140 prints D using the numeric field ## which allows for only two digits. Since the value of D is 213, it can't fit in that field. D is accordingly printed as %213, spoiling the column alignment.

This example makes one thing clear. When you design a numeric field, consider the size of the numbers that will be printed in it. How many digits will they have to the left of the decimal point? Since the "cost" of making a numeric field too large is printing extra blanks, while the "cost" of making a numeric field too small is spoiling the column alignment, it is better to be safe and make the numeric field one or two digits larger than you think you might need.

Notice, however, that when you are specifying what happens to the right of the decimal point, you should put in only as many #s as you wish to have printed. A value that has more digits than that will not cause BASIC to print a %. Instead, as we saw in the printing of C, the value will be rounded which is often desirable.

PRINTING STRING VARIABLES

String variables may also be printed with the PRINT USING statement. In Program 6.3, line 130 shows the coding for a format string to print four string variables. Backslashes, \, are used to define a string field. The first backslash indicates the start of the string field and the second backslash the end of the field. The number of characters printed is equal to the number of spaces between the backslashes plus 2. So two backslashes next to each other, \\, will print two characters, two backslashes separated by one space, \ \, will print three characters, etc.

Left-justified
Printed as far to the left in a field as possible.

String variables are always **left-justified**, which means that the string is printed as far to the left as possible. If the string variable to be printed contains fewer characters than the field provides for, blanks for the extra characters are printed at the end. If the string variable contains more characters than the field provides for, as many characters as will fit are printed and the extra characters are ignored.

For example, the first two fields in line 130 have 8 spaces between the backslashes, so they will print 10 characters. Line 140 prints A$ using this field. Since A$ contains the 6 characters STRING, it is left-justified in the field, and blanks are printed in the remaining 4 columns. Line 140 also prints B$ using an identical field. But B$ contains 15 characters, so only the first 10—VERY BIG S—are printed. Notice that unlike the % that is printed when a number is too large for its field, BASIC does not give any indication that only part of B$ was printed.

In addition to backslashes, two other characters may be used to define string fields. The exclamation point, !, specifies that only the first character of the string variable should be printed. Line 140 prints A$ using an exclamation point; you can see how only the first character of A$, an S, was printed.

The ampersand, &, prints the complete string. Line 140 prints C$ using an &, and you can see that all of C$ is printed. Printing a string variable using an ampersand field gives the same output you would get if you used

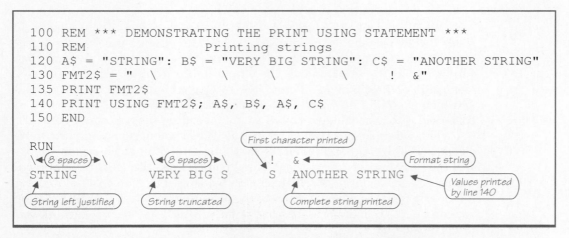

```
100 REM *** DEMONSTRATING THE PRINT USING STATEMENT ***
110 REM               Printing strings
120 A$ = "STRING": B$ = "VERY BIG STRING": C$ = "ANOTHER STRING"
130 FMT2$ = "  \        \     \          \      !  &"
135 PRINT FMT2$
140 PRINT USING FMT2$; A$, B$, A$, C$
150 END
```

PROGRAM 6.3   **Printing strings with the PRINT USING statement.**

an ordinary PRINT statement. That is, the ampersand prints a variable number of characters. Of course, with a variable number of characters printed, it is impossible to maintain column alignment. Also, the ampersand leaves no spaces before or after the string.

OTHER FORMAT CHARACTERS

In Program 6.4, the first numeric field defined in line 130 shows that to print a $ in front of a number you simply code a $ at the beginning of the numeric field. But sometimes, especially on checks, a blank between the $ and the first digit is not desirable. The second numeric field in line 130 shows that to eliminate that blank you code *two* dollar signs, $$, at the beginning of the numeric field. Coding $$ at the beginning of the numeric field causes the $ to be printed next to the first digit. One of the $s represents a position for a digit, so the field $$####.## could correctly print numbers as large as 99999.99.

Another way to eliminate blanks when numbers are printed is to code two asterisks, **, at the beginning of the numeric field, as shown in the first numeric field defined in line 150. Coding ** at the beginning of the numeric field causes leading spaces in the printed numeric field to be replaced by asterisks. You can also combine the two dollar signs and two asterisks by coding **$ at the beginning of the numeric field, as shown in the second numeric field defined in line 150. The output shows that this combination causes the dollar sign to be printed next to the first digit and the leading spaces to be replaced by asterisks.

When a PRINT USING statement is executed, only the characters used to define numeric and string fields in the format string are replaced by numbers and characters. All other characters are printed exactly as they appear

```
100 REM *** DEMONSTRATING THE PRINT USING STATEMENT ***
110 REM          Additional Formatting Characters
120 A = 150: B = 20.25
130 FMT1$ = "  $####.##   $$####.##"
135 PRINT FMT1$
140 PRINT USING FMT1$; A, B
150 FMT2$ = "  **####.##   **$####.##"
155 PRINT FMT2$
160 PRINT USING FMT2$; A, B
170 FMT3$ = "  Total Sales This Month   $$###.##"
175 PRINT FMT3$
180 PRINT USING FMT3$; B
190 END

RUN
  $####.##     $$####.##        ◄── Format string
  $ 150.00       $20.25         ◄── Values printed by line 140
  ▲              ▲
  $ printed      $ printed with no blanks
  **####.##    **$####.##       ◄── Format string
  ***150.00    ****$20.25       ◄── Values printed by line 160
  ▲            ▲
  Asterisk fill  Asterisk fill with $
Total Sales This Month   $$###.##      ◄── Format string
Total Sales This Month     $20.25      ◄── Values printed by line 180
```

PROGRAM 6.4 Demonstrating PRINT USING with additional formatting characters.

in the format string. This is illustrated in the format string defined in line 170. The output shows that the whole string constant Total Sales This Month was printed, as well as the edited number.

Sometimes you might want to print a character that is used to define a format string. For example, suppose you want to print the words Student ID# followed by the actual number. If you write the PRINT USING statement as

```
PRINT USING "Student ID# ####"; STUD.NO
```

BASIC will assume that you have defined two numeric fields, # and ####. If the value of STUD.NO is 1234, this statement will print

```
Student ID%1234
```

which is not what you want. The solution is to use an underscore character (_) in the format string, as follows:

```
PRINT USING "Student ID_# ####"; STUD.NO
```

The underscore character tells BASIC to print the next character as it stands and not to interpret it as part of a field definition. This statement will print what you want:

```
Student ID# 1234
```

CONTROLLING PLUS AND MINUS SIGNS

Like the ordinary PRINT statement, the PRINT USING statement prints positive numbers with no sign and negative numbers with a leading minus sign. For example, consider line 140 in Program 6.5, where C (which is set equal to -14.7 in line 120) is printed using the format field ###.#. We can control the printing and placement of the sign using plus and minus signs in the format field. A plus sign, +, may be coded at the beginning or the end of the format field, as shown in the last four format fields defined in line 130. The output produced by this format shows that a plus sign causes a positive number to

```
100 REM *** DEMONSTRATING THE PRINT USING STATEMENT ***
110 REM          Plus and Minus Signs
120 C = -14.7: D = 39.4: E = -23.9
130 FMT1$ = "  ###.#  +###.#  +###.#  ###.#+  ###.#+"
135 PRINT FMT1$
140 PRINT USING FMT1$; C, D, E, D, E
150 FMT2$ = "  ###.#-  ###.#-"
155 PRINT FMT2$
160 PRINT USING FMT2$; C, D
170 END

RUN
  ###.#  +###.#  +###.#  ###.#+  ###.#+          Format string
  -14.7  +39.4   -23.9   39.4+   23.9-           Values printed by line 140

  - printed      + and - printed before and after numbers

  ###.#-  ###.#-          Format string
  14.7-   39.4            Values printed by line 140

  Only - printed after number
```

PROGRAM 6.5   **Demonstrating PRINT USING with plus and minus signs.**

be printed with a plus sign and a negative number to be printed with a minus sign. The sign is printed before or after the number, depending on whether the plus sign was coded at the beginning or the end of the field.

A negative sign may be coded only at the end of a numeric field, as shown in line 150. The output produced using this format shows that negative numbers are printed with a minus sign and positive numbers are printed with no sign.

You can mix string and numeric field definitions in the same format field, for example,

```
PRINT USING "\      \   ###"; PATIENT.NAME$, AGE
```

When you do so, though, you must be careful to print string variables using string format fields and numbers using numeric format fields.

ADDITIONAL NOTES

Format strings need not always appear in the order and style you have just seen. For example, it is not necessary that a format string be defined in the line just before the line in which it is used. A format string may be defined anywhere in the program; the only requirement is that the line in which it is defined must be executed before the line in which it is used is executed.

Usually, but not necessarily, the number of fields defined in the format string is the same as the number of variables in the print list. For example, consider the statement:

```
PRINT USING " ### ##.###"; A, B, C, D
```

Under these conditions, the format string is reused from the beginning. In this example, A and C will be printed using the number field ###, and B and D will be printed using the number field ##.###.

Table 6.1 summarizes the functions of the formatting characters we have discussed.

Printing Headings

In our earlier examples, you saw how to print a simple title, plus a column heading in each print zone. In this section, you will learn how to print more elaborate headings and how to design format strings to go with them.

Before you can print a heading you have to design it, and for that a **spacing chart**, like that shown in Figure 6.4, is helpful. Your instructor may supply spacing charts, or you may be able to buy them in the bookstore.

Figure 6.4 shows a title, column headings, and format string that could be used with the overtime pay problem in Program 6.1. After designing column headings, you should design the format string on the spacing chart to make sure that values will be printed under their column headings. When the spacing chart is complete, the title, column headings, and format string can be translated, spaces and all, into TAB functions and heading and format strings, as shown in lines 30 through 70 in Program 6.6.

Program 6.6 also uses a little trick that you may find helpful. If you look carefully, you will see in lines 40 and 50 two spaces between the equal sign and the quotation mark. The extra spaces allow the two heading strings and the format string in line 60 to start in the same column. This in turn simplifies typing the strings. Once you have carefully typed HEAD1$, counting spaces between words, you can easily type HEAD2$ by lining up its words with the words in HEAD1$. For example, Figure 6.4 shows that the R of Rate in

Spacing chart
A chart used to design printed reports and screens.

TABLE 6.1   **Formatting characters used with PRINT USING**

Character	Description
	String-Printing Characters
!	Prints only the first character of the string.
\ \	Prints two more than the number of spaces between the two backslashes. The string is left-justified in the field; if the string is longer than the field, it is truncated.
&	Prints the whole string.
_	Causes the following character to be printed "as is" and not to be interpreted as part of a field definition.
	Number-Printing Characters
#	Specifies a numeric field. Each # represents a digit position. The number is right-justified in the field. If the number is larger than the number of digits allowed for, a % is printed.
.	Specifies the position of the decimal point in the numeric field. The decimal point in the numeric value is aligned with the decimal point in the field.
$	Prints as a $.
$$	Prints a single $ to the immediate left of the number.
**	Prints asterisks in the leading spaces of the numeric field.
**$	Combines the effects of $$ and **. Leading spaces of the numeric field are filled with asterisks, and a $ is printed to the immediate left of the number.
+	Prints the sign of the number. The sign is printed before the number if the + is at the beginning of the numeric field, or after the number if the + is at the end of the field.
-	Must be used at the end of a numeric field, where it prints a minus sign if the number is negative and nothing if the number is positive.

HEAD2$ should start one column before the P of Pay in HEAD1$. Instead of counting spaces, you can simply hold down the space bar until the cursor is in the correct column and then type the word Rate. Similarly, instead of counting spaces when you type FORMAT$, you can visually line up the format strings with the words in HEAD2$ according to the layout in Figure 6.4.

You may be surprised to see that values are assigned to the variables in line 20 of this program. The purpose of assigning these values is to let us test the program. Eventually, we will eliminate line 20. In fact, this entire program will eventually become a routine in the overtime pay program. The advantage of a separate routine is that the program may be run—and quickly corrected—on its own, without involving the complete program of which it will become a part. Because this program will become part of another program, it does not contain an END statement.

The MERGE Command

Once the heading routine is working properly, we would like to incorporate it into Program 6.1. Unless you are unusually fond of typing, you will be glad to know that BASIC can merge the two programs if you make a few

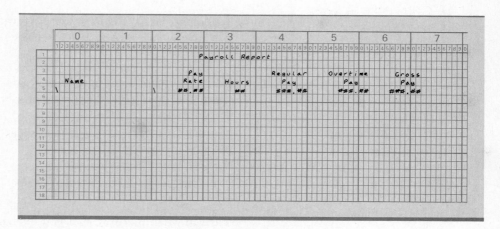

FIGURE 6.4   **Printer spacing chart for Bat-O program with overtime.**

simple changes. First, delete the unwanted line 20 from Program 6.6 and use the Editor to change all the PRINT statements to LPRINT. Then examine Program 6.1 to determine where the heading routine could fit in. The line numbers between 200 and 299 are not being used. To fit in this space, you must renumber Program 6.6 with an increment of 5 by using the command

RENUM 200, , 5

Next, you must save Program 6.6. However, an ordinary SAVE won't do. Eventually we want to merge this program with Program 6.1, and for BASIC

```
10 REM *** Heading routine
20 EMP.NAME$ = "Joe Tinker": PAY.RATE = 6.75: HOURS = 50: REGULAR.PAY = 270:
      OVERTIME.PAY = 101.25: GROSS.PAY = 371.25
30   TITLE$ = "Payroll Report"
40   HEAD1$ = "                          Pay             Regular    Overtime
  Gross"
50   HEAD2$ = "  Name                    Rate    Hours     Pay         Pay
  Pay"
60   FORMAT$ = "\                    \    ##.##     ##      ###.##      ###.##
 ###.##"
70   PRINT TAB(29); TITLE$
80   PRINT
90   PRINT HEAD1$
100   PRINT HEAD2$
110   PRINT USING FORMAT$; EMP.NAME$, PAY.RATE, HOURS, REGULAR.PAY,
                    OVERTIME.PAY, GROSS.PAY
120 REM *** End of heading routine
130 '
RUN
                 Payroll Report

                 Pay             Regular    Overtime    Gross
   Name          Rate    Hours     Pay         Pay        Pay
Joe Tinker       6.75     50      270.00      101.25     371.25
Ok
```

PROGRAM 6.6   **Program to print headings.**

to be able to merge a file, the file must be saved in ASCII format. To save the program in ASCII format, you must use the command

                    SAVE "HEADING", A

The A after the filename causes the program to be saved in ASCII format.

  Now we can merge HEADING and Program 6.1. First, load Program 6.1, using the command

                    LOAD "OVERTIME"

Then use the command

                    MERGE "HEADING"

to merge the two files.

  Be careful when merging that you have no overlapping line numbers in the two files. If any line in OVERTIME (Program 6.1) had the same line number as a line in HEADING (Program 6.6), the line from HEADING would replace the matching line in OVERTIME. The way we numbered HEADING, there are no matching line numbers. When you use MERGE for other problems, however, you will need to remember how MERGE deals with overlapping line numbers.

  The MERGE command is useful because it allows you to create a library of subroutines that perform generally useful functions and to combine a subroutine with a main program whenever you need one of those functions.

  At this point, our improved program is almost complete. But you must still make a few more changes. First, to execute the heading subroutine, change line 110 to GOSUB 200. Then use the Editor to change the line number of the LPRINT USING statement from 245 to 150. Doing so also deletes the old LPRINT statement that was in line 150. Finally, you must add the RETURN statement at line 245, replacing the LPRINT statement there.

  The improved overtime program and the output it produces are shown in Program 6.7. Notice how attractive the output looks and especially how the decimal points in the money fields line up.

Syntax Summary

PRINT USING Statement
Form: PRINT USING format string; expression, . . .
Example: PRINT USING "\   \ ###,### sq. miles"; STATE$, AREA
Interpretation: The values of the expressions are displayed
                  on the screen as specified in the format
                  string. For a description of the formatting
                  string characters, see Table 6.1.
                  Note: The LPRINT USING statement functions
                  exactly the same way, but sends the output to the
                  printer instead of the screen.

Getting the Bugs Out

Problem: During execution, BASIC stops and displays the message

                    Type mismatch in nn

where nn is the line number of a PRINT USING statement.

Reason: You are trying to print a string variable using a numeric format field or a numeric variable using a string format field, for example, PRINT USING "\   \ ###"; AGE, PATIENT.NAME$ instead of PRINT USING "\   \ ###"; PATIENT.NAME$, AGE.

Solution: Correct the format field or the variable.

```
100 REM *** IMPROVED BAT-O PROGRAM WITH OVERTIME ***
110 GOSUB 200                      'Print headings
120 GOSUB 300                      'Obtain input
130   IF HOURS > 40
         THEN GOSUB 500
         ELSE GOSUB 600
140   GROSS.PAY = REGULAR.PAY + OVERTIME.PAY
150   LPRINT USING FORMAT$; EMP.NAME$, PAY.RATE, HOURS, REGULAR.PAY,
                           OVERTIME.PAY, GROSS.PAY
160 GOTO 120
170 PRINT "Normal end of program"
180 STOP
190 '
200 REM *** Heading routine
205   TITLE$ = "Payroll Report"
210   HEAD1$ = "                         Pay              Regular    Overtime
   Gross"
215   HEAD2$ = " Name                    Rate    Hours      Pay        Pay
   Pay"
220   FORMAT$ = "\                 \    ##.##      ##      ###.##      ###.##
   ###.##"
225   LPRINT TAB(29); TITLE$
230   LPRINT
235   LPRINT HEAD1$
240   LPRINT HEAD2$
245 RETURN
250 REM *** End of heading routine
255 '
300 REM *** Input Routine
310   READ EMP.NAME$, PAY.RATE
320   IF EMP.NAME$ = "Stop"
         THEN RETURN 170
330   PRINT "Enter hours for employee "; EMP.NAME$;
340   INPUT HOURS
350 RETURN
360 REM *** End of input routine
370 '
500 REM *** Overtime pay routine
510   REGULAR.PAY = PAY.RATE * 40
520   OVERTIME.PAY = 1.5 * PAY.RATE * (HOURS - 40)
530 RETURN
540 REM *** End of overtime pay routine
550 '
600 REM *** Regular pay routine
610   REGULAR.PAY = PAY.RATE * HOURS
620   OVERTIME.PAY = 0
630 RETURN
640 REM *** End of regular pay routine
650 '
700 REM *** Data used by input routine
710 DATA Joe Tinker, 6.75
720 DATA John Evers, 6.00
730 DATA Frank Chance, 5.75
740 DATA Stop, 0                              : REM Trailer data
750 END

RUN
Enter hours for employee Joe Tinker? 50
Enter hours for employee John Evers? 30
Enter hours for employee Frank Chance? 43
Normal end of program
Break in 180
```

		Payroll Report			
Name	Pay Rate	Hours	Regular Pay	Overtime Pay	Gross Pay
Joe Tinker	6.75	50	270.00	101.25	371.25
John Evers	6.00	30	180.00	0.00	180.00
Frank Chance	5.75	43	230.00	25.88	255.88

PROGRAM 6.7   **Bat-O Program with overtime and headings.**

Problem: During execution, BASIC displays the error message

```
Illegal function call in nn
```

where nn is the line number of a PRINT USING statement.

Reason: Your format string does not contain a field definition. The most likely cause of this error is that you used a slash, /, instead of a backslash, \, to define a string field.

Problem: A PRINT or LPRINT statement that contains a TAB or SPC function prints an unexpected zero.

Reason: You left a space between TAB or SPC and the left parenthesis.

Solution: Delete the space.

Problem: During execution, BASIC stops and displays the message

```
Subscript out of range in nn
```

where nn is the line number of a PRINT or LPRINT statement that contains a TAB or SPC function.

Reason: You left a space between TAB or SPC and the left parenthesis. (This seems to be the same as the previous error, but you get this message when the argument of the TAB or SPC function is greater than 10; you get the earlier message when the argument is less than or equal to 10.)

Solution: Delete the space.

Problem: You try to perform a merge, and BASIC displays the error message

```
Bad file mode
```

Reason: The file you are merging was not saved in ASCII format.

Solution: Save your current program, then load the program you want to merge and save it using the command SAVE "filename", A. Load the original program and issue the MERGE command again.

EXERCISES

....

6.5 Explain the difference between the TAB and SPC functions.

6.6 Write a PRINT statement with a TAB function to print the message Please enter your name starting in column 40.

*6.7 Consider the following PRINT USING statement:

```
PRINT USING"\       \ $##.##"; ITEM$, PRICE
```

(There are nine blanks between the \s and three blanks between the right \ and the $.) What output will this statement produce if ITEM$ = Peaches and PRICE = 1.35? Indicate blanks on the output by the letter "b."

6.8 Consider the following PRINT USING statement:

```
PRINT USING FMT$; STUDENT.NAME$,
          COURSE.CREDITS, GPA
```

(STUDENT.NAME$ may have up to 25 characters, COURSE.CREDITS is a whole number in the range 0 to 200, and GPA has two decimal positions and is in the range 0.00 to 4.00.) Write the LET statement to define FMT$.

6.9 Suppose you have written a routine that analyzes statistics and predicts the winner of a ball game, and that the routine contains 18 lines. Now you want to merge it to occupy the lines in the range 500 to 599 in a program named GAME.

a) Write the command to renumber the routine.
b) Write the command to save the routine with the name WINNER.
c) Write the command to merge WINNER with GAME.

*6.10 Consider the following PRINT USING statement:

    PRINT USING PRICE.FMT$; PRICE

(PRICE will be in the range 5,000 to 35,000.) Write the LET statement to define PRICE.FMT$ so that, for example, if PRICE = 8632 the statement will print

    Sticker price......$ 8,632.00

(Notice the comma in the price.)

PROGRAMMING ASSIGNMENTS

6.6 Write a program that accepts two whole numbers, A and B. Perform the following operations:

    C = (B + 1) / A
    D = (C + 1) / B
    E = (D + 1) / C
    F = (E + 1) / D

Print A, B, and F using a PRINT USING statement with a format string that prints these variables as whole numbers. Are you surprised? Run the program with different values of A and B.

*6.7 Write a program to print the following rectangle:

The right edge of the rectangle is in column 10. Hint: Use the TAB and SPC functions.

6.8 Resolve Programming Assignment 5.12 printing headings and using PRINT USING statements to make your output attractive. Print the test marks as integers and the averages with one decimal place.

CONTROLLING THE SCREEN

In our work so far, we have treated the PC screen as though it were a piece of paper in a typewriter; each new line of output was printed on the next line. In fact, you can specify exactly where on the screen you want output printed and the colors to be used when the output is printed. By using these features, you make your programs much more professional looking.

Clearing the Screen: The CLS and KEY Statements

To control the screen, you must first clear it. You will need two statements to do that. The CLS statement clears the screen and places the cursor in the upper left corner of the screen. This is the same as the Ctrl + Home keys we have been using up to now, but CLS has an advantage over the Ctrl + Home keys because it allows you to clear the screen from within a program. The CLS statement does not clear the bottom line, where the meanings of the function keys are displayed. To clear the bottom line, you must use the KEY OFF statement. The KEY OFF statement turns off the display, but does not disable the function keys; they still have the same meanings they had before. You can turn the display back on by using the KEY ON statement. Because the

CLS and KEY OFF statements are so closely related, they are frequently coded on the same line, as in

111 CLS: KEY OFF

Using the Alt + K keys is equivalent to typing the word KEY. You can also type KEY by pressing the F9 function key.

Positioning Output on the Screen: The LOCATE Statement

Menu
A list of values from which the user may choose.

To design a screen, you again use a spacing chart. Figure 6.5 shows the design of a screen that we will use in a new version of the Sound Value record store program. On this screen, the program will display a **menu**, which is a list of values from which a user may choose.

As the numbering at the left edge of Figure 6.5 shows, the screen is divided into 25 rows. The top row is row 1, and the bottom row is row 25. Rows are often called lines, so row 15 and line 15 mean the same thing. Figure 6.5 also shows that the screen is divided into 80 columns. The leftmost column is column 1, and the rightmost column is column 80.

Once you have completed a spacing chart, you must instruct BASIC to display output in the appropriate row and column. To do so, use the LOCATE statement, which positions the cursor on the screen. The syntax of the LOCATE statement is

LOCATE [row] [,column] [,cursor]

where row specifies the row where you want to begin printing, and column specifies the column. Using the Alt + L keys is equivalent to typing the word LOCATE. After a LOCATE statement is executed, any statement that writes to the screen begins at the specified cursor position. The value chosen for cursor is used to make the cursor visible or invisible. If cursor is 1, the cursor is visible; if cursor is 0, it is invisible. When a program is run, the cursor is normally invisible. You may not have realized that, because the INPUT statement also makes the cursor visible.

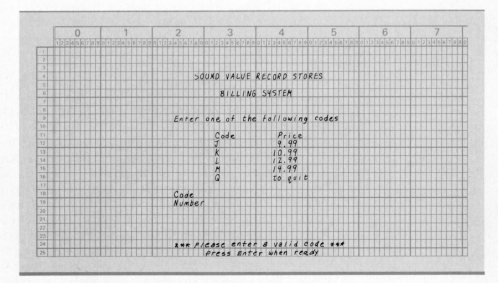

FIGURE 6.5   **Screen layout chart for Sound Value record store program.**

Parameter
A value used with a statement that affects the statement's operation.

LOCATE is the first statement we have discussed that uses parameters— in this case row, column, and cursor. A **parameter** is a value (a constant, a variable, or an expression) that is coded with a statement and that affects the statement's operation. In fact, a parameter is very similar to an argument, but traditionally functions are said to use arguments and statements parameters.

All three parameters in a LOCATE statement are optional. An omitted parameter is not changed. Consider the statement

LOCATE ,60

The comma indicates that the row parameter was omitted. By omitting the row parameter, we tell BASIC to position the cursor at column 60 in whichever row the cursor is currently located. Similarly, the statement

LOCATE ,,1

makes the cursor visible, without changing its position.

Both ROW and COLUMN may be constants, as in our examples, or they may be variables or numeric expressions. The statement

LOCATE ROW,COLUMN

is legal and even useful. In this statement, ROW and COLUMN are variables and must be assigned values before being used in the LOCATE statement. ROW must have a value between 1 and 25, and COLUMN must have a value between 1 and 80.

As an example of how you can use the LOCATE statement, consider Figure 6.5, which shows that we want to print the title, SOUND VALUE RECORD STORES, starting in row 4, column 28. The corresponding LOCATE statement is

LOCATE 4, 28

The LOCATE statement specifies only where printing is to begin; it does not itself cause anything to be printed. To print the title, we would use the statement

PRINT "SOUND VALUE RECORD STORES"

immediately after the LOCATE statement.

Using Color

In addition to position, you can also control the color of output on the screen. You can get the full range of colors if your PC has a color/graphics adapter and a color monitor. If your PC has only a monochrome adapter, you can get only a limited range of colors. Your instructor will tell you the kind of adapter installed on your PC.

THE SCREEN STATEMENT

Before you can use color, you must tell BASIC that you want color. If you have a color/graphics adapter, you can use the SCREEN statement to tell BASIC you want color.* The SCREEN statement is not needed to use the limited colors available with the monochrome adapter.

---

*As discussed in Chapters 13 and 14, the SCREEN statement is also used to switch between text mode and the graphics mode.

The syntax of the SCREEN statement is

SCREEN [mode] [,burst]

Using the Alt + S keys is equivalent to typing the word SCREEN. Here, mode specifies the type of screen you want to use. A value of 0 specifies text mode, which is the mode BASIC starts in and what we have been using all along. If you are using text mode, the only reason to code a SCREEN statement is because a previously executed program might have changed the mode or turned off color. A value of 1 specifies medium-resolution graphics mode, and a value of 2 specifies high-resolution graphics mode. (The graphics modes are discussed in Chapter 13.)

The value assigned to burst turns color on and off on some monitors (on most monitors, color is always on). In text mode (mode = 0), a burst value of 1 turns color on, and a burst value of 0 turns color off. So the statement

SCREEN 0,1

specifies text mode with color turned on.

THE COLOR STATEMENT

When a character is printed on the screen, the color in which it is printed is called the **foreground color**, and the color against which it appears is called the **background color**. These colors may be specified using the COLOR statement. In text mode, the syntax of the COLOR statement is

COLOR [foreground] [,background] [,border]

Foreground color
The color used to display text.

Background color
The color of the background against which text is displayed.

Using the Alt + C key is equivalent to typing the word COLOR. Here, foreground specifies the foreground color, background specifies the background color, and border specifies the color of the border that surrounds the screen.

If your PC has a color/graphics adapter, refer to Table 6.2 to find the values for foreground and the colors they represent. If your PC has only the monochrome adapter, refer to Table 6.3 to find the values for foreground and the colors they represent. (For quick reference, Tables 6.2 and 6.3 are reproduced in Appendix C.) If you add 16 to the appropriate values for your machine, the colors will blink. For example, a value of 23 gives blinking white on PCs with color adapters, while a value of 17 gives blinking underlined white on PCs with monochrome adapters.

For background, with a color/graphics adapter you may use any value from 0 through 7. With the monochrome adapter, the only values you may use for background are 0 and 7, and 7 may be used only when foreground is 0 or 16.

TABLE 6.2   **Colors allowed for Foreground in text mode with the color/graphics monitor adapter**

0	Black	8	Grey
1	Blue	9	Light Blue
2	Green	10	Light Green
3	Cyan	11	Light Cyan
4	Red	12	Light Red
5	Magenta	13	Light Magenta
6	Brown	14	Yellow
7	White	15	High-intensity White

TABLE 6.3   **Colors allowed for foreground in text mode
with the monochrome adapter**

0	Black
1	Underlined white characters
7	White
9	Underlined high-intensity white characters
15	High-intensity white

For border, with a color/graphics adapter you may use values 0 through 15. The border feature is available only with a color/graphics adapter.

Once a COLOR statement is executed, all characters sent to the screen thereafter are printed in the specified colors. Characters may be sent to the screen by a PRINT statement, or they may be entered at the keyboard in response to an INPUT statement. Any characters that were on the screen before the COLOR statement was executed retain their original colors. We will exploit this feature to print an error message in striking colors, while not affecting the rest of the output on the screen. Some examples may clarify how the color statement is used.

COLOR Statement

COLOR 7, 0

Effect

Creates "white" (green on an IBM monochrome display) characters on a black background. This is the default setting.

COLOR Statement

COLOR 0, 7

Effect

Creates black characters on a "white" background—a display called a **reverse image**.

COLOR Statement

COLOR 16, 7

Effect

Creates a blinking reverse image.

COLOR Statement

COLOR 0, 0

Effect

Creates black characters on a black background, making the characters invisible.

COLOR Statement

COLOR 7, 1, 4

Effect

On machines with color adapters, creates white characters on a blue background with a red border.

Reverse image
A display in which black characters appear against a white background.

Any of the three parameters in a COLOR statement — foreground, background, or border — may be constants (as in our examples), variables, or numeric expressions. So statements like

COLOR FOREGROUND, BACKGROUND, BORDER

are legal, providing the variables FOREGROUND, BACKGROUND, and BORDER are assigned legal values before the statement is executed.

■ *Sound Value Billing Program Revisited*

Let's rewrite the Sound Value billing program using the new BASIC statements you have just learned. This program will use the same variables we used earlier, but it is more complicated and needs a new algorithm:

1. Display the menu of codes.
2. Accept the CODE$ of the item purchased.
3. If this is the trailer data, go to step 10.
4. Test the CODE$ to determine the PRICE of the item.
5. If an invalid CODE$ was entered, display an error message and go to step 2.
6. Accept the NUMBER of items purchased.
7. Calculate the BILL, using the appropriate PRICE.
8. Print NUMBER, CODE$, PRICE, and BILL.
9. Repeat steps 2 through 8 for all customers.
10. Stop execution.

Figure 6.6 (see pgs. 156–57) shows a flowchart that implements this algorithm. Because displaying the menu and printing the error messages are a little complicated, these functions have been coded as subroutines. Since some of the functions are coded as subroutines in this program, we will code the case structure that determines the price of a subroutine, too. This flowchart introduces two new symbols:

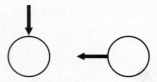

The symbol on the left is called the **output connector**, and the symbol on the right is called the **input connector**. Connectors are used in place of flowlines when drawing the flowlines would make the flowchart cluttered and hard to read or when the flowchart extends over more than one page. In Figure 6.6, output connector A simply means that the program continues at input connector A. Although Figure 6.6 has only one pair of connectors, in general a flowchart may have several pairs. To distinguish them, you put different letters inside the connectors.

To better understand how connectors work, consider Program 6.8 (see pgs. 158–59), which is based on Figure 6.6. In line 110, the statement

Output connector
A flowchart symbol in the shape of a circle with a letter inside and a flowline entering it. It is used to replace a flowline to the input connector with the same letter inside.

Input connector
A flowchart symbol in the shape of a circle with a letter inside and a flowline leaving it. It is used to show the destination of an output connector.

SCREEN 0, 1 sets the screen for text mode with color on. The statement COLOR 7, 1, 1 selects white characters on a blue background with a blue border (if you have a monochrome adapter, you would use COLOR 7, 0, the default white characters on a black background).

Also in line 110, CLS clears the screen, and KEY OFF erases the function-key display on line 25. As you learned earlier, the COLOR statement affects only the colors of output displayed after it is executed. By coding the CLS statement after the COLOR statement, the whole screen is cleared to the blue background color. Line 120 executes the menu display subroutine, which we will examine in a moment.

THE INPUT$ FUNCTION

Line 130 locates the cursor at row 18 and column 24 and makes it visible. Line 140 prints a prompt, and line 150 uses the INPUT$ function to accept a value for CODE$. The INPUT$ function accepts data entered from the keyboard, without requiring the user to press the Enter key. The syntax of the INPUT$ function is

```
string variable = INPUT$(n)
```

where n is the argument of the INPUT$ function. It specifies the number of string characters to be accepted from the keyboard and must be between 1 and 255. Thus, line 150 of Program 6.8, the statement CODE$ = INPUT$(1), specifies the value of n as 1. That is, when a user types 1 character, that character is assigned to CODE$.

Functions may return strings or numbers. If the function's name ends with $—for example, INPUT$—it returns a string; otherwise, it returns a number.

INPUT$ is convenient for the user, who does not have to press the Enter key. But you cannot always use INPUT$. For example, we couldn't use INPUT$ in most of our earlier programs, because we didn't know how many characters of data would be entered. We couldn't know whether the user entering data for PAY.RATE would enter one character (such as 5), two characters (such as 12), or perhaps four characters (such as 6.25). When INPUT$ is used, we must specify, by its argument, how many characters of data will be entered.

In addition to the need to specify an argument, the INPUT$ function differs from the INPUT statement in two important ways. First, the INPUT$ function does not provide a way to print a prompt. Second, it does not automatically display input value on the screen. To achieve those effects, you must add PRINT statements like those in lines 140 and 160. Moreover, if you want the input value to be displayed next to the prompt, the way it is when the INPUT statement is used, you must end the PRINT statement that prints the prompt with a semicolon (as in line 140).

Line 170 tests for trailer data, and line 180 executes the price determination subroutine, which we will discuss momentarily. Line 190 locates the cursor to position the prompt produced by the INPUT statement in line 200. This INPUT statement uses a comma between the prompt and the variable NUMBER, instead of the semicolon you are used to seeing. Using a comma in place of a semicolon eliminates the question mark that is usually displayed after the prompt. Line 210 calculates BILL, and lines 220 and 230 print it.

THE SPACE$ FUNCTION

Lines 240 through 270 erase the values of CODE$ and NUMBER that were just entered to get ready for the next set of data. The LOCATE statements (lines 240 and 260) position the cursor for the PRINT statements (lines 250 and 270), which use the SPACE$ function to print spaces to erase the old data.

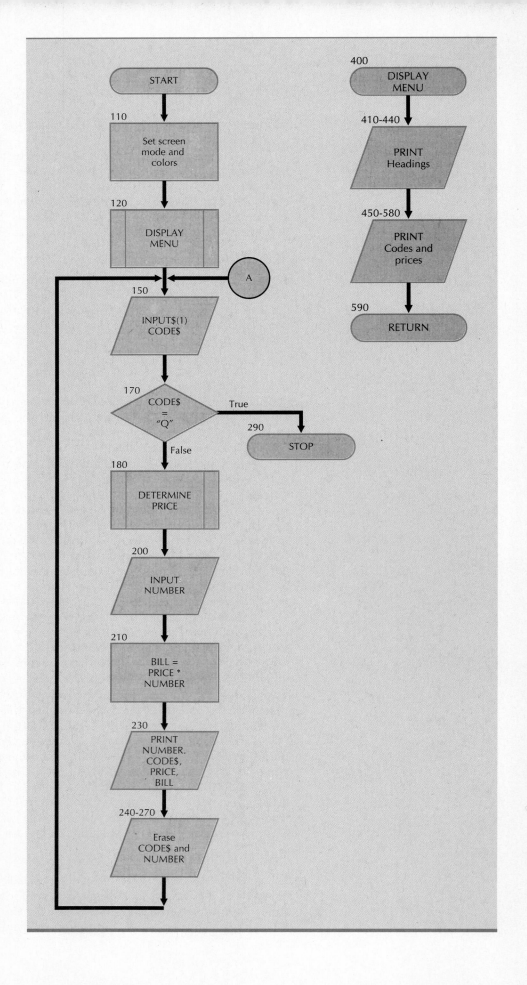

FIGURE 6.6

**Flowchart for improved
Sound Value program.**

156

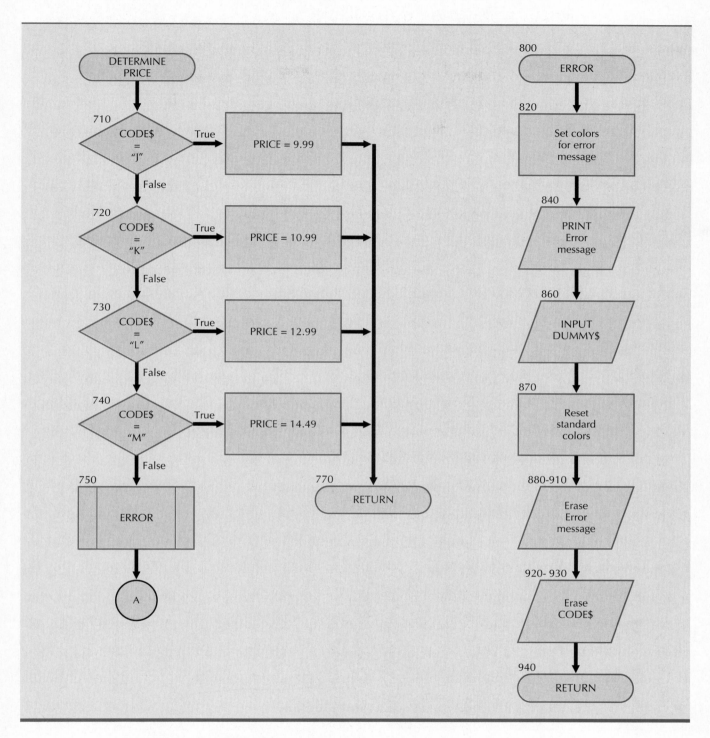

FIGURE 6.6 **(Continued).**

```
100 REM *** SOUND VALUE BILLING PROGRAM ***          Select text mode with color,
110 SCREEN 0, 1: COLOR 7, 1, 1: CLS : KEY OFF        set white on blue, clear the screen,
                                                     and erase function key display
120 GOSUB 400                         'Display menu
130 LOCATE 18, 24, 1                                 Position cursor and make it visible
140    PRINT "Code    ";
150    CODE$ = INPUT$(1)
160    PRINT CODE$
170    IF CODE$ = "Q"
          THEN GOTO 290
180    GOSUB 700                       'Get price
190    LOCATE 19, 24
200    INPUT "Number ", NUMBER
210    BILL = PRICE * NUMBER
220    LOCATE 21, 20
230    PRINT USING "### code ! items at ##.## each total $###.##";
                    NUMBER; CODE$; PRICE; BILL
240    LOCATE 18, 31              'Clear
250    PRINT SPACE$(1)            'previous
260    LOCATE 19, 31              'code and
270    PRINT SPACE$(3)            'number
280 GOTO 130
290 STOP
300 '
400 REM *** Start of subroutine to display menu
410    LOCATE 4, 28
420    PRINT "SOUND VALUE RECORD STORES"
430    LOCATE 6, 33
440    PRINT "BILLING SYSTEM"
450    LOCATE 9, 24
460    PRINT "Enter one of the following codes"
470    LOCATE 11, 32
480    PRINT "Code        Price"
490    LOCATE 12, 31
500    PRINT " J          9.99"
510    LOCATE 13, 31
520    PRINT " K         10.99"
530    LOCATE 14, 31
540    PRINT " L         12.99"
550    LOCATE 15, 31
560    PRINT " M         14.49"
570    LOCATE 16, 31
580    PRINT " Q         to quit"
590 RETURN
600 REM *** End of routine to display menu
610 '
```

PROGRAM 6.8   Improved Sound Value program.

```
700 REM *** Start of subroutine to determine price
710    IF CODE$ = "J"
          THEN PRICE = 9.99: GOTO 770
720    IF CODE$ = "K"
          THEN PRICE = 10.99: GOTO 770
730    IF CODE$ = "L"
          THEN PRICE = 12.99: GOTO 770
740    IF CODE$ = "M"
          THEN PRICE = 14.49: GOTO 770
750    GOSUB 800                      'Wrong code, call error subroutine
760    RETURN 130                     'Obtain new code
770 RETURN
780 REM *** End of price routine
790 '
800 REM *** Start of error subroutine
810    BEEP
820    COLOR 31, 4                    'Set blinking white on red
830    LOCATE 24, 24
840    PRINT "*** Please enter a valid code ***";
850    LOCATE 25, 30
860    INPUT ; "Press Enter when ready", DUMMY$
870    COLOR 7, 1                     'Reset standard colors
880    LOCATE 24, 24                  'Erase
890    PRINT SPACE$(33);              'error  message
900    LOCATE 25, 30                  'on both
910    PRINT SPACE$(24);              'lines
920    LOCATE 18, 31                  'Clear
930    PRINT SPACE$(1)                'previous code
940 RETURN
950 REM *** End of error routine
960 END

RUN
```

(annotation: Hanging semicolon prevents scrolling — pointing to line 840)

(annotation: Semicolon prevents scrolling — pointing to line 860)

```
                    SOUND VALUE RECORD STORES

                          BILLING SYSTEM


               Enter one of the following codes

                    Code          Price
                    J             9.99
                    K             10.99
                    L             12.99
                    M             14.49
                    Q             to quit

          Code    W
          Number
```

(annotation: Invalid code caused error message to be printed)

```
          *** Please enter a valid code ***
                Press Enter when ready
```

PROGRAM 6.8   (Continued).

The syntax of the SPACE$ function is

SPACE$(n)

where the argument, n, specifies the number of spaces to generate and may have any value between 0 and 255. In line 250, the argument is 1, because CODE$ is only one character; in line 270, the argument is 3 because we allow someone to buy up to 999 items. Unlike the SPC function, which may be used only in PRINT and LPRINT statements, the SPACE$ function may be used anywhere a string can be used. Line 280 returns to the top of the loop. Notice that we must return to the LOCATE statement in line 130, to position the cursor properly for the PRINT statement in line 140.

The menu display subroutine which starts in line 400, uses LOCATE and PRINT statements to produce the screen you see in Program 6.8. This is a much more professional-looking screen than the simple prompt we used in Program 5.4. The screen is shown after an invalid value was entered for CODE$.

The price determination subroutine starts in line 700. It is similar to the case structure in Program 5.4, except that instead of printing an error message if all the case IFs are false, line 750 executes the error subroutine. The error subroutine starts in line 800, where line 810 BEEPs the user. Line 820 sets the colors with a color adapter to blinking white on red (if you have a monochrome adapter, you would use COLOR 16, 7, which is blinking reverse image). Line 830 positions the cursor on row 24, and line 840 prints an error message. Notice that the PRINT statement in line 840 ends with a hanging semicolon, to prevent scrolling. In general, scrolling does not cause any problems, but here we have displayed a menu, and scrolling would spoil it. To prevent scrolling, we must be aware of two things. First, any PRINT statement that writes on lines 24 or 25 must end with a hanging semicolon or comma. Second, you must not print in column 80 of line 24 or 25.

Line 850 positions the cursor to display the prompt of the INPUT statement in line 860 on row 25. Using an INPUT statement here forces the program to pause. After reading and understanding the error message, the user can simply press the Enter key to continue.

If an INPUT statement prints a prompt on rows 24 or 25, when the user presses the Enter key to signal that all the data have been typed, the screen will scroll. This INPUT statement has a semicolon immediately following the word INPUT that prevents this scrolling.

Because the COLOR statement affects only the colors of output generated after it is executed, only the error message in line 840 and the prompt in line 860 are printed in blinking white on red as specified in the COLOR statement in line 820. The rest of the screen keeps its normal white characters on a blue background. Line 870 sets the colors back to normal on machines with a color adapter (if you have a monochrome adapter, use COLOR 7, 0, to restore white characters on a black background). Thus, the PRINT statements in lines 890, 910, and 930 print spaces to erase the error message, the prompt, and the invalid CODE$ in the normal white on blue.

When we return from the error subroutine, line 760 executes the statement RETURN 130. In the flowchart in Figure 6.6, this RETURN statement is represented by the output connector. The purpose of this RETURN statement is to return to line 130, where we will position the cursor, print a prompt (per line 140), and accept a new value of CODE$ (per line 150).

The INKEY$ Function

In addition to INPUT and INPUT$, we can also use the INKEY$ function to obtain input from the keyboard. The syntax of INKEY$ is

string variable = INKEY$

Like INPUT$, INKEY$ does not provide a way to print a prompt, nor does it display the entered data on the screen. Unlike INPUT$, however, you do not need to specify the size of the string to be read by INKEY$, since INKEY$ reads only one character. The other difference between INKEY$ and INPUT$ (and INPUT) is that INKEY$ does not pause and wait for you to enter a value. It simply checks to see if you have typed a value. If you have, it assigns that value to the string variable on the left side of the equal sign. If you haven't typed a value, it assigns the **null string**, a string that contains no characters, to the string variable on the left side of the equal sign.

> **Null string**
> The string that contains no characters.

As you can see, you should use INKEY$ *only* when the user must enter just one character *and* you want processing to continue while the user is thinking about a response.

To give you an idea of how INKEY$ works, consider Program 6.9, which repeatedly displays a sentence from the Declaration of Independence—first in red, then in white, and finally in blue, until the user presses a key. In line 120, we use INKEY$ to assign a value to HALT$. In line 130, which is essentially a test for trailer data, BASIC tests HALT$ to see if it does not contain the null string. Notice that we code the null string in the condition as two quotation marks right next to each other. If the user types a value, HALT$ will not contain the null string, the condition will be true, and BASIC will end execution by branching to the STOP statement in line 210. If the user does not type a value, HALT$ will contain the null string, the condition will be false, and BASIC will fall through the IF statement and execute line 140. This line sets the foreground color to red, so when line 150 executes the subroutine that displays the sentence from the Declaration, it is displayed in red. When we return from the subroutine, line 160 sets the foreground color to white, so when line 170 executes the subroutine, the sentence is displayed in white. Finally, line 180 sets the foreground color to blue, so when line 190 executes the subroutine, the sentence is displayed in blue. This loop continues until the user presses any key.

```
100 REM *** DEMONSTRATING INKEY$ ***
110 SCREEN 0, 1: CLS: KEY OFF
120 HALT$ = INKEY$                'Check if a key was pressed
130    IF HALT$ <> ""
          THEN GOTO 210           'Test for trailer data
140    COLOR 12                   'Print red
150    GOSUB 300                  'Print selection
160    COLOR 15                   'Print white
170    GOSUB 300                  'Print selection
180    COLOR 9                    'Print blue
190    GOSUB 300                  'Print selection
200 GOTO 120
210 STOP
300 REM *** Printing subroutine
310    CLS
320    LOCATE 6, 20: PRINT "We hold these truths to be self-evident,"
330    LOCATE 7, 20: PRINT "that all Men are created equal,"
340    LOCATE 8, 20: PRINT "that they are endowed by their Creator"
350    LOCATE 9, 20: PRINT "with certain unalienable Rights,"
360    LOCATE 10, 20: PRINT "that among these are Life, Liberty, "
370    LOCATE 11, 20: PRINT "and the pursuit of Happiness."
380 RETURN
390 REM *** End of printing subroutine
400 END
```

PROGRAM 6.9   Demonstrating INKEY$.

Syntax Summary

CLS Statement
Form: `CLS`
Example: `CLS`
Interpretation: Clears the screen.

KEY OFF Statement
Form: `KEY OFF`
Example: `KEY OFF`
Interpretation: Erases the function key display on line 25.

LOCATE Statement
Form: `LOCATE [row] [,column] [,cursor]`
Example: `LOCATE 5, 30, 1`
Interpretation: Positions the cursor on the screen for
                  subsequent output. A value of 1 for cursor
                  makes the cursor visible, and a value of 0
                  makes it invisible.

SCREEN Statement
Form: `SCREEN [mode] [,burst]`
Example: `SCREEN 1, 0`
Interpretation: Sets the screen attributes. A value of 0 for
                  mode selects text mode, 1 selects medium-
                  resolution graphics mode, and 2 selects high-
                  resolution graphics mode. In text mode, a
                  value of 1 for burst turns color on, but on
                  most color monitors color is always on.

COLOR Statement
Form: `COLOR [foreground] [,background] [,border]`
Example: `COLOR 8, 3, 1`
Interpretation: Sets the colors used for subsequent output.

INPUT$ Function
Form: `string variable = INPUT$(n)`
Example: `DEPT$ = INPUT$(2)`
Interpretation: Reads n characters from the keyboard and
                  assigns them to the string variable on the
                  left of the equal sign. The user does not have
                  to press the Enter key.

INKEY$ Function
Form: `string variable = INKEY$`
Example: `CONTINUE$ = INKEY$`
Interpretation: If a character has been typed, reads the character
                  and assigns it to the string variable on the left
                  of the equal sign. If no character has been
                  typed, assigns the null string to the
                  string variable.

Getting the Bugs Out

Problem: During execution, BASIC stops and displays the message

`Illegal function call`

Reason: A parameter or argument is outside the legal range. The legal ranges are

LOCATE row must be between 1 and 25, and `column` must be between 1 and 80.

SCREEN mode must be 0, 1, or 2, and burst must be 0 or 1.

COLOR foreground must be between 0 and 31, background must be between 0 and 7, and border must be between 0 and 15.

SPACE$ The argument must be in the range 0 to 255.

Solution: Correct the illegal parameter or argument.

EXERCISES

6.11 A program accepts the following data:

a) Address
b) Sex (M/F)
c) Social security number
d) Married (Y/N)

Which of these values could be accepted using an INPUT$ function? Which could be accepted using an INKEY$ function?

6.12 Write a statement that puts the screen in text mode and enables color.

*6.13 Write a statement(s) to print the message How many tickets please? in row 20 starting in column 10.

6.14 Write LOCATE and INPUT statements that will print the prompt Enter your name in row 6 starting in column 15.

*6.15 Write a statement(s) to put the screen in text mode, enable color, and print blue letters on a yellow background.

6.16 Write a statement(s) to print 33 spaces starting at row 5 column 10.

*6.17 Write a statement to use INKEY$ to assign a value to the variable GO$.

6.18 Write a statement to test the variable GO$ in Exercise 6.17 and branch to line 300 if a key has been pressed.

6.19 Program 6.10 shows a program that is supposed to accept two words and print them in alphabetical order. As you can see, the output is not correct. Find and correct the error.

```
10 REM *** PRINTING WORDS IN ALPHABETICAL ORDER ***
15 FMT$ = "In alphabetical order the words are /      /  /      /"
20 INPUT "Enter two words, STOP to stop"; WORD1$, WORD2$
30    IF WORD1$ = "STOP"
         THEN GOTO 90
40    IF WORD1$ < WORD2$
         THEN PRINT USING FMT$; WORD1$, WORD2$
         ELSE PRINT USING FMT$; WORD2$, WORD1$
50 GOTO 20
90 END

RUN
Enter two words, STOP to stop? DOG, CAT
In alphabetical order the words are /      /  /      /
Illegal function call in 40
Ok
```

PROGRAM 6.10   **An attempt to print words in alphabetical order.**

SUMMARY

In this chapter you have learned that

☐ The READ statement obtains values from DATA statements and assigns them to variables. DATA statements may be placed anywhere in a program, but usually they are best placed just before the END statement.

☐ A comment may be added to the end of a line by starting the comment with an apostrophe.

☐ The TAB and SPC functions are used with a PRINT or LPRINT statement. TAB skips to the specified column, while SPC skips the specified number of columns.

☐ The PRINT USING and LPRINT USING statements require a format string. In a format string, number signs, #, are used to define numeric fields. Numeric fields may also contain periods, commas, and dollar signs. Backslashes, \, are usually used to define string fields, but an ampersand, &, prints the complete string and an exclamation point, !, prints just the first character of a string.

☐ A spacing chart is used to design a screen and to help devise appropriate spacing for titles, column headings, and format strings in a printed report.

☐ The MERGE command is used to combine a program saved on disk into the active program. The program on disk must have been saved in ASCII format.

☐ The CLS statement is used to clear the screen.

☐ The KEY OFF statement is used to erase the function-key display on line 25.

☐ The LOCATE statement is used to position output on the screen.

☐ The SCREEN statement is used to specify whether you want text or graphics mode and whether you want color.

☐ In text mode, the COLOR statement is used to specify the foreground, background, and border colors.

☐ The INPUT$ function is used to accept input from the keyboard, without requiring the user to press the Enter Key.

☐ The SPACE$ function is used to generate up to 255 spaces.

☐ The INKEY$ is used to accept one character from the keyboard. It does not stop execution while it waits for input.

KEY TERMS IN THIS CHAPTER

QUESTIONS FOR REVIEW

6.1 In a format string, which character causes a complete string to be printed, no matter how long the string is?

6.2 What punctuation mark separates the values listed in a DATA statement?

6.3 True or false: In a format string, the field $$####.## causes two $ to be printed.

6.4 When must string data listed in a DATA statement be enclosed by quotation marks?

6.5 Write the statement to turn off the function-key display on line 25. Write the statement to turn it back on.

6.6 Does the INPUT$ function return a string or a number?

6.7 In the format string of a PRINT USING statement, which character is used to indicate the printing of numeric variables? Which characters are used to indicate the printing of string variables?

6.8 True or false: DATA statements must be placed before their READ statements.

6.9 How is the number of characters returned by the INPUT$ function determined?

6.10 In a PRINT USING statement, what punctuation must separate the format string from the list of variables to be printed?

6.11 Which statement is used to clear the screen?

6.12 In a format string, if there are five spaces between two \s, how many characters can be printed?

6.13 True or false: If a program contains a READ statement, it must also contain at least one DATA statement.

6.14 What does the statement COLOR 1, 0 do if you are using the monochrome adapter? What does it do if you are using a color/graphics adapter?

6.15 How can you add a comment at the end of a line?

6.16 How many characters are read by the INKEY$ function?

6.17 True or false: A LOCATE statement may be used to display a message on the screen.

ADDITIONAL PROGRAMMING ASSIGNMENTS

6.9 Re-solve Programming Assignment 5.12, but now *read* each student's name, display the name in a prompt, and accept three test marks.

*6.10 Re-solve Programming Assignment 5.15, but now design a screen to accept data. Use an INPUT$ function to accept the Call Area and verify that a valid value was entered. If an invalid value is entered, print an error message on line 25 in blinking colors.

6.11 Modify your solution to Programming Assignment 4.11, so the prompt that asks the user to enter a name is printed on a clear screen on row 5 starting in column 20. Then the screen should be cleared, the message Good Morning should be printed on line 10 starting in column 30, the name should follow, printed in reverse image, and the message Have a good day should be printed two lines down in blinking reverse image. (Note: To hold the display on the screen between cases, add the following statement just before the GOTO statement that branches to the top of the loop:

```
DUMMY$ = INPUT$(1)
```

The program will pause when it comes to this statement so you can admire the screen. To continue, simply press any key.)

6.12 The Beeline Travel Agency offers the following tours

Code	Destination	Price
E	Europe	$3,500
H	Hawaii	$2,500
C	Caribbean	$2,000
A	Australia	$4,600
J	Japan	$4,800

Write a program that displays a menu of these choices, accepts a code and the number of people making the trip, and calculates and prints the total bill. If an invalid code is entered, print an error message in blinking blue on a white background.

6.13 Write a program that clears the screen and then prints 2, 4, 6, and so on, until the user presses a key. The numbers should be printed in the same location at the approximate center of the screen. Depending on how fast your computer is, it can be a challenge to press a key to stop the program when a particular number, say 100, is displayed. Hint: If J is used to print the numbers, successive values of J may be calculated using the statement

$$J = J + 2$$

BEYOND THE BASICS

6.1 Write a program that draws a class schedule on the screen. Assume classes meet between 8 AM and 5 PM, Monday through Friday. The program should begin by printing MON, TUE, WED, THU, and FRI across the screen, and the times 8, 9, 10, and so on, down the screen. The program should next accept the name of a course and then ask for the day, hour, and room where the course will meet. The course name and room should be plotted in reverse image on the screen at the intersection of the day and hour. The program should continue to request a meeting day, hour, and room for a course, until the user enters an X for the day, indicating that all the meetings for that course have been entered. At that point, the program should request another course name and accept and plot the meetings for that course.

6.2 Write a program that draws a tic-tac-toe board on the screen. The lines may be drawn using Xs, and the legs should be about 20 Xs long. Hint: Do not use more than four PRINT statements and consider the usefulness of statements of the form

$$ROW = ROW + 1$$

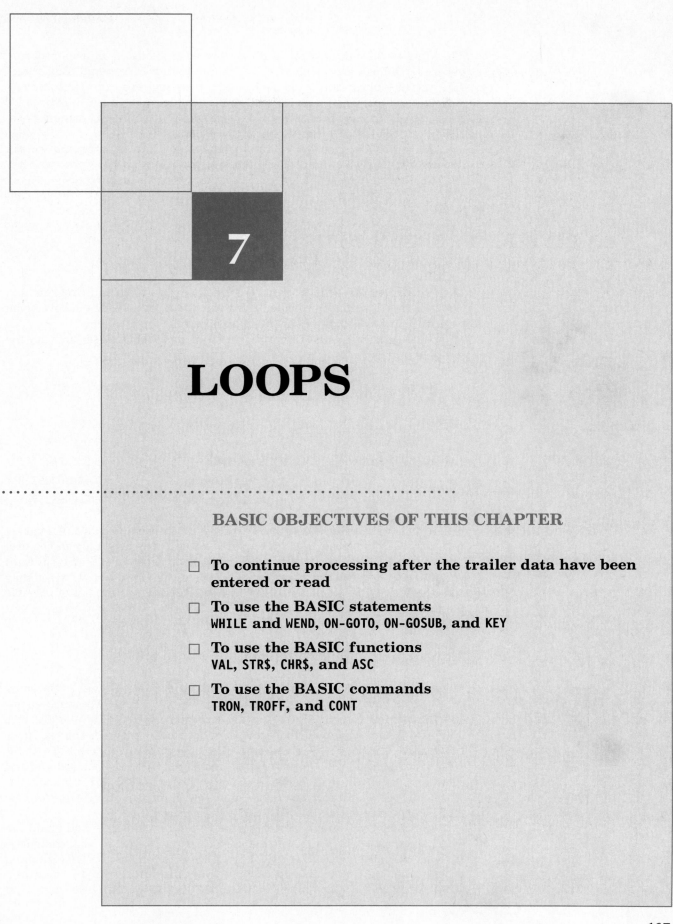

7

LOOPS

Thus far, we have dealt with relatively simple problems in which a program generally stopped executing after the trailer data were entered. But in real life, we sometimes want to do additional processing. For example, after calculating and printing gross pay for employees, we might want to print total gross pay. In this chapter, we will explore different ways of continuing execution and also of stopping execution in a loop.

Moreover, because you will be writing more complex programs, we will discuss some more powerful commands and functions and how you can alter the function keys of your computer to reflect *your* needs.

A PAYROLL PROBLEM WITH TOTALS

Let's return to the simplest Bat-O Boats Company program, Program 4.2. Suppose that in addition to calculating the gross pay of each employee, you want to know the total and average gross pay for the company.

In keeping with step 1 of our structured approach, we use the following variable names:

Input variables	Employee name	`EMP.NAME$`
	Pay rate	`PAY.RATE`
	Hours worked	`HOURS`
Internal variable	Counter	`EMPLOYEES`
Output variables	Gross pay	`GROSS.PAY`
	Total gross pay	`TOTAL.GROSS.PAY`
	Average gross pay	`AVE.GROSS.PAY`

Internal variable
A variable that is used in a program but is not input into it or output from it.

Notice that we have a new kind of variable, an internal variable. An **internal variable** is neither read in nor printed out. It is used only in the program. Sometimes you may not realize you need an internal variable until you start to develop the algorithm and draw the flowchart. If so, simply come back and add the names of the internal variables to the list of variable names.

◼ *Developing the Program*

Much of step 2—developing the algorithm for the problem—will be the same as for Program 4.2. The difference is that this time we must calculate the total and average gross pay. Clearly, we can print `TOTAL.GROSS.PAY` only after the data for all the employees have been entered, that is, after the trailer data have been entered. But how can we do that? To print `TOTAL.GROSS.PAY`, BASIC must recall all the `GROSS.PAY`s it calculated and add them up. But BASIC can "remember" only the last `GROSS.PAY` it calculated. The `GROSS.PAY` location box holds only one number; every time a new `GROSS.PAY` is calculated, the old `GROSS.PAY` is erased.

Obviously, we cannot wait until the end of processing to add up all the `GROSS.PAY`s, because by that time they are no longer in the computer. Instead, we must add each `GROSS.PAY` to the total as we go. This totalling process requires a variable to act as an **accumulator**, in this program, `TOTAL.GROSS.PAY`. Once we have found `TOTAL.GROSS.PAY`, we can find

Accumulator
A variable used to accumulate the values of another variable.

AVE.GROSS.PAY by dividing TOTAL.GROSS.PAY by the number of EMPLOYEES. But how can we determine how many EMPLOYEES we have processed? The answer lies in the use of a variable called a **counter**. Like all counters, EMPLOYEES is a variable that increases each time a set of data is processed. We will discuss exactly how to use an accumulator and a counter when we develop the flowchart and program. For now, though, it may help to think of a counter as a computerized version of the hand-held devices used by shoppers and the attendants who count entrants coming through the gate at a free concert.

Counter
A variable used to count some number, such as the number of times a loop is executed.

To solve this problem, we can use the following algorithm:

1. Set TOTAL.GROSS.PAY and EMPLOYEES equal to zero.
2. Accept EMP.NAME$, PAY.RATE, and HOURS for an employee.
3. If these are the trailer data, go to step 9.
4. Calculate GROSS.PAY.
5. Accumulate GROSS.PAY into TOTAL.GROSS.PAY.
6. Increment EMPLOYEES.
7. Print EMP.NAME$, PAY.RATE, HOURS, and GROSS.PAY.
8. Repeat steps 2–7 for all employees.
9. Print TOTAL.GROSS.PAY.
10. Calculate and print AVE.GROSS.PAY.
11. Stop execution.

We will consider why step 1 is necessary and how steps 5 and 6 are done in BASIC when we trace the program.

Figure 7.1 shows a flowchart based on this algorithm. Step 3 of our structured approach calls for us to calculate answers by hand, which we do as follows:

Employee No.	Employee Name	Rate of Pay	Hours Worked	Gross Pay
1	Joe Tinker	6.75	40	270.00
2	John Evers	6.00	30	180.00
3	Frank Chance	5.75	25	143.75
				Total = 593.75
				Average = 197.92

Program 7.1 shows a listing and execution of the BASIC program and the output produced.

Tracing the Program

Initialize
To assign an initial value to a variable.

To make sure you understand exactly how this program works, let's trace it. When BASIC executes line 110, it puts 0 in the TOTAL.GROSS.PAY box, as shown in Figure 7.2(a). That is, line 110 **initializes** TOTAL.GROSS.PAY, assigning it the value 0. Likewise, line 120 initializes EMPLOYEES to zero.

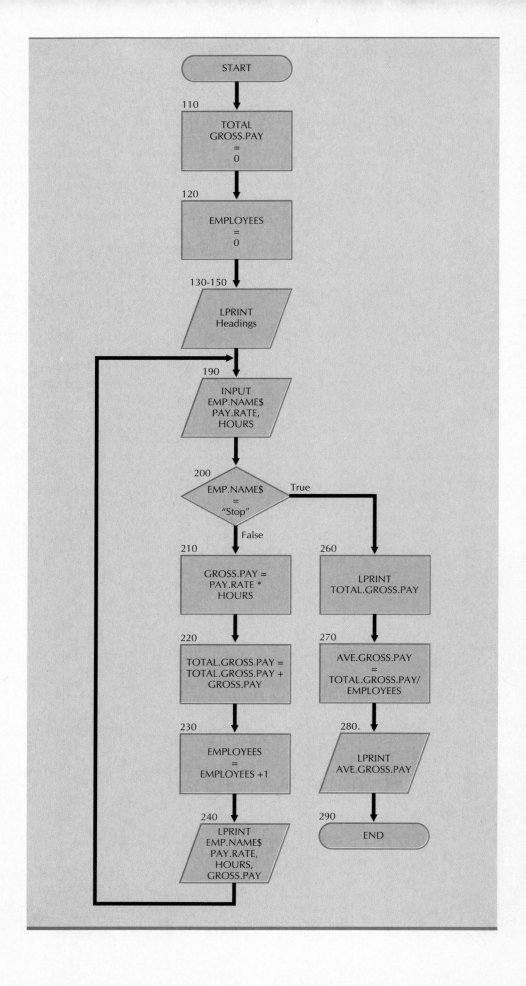

START

110 TOTAL GROSS.PAY = 0

120 EMPLOYEES = 0

130-150 LPRINT Headings

190 INPUT EMP.NAME$ PAY.RATE, HOURS

200 EMP.NAME$ = "Stop"   True   False

210 GROSS.PAY = PAY.RATE * HOURS

220 TOTAL.GROSS.PAY = TOTAL.GROSS.PAY + GROSS.PAY

230 EMPLOYEES = EMPLOYEES +1

240 LPRINT EMP.NAME$ PAY.RATE, HOURS, GROSS.PAY

260 LPRINT TOTAL.GROSS.PAY

270 AVE.GROSS.PAY = TOTAL.GROSS.PAY/ EMPLOYEES

280. LPRINT AVE.GROSS.PAY

290 END

FIGURE 7.1

Flowchart for Bat-O problem with total pay.

```
100  REM *** BAT-O PROGRAM WITH TOTAL PAY ***
110  TOTAL.GROSS.PAY = 0              ⟵  ( TOTAL.GROSS.PAY initialized to 0 )
120  EMPLOYEES = 0                    ⟵  ( EMPLOYEES initialized to 0 )
130  LPRINT      "           PAYROLL REPORT"
140  LPRINT
150  LPRINT      "Employee Name   Pay Rate    Hours    Gross Pay"
160  FORMAT1$ = "\              \    ##.##       ##       ###.## "
170  FORMAT2$ = "                    Total Gross Pay $#,###.##"
180  FORMAT3$ = "                    Average Gross Pay  $ ###.##"
190  INPUT "Enter Name, Rate, Hours, Stop to end ";EMP.NAME$, PAY.RATE, HOURS
200    IF EMP.NAME$ = "Stop"
          THEN GOTO 260                       ( TOTAL.GROSS.PAY used
210    GROSS.PAY = PAY.RATE * HOURS             as an accumulator )
220    TOTAL.GROSS.PAY = TOTAL.GROSS.PAY + GROSS.PAY  ⟵
230    EMPLOYEES = EMPLOYEES + 1    ⟵  ( EMPLOYEES incremented )
240    LPRINT USING FORMAT1$; EMP.NAME$, PAY.RATE, HOURS, GROSS.PAY
250  GOTO 190
260  LPRINT USING FORMAT2$; TOTAL.GROSS.PAY
270  AVE.GROSS.PAY = TOTAL.GROSS.PAY / EMPLOYEES
280  LPRINT USING FORMAT3$; AVE.GROSS.PAY
290  END


RUN
Enter Name, Rate, Hours, Stop to end ? Joe Tinker,6.75,40
Enter Name, Rate, Hours, Stop to end ? John Evers,6,30
Enter Name, Rate, Hours, Stop to end ? Frank Chance,5.75,25
Enter Name, Rate, Hours, Stop to end ? Stop,0,0
Ok
```

```
              PAYROLL REPORT

Employee Name    Pay Rate    Hours    Gross Pay
Joe Tinker         6.75        40       270.00
John Evers         6.00        30       180.00
Frank Chance       5.75        25       143.75
                    Total Gross Pay $  593.75
                    Average Gross Pay  $ 197.92
```

PROGRAM 7.1   **Bat-O program with total and average gross pay.**

Lines 130 through 180 print the headings and define the format strings to be used later in the LPRINT USING statements. When BASIC executes line 190, in response to our input it puts Joe Tinker in the EMP.NAME$ box, 6.75 in the PAY.RATE box, and 40 in the HOURS box, as shown in Figure 7.2(c). The condition in line 200 is false, so BASIC falls through to line 210. When this line is executed, 270 (6.75 * 40) is put in the GROSS.PAY box, as shown in Figure 7.2(d).

Line 220 introduces something new. Remember how a LET statement works. First BASIC does the arithmetic specified in the expression on the right of the equal sign. In this case, it takes the 0 from the TOTAL.GROSS.PAY box and adds to it the 270 from the GROSS.PAY box, getting 270 as the answer. That number is then put into the box of the variable on the left, TOTAL.GROSS.PAY, as shown in Figure 7.2(e).

Statement	EMP.NAME$	PAY.RATE	HOURS	GROSS.PAY	TOTAL.GROSS.PAY	EMPLOYEES
a) 110 TOTAL.GROSS.PAY = 0					0	
b) 120 EMPLOYEES = 0					0	0
c) 190 INPUT EMP.NAME$, PAY.RATE, HOURS	Joe Tinker	6.75	40		0	0
d) 210 GROSS.PAY = PAY.RATE * HOURS	Joe Tinker	6.75	40	270	0	0
e) 220 TOTAL.GROSS.PAY= TOTAL.GROSS.PAY + GROSS.PAY	Joe Tinker	6.75	40	270	270	0
f) 230 EMPLOYEES = EMPLOYEES + 1	Joe Tinker	6.75	40	270	270	1
.						
.						
.						
g) 210 GROSS.PAY = PAY.RATE * HOURS	John Evers	6.00	30	180	270	1
h) 220 TOTAL.GROSS.PAY= TOTAL.GROSS.PAY + GROSS.PAY	John Evers	6.00	30	180	450	1
i) 230 EMPLOYEES = EMPLOYEES + 1	John Evers	6.00	30	180	450	2

FIGURE 7.2   **Tracing Program 7.1.**

As noted earlier, in this program TOTAL.GROSS.PAY is acting as an accumulator. The LET statement for an accumulator is written as follows:

accumulator = accumulator + something else

Notice that the accumulator variable must appear on both sides of the equal sign. Each time the accumulator is executed, it accumulates the value of the something else variable. In Program 7.1, the accumulator is TOTAL.GROSS.PAY and the something else is GROSS.PAY.

Having completed this step, BASIC goes to line 230, where it encounters a special type of accumulator called a counter, in this case, EMPLOYEES. In this counter/accumulator, EMPLOYEES is the accumulator and 1 is the "something else." That is, the LET statement for a counter variable is written as

counter = counter + 1

Thus, when BASIC executes line 230, it adds the 0 that is in the EMPLOYEES box to 1 and puts that answer, 1, back in the EMPLOYEES box, as shown in Figure 7.2(f).

At this point, BASIC repeats lines 190 through 210 for the second set of data, with the results shown in Figure 7.2(g). Can you figure out what the value of TOTAL.GROSS.PAY will be after line 220 is executed for the second time? BASIC adds the number in the TOTAL.GROSS.PAY box (270) to the number in the GROSS.PAY box (180) and puts the total (450) in the TOTAL.GROSS.PAY box, as shown in Figure 7.2(h). Then, when BASIC executes line 230 the second time, it adds the existing 1 in the EMPLOYEES box to 1 and puts the answer, 2, in the EMPLOYEES box, as shown in Figure 7.2(i). Hence, after executing lines 220 and 230 for the third time, the value of TOTAL.GROSS.PAY will be 593.75 and the value of EMPLOYEES will be 3.

On its fourth pass, BASIC encounters the trailer data, which make the condition in the IF statement in line 200 true and cause a branch to line 260. Line 260 prints the value of TOTAL.GROSS.PAY (593.75). Notice that when we get to line 260, no calculations are required, TOTAL.GROSS.PAY is ready to be printed. This is not true for AVE.GROSS.PAY, which is calculated in line 270 by dividing TOTAL.GROSS.PAY by EMPLOYEES and printed in line 280. At this point, program execution stops.

EXERCISES

7.1 Suppose Program 7.1 were run with 25 employees (in addition to the trailer employee). How many times would line 120 be executed? How many times would line 190 be executed?

7.2 Trace Program 7.1 to determine what output will be produced if the following changes are made. Before making each new change, assume the program is restored back to its original form.

   a) The GOTO statement in line 250 is changed to

                   250 GOTO 110

   b) Lines 210 and 220 are interchanged.
   c) Lines 220 and 230 are interchanged.
   d) Lines 220 and 230 are moved to lines 242 and 244.

*7.3 Write the LET statement to accumulate AREA into TOTAL.AREA.

PROGRAMMING ASSIGNMENTS

7.1 Modify Programming Assignment 5.5 to print the total of all the bills.

*7.2 Modify Program 6.1 to print TOTAL.REGULAR.PAY, TOTAL.OVERTIME.PAY, and TOTAL.GROSS.PAY.

7.3 Write a program that accepts a series of numbers and prints their average. Use 9999 as the trailer data.

7.4 Write a program that reads a series of ages and prints the average age and the number of ages in each of these brackets: 0 to 19, 20 to 39, 40 to 59, and 60 and above. Use −1 as trailer data. You may merge A07–04.DAT into your program to supply the data.

FINDING THE HIGHEST SALES

As another example of continuing processing after all the data have been entered, consider the following problem. The Dancer Fan Company wants a program that will read a series of salespersons' names and sales, then find and print the highest sales.

We will use the following variable names:

Input variables	Salesperson's name	SALES.NAME$
	Sales	SALES
Output variable	Highest sales	HIGHEST.SALES

If we use the following data,

Salesperson's Name	Sales
Hart, M.	300
Lee, G. R.	700
Rand, S.	200

Our program *should* print 700 as the highest sales. For a change, let's use FINISHED as the name in the trailer data.

The algorithm for this problem involves a technique that is easier to explain when the program is traced. For now, let's just state the algorithm.

---

1. Set HIGHEST.SALES to 0.
2. Read SALES.NAME$ and SALES.
3. If these are the trailer data, go to step 6.
4. If this SALES is higher than HIGHEST.SALES, set HIGHEST.SALES equal to SALES. Otherwise, do nothing.
5. Repeat steps 2 through 4 for all salespeople.
6. Print HIGHEST.SALES.
7. Stop execution.

The flowchart for this problem is shown in Figure 7.3, and a program based on this algorithm is shown in Program 7.2.

As you can see, Program 7.2 erroneously printed 300 as the highest sales. Since BASIC did not flag any syntax errors, the program must contain a logic error. Although you already may have spotted the error, this is a good chance to talk about additional debugging tools.

Debugging with TRON and TROFF

Program 7.2 shows the effects of typing the command TRON (which stands for "trace on") and then typing RUN. As you can see, each time a line is executed, the line number is displayed on the screen, enclosed in square brackets. The trace output shows that lines 100 through 160 were executed, and the incorrect output was printed. Then lines 170 through 240 were executed. Clearly, the error is a missing GOTO statement between lines 140 and 150.

The missing statement can be added as line 145. Then the TROFF command is entered to turn off tracing, and the program is listed. The listing of lines 140 through 150 shows that statement 145 was added in its proper position. Finally, the program is run again, and now produces the correct output.

Function key F7 means TRON←and F8 means TROFF←, where ←stands for the Enter key. So the easiest way to turn tracing on is to press the F7 key, and the easiest way to turn it off is to press the F8 key.

Tracing the Program

Now that the program is working properly, let's trace it manually to see how it works. When BASIC executes line 110, it puts a 0 in the HIGHEST.SALES box, as shown in Figure 7.4(a). When line 120 is executed, it reads the first set of data and puts Hart, M. in the SALES.NAME$ box and 300 in the SALES box, as shown in Figure 7.4(b). SALES.NAME$ is not equal to FINISHED, so the program falls through line 130 to line 140. Since SALES is greater than HIGHEST.SALES, the THEN clause of line 140 is executed, which causes BASIC to put the number in the SALES box, 300, in the HIGHEST.SALES box (Figure 7.4c). Executing line 145 returns BASIC to the READ statement in line 120.

The second set of data follows the same path. Because 700 is higher than 300, BASIC puts 700 in the HIGHEST.SALES box when it executes line 140 (Figure 7.4e).

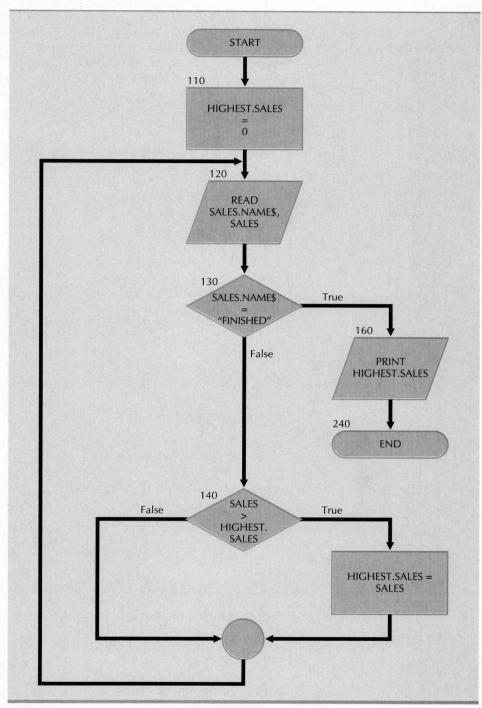

FIGURE 7.3   **Flowchart to find highest sales for Dancer Fan Co.**

But for the third set of data, when BASIC reaches line 140, SALES is not greater than HIGHEST.SALES. Thus, as shown in Figure 7.4g, BASIC does not execute the THEN clause; HIGHEST.SALES remains 700. Instead, BASIC falls through to line 145, which returns it to the READ statement. Finally, BASIC reads the trailer data and finds the condition in line 130 is true. The THEN branch of line 130 sends control to line 150, which prints the value of HIGHEST.SALES.

```
100 REM *** FINDING THE HIGHEST SALES ***
110 HIGHEST.SALES = 0
120 READ SALES.NAME$, SALES
130    IF SALES.NAME$ = "FINISHED"
          THEN GOTO 150
140    IF SALES > HIGHEST.SALES
          THEN HIGHEST.SALES = SALES
150 REM *** Print highest sales
160 PRINT "Highest sales", HIGHEST.SALES
170 '
180 REM *** Data used by program
190 DATA "Hart, M.", 300
200 DATA "Lee, G. R.", 700
210 DATA "Rand, S.", 200
220 REM Trailer data follow
230 DATA FINISHED, 0
240 END


RUN
Highest sales  300  ◄─ (Incorrect answer)
Ok
TRON ◄─ (Turn tracing on)
Ok                        (Trace output)
RUN
[100][110][120][130][140][150][160]Highest sales          300
[170][180][190][200][210][220][230][240]
Ok
145    GOTO 120 ◄─ (Insert missing statement)
TROFF ◄─ (Turn tracing off)
Ok
LIST 140-150 ◄─ (List lines 140 through 150)
140    IF SALES > HIGHEST.SALES
          THEN HIGHEST.SALES = SALES
145    GOTO 120 ◄─ (Line 145 inserted in proper position)
150 REM *** Print highest sales
Ok
RUN
Highest sales  700 ◄─ (Correct answer)
Ok
```

PROGRAM 7.2   Program to find highest sales for Dancer Fan Co.

Now you can see the basic idea behind this algorithm: When SALES is greater than HIGHEST.SALES, BASIC saves that value of SALES in the HIGHEST.SALES box; when SALES is not greater than HIGHEST.SALES, it ignores that value of SALES.

For this scheme to work, HIGHEST.SALES must be given an initial value *less* than the highest sales. The easiest way to do that is to give HIGHEST.SALES an initial value of 0, since sales can never be less than zero. If we wanted to find the lowest sales, we might let LOWEST.SALES stand for lowest sales. We would then have to give LOWEST.SALES an initial value *greater* than the lowest sales. To do that, we would have to know how high sales could be. If sales are always less than $1000, for example, we could give LOWEST.SALES an initial value of 1000.

Statement	SALES.NAME$	SALES	HIGHEST.SALES
a) 110 HIGHEST.SALES = 0			0
b) 120 READ SALES.NAME$, SALES	Hart, M.	300	0
c) 140 IF SALES > HIGHEST.SALES THEN HIGHEST.SALES = SALES	Hart, M.	300	300
d) 120 READ SALES.NAME$, SALES	Lee, G. R.	700	300
e) 140 IF SALES > HIGHEST.SALES THEN HIGHEST.SALES = SALES	Lee, G. R.	700	700
f) 120 READ SALES.NAME$, SALES	Rand, S.	200	700
g) 140 IF SALES > HIGHEST.SALES THEN HIGHEST.SALES = SALES	Rand, S.	200	700

FIGURE 7.4 **Tracing Program 7.2.**

EXERCISES

7.4 What output would be produced by Program 7.2 if the following changes were made (assume the program is restored to its original state before each change)?

a) Line 110 is changed to

    110 HIGHEST.SALES = 1000

b) Line 145 is changed to

    145 GOTO 110

c) Lines 130 and 140 are interchanged.

*7.5 In the DATA statements in Program 7.2, the salespersons' names are enclosed in quotation marks, but FINISHED is not. Why?

PROGRAMMING ASSIGNMENTS

7.5 Modify Program 7.2 to find and print the name of the salesperson with the highest sales, along with the numerical value of the highest sales. Assume there is not a tie for highest sales.

7.6 Chlora Strohl is considering several brands of cooking oil for use in her diner. Write a program to read a set of names and prices and find and print the lowest price. Assume that the prices are less than $10.

*7.7 Modify Program 7.2 to find and print both the highest and the lowest sales.

HOW TO BECOME A MILLIONAIRE

Up to now, we have entered trailer data when we wanted to exit from a loop. But sometimes you want BASIC to exit when a variable reaches a certain value. For example, consider the problem of Michael Anthony, who hired you to help build his fortune. He is willing to invest a certain amount of money each year, but he expects to end up with a million dollars. You have decided to deposit his money in a bank. Given the size of Mr. Anthony's DEPOSIT and the interest RATE being offered by the local bank, how many years (NO.YEARS) will it take for the TOTAL in his account to be $1 million?

Clearly, RATE and DEPOSIT are the input variables, and NO.YEARS and TOTAL are the output variables. For your reference, the equation for this problem is*

$$TOTAL = DEPOSIT * ((1 + RATE) \wedge NO.YEARS - 1) / RATE$$

If you had to do this calculation by hand, using only a calculator, you would probably decide to start with a small value for NO.YEARS and gradually increase it until the TOTAL equals $1 million. We will do much the same in BASIC. Thus, the algorithm for this problem is

1. Accept RATE and DEPOSIT.
2. If these are the trailer data, go to step 9.
3. Set TOTAL and NO.YEARS equal to 0.
4. While TOTAL is less than 1 million, execute steps 5 and 6.
5. Increment NO.YEARS by 1.
6. Calculate TOTAL.
7. Print NO.YEARS and TOTAL.
8. Repeat steps 1 through 7 until all sets of RATE and DEPOSIT have been processed.
9. Stop execution.

Notice that in step 4 we refer to steps 5 and 6. When you first write the algorithm, you will not know which step numbers you must repeat. Just use question marks to represent those line numbers; at the end of the algorithm, you can go back and replace the question marks with the correct step numbers.

Figure 7.5 shows a flowchart of this algorithm. This flowchart introduces a new structure called the WHILE **loop**. In the WHILE loop, a condition is tested. In Figure 7.5, the condition is TOTAL < 1000000. While the condition is true, statements in the loop are executed. If the program has been designed properly, eventually the condition will become false; instead of executing the statements in the loop, BASIC will execute the statements following the loop.

The flowchart clearly shows the loop consisting of boxes 150, 160, and 170. TOTAL is tested in box 150. If TOTAL is less than 1 million, NO.YEARS is increased by 1 in box 160, TOTAL is calculated in box 170, and the loop is repeated. Sooner or later, we will get up to a NO.YEARS that causes TOTAL to become greater than or equal to 1 million, and then we will follow the "False" branch and print NO.YEARS and TOTAL.

The flowchart shows that TOTAL is tested before the statements in the loop are calculated. If TOTAL is greater than 1 million the first time box 150 is executed, then the statements in the loop will not be executed. That is why TOTAL is set to 0 in box 130. You might think that instruction is not necessary, because you know that if BASIC uses an uninitialized variable it will

WHILE loop
A loop, defined by a WHILE and a WEND statement, that is executed while the condition in the WHILE statement is true.

---

*This is the standard formula for an amount of an annuity and assumes that the deposits are made at the end of each year.

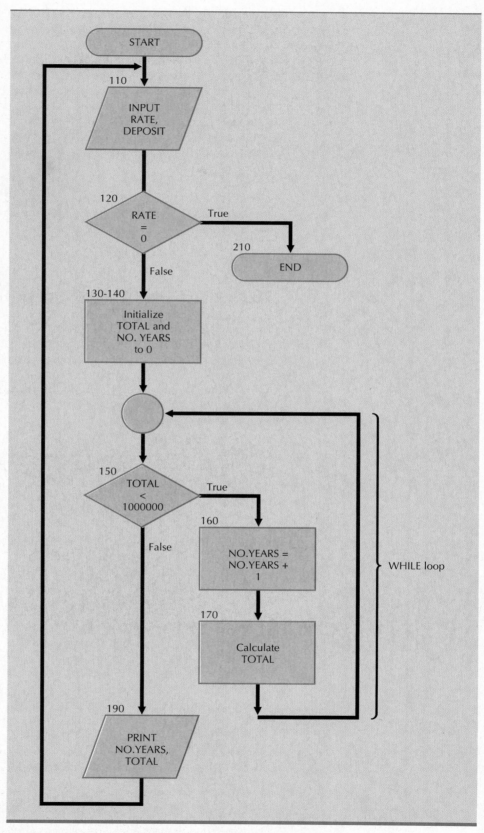

FIGURE 7.5   **Flowchart to make Michael Anthony a millionaire.**

automatically assign it a value of 0. However, that would be true only the first time line 150 was executed. After we print NO.YEARS and TOTAL for the first set of DEPOSIT and RATE values, we return to box 110 to accept the next set of DEPOSIT and RATE values. If we didn't reset TOTAL and NO.YEARS back to 0 in boxes 130 and 140, TOTAL would have the value greater than 1000000 left over from the first case, the condition in box 150 would be false, and the loop statements would not be executed. Instead, the PRINT instruction in box 190 would be executed, printing the old values for NO.YEARS and TOTAL. This error emphasizes the rule that if you want a variable initialized to zero, you should use a LET statement to set it to zero and not depend on BASIC to do it for you.

Notice the words "Calculate TOTAL" in box 170. The whole equation to calculate TOTAL does not fit in this little box, so "Calculate TOTAL" reminds us to calculate TOTAL at this point. Of course, the complete equation must be used when the program is written.

The WHILE and WEND Statements

The program based on Figure 7.5 is shown in Program 7.3. The WHILE loop is implemented by the WHILE statement in line 150 and the WEND statement in line 180. The WHILE statement indicates the top of the loop, and the WEND statement indicates the end of the loop. The WHILE and WEND statements are *always* used together. Notice that in Program 7.3 the statements in the WHILE loop are indented (except for the STOP statement, which, as will be explained shortly, is special). BASIC does not require this indentation, but it makes the loop easier to see. You should follow the same convention in your programs.

The syntax of the WHILE and WEND statements is

```
WHILE condition
            .
            .
loop statements
            .
            .
            .
WEND
```

As noted in the discussion of the flowchart, the condition in the WHILE statement, which may be either a simple condition or a compound condition, is tested. If the condition is true, the statements between the WHILE and WEND statements are executed. The WEND statement actually has two functions: It not only marks the end of the WHILE loop, it also branches back to the WHILE statement, where the condition is tested again. When the condition is false, BASIC branches to the statement following the WEND statement. In Program 7.3, as long as TOTAL is less than 1 million, lines 160 through 180 will be executed. When TOTAL equals or exceeds 1 million, line 190 will be executed.* Other examples of WHILE loops include:

_____

*BASIC added an ! to the 1000000 in line 150. The ! is related to the fact that BASIC can store numbers in integer, single-precision and double-precision forms. These different forms are discussed briefly in Chapter 12, but for now you may safely ignore the !.

```
100 REM *** HOW TO BECOME A MILLIONAIRE ***
110 INPUT "Enter Interest Rate and Annual Deposit, 0 to stop "; RATE, DEPOSIT
120    IF RATE = 0
          THEN GOTO 210
130    TOTAL = 0
140    NO.YEARS = 0
150    WHILE TOTAL < 1000000!  ◄───( Ignore exclamation point )
160       NO.YEARS = NO.YEARS + 1
170       TOTAL = DEPOSIT * ((1 + RATE) ^ NO.YEARS - 1) / RATE
175 STOP ◄──( Stop statement used for checking )
180    WEND
190    PRINT USING "After ### years, you will have $#,###,###"; NO.YEARS, TOTAL
200 GOTO 110
210 END


RUN
Enter Interest Rate and Annual Deposit, 0 to stop ? .10, 1000
Break in 175 ◄──( Break caused by STOP statement )
Ok
PRINT NO.YEARS, TOTAL ◄──( PRINT statement entered in direct mode )
 1              1000 ◄──( Values are correct )
Ok
CONT ◄──( CONT command resumes execution )
Break in 175
Ok
PRINT NO.YEARS, TOTAL
 2              2100 ◄──( Second set of values is correct )
Ok
CONT
Break in 175
Ok
PRINT NO.YEARS, TOTAL
 3              3310.001 ◄──( Third set of values is correct )
Ok
175 ◄──( Delete line 175 )
RUN ◄──( Execute again )
Enter Interest Rate and Annual Deposit, 0 to stop ? .10, 1000
After  49 years, you will have $1,057,190
Enter Interest Rate and Annual Deposit, 0 to stop ? 0,0
Ok
```

PROGRAM 7.3   **Program to make Michael Anthony a millionaire.**

Statement

```
10 A = 1
20 WHILE A < 5
30    PRINT "GO TEAM"
40    A = A + 1
50 WEND
60 END
```

Effect

GO TEAM is printed 4 times: when A is equal to 1, 2, 3, and 4. When A is 5, the condition in line 20 is false, and BASIC branches to line 60.

Statement

```
10 A = 1
20 WHILE A = 5
30    PRINT "GO TEAM"
40    A = A + 1
50 WEND
60 END
```

Effect

GO TEAM is not printed at all because the first time line 20 is executed, the condition is false, and BASIC branches to line 60.

■ *Using STOP and CONT to Debug a Program*

It would be difficult to calculate an answer to this problem by hand. Fortunately, we don't have to. We can reason that the critical step is the calculation of TOTAL. If we can be sure that TOTAL is calculated properly, and if, when we exit from the loop and print NO.YEARS and TOTAL, we see that TOTAL is in fact greater than or equal to 1 million, we can have confidence in our program.

We can be sure that TOTAL is calculated properly by checking BASIC's calculation against a hand calculation. Let's pick RATE = .10 (10% interest) and DEPOSIT = 1000 and calculate TOTAL for NO.YEARS = 1, 2, and 3. That is not very hard, particularly if we use a calculator. The answers are

NO.YEARS	TOTAL
1	1000
2	2100
3	3310

But this doesn't do us any good, since the program doesn't print the TOTAL it calculated when NO.YEARS was 1, 2, or 3. It only prints NO.YEARS and TOTAL when TOTAL becomes greater than or equal to 1 million.

This kind of problem occurs from time to time. The solution is to add a STOP statement to the program. In Program 7.3, line 175 contains a STOP statement. When the STOP statement is executed in this program, BASIC prints the message Break in 175 and stops. At that point, you can print the values of NO.YEARS and TOTAL by executing a PRINT statement in direct mode. You then can continue execution by typing the command CONT, which resumes execution at the statement following STOP. As you can see in Program 7.3, except for a small round-off error, the values of TOTAL for years 1, 2, and 3 agree with the values calculated previously, so this part of the program is correct.

To eliminate the STOP statement after you know the program is correct, type its line number, 175, and press the Enter key. To resume execution after a program is changed, you cannot use the CONT command, but instead must use the RUN command. As you can see in Program 7.3, RUN caused BASIC to execute the program from the beginning until TOTAL was greater than 1 million. Program 7.3 shows that it will take only 49 years for TOTAL to become $1,057,190.

The CONT command can also be used to resume execution after a program halt caused by typing Ctrl + Break or by an END statement. Function key F5 means CONT←, so the easiest way to continue is to press the F5 key.

■ *The WHILE and WEND Statements Revisited*

The WHILE loop is the most complicated construction we have discussed so far, so it is worthwhile to examine it again. Many beginners have the mistaken idea that each time any statement in the loop is executed, BASIC checks to see if the condition in the WHILE statement is still true. That is absolutely wrong! As the flowchart of the WHILE loop in Figure 7.5 shows, the condition is checked only when the WHILE statement is executed.

Because the condition is checked only when the WHILE statement is executed, the statement that affects the condition is almost always the last statement in the loop. For example, in Figure 7.5 the statement that affects the condition is the calculation of TOTAL in line 170, and that statement is the last in the loop.

We can use WHILE loops in many situations, for example, with trailer data to control program execution. Program 7.4 shows a modification of Program 3.3 (the first program in which we used trailer data to control execution) that uses a WHILE loop. In Program 3.3, line 30 was an IF statement that branched out of the loop if PAY.RATE was equal to −1. In Program 7.4, line 30 is a WHILE statement that keeps executing the statements in the loop if PAY.RATE is *not* equal to −1. In Program 3.3, line 60 was a GOTO statement that branched to the top of the loop. In Program 7.4, line 60 is a WEND statement that returns control to the top of the loop.

These two changes are straightforward, but Program 7.4 also contains an INPUT statement in new line 55 that is identical to the INPUT statement in

```
10 REM  *** BAT-O PROGRAM ***
20 INPUT "Enter Pay Rate and Hours Worked, -1 to stop"; PAY.RATE, HOURS
30 WHILE PAY.RATE <> -1
40   GROSS.PAY = PAY.RATE * HOURS
50   LPRINT PAY.RATE, HOURS, GROSS.PAY
55   INPUT "Enter Pay Rate and Hours Worked, -1 to stop"; PAY.RATE, HOURS
60 WEND
70 END

RUN
Enter Pay Rate and Hours Worked, -1 to stop? 6.75,40
Enter Pay Rate and Hours Worked, -1 to stop? 6,30
Enter Pay Rate and Hours Worked, -1 to stop? 5.75,25
Enter Pay Rate and Hours Worked, -1 to stop? -1,0
Ok
```

```
6.75          40          270
6             30          180
5.75          25          143.75
```

PROGRAM 7.4   **Resolving Program 3.3 using a WHILE loop.**

line 20 of both programs. Why this seeming duplication? The INPUT statement in line 20 is used to accept just the first set of data, so that we will have a value of PAY.RATE to test in line 30. The INPUT statement in line 55 is used to accept the second and all subsequent sets of data. This INPUT statement will eventually accept the trailer data, which will make the condition in the WHILE statement false and cause the program to stop executing the loop. Notice that, as we said above, the statement that affects the condition in the WHILE statement is the last statement in the loop.

WHILE loops can also be used to validate input, as shown in the following program fragment:

```
INPUT "Enter Y or N"; RESPONSE$
WHILE NOT (RESPONSE$ = "Y" OR RESPONSE$ = "N")
    BEEP
    INPUT "Please enter only a Y or N"; RESPONSE$
WEND
```

If the user enters anything but a Y or an N, the condition in the WHILE statement will be true, and the statements in the loop will be executed. The statements in the loop will continue to be executed until the user enters a Y or an N. Notice that this logic also requires that we code two INPUT statements, one before the loop and one inside it.

Syntax Summary   WHILE and WEND statement
                         Form: WHILE condition

                                        ·
                                        loop statements
                                        ·

                                        WEND
                         Example: N = 1
                                        WHILE N < 10
                                          PRINT N
                                          N = N + 1
                                        WEND
                         Interpretation: If condition is true, the loop statements are
                                          executed. WEND returns control to WHILE,
                                          where condition is tested again. If
                                          condition is still true, the process is
                                          repeated. When condition becomes false,
                                          control is passed to the statement following
                                          WEND.

***Getting the
Bugs Out***

Problem: During execution, BASIC displays the error message

                                    WEND without WHILE

Reason: Your program executed a WEND statement before it executed a
                 WHILE statement. You may have branched into the middle of a
                 WHILE loop, or you may have a WEND statement without a
                 matching WHILE statement.

Solution: Eliminate any branch into the middle of the WHILE loop and
                 make sure that every WEND statement has a matching WHILE.

Problem: During execution, BASIC displays the error message

                                    WHILE without WEND

Reason: Your program executed a WHILE statement, but BASIC could not find a matching WEND statement before the physical end of the program.

Solution: Make sure every WHILE statement has a matching WEND statement.

Problem: While executing a program that contains a WHILE loop, BASIC goes into an endless loop.

Reason: The condition in the WHILE statement never became false.

Solution: Make sure that the statements in the WHILE loop will eventually cause the condition to become false and that the WHILE condition is coded correctly.

Problem: A program requests less input and produces less output than was expected.

Reason: The condition in the WHILE statement was never true. Remember, if the condition is false the first time the WHILE statement is executed, the WHILE loop is never executed.

Solution: Make sure the condition in the WHILE statement is true initially and that the WHILE condition is coded correctly.

EXERCISES

7.6 A student objects to typing the INPUT statement twice, so he has written his version of Program 7.4 as follows:

```
10 REM *** WRONG PROGRAM ***
20 WHILE PAY.RATE <> -1
30    INPUT "Enter Pay Rate and Hours Worked,
            -1 to stop"; PAY.RATE, HOURS
40    GROSS.PAY = PAY.RATE * HOURS
50    LPRINT PAY.RATE, HOURS, GROSS.PAY
60 WEND
70 END
```

Trace this program using the following data: 6.75, 40; 6, 30; 5.75, 25; and −1, 0.

7.7 The following two programs are supposed to print the sum of the numbers 1 through 5. Trace the programs to determine the output and comment on your results.

a)
```
10 SUM = 0
20 NUMBER = 1
30 WHILE NUMBER <= 5
40    SUM = SUM + NUMBER
50    NUMBER = NUMBER + 1
60 WEND
70 PRINT SUM
80 END
```

b)
```
10 SUM = 0
20 NUMBER = 1
30 WHILE NUMBER <= 5
40    NUMBER = NUMBER + 1
50    SUM = SUM + NUMBER
```

```
60 WEND
70 PRINT SUM
80 END
```

*7.8 How many times will HELLO be printed by the following program?

```
10 A = 10
20 WHILE A < 10
30    PRINT "HELLO"
40    A = A + 1
50 WEND
60 END
```

Modify line 20 to print HELLO just once.

7.9 How many times will GOODBYE be printed by the following program?

```
10 B = 1
20 WHILE B < 5
30    PRINT "GOODBYE"
40 WEND
50 END
```

Modify the program to print GOODBYE five times.

*7.10 What output is produced by the following program?

```
10 M = 2
20 WHILE M < 50
30    M = 2 * M
40    PRINT M
50 WEND
60 END
```

PROGRAMMING ASSIGNMENTS

7.8 Re-solve Programming Assignment 5.5 to use a WHILE loop to control program termination.

7.9 The ozone concentration in the upper atmosphere is 450 ppm. If the fraction lost each year is LOSS.RATE, then the amount lost each year is

$$LOSS = LOSS.RATE * OZONE$$

and the ozone at the end of the year is

$$OZONE = OZONE - LOSS$$

Write a program that will accept a value for LOSS.RATE (try .05, .1, and .20) and determine how many years it will take for the ozone concentration to fall below 200 ppm. (Hint: You will need a counter to keep track of the years.)

7.10 Suppose you have a business deal that will double your money each month, and further suppose you start with $1. Write a program that will determine how many months it will take for your money to grow to more than $1000. (Hint: You will need a counter to keep track of the months.)

*7.11 Chancy Wynn won $100,000 in a lottery. She put the money in a savings account that pays 8% interest. At the end of each year, she withdraws $15,000 from the account and spends it on a big bash. Write a program to determine how many years she can do this before her account balance is down to or below zero.

To be sure you understand the problem, let's examine what happens during the first two years. During the first year, the full $100,000 is on deposit, so the interest earned is 0.08 × $100,000 = $8,000. On December 31, therefore, the balance is $100,000 + 8,000 = $108,000. However, Chancy now withdraws $15,000, so her balance goes down to $108,000 − 15,000 = $93,000. During the second year, interest is earned on $93,000 and is only 0.08 × $93,000 = $7,440. When at the end of the second year Chancy withdraws her usual $15,000, her balance is reduced to $93,000 + 7,440 − 15,000 = $85,440. This process continues until her balance becomes less than or equal to 0.

A SALES PROBLEM WITH SUBTOTALS

Now that you know how to write WHILE and WEND statements, we can use them to solve more complex problems. For example, Basic Goods Department Store wants to keep track of its sales by department number. The management of the store would like to have a BASIC program that prints every sale and the total of all the sales. In addition, the program must print the subtotal of sales for each department.

Assume that one day you are sent the following data:

Department No.	Amount of Sale
46	500
46	200
49	150
57	200
57	600
57	50

What is particularly significant about the data is that the number of sales for each department is variable. Notice that department 46 has two sales, department 49 has only one sale, and department 57 has three sales. If you hand-calculate answers for this problem, you will find that the total sales for department 46 are 700, for department 49 are 150, for department 57 are 850, and the grand total for all departments is 1700.

Although we had no trouble calculating answers by hand, how can we do it in a BASIC program? The problem comes in determining when to print the subtotal for a department. How does BASIC know when we have processed all the sales for department 46 and are therefore ready to print the subtotal for that department? If, as above, the sales for each department are grouped together, then a change in the department number means that we must have finished reading the data for the previous department and that BASIC should print the subtotal of its sales. The change in department number is called a **control break.**

Control break
A change in the value of a control variable, which means that some special processing, such as printing subtotals, should be performed.

Variable Names and Algorithm

As always, we begin by assigning names to the variables we will use:

Input variables	Department number	DEPT.NO
	Sales	SALES
Internal variable	Previous department number	PREVIOUS.DEPT.NO
Output variables	Total sales for a department	DEPT.TOTAL
	Total sales for all departments	GRAND.TOTAL

We will use a department number equal to 9999 as the trailer data.

Thus, the algorithm we will use is

1. Initialize DEPT.TOTAL and GRAND.TOTAL to 0.
2. Accept the first DEPT.NO and SALES.
3. Set PREVIOUS.DEPT.NO equal to DEPT.NO.
4. While DEPT.NO is not 9999, perform steps 5 through 8.
5. If DEPT.NO is different from previous DEPT.NO:
   Print the subtotal for the previous department.
   Accumulate DEPT.TOTAL into GRAND.TOTAL.
   Set DEPT.TOTAL to 0.
   Set PREVIOUS.DEPT.NO equal to DEPT.NO.
6. Accumulate SALES into DEPT.TOTAL.
7. Print DEPT.NO and SALES.
8. Accept the next DEPT.NO and SALES.
9. Print the subtotal for the last department.
10. Print GRAND.TOTAL.
11. Stop run.

Let's look at steps 5 and 9 more closely. In step 5, how is BASIC to know whether DEPT.NO is different from the previous DEPT.NO? It must compare DEPT.NO with the previous DEPT.NO. Therefore, we must save the previous DEPT.NO, which we will do in a variable named PREVIOUS.DEPT.NO.

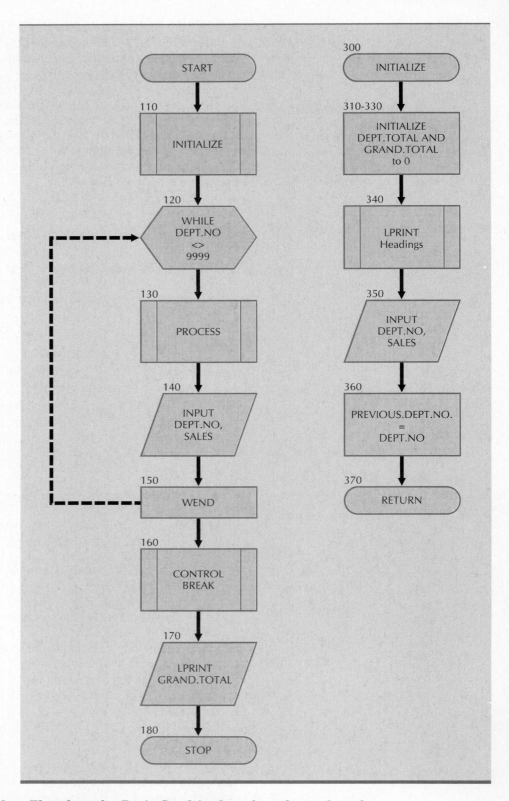

FIGURE 7.6   **Flowchart for Basic Goods' subtotals and grand total.**

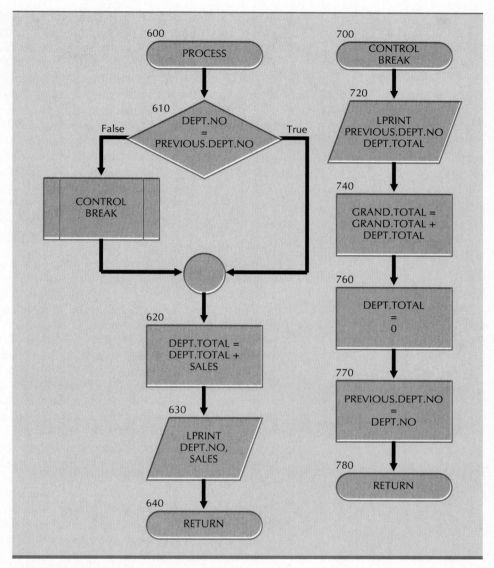

FIGURE 7.6   **(Continued).**

You might also wonder why we included step 9 to print the subtotal for the last department after BASIC accepts the trailer data. Students often assume that BASIC will already have printed this subtotal and is ready to print the grand total. But if you look closely, you will see that BASIC would have to return to step 5 to print the subtotal—something it will not do after receiving the trailer data in step 8. Hence the need for step 9.

The Flowchart

Figure 7.6 shows the flowchart for this algorithm (the subroutine that prints the headings is very simple and is not shown). The first step is the INITIALIZE subroutine, which sets the accumulators to zero, prints the headings, and accepts the first set of data. Just like Program 7.4, this program contains two INPUT statements: one in the INITIALIZE subroutine and one that is the last statement in the WHILE loop. The variable PREVIOUS.DEPT.NO is supposed to contain the previous department number. When we start, however, there is no previous department number. Therefore, after BASIC accepts the first set of DEPT.NO and SALES in line 350, it sets PREVIOUS.DEPT.NO equal to the first DEPT.NO entered in line 360. Once PREVIOUS.DEPT.NO has a value, BASIC can proceed to the main part of the program.

The main part of the program is a WHILE loop, which will be executed repeatedly as long as the DEPT.NO is not 9999. That is to say, the loop will be executed until the trailer data, giving a DEPT.NO of 9999, are entered.

Notice the simplified presentation of the WHILE loop in this flowchart. In Figure 7.5, we showed exactly how a WHILE loop works, for example, what would happen if the condition in the WHILE statement were false the first time the WHILE statement was executed. However, now that you understand how a WHILE loop works, showing all the details is not necessary; in fact, by making the flowchart more complicated, it actually makes the flowchart harder to understand and less useful. Therefore, this and all future flowcharts will use the simplified symbols shown in Figure 7.6. These symbols consist of a hexagon to represent the WHILE statement and a rectangle to represent the WEND statement. To show the loop clearly, the WHILE and WEND symbols are connected with a flowline that is dotted, to emphasize that it does not represent a GOTO statement.

In the main loop, BASIC executes the processing subroutine, which processes one set of data, and then line 140 accepts the next set of data. In the processing subroutine, BASIC first checks to see whether the department number has changed. If it has, BASIC executes the subroutine to process a control break. Whether or not the department number has changed, BASIC next accumulates the current sales and prints the current data. The next set of data is accepted, and BASIC then returns to the main loop.

Line 720 in the subroutine to process a control break prints the subtotal for the previous department. Note that in doing so BASIC uses PREVIOUS.DEPT.NO, not DEPT.NO. Why? Because PREVIOUS.DEPT.NO contains the department number of the previous department; DEPT.NO contains the department number of the current department. BASIC then accumulates the departmental subtotal into the grand total, resets the department subtotal back to 0, and sets the previous department number equal to the current department number.

There is one small point that deserves discussion. In the list of the variables used in this problem, PREVIOUS.DEPT.NO was listed as an internal variable, but the flowchart shows it being printed. It is listed as an internal variable because its primary use in this problem is to indicate when the department number has changed. In fact, PREVIOUS.DEPT.NO could correctly be listed as either an internal variable or an output variable, depending on which you think is its primary use.

Program 7.5 is a straightforward implementation of the flowchart. Note the documentation in the main program; comments at the end of several statements make the logic of the program easier to follow. Also notice the STOP statement in line 180. Without that statement, after BASIC executed the LPRINT statement in line 170, it would fall into the initialization routine. Then when BASIC executed the RETURN statement in line 370, it would print the message RETURN with no GOSUB.

```
100 REM *** A REPORT WITH SUBTOTALS AND GRAND TOTAL ***
110 GOSUB 300                          'Perform initialization
120 WHILE DEPT.NO <> 9999              'Execute loop until trailer data are entered
130   GOSUB 600                        'Process one set of data
140   INPUT "Enter Dept No and Sales, Dept No 9999 to end"; DEPT.NO, SALES
150 WEND
160 GOSUB 700                          'Print subtotal for last department
170 LPRINT USING GRAND.TOTAL.FORMAT$; GRAND.TOTAL
180 STOP
190 '
300 REM *** Initialization routine =============================================
310   REM *** Initialize accumulators
320   DEPT.TOTAL = 0
330   GRAND.TOTAL = 0
340   GOSUB 500                        'Print headings
350   INPUT "Enter Dept No and Sales, Dept No 9999 to end"; DEPT.NO, SALES
360   PREVIOUS.DEPT.NO = DEPT.NO   'Initialize PREVIOUS.DEPT.NO
370 RETURN
380 REM *** End of initialization routine
390 '
500 REM ***  Routine to print headings and set up format strings
510   LPRINT TAB(15);"SALES REPORT"
520   LPRINT TAB(26);"Dept No.       Sales"
530   DETAIL.LINE.FORMAT$ = "                            ##        #,###"
540   DEPT.TOTAL.FORMAT$ =  "Total Sales for Department  ##       ##,###"
550   GRAND.TOTAL.FORMAT$ = "Grand Total for All Departments     ###,###"
560 RETURN
570 REM ***  End of heading routine
580 '
600 REM ***  Routine to process one set of data ==================================
610   IF DEPT.NO = PREVIOUS.DEPT.NO
         THEN GOTO 620
         ELSE GOSUB 700         'Control break
620   DEPT.TOTAL = DEPT.TOTAL + SALES
630   LPRINT USING DETAIL.LINE.FORMAT$; DEPT.NO, SALES
640 RETURN
650 REM ***  End of routine to process one set of data
660 '
700 REM ***  Routine to process a control break
710   LPRINT
720   LPRINT USING DEPT.TOTAL.FORMAT$; PREVIOUS.DEPT.NO, DEPT.TOTAL
730   LPRINT
740   GRAND.TOTAL = GRAND.TOTAL + DEPT.TOTAL
750   REM *** Get ready for new department
760   DEPT.TOTAL = 0
770   PREVIOUS.DEPT.NO = DEPT.NO
780 RETURN
790 REM ***  End of routine to process a control break
800 END


RUN
Enter Dept No and Sales, Dept No 9999 to end? 46,500
Enter Dept No and Sales, Dept No 9999 to end? 46,200
Enter Dept No and Sales, Dept No 9999 to end? 49,150
Enter Dept No and Sales, Dept No 9999 to end? 57,200
Enter Dept No and Sales, Dept No 9999 to end? 57,600
Enter Dept No and Sales, Dept No 9999 to end? 57,50
Enter Dept No and Sales, Dept No 9999 to end? 9999,0
Break in 180
Ok
```

PROGRAM 7.5   **Program for Basic Goods' subtotal and grand total.**

```
        SALES REPORT
                      Dept No.        Sales
                        46             500
                        46             200

Total Sales for Department  46         700

                        49             150

Total Sales for Department  49         150

                        57             200
                        57             600
                        57              50

Total Sales for Department  57         850

Grand Total for All Departments      1,700
```

PROGRAM 7.5   (Continued).

EXERCISES

7.11 Suppose Program 7.5 were executed for 27 values of SALES (in addition to the trailer data). How many times would the INPUT statement in line 140 be executed? How many times would the INPUT statement in line 350 be executed?

*7.12 How would the output in Program 7.5 change if line 160 were deleted?

PROGRAMMING ASSIGNMENTS

7.12 The Sole Supplier Fish Market uses a computer to keep track of how much of each kind of fish, shrimp, clams, salmon, tuna, swordfish, flounder, monkfish, bluefish, and lobster, they sell. Their sales for one day have been arranged in order by type of fish and recorded in DATA statements in A07-12.DAT. The format of the DATA statements is

DATA fishkind, weight

where fishkind is a string and weight is a number. Write a program that will read and print these data and calculate and print the total weight of each kind of fish.

*7.13 Blanche Czech, social worker, uses a computer to keep track of the earnings of her clients that affect their welfare payments. Many of her clients receive welfare for only a few months; others are long-term beneficiaries. Typical data for a given

quarter might be:

Annette	385
Annette	260
Annette	250
Darlene	85
Darlene	85
Jimmy	45
Roy	225
Roy	260
Roy	115
Cubby	95

Write a program that will accept and print these data and calculate and print the total earnings and average earnings per month for each client, as well as a grand total and average for all clients.

THE ON-GOTO AND ON-GOSUB STATEMENTS

In Chapter 5, you learned how to use IF statements to implement the case structure. BASIC provides two conditional branching instructions that, under certain circumstances, can offer a more convenient way of implementing the case structure: the ON-GOTO and ON-GOSUB statements.

Consider the following statement:

```
ON X GOTO 300, 150, 200
```

In this example, X is the name of a variable, and the numbers 300, 150, and 200 are line numbers in the program. If X is 1, BASIC branches to line number 300 because 300 is the first line number listed. If X is 2, BASIC branches to the second line number listed, 150. Finally, if X is 3, BASIC branches to the third line number listed, 200. If X is not 1, 2, or 3, the next statement is executed.

The syntax of the ON-GOTO statement is

```
ON variable GOTO line[, line] ...
```

where variable may be a variable name or a numeric expression. If variable is not an integer, it is rounded before the statement is executed. If variable is 0 or greater than the number of line numbers listed, the next statement is executed. For example,

Statement

ON N GOTO 65, 150, 130, 99

Effect

If N is 1, BASIC branches to line 65; if N is 2, BASIC branches to line 150; if N is 3, BASIC branches to line 130; and if N is 4, BASIC branches to line 99. If N is 0 or greater than 4, BASIC falls through the ON GOTO to the next statement.

Statement

ON J/K GOTO 100, 200, 300

Effect

If J/K (rounded if necessary) is 1, BASIC branches to line 100; if J/K is 2, BASIC branches to line 200; and if J/K is 3, BASIC branches to line 300. If J/K is 0 or greater than 3, BASIC falls through the ON GOTO to the next statement.

The ON-GOSUB statement works exactly the same way, except that a GOSUB to the specified line is executed, rather than a GOTO.

As an example of when an ON-GOTO statement could be used, consider the following problem. The No Bum Steer fast-food chain has assigned a code number to each possible order, as follows:

Code No.	Order	Price
1	Hamburger	1.25
2	Fries	.90
3	Shake	1.00
4	Hamburger and Fries	2.00
5	Hamburger and Shake	2.15
6	Fries and Shake	1.75
7	Hamburger, Fries, and Shake	2.95

No Bum Steer's management wants a BASIC program that will accept as input the code number of a customer's order and calculate and print the customer's bill.

Developing the Program

In keeping with the first step in our structured approach, we begin by assigning the following names for the variables:

Input variables	Code number of the order, string	CODE$
	Code number of the order, number	CODE
Output variable	Customer's bill	BILL

From these variables we can develop the following algorithm:

1. Display the menu of orders.
2. Accept CODE$.
3. Convert CODE$ to CODE.
4. If CODE equals 8, stop.
5. Calculate and print BILL.
6. Repeat steps 2 through 5 for all customers.

Figure 7.7 shows a flowchart for this algorithm. The subroutines that display the menu and error message are similar to those you have seen before and are not shown. We will examine the purpose of box 170 in a minute. First, let's see how the ON-GOTO works.

This problem could be solved using eight IF statements to implement a case structure, but it is much easier to use an ON-GOTO statement. Look at boxes 180 and 210 to 360. They represent the ON-GOTO statement. The flowchart symbol for the ON-GOTO statement is a diamond, because ON-GOTO is a *conditional* branching instruction. However, the many branches leaving the diamond show immediately that the diamond does not represent an IF statement. To make the flowchart as clear as possible, each branch is labeled with the value of the variable that causes BASIC to take that branch.

This flowchart, in turn, leads to Program 7.6. Notice that if the user enters a number outside the range 1 to 8, the ON-GOTO statement in line 180 falls through to line 190, which executes the error subroutine. The error

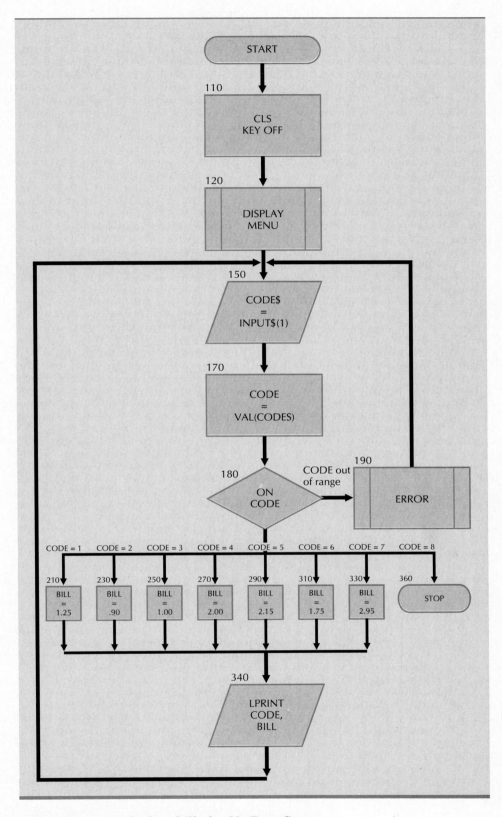

FIGURE 7.7   Flowchart to calculate bills for No Bum Steer.

```
100 REM *** CUSTOMERS' BILLS FOR NO BUM STEER ***
110 CLS : KEY OFF
120 GOSUB 400                                    'Display menu
130 LOCATE 16, 16, 1
140 PRINT "Enter Code Number of Customer's Bill ";
150    CODE$ = INPUT$(1)
160    PRINT CODE$
170    CODE = VAL(CODE$)
180    ON CODE GOTO 210, 230, 250, 270, 290, 310, 330, 360
190    GOSUB 700                                 'Error routine
200    GOTO 130
210    BILL = 1.25
220    GOTO 340
230    BILL = .9
240    GOTO 340
250    BILL = 1
260    GOTO 340
270    BILL = 2
280    GOTO 340
290    BILL = 2.15
300    GOTO 340
310    BILL = 1.75
320    GOTO 340
330    BILL = 2.95
340    LPRINT USING " Code  #   Bill ##.##"; CODE; BILL
350 GOTO 130
360 STOP
370 '
400 REM  *** Start of subroutine to display menu
410    LOCATE 2, 25
420    PRINT "WELCOME TO NO BUM STEER"
430    LOCATE 4, 16
440    PRINT "Enter the number that corresponds to order"
450    LOCATE 6, 17
460    PRINT "Code    Order                       Price"
470    LOCATE 7, 17
480    PRINT " 1       Hamburger                  1.25"
490    LOCATE 8, 17
500    PRINT " 2       Fries                       .90"
510    LOCATE 9, 17
520    PRINT " 3       Shake                      1.00"
530    LOCATE 10, 17
540    PRINT " 4       Hamburger and Fries        2.00"
550    LOCATE 11, 17
560    PRINT " 5       Hamburger and Shake        2.15"
570    LOCATE 12, 17
580    PRINT " 6       Fries and Shake            1.75"
590    LOCATE 13, 17
600    PRINT " 7       Hamburger, Fries, and Shake  2.95"
610    LOCATE 14, 17
620    PRINT " 8                   To quit"
630 RETURN
640 REM *** End of routine to display menu
650 '
700 REM *** Start of error routine
710    BEEP
720    LOCATE 17, 16
730    PRINT "Enter a value between 1 and 8 please"
740 RETURN
750 REM *** End of Error Routine
760 END
RUN
```

```
                    WELCOME TO NO BUM STEER

        Enter the number that corresponds to order

           Code    Order                        Price
            1       Hamburger                    1.25
            2       Fries                         .90
            3       Shake                        1.00
            4       Hamburger and Fries          2.00
            5       Hamburger and Shake          2.15
            6       Fries and Shake              1.75
            7       Hamburger, Fries, and Shake  2.95
            8               To quit

        Enter Code Number of Customer's Bill  3


   _____


 Code   3    Bill   1.00
```

PROGRAM 7.6   **(Continued).**

subroutine beeps the speaker, prints an error message, and returns to line 200, which branches to line 130, which prints the prompt.

As you can see, implementing a case structure with one ON-GOTO statement is more convenient than writing several IF statements. However, the ON-GOTO statement can be used only when the case structure depends on determining which value of several possible *integer* values a variable has. In this problem, CODE could only be an integer between 1 and 8. In many other cases, the ON-GOTO cannot be used, and IF statements must be used. For example, we could not use an ON-GOTO statement in the Re-Bait commission program (Program 5.3), since the commission rate depends on the value of SALES, which may range from zero to several thousand dollars. Similarly, in the Sound Value billing program (Programs 5.4 and 6.8), the user makes a selection by entering J, K, L, M, or Q, values that cannot be used with an ON-GOTO statement.

■ *The VAL and STR$ Functions*

Program 7.6 also contains one complication that must be explained. It uses the INPUT$ function to accept input so that the employees of No Bum Steer will not have to press the Enter key. But there is an incompatibility between the INPUT$ function and the ON-GOTO statement. The INPUT$ function returns a string, but the ON-GOTO statement requires a numeric variable. Fortunately, BASIC provides the VAL function to convert a string to a number. In line 170, the VAL function converts CODE$, which is the string variable assigned a value by INPUT$, to CODE, which is the numeric variable used in the ON-GOTO statement. So, for example, if CODE$ is equal to "5", CODE will be equal to 5.

The syntax of the VAL function is

```
variable = VAL (string$)
```

Although the argument of VAL must be a string, the value of the string should be a number. The argument may also contain leading blanks (blanks before the first character), a + or − sign, and a decimal point, all of which are considered numeric characters. So, for example:

Statement

```
X = VAL("5280")
```

Effect

X = 5280 because VAL converts the string "5280" to the number 5280.

Statement

```
X = VAL("-12.5")
```

Effect

X = −12.5 because the − sign is a valid numeric character.

Statement

```
X = VAL("4th of July")
```

Effect

X = 4 because VAL stops converting when it reaches a nonnumeric character.

Statement

```
X = VAL("July 4")
```

Effect

X = 0 because VAL returns a 0 if the first character of its argument is nonnumeric.

The STR$ function is the complement of the VAL function and is used to convert a number to a string. The syntax of the STR$ function is

```
string$ = STR$ (variable)
```

If the argument of the STR$ function is positive, the string it returns contains a leading blank. If the argument is negative, the string contains a leading minus sign. For example:

Statement

```
A$ = STR$(14.7)
```

Effect

A$ = " 14.7"

Statement

```
A$ = STR$(-29.2)
```

Effect

A$ = "-29.2"

Syntax Summary

```
ON-GOTO Statement
Form:      ON variable GOTO line, ...
Example:   ON NUM GOTO 40, 30, 90
Function:  If the value of variable is 1, BASIC executes a GOTO to
           the first line number; if variable is 2, BASIC executes
           a GOTO to the second line number; and so on. If variable
           is 0 or is greater than the number of line numbers listed,
           the next line is executed. The ON-GOSUB statement is
           similar except that BASIC executes a GOSUB, rather than
           a GOTO, to the appropriate line.
```

Getting the Bugs Out

Problem: During execution, BASIC displays the error message

```
Illegal function call in line nn
```

where nn is the line number of an ON-GOTO or ON-GOSUB statement.

Reason: The value of variable is outside the range 0 to 255.

Solution: Check the calculation of variable.

Problem: During execution, BASIC displays the error message

```
Undefined line number in line nn
```

where nn is the line number of an ON-GOTO or ON-GOSUB statement.

Reason: The line number to which you want to branch does not exist in the program.

Solution: Either change the line number in the ON statement or add the missing statement.

 EXERCISES

....

*7.13 Consider the following ON-GOTO statement

```
ON F GOTO 30, 50, 40, 20, 80
```

What line number will be branched to if F has the following values?

a) 5
b) 1
c) 40

7.14 Consider the statement

```
J = VAL(P$)
```

What value is assigned to J when P$ has the following values?

a) 9
b) -1
c) Fourth of July
d) 500 Fifth Avenue

 PROGRAMMING ASSIGNMENTS

....

7.14 Modify Program 7.6 to print the number of customers who requested each of the seven different orders. (Hint: Introduce seven counters, one for each type of order. When a particular order is entered, in addition to printing the bill, increment the counter for that order. When an 8 is entered, print the values of all seven counters.)

*7.15 Program 7.6 assumes that each customer requests only one order, but it is more likely that a customer will request several orders. Modify Program 7.6 so that a code of 8 means to print the total bill for a customer, and a code of 9 means to end the program.

7.16 Write a program to print fortunes like those you get in fortune cookies. Ask the user to enter a "lucky" number in the range 1 to 9 and use an ON-GOTO statement to print the fortune. When 0 is entered, end the program.

DEFINING THE FUNCTION KEYS

Now that you are writing more complex programs, it will be useful to learn how to define the function keys to make them mean what you want. Because their meanings can be changed, the function keys are called "soft keys."

You already know how to use KEY OFF and KEY ON to erase and display the meanings of the function keys on line 25. A different version of the KEY statement changes the meanings of the function keys. For example, the following statement changes the meaning of function key F6 to AUTO 100:

```
KEY 6, "AUTO 100"
```

Then, instead of typing AUTO 100, you can just press the F6 key.

The syntax for defining function keys is

```
KEY n,string
```

where n is the number of the function key whose meaning you want to change, and string is the new meaning you want to give it. If you have the enhanced keyboard, be aware that to assign a value to function key 11 you must use n = 30, and for function key 12 you must use n = 31.

If the function key display is on, the new meaning of the key will be displayed on line 25. Up to 15 characters may be assigned to a function key (not counting the quotation marks), but the function key display shows only the first 6 characters. To see all the characters assigned to all the keys, use the command KEY LIST. This command lists all 15 characters assigned to all the function keys.

With the F6 key redefined as AUTO 100, to automatically generate line numbers, you would only have to press the F6 and Enter keys. In fact, you can even avoid pressing the Enter key if you use the CHR$ function.

The CHR$ Function

The CHR$ function is used with a numeric argument, n,

```
CHR$(n)
```

and returns the character whose ASCII code is n. The ASCII codes are listed in Appendix C. For example, the statement

```
LETTER$ = CHR$(65)
```

assigns the letter A to LETTER$. Similarly, the statement

```
PRINT CHR$(68)CHR$(79)CHR$(71)
```

prints the word DOG. Of course, that is a hard way to print DOG. The advantage of the CHR$ function is that it allows you to use characters that cannot be typed directly from the keyboard. For example, the following PRINT statement will display on the screen happy faces whose ASCII codes are 1 and 2:

```
PRINT CHR$(1), CHR$(2)
```

(Unfortunately, while you can display these symbols on the screen, many printers will not print them.)

The CHR$ function also allows you to include the Enter key as part of a function key definition. For example, to make the Enter key part of the revised definition of the F6 key, you cannot simply type

```
KEY 6, "AUTO 100"
```

and then press the Enter key. Pressing the Enter key ends the command; it does become part of the string. But you can simulate pressing the Enter key at the end of the command by using the CHR$ statement as follows

```
KEY 6, "AUTO 100" + CHR$(13)
```

because the ASCII code for a carriage return is 13 (see Appendix C).

The CHR$ function can also be used to print a string that contains quotation marks. The ASCII code for the quotation mark is 34. Thus, to print the string

```
Mary said, "Use the CHR$ function".
```

you would code

```
PRINT "Mary said, "; CHR$(34);
       "Use the CHR$ function"; CHR$(34); "."
```

Finally, the CHR$ function can be used to send special characters to the printer. The ASCII code for a form feed is 12, so the statement

```
LPRINT CHR$(12)
```

causes the printer to advance the paper to a new page. On IBM and some other printers, CHR$(15) causes the printer to produce compressed (small) letters, while CHR$(14) results in expanded letters. Unfortunately, these special characters are not standardized and are not recognized by all printers.

The ASC Function

The ASC function is the opposite of the CHR$ function. It is used with a string argument and returns the ASCII code of the first character of the string. For example, the statement

```
NUMBER = ASC("BASIC")
```

assigns 66 to NUMBER, because the ASCII code of B is 66.

The ASC function permits us to manipulate strings in interesting ways. For example, the ASCII code for a lowercase letter is 32 more than the code for the corresponding uppercase letter. That is, the code for a is 97, while the code for A is 65. Therefore, if UPPER.LETTER$ contains an uppercase letter, we can convert it to lowercase by the statements

```
ASCII.LOWER = ASC(UPPER.LETTER$) + 32
LOWER.LETTER$ = CHR$(ASCII.LOWER)
```

EXERCISES

....

7.15 What output is produced by the following statements?

a) PRINT VAL("65")
b) PRINT STR$(65)
c) PRINT ASC("65")
d) PRINT CHR$(65)

7.16 Write the KEY statement to assign the string SAVE "GRADES" followed by the Enter key to function key F8.

*7.17 What is printed by the following statement?

> PRINT CHR$(3)

7.18 What value is assigned to NUM by the following statement?

> NUM = ASC("$")

7.19 What value is assigned to A by the following statement?

> A = ASC(CHR$(90))

*7.20 Simple Simon says the string

> Mary said, "Use the CHR$ function".

could be coded as follows

> "Mary said, CHR$(34)Use the CHR$
> function CHR$(34)."

Comment.

7.21 What value is assigned to A$ by the following statement?

> 10 A$ = CHR$(ASC("7"))

7.22 Suppose LOWER.LETTER$ contains a lowercase letter. Write the statements that will convert it to uppercase and store the value in UPPER.LETTER$.

7.23 Program 7.7 shows an attempt to use a WHILE loop to control Program 5.3. There must be an error because the figure shows all the output the program produced. Find and correct the error.

```
100 REM *** RE-BAIT TACKLE PROBLEM ***
110 LPRINT "Name", "Sales", "Rate", "Commission"
116 WHILE MORE$ = "Y" OR MORE$ = "y"
120    INPUT "Enter name and sales "; SALES.NAME$, SALES
130    REM Start of case structure to determine commission rate
140    IF SALES < 100
          THEN RATE = .1: GOTO 190
150    IF SALES >= 100 AND SALES < 500
          THEN RATE = .2: GOTO 190
160    IF SALES >= 500 AND SALES < 1000
          THEN RATE = .3: GOTO 190
170    IF SALES >= 1000
          THEN RATE = .4: GOTO 190
180    REM End of case structure
190    COMMISSION = RATE * SALES
200    LPRINT SALES.NAME$, SALES, RATE, COMMISSION
210    INPUT "Are there more salespeople (Y or N)"; MORE$
220 WEND
230 END

RUN
Ok
```

PROGRAM 7.7   **An incorrect modification of Program 5.3.**

SUMMARY

In this chapter you have learned that

☐ Accumulators allow you to add the values of a variable, while counters tally the number of times a statement is executed.

☐ The TRON command turns tracing on, which is very useful when you debug programs. The TROFF statement turns tracing off.

☐ The WHILE and WEND statements are used to create a WHILE loop. The statements in a WHILE loop are executed while the condition coded in the WHILE statement is true.

☐ The CONT command is used to continue execution after a program has stopped because of a STOP or END statement or because a user has entered a Ctrl + Break.

☐ Using control breaks allows you to print minor totals.

☐ Under some conditions, the ON-GOTO and ON-GOSUB statements are used to implement a case structure.

☐ The VAL function converts a string to a number.

☐ The STR$ function converts a number to a string.

☐ The KEY statement redefines the function keys.

☐ The CHR$ function converts an ASCII code to its corresponding character.

☐ The ASC function converts a character to its corresponding ASCII code.

KEY TERMS IN THIS CHAPTER

accumulator 168   **counter** 169   **internal variable** 168
control break 187   **initialize** 169   **WHILE loop** 178

QUESTIONS FOR REVIEW

7.1 What command is used to turn tracing on? What command turns it off?

7.2 If a program contains a WHILE statement, it must also contain a _____ statement.

7.3 What does the CONT statement do? Which function key means CONT?

7.4 What does the STR$ function do?

7.5 When the statement

            150 ON N GOTO 200, 300, 400

is executed, BASIC branches to line 400 when N has what value? What line is executed if N has the value 200?

7.6 Why are the function keys also called the soft keys?

7.7 Does the VAL function return a number or a string?

7.8 What does the CHR$ function do?

7.9 Which statement is used to redefine the function keys?

7.10 In a WHILE statement you code a condition, and the WHILE loop is executed as long as the condition is _____ .

7.11 What does the STR$ function do?

7.12 True or false: A counter variable must be used in an IF statement.

7.13 In the following statement, which variable is used as an accumulator?

$$P = P + Q$$

7.14 What is the likely cause of the error if, during execution of a program, BASIC displays the error message WEND without WHILE?

7.15 What is the likely cause of the error if, during execution of a program that contains a WHILE loop, BASIC goes into an endless loop?

7.16 What is the likely cause of the error if, during execution of a program, BASIC displays the error message Undefined line number in 60, where 60 is the line number of an ON-GOTO statement?

ADDITIONAL PROGRAMMING ASSIGNMENTS

7.17   Write a program that calculates the sum of the numbers $1 + 2 + 3 + \ldots$ and keeps adding numbers until the sum is greater than 1000. The program should then print the last number added to the sum and the sum.

7.18   Write a program that accepts a single character at a time. If the user enters an uppercase letter, convert it to lowercase and print it; if the user enters a lowercase letter, convert it to uppercase and print it. If the character entered is not a letter, print it unaltered.

*7.19   Re-solve Programming Assignment 5.8 to include calculation and printing of the average number of days skis are rented and the average bill.

7.20   Write a program that accepts a number, call it MAX, and then finds the largest integer whose square is less than MAX.

*7.21   The population of the world is now 3.5 billion (you can write that number in a program as 3.5E9). If the population now is represented by POP and the rate of increase (as a decimal) as RATE, then the growth in population in one year is

GROWTH = RATE * POP

and the population at the end of the year is

POP = POP + GROWTH

Write a program that accepts a value for RATE (suggested values are 1, 2, and 3 percent) and determines how long at that RATE it will take for the population to reach 6 billion people.

7.22   Seymour's Videos rents video cassettes for $4.50 per day, or $2.75 per day if you pay $35 to join a rental club. Write a program that determines the number of cassettes you have to rent in order to save money by joining the club.

7.23   Re-solve Programming Assignment 5.15 using an ON-GOTO statement. (Hint: To use an ON-GOTO statement, you will have to convert the call areas A through D to the numbers 1 through 4. The easiest way to do that is to notice that the ASCII codes of the letters A through D are the numbers 65, 66, 67, and 68. Therefore, introduce a new variable, CALL.AREA, which is calculated by the equation

CALL.AREA = ASC(CALL.AREA$) - 64

You can verify that CALL.AREA is 1 when CALL.AREA$ is A, that it is 2 when CALL.AREA$ is B, etc.)

7.24   Frank Grinder uses a computer to keep track of his school performance. Every time he takes a test, he records the name of the class and the test mark. Typical data might be

Class	Mark
English	76
English	84
Math	92
Math	95
Psyc	71
Psyc	65
Psyc	54

Write a program that will accept and print these data and calculate and print the average mark in each class.

BEYOND THE BASICS

7.1   A bug is crawling from one end of a rubber band to the other. The rubber band is 10 inches long, and the bug crawls 1 inch per minute. At the end of the first minute, the rubber band stretches to 20 inches. During the stretching, the bug holds on tightly and is carried along by the stretching. The bug keeps crawling at the same rate, and at the end of each subsequent minute the rubber band is stretched an additional 10 inches. The situation after the first few minutes is as follows:

At the End of Minute	Position After Crawling	Position After Stretching	Length of Rubber Band
1	1	2	20
2	3	4.5	30
3	5.5	7.333	40

Write a program to determine how long it takes the bug to reach the end of the rubber band.

7.2 Write a program that draws a vertical line down column 70. You can use the ¦ symbol, which is on the \ key, to draw the line. Then draw an arrow on rows 12, 13, and 14, starting in column 1. A reasonable arrow can be drawn using the \ and / keys for the point and the hyphen for the shaft. Next fly the arrow across the screen, stopping when the user presses any key. The object of the game is for the user to stop the arrow as close to the line as possible, but before it smashes through the line.

7.3 The greatest common divisor (GCD) of two integers is the largest integer that evenly divides both integers. The GCD of the integers a and b can be found using Euclid's algorithm, which goes like this. Divide a by b and note the remainder, r. If r is 0, then b is the GCD. If the r is not 0, then make the following substitution:

$$a = b$$

$$b = r$$

and again divide a by b and note the remainder. Repeat this procedure until you get a remainder of 0; the last b you used is the GCD. For example, to find the GCD of 147 and 70, the steps are

Step Number	a	b	r
1	147	70	7
2	70	7	0

Since r is 0 when b is 7, 7 is the GCD of 147 and 70.

Once the GCD is found, the least common multiple (LCM), also known as the least common denominator, may be calculated using the equation

$$\text{LCM} = \frac{a \cdot b}{\text{GCD}}$$

Write a program that will accept two integers and calculate their GCD and LCM.

7.4 Write a program that does integer arithmetic with fractions. The program should accept the numerator and denominator of the first fraction and the numerator and denominator of the second fraction and then add the two fractions. The answer should be expressed in simplest form, so that, for example, if the numbers entered are 3, 4 and 5, 12, the program should print

$$\frac{3}{4} + \frac{5}{12} = 1\frac{1}{6}$$

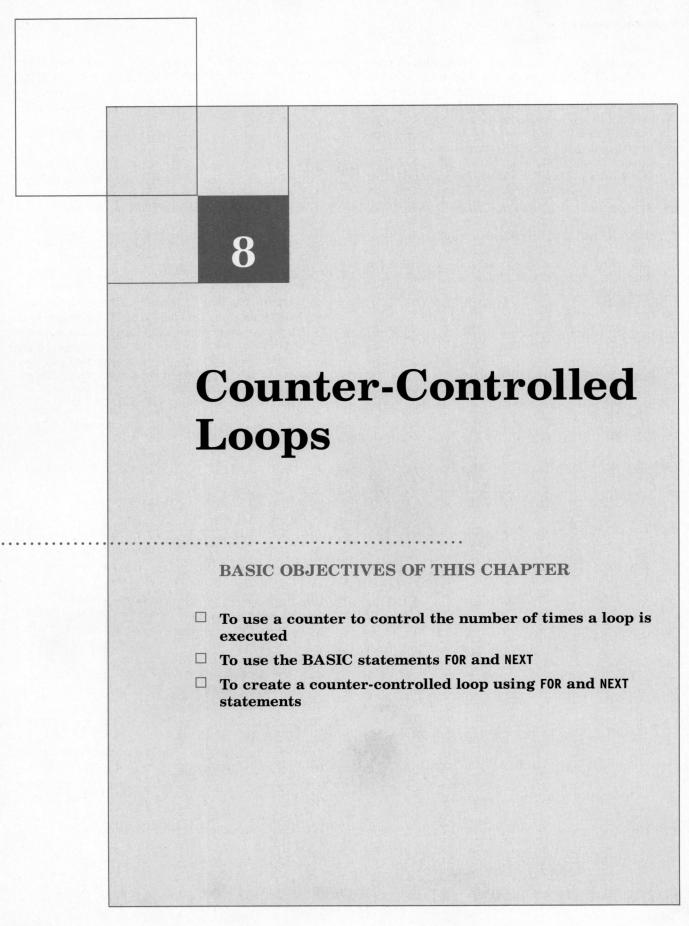

8

Counter-Controlled Loops

BASIC OBJECTIVES OF THIS CHAPTER

☐ To use a counter to control the number of times a loop is executed

☐ To use the BASIC statements FOR and NEXT

☐ To create a counter-controlled loop using FOR and NEXT statements

Counter-controlled loop
A loop that has a counter that
controls the number of times it
is executed.

In the problems we discussed in Chapter 7, we exited from the loop when trailer data were entered or read or when the condition in a WHILE statement became false. In many instances, however, we want to exit from a loop when it has been executed a certain number of times. Such loops are called **counter-controlled loops**.

A SIMPLE COUNTER-CONTROLLED LOOP

The flowchart in Figure 8.1 shows a counter-controlled loop. Before you read further, determine what output will be produced by a program based on this flowchart. You should be able to trace the flowchart and figure out that it will print the numbers 1 through 10.

Let's see why the loop in Figure 8.1 is called a counter-controlled loop. The variable COUNTER is the counter. In box Ⓐ, COUNTER is initialized at 1. In box Ⓑ, COUNTER is tested. If COUNTER is greater than 10, BASIC exits from the loop. If COUNTER is not greater than 10, BASIC executes the statements in the loop. The loop may contain any BASIC statements you want. To keep this example simple, the only statement in the loop is the PRINT statement in box Ⓒ. In box Ⓓ, 1 is added to COUNTER. The loop then continues.

Every counter-controlled loop must contain three steps: (1) the counter must be initialized; (2) the counter must be tested; and (3) the counter must be incremented.

The FOR and NEXT Statements

Counter-controlled loops are so important that BASIC provides the FOR and NEXT statements to make writing them easy. In fact, the FOR and NEXT statements do all the work for you. They initialize the counter, they test the counter, and they increment the counter. Program 8.1 uses the FOR and NEXT statements to create the counter-controlled loop flowcharted in Figure 8.1. We will examine the syntax of the FOR and NEXT statements shortly, but for now you should know that, like the WHILE and WEND statements, the FOR and NEXT statements are always used together. They define a counter-controlled loop, with the FOR statement indicating the start of the loop and the NEXT statement indicating the end of the loop. The FOR statement in line 30 essentially says to BASIC, "Execute all the statements between here and the NEXT statement, first with COUNTER equal to 1, then with COUNTER equal to 2, and so on, and finally with COUNTER equal to 10."

Notice that in Program 8.1 the PRINT statement is indented two spaces. BASIC doesn't require this indentation, but the indents make it easier to see the beginning and the end of the loop. You should follow the same convention.

To give you a better understanding of how the FOR and NEXT statements work, let's trace Program 8.1. The first time BASIC executes the FOR statement in line 30, it sets COUNTER equal to 1 and checks to see if COUNTER is greater than 10, which is the upper limit. Since COUNTER is not greater than 10, BASIC executes the PRINT statement in line 40 and prints the 1. When it executes the NEXT statement in line 50, BASIC first sets COUNTER equal to the next value, which is 2, and then branches back to the FOR statement in line 30. When it executes the FOR statement, BASIC again checks to see if COUNTER is greater than 10. Since COUNTER is not greater than 10, BASIC executes the

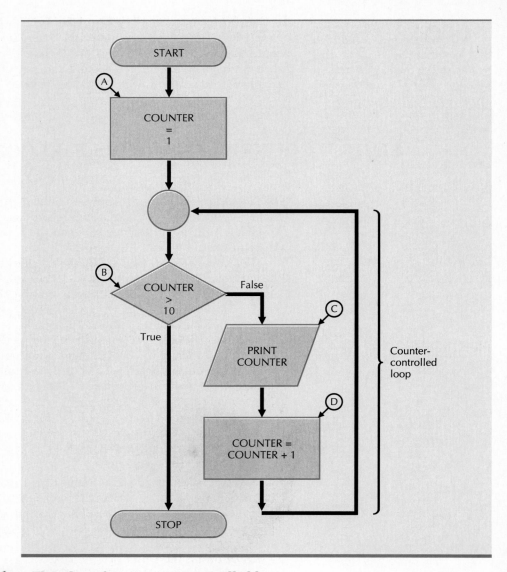

FIGURE 8.1   **Flowchart for a counter-controlled loop.**

loop again, this time with COUNTER equal to 2. This procedure is repeated until the loop is executed with COUNTER equal to 10.

When COUNTER is 10 and BASIC executes the NEXT statement in line 50, it sets COUNTER equal to the next value, which is 11. Now when COUNTER is checked in the FOR statement, BASIC finds that COUNTER is greater than 10. Instead of executing the loop again, BASIC exits from the loop by branching to the statement following the NEXT statement, line 60, and ends execution.

Now that you understand a bit about FOR and NEXT statements, let's use them to solve a problem.

Calculating Population Growth

The town of Malthus has experienced a tremendous growth in its population over the last few years. In preparation for expanding its school system, the town has asked you to write a program that will calculate the increase and

```
10 REM *** USING FOR-NEXT STATEMENTS TO CREATE ***
20 REM ***       A COUNTER-CONTROLLED LOOP       ***
30 FOR COUNTER = 1 TO 10
40   PRINT COUNTER
50 NEXT COUNTER
60 END

RUN
 1
 2
 3
 4
 5
 6
 7
 8
 9
 10
Ok
```

PROGRAM 8.1   **Using the FOR and NEXT statements to create a counter-controlled loop.**

total population at the end of each of the next five years, given that the rate of growth remains constant.

The clue that you should use a counter-controlled loop in this problem is that you will need to repeat the calculation for each of the next five years. Thus, you must set up a loop that is executed five times.

As always, you should begin with step 1 of our structured programming procedure and assign variable names. Let's use the following:

Input variables	Initial population	INITIAL.POPULATION
	Growth rate	RATE
Output variables	Growth in population	GROWTH
	Population	POPULATION
	Year counter	YEAR

Again, step 2 of our standard procedure calls for you to develop an algorithm for the problem. In this case, the algorithm is

1. Input INITIAL.POPULATION and RATE.
2. Set POPULATION equal to INITIAL.POPULATION.
3. Repeat steps 4 through 6 for five YEARs.
4. Calculate GROWTH.
5. Add GROWTH to POPULATION.
6. Print YEAR, GROWTH, and POPULATION.
7. Stop execution.

The only complicated part of the program is the loop. Since the FOR and NEXT statements take care of all the complications for you, it is not necessary to draw a flowchart for this program.

To complete step 3 of our standard approach, you need to calculate answers by hand only for the first two years. If the computer-calculated answers for the first two years agree with your hand-calculated answers, you may assume the program is correct. Let's say that the town's current population is 40,000 and the growth rate is 10 percent. The results for the first two years are as follows:

Year	Growth	Population at End of Year
1	4,000	44,000
2	4,400	48,400

Program 8.2 shows these calculations as performed by BASIC. Notice that the first time BASIC executes line 160 it multiplies a POPULATION of 40000 by a RATE of .10 and puts the result, 4000, in the GROWTH box. Adding this first year's GROWTH to the initial POPULATION of 40000 in line 170 produces a new POPULATION of 44000 at the end of the first year.

The second time BASIC executes line 160, it applies the RATE of .10 to the new POPULATION of 44000, which gives a GROWTH of 4400. Line 170 adds this GROWTH to the POPULATION of 44000 to determine that POPULATION = 48400 at the end of the second year. As Program 8.2 shows, BASIC repeats this procedure for years 3, 4, and 5.

```
100 REM *** CALCULATE POPULATION GROWTH ***
110 INPUT "Enter initial population and growth rate"; INITIAL.POPULATION, RATE
120 POPULATION = INITIAL.POPULATION
130 PRINT      "Year        Growth       Population"
140 FORMAT$ = " ##          #,###        ###,###"
150 FOR YEAR = 1 TO 5
160    GROWTH = RATE * POPULATION
170    POPULATION = POPULATION + GROWTH
180    PRINT USING FORMAT$; YEAR, GROWTH, POPULATION
190 NEXT YEAR
200 END

RUN
Enter initial population and growth rate? 40000,.10
Year        Growth       Population
  1         4,000        44,000
  2         4,400        48,400
  3         4,840        53,240
  4         5,324        58,564
  5         5,856        64,420
Ok
```

PROGRAM 8.2   **Calculating population growth in Malthus.**

Comparing FOR-NEXT Loops with WHILE Loops

Students are often confused about when they should use a FOR-NEXT loop and when they should use a WHILE loop. In general, if you know the number of times you want to execute a loop, as we did in Program 8.2, use a FOR-NEXT loop. If you don't know how many times you want to execute a loop, as in Program 7.3, where we executed the loop until TOTAL was greater than 1 million, use a WHILE loop. In fact, not only didn't we know how many times we would have to execute the loop before we solved the problem in Program 7.3, finding this number is why we wrote the program.

EXERCISES

. . . .

*8.1 Would the output of Program 8.2 be changed if lines 120 and 130 were interchanged? What if lines 160 and 170 were interchanged?

8.2 In every counter-controlled loop, the counter is initialized, tested, and incremented. Which of these operations is performed by the FOR and NEXT state-

ments, and which must be separately coded by the programmer?

8.3 How many times will BASIC execute a FOR-NEXT loop that starts with the statement

```
FOR P = 1 TO 30
```

PROGRAMMING ASSIGNMENTS

. . . .

8.1 The Baker's Man sells rolls for $0.35 each. To help its salespeople, the company would like a table showing the cost of rolls for orders of 1 to 12 rolls. (Hint: This program does not require any input.)

8.2 Write a program to calculate the balance in a savings account at the Cache National Bank. The program should accept a deposit and interest rate and calculate and print for each of the next 10 years the interest earned and the balance at the end of the year.

*8.3 Program 8.2 assumes that the growth rate stays constant. We might suppose that as the town grows, the new residents attract additional people, so that each year the growth rate increases by 5 percent. Write a program to calculate the population growth under this assumption.

8.4 a) One morning Queen Doyenna set out from the castle and gave 1 ounce of gold to the first person she met, 2 ounces of gold to the second person she met, 3 ounces of gold to the third person, and so on, stopping when she had given 100 ounces of gold to the one hundredth person she met. How much gold did she give away?

b) That same day, King Khan gave 1 pound of gold to the first person he met, ½ pound of gold to the second person he met, ⅓ pound of gold to the third person, and so on, stopping when he had given ¹⁄₁₀₀ of a pound of gold to the one hundredth person he met. How much gold did he give away?

MORE COMPLEX FOR AND NEXT STATEMENTS

. . . .

Now that you have used FOR and NEXT statements, you may think them quite simple. They can, however, be more complex. In this section, we will examine these statements in detail.

The syntax of the FOR statement is

```
FOR counter variable = starting value TO final value [STEP step size]
```

In a FOR statement, counter variable may be any legal BASIC numeric variable name. The starting value and the final value may be constant numbers—as in line 150 of Program 8.2, where these values were 1 and 5 respectively—or they may be variables or even expressions. The meaning of the STEP clause will be discussed shortly. Using the Alt + F keys is equivalent to typing the word FOR.

```
10 REM *** FOR STATEMENT WITH VARIABLE STARTING AND FINAL VALUES ***
20 INPUT "Enter Starting and Final Values "; START,FINAL
30 FOR COUNTER = START TO FINAL
40   PRINT COUNTER
50 NEXT COUNTER
60 END

RUN
Enter Starting and Final Values ? 6,13
  6
  7
  8
  9
  10
  11
  12
  13
Ok
```

PROGRAM 8.3   **A FOR-NEXT loop with variable starting and final values.**

Program 8.3, a generalized version of Program 8.1, uses START for starting value and FINAL for final value, so that this program can print the numbers between any two numbers we like.

As in Program 8.1, the NEXT statement in Program 8.3 is NEXT COUNTER. The syntax of the NEXT statement is simply

NEXT counter variable

where counter variable must be the same as counter variable in the FOR statement. Using the Alt + N keys is equivalent to typing the word NEXT.

As you will see later, there may be more than one FOR-NEXT loop in a program. In such cases, BASIC pairs a NEXT statement with the FOR statement that has the same counter variable.

■ *Rules About FOR-NEXT Statements*

As you can see, using a FOR-NEXT loop is not difficult, but there are a few rules you should know. First, each time you go through a FOR-NEXT loop, be sure that the last statement you execute is the NEXT statement. You may not understand the reason for this rule, because our examples have been rather simple. However, if a loop contains complicated logic, when you finish processing a case you may be tempted to branch to the INPUT statement or to the FOR statement, either of which would be wrong. You must branch to the NEXT statement, because when you use a FOR-NEXT loop, the FOR and NEXT statements control the loop. The NEXT statement increments the counter and branches back to the top of the loop, where the counter is tested. If you branch to an INPUT statement or to a FOR statement, the value of the counter will be incorrect.

You must never branch into a FOR-NEXT loop; always start the loop by executing the FOR statement. As you will see later, however, it is legal and sometimes useful to branch *out* of a FOR-NEXT loop. Once inside the loop, though, do not change the value of the starting variable, the final variable, or the step variable. The reason for this rule should be clear; if you change any of these variables, the loop will not be executed the correct number of times.

■ The STEP Clause

In our examples thus far, when we executed the NEXT statement, we calculated the next value of the counter variable by adding 1 to the old value. But you may not always want to go up in steps of 1. The STEP clause of the FOR statement lets you use any step size you like.

Like starting value and final value, step size may be a number, a variable, or an expression. We did not have to use the STEP clause in our earlier problems because we were using a step size of 1. If you omit the STEP clause, BASIC uses a default step size of 1.

Suppose you want to print only the odd numbers from 1 through 10. Program 8.4 shows a modification of Program 8.1 that achieves this goal by adding a STEP clause to the FOR statement. The FOR statement in line 20 of this program instructs the computer to give COUNTER the values 1 through 10, going up in steps of 2.

Let's trace the program. The first time it executes line 20, BASIC sets COUNTER = 1. Line 30 prints the 1. In the NEXT statement in line 40, the next value of COUNTER is calculated by adding step size to the current value of COUNTER. In this case, step size is 2, so the next value of COUNTER is calculated to be 3. Since the new value of COUNTER is not greater than the final value of 10 specified in the FOR statement, the loop is repeated with COUNTER equal to 3.

This process is repeated with COUNTER equal to 5, 7, and 9. When a COUNTER of 9 is printed and the NEXT statement is executed, the next value of COUNTER is calculated to be 11. Since 11 is greater than the final value of 10, BASIC does not execute the loop again, but branches to the END statement that follows the NEXT statement.

NONINTEGER AND NEGATIVE STEP SIZE

The step size doesn't have to be an integer. It doesn't even have to be positive. For example, the FOR statement

FOR X = 0 TO 1 STEP 0.25

```
10 REM *** USE OF STEP CLAUSE ***
20 FOR COUNTER = 1 TO 10 STEP 2
30    PRINT COUNTER
40 NEXT COUNTER
50 END
Ok

RUN
 1
 3
 5
 7
 9
Ok
```

PROGRAM 8.4   **Using the STEP clause to print only odd numbers.**

causes X to have the values 0, 0.25, 0.50, 0.75, and 1. Nothing new is involved here; we still get the next X by adding the step size to the old X.

To show the use of a negative step size, consider the following FOR statement:

```
FOR COUNTDOWN = 10 TO 1 STEP -1
```

If this statement replaced the FOR statement in line 20 of Program 8.4,* the program would print the numbers 10, 9, 8, 7, 6, 5, 4, 3, 2, and 1. We still add the step size to the old COUNTDOWN to get the next COUNTDOWN, but when we add −1 to 10 we get 9, and when we add −1 to 9 we get 8, and so on, until we add −1 to 2 and get 1. When a negative step size is used, BASIC exits from the loop when the calculated value of the counter variable becomes *less* than the final value specified in the FOR statement. In this case, BASIC exits from the loop when the counter variable becomes 0. So for a negative step size to work properly, the final value must be less than the starting value.

The flowchart in Figure 8.2 shows how the FOR and NEXT statements work. (This flowchart assumes that step size is positive. If step size is negative, the relational symbol in the decision box must be changed to <.) Refer to this flowchart to verify the effects of the following FOR-NEXT loops:

Statement
```
20 FOR J = 11 TO 6 STEP -2
30    PRINT J
40 NEXT J
```

Effect
The numbers 11, 9, and 7 are printed. The next J is obtained by adding the step size to the previous J.

Statement
```
20 FOR J = 1 TO 7 STEP 3
30 NEXT J
40 PRINT J
```

Effect
The number 10 is printed. The flowchart shows that when BASIC exits from the loop, the counter variable has the value that caused the exit. In this case, the loop is executed when J is 1, 4, and 7 and exited when J is 10.

Statement
```
20 FOR J = 10 TO 5
30    PRINT J
40 NEXT J
```

Effect
Nothing is printed. The flowchart shows that if the starting value is greater than the final value, the loop is not executed at all.

---

*And the NEXT statement is changed to NEXT COUNTDOWN.

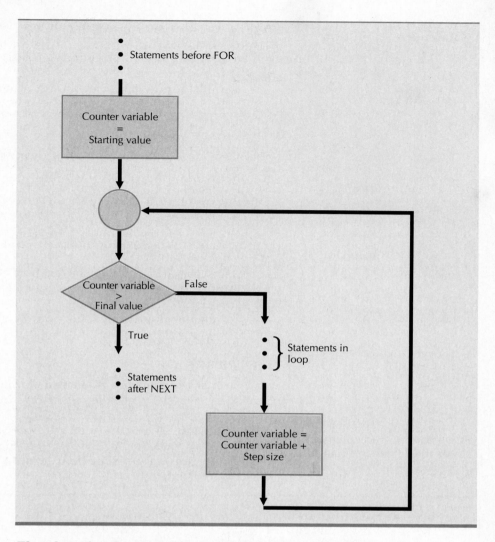

FIGURE 8.2 **Flowchart for the FOR-NEXT statements with a positive step size.**

Controlling Loop Execution with FOR-NEXT Statements

When you know in advance the number of cases you want to process, you can use a FOR-NEXT loop instead of trailer data to control the number of times the loop is executed. To give you a clearer understanding of these ideas, let's re-solve Program 3.3, (which we re-solved using a WHILE loop in Chapter 7), using a FOR-NEXT loop.

Following the first step of our structured approach, we will assign the following variable names:

Input variables	Pay Rate	PAY.RATE
	Hours worked	HOURS
	Number of employees	NO.EMPLOYEES
Internal variable	Employee counter	EMPLOYEES
Output variables	Gross Pay	GROSS.PAY

As you can see, there are two new variables: NO.EMPLOYEES, for the number of employees, and EMPLOYEES, for the employee counter. NO.EMPLOYEES will be used as the final value in the FOR statement, and EMPLOYEES will be used as the counter variable.

Again, step 2 is to develop an algorithm. In this case, we will use

---

1. Accept NO.EMPLOYEES.
2. Repeat steps 3 through 5 NO.EMPLOYEES times.
3. Accept PAY.RATE and HOURS.
4. Calculate GROSS.PAY.
5. Print PAY.RATE, HOURS, and GROSS.PAY.
6. Stop execution.

Once again, the only complicated part of the program is the loop. Since the FOR and NEXT statements take care of all the complications for you, it is not necessary to draw a flowchart.

For our hand-calculated answers, we should get the same results we got in Program 3.3.

THE PROGRAM

Header data
Data that specify the number of cases to be processed and that are entered before the rest of the data.

Look first at the comment at the end of line 12 in Program 8.5, which was developed from the preceding algorithm. In this program, we do not use trailer data to control the number of times the loop is executed. Instead, we use the variable NO.EMPLOYEES as the final value in a FOR statement. Since BASIC reads a value for NO.EMPLOYEES ahead of reading any actual employee data, we say that we are using **header data** to control the number of times the loop is executed.

```
10 REM  *** BAT-O PROGRAM ***
12 INPUT "Enter number of employees"; NO.EMPLOYEES           'Header data
14 FOR EMPLOYEES = 1 TO NO.EMPLOYEES
20   INPUT "Enter Pay Rate and Hours Worked"; PAY.RATE, HOURS
40   GROSS.PAY = PAY.RATE * HOURS
50   LPRINT PAY.RATE, HOURS, GROSS.PAY
60 NEXT EMPLOYEES
70 END

RUN
Enter number of employees? 3  ◄─────────────  (Entering header data)
Enter Pay Rate and Hours Worked? 6.75,40
Enter Pay Rate and Hours Worked? 6,30
Enter Pay Rate and Hours Worked? 5.75,25
Ok
```

```
6.75           40             270
6              30             180
5.75           25             143.75
```

PROGRAM 8.5   Re-solving Program 3.3 using a FOR-NEXT loop.

Looking at line 14, you might wonder why we did not simply write

```
14 FOR EMPLOYEES = 1 TO 3
```

Writing the FOR statement this way would simplify the program, but then the program could be used only with three employees. By writing the program as we did, the program can still be used if the company's workforce expands or shrinks. Good programmers design their programs to be flexible.

It is important that you understand the difference between NO.EMPLOYEES and EMPLOYEES. NO.EMPLOYEES is the number of employees we want BASIC to process. It is set once during each run of the program. EMPLOYEES is the number of employees BASIC has processed. EMPLOYEES starts out as one and increases by one each time an EMPLOYEE is processed. When EMPLOYEES becomes equal to NO.EMPLOYEES, the number of employees processed is equal to the number of employees we want processed, and the loop is finished.

Syntax Summary

FOR and NEXT statements

Form: FOR counter variable = starting value TO final value [STEP step size]

        .

        loop statements

        .

        NEXT counter variable

Example: FOR J = 10 TO 0 STEP −2
            PRINT J
         NEXT J

Interpretation: counter variable is set equal to starting value, and the loop statements are executed. When the NEXT statement is executed, counter variable is incremented by step size. (If STEP is omitted, the increment is 1.) Control is transferred to the FOR statement, where counter variable is compared with final value. If counter variable is less than final value, the loop statements are executed again. When counter variable becomes greater than final value, control is passed to the statement following the NEXT statement. If step size is negative, the loop statements are executed until counter variable becomes less than final value.

Getting the Bugs Out

Problem: During execution, BASIC displays the error message

```
NEXT without FOR
```

Reason: A NEXT statement was executed before a FOR statement. You may have omitted the FOR statement, branched into the middle of a FOR-NEXT loop, or executed a NEXT statement with a counter variable that was not the counter variable named in the FOR statement.

Solution: Eliminate any branch into the middle of the loop and make sure that the NEXT and FOR statements name the same counter variable.

Problem: During execution, BASIC displays the error message

FOR without NEXT

Reason: Your program executed a FOR statement, but BASIC could not find a NEXT statement before the physical end of the program.

Solution: Make sure that every FOR statement has a matching NEXT statement.

EXERCISES

8.4 Consider the following program

```
10 FOR C = 11 TO 21 STEP 3
20    PRINT C
30 NEXT C
40 END
```

a) What output is produced?
b) What is the value of C when line 40 is executed?
c) What output is produced if line 10 is changed to

```
10 FOR C = 7 TO 8 STEP .2
```

d) What output is produced if line 10 is changed to

```
10 FOR C = 30 TO 20 STEP -2
```

*8.5 Consider the following program.

```
10 READ J, K, L
20 FOR I = J TO K STEP L
30    PRINT I
40
50 DATA 2, 10, 3
60 END
```

a) What statement belongs in line 40?
b) What output is produced by this program?
c) What output is produced if line 20 is changed to

```
20 FOR I = L TO K STEP J
```

8.6 What output is produced by the following program?

```
10 FOR K = 3 TO 8 STEP 2
20 NEXT K
30 PRINT K
40 END
```

8.7 We want to write a program that accepts 10 numbers and prints the numbers that are not negative. Will the following coding work? If it won't work, show how to fix it.

```
10 FOR J = 1 TO 10
20    INPUT W
30    IF W < 0
         THEN GOTO 10
         ELSE PRINT W
40 NEXT J
50 END
```

*8.8 Will the following program print the numbers from 30 to 40? If it won't, show how to fix it.

```
10 FOR M = 30 TO 40
20    PRINT M
30    M = M + 1
40 NEXT M
50 END
```

PROGRAMMING ASSIGNMENTS

8.5 Write a program that uses a FOR-NEXT loop to print the numbers 4, 7, 10, 13, 16, and 19.

8.6 Write a program that accepts a number, n, and calculates and prints the sum $1 + 2 + \ldots + n$.

8.7 In 1626 Manhattan Island was sold for $24. Write a program that accepts today's year, and calculates and prints how much that $24 would be worth today if it had been deposited in a savings account paying 6% interest compounded annually. (Hint: Use a FOR-NEXT loop, with a starting value of 1626.)

8.8 Write a program that uses a FOR-NEXT loop to print:

```
10 - 9 - 8 - 7 - 6 - 5 - 4 - 3 - 2 - 1 - BLASTOFF!
```

8.9 Re-solve Programming Assignment 5.3 using a FOR-NEXT loop instead of trailer data to control the program execution.

*8.10 The factorial of a number, n, is defined as

$$1 * 2 * \ldots * (n - 1) * n$$

Write a program that accepts a number between 1 and 30 and calculates and prints the factorial of that number.

8.11 Write a program that will accept a starting character and an ending character and then print them and all the characters between. (Hint: You will find both the ASC and the CHR$ functions useful.)

NESTED FOR-NEXT LOOPS

Independent loops
FOR-NEXT loops that do not intersect (see Figure 8.3).

Nested loops
FOR-NEXT loops in which an inner loop is completely enclosed in an outer loop (see Figure 8.3).

As noted earlier, a program may have more than one FOR-NEXT loop. Figure 8.3(a) shows a simple example in which the A loop and the B loop are completely separate. When the program is executed, first the A loop is executed and then the B loop. FOR-NEXT loops used this way are called **independent loops**.

Figure 8.3(b) also shows two FOR-NEXT loops, but in this case the B loop is completely inside the A loop. FOR-NEXT loops used this way are called **nested loops**. When FOR-NEXT loops are nested, the inner loop is completely executed on every pass through the outer loop. Although the figure shows two FOR-NEXT loops, you may nest as many as you like, as long as each inner loop is completely contained within the outer loop in which it starts.

Not all combinations of FOR-NEXT loops are legal in BASIC, however. The loops in Figure 8.3(c) are said to be *crossed* and are illegal. In addition, the counter variable in nested FOR-NEXT loops must be different in the two loops. Therefore, the nested loops shown in Figure 8.3(d) are also illegal.

To help you understand nested FOR-NEXT loops better, consider Program 8.6. When BASIC executes Program 8.6, the outer loop (the A loop) will be executed 3 times. And in each execution, the inner loop (the B loop) will be executed 2 times. Let's trace Program 8.6 to make these ideas clearer.

When BASIC executes line 20, it puts 1 in the A box, as in Figure 8.4(a). When it executes line 30, it puts 1 in the B box, as in Figure 8.4(b). When it executes line 40, it multiplies A and B and puts 1 in the C box, as in Figure 8.4(c). Line 50 prints these values. When BASIC executes the NEXT B statement in line 60, it puts 2 in the B box, as in Figure 8.4(d), and branches back to line 30. Notice that the number in the A box has not changed. In line 30, BASIC tests the value of B, but since it is not greater than 2, the loop continues. When BASIC executes line 40, it multiplies 1 by 2 and puts the result, 2, in the C box, as in Figure 8.4(e); in line 50 it prints these values.

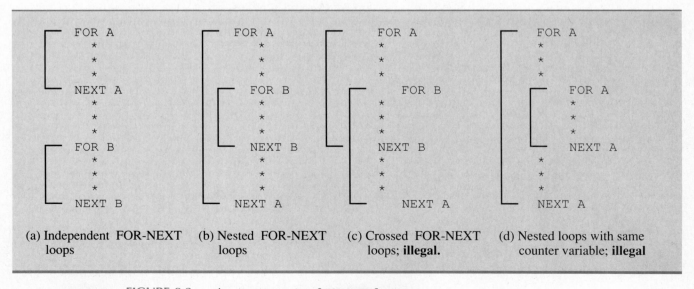

(a) Independent FOR-NEXT loops

(b) Nested FOR-NEXT loops

(c) Crossed FOR-NEXT loops; **illegal.**

(d) Nested loops with same counter variable; **illegal**

FIGURE 8.3   **Arrangements of FOR-NEXT loops.**

```
10 REM *** NESTED FOR-NEXT LOOPS ***
20 FOR A = 1 TO 3
30    FOR B = 1 TO 2
40      C = A * B
50      PRINT USING "A = #  B = #  C = #"; A, B, C
60    NEXT B
70 NEXT A
80 END

RUN
A = 1  B = 1  C = 1
A = 1  B = 2  C = 2
A = 2  B = 1  C = 2
A = 2  B = 2  C = 4
A = 3  B = 1  C = 3
A = 3  B = 2  C = 6
Ok
```

PROGRAM 8.6   **Illustration of nested FOR-NEXT loops.**

When BASIC executes the NEXT B statement in line 60, it puts a 3 in the B box and branches to the FOR statement in line 30. Now when BASIC tests B, it finds that B is larger than the final value of 2, so instead of continuing the loop, BASIC exits from the B loop by branching to line 70.

When BASIC executes the NEXT A statement in line 70, it puts 2 in the A box, as in Figure 8.4(f), and branches back to line 20. Since A is not greater than the final value of 3, the loop continues. When BASIC executes line 30, it puts 1 in the B box, as in Figure 8.4(g), and starts the B loop again. At this point, you should continue tracing the program to make sure you understand how the rest of the output was generated.

Printing a Balance Table

To further illustrate nested FOR-NEXT loops, consider the problem of the Common Cents Savings and Loan Company. To attract new customers, Common Cents is considering offering higher interest rates to customers who make

Statement	A	B	C
a) 20 FOR A = 1 TO 3	1		
b) 30 FOR B = 1 TO 2	1	1	
c) 40 C = A * B	1	1	1
d) 60 NEXT B	1	2	1
e) 40 C = A * B	1	2	2
f) 70 NEXT A	2	2	2
g) 30 FOR B = 1 TO 2	2	1	2

FIGURE 8.4   **Tracing Program 8.6.**

long-term deposits (5, 10, 15, or 20 years). The interest rates it is contemplating are 8%, 10%, and 12%. The bank needs a program that will calculate the balances in these accounts.

Let's use the following variable names:

Input variable	Deposit	DEPOSIT
Internal variables	Interest rate	RATE
	Year counter	YEAR
Output variable	Balance	BALANCE

We can calculate the balance in the account using the compound interest formula:

$$BALANCE = DEPOSIT * (1 + RATE) \char`\^ YEAR$$

The algorithm for this problem is

1. Accept DEPOSIT.
2. Repeat steps 3 and 4 for YEAR equal to 5, 10, 15, and 20.
3. Repeat step 4 for RATE equal to 8%, 10%, and 12%.
4. Calculate and print BALANCE.
5. Stop execution.

Because the logic is so simple, pseudocode is more useful than a flowchart for this program. The pseudocode is

```
Calculate a Balance Table
INPUT DEPOSIT
IF DEPOSIT = 0 stop execution
FOR YEARS = 5, 10, 15, and 20
   FOR RATE = 8%, 10%, and 12%
      Calculate BALANCE using the compound interest formula
      Print BALANCE
   NEXT RATE
NEXT YEAR
```

Using a hand calculator and the compound interest formula, we find that $1000 deposited for 5 years at 10% interest grows to $1610.51.

Just a few of the statements in Program 8.7, which is based on this algorithm, require discussion. In line 160, we print the value of YEAR, so that each row in the table will be labeled with its year number. Lines 160 and 190, in which we print BALANCE, both use hanging semicolons. As noted earlier, if a print list ends with hanging punctuation, the next PRINT or PRINT USING statement executed continues printing on the same line. Using hanging semicolons in lines 160 and 190 causes YEAR and the three BALANCEs that belong to that YEAR to be printed on one line, generating a nice table. Hanging commas would work as well.

After YEAR and three BALANCEs have been printed on one line, you must escape from the hanging semicolon if the next YEAR and its three BALANCEs are to print on a new line. The PRINT statement in line 210 provides the escape from the hanging semicolon. Since no print list is associated with the PRINT statement in line 210, nothing is printed when it is executed. Since line 210 does not contain hanging punctuation, the next PRINT statement executed (line 160) will start a new line, which is exactly what we want.

```
100 REM *** PRINTING A BALANCE TABLE ***
110 INPUT "Enter Deposit, 0 to stop "; DEPOSIT
120    IF DEPOSIT = 0
          THEN GOTO 240
130    PRINT "                  Interest Rate"
140    PRINT "Year        8%             10%              12%"
150    FOR YEAR = 5 TO 20 STEP 5
160       PRINT USING " ##    ";YEAR;
170       FOR RATE = .08 TO .12 STEP .02
180          BALANCE = DEPOSIT * (1 + RATE) ^ YEAR
190          PRINT USING "##,###.##    ";BALANCE;
200       NEXT RATE
210       PRINT
220    NEXT YEAR
230 GOTO 110
240 END

RUN
Enter Deposit, 0 to stop ? 1000
              Interest Rate
Year        8%             10%             12%
  5     1,469.33      1,610.51      1,762.34
 10     2,158.93      2,593.74      3,105.85
 15     3,172.17      4,177.25      5,473.57
 20     4,660.96      6,727.50      9,646.29
Enter Deposit, 0 to stop ? 0
Ok
```

PROGRAM 8.7   **Program to print a balance table for Common Cents Savings and Loan Company.**

EXERCISES

*8.9 Correct the error in the following program and then determine the output it will produce.

```
10 FOR J = 3 TO 5
20    FOR K = 1 to 3
30       P = J + K
40          PRINT P
50    NEXT J
60 NEXT K
70 END
```

8.10 What output is produced by the following program?

```
10 FOR A = 1 TO 2
20    FOR B = 3 TO 1 STEP -1
30       C = A * B
40          PRINT C
50    NEXT B
60 NEXT A
70 END
```

PROGRAMMING ASSIGNMENTS

8.12 Every year, Harriet Stowe DEPOSITs a certain amount of money at a given interest RATE. At the end of NO.YEARS, the TOTAL in Harriet's account can be calculated by the equation

```
TOTAL = DEPOSIT * ((1 + RATE) ^
        NO.YEARS - 1) / RATE
```

Write a program that will accept DEPOSIT and print TOTAL after 5, 10, 15, and 20 years for RATEs of 10%, 12%, and 14%.

8.13 The song "The Twelve Days of Christmas" speaks of the gifts "my true love gave to me." On the first day, the singer got a partridge in a pear tree; on the second day, two turtle doves and a partridge in a pear tree, for a total of three gifts; on the third day, three French hens, two turtle doves, and a partridge in a pear tree, for a total of six gifts; and so on. Write a program to determine the total number of gifts received in twelve days.

*8.14 The relative damage done by an earthquake that measures RICHTER on the Richter scale at DISTANCE miles from the center of the earthquake can be calculated by the equation

$$\text{DAMAGE} = \frac{0.8 * \text{RICHTER} \wedge 3}{\text{DISTANCE} \wedge 2}$$

Write a program that will print a table of DAMAGE values for RICHTER equal to 4, 5, 6, 7, and 8 and distances of 5, 10, 15, and 20 miles.

8.15 The cost of running an air conditioner depends on the temperature and humidity in the following way:

$$\text{COST} = \frac{1.5 * (\text{TEMPERATURE} - 70)}{(120 - \text{HUMIDITY}) \wedge .5}$$

Write a program that will print a table of COSTs for TEMPERATUREs of 70, 80, 90, and 100 degrees and HUMIDITY levels of 60, 70, 80, 90, and 100. If your program is correct, you should find that at 80 degrees and 70 percent humidity the cost is $2.12.

SEARCHING FOR A SOLUTION

In some problems, we can use a FOR-NEXT loop to search for a solution. Consider this problem. The Happy Heifer hamburger stand is trying to decide on the best price for its hamburgers. A consultant has told the company that the relationship between the price of hamburgers and the number sold can be calculated by the equation

$$\text{Sales} = \frac{550}{\text{Price}^2 + .2}$$

Happy Heifer wants you to write a program using this equation to find the price it should charge to maximize its profit. Happy Heifer defines profit as

Profit = Sales (Price per hamburger − Cost per hamburger)

In keeping with the first step of our structured approach, you should assign names to the variables. Let's use the following:

Input variable	Cost per hamburger	COST
Internal variables	Number of hamburgers sold	SALES
	Price per hamburger	PRICE
	Profit	PROFIT
Output variables	Price that maximizes profit	BEST.PRICE
	Highest profit	HIGHEST.PROFIT

The second step of our structured approach calls for you to develop an algorithm to solve the problem. Let's use the following:

1. Initialize HIGHEST.PROFIT to 0.
2. Accept COST.
3. Repeat steps 3 through 6 for each PRICE in the range
   COST + .01 to 2.00.
4. Calculate SALES.
5. Calculate PROFIT.
6. If this PROFIT is higher than HIGHEST.PROFIT, set
   HIGHEST.PROFIT equal to PROFIT and BEST.PRICE equal to
   PRICE. Otherwise, do nothing.
7. Print HIGHEST.PROFIT and BEST.PRICE.
8. Stop execution.

As you can see, this search for the best price involves trying each price in the range of interest and "remembering" the price that gave the highest profit. Notice that in step 3 of this algorithm the search starts at a price only one cent above the cost and stops at two dollars. The two-dollar maximum is arbitrary; if the program showed that the best price is two dollars, that would be an indication that the search might have stopped at too low a price and that prices above two dollars should be examined.

Although the next step in our structured approach calls for you to calculate answers by hand, in this case you can let the computer do some of the work for you. Program 8.8 shows that BASIC found $1.08 to be the best price and $253.59 to be the highest profit. To check the accuracy of the program, you need only temporarily insert between lines 150 and 160 a debugging statement to print PRICE, SALES, and PROFIT. By checking the arithmetic on any one calculation, you can be sure that SALES and PROFIT are calculated correctly. The easiest way to verify that HIGHEST.PROFIT is calculated correctly is to execute the program with the debugging PRINT statement in place and with the final value of the FOR statement changed to COST + .05. By inspecting the limited output, you can see if the HIGHEST.PROFIT printed is indeed the highest profit found. If it is, you can delete the debugging

```
100 REM *** BEST PRICE FOR HAMBURGERS ***
110 INPUT "Enter the cost of a hamburger"; COST
120 HIGHEST.PROFIT = 0
130 FOR PRICE = COST + .01 TO 2 STEP .01
140    SALES = 550 / (PRICE ^ 2 + .2)
150    PROFIT = SALES * (PRICE - COST)
160    IF PROFIT > HIGHEST.PROFIT
          THEN HIGHEST.PROFIT = PROFIT: BEST.PRICE = PRICE
170 NEXT PRICE
180 PRINT USING "The highest profit is $###.##, which occurs at price $#.##";
              HIGHEST.PROFIT, BEST.PRICE
190 END

RUN
Enter the cost of a hamburger? .45
The highest profit is $253.59, which occurs at price $1.08
Ok
```

PROGRAM 8.8   **Program to find the best hamburger price for the Happy Heifer.**

PRINT statement, change the final value of the FOR statement back to 2, and run the program again.

Using Nested Loops to Search for a Solution

Sometimes you will have to use nested loops to search for a solution, as in the following problem. Dee Posit cashed a check that was drawn for less than $100. The teller accidentally gave her as many dollars as there should have been cents and as many cents as there should have been dollars. Ms. Posit spent 68 cents and then noticed that she had twice as much money as the check was written for. What was the original amount of the check?

Let's use the following variable names:

Internal variables	The number of dollars the check was written for	DOLLARS
	The number of cents the check was written for	CENTS
	The amount paid by the teller	PAID.BY.TELLER
	The amount left after spending 68 cents	AMOUNT.LEFT
Output variable	The amount of the check	AMOUNT.OF.CHECK

The algorithm we can use is

1. Repeat steps 2 through 4 for each DOLLARS in the range 1 through 99.
2. Repeat steps 3 and 4 for each CENTS in the range DOLLARS through 99.
3. Calculate AMOUNT.OF.CHECK, PAID.BY.TELLER, and AMOUNT.LEFT.
4. If AMOUNT.LEFT is two times AMOUNT.OF.CHECK, print AMOUNT.OF.CHECK and go to step 5.
5. Stop execution.

The logic behind this algorithm is straightforward: We simply try every possible amount until we find the one that solves the problem. The only point that is a little subtle occurs in step 2, where the starting value for CENTS is DOLLARS instead of 0 as you might have anticipated. Since after the mixup Ms. Posit had more money than she should have had, we know that the CENTS she should have received must have been greater than DOLLARS. Note, though, that if we started CENTS at 0 instead of at DOLLARS, the program would merely take a little longer to find the solution.

Program 8.9 shows a BASIC version of this algorithm. You may wonder about the purpose of line 120. Searching for a solution may take a long time, and it is disconcerting to stare at the screen while nothing seems to be happening. Printing a message each time a new value of DOLLAR is examined lets you know that the program is working and how far it has progressed in its task.

Also notice lines 140 and 170. When doing the calculations, it is convenient to express the amount in pennies. For example, when we calculate the

```
100 REM *** MIXED-UP CHECK PROBLEM ***
110 FOR DOLLARS = 1 TO 99
120   PRINT USING "Now trying ### dollars"; DOLLARS
130   FOR CENTS = DOLLARS TO 99
140     AMOUNT.OF.CHECK = 100 * DOLLARS + CENTS
150     PAID.BY.TELLER = 100 * CENTS + DOLLARS
160     AMOUNT.LEFT = PAID.BY.TELLER - 68
170     IF AMOUNT.LEFT = 2 * AMOUNT.OF.CHECK
           THEN PRINT USING "Check was for $###.##"; AMOUNT.OF.CHECK / 100:
               GOTO 200
180   NEXT CENTS
190 NEXT DOLLARS
200 END

RUN
Now trying    1 dollars
Now trying    2 dollars
Now trying    3 dollars
Now trying    4 dollars
Now trying    5 dollars
Now trying    6 dollars
Now trying    7 dollars
Now trying    8 dollars
Now trying    9 dollars
Now trying   10 dollars
Check was for $ 10.21
Ok
```

PROGRAM 8.9   **Using nested FOR-NEXT loops to search for a solution.**

amount of the check in line 140, we write 100 * DOLLARS + CENTS. However, we want to print the amount of the check in dollars and cents, so in line 170 we divide AMOUNT.OF.CHECK by 100.

EXERCISES

8.11 If Program 8.8 were modified so that the highest price examined were $1.00 instead of $2.00, what price do you think would be selected as the best price?

8.12 Even though they both contain an IF statement, the structures of Programs 8.8 and 8.9 are quite different. In Program 8.9, the first time the IF statement is true, we print the answer and exit from the loop.

In Program 8.8, no matter how many times the IF statement is true, the complete FOR-NEXT loop is executed and then the answer is printed. Explain why.

8.13 Program 8.10 shows the execution of a program that is supposed to accept an integer, N, and print the sum 1 + 2 + ... + N. Something is wrong, since the answer printed, 25, should be 15. Find and correct the error.

PROGRAMMING ASSIGNMENTS

*8.16 John Silver was swimming one day and found a treasure map. The map must have been drawn by a mathematically inclined pirate, because it says

that to find the treasure you must start at the hanging tree and walk north by northwest a certain number of feet. The number of feet is such

```
100  REM CALCULATING THE SUM OF THE FIRST N INTEGERS
110  INPUT "Enter the final number, 0 to stop"; N
120  SUM = 0
130    IF N = 0
            THEN GOTO 190
140    FOR J = 1 TO N
150      SUM = SUM + N
160    NEXT J
170   PRINT "The sum from 1 to"; N; "is"; SUM
180  GOTO 110
190  END

RUN
Enter the final number, 0 to stop? 5
The sum from 1 to 5 is 25
Enter the final number, 0 to stop? 0
Ok
```

PROGRAM 8.10   **A program that is supposed to calculate the sum of the first N integers.**

that when it is divided by 5 it gives a remainder of 4, when it is divided by 6 it gives a remainder of 5, and when it is divided by 7 it gives a remainder of 6. John knows that the distance must be less than 300 feet, because at 300 feet you arrive at the water. Write a program to help John find the treasure. (Hint: Remember that the MOD operator gives the remainder.)

8.17 A company that manufactures tin cans wants to make cans that use the least amount of metal while having a specified volume. The volume of a cylindrical can is

$$V = 2\pi R^2 h$$

and the surface area (including the top and bottom) is

$$S = 2\pi(R^2 + Rh)$$

Write a program to find the R and h that give the minimum surface for volumes between 10 and 50. Search for the best R to the nearest .01 in the range between 1 and 2. Print R and h and their ratio. Examine your results and draw a conclusion about the best ratio of h to R. (Hint: Input V, and in a FOR-NEXT loop try different Rs. For each R use the volume (V) equation to calculate h and then use the surface area (S) equation to calculate S.)

8.18 Emma Nesiak is hopelessly absent-minded. She spent half her money and then lost $1. She spent half of what she had left, then lost $2. She once more spent half of what she had left and then lost $3. At that time, she had $1 left. If she never broke a bill and started with less than $100, how much did she start with?

*8.19 Three sailors were shipwrecked on a deserted island. They gathered less than 100 coconuts into a pile to share the next day. However, during the night one sailor secretly divided the pile into thirds and found one coconut left over, which he gave to a friendly monkey. He then hid his share and went to sleep. Later the other two sailors did the same thing, each one finding one coconut left over when the pile was divided into thirds and giving it to the monkey. The next morning, all three sailors divided the pile into thirds and found one coconut left over, which they again gave to the monkey. How big was the original pile?

8.20 Chuck Wagoner wants to fence a cattle pen along a river, as shown below. He has 100 feet of fencing, so the depth and length have the relationships shown on the drawing. If he wants the pen to have the maximum area, what should the depth be?

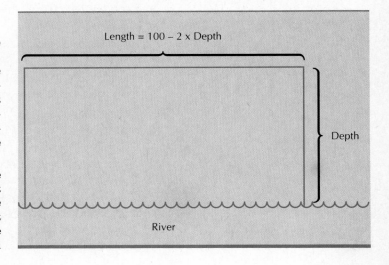

8.21 You have just driven to the Tradewinds Shopping Mall and are looking for a place to park. The mall is not crowded, so you can park anywhere you like along the line shown below. You want to visit Pig in a Poke and Cash and Carry. Where should you park to minimize the total distance you have to walk? Use the formulas

$$L1 = (40^2 + Parking^2)^{1/2}$$

and

$$L2 = (20^2 + (100 - Parking)^2)^{1/2}$$

to figure the distances to Pig in a Poke and Cash and Carry, respectively. (Hint: No matter where you park, you will have to walk from one store to the other, so that distance doesn't enter into the calculation of the best parking position.)

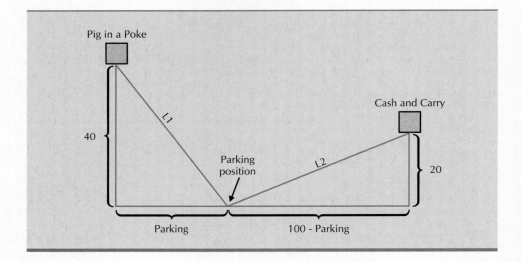

 SUMMARY

In this chapter you have learned that

☐ Loops that are executed a specified number of times are called counter-controlled loops.

☐ The FOR and NEXT statements are used to create counter-controlled loops.

☐ The STEP clause is used to set step sizes other than 1.

☐ Each time a FOR-NEXT loop is executed, the last statement executed must be the NEXT statement.

☐ You must never branch into a FOR-NEXT loop; the loop must always be started by executing the FOR statement.

☐ Once inside a FOR-NEXT loop, you must not change the values of the starting value, the final value, or the step size.

☐ Instead of using trailer data, the number of cases to be processed can be entered as header data. The header data are used as the final value in a FOR statement.

☐ When two FOR-NEXT loops are separate, they are said to be independent. Independent loops may use the same counter variables.

☐ In nested FOR-NEXT loops, the inner loop must be completely inside the outer loop. Nested loops must use different counter variables.

KEY TERMS IN THIS CHAPTER

counter-controlled loops 207   header data 216
independent loops 219   nested loops 219

QUESTIONS FOR REVIEW

8.1 When nested FOR-NEXT loops are used, is it necessary that the loops use the same or different variables for their counter variables?

8.2 Is the following a valid FOR statement?

        FOR Z = 25 TO 35 STEP .1

8.3 Name the three steps that every counter-controlled loop must contain.

8.4 To have a FOR-NEXT loop work properly, if the step size is positive, must the final value be greater or less than the starting value? If the step size is negative, must the final value be greater or less than the starting value?

8.5 What step size is used if the STEP clause is omitted?

8.6 How many times will the following loop be executed?

        10 FOR P = 16 TO 7
        20 NEXT P
        30 END

8.7 When you write a FOR statement, which of the following 1) must be a variable; 2) must be a constant; or 3) may be either a variable or a constant?

    a) counter variable
    b) starting value
    c) ending value
    d) step size

8.8 What errors would you look for if, during execution of a program, BASIC displayed the error message NEXT without FOR?

ADDITIONAL PROGRAMMING ASSIGNMENTS

*8.22 Write a program that accepts an integer, N, and if N is odd calculates and prints the sum 1 + 3 + 5 + . . . + N, and if N is even calculates and prints the sum 2 + 4 + 6 + . . . + N.

8.23 The series of numbers

$$1, 1, 2, 3, 5, 8, 13, \ldots$$

is known as the Fibonacci series. The first two terms in this series are 1, and the remaining terms are calculated by adding the preceding two terms. For example, 2 = 1 + 1, and 3 = 2 + 1. Write a program that prints the first 25 terms in the Fibonacci series.

8.24 In an ancient Chinese tale, a man who saved the emperor's life was told he could ask anything for a reward. He requested a checkerboard. He then asked that one grain of rice be placed on the first square, two grains on the second square, four grains on the third square, and so on, doubling the number of grains on each square. There are 64 squares on a checkerboard. Write a program that will determine how many grains of rice were put on the last square and how many grains altogether.

8.25 Write a program that uses the SOUND statement to generate tones with frequencies between 220 and 880 hertz in steps of 20 hertz. Hold each tone for 0.1 second. Generate an ascending series of tones, followed by a descending series, then repeat the whole process three times.

8.26 Write a program to test students' mastery of multiplication tables. The program should accept a number and then ask the student to enter the product of that number and 1, that number and 2, on through the product of that number and 12. The program should print a message telling the student whether the answer was right or wrong. The program should also keep track of how many problems were right and how many were wrong. When the table is finished, the number right and the number wrong should be printed.

BEYOND THE BASICS

8.1 The Slice of Life Pizza Parlor sells plain cheese pizza for $9.00. For additional toppings, its charges are as follows: mushrooms, $.50; anchovies, $.75; sausage, $1.25; and pepperoni, $1.50. Write a program that will produce the following cost table:

PEPPERONI	SAUSAGE	ANCHOVIES	MUSHROOMS	PRICE
NO	NO	NO	NO	9.00
NO	NO	NO	YES	9.50
NO	NO	YES	NO	9.75
NO	NO	YES	YES	10.25
NO	YES	NO	NO	10.25
NO	YES	NO	YES	10.75
NO	YES	YES	NO	11.00
NO	YES	YES	YES	11.50
YES	NO	NO	NO	10.50
YES	NO	NO	YES	11.00
YES	NO	YES	NO	11.25
YES	NO	YES	YES	11.75
YES	YES	NO	NO	11.75
YES	YES	NO	YES	12.25
YES	YES	YES	NO	12.50
YES	YES	YES	YES	13.00

8.2 A number, N, is classified as being deficient, perfect, or abundant depending on whether the sum of the divisors of N is less than, equal to, or greater than N. In summing the divisors, 1 is included, but N itself is not. For example, the divisors of 4 are 1 and 2, and since 1 + 2 = 3, 4 is a deficient number. The divisors of 6 are 1, 2, and 3, and since 1 + 2 + 3 = 6, 6 is a perfect number. The divisors of 12 are 1, 2, 3, 4, and 6, and since 1 + 2 + 3 + 4 + 6 = 16, 12 is an abundant number. Write a program that accepts a number and determines and prints its classification.

8.3 Write a program that prints a big triangle made up of asterisks. The triangle should consist of 22 rows: the first row should contain 1 asterisk, the second row 3 asterisks, the third row 5 asterisks, and so on. The first row should be printed in the top row on the screen, starting in column 40. The second row should be printed in the second row on the screen, starting in column 39, and so on.

8.4 You want to walk across some fields to visit a friend's house. You know that a straight line is the shortest distance between two points, but you want to minimize not the distance you walk, but the time it takes you. As shown below, you must first walk through a thicket (in which you can walk at only 2 miles per hour) and then a field (in which you can walk at 3 miles per hour). Find the POSITION to the nearest .01 mile that minimizes the total time of your trip. DISTANCE1, through the thicket, can be calculated as

$$\text{DISTANCE1} = (1^2 + \text{POSITION}^2)^{1/2}$$

DISTANCE2, through the field, can be calculated as

$$\text{DISTANCE2} = (2^2 + (1 - \text{POSITION})^2)^{1/2}$$

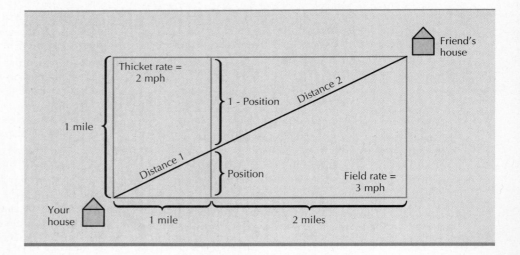

9

Numeric and String Functions

BASIC OBJECTIVES OF THIS CHAPTER

- ☐ To use BASIC's numeric and string functions
- ☐ To perform a simulation
- ☐ To use the BASIC statements RANDOMIZE, MID$, LINE INPUT, and DEF FN
- ☐ To use the BASIC numeric functions LOG, EXP, SQR, COS, SIN, TAN, ATN, SGN, ABS, FIX, INT, CINT, RND, and TIMER
- ☐ To use the BASIC string functions DATE$, TIME$, LEN, LEFT$, RIGHT$, MID$, INSTR, and STRING$

In earlier chapters, you learned how to use some BASIC functions. In this chapter, we will discuss a great many more, including numeric functions, string functions, and functions you define. You will learn how functions can be used to simulate a variety of systems, from casino games to the national economy.

NUMERIC FUNCTIONS

BASIC provides many numeric functions in addition to those we examined earlier. Table 9.1 lists the functions we will examine in this chapter.

◼ *The Exponentiation Functions*

Three functions, LOG, EXP, and SQR, are classified as exponentiation functions.

THE LOG AND EXP FUNCTIONS

The LOG function returns the natural logarithm of its argument, which must be greater than 0. The EXP function raises the mathematical constant e, 2.71828..., to the power of its argument, which must be less than 88.02969.

THE SQR FUNCTION

The SQR function returns the square root of its argument, as long as the argument is positive or zero. For example, SQR(16) is 4. (We could also calculate the square root by raising to the .5 power, as in 16 ^ .5, but the SQR function is about twice as fast.)

TABLE 9.1   **Numeric functions discussed in this chapter**

Function	Purpose
ABS(x)	Returns the absolute value of x.
ATN(x)	Returns the arctangent (in radians) of x.
CINT(x)	Rounds x to the nearest integer; x must be between −32,768 and 32,767.
COS(x)	Returns the cosine of angle x, where x is in radians.
EXP(x)	Raises e (2.71828...) to the x power; x must be less than 88.02969.
FIX(x)	Truncates x to an integer.
INT(x)	Returns the largest integer less than or equal to x.
LOG(x)	Returns the natural logarithm of x; x must be greater than 0.
RND	Returns a random number.
SGN(x)	Returns -1 if x is negative, 0 if x is 0, and +1 if x is positive.
SIN(x)	Returns the sine of angle x, where x is in radians.
SQR(x)	Returns the square root of x; x must be greater than or equal to 0.
TAN(x)	Returns the tangent of angle x, where x is in radians.
TIMER	Returns the time, in seconds, according to the computer's internal clock.

The Trigonometric Functions

The arguments of the trigonometric functions COS, SIN, and TAN must be in radians. To convert from degrees to radians, multiply the number of degrees by 0.01745329 (that is, $2\pi/360$). For example, if you want A to equal the sine of 30 degrees, you must code

$$A = SIN(30 * 0.01745329)$$

The ATN function returns the arctangent, in radians, of its argument. To convert from radians to degrees, multiply by 57.29578 (that is, $360/2\pi$). So if you want B to be the arctangent of 1, expressed in degrees, you must code

$$B = 57.29578 * ATN(1)$$

If you are not a math major, you may think you have no use for trigonometric functions. But as you will see in Chapter 14, such functions are important in creating graphics on your computer.

The Algebraic Functions

Five functions: SGN, ABS, FIX, INT, and CINT are classified as algebraic functions.

THE SGN FUNCTION

The SGN function is called the sign function. As Table 9.1 shows, if its argument is negative, the SGN function returns -1; if its argument is 0, it returns 0; and if its argument is positive, it returns +1.

THE ABS FUNCTION

The ABS function returns the absolute value of its argument. The absolute value is always positive or zero. For example, both ABS(5.5) and ABS(-5.5) equal 5.5. The ABS function is useful when you want to calculate the difference between two numbers but you do not know which is greater. That is, if you want to know the difference between M and N, the equation ABS(M - N) will give you the correct answer whether M is greater than, less than, or equal to N.

THE FIX FUNCTION

The FIX function discards digits to the right of the decimal point of its argument. For example, the statements

```
A = FIX(27.6)
B = FIX(-43.2)
```

assign the value 27 to A and -43 to B.

THE INT FUNCTION

The INT function returns the largest integer that is less than or equal to its argument. Thus, the statements

```
A = INT(27.6)
B = INT(-43.2)
```

assign the value 27 to A and -44 to B. Notice that for positive arguments, the FIX and INT functions return the same value.

When would you use the INT or FIX function? Suppose you wanted a user to enter an integer in response to an INPUT statement. Line 150 below determines whether INT(A) is equal to A. If it is, then A is an integer; if it is not equal, A is not an integer.

```
140 INPUT "Enter an integer"; A
150 IF INT(A) <> A
        THEN PRINT "Enter an integer please": GOTO 140
```

THE CINT FUNCTION

The CINT function rounds its argument to the nearest integer. For example, the statements

```
A = CINT(27.6)
B = CINT(-43.2)
```

assign the value 28 to A and -43 to B. Table 9.2 compares the FIX, INT, and CINT functions for both negative and positive arguments.

The RND Function

Random number
A number that cannot be predicted.

The RND function returns a **random number**, that is, a number that cannot be predicted. The RND function is used as follows:

```
A = RND
```

Notice that the RND function does not need an argument. The RND function returns a random number between 0 and 0.9999999. (Because 0.9999999 is so close to 1, for convenience we will often assume the upper limit is 1.) All the numbers between 0 and 0.9999999 are equally likely to be returned. For example, if you executed the preceding LET statement three times, A might be assigned the values 0.469215, 0.917527, and 0.361473. Another time A might be assigned three completely different values.

HOW THE RND FUNCTION WORKS

Before you can use the RND function, you should have a better understanding of how it works. Although our definition of the RND function said that it returns *unpredictable* random numbers, the numbers are not really totally unpredictable. In any one run, the first time the RND function is executed,

TABLE 9.2   **Comparing the FIX, INT, and CINT functions**

N	FIX(N)	INT(N)	CINT(N)
−9.3	−9	−10	−9
−9.5	−9	−10	−10
−9.7	−9	−10	−10
9.3	9	9	9
9.5	9	9	10
9.7	9	9	10

Random number seed
The number used to start generating a sequence of random numbers.

Random number generator
The mathematical function used to generate random numbers.

BASIC starts with a number, called the **random number seed**, and performs some involved mathematical operations on the seed to generate the first random number. The part of BASIC that does the involved mathematical operations is called the **random number generator**. The random number generator produces the second random number by operating on the first random number. Then it generates each succeeding random number by operating on the previous random number.

Because the random numbers generated depend on the seed used to generate the first random number, you need to know where BASIC gets the seed. When the RND function is used without an argument, it always starts with the same seed, and therefore it generates the same series of "random" numbers every time it is used. It may seem pointless to generate the same series of "random" numbers; if they are always the same, they are predictable and not random. However, when you are debugging a program you may find it easier to trace the program if the RND function returns the same series of "random" numbers.

THE RANDOMIZE STATEMENT

Once you have debugged a program you can use the RANDOMIZE statement, which causes the RND function to use a new seed, that is, the RANDOMIZE statement "reseeds" the random number generator. The simplest use of the RANDOMIZE statement is

```
RANDOMIZE
```

When BASIC executes this statement, the program halts, prints the prompt Random number seed (-32,768 to 32,767)?, and waits for the user to enter a number to be used as the random number seed. If you enter the same seed in two runs, BASIC will generate the same sequence of random numbers. To supply a "random" seed automatically, you can use the TIMER function:

```
RANDOMIZE TIMER
```

The TIMER function returns the time, according to the computer's internal clock, to the nearest hundredth of a second. TIMER thus returns one of hundreds of thousands of rapidly changing values. As a result, every time BASIC executes the program, it uses a different seed and generates a different, unpredictable sequence of random numbers.

The TIMER function can also be used on its own. For example, it can be used to determine how long a program takes to execute, as you will see in Programming Assignment 9.2.

You can also use the TIMER function to introduce a measured delay into a program. The statements

```
NOW = TIMER
WHILE TIMER < NOW + 5
WEND
```

will cause a five-second delay.

The "Guess the Number" Program

Now that you know how to generate truly random numbers, let's write an easy game program that uses numeric functions. In "Guess the Number," the program should randomly select an integer between 1 and 100, and a player should try to guess the integer. Each time the player enters a guess, the program should indicate whether the guess was correct, too high, or too low. If the player doesn't guess the integer in ten tries, the program should print the answer.

In keeping with our systematic procedure, we begin by choosing variable names.

Input variable	Number guessed	GUESS
Internal variables	Number to be guessed	NUMBER
	Counter for guesses	TRIAL

The algorithm we can use is

---

1. Assign to NUMBER a random integer between 1 and 100.
2. Repeat steps 3 through 5 10 times.
3. Accept GUESS.
4. If GUESS equals NUMBER, print a message and go to step 6.
5. If GUESS does not equal NUMBER, print the appropriate message, either Too high or Too low.
6. Ask whether the player wants to play again.

Much of this program, like many of the programs in this chapter, is so easily written that we can dispense with a flowchart. But step 1 poses a problem. You want to assign to NUMBER a random integer between 1 and 100, but the RND function returns a number between 0 and 0.9999999. To get integers in the range 1 to 100, you must first multiply the RND function by 100:

$$NUMBER = 100 * RND$$

Since RND returns a value between 0 and 0.9999999, NUMBER will have a value between 0 and 99.99999. Next use the INT function

$$NUMBER = INT(100 * RND)$$

Now NUMBER will have integer values between 0 and 99. Finally, to get NUMBER to the range 1 to 100, add 1, producing the statement

$$NUMBER = 1 + INT(100 * RND)$$

With this statement, NUMBER will have integer values between 1 and 100, and each integer is equally likely to be returned.

We can generalize this result. To get a variable, M, to have random integer values in the range A to B, use the statement

$$M = A + INT((B - A + 1) * RND)$$

Program 9.1 plays "Guess the Number." The RANDOMIZE statement in line 110 randomly reseeds the random number generator. Line 150 generates a random integer between 1 and 100. The FOR-NEXT loop in lines 160 through 200 keeps track of the number of guesses. In line 230, the INPUT$ function is used to determine if the player wants to play another game. In line 240, a response of Y or y causes the game to be replayed.

```
100 REM *** GUESS THE NUMBER GAME ***
110 RANDOMIZE TIMER
120 CLS: KEY OFF
130 PRINT "Guess the number between 1 and 100 the computer picked."
140 PRINT "You get 10 guesses - Good Luck!"
150 NUMBER = 1 + INT (100 * RND)
160 FOR TRIAL = 1 TO 10
170    INPUT "Guess "; GUESS
180    IF GUESS = NUMBER
          THEN PRINT "Congratulations, you took only ";TRIAL;"guesses":
             GOTO 220
190    IF GUESS > NUMBER
          THEN PRINT "Too high"
          ELSE PRINT "Too low"
200 NEXT TRIAL
210 PRINT "Sorry, you used 10 guesses.  The number was"; NUMBER
220 PRINT "Do you want to play again? (Y or N)"
230 RESPONSE$ = INPUT$(1)
240 IF RESPONSE$ = "Y" OR RESPONSE$ = "y"
       THEN GOTO 120
250 END

RUN
Guess the number between 1 and 100 the computer picked.
You get 10 guesses - Good Luck!
Guess ? 50
Too high
Guess ? 25
Too high
Guess ? 13
Too high
Guess ? 6
Congratulations, you took only  4 guesses
Do you want to play again? (Y or N)
Ok
```

PROGRAM 9.1   A program that plays "guess the number."

Syntax Summary

RANDOMIZE Statement
Form: `RANDOMIZE [expression]`
Example: RANDOMIZE TIMER
Interpretation: Initializes the random number generator. If
                expression is omitted, BASIC will pause and
                ask you to enter a seed. If you enter the
                same seed, the RND function will return the
                same series of random numbers. Coding TIMER,
                as in the example, uses the system time as
                the seed and causes RND to generate a series
                of unpredictable random numbers.

Getting the Bugs Out

Problem: During execution, BASIC displays the error message

`Illegal function call`

Reason: The argument of a SQR or LOG function was outside the acceptable limits.

Solution: Make sure the argument of the function is within the acceptable range: positive or zero for SQR and greater than zero for LOG.

Problem: During execution, BASIC displays the error message

Overflow

Reason: The argument of a CINT or EXP function was outside the acceptable range.

Solution: Make sure the argument of the function is within the acceptable range: −32,768 to 32,767 for CINT and less than 88.02969 for EXP.

EXERCISES

9.1 What value is assigned to A in each of the following statements?

```
   a)  A = SGN(-4)
   b)  A = ABS(-37.3)
  *c)  A = INT(17.9)
   d)  A = INT(-17.9)
  *e)  A = FIX(17.9)
   f)  A = FIX(-17.9)
   g)  A = CINT(17.9)
 h )  A = CINT(-17.9)
  *i)  A = SQR(36)
   j)  A = SQR(225)
```

9.2 Under what conditions will the following statements print the word EQUAL?

```
   a)  IF ABS(X - Y) = ABS(Y - X)
          THEN PRINT "EQUAL"
   b)  IF X - Y = ABS(X - Y)
          THEN PRINT "EQUAL"
```

9.3 Write the statements to calculate the following trigonometric functions:

a) The cosine of 30 degrees.
b) The tangent of 45 degrees.
c) The arctangent, in degrees, of 1.0.

9.4 a) Write a BASIC statement to generate random integers between 5 and 30.
  *b) Write a BASIC statement to generate random integers between 1 and 7.

9.5 What are the possible values of INT(RND)?

9.6 Modify Program 9.1 so that it prints You only have 5 guesses left after the user has entered the fifth wrong guess.

*9.7 Modify Program 9.1 so that, in addition to printing Too high and Too low, the program will also print You are getting close whenever the guess is within 5 of the number. (Hint: You will find the ABS function helpful.)

PROGRAMMING ASSIGNMENTS

*9.1 a) Write a program to help your kid brother improve his addition. The program should randomly select two integers between 1 and 10. For example, if the integers are 6 and 2, BASIC should print the message WHAT IS THE SUM OF 6 AND 2? The program should accept your brother's answer as input, check to see if his answer is correct, and print an appropriate message, either THAT'S RIGHT or SORRY, THE CORRECT ANSWER IS 8. Use a FOR-NEXT loop to propose 10 problems and keep track of how many problems are answered correctly. After all 10 problems have been an-

swered, print the number which were answered correctly.
b) Use the TIMER function to determine how long it took to enter the answer. If the correct answer is entered, print the elapsed time as well as the message THAT'S RIGHT. If the incorrect answer is entered, do not print the elapsed time.

9.2 The TIMER function may be used to determine how long a program or a part of a program takes to execute. At the beginning of the program, add a statement like START = TIMER, and at the end of the program add a statement like FINISH = TIMER. The difference FINISH - START gives the elapsed time in seconds. Use the TIMER function to verify that using the SQR function to calculate square roots is faster than raising to the .5 power. Use two FOR-NEXT loops to calculate the square roots of the integers between 1 and 1000. In one loop, use the SQR function; in the other, raise to the .5 power. Don't print the square roots; printing is so slow that it will swamp the differences in calculation.

9.3 In Programming Assignment 4.1, you used the compound interest equation to calculate the BALANCE after NO.YEARS of a DEPOSIT that earns interest RATE, if interest is compounded M times a year. If the interest is compounded continuously, the equation is

    BALANCE = DEPOSIT * EXP(NO.YEARS * RATE)

Write a program that accepts DEPOSIT, RATE, and NO.YEARS and calculates two BALANCEs: one assuming

quarterly compounding and one assuming continuous compounding.

9.4 In Program 7.3, we let the program find the NO.YEARS it takes for a DEPOSIT made annually at a given interest RATE to become $1 million. We could solve the equation for NO.YEARS and calculate it directly. The equation is

    NO.YEARS = LOG(1 + 1000000 * RATE / DEPOSIT)
                    / LOG(1 + RATE)

Write a program that accepts DEPOSIT and RATE and calculates NO.YEARS.

SIMULATION

Simulation Modeling the behavior of a system.	Numerical functions are also the basis for many simulation programs. **Simulation** programs attempt to recreate on a computer the behavior of a system. All kinds of systems may be simulated, for example, the national economy, telephone networks, and warehouse inventories.

Simulations allow users to experiment by varying particular factors and then studying the reaction of the system to those variations. Often it is possible to perform such experiments on a computer when it would be impossible, dangerous, or too expensive to perform the same experiment on the system itself. Simulations allow users to ask "What if" questions. For example, a computer simulation of the national economy can enable economists to ask, "What if taxes were cut 10%?" The telephone company can get the answer to "What if telephone traffic increased 20%?" You can ask, "What if I use my favorite system at a roulette table?"

 "Heads You Win"

Monte Carlo simulation A simulation that involves random elements.	Very often a simulation involves random factors; such simulations are called **Monte Carlo simulations**. As an example of a simple simulation, let's write a program that simulates tossing a coin 30 times. We can use the following variable names:

Internal variables	A random number between 0 and .9999999.	X
	A counter for the number of tosses.	TOSS
Output variables	The number of heads that came up.	HEADS
	The number of tails that came up.	TAILS

The algorithm we can use is

1. Initialize HEADS and TAILS to 0.
2. Repeat the following step 30 times.
3. If a head comes up, print an H and increment HEADS; otherwise, print a T and increment TAILS.
4. Print HEADS and TAILS.
5. Stop execution.

How do we decide whether the coin has come up heads or tails? A fair coin should come up heads about half the time and tails about half the time. Since half the numbers generated by the RND function are below .5 and half are above .5, we can consider any random number greater than .5 to mean that the coin came up heads, and any below .5 to mean that the coin came up tails.

This logic is implemented in line 150 of Program 9.2, which also shows two executions of the program. These two executions illustrate an important fact about random simulations: Although on the average we expect to get 15 heads and 15 tails, in any particular run we may get substantial deviations from the expected results. In Program 9.2, the first execution gave 18 heads and only 12 tails, while in the second execution we got 13 heads and 17 tails.

Since there is no one "correct" answer for this problem, how can we know that the program is correct? We could let the computer help us by temporarily inserting a print statement like the following:

155 PRINT X; HEADS; TAILS

We could then verify that when X was greater than .5, an H was printed and HEADS was incremented, and when X was less than .5, a T was printed and TAILS was incremented.

```
100 REM *** SIMULATING A COIN TOSS ***
110 RANDOMIZE TIMER
120 HEADS = 0: TAILS = 0
130 FOR TOSS = 1 TO 30
140   X = RND
150   IF X > .5
         THEN PRINT "H ";: HEADS = HEADS + 1
         ELSE PRINT "T ";: TAILS = TAILS + 1
160 NEXT TOSS
170 PRINT: PRINT USING "We have ## heads and ## tails"; HEADS, TAILS
180 END

RUN
T H H H H H H H T T T T H T T T H T H T H H H H H H T T H H T
We have 18 heads and 12 tails
Ok
RUN
T T H H T H T H T H T T H T T H H T T T H H T H T T T T H H T H
We have 13 heads and 17 tails
Ok
```

PROGRAM 9.2   **A program that simulates tossing a coin.**

In Program 9.2, only 30 cases are simulated. In other problems where many more cases are simulated, if you print all the values calculated for all the cases, you will be overwhelmed by output. In those situations, it is a good idea to use a small number of cases while you are debugging the program.

Alternatively, you can print periodically. The following statement:

```
IF TRIAL MOD 10 = 0
    THEN PRINT (any data you like)
```

prints every tenth trial.

▪ A Business Simulation

As a more practical application, consider the problem of Frank Furter. Every week Frank sells hot dogs at the local ball field. They cost him $.60 each, and he sells them for $1.25 each. His problem is to decide how many hot dogs to bring to a game. If he brings too few, he loses sales and profits, but if he brings too many, the unsold hot dogs must be thrown away, which also hurts his profits. (We will disregard the unappetizing possibility that Frank reheats the unsold hot dogs and sells them the next week.)

Based on past experience, Frank estimates that the demand for hot dogs is roughly as follows:

Number of hot dogs	Percent of the time
100	10
110	20
120	30
130	30
140	10
	100

As always, we begin by choosing variable names:

Internal variables	Number of hot dogs brought to game	SUPPLY
	Cost of hot dogs brought to game	COST
	Demand for hot dogs	DEMAND
	Revenue from selling hot dogs	REVENUE
	Profit in one game	PROFIT
	Total profit for all games at a particular SUPPLY	TOTAL.PROFIT
	Counter for the number of games	GAMES
	Random number between 0 and .9999999	X
	Average profit for all trials at a particular SUPPLY	AVERAGE.PROFIT

Output variables	Highest profit	`HIGHEST.PROFIT`
	Supply that gave the highest profit	`BEST.SUPPLY`

To determine the best `SUPPLY` for Frank to bring, we must simulate the operation of the hot dog stand. Thus, we will use the following algorithm:

1. Initialize `HIGHEST.PROFIT` to 0.
2. Repeat steps 3 through 9 for values of `SUPPLY` in the range of interest.
3. Calculate the `COST` of this `SUPPLY` of hot dogs.
4. Initialize `TOTAL.PROFIT` to 0.
5. Repeat steps 6 and 7 100 times.
6. Generate a random `DEMAND` according to the percentages given above.
7. Calculate the `REVENUE` and `PROFIT` and accumulate `PROFIT` into `TOTAL.PROFIT`.
8. Calculate the `AVERAGE.PROFIT` at this `SUPPLY`.
9. If this `AVERAGE.PROFIT` is higher than `HIGHEST.PROFIT`, set `HIGHEST.PROFIT` equal to `AVERAGE.PROFIT` and `BEST.SUPPLY` equal to `SUPPLY`. Otherwise, do nothing.
10. Print `HIGHEST.PROFIT` and `BEST.SUPPLY`.
11. Stop execution.

The idea behind this algorithm is to pick a value of `SUPPLY`, simulate bringing that `SUPPLY` to 100 games, and see what the `AVERAGE.PROFIT` would be. We then repeat the calculation for all the values of `SUPPLY` in which we are interested. Finally, we use the same technique to find the `HIGHEST.PROFIT` and the `SUPPLY` that gave that profit, as we did to find `HIGHEST.SALES` in Program 7.2.

You may wonder why we are using 100 as the number of games to simulate in step 5. In some situations, you may need to use complicated equations to determine the number of cases to try, but for this problem an intuitive approach suffices. Ten games are probably too few to give reliable answers. One thousand games would take too long to calculate. In essence, 100 seems both big enough to give reliable answers and small enough not to take too long.

If you have doubts about the number chosen, you can always run the program more than once and check for a difference in results. Keep in mind, though, that this problem does not need a mathematically exact answer, but rather a *useful* answer. After all, the whole calculation depends on Frank's estimate of the demand, which is not exact. It is pointless to carry out a calculation that is more accurate than the basic data on which the calculation is based.

THE PROGRAM

Program 9.3 shows an implementation of this algorithm. In line 130, we use a step size of 5, because we feel that finding the best `SUPPLY` to the nearest 5 hot dogs is as accurate as the estimates of `DEMAND` warrant.

If you think about it, you will realize that the number of hot dogs Frank can sell is the lower of `SUPPLY` and `DEMAND`. When `DEMAND` is less than `SUPPLY`,

```
100 REM *** SELLING HOT DOGS ***
110 RANDOMIZE TIMER
120 HIGHEST.PROFIT = 0
130 FOR SUPPLY = 100 TO 140 STEP 5
140    COST = .6 * SUPPLY
150    TOTAL.PROFIT = 0
160    FOR GAME = 1 TO 100
170       GOSUB 300                         'Generate random DEMAND
180       IF SUPPLY < DEMAND
             THEN REVENUE = 1.25 * SUPPLY
             ELSE REVENUE = 1.25 * DEMAND
190       PROFIT = REVENUE - COST
200       TOTAL.PROFIT = TOTAL.PROFIT + PROFIT
210    NEXT GAME
220    AVERAGE.PROFIT = TOTAL.PROFIT / 100
230    PRINT USING "With ### hot dogs, the average profit is ###.##";
                 SUPPLY, AVERAGE.PROFIT
240    IF AVERAGE.PROFIT > HIGHEST.PROFIT
          THEN HIGHEST.PROFIT = AVERAGE.PROFIT: BEST.SUPPLY = SUPPLY
250 NEXT SUPPLY
260 PRINT USING "The highest profit, $##.##, occurs at supply of ### hot dogs";
                 HIGHEST.PROFIT, BEST.SUPPLY
270 STOP
280 '
300 REM *** Routine to generate random DEMAND
310    X = RND
320    IF X >= 0 AND X < .1
          THEN DEMAND = 100: GOTO 370
330    IF X >= .1 AND X < .3
          THEN DEMAND = 110: GOTO 370
340    IF X >= .3 AND X < .6
          THEN DEMAND = 120: GOTO 370
350    IF X >= .6 AND X < .9
          THEN DEMAND = 130: GOTO 370
360    IF X >= .9 AND X < 1
          THEN DEMAND = 140: GOTO 370
370 RETURN
380 REM *** End of routine to generate random DEMAND
390 END


RUN
With 100 hot dogs, the average profit is  65.00
With 105 hot dogs, the average profit is  67.81
With 110 hot dogs, the average profit is  70.13
With 115 hot dogs, the average profit is  72.00
With 120 hot dogs, the average profit is  73.13
With 125 hot dogs, the average profit is  73.81
With 130 hot dogs, the average profit is  72.13
With 135 hot dogs, the average profit is  69.81
With 140 hot dogs, the average profit is  68.38
The highest profit, $73.81, occurs at supply of 125 hot dogs
Break in 270
Ok
```

PROGRAM 9.3   A program to calculate the best hot dog supply.

Frank can sell only DEMAND hot dogs, while if SUPPLY is less than DEMAND, he can sell only SUPPLY hot dogs. REVENUE is calculated according to this logic in line 180. The purpose of line 230 is to permit us to follow the progress of the calculation. The highest profit and the supply that gave it are printed in line 260.

The complicated part of the program appears in the subroutine beginning at line 300. Here we must calculate DEMAND according to Frank's estimates of the percentages. We have to relate the random number X to DEMAND. X will be in the range 0 to .9999999, with all values equally likely. Therefore, the percent of the time that X will be between two values, say a and b, is

$$\text{Percent} = 100 * (b - a)$$

For example, the percent of the time that X will be between .0 and .1 is

$$\text{Percent} = 100 * (.1 - 0) = 10\%$$

This equation lets us write line 320, knowing that it reflects the fact that 10 percent of the time DEMAND is 100. Similarly, we can determine that 20 percent of the time X will be between .1 and .3 and write line 330. We continue this way, assigning intervals of X to values of DEMAND, until the interval of X that ends at X = .9999999 is assigned to the last value of DEMAND.

The output shows that AVERAGE.PROFIT peaks when SUPPLY is 125 hot dogs. So 125 is the number of hot dogs Frank should bring to each game.

EXERCISES

9.8 What output would have been generated by Program 9.2 if the relational operator in line 150 had been < instead of >?

*9.9 On the average, what value will be printed for COUNTER when the following program is run?

```
10 RANDOMIZE TIMER
20 COUNTER = 0
30 FOR J = 1 TO 100
40    X = RND
50    IF X > .2 AND X < .7
          THEN COUNTER = COUNTER + 1
60 NEXT J
70 PRINT COUNTER
80 END
```

9.10 Someone might complain that in Program 9.3 we did not allow for the possibility that SUPPLY and DEMAND are equal. Explain why that is not true.

9.11 The following table shows the number of thwigs sold in a month. Write a subroutine to generate the variable SOLD that follows this pattern:

Number sold	Percent of the time
1000	20
2000	40
3000	40

PROGRAMMING ASSIGNMENTS

9.5 Write a program to play the following dice game. Two dice are thrown and your score is the higher number showing. If your score is a 5 or a 6, you win a dollar; otherwise, you lose a dollar. Start with $100, play 100 games, and print the amount of money you have left. Since a die may show any number from 1 to 6, you can simulate throwing a die by generating a random integer between 1 and

6. After 100 games, the original $100 should have grown to about $110.

9.6 Write a program that plays the carnival game Chuck-a-luck, which is played with three dice. You bet on a number, and the dice are tossed. If none of the dice show your number, you lose your bet. If one die shows your number, you win your bet. If two dice show your number, you win twice your bet, and if all three dice show your number, you win three times your bet. Your program should start the player out with $100 and ask how much she wants to bet and which number she wants to bet on. If a player tries to bet more than she has, print a message and bet all her money. At the end of each play, display the three numbers that came up and the player's current money. If the player is bankrupt, end the game; otherwise, ask if the player wants to play again.

*9.7 Diskettes have 40 tracks. To read the data on a track, the arm must move to position the read/write head over the track. Assuming that all tracks are equally likely to be read, write a program that will find the average number of tracks the arm must move for each read. Your answer should be near 13.3.

9.8 Write a program to play Sink the Sub. The program should place a submarine at a randomly chosen point on a grid in which X and Y run from 0 to 10. X runs east-west, with 0 being farthest west and 10 farthest east. Y runs north-south, with 0 being farthest south and 10 farthest north. Ask the player to enter the X and Y coordinates where the depth charge will be dropped. If the player enters the sub's coordinates, the sub is sunk, and the player wins. If the player misses the sub, have the program tell him in which direction he should move. For example, if YSUB = 5 and XSUB = 5, and the user guesses Y = 3, X = 7, the program should say Move North West. Give the user 5 tries, and if the sub is still not sunk, announce its position. (Hint: You can analyze the Y and X guesses separately. For example, if Y is less than YSUB, you can tell the player to move north, independent of whether the X guess is too low, too high, or correct.)

9.9 Plane Dealing Airlines serves chicken and beef dinners. Past experience shows that half of Plane Dealing's passengers order chicken and half order beef. Each plane carries 50 passengers, so it carries 25 of each kind of dinner. We can expect, however, that on some flights more than 25 passengers will want chicken, while on other flights more than 25 will want beef. Simulate 100 flights

to determine the percentage of passengers who will not receive their choice of dinner. (Hint: You'll need nested FOR-NEXT loops: the outer to simulate flights and the inner to simulate the passengers making their selections. Simulating the making of a selection is like simulating tossing a coin. You should find that about 5.8 percent of the passengers are disappointed.)

*9.10 Write a program to play an oil well investment game. With oil wells, you lose your investment 50 percent of the time, double it 40 percent of the time, and get a tenfold return 10 percent of the time. Start the player with $10,000 and ask how much the player wants to invest on this turn. Simulate the return made by an oil well and report the result to the player. Let the player stop the game at any time by entering 0 for the amount to be invested. If the player tries to invest more than there is left, print a message and invest all the money available.

9.11 The people at the Anything Doughs Bakery would like some help determining the number of cakes they should bake for the weekend. Their past experience shows that the demand for cakes is as follows:

Number of cakes	Percent of the time
30	10
35	25
40	25
45	20
50	20

Assume that cakes cost $4 each to make and that they sell for $8 each. Also assume that any cakes not sold must be thrown away. Write a program to find the best number of cakes to bake.

STRING FUNCTIONS

So far in this chapter, we have considered only numeric functions, but BASIC also provides a number of string-related functions. Table 9.3 lists the string functions we will explore in this chapter. As you can see, some of the functions listed return a string, while others return a number.

TABLE 9.3   **String functions discussed in this chapter**

Function	Purpose
DATE$	Returns the date, in the form mm-dd-yyyy.
INSTR(n, x$, y$)	Returns the position of y$ in x$. n specifies the position in x$ where the search is to begin.
LEN(x$)	Returns the length of x$.
LEFT$(x$, n)	Returns the n leftmost characters of x$.
MID$(x$, n, m)	Returns m characters of x$ starting with the nth character.
RIGHT$(x$, n)	Returns the n rightmost characters of x$.
STRING$(n, x$)	Returns a string of n characters, all consisting of the first character of x$.
STRING$(n, m)	Returns a string of n characters, all consisting of the character whose ASCII code is m.
TIME$	Returns the time of day, in the form hh:mm:ss.

The DATE$ and TIME$ Functions

The DATE$ function returns the date obtained from the system. For example, on March 21, 1991, the statement

```
PRINT DATE$
```

would print 03-21-1991.

Similarly, the TIME$ function returns the time obtained from the computer's internal clock. For example, at 10:53:07 p.m., the statement

```
PRINT TIME$
```

would print 22:53:07 (remember that BASIC uses a 24-hour clock). Thus, you might use the DATE$ and TIME$ functions to print the date and time on a report or letter.

As noted in Chapter 1, some computers have a built-in clock calendar, so they automatically know the date and time. Other computers require you to enter the date and time when you are in DOS. As an alternative, you can set these values in BASIC. For example, you can set the date 3/21/91 and the time 10:53:07 p.m. by coding

```
DATE$ = "3-21-91"
TIME$ = "22:53:07"
```

The STRING$ Function

The STRING$ function has two forms that produce the same results. The statement

```
ASTERISKS$ = STRING$(30, "*")
```

assigns 30 asterisks to the variable ASTERISKS$. You can achieve the same result with the statement

```
ASTERISKS$ = STRING$(30, 42)
```

because the ASCII code for an asterisk is 42.

■ *The LEN Function*

In the LET statement,

$$P = LEN(A\$)$$

LEN stands for "length." This statement assigns to the variable P the number of characters in the string variable A\$. So if A\$ = "HELLO, I MUST BE GOING", then P would be 22, because the comma and the spaces count as characters, but the quotation marks do not. Notice that since the LEN function returns a number, the variable on the left side of the equal sign must be a numeric variable.

We will use the LEN function many times later in this chapter. For now, let's consider a simple application of it. If you are printing a report and want to center the title on a line 65 characters long, you could code the following statement:

$$PRINT\ SPC((65\ -\ LEN(TITLE\$))\ \backslash\ 2);\ TITLE\$$$

In this case, the argument of the SPC function is the number of blanks that should be printed before the title, calculated as half the difference between 65 and the length of TITLE\$.

The argument of the LEN function may also be a **string expression**, which is the string equivalent of a numeric expression. Just as the result of evaluating a numeric expression is a number, so the result of evaluating a string expression is a string.

String expression
A combination of string variables, constants, and functions and the concatenation operator that evaluates to a string.

■ *The SUBSTRING Functions*

Three functions, LEFT\$, RIGHT\$, and MID\$, are used to extract parts of a string. When you extract part of a string, you create what is known as a **substring**. Let's consider first the LEFT\$ function.

Substring
Part of a string.

THE LEFT\$ FUNCTION
Using the LEFT\$ function, the statement

$$B\$ = LEFT\$(A\$, 3)$$

causes 3 characters of A\$, starting from the left (that's how the function gets its name), to be assigned to B\$. So if A\$ were equal to ORANGE, B\$ would be equal to ORA. Notice that the LEFT\$ function requires two arguments, which must be separated by a comma. The first argument is the string from which a substring is to be extracted, and the second argument is the number of characters of the first argument that are to be extracted. Since LEFT\$ returns a string, the variable on the left of the equal sign must be a string variable.

THE RIGHT\$ FUNCTION
The RIGHT\$ function is similar to the LEFT\$ function, except that it extracts characters starting from the right. So if A\$ were equal to ORANGE, the statement

$$B\$ = RIGHT\$(A\$, 3)$$

would cause B\$ to be assigned the string NGE.

To get a better feel for how the LEFT\$ and RIGHT\$ functions work, look at Program 9.4. We start by setting ANIMAL\$ equal to HIPPOPOTAMUS and L equal to the length of ANIMAL\$. Then, in the FOR-NEXT loop, when J is 1, the program

```
10 REM *** DEMONSTRATING THE LEFT$ AND RIGHT FUNCTIONS ***
20 PRINT "LEFT PART",, "RIGHT PART"
30 ANIMAL$ = "HIPPOPOTAMUS"
40 L = LEN(ANIMAL$)
50 FOR J = 1 TO L
60   LEFT.PART$ = LEFT$(ANIMAL$,J)
70   RIGHT.PART$ = RIGHT$(ANIMAL$,J)
80   PRINT LEFT.PART$,, RIGHT.PART$
90 NEXT J
100 END


RUN
LEFT PART                       RIGHT PART
H                               S
HI                              US
HIP                             MUS
HIPP                            AMUS
HIPPO                           TAMUS
HIPPOP                          OTAMUS
HIPPOPO                         POTAMUS
HIPPOPOT                        OPOTAMUS
HIPPOPOTA                       POPOTAMUS
HIPPOPOTAM                      PPOPOTAMUS
HIPPOPOTAMU                     IPPOPOTAMUS
HIPPOPOTAMUS                    HIPPOPOTAMUS
Ok
```

PROGRAM 9.4   **Demonstrating the LEFT$ and RIGHT$ functions.**

extracts and prints the first and last letter of ANIMAL$. When J is 2, it extracts and prints the first and last 2 letters of ANIMAL$. This continues until J is finally equal to L, when the program extracts and prints all the characters of ANIMAL$.

THE MID$ FUNCTION

Finally, the MID$ function extracts substrings from the middle of a string. For example, if A$ = "ORANGE",

$$B\$ = MID\$(A, 2, 3)$$

tells BASIC to start extracting at the second character of A$ and to extract 3 characters. Therefore, B$ equals RAN. Note that if you omit the last argument, for example,

$$B\$ = MID\$(A\$, 2)$$

all the characters starting with the second will be assigned to B$—in this case, RANGE.

The MID$ function is the most powerful string-extraction function because it can be used to perform the same functions as LEFT$ and RIGHT$. If MID$ is used with a starting position of 1, it functions exactly like the LEFT$ function. In other words, the statement

$$B\$ = LEFT\$(A\$, N)$$

is equivalent to

$$B\$ = MID\$(A\$, 1, N)$$

Similarly, the statement

```
B$ = RIGHT$(A$, N)
```

is equivalent to

```
L = LEN(A$)
B$ = MID$(A$, L - N + 1)
```

In fact, we can write these last two statements together as one more complicated statement:

```
B$ = MID$(A$, LEN(A$) - N + 1)
```

THE MID$ STATEMENT

Besides being used as a function, MID$ can also be used as a statement, that is, it can be used on the left side of an equal sign in a LET statement. The first argument of the MID$ statement is the string in which characters are to be replaced. The second argument specifies the position at which replacement is to start, and the third argument specifies the number of characters to be replaced.

Program 9.5 uses the MID$ statement to replace the hyphens the DATE$ function returns with slashes. Line 30 replaces the hyphen in position 3 with a slash, and line 40 replaces the hyphen in position 6 with a slash.

The INSTR Function

The INSTR function searches for the appearance of one string in another. For example, if A$ = STRING PROCESSING, the statement

```
J = INSTR(1, A$, "R")
```

causes A$ to be searched, starting from position 1, for the string R. Since R appears in position 3 of A$, J is set equal to 3. Notice that the second R is ignored. INSTR stops searching as soon as it finds an R. This statement could also have been coded as

```
J = INSTR(A$, "R")
```

because if the first argument is not coded, BASIC automatically starts searching from position 1.

Next consider the statement

```
J = INSTR(6, A$, "R")
```

```
10 REM *** USING THE MID$ STATEMENT TO PRINT THE DATE ***
20 TODAY$ = DATE$
30 MID$(TODAY$,3,1) = "/"
40 MID$(TODAY$,6,1) = "/"
50 PRINT TODAY$
60 END

RUN
03/21/1991
Ok
```

PROGRAM 9.5   Using the MID$ statement to print the date.

This statement sets J to 9 because BASIC starts it search from position 6. Notice that J is the position of the R measured from the start of A$, not from the starting position of the search.

When INSTR does not find the string it is searching for, it returns a zero. So, for example, the statement

$$J = INSTR(11, A\$, "R")$$

sets J equal to 0, because no R appears in A$ after the starting position, 11.

The INSTR function can also search for the appearance of strings of more than one character. Thus, the statement

$$J = INSTR(A\$, "RING")$$

sets J equal to 3. Notice that J is set equal to the position in A$ where RING *starts*.

The INSTR function offers a convenient way to validate input data. Program 9.6 shows a modification of the Sound Value billing program from Chapter 5 (Program 5.4). That program requested users to enter J, K, L, M, or Q and used a case structure to detect invalid data. An alternative would be to use the INSTR functions, as shown in line 120 in Program 9.6. In this line, BASIC searches the string "JKLMQ" for whatever value CODE$ has. If CODE$ is not J, K, L, M, or Q, then VALID will be set to 0. When VALID is tested in line 130, BASIC BEEPS, prints the error message, and branches to line 110 to get a new value for CODE$. If VALID is not 0, BASIC falls through the IF statement and arrives at line 140. We know when we get to line 140 that CODE$ must contain a valid value, so in the rest of the program we don't have to worry about trapping invalid values.

As a further refinement, VALID allows us to use an ON-GOTO statement to code the case structure. Notice that in line 120 if CODE$ were J, then VALID would be 1; if CODE$ were K, VALID would be 2, and so on. Based on these observations, line 140 shows how one ON-GOTO statement implements the case structure that in Program 5.4 requires four IF statements.

Before proceeding, make sure you understand the following examples of string functions:

Statement

X = LEN("STARLIGHT")

```
100 REM *** SOUND VALUE BILLING PROGRAM USING INSTR ***
110 INPUT "Enter code, J, K, L or M, and number, Q to quit"; CODE$, NUMBER
120    VALID = INSTR("JKLMQ", CODE$)
130    IF VALID = 0
          THEN BEEP: PRINT "Valid codes are J, K, L, M, or Q": GOTO 110
140    ON VALID GOTO 150, 160, 170, 180, 220
150    PRICE = 9.99: GOTO 190
160    PRICE = 10.99: GOTO 190
170    PRICE = 12.99: GOTO 190
180    PRICE = 14.49: GOTO 190
190    BILL = PRICE * NUMBER
200    PRINT NUMBER; "code "; CODE$; " items at"; PRICE; "each total"; BILL
210 GOTO 110
220 END
```

PROGRAM 9.6   **Using INSTR to validate input data.**

Effect

X is 9, the number of characters in STARLIGHT.

Statement

X$ = STRING$(4, "STARLIGHT")

Effect

X$ is SSSS, the first character of STARLIGHT repeated 4 times.

Statement

X$ = STRING$(2, 36)

Effect

X$ is $$, 2 copies of the string whose ASCII code is 36.

Statement

X$ = LEFT$("STARLIGHT", 4)

Effect

X$ is STAR, the leftmost 4 characters of STARLIGHT.

Statement

X$ = RIGHT$("STARLIGHT", 5)

Effect

X$ is LIGHT, the rightmost 5 characters of STARLIGHT.

Statement

X$ = MID$("STARLIGHT", 5, 3)

Effect

X$ is LIG, the 3 characters of STARLIGHT starting with the 5th character.

Statement

X = INSTR(3, "STARLIGHT", "T")

Effect

X is 9, the position of T in STARLIGHT searching from the 3rd character.

Getting the Bugs Out

Problem: During execution, BASIC displays the error message

String too long

Reason: You generated a string that contained more characters than the maximum 255 that BASIC allows.

Solution: You probably made a mistake in a string expression. If your program really does require a string that is longer than 255 characters, you will have to modify your algorithm to stay within the 255-character limit.

EXERCISES

9.12 What is the value assigned to L in Program 9.4?

9.13 What is the value of B$ after the following statements are executed?

```
B$ = LEFT$("BANANA", 3)
B$ = RIGHT$("BANANA", 3)
```

*9.14 How would you modify Program 9.4 so that the results would be printed in reverse order? That is, the output on the left should be

```
HIPPOPOTAMUS
HIPPOPOTAMU
HIPPOPOTAM
     .
     .
     .
     H
```

9.15 Suppose that line 20 in Program 9.4 were changed to

```
20 ANIMAL$ = "GIRAFFE"
```

Consider that HIPPOPOTAMUS has twelve letters and GIRAFFE has only seven letters, would the program still work properly?

9.16 What is the value of W$ after each of the following statements is executed?

a) W$ = MID$("MISINFORMATION", 2, 3)
*b) W$ = MID$("MISINFORMATION", 3, 2)

c) W$ = MID$("MISINFORMATION", 4, 6)
d) W$ = MID$("MISINFORMATION", 6, 3)
*e) W$ = MID$("MISINFORMATION", 6, 9)
f) W$ = MID$("MISINFORMATION", 9, 4)
g) W$ = MID$("MISINFORMATION", 10, 2)
*h) W$ = MID$("MISINFORMATION", 13, 2)

9.17 If the initial value of A$ is TIN, what will its value be after each of the following statements is executed?

a) MID$(A$, 1, 1) = "S"
b) MID$(A$, 2, 1) = "A"
*c) MID$(A$, 2, 2) = "ED"

9.18 Determine the value of J after each of the following statements is executed:

a) J = INSTR(1, "ANTISEPTIC", "T")
*b) J = INSTR(4, "ANTISEPTIC", "T")
c) J = INSTR(9, "ANTISEPTIC", "T")
d) J = INSTR(1, "ANTISEPTIC", "PIC")
*e) J = INSTR(1, "ANTISEPTIC", "SEP")

9.19 What will the following statement print?

```
PRINT STRING$(13, 47)
```

9.20 If B$ = "LOOK" and F$ = "OUT", what will be the value of M$ after each of the following statements is executed?

a) M$ = B$ + F$
*b) M$ = F$ + B$

PROGRAMMING ASSIGNMENTS

9.12 Write a program using the MID$ function to create a "triangular" HIPPOPOTAMUS like the following:

```
     PO
    OPOT
   POPOTA
  PPOPOTAM
 IPPOPOTAMU
HIPPOPOTAMUS
```

(Be sure to center the "triangle" on the screen or page.)

9.13 Write a program that accepts string input of up to 80 characters and displays it right-justified, that is, so the last character is displayed in column 80.

*9.14 Write a program that accepts a word with up to 11 letters and prints the word down the screen,

with each letter separated from the next by two spaces.

9.15 You know that if in response to an INPUT prompt you enter a nonnumeric character for a numeric variable BASIC will display the infamous ?Redo from start error message. Nonprogrammers who see that message are likely to throw up their hands and turn the computer off. Write a polite program that accepts numeric data into a string and checks that the string contains only the digits 0 through 9. If the string contains any invalid character, print a *gentle* message asking the user to reenter the data correctly. (Your program will not be able to accept numbers that contain commas.)

USING STRING FUNCTIONS

Now that you understand string functions, let's use them to solve some interesting problems.

The Name Game

AKA, Inc. wants to read a name in the format

first-name space last-name

(for example, Mark Twain) and to print it in the format

last-name comma space first-name

(for example, Twain, Mark).

VARIABLES AND ALGORITHM

We begin, of course, by picking variable names. Let's use

Input variable	Name	NAME.IN$
Internal variables	Position of blank in NAME.IN$	BLANK.POS
Output variables	First name	FIRST.NAME$
	Last name	LAST.NAME$

To solve this problem, we will use the following algorithm:

1. Read NAME.IN$.
2. If this is the trailer data, stop.
3. Search NAME.IN$ for a blank.
4. If no blank is found, print an error message.
5. If a blank is found, extract the FIRST.NAME$ and LAST.NAME$ and print them.
6. Repeat steps 1 through 5 for all values of NAME.IN$.

Only steps 3 and 5 of this algorithm are complicated. We will discuss them in detail when we examine the program.

THE PROGRAM

This algorithm produced Program 9.7. Step 3 of the algorithm is carried out in line 150, where we use the INSTR function to search for a blank in NAME.IN$. In line 160 we determine whether BLANK.POS is 0. If it is, then a blank was not found, and NAME.IN$ is not in the correct format. We print an error message and go on to the next name.

```
100 REM *** REARRANGING NAMES ***
110 PRINT  "   First Last          Last, First"
120 FMT$ = "\                  \     \                    \"
130 READ NAME.IN$
140   IF NAME.IN$ = "FINISHED"
        THEN GOTO 190
150   BLANK.POS = INSTR(NAME.IN$," ")
160   IF BLANK.POS = 0
        THEN NAME.OUT$ = "No blank in name"
        ELSE GOSUB 300               'Extract first and last names
170   PRINT USING FMT$; NAME.IN$, NAME.OUT$
180 GOTO 130
190 STOP
200 '
300 REM *** Extract names routine
310   FIRST.NAME$ = LEFT$(NAME.IN$,BLANK.POS-1)
320   LAST.NAME$ = MID$(NAME.IN$,BLANK.POS+1)
330   NAME.OUT$ = LAST.NAME$ + ", " + FIRST.NAME$
340 RETURN
350 REM *** End of extract names routine
360 '
400 REM *** Data used in program
410 DATA "Mark Twain"
420 DATA "Lewis Carroll"
430 DATA "GeorgeSand"
440 DATA "Nelly Bly"
450 DATA "Isak Dinesen"
460 DATA FINISHED
470 END

RUN
   First Last            Last, First
Mark Twain            Twain, Mark
Lewis Carroll         Carroll, Lewis
GeorgeSand            No blank in name
Nelly Bly             Bly, Nelly
Isak Dinesen          Dinesen, Isak
Break in 190
Ok
```

PROGRAM 9.7   **A program to rearrange names.**

If BLANK.POS is not 0, we have found a blank. We must then implement step 5 of the algorithm and extract the first and last names from NAME.IN$, using the subroutine that starts at line 300. The statement

```
310 FIRST.NAME$ = LEFT$(NAME.IN$, BLANK.POS - 1)
```

extracts the first name from NAME.IN$. How does this statement work? Recall that when we execute this statement BLANK.POS is equal to the position of the blank in NAME.IN$. We call BLANK.POS a **pointer** because it points to the blank. For example, if NAME.IN$ were equal to Mark Twain, BLANK.POS would be equal to 5. Then the above statement would assign the BLANK.POS - 1 = 5 - 1 = 4 leftmost characters of NAME.IN$, that is, Mark, to FIRST.NAME$, which is exactly what we want.

Pointer
A variable that indicates the location of an item of data.

The next statement,

```
320 LAST.NAME$ = MID$(NAME.IN$, BLANK.POS + 1)
```

extracts the last name from NAME.IN$. For Mark Twain, BLANK.POS + 1 = 5 + 1 = 6. Notice that the third parameter of the MID$ function is not coded. Thus, this statement assigns all the characters beginning with the sixth character of NAME.IN$—that is, Twain—to LAST.NAME$, which again is exactly what we want.

Word Processing

Word processing
Using a computer to create written material and to simplify making changes to it.

String functions are also fundamental to word processing. In **word processing**, computers simplify creating and revising written materials—reports, stories, or even whole books. In fact, word processing is one of the most popular ways to use computers. To give you some idea of how word processing works, let's assume we have typed in some text already, and let's write a program that will allow us to replace any string in that text by another string.

VARIABLES AND ALGORITHM

As usual, we begin by naming the variables. In this case, they are

Input variables	A line of the text to be modified	TEXT$
	String to be replaced	ORIGINAL$
	Replacement string	REPLACE$
Internal variables	Length of ORIGINAL$	LEN.ORIGINAL
	Starting point for search of ORIGINAL$ in TEXT$	START
	Position of start of ORIGINAL$ in TEXT$	POSITION
	Part of TEXT$	PART$
Output variable	A line of new text	NEW.TEXT$

In keeping with step 2 of our structured procedure, we must develop an algorithm like the following:

> 1. Accept ORIGINAL$ and REPLACE$.
> 2. Initialize NEW.TEXT$ to the null string.
> 3. Read TEXT$.
> 4. If these are the trailer data, stop.
> 5. Repeat step 6 for all occurrences of ORIGINAL$ in TEXT$.
> 6. Replace ORIGINAL$ by REPLACE$ and assign the altered text to NEW.TEXT$.
> 7. Print NEW.TEXT$.
> 8. Repeat steps 2 through 7 for all lines of text.

The only complicated part of this algorithm is step 6. We will discuss that step in detail as we examine the program.

```
100 REM *** WORD PROCESSING PROGRAM ***
110 INPUT "Enter text to be changed"; ORIGINAL$
120 LEN.ORIGINAL = LEN(ORIGINAL$)
130 INPUT "Enter replacement text"; REPLACE$
140 NEW.TEXT$ = ""
150   READ TEXT$
160   IF TEXT$ = "XXX"
         THEN GOTO 200
170   GOSUB 300
180   LPRINT NEW.TEXT$
190 GOTO 140
200 STOP
210 '
300 REM *** Routine to replace text
310   START = 1
320   POSITION = INSTR(START,TEXT$,ORIGINAL$)
330   WHILE POSITION <> 0
340     PART$ =  MID$(TEXT$,START,POSITION-START)
350     NEW.TEXT$ = NEW.TEXT$ + PART$ + REPLACE$
360     START = POSITION + LEN.ORIGINAL
370     POSITION = INSTR(START,TEXT$,ORIGINAL$)
380   WEND
390   NEW.TEXT$ = NEW.TEXT$ + MID$(TEXT$,START)
400 RETURN
410 REM *** End of routine to replace text
420 '
500 REM *** Data used as text to be changed
510 DATA "In the theory of colour, there are three primary colours: red, blue"
520 DATA "and yellow.  Using these colours, we can create any colour we wish."
530 DATA XXX
540 END

RUN
Enter text to be changed? colour
Enter replacement text? color
Break in 200
Ok
```

```
In the theory of color, there are three primary colors: red, blue
and yellow.  Using these colors, we can create any color we wish.
```

PROGRAM 9.8   **A word processing program.**

THE PROGRAM

In Program 9.8, which is based on this algorithm, the text in lines 510 and 520,

```
510 DATA "In the theory of colour, there are three primary colours: red, blue"
520 DATA "and yellow. Using these colours, we can create any colour we wish."
```

might be from a physics textbook. The objective is to change the English spelling colour to the American spelling color.

The program begins by asking the user to enter the string to be replaced and assigns the string entered to ORIGINAL$. In the example, ORIGINAL$ is equal to colour. LEN.ORIGINAL is then set equal to the length of ORIGINAL$, which in this case is 6. The program then asks for the replacement string and assigns the string entered to REPLACE$. In the example, REPLACE$ is equal to color. In the main loop, the program first sets NEW.TEXT$ to the null string. In line 350, NEW.TEXT$ will be used as a string accumulator, and just as numeric accumulators must be initialized to 0, so string accumulators must be initialized to the null string.

The program then reads TEXT$, and in line 160 checks to see if the trailer data, consisting of XXX, have been read. If they have, the program is finished, and it branches to the STOP statement in line 200. If the trailer data have not been read, the program executes the subroutine that starts at line 300. This subroutine does the actual replacement.

In line 310, START is set to 1. In line 320, the INSTR function is used to search for ORIGINAL$ in TEXT$, starting from the first character. If POSITION is 0, then ORIGINAL$ was not found in TEXT$, and the WHILE loop is not executed. If POSITION is not zero, ORIGINAL$ was found in TEXT$, and POSITION points to the character in TEXT$ where ORIGINAL$ starts. In Program 9.8, the c of the first colour is the eighteenth character of TEXT$, so POSITION is set to 18. All that needs to be done now is to delete ORIGINAL$ from TEXT$ and to insert REPLACE$ in its place, which is done in the WHILE loop.

In line 340,

```
340 PART$ = MID$(TEXT$, START, POSITION - START)
```

PART$ is assigned the value of the characters in TEXT$ up to the first character of ORIGINAL$. Let's examine this statement closely. START is 1, and POSITION - START is 17, so this statement is equivalent to

```
PART$ = MID$(TEXT$, 1, 17)
```

This statement assigns 17 characters of TEXT$, starting from the first character, to PART$. Therefore, PART$ contains "In the theory of ". In line 350, three items—NEW.TEXT$ (which contains the null string), PART$, and REPLACE$—are concatenated and assigned to NEW.TEXT$. NEW.TEXT$ now contains "In the theory of color".

In line 360, a new value of START is calculated, equal to POSITION plus LEN.ORIGINAL. In this case, START becomes 18 + 6 = 24 and points to the comma following colour. In line 370, the INSTR function tells BASIC to search for ORIGINAL$ in the section of TEXT$ from character 24 to the end. The c of the second colour is the fiftieth character of TEXT$, so POSITION is set to 50. Since POSITION is not 0, the WHILE loop continues.

Let's study the second execution of line 340. Recall that START is 24 and POSITION is 50, so line 340 is now equivalent to

```
PART$ = MID$(TEXT$, 24, 26)
```

This statement assigns 26 characters of TEXT$, starting from the twenty-fourth character, to PART$. PART$ is therefore ", there are three primary ". Then, in line 350, NEW.TEXT$, PART$, and REPLACE$ are concatenated and assigned to NEW.TEXT$. As a result, NEW.TEXT$ becomes "In the theory of color, there are three primary color".

START is updated in line 360 and becomes 56. Then, when BASIC executes line 370, the INSTR function returns a 0, because colour does not occur beyond character 56 of TEXT$. Because POSITION is now 0, we exit from the WHILE loop. We are not quite finished with TEXT$, however, because NEW.TEXT$ does not contain characters beyond the fifty-sixth character of TEXT$. Line 390 extracts the characters of TEXT$ from the fifty-sixth character to the end of TEXT$, concatenates them to NEW.TEXT$, and assigns the whole string to NEW.TEXT$. At this point NEW.TEXT$ contains all of TEXT$, with every occurrence of colour replaced by color, so BASIC returns to the main routine and prints NEW.TEXT$.

BASIC then branches to the top of the loop, reads the next line of text, and repeats the whole process. In this way, each line of text is processed until BASIC reads the trailer data (XXX) and branches to the STOP statement in line 200.

EXERCISES

9.21 How would you modify Program 9.7 so that a space is not printed after the comma?

9.22 In line 360 in Program 9.8, START is calculated as POSITION + LEN.ORIGINAL. How would the output change if START were calculated as POSITION + 1?

9.23 Trace Program 9.8 when the second line of TEXT$ is processed.

*9.24 Trace Program 9.8, assuming that the value entered for ORIGINAL$ is purple and the value entered for REPLACE$ is violet.

PROGRAMMING ASSIGNMENTS

9.16 Write a program that accepts a string that includes a pair of parentheses with some characters inside them as well as characters outside the parentheses. The program should delete the parentheses and the characters inside them and print the resulting string.

*9.17 Stock prices are often quoted using fractions, that is, 37⅜. In the fractions used, both the numerator and denominator have only one digit. Write a program that will accept a price in this form and print it in dollars and cents.

9.18 A BASIC expression is balanced if a) it contains the same number of left and right parentheses and b) while it is scanned from left to right, the number of left parentheses is always greater than or equal to the number of right parentheses. Write a program that accepts an expression and reports whether it is balanced.

*9.19 Write a program to read a phrase and print each word backward. If your phase is

HAPPY BIRTHDAY

your program should produce

YPPAH YADHTRIB

9.20 Write a program that accepts a string and changes a run of multiple blanks into a single blank. For example, it should change This   is   a   test to This is a test.

*9.21 Assume that your keyboard's space bar malfunctions and every time it is pressed it prints an asterisk instead of a space. Write a program that will replace every asterisk with a space. (Hint: Of course, Program 9.8 could be used, but you can write a better program if you exploit the fact that the original and replacement strings are the same size—that is, they both consist of one character. Therefore, use the MID$ *statement* to make the replacement directly in the original text; do not define a NEW.TEXT$ variable.)

MAKING A CODE

Some years ago, it was reported that within the federal government the National Security Agency (NSA) made the greatest use of computers. Most governments use computer programs to put their messages into code and to break the codes of other countries. The programs used by governments are quite sophisticated, but you can write a rather simple BASIC program to encode a message.

To keep the problem manageable, we will use a simple substitution code in which every letter in the original English message is replaced by a different letter in the coded message. Moreover, we will assume that the English message is written in capital letters.

Variables and Algorithm

We begin, of course, by naming the variables we will use:

Input variable	English message	ENGLISH$
Internal variables	Alphabet string	ALPHA$
	Translating string	TRANS$
	Current character	CHAR$
	Pointer	SEARCH
	Length of ENGLISH$	LENGTH
	Counter variable	CHANGE
Output variable	Coded message	CODE$

We may then use the following algorithm:

1. Initialize ALPHA$ to the alphabet, TRANS$ to a translation string, and CODE$ to the null string.
2. Accept a message for ENGLISH$.
3. Repeat step 4 for each character in ENGLISH$.
4. Translate the character and concatenate it to CODE$.
5. Print the coded message.
6. Stop execution.

The Program

In Program 9.9, which is based on this algorithm, line 110 sets ALPHA$ equal to the uppercase letters of the alphabet, in their normal order. In line 120, the translation string, TRANS$, causes the letters in the English message to be replaced by different letters in the coded message, in this case, the alphabet in backward order. That is, TRANS$ will cause an A in the original English message to be changed to a Z in the coded message, a B to be changed to a Y, a C to an X, and so on, with a Z being changed to an A. You should understand, however, that the letters in TRANS$ can be in any order. Different orders just produce different codes. The only requirement is that TRANS$ contain every letter exactly once.

All the work of encoding is done in the FOR-NEXT loop in lines 160 through 200. In line 170, the MID$ function extracts a character from ENGLISH$ and assigns it to CHAR$. When CHANGE is 1, the first character of ENGLISH$ is extracted, when CHANGE is 2, the second character is extracted, and so on.

In line 180, the INSTR function is used to search ALPHA$ for CHAR$. If SEARCH is equal to 0, it means that CHAR$ does not appear in ALPHA$ (it might be a space or a punctuation mark). In that case, CHAR$ is just concatenated to CODE$. If SEARCH is not 0, it points to the position in ALPHA$ where CHAR$ ap-

```
100 REM *** ENCODING A MESSAGE ***
110 ALPHA$ = "ABCDEFGHIJKLMNOPQRSTUVWXYZ"          'Initialize alphabet,
120 TRANS$ = "ZYXWVUTSRQPONMLKJIHGFEDCBA"          'translate, and
130 CODE$ = ""                                     'code strings
140 INPUT "English message"; ENGLISH$              'Accept English string
150 LENGTH = LEN(ENGLISH$)                          'and get its length
160 FOR CHANGE = 1 TO LENGTH                        'Translate each character
170   CHAR$ = MID$(ENGLISH$,CHANGE,1)              'Extract the character
180   SEARCH = INSTR(ALPHA$,CHAR$)                 'Search for it in alphabet
190   IF SEARCH = 0
        THEN CODE$ = CODE$ + CHAR$
        ELSE CODE$ = CODE$ + MID$(TRANS$,SEARCH,1) 'Translate character
200 NEXT CHANGE
210 PRINT "Encoded message:  "; CODE$              'Print coded message
220 END

RUN
English message? "ONE IF BY LAND, TWO IF BY SEA"
Encoded message:  LMV RU YB OZMW, GDL RU YB HVZ
Ok
```

PROGRAM 9.9   **A program to encode a message.**

pears. The ELSE branch of line 190 causes the corresponding character from TRANS$ to be concatenated to CODE$.

To see exactly how this works, assume that CHAR$ equals E. When BASIC searches ALPHA$ for CHAR$, it sets SEARCH to 5, because E is the fifth character in ALPHA$. Then in line 190 the fifth character of TRANS$, V, will be concatenated to CODE$. In this way, the E in the original English message is changed to a V in the coded message.

When BASIC falls through the FOR-NEXT loop, all the characters in ENGLISH$ have been encoded, so in line 210 it prints CODE$.

The LINE INPUT Statement

It would be nice to modify Program 9.9 to accept a sentence without the user having to type quotation marks. The LINE INPUT statement allows you to do just that. Furthermore, if you use the LINE INPUT statement, the entered sentence may contain embedded quotation marks. The difference between a LINE INPUT statement and an ordinary INPUT statement is that the LINE INPUT statement reads a whole line at a time. That is, the LINE INPUT statement ignores commas and quotation marks and reads all the characters entered at the keyboard until you press the Enter key.

The format of the LINE INPUT statement is

LINE INPUT [;] ["prompt";] string variable

Notice that only one string variable is coded; all the characters read are assigned to that one string variable. Like the optional semicolon in the INPUT statement, the optional semicolon that follows LINE INPUT prevents BASIC from scrolling the screen when the input is entered on line 24 or 25.

To use a LINE INPUT statement in Program 9.9, you need only alter line 140 by changing INPUT to LINE INPUT.

User-Defined Functions

You have seen that the functions BASIC supplies can be useful. But BASIC also permits you to define your own functions by using the DEF FN statement.

The syntax for DEF FN is

DEF FNname[(arg,...)] = expression

where name is the name of the function and must be a valid variable name, and arg is an argument. You may have as many arguments as you want. Like other BASIC functions, user-defined functions must end with a $ if you want them to return a string. Because DEF FN statements must be executed before the function is used, it is customary to place them near the beginning of a program or in an initialization routine.

Since DEF FN is a complicated statement, let's define a simple function to see how it works. For example,

DEF FNDIVIDE(X,Y) = (X + 2) / Y

defines a function named FNDIVIDE that adds 2 to the first argument and divides the sum by the second argument. The following LET statement executes this function:

A = FNDIVIDE(V,L)

Dummy variable
A variable that has meaning only within the function in which it is defined.

In this statement, V and L take on the roles of X and Y. So if V equals 19 and L equals 4, A = (19 + 2)/4 = 5.25. Because X and Y have no values, but just "hold the place" of real variables, they are sometimes called **dummy variables**. In fact, there may be variables in the program named X and Y, but these variables have no relation to the dummy variables X and Y.

You can also use constants instead of variables when executing a function. For example, the statement

VALUE = FNDIVIDE(37,5)

assigns the value 7.8 to VALUE.

Syntax Summary

LINE INPUT Statement
Form: LINE INPUT [;] ["prompt";] string variable
Example: LINE INPUT "Enter the message to encode"; CODE$
Interpretation: Accepts a complete line of input from the keyboard, ignoring commas and quotation marks.

DEF FN Statement
Form: DEF FNname [(argument,...)]
Example: DEF FNCELSIUS(FAHRENHEIT) = 5 * (FAHRENHEIT - 32) / 9
Interpretation: Creates a user-defined function. After the function has been defined, it may be used just like a BASIC function.

Getting the Bugs Out

Problem: During execution, BASIC displays the error message

Undefined user function in nn

where nn is the line number where you referenced a user-defined function.

Reason: You tried to execute a user-defined function before you defined it.

Solution: Make sure you execute the DEF FN statement before you try to execute the user-defined function. If you did execute the DEF FN statement, make sure you spelled the user-defined function the same where you defined it and where you used it.

EXERCISES

9.25 What output would Program 9.9 produce if the ELSE clause of line 190 were changed to

```
ELSE CODE$ = CODE$ + MID$ (ALPHA$, SEARCH, 1)
```

*9.26 In Program 9.9, what would happen if a letter appeared twice in TRANS$?

9.27 How would you change Program 9.9 if you wanted a blank space to be translated into a Z and a Z translated into a blank space?

*9.28 How would you change Program 9.9 to encode messages written in both uppercase and lowercase letters?

*9.29 What value is printed by the following program?

```
10 DEF FNTEST(A,B) = (A ∧ B)/(B ∧ A)
20 P = 2
```

```
30 Q = 3
40 R = FNTEST(P,Q)
50 PRINT R
60 END
```

9.30 Write a user-defined function to calculate the volume of a cylinder from the radius and the height. The formula is

```
VOLUME = 3.14159 * RADIUS ∧ 2 * HEIGHT
```

9.31 Program 9.10 shows a program that is supposed to accept a word and print the word across the screen with each letter separated from the next by five spaces. As you can see, the output is not correct. Find and correct the error.

```
10 REM *** PRINTING CHARACTERS ACROSS THE SCREEN ***
20 INPUT "Enter a word with up to 12 letters"; WORD$
30   FOR J = 1 TO LEN(WORD$)
40     LETTER$ = MID$(WORD$,J)
50     PRINT SPC(5); LETTER$;
60   NEXT J
70 END

RUN
Enter a word with up to 12 letters? hello
     hello     ello     llo     lo     o
Ok
```

PROGRAM 9.10   **An attempt to print a word across the screen.**

PROGRAMMING ASSIGNMENTS

9.22 The following message was encoded by Program 9.9:

DV SZEV NVG GSV VMVNB ZMW SV RH FH

Write a program that will decode this message.

*9.23 To detect typing errors when data are entered into computer systems, businesses often include in account numbers and employee numbers a last digit called a check digit. One system works like this: First, the digits in the units position and in every second position are assigned a weight of 2. The remaining digits are assigned a weight of 1. Each digit is multiplied by its weight, and the products are added. For example, if the number is 93728, the operation is:

Digit position	1	2	3	4	5
Original number	9	3	7	2	8
Weight	2	1	2	1	2
Product	18	3	14	2	16

The sum of the products is $18 + 3 + 14 + 2 + 16 = 53$. Now, the sum is divided by 10 and the remainder noted. If the remainder is 0, the check digit is 0; otherwise, the check digit is obtained by subtracting the remainder from 10. In the exam-

ple, when 53 is divided by 10, the remainder is 3; when 3 is subtracted from 10, we obtain the check digit of 7. Finally, the check digit is incorporated into the original number, which becomes 937287. When this number is entered into a computer system, the computer can calculate the check digit. If an error was made, the check digits will not agree, and the error will be detected. Write a program that will accept a six-digit number consisting of a five-digit number and a check digit. Calculate the check digit and compare it against the entered check digit, to determine whether an error has been made. Your program should find that the number 937287 is correct and the number 748245 is an error.

SUMMARY

In this chapter you have learned that

- The LOG function returns the natural logarithm of its argument.
- The EXP function returns *e* raised to the power of its argument.
- The SQR function returns the square root of its argument.
- The COS function returns the cosine of its argument, the SIN function returns the sine of its argument, the TAN function returns the tangent of its argument, and the ATN function returns the arctangent of its argument.
- The SGN function returns −1 if its argument is negative, +1 if its argument is positive, and 0 if its argument is 0.
- The ABS function returns the absolute value of its function.
- The FIX function truncates its argument to an integer, the INT function returns the largest integer that is less than or equal to its argument, and the CINT function rounds its argument to the nearest integer.
- The RND function generates random numbers.
- The RANDOMIZE statement reseeds the random number generator.
- The TIMER function returns the time, in seconds, according to the computer's internal clock and may be used to provide a seed for the RANDOMIZE statement.
- Simulation programs allow users to study the behavior of systems on a computer.
- The DATE$ function returns the date.
- The TIME$ function returns the time of day.
- The STRING$ function returns a string of any desired length consisting of any chosen character.
- The LEN function returns the length of its argument.
- The LEFT$, RIGHT$, and MID$ functions extract substrings.
- The MID$ statement replaces characters in a string.
- The INSTR function searches a string for the occurrence of another string.
- Word processing allows users to create and to easily modify written material.
- The LINE INPUT statement accepts a complete line of input.
- The DEF FN statement defines user-defined functions.

KEY TERMS IN THIS CHAPTER

dummy variable 261
Monte Carlo simulation 239
pointer 254
random number 234

random number generator 235
random number seed 235
simulation 239

string expression 247
substring 247
word processing 255

QUESTIONS FOR REVIEW

9.1 Why are systems simulated?

9.2 Explain the purpose of the RANDOMIZE statement.

9.3 How many variables may be listed in a LINE INPUT statement?

9.4 How many arguments may a user-defined function use?

9.5 What statement is used to define a user-defined function?

9.6 The RND function returns a random number between _____ and _____.

9.7 What rule governs the placement of the DEF FN statement?

9.8 If you want to use the SIN function, in what units must the angle be measured?

9.9 Match each function in the first column with its action listed in the second column.

A. LEFT$ (1) Returns the time in the form hh:mm:ss.

B. TIMER   (2) Extracts a substring starting from the right.

C. FIX   (3) Searches for one string in another.

D. TIME$ (4) Extracts a substring starting from the left.

E. MID$ (5) Discards digits to the right of the decimal point.

F. CINT   (6) Returns a random number.

G. INSTR   (7) Returns the length of its argument.

H. INT   (8) Returns the largest integer less than or equal to its argument.

I. RND   (9) Returns the time in seconds.

J. RIGHT$ (10) Extracts an arbitrary substring.

K. DATE$ (11) Returns the date.

L. LEN   (12) Rounds its argument to the nearest integer.

9.10 What error would you look for if, during the execution of a program that uses the SQR function, BASIC displayed the error message

```
Illegal function call?
```

ADDITIONAL PROGRAMMING ASSIGNMENTS

*9.24 Mathematicians study a class of problems known as random walk problems, of which the following is an example. The bridge over the river Chi is 10 steps across and 6 steps wide. After having a few too many at a nearby pub, Sherry Tipler tries to cross this bridge. Each time Sherry takes one step forward, she also lurches to the side. She lurches to the right and to the left with equal probability. Sherry steps on the bridge at the center line, but if she ever gets more than 3 steps from the center she falls in the river. If she manages to take 10 steps without falling in, she is safe. Simulate 100 attempted crossings of the bridge and keep track of how many times Sherry makes it across and how many times she falls in. (Hint: Use a FOR-NEXT loop to simulate the attempted crossings, and inside that loop, use a WHILE loop that continues executing as long as Sherry is on the bridge. You should find that she falls in about 35 percent of the time.)

9.25 Suppose you are waiting for your luggage to come off an airplane. If you are waiting for one piece of luggage, then on the average, half the luggage must come out of the plane before yours does. How many pieces must come out if you are waiting for two pieces? Assume there are 120 pieces of luggage on the plane. You should find you wait for about 80 bags.

9.26 Charlie Dunkin and Paul Fowler are playing a game in which the first one to sink a basket wins. Paul sinks 40 percent of his shots, but Charlie sinks only 30 percent of his, so to make the game fairer, Charlie is allowed to shoot first. Simulate 100 games and determine how many games Charlie wins and how many games Paul wins. (Hint: Use a FOR-NEXT loop to simulate the games, and a WHILE loop that continues executing until somebody sinks a basket. You should find they each win about half the games.)

9.27 Write a program that allows the user to enter a number with none, one, or more commas. Strip the commas from the number and print the original number and two times the number. Use the LINE INPUT statement to accept the number.

*9.28 Write a program to perform the following operations. Start with any positive integer. Calculate the sum of the squares of its digits. For example, starting with 7639, we calculate 49 + 36 + 9 + 81 = 175. Now apply the same operation to 175. Keep repeating this procedure until you reach either the number 4 or the number 1. Print the values generated on the way to 4 or 1. Starting with 7639, the values are 175 75 74 65 61 37 58 89 145 42 20 4.

9.29 Write a program that will search for a string in some text. The program should accept a search string, read several lines of text from DATA statements, and display the text with the search string in blinking color. You may merge the data in A09-29.DAT, in which case you should search for the string crooked and use XXX as the trailer data.

9.30 Write a program to play Buzz. In Buzz, you count starting from 1, but whenever you come to a number that is either a multiple of 6 or contains 6 in its name, as in 16, instead of saying the number you say "Buzz." Count from 1 to 100.

9.31 a) Write a program that will encode a message by interchanging the order of pairs of characters. For example, if the message is HAVE A GOOD DAY, the coded message is AHEVA G OO DADY. (Remember that a space counts as a character.)

    *b) Another code uses the scheme of printing alternately a character from the first half of the message and a character from the second half. For example, if the message is HAVE A GOOD DAY the coded message is HOAOVDE DAA YG. (Hint: If L is the length of the message, you can calculate the halfway point using the equation H = L \ 2 + L MOD 2. This equation gives the correct value whether L is even or odd.)

BEYOND THE BASICS

9.1 A particularly simple type of substitution code is known as a Caesar code, after Julius Caesar, who supposedly used it. In terms of Program 9.9, the TRANS$ string is in normal alphabetical order, but it is shifted to the left by an arbitrary number of letters. The letters that are pushed out of the front end of TRANS$ are added to the back. For example, if we shifted TRANS$ by four letters, it would be

    TRANS$ = "EFGHIJKLMNOPQRSTUVWXYZABCD"

    With this TRANS$, every letter in the original English message is replaced by the letter four letters after it in the alphabet. (We understand that, for example, the letter four letters "after" Z is D.) Since the shift can be any number from 1 to 25, there are 25 different Caesar codes.

    Suppose you have found a coded message that was encoded using one of the Caesar codes, but of course, you don't know which one. Write a program that will decode the message by systematically trying all 25 Caesar codes. Try your program on the following message:

    JVUNYHABSHAPVUZ, FVB JHU HWWSF
    AV AOL UZH MVY H QVI

9.2 In spreadsheets, columns are named with letters. The sequence of letter names is A, B, C, ..., Z, AA, AB, ..., AZ, BA, BB, ... Many spreadsheets have 256 columns, and therefore the last column is named IV. Write a program that accepts a column's number and determines and prints the column's name.

9.3 Write a program that accepts an English sentence and translates each word into pig Latin. If the first letter of the English word is a vowel, the word is translated into pig Latin by adding WAY to the end of the word. Thus, for example, APPLE becomes APPLEWAY. If the first letter of the English word is not a vowel, the word is translated by moving the first letter of the word to the end of the word and adding AY to the end of the word. So PIG LATIN becomes IGPAY ATINLAY. (Consider only A, E, I, O, and U vowels.)

9.4 Write a program that accepts a number and displays that number in big digits on the screen. For example, if the user enters 468, the program should display

9.5   Modify Program 9.2 to plot the results on the screen. Draw the horizontal and vertical axes. After each toss, plot an asterisk one column to the right of the previous asterisk. If a head comes up, plot the asterisk one row higher than the last asterisk; if a tail comes up, plot it one row lower.

9.6   Write a program to play Hangman. The program should allow one player to enter a word, then erase the word and ask the second player to guess the word by entering one letter at a time. The program should print underscores to represent the unknown letters. When a letter is guessed, the underscore should be replaced by the correct letter. If the letter occurs more than once, all occurrences should be shown. Give the player ten guesses and count only the wrong guesses.

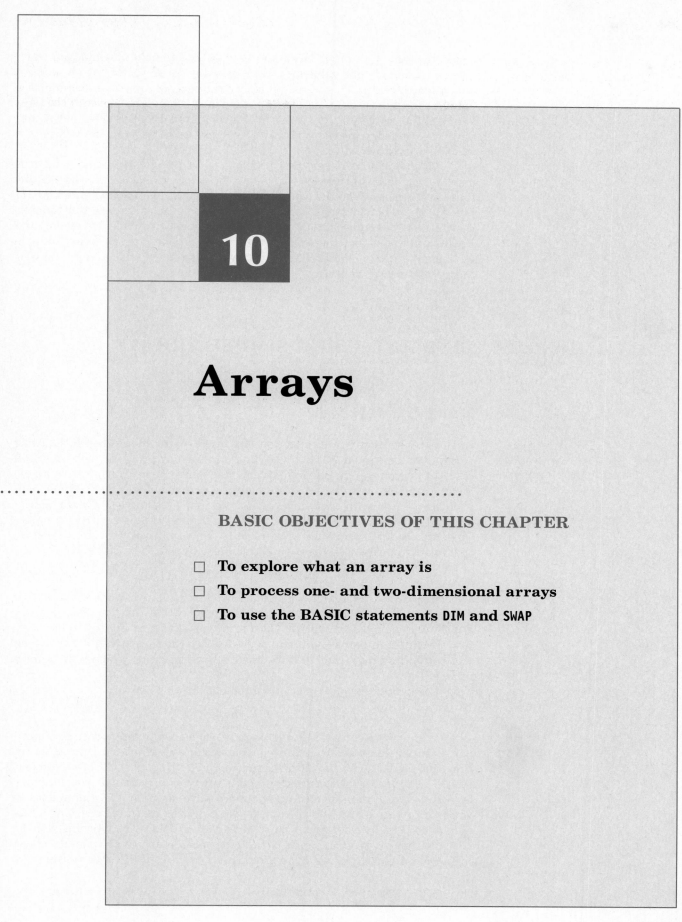

10

Arrays

BASIC OBJECTIVES OF THIS CHAPTER

☐ To explore what an array is

☐ To process one- and two-dimensional arrays

☐ To use the BASIC statements DIM and SWAP

You know that the storage boxes set up by BASIC to hold the value of a variable can hold only one value at a time. By using accumulators, we have been able to work within this restriction. For example, we used an accumulator in calculating total gross pay and thus avoided the need to have all the individual values of gross pay stored in the computer. But this device does not always serve; some problems really do require us to have all the values of a variable stored in the computer.

For example, consider this problem: Given students' names and test marks, calculate the average test mark. Then print each mark and the difference between it and the average. Calculating the average test mark would present no difficulty; we solved similar problems in Chapter 7. But to print the differences requires that the original marks be available. Using only the BASIC you know now, you could not solve this problem, but it is easy to solve by using an array. In this chapter you will learn how to use arrays and how to sort and search them.

UNDERSTANDING AND USING SIMPLE ARRAYS

What Is an Array?

Array
A collection of storage locations that have the same name.

In BASIC, an **array** is a collection of storage locations that have the same variable name. If you want to use an array in your program, you must tell BASIC that you want a particular variable to be an array, rather than an ordinary variable, and you must indicate the number of storage locations you want associated with that variable. You do that by using a DIM statement.

DIM is short for "dimension," and the DIM statement gets its name because we use it to specify the size—that is, the number of storage locations—that should be reserved for each array. For example,

```
DIM DWARFS$(7), GOLD(12)
```

tells BASIC that you want DWARFS$ and GOLD to be arrays, not ordinary variables, and that BASIC should set up 7 storage locations for the DWARFS$ array and 12 storage locations for the GOLD array, as shown in Figure 10.1(a).

From their names, you can tell that DWARFS$ is a string array, which will contain strings, and that GOLD is a numeric array, which will contain numbers.

The syntax for a simple DIM statement is

```
DIM variable (number)[,...]
```

where variable is either a string or numeric variable and number is a number, numeric variable, or expression indicating the number of storage locations you want BASIC to set up for that variable.* If number is not an integer, BASIC rounds it to the nearest integer. As many variables as you like may be listed in a DIM statement, and you can have as many DIM statements as you like in a program, but of course, you can dimension a particular array only once. The DIM statement must be executed before the first instruction that uses an array variable. It is therefore customary to put the DIM statement near the beginning of the program or in an initialization routine.

---

*In fact, it is not necessary to dimension any array that has 10 or fewer storage locations. Programs are much clearer, however, when you do so.

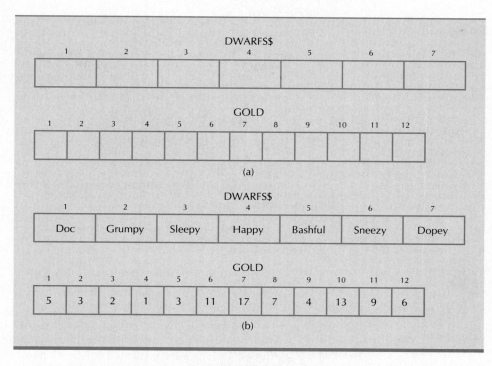

FIGURE 10.1   **(a) Storage locations for the DWARFS$ and GOLD arrays. (b) DWARFS$ and GOLD arrays with values assigned to the elements.**

The individual storage boxes specified in a DIM statement are called **elements**. Since we want to be able to reference the elements of an array, they are numbered, as shown in Figure 10.1(a).* To print, for example, the value of the third element of the DWARFS$ array, you need only write

Elements
The individual components of an array.

PRINT DWARFS$(3)

Subscript
A numeric constant, variable, or expression that specifies a particular element of an array.

We say that DWARFS$(3) is a subscripted variable and that 3 is the **subscript**. The subscript is always enclosed in parentheses immediately following the variable name. For example:

DIM Statement
DIM VOWEL$(5)

Effect
Assigns 5 storage locations to VOWEL$.

DIM Statement
PRINT VOWEL$(4)

Effect
Prints the 4th element of VOWEL$ (0 if the vowels are assigned in the order A, E, I, O, U).

DIM Statement
DIM ODD.NUMBER(100)

Effect
Assigns 100 storage locations to ODD.NUMBER.

*In fact, BASIC sets up a zero element. However, the zero element is not often used, and in this discussion we will ignore it.

DIM Statement

PRINT ODD.NUMBER(6)

Effect

Prints the 6th element of ODD.NUMBER (11 if odd numbers are assigned sequentially starting with 1).

DIM Statement

DIM STATE$(50), AREA(50)

Effect

Assigns 50 locations each to STATE$ and AREA.

DIM Statement

PRINT STATE$(50), AREA(50)

Effect

Prints the 50th element in both STATE$ and AREA (Wyoming and 97,809 if states and their areas are assigned alphabetically).

As long as you specify a subscript, you may use an array variable anywhere that you could use an ordinary variable. Suppose the values shown in Figure 10.1(b) were assigned to the elements of the DWARFS$ and GOLD arrays. (For now, don't worry about how the values were assigned; you will see that later.) The following statement is legal:

TEAM$ = DWARFS$(3) + " and " + DWARFS$(5)

Before reading further, can you determine the value of TEAM$? BASIC will evaluate the LET statement by concatenating the value of the 3rd element of DWARFS$, which is Sleepy, with " and " and the 5th element of DWARFS$, which is Bashful, and assigning the result, Sleepy and Bashful, to TEAM$.

These examples used numbers as subscripts, but variables and even expressions may be used as subscripts. Consider the statements

```
100 J = 4
110 K = 11
120 X = GOLD(K) + GOLD(K - J)
```

When BASIC evaluates line 120, it requires the value of GOLD(K). Since line 110 just assigned 11 to K, BASIC evaluates GOLD(K) as GOLD(11). Similarly, BASIC evaluates GOLD(K - J) as GOLD(11 - 4) = GOLD(7). Using the values for GOLD(11) and GOLD(7) in Figure 10.1(b), we see that X will be equal to 26 (9 + 17 = 26).

Notice especially that GOLD(K - J) is *not* evaluated as GOLD(K) - GOLD(J). BASIC first evaluates the subscript, K - J, and then references that element of the array.

Assigning Values to an Array

Now that you know the fundamentals of arrays, let's consider how values are assigned to the elements of an array.

We could use READ and DATA statements to assign the values shown in Figure 10.1(b) to the DWARFS$ array, as follows:

```
10 DIM DWARFS$(7)
20 READ DWARFS$(1), DWARFS$(2), DWARFS$(3), DWARFS$(4),
      DWARFS$(5), DWARFS$(6), DWARFS$(7)
         .
         .
         .
90 DATA Doc, Grumpy, Sleepy, Happy, Bashful, Sneezy, Dopey
```

But what if DWARFS$ were larger—if, for example, it had 100 or 500 elements. This scheme would be inconvenient, to say the least.

The following statements provide a more convenient way to assign values to the elements of the DWARFS$ array:

```
10 DIM DWARFS$(7)
20 FOR J = 1 TO 7
30   READ DWARFS$(J)
40 NEXT J
      .
      .
      .
90 DATA Doc, Grumpy, Sleepy, Happy, Bashful, Sneezy, Dopey
```

Let's trace these statements to see how they work. The first time line 30 is executed, J is 1, so BASIC evaluates READ DWARFS$(J) as READ DWARFS$(1) and assigns the first value listed in the DATA statement, Doc, to DWARFS$(1). The second time line 30 is executed, J is 2, so BASIC evaluates READ DWARFS$(J) as READ DWARFS$(2) and assigns the second data value, Grumpy, to DWARFS$(2). In this way, the loop assigns a value to all 7 elements of the DWARFS$ array.

This is the fundamental idea behind the use of arrays: Write one or more statements that use subscripted variables (like the READ statement in the previous example), put these statements inside a FOR-NEXT loop, and use the counter variable of the FOR-NEXT loop as the subscript. BASIC will then execute the statements as many times as you wish. Note that the DIM statement is *not* inside the FOR-NEXT loop.

Another advantage of this approach is that if the DWARFS$ array were dimensioned with 500 elements, we would just change the final value of the FOR statement from 7 to 500 and add additional DATA statements. The executed section of the program, lines 20 to 40, would be no longer and no more complicated. The size and complexity of a program does not depend on how many elements the array contains.

You can also use a PRINT statement inside a FOR-NEXT loop to print an array, for example,

```
20 FOR K = 1 TO 7
30   PRINT DWARFS$(K)
40 NEXT K
```

Notice that this PRINT statement uses K as the subscript, even though the READ statement above uses J. There is no connection between the variables J or K and the DWARFS$ array; what is important is the value of the subscript. If J and K and a new variable ZZZ all have the value 5, then DWARFS$(J), DWARFS$(K), and DWARFS$(ZZZ) all refer to the fifth element of the DWARFS$ array.

We are not restricted to using READ and PRINT statements in FOR-NEXT loops; we can use any BASIC statement. Thus, we can add the corresponding elements of two arrays, A and B, and assign the sum to the elements of the C array, as follows:

```
10 DIM A(50), B(50), C(50)
20 FOR J = 1 TO 50
30    C(J) = A(J) + B(J)
40 NEXT J
```

Errors

When working with arrays, you may make some new kinds of errors. For example, students frequently write the previous example as

```
10 DIM DWARFS$(7)
20 READ DWARFS$(J)
```

and leave out the FOR and NEXT statements. You can avoid this kind of error if you remember that you want the READ statement to be executed many times. The READ statement in line 20 will be executed only once.

Another kind of error you might make is shown in the following example:

```
10 DIM GOLD(12)
20 K = 20
30 GOLD(K) = 10
```

The value coded in a DIM statement for an array determines the maximum subscript that you may use with that array. In this case, when BASIC executes line 30 it tries to put 10 into GOLD(20). Since the maximum subscript that may be used with GOLD is 12, there is no GOLD(20). BASIC accordingly prints the message Subscript out of range and stops executing. This message indicates either that a DIM statement is wrong or that you assigned the subscript an incorrect value.

You might also forget to specify a subscript when using an array variable. For example, writing

```
PRINT DWARFS$
```

is wrong. We set up seven storage locations for DWARFS$, but in this statement we have not specified which one we want printed.* In fact, it is legal, but poor practice, for a program to contain a subscripted variable and an ordinary variable with the same name. In executing this statement, BASIC would think we were referring to an ordinary variable named DWARFS$. Since we never assigned a value to the ordinary variable DWARFS$, BASIC would print the null string. Likewise, GOLD(3) and GOLD3 are completely different variables. GOLD(3) refers to the third element of GOLD, while GOLD3 is an ordinary variable.

Printing the Difference from the Average

Now that you know something about arrays, we can use them to solve some problems. Let's return to the problem mentioned at the beginning of this chapter: Given students' names and test marks, calculate and print the average test mark; also calculate and print each mark and the difference between that mark and the average.

---

*We will discuss an exception to this rule in Chapter 14.

VARIABLES AND ALGORITHM

As always, we begin our structured procedure by naming the variables:

Input variables	Student names array	STUDENT.NAMES$
	Test marks array	TEST.MARKS
	Number of students	NO.STUDENTS
Internal variables	Subscript	STUDENT.COUNTER
	Test mark accumulator	TOTAL.TEST.MARK
Output variables	Average test mark	AVERAGE
	Difference, test mark minus average	DIFFERENCE

Parallel arrays
Two or more arrays in which the data stored in a particular element of one array correspond to data in the same element of the other(s).

The STUDENT.NAMES$ and TEST.MARKS arrays are called **parallel arrays**, because of the correspondence between the data they contain. For instance, STUDENT.NAMES$(1) will contain a student's name, and TEST.MARK(1) will contain that student's test mark.

In keeping with step 2, we can use the following algorithm for this problem:

1. Set TOTAL.TEST.MARK to 0.
2. Accept NO.STUDENTS.
3. Repeat steps 4 and 5 NO.STUDENTS times.
4. Accept STUDENT.NAMES$ and TEST.MARKS.
5. Accumulate TEST.MARKS.
6. Calculate and print AVERAGE.
7. Repeat steps 8 and 9 NO.STUDENTS times.
8. Calculate DIFFERENCE.
9. Print STUDENT.NAMES$, TEST.MARKS, and DIFFERENCE.
10. Stop execution.

HAND-CALCULATION AND FLOWCHART

To hand-calculate an answer, let's use the following data:

Student name	Test mark
Melita	90
Benito	80
Angela	86
Mickey	74

From this data, we can quickly determine that the average test mark is 82.5 and that Melita, Benito, Angela, and Mickey have grades that differ from this average by 7.5, −2.5, 3.5, and −8.5, respectively.

The flowchart in Figure 10.2 contains what may at first appear as strange notation: The array names are written with parentheses, but without a subscript inside the parentheses. For example, in the INPUT subroutine, the arrays are written as STUDENT.NAMES$() and TEST.MARKS(). The parentheses are there to remind you that STUDENT.NAMES$ and TEST.MARKS are arrays and to represent the missing subscript, STUDENT.COUNTER. You can always determine the missing subscript because it is the counter variable of

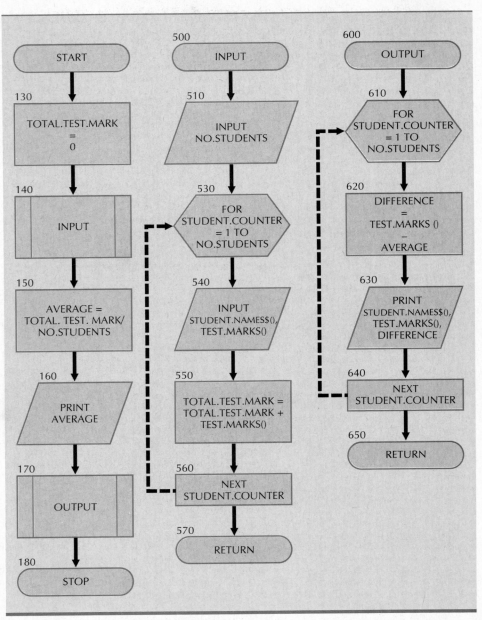

Flowchart to print the average test mark and the differences from the average.

the FOR-NEXT loop in which the statement appears. In the program, of course, the array names will be written with the subscripts.

The flowchart also contains two subroutines, both of which contain a FOR-NEXT loop. Since these FOR-NEXT loops are independent (not nested), we can use the same counter variable, STUDENT.COUNTER, in both loops. Notice that this flowchart contains simplified symbols for the FOR-NEXT loop (similar to the simplified symbols we used for the WHILE loop). Now that you know how a FOR-NEXT loop works, showing all the details just makes the flowchart more complicated and harder to understand. After all, the point of drawing a flowchart is to make it easier to write the program.

PROGRAM

Our algorithm and flowchart in turn produce Program 10.1. Notice that in the DIM statement in line 120, the maximum subscript chosen for STUDENT.NAMES$ and TEST.MARKS is 40, since it seems unlikely that this program would be used to process more than 40 students. But the REM state-

```
100 REM *** CALCULATE AVERAGE TEST MARKS AND DIFFERENCE FROM AVERAGE ***
105 REM ***    If more than 40 students are to be processed,
110 REM ***    the DIM statement in line 120 must be changed.
120 DIM STUDENT.NAMES$(40), TEST.MARKS(40)
130 TOTAL.TEST.MARK = 0
140 GOSUB 500          'Accept names and marks and accumulate marks
150 AVERAGE = TOTAL.TEST.MARK / NO.STUDENTS
160 PRINT "Average test mark is "; AVERAGE
170 GOSUB 600          'Calculate differences and print results
180 STOP
190 '
500 REM *** Routine to read names and marks, and accumulate marks
510   INPUT "Enter the number of students"; NO.STUDENTS
520   PRINT "Enter each student's name and test mark"
530   FOR STUDENT.COUNTER = 1 TO NO.STUDENTS
540     INPUT STUDENT.NAMES$(STUDENT.COUNTER), TEST.MARKS(STUDENT.COUNTER)
550     TOTAL.TEST.MARK = TOTAL.TEST.MARK + TEST.MARKS(STUDENT.COUNTER)
560   NEXT STUDENT.COUNTER
570 RETURN
580 REM *** End of input routine
590 '
600 REM *** Routine to calculate differences and print results
610   FOR STUDENT.COUNTER = 1 TO NO.STUDENTS
620     DIFFERENCE = TEST.MARKS(STUDENT.COUNTER) - AVERAGE
630     PRINT STUDENT.NAMES$(STUDENT.COUNTER), TEST.MARKS(STUDENT.COUNTER),
              DIFFERENCE
640   NEXT STUDENT.COUNTER
650 RETURN
660 REM *** End of output routine
670 END

RUN
Enter the number of students? 4
Enter each student's name and test mark
? Melita,90
? Benito,80
? Angela,86
? Mickey,74

Average test mark is  82.5
Melita          90              7.5
Benito          80             -2.5
Angela          86              3.5
Mickey          74             -8.5
Break in 180
Ok
```

PROGRAM 10.1   **A program to calculate the average test mark and the difference from the average.**

ments in lines 105 and 110 warn users of this restriction and tell them how the program can be modified to process more students.

If, when we execute the program, the number of students is less than 40, some of the elements of STUDENT.NAMES$ and TEST.MARKS will not be assigned values. Since we will never use those elements, the fact that they have not been assigned values will not cause any problems. BASIC simply ignores the empty boxes.

The rest of the program follows directly from the flowchart and should not be difficult to understand. Notice that BASIC's answers agree with our hand-calculated answers.

Customers' Bills for No Bum Steer

For another example of using arrays, let's return to the problem of the No Bum Steer fast-food chain (see Program 7.6). This time, let's use arrays to display the menu, calculate the bills, and, as a new feature, keep track of the number of customers who buy each of the seven different kinds of orders.

VARIABLES AND ALGORITHM

As always, we begin by choosing variable names:

Input variables	Code number of the order, string	CODE$
	Code number of the order, number	CODE
Internal variables	Cost of orders array	COST
Output variables	Customer's bill	BILL
	Name of orders array	ORDER$
	Array to count the number of customers who ordered each kind of order	COUNTER

Notice that this list includes three array variables, which were not used in Chapter 7: COST, ORDER$, and COUNTER. You will see how these array variables are used when we examine the program.

In keeping with step 2 of our structured approach, we can modify the algorithm used in Chapter 7 by adding steps to count and print the number of customers buying each kind of order.

1. Initialize COUNTER array to 0, the ORDER$ array to the names of the orders, and COST array to the costs of the orders.
2. Display the menu of orders.
3. Accept CODE$.
4. Convert CODE$ to CODE.
5. If CODE is invalid, go to step 3.
6. If CODE is 8, go to step 10.
7. Calculate and print BILL.
8. Count this order by incrementing the CODE element of COUNTER.
9. Repeat steps 3 through 8 for all customers.
10. Print COUNTER array.
11. Stop execution.

PROGRAM

This algorithm is not so complicated that you need a flowchart to understand it, so let's go directly to Program 10.2. In line 130, BASIC executes the initialization subroutine, which starts at line 400. In this subroutine, the COUNTER array is initialized to 0, the ORDER$ array is initialized to the names of the orders, and the COST array is initialized to the costs of the orders. When BASIC returns from this subroutine, COST(J) contains the cost of the Jth order. That is, COST(1) contains the cost of order number 1 (which is 1.25), COST(2) contains the cost of order number 2 (which is .90), and so on. Similarly, ORDER$(1) contains the name of order number 1 (Hamburger), ORDER$(2) contains the name of order number 2 (Fries), and so on. You will see how the COST and ORDER$ arrays are used in a minute.

In line 140, BASIC executes the subroutine that displays the menu, which begins at line 600. The appearance of the menu will be the same as that created by Program 7.6. However, Program 10.2 uses the ORDER$ and COST arrays to display the menu.

This approach has two advantages over the method used on Program 7.6. First, it results in a shorter subroutine than we had in Program 7.6. But more important, the costs and names of the orders are now stored in one place—the COST and ORDER$ arrays. If we wanted to change the price of, for example, order 1, we have to change only the DATA statement in line 450. The new cost is then automatically reflected in both the menu and the bill calculation. In Program 7.6, in contrast, we would have to change the price in both the menu subroutine and the bill calculation. Having to make a change in two places in a program is poor practice because it is easy to mistakenly make a change in only one place. If we made that mistake, the price displayed in the menu and the price used in the bill calculation would not be the same, and the program would be wrong. You want to make your programs as easy as possible to modify.

The FOR-NEXT loop that starts at line 670 displays the codes, names, and costs of the orders. Notice how the lines of the menu are positioned on the screen. Line 650 tells BASIC to LOCATE the heading at row 6, column 17. To get order number 1 to print on row 7, order number 2 on row 8, and so on, we thus need the LOCATE statement in line 680—

```
680 LOCATE J + 6, 17
```

which adds 6 to J to accomplish this positioning.

In the main routine, BASIC accepts a value for CODE$ (line 170), converts it to CODE (line 190), and checks to see if it is valid (line 200). If CODE$ is not valid, the error subroutine that starts at line 800 is executed. If CODE$ is valid, line 210 tests whether CODE is 8; if it is, BASIC branches to line 280, which we will discuss in a minute. If CODE is between 1 and 7, the bill for this customer is calculated in line 220:

```
220 BILL = COST(CODE)
```

This statement is complicated, so make sure you understand how it works. If CODE is 4, for example, BASIC interprets this statement as

```
220 BILL = COST(4)
```

and assigns the correct value to BILL—2.00. Because of the way we initialized COST, the correct value will be assigned to BILL for all values of CODE.

Line 230 counts this order, which BASIC interprets as

```
230 COUNTER(4) = COUNTER(4) + 1
```

That is, if a customer chooses order number 4, then COUNTER(4) is incremented.

```
100 REM *** CUSTOMERS' BILLS FOR NO BUM STEER ***
110 DIM COUNTER(7), COST(7), ORDER$(7)
120 CLS : KEY OFF
130 GOSUB 400                        'Initialize COUNTER, COST, and ORDER$ arrays
140 GOSUB 600                        'Display menu
150 LOCATE 16, 16, 1
160 PRINT "Enter Code Number of Customer's Bill ";
170   CODE$ = INPUT$(1)
180   PRINT CODE$
190   CODE = VAL(CODE$)
200   IF CODE < 1 OR CODE > 8
        THEN GOSUB 800: GOTO 250                    'Execute error routine
210   IF CODE = 8
        THEN GOTO 280                              'Finished, print totals
220   BILL = COST(CODE)
230   COUNTER(CODE) = COUNTER(CODE) + 1
240   LPRINT USING " Code  # \              \ Bill  $##.##";
                CODE, ORDER$(CODE), BILL
250   LOCATE 16, 53
260   PRINT SPACE$(1)
270 GOTO 150
280 REM *** Print the number of customers who bought each of the 7 orders
290 LPRINT: LPRINT: LPRINT "Code       Order               Number"
300 FOR J = 1 TO 7
310   LPRINT USING " # \                    \   #";J, ORDER$(J), COUNTER(J)
320 NEXT J
330 STOP
340 '
400 REM *** Initailization routine
410   FOR J = 1 TO 7
420     COUNTER(J) = 0
430     READ ORDER$(J), COST(J)
440   NEXT J
450   DATA Hamburger, 1.25
460   DATA Fries, .90
470   DATA Shake, 1.00
480   DATA Hamburger and Fries, 2.00
490   DATA Hamburger and Shake, 2.15
500   DATA Fries and Shake, 1.75
510   DATA "Hamburger, Fries, and Shake", 2.95
520 RETURN
530 REM *** End of initialization routine
540 '
600 REM  *** Start of subroutine to display menu
610   LOCATE 2, 25
620   PRINT "WELCOME TO NO BUM STEER"
630   LOCATE 4, 16
640   PRINT "Enter the number that corresponds to order"
650   LOCATE 6, 17
660   PRINT "Code   Order                     Price"
670   FOR J = 1 TO 7
680     LOCATE J + 6, 17
690     PRINT USING "   #   \                    \    #.##";
                J, ORDER$(J), COST(J)
700   NEXT J
710   LOCATE 14, 17
720   PRINT "  8     To quit"
730 RETURN
740 REM *** End of routine to display menu
750 '
```

PROGRAM 10.2   **A program to calculate bills for No Bum Steer.**

```
800 REM *** Start of error routine
810   BEEP
820   LOCATE 17, 16
830   PRINT "Enter a value between 1 and 8 please"
840 RETURN
850 REM *** End of Error Routine
860 END
RUN
```

```
Code  4  Hamburger and Fries               Bill  $ 2.00
Code  1  Hamburger                         Bill  $ 1.25
Code  3  Shake                             Bill  $ 1.00
Code  7  Hamburger, Fries, and Shake Bill  $ 2.95
Code  5  Hamburger and Shake               Bill  $ 2.15
Code  6  Fries and Shake                   Bill  $ 1.75
Code  2  Fries                             Bill  $ 0.90
Code  4  Hamburger and Fries               Bill  $ 2.00


Code        Order                 Number
1 Hamburger                        1
2 Fries                            1
3 Shake                            1
4 Hamburger and Fries              2
5 Hamburger and Shake              1
6 Fries and Shake                  1
7 Hamburger, Fries, and Shake  1
```

PROGRAM 10.2 **(Continued).**

When the user enters an 8, indicating that all data have been entered, the FOR-NEXT loop that starts at line 300 prints all the elements of the COUNTER array, showing us the number of customers who chose each kind of order.

If you solved Programming Assignment 7.14, which asked you to solve this problem before you learned about arrays, you will agree that Program 10.2 is simpler.

Syntax Summary	DIM Statement	
	Simple Form:	DIM variable(subscript), ...
	Example:	DIM STATES$(50), AREA(50)
	Interpretation:	Allocates area for array variables and specifies the maximum value that the subscripts may have.

Getting the Bugs Out

Problem: During execution, BASIC displays the error message

Subscript out of range

Reason: A subscript has a value larger than the maximum allowed as specified in the DIM statement, you did not code a DIM statement, or the DIM statement was not executed.

Solution: If the subscript was assigned too large a value, correct the error. If the subscript is correct, change or add the DIM statement. If the DIM statement was not executed, change its location so that it is executed.

Problem: During execution, BASIC displays the error message

Illegal function call in nn

where nn is the line number of a statement that uses a dimensioned variable.

Reason: The subscript was negative.

Solution: Correct the calculation of the subscript.

Problem: During execution, BASIC displays the error message

Duplicate definition

Reason: You dimensioned a variable twice. Or you used a variable with a subscript less than 10, so BASIC assigned the default dimension of 10 to the variable, and you later used a larger dimension.

Solution: Dimension each variable once and make sure the DIM statement is executed before the variable is used.

EXERCISES

10.1 Write a DIM statement to allocate 15 storage locations to the array A and 30 to the array B$.

10.2 Assume that STATE.NAME$ has been dimensioned with 50 elements and that all 50 elements have been assigned values. What will be printed by the following statement?

PRINT STATE.NAME$

10.3 Suppose A has been dimensioned with 10 elements and that the program contains a DATA statement with 10 values. Will the following statement assign values to all 10 elements?

READ A(10)

10.4 The array DAYS$ is defined to have seven elements, which have the values Sunday, Monday, Tuesday, Wednesday, Thursday, Friday, Saturday.

a) What is printed by the statement

PRINT DAYS$(2), DAYS$(6)

b) What value is assigned to LONG.WEEKEND$ by the statement

LONG.WEEKEND$ = DAYS$(6) + ", "
   + DAYS$(7) + ", " + DAYS$(1)

*10.5 The array V is defined to have eight elements, 6, 2, 1, 7, 4, 3, 9, 6. Suppose J is equal to 3, K is equal to 4, and L is equal to 6. What value is assigned to A when each of the following LET statements is executed?

a) A = V(J) - V(K)
b) A = V(L) * V(K - J)
c) A = V(K) - V(J - K)

(Hint: Draw a set of numbered storage boxes like those in Figure 10.1 and insert the values of V in sequence.)

10.6 What values are assigned to A by the following FOR-NEXT loops?

a) 20 FOR K = 1 TO 5
    30   A(K) = K
    40 NEXT K

b) 20 FOR J = 1 TO 5
    30   A(J) = J
    40 NEXT J

c) 20 FOR J = 1 TO 5
    30   A(6 - J) = J
    40 NEXT J

d) 20 FOR J = 5 TO 1 STEP -1
    30   A(J) = J
    40 NEXT J

e) 20 A(1) = 5
    30 FOR J = 2 TO 5
    40   A(J) = J * A(1)
    50 NEXT J

*10.7 What output is produced by the following program?

10 DIM P(5)
20 FOR J = 1 TO 5
30   READ P(J)
40 NEXT J
50 FOR J = 5 TO 1 STEP -1
60   PRINT P(J);
70 NEXT J
80 DATA 6, 4, 2, 9, 5
90 END

10.8 Assume A has been defined with 12 elements. Write the statements to add 1 to each element of A.

10.9 Consider the following program:

```
10 DIM X(16)
20 FOR J = 1 TO 16
30   X(J) = J
40 NEXT J
50 FOR J = 2 TO 4
60   IF X(J) = 0
        THEN GOTO 100
70   FOR K = 2 * J TO 16 STEP J
80     X(K) = 0
90   NEXT K
100 NEXT J
110 FOR J = 1 TO 16
120   IF X(J) < > 0
        THEN PRINT X(J);
130 NEXT J
140 END
```

a) What are the values of X when the FOR-NEXT loop in lines 20 to 40 completes executing?
b) What output is produced?

*10.10 Simple Simon says that since Program 10.2 does not use an ON-GOTO statement, there is no reason to use the VAL function to change CODE$ to CODE. Why is he wrong?

10.11 How would you modify Program 10.2 to print, along with the order number and the number of customers who chose that order, the total income from that order number?

PROGRAMMING ASSIGNMENTS

10.1 Write a program like Program 10.1, but have all marks greater than the average printed first, along with students' names, followed by grades less than or equal to the average, along with those students' names.

10.2 Write a program that accepts the number of different stocks an investor owns and then accepts the name, number of shares held, and price of each stock. Print a report that includes the input data and the value of each stock (number of shares times price) and the percent of total value contributed by each stock.

*10.3 Write a program that allows a user to enter a number N and then N numbers, and then prints the numbers in reverse order.

10.4 Write a program that allows a user to enter a day number in the range 1 to 7 and prints the name of the day, where day 1 is Sunday, day 2 is Monday, and so on. *Hint:* This program does not require an IF statement.

10.5 Write a program that can be used to mark multiple-choice tests. The program should accept ten correct answers into a key array. The program should also accept a student's name and ten answers into an answer array. The key and answer arrays should be compared, and the student's grade calculated.

10.6 Re-solve Programming Assignment 6.12, using arrays to store the tour codes, destinations, and prices. Also keep track of the number of clients who purchase each tour.

10.7 Write a program that generates 1000 random integers in the range 1 to 10 and then prints the number of 1s generated, the number of 2s generated, and so on.

*10.8 Write a program that will read some text and count and print the number of times each letter is used. To make the program interesting, have the text extend over several DATA statements and use a DATA statement containing the word XXX as trailer data. As an alternative, use the data in A10-08.DAT. In either case, enter the text in all capital letters. (Hint: It will be useful to set up an alphabet string ALPHA$, like the one used in Program 9.9. In addition, you should set up a counter array, COUNTER, with 26 elements, corresponding to the 26 letters. Examine the text, and whenever you find a letter in the text, add 1 to the corresponding element of COUNTER.)

10.9 Calculate the odds of getting each of the possible scores when two dice are tossed. Do not simulate tossing the dice; rather use a nested FOR-NEXT loop to calculate the number of ways each of the scores can be obtained. The odds of getting a score is just the number of ways the score can be obtained divided by 36 (the number of possible outcomes).

10.10 Write a program that will allocate seats at a theater. The program should display a seating plan like the following:

```
*******************************************************
*                  GLOBE THEATRE                      *
*                                                     *
* Orchestra        1  2  3  4  5  6  7  8  9  10       *
*                 11 12 13 14 15 16 17 18 19 20        *
*                                                     *
*                                                     *
* Balcony    1  2  3  4  5  6  7  8  9 10 11 12 13 14 15 *
*           16 17 18 19 20 21 22 23 24 25 26 27 28 29 30 *
*******************************************************
```

You should then ask which section and how many seats the customer wants. Customers may *not* request specific seats. Instead, the program should allocate seats sequentially, starting with the lowest numbered seat available in the desired section. As seats are allocated, the program should replace those seat numbers with Xs and then update the seating plan, so the screen always shows the current status of seats sold. (Hint: Use two string arrays, one for the orchestra seats and the other for the balcony seats, and initialize them with seat numbers. When a seat is sold, change the corresponding seat array element to X.)

THE BUBBLE SORT

Problems frequently call for sorting arrays. For example, if we print a report consisting of student names and grade point averages, the report will be more useful if it is printed either in alphabetical order by student name or in numerical order by grade point average. To print a report in order, the data must first be sorted.

There are many sorting techniques; in this section, you will learn a technique known as the **bubble sort**. This technique got its name because the elements of the array gradually move, that is, bubble, toward their final position. Other sorting methods are faster than the bubble sort,* but the bubble sort is easy to understand and program, and for small arrays the differences in execution speed are not significant.

The elements of an array may be sorted into ascending or descending order, but in this discussion we will assume we want to sort in ascending order. When the array is sorted, the first element will be less than or equal to the second element, the second will be less than or equal to the third, and so on. In the bubble sort, we compare adjacent elements of the array. If the first element is greater than the second element (that is, if the two elements are in the "wrong" order), we swap them. If the first element is less than or equal to the second element (that is, if the two elements are in the "right" order), we leave them alone. Every time we swap two elements, the array gets a little closer to being sorted, and if we continue swapping long enough, eventually the whole array will be sorted. We will discuss exactly how to determine when the array is completely sorted later in this chapter.

Bubble sort
A method of sorting an array in which adjacent elements are compared and swapped if necessary, so that elements move slowly toward their final positions.

■ *A Small Example*

Let's clarify this procedure by applying it to an actual example. Suppose we have an array, A, whose elements are in any mixed-up order, and we want to sort A so that its elements are in ascending order. The procedure works for both string and numeric arrays of any size. To keep this discussion to a reasonable length, however, let's assume that A contains only five elements and that initially they have the values shown in Figure 10.3(a).

We begin by comparing A(1) with A(2). A(1), which is 3, is less than A(2), which is 7. Thus, these elements are in the "right" order, so we leave them alone. Next we compare A(2) with A(3). A(2), which is 7, is greater than A(3), which is 1. So these elements are in the "wrong" order and we swap them. Comparing the new A(3), which is 7, with A(4), which is 9, we see that these elements are in the "right" order. Hence, we leave them alone. Finally, we compare A(4), which is 9, and A(5), which is 6. Since these elements are in

*See Beyond the Basics 10.8 for one alternative sort.

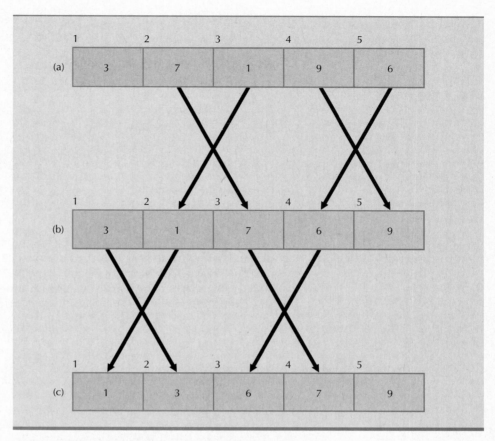

FIGURE 10.3 **Sorting using the bubble sort method. (a) Initial values of A. (b) Values of A after first pass. (c) Values of A after second pass.**

the "wrong" order, we swap them. After the first pass, A has the values shown in Figure 10.3(b).

It may seem that we have done a lot of work and have little to show for it, since A is still pretty mixed up. But if we repeat the procedure just once, we get the results shown in Figure 10.3(c)—A has been sorted. (Be sure you understand how Figure 10.3(c) is obtained from Figure 10.3(b).) In this case, sorting A required only two passes; in other cases, it might require more or fewer. The number of passes required to sort an array depends on two things: the size of the array and how mixed up it is at the start.

Programming a Bubble Sort

Now that you understand the principles behind a bubble sort, let's consider how to program one in BASIC. Following the first step of our structured procedure, we must choose variable names. For this problem, we can use

Input variables	Array to be sorted	A
	Number of elements of A to be sorted	NUMBER
Internal variables	Subscript	K
	Flag to indicate the sort is finished	SORTED.FLAG$
Output variable	Sorted array	A

We will discuss the variable SORTED.FLAG$ later in this section. For now, let's examine the algorithm for this program.

ALGORITHM AND FLOWCHART

The algorithm for the bubble sort is quite simple:

1. Accept data into A.
2. Swap elements of A that are out of order until A is sorted.
3. Print A.
4. Stop execution.

Figure 10.4 shows part of the flowchart for this algorithm. (The INPUT and OUTPUT subroutines consist of simple FOR-NEXT loops, so their flowcharts are not shown.) We start by accepting NUMBER, the number of elements of A that are to be sorted. After executing an input routine that assigns values to the first NUMBER elements of A, we are ready to begin the actual sorting.

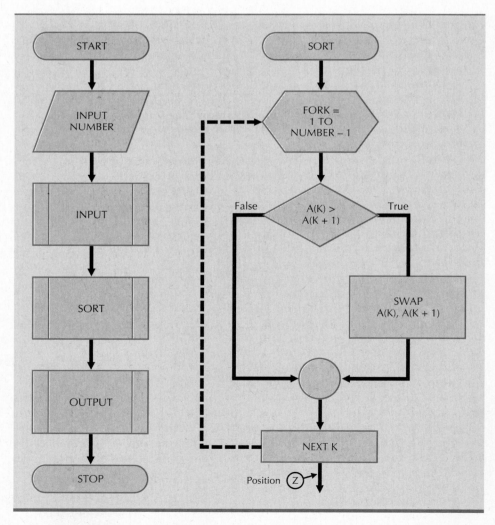

FIGURE 10.4   **Flowchart for the bubble sort, showing the start of the sort subroutine.**

The bubble sort requires that we compare adjacent elements of A: A(1) with A(2), A(2) with A(3), and so on. How can we perform all these comparisons? Naturally, we don't want to write separate IF statements; if we did, our program would be much too complicated. We can use only one IF statement if we compare A(K) with A(K + 1). We can put this IF statement inside a FOR-NEXT loop in which K is the counter variable. Then when K is 1, BASIC will compare A(1) with A(2). When K is 2, it will compare A(2) with A(3), and so on. Notice, however, that the highest value K should have is NUMBER − 1. If we allow K to have the value NUMBER, BASIC will try to compare A(NUMBER) with A(NUMBER + 1). Since we are sorting only NUMBER elements of A, a reference to A(NUMBER + 1) would be incorrect.

If the condition A(K) > A(K + 1) is true, we want to swap A(K) and A(K + 1). As you will see when we examine the program, BASIC has a special instruction named SWAP, which we will use to swap A(K) and A(K + 1). If the condition A(K) > A(K + 1) is false, we do nothing.

USING A FLAG

We have one last problem to solve: How do we know when to stop? Suppose we are at position Ⓩ in Figure 10.4. If all the pairs of elements of A are in the "right" order, we want the sort to stop and BASIC to go on to the next step.

How can BASIC know when all the pairs of elements are in the "right" order? Clearly, if during a particular pass through A, the condition A(K) > A(K + 1) were never true, then all the pairs of elements would be in the "right" order, and the sort would be complete. To tell BASIC that on the previous pass the condition was never true, we introduce a flag, in this case a variable named SORTED.FLAG$.

A **flag** is a variable introduced into a program for the sole purpose of controlling the execution of the program by indicating the presence or absence of some condition. That definition may sound complicated, but a flag is not really very different from trailer data. When we use trailer data, we set one of the program's variables to a particular value to indicate that we have reached the end of the data. When we use a flag, we introduce a new variable and set it to a particular value to indicate some condition.

In this problem, we will assign SORTED.FLAG$ the value YES if the sort is finished and NO if it is not. Figure 10.5 is an expanded flowchart for the SORT subroutine. As the figure shows, we set SORTED.FLAG$ to YES just before the FOR-NEXT loop, and we set it to NO in the "True" branch of the decision.

Suppose that on a pass through A, the condition A(K) > A(K + 1) is true, even once. Then the LET statement at position Ⓨ will set SORTED.FLAG$ to NO. When BASIC completes the FOR-NEXT loop and gets to position Ⓩ, SORTED.FLAG$ will have the value NO. BASIC must repeatedly execute the FOR-NEXT loop as long as, when it gets to position Ⓩ, SORTED.FLAG$ has the value NO. Obviously, we must put the FOR-NEXT loop in a WHILE loop, as shown in Figure 10.5. We must make sure that the WHILE loop is executed at least once, so in box 610 we set SORTED.FLAG$ equal to NO before entering the WHILE loop.

Notice that this logic requires BASIC to make an additional pass after the array is sorted. It is this final pass that leaves SORTED.FLAG$ equal to YES and ends the sort.

THE PROGRAM

Program 10.3 shows the bubble sort in BASIC. The only new element is the SWAP statement used in line 650. The syntax of the SWAP statement is quite simple:

```
SWAP variable1,variable2
```

Flag
A variable whose purpose is to control the execution of a program by indicating that some condition has or has not occurred.

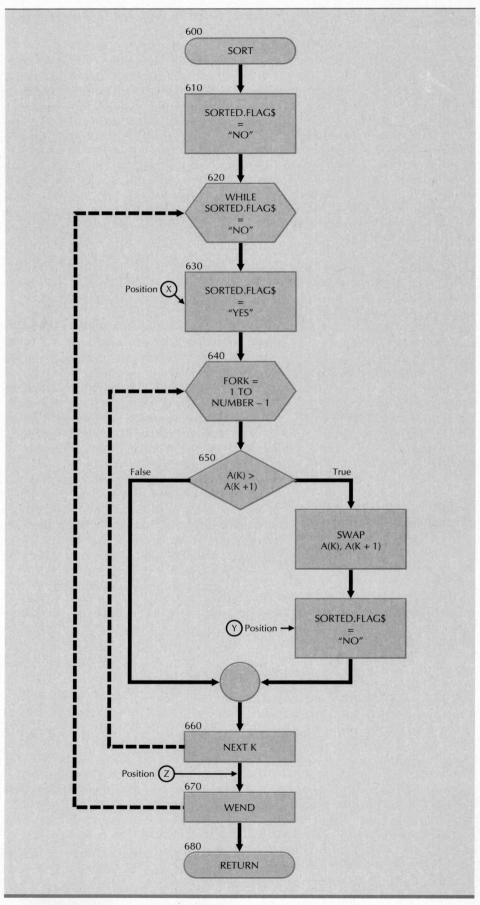

FIGURE 10.5 **Complete flowchart for the bubble sort subroutine.**

```
100 REM *** BUBBLE SORT ***
110 INPUT"Enter the number of numbers to be sorted"; NUMBER
120 DIM A(NUMBER)
130 GOSUB 500         'Accept data into A
140 GOSUB 600         'Sort A
150 GOSUB 800         'Print sorted A
160 STOP
170 '
500 REM *** Input routine
510  PRINT "Enter the numbers to be sorted, one at a time"
520   FOR K = 1 TO NUMBER
530     INPUT A(K)
540   NEXT K
550 RETURN
560 REM *** End of input routine
570 '
600 REM *** Sorting routine
610    SORTED.FLAG$ = "NO"
620    WHILE SORTED.FLAG$ = "NO"
630      SORTED.FLAG$ = "YES"
640      FOR K = 1 TO NUMBER - 1
650        IF A(K) > A(K+1)
              THEN SWAP A(K),A(K+1): SORTED.FLAG$ = "NO"
660      NEXT K
670    WEND
680 RETURN
690 REM *** End of sorting routine
700 '
800 REM *** Routine to print sorted A
810   FOR K = 1 TO NUMBER
820     PRINT A(K);
830   NEXT K
840 RETURN
850 REM *** End of output routine
860 END

RUN
Enter the number of numbers to be sorted? 8
Enter the numbers to be sorted, one at a time
? 7
? 12
? 6
? 9
? 17
? 4
? 6
? 3
 3  4  6  6  7  9  12  17
Break in 160
Ok
```

PROGRAM 10.3   A program for a bubble sort.

When the SWAP statement is executed, the values of the two variables are exchanged. Any type of variables may be swapped, but the two variables must be of the same type: both numeric or both string.

The following examples show how the SWAP statement is used:

SWAP Statement
```
SWAP P, Q
```

Effect
Interchanges the values of P and Q.

SWAP Statement
```
SWAP NAME1$, NAME2$
```

Effect
Interchanges the values of NAME1$ and NAME2$.

SWAP Statement
```
SWAP W, P(7)
```

Effect
Interchanges the values of W and P(7).

Sorting Parallel Arrays

Program 10.3 sorts the single array A, but often we have to sort two or more parallel arrays simultaneously. For example, suppose we have two arrays, STUDENT.NAME$, which contains student's names, and GPA, which contains their grade point averages. We want to sort STUDENT.NAME$ to put the names in alphabetical order, but while we are doing that we must also move around the elements of GPA so they stay in correspondence with the elements of STUDENT.NAME$. Program 10.4 sorts such parallel arrays, using much the same logic as Program 10.3. The only significant change is line 650:

```
650 IF STUDENT.NAME$(K) > STUDENT.NAME$(K + 1)
        THEN SWAP STUDENT.NAME$(K), STUDENT.NAME$(K + 1):
            SWAP GPA(K), GPA(K + 1): SORTED.FLAG$ = "NO"
```

in which whenever we tell BASIC to SWAP elements of STUDENT.NAME$ we also have it SWAP the corresponding elements of GPA.

Shuffling and Selecting from an Array

Sometimes instead of sorting the elements of an array, we want to mix them up, that is, shuffle them. An easy way to shuffle an ARRAY that contains N elements is

```
20 FOR J = 1 TO N
30   K = 1 + INT(N * RND)
40   SWAP ARRAY(J), ARRAY(K)
50 NEXT J
```

By the time we exit from the FOR-NEXT loop, the elements of ARRAY are completely shuffled. To use this scheme, substitute the values from your problem for N and ARRAY. (Of course, if your problem involves a string array, you must use a legal string variable name for your array instead of ARRAY.)

Another operation frequently performed is randomly selecting elements from an array. Suppose the debating club has 10 members and wants

```
100 REM *** BUBBLE SORT OF PARALLEL ARRAYS ***
110 INPUT"Enter the number of students "; NUMBER
120 DIM STUDENT.NAME$(NUMBER), GPA(NUMBER)
130 GOSUB 500        'Accept data into arrays
140 GOSUB 600        'Sort arrays
150 GOSUB 800        'Print sorted arrays
160 STOP
170 '
500 REM *** Input routine
510   PRINT "Enter the students' names and GPAs, one at a time"
520   FOR K = 1 TO NUMBER
530     INPUT STUDENT.NAME$(K), GPA(K)
540   NEXT K
550 RETURN
560 REM *** End of input routine
570 '
600 REM *** Sorting routine
610   SORTED.FLAG$ = "NO"
620   WHILE SORTED.FLAG$ = "NO"
630     SORTED.FLAG$ = "YES"
640     FOR K = 1 TO NUMBER - 1
650       IF STUDENT.NAME$(K) > STUDENT.NAME$(K+1)
              THEN SWAP STUDENT.NAME$(K), STUDENT.NAME$(K+1):
                   SWAP GPA(K), GPA(K+1): SORTED.FLAG$ = "NO"
660     NEXT K
670   WEND
680 RETURN
690 REM *** End of sorting routine
700 '
800 REM *** Routine to print sorted arrays
810   PRINT "Student Name         GPA"
820   FOR K = 1 TO NUMBER
830     PRINT USING "\                    \    #.##"; STUDENT.NAME$(K), GPA(K)
840   NEXT K
850 RETURN
860 REM *** End of output routine
870 END

RUN
Enter the number of students ? 5
Enter the students' names and GPAs, one at a time
? Rick, 2.6
? Ilsa, 3.4
? Victor, 2.3
? Louis, 1.9
? Sam, 3.8
Student Name         GPA
Ilsa                 3.40
Louis                1.90
Rick                 2.60
Sam                  3.80
Victor               2.30
Break in 160
Ok
```

PROGRAM 10.4   **A program that performs a bubble sort on two parallel arrays.**

to randomly select a member to be president. The 10 members' names could be entered into a MEMBER$ array. Then a random number between 1 and 10 could be generated and used as the subscript for MEMBER$ to select the president. This process is straightforward, but now suppose the club wants to randomly select 3 members to send to a debate. Following the procedure we used to select the president, we might plan to generate three random numbers between 1 and 10 and use these numbers as subscripts for MEMBER$. That would work, but with the complication that we must make sure we don't choose the same number more than once. We can avoid that complication by using the following statements:

```
110 K = 1
120 SELECT = NO.PICK
130 REMAINING = NO.POOL
140 FOR J = 1 TO NO.POOL
150    IF RND < SELECT / REMAINING
           THEN PICK$(K) = POOL$(J): K = K + 1: SELECT = SELECT - 1
                 REMAINING = REMAINING - 1
160 NEXT J
```

NO.POOL is the size of the pool from which we are choosing, and NO.PICK is the number we want to choose. In our example, NO.POOL is the number of members in the debating club (10), and NO.PICK is the number we are choosing to send to the conference (3). POOL$ is the array that contains the elements we are choosing from, which in our example would be MEMBER$. When we finish, the PICK$ array will contain NO.PICK elements randomly chosen from POOL$ with no element chosen more than once. As a bonus, if the elements of POOL$ are in order, then the elements of PICK$ will also be in order. Of course, if your problem involves a numeric array, you would use legal numeric variable names for your arrays in place of POOL$ and PICK$.

Syntax Summary

SWAP Statement
Form: `SWAP variable1, variable2`
Example: `SWAP SALES(7), SALES(21)`
Interpretation: The values of the two variables are exchanged.

Getting the Bugs Out

Problem: During execution, BASIC displays the error message

`Type mismatch in nn`

where nn is the line number of a statement that contains a SWAP statement.

Reason: The two variables named in the SWAP statement are not the same type. They must both be numeric variables or string variables.

Solution: Change one of the variables.

EXERCISES

10.12 Suppose P = 15 and Q = 28. What are the values of these variables after executing the statement

`SWAP P,Q`

10.13 The bubble sort in Program 10.3 sorts in ascending order. How would you change it to sort in descending order?

*10.14 Trace Program 10.3 to determine what would happen if

a) Line 610 were omitted.
b) Line 610 were restored and line 630 were omitted.
c) Line 640 were changed to

      640 FOR K = NUMBER -1 TO 1 STEP -1

10.15 a) What output would be produced by Program 10.4 if line 650 swapped only STUDENT.NAME$?

b) How would you change Program 10.4 to sort by GPA, with the highest GPA printed first?

*10.16 Write the statements to swap elements A(K) and A(K + 1), without using the SWAP statement. Hint: The following two LET statements don't work:

$$A(K) = A(K + 1)$$
$$A(K + 1) = A(K)$$

PROGRAMMING ASSIGNMENTS

*10.11 Write a program that finds and prints the median of a set of numbers. To find the median, the numbers must be sorted. If the number of numbers in the set is odd, the median is the middle number; if the number of numbers is even, the median is the average of the two middle numbers.

10.12 Write a program that accepts a student's name and five test marks, then calculates the average mark after dropping the lowest and highest test marks. (Hint: Sort the test marks.)

10.13 A10-13.DAT contains the following data for each of the fifty states:

      DATA ABBREVIATION, AREA

Write a program that will read these data and print a list in order by area, with the largest area first.

*10.14 Unlike many computerized dating services, Chance Encounters, Inc., doesn't promise to match people according to their likes and dislikes—chess players with chess players or hockey fans with hockey fans. Their only guarantee is that all dates will pair one woman and one man. To help them, read ten men's names into an array and ten women's names into a second array. Then shuffle each of the arrays and print ten pairs of names.

*10.15 Sometimes parents have a hard time selecting names for a baby. It might be helpful to let the computer choose a name randomly. Write a program that allows a user to enter a number N and then N names. Then have the program randomly select and print one of the names.

10.16 What's the Scoop ice cream parlor sells 12 different flavors of ice cream. Write a program that will randomly select three different flavors for a sundae.

SEARCHING AN ARRAY

As you have seen, arrays are often used to store data. For example, in Program 10.2 the COST array stored the cost of the various orders. In that program, it was easy to extract the data we needed from the array because, for example, COST(3) is the cost of order 3. But often it is not so easy to extract the data we need; we must search the array. As an example, consider the problem of Polly Glotte, who wants a program to translate English words into Spanish. (Although we will discuss only the searching of string arrays, numerical arrays can also be searched.)

Variable Names and Algorithm

As always, the first step in our structured procedure is to choose variable names. We will use

Input variable	Word to be translated	WORD$
Internal variables	English words array	ENGLISH$
	Subscript	J
	Flag to indicate whether search was successful	FOUND$
Output variable	Spanish words array	SPANISH$

In this algorithm, we once again are using parallel arrays: ENGLISH$, which contains English words, and SPANISH$, which contains Spanish words. We will initialize the arrays so that the Jth element of SPANISH$ contains the Spanish translation of the Jth element of ENGLISH$. In other words, if ENGLISH(1) is BLACK, then SPANISH$(1) is NEGRO, the Spanish translation of "black."

The algorithm for this problem may be stated quite simply:

1. Initialize ENGLISH$ and SPANISH$.
2. Accept an English WORD$.
3. If this is the trailer data, stop.
4. Search ENGLISH$ for WORD$.
5. If WORD$ was found in ENGLISH$, display the corresponding word from SPANISH$; otherwise, display an error message.
6. Repeat steps 2 through 5 for all words.

At the heart of this algorithm is step 4, the search, which we will examine in a minute. Notice, however, that in step 5 we allow for the possibility that the search was unsuccessful. This provides for misspelled English words and words beyond the translator program's vocabulary.

A Sequential Search

The only part of the algorithm that requires a flowchart is the search subroutine, shown in Figure 10.6. This particular search method is called a **sequential search**, because it examines all the elements in order, one after the other.

Sequential search
A method of searching an array in which the elements of the array are examined in sequence.

The logic of a sequential search is straightforward. We start by setting the flag FOUND$ equal to NO because we have not yet found the word. Then in a FOR-NEXT loop we compare each element of ENGLISH$ with WORD$. If we find a match, the search has been successful. We set FOUND$ to YES and branch to the RETURN statement. (Notice that J automatically contains the value for which the condition ENGLISH$(J) = WORD$ is true. We say that J *points to* the element of ENGLISH$ that equals WORD$). On returning to the main program, BASIC will print SPANISH$(J) as the translation of WORD$.

If none of the elements of ENGLISH$ equals WORD$, the search has been unsuccessful. BASIC falls through the FOR-NEXT loop without executing the

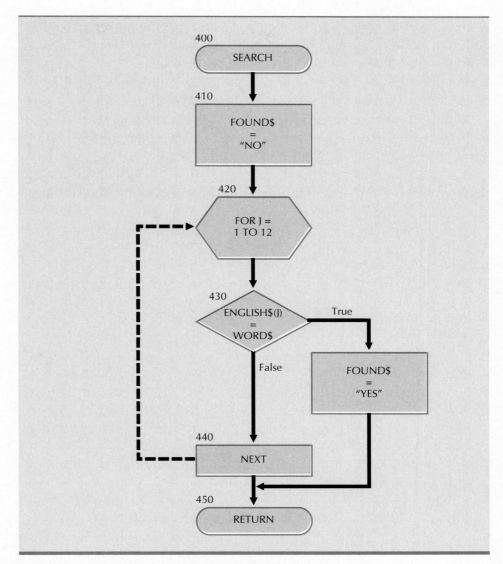

FIGURE 10.6   **Flowchart for the sequential search subroutine.**

statement that sets FOUND$ to YES, so FOUND$ will still have the value NO that we initially assigned to it.

Program 10.5 follows directly from the flowchart and uses only statements you already know, so you should not have any trouble understanding it.

A Binary Search

For small arrays, the sequential search is satisfactory. But for larger arrays that are arranged in numeric or alphabetical order, we can devise a much faster search method.

Imagine you are looking for a name in a telephone book. If you sequentially searched for the name, you would start looking for it on page one and look at each page in turn until you found the name you were looking for. Of course, you would never do such a thing; it would be too slow. What you

```
100 REM *** TRANSLATING ENGLISH INTO SPANISH ***
110 DIM ENGLISH$(12), SPANISH$(12)
120 GOSUB 200                      'Initialize ENGLISH$ and SPANISH$
130 INPUT "Enter English word to be translated into Spanish, Enter to end";
          WORD$
140   IF WORD$ = ""
         THEN GOTO 180             'Test for trailer data
150   GOSUB 400                    'Search for WORD$ in ENGLISH$
160   IF FOUND$ = "YES"
         THEN PRINT WORD$; " in Spanish is "; SPANISH$(J)
         ELSE PRINT "Sorry, "; WORD$; " is not one of the words I can translate"
170 GOTO 130
180 STOP
190 '
200 REM *** Initialization routine
210   FOR J = 1 TO 12
220     READ ENGLISH$(J), SPANISH$(J)
230   NEXT J
240   DATA BLACK, NEGRO
250   DATA BLUE, AZUL
260   DATA BROWN, PARDO
270   DATA GREEN, VERDE
280   DATA GREY, GRIS
290   DATA ORANGE, NARANJA
300   DATA PINK, ROSADO
310   DATA PURPLE, MORADO
320   DATA RED, ROJO
330   DATA TURQUOISE, TURQUESA
340   DATA WHITE, BLANCO
350   DATA YELLOW, AMARILLO
360 RETURN
370 REM ***End of initialization routine
380 '
400 REM *** Sequential search routine
410   FOUND$ = "NO"
420   FOR J = 1 TO 12
430     IF ENGLISH$(J) = WORD$
           THEN FOUND$ = "YES": GOTO 450
440   NEXT J
450 RETURN
460 REM *** End of sequential search routine
470 END
RUN

Enter English word to be translated into Spanish, Enter to end? BLUE
BLUE in Spanish is AZUL
Enter English word to be translated into Spanish, Enter to end? INDIGO
Sorry, INDIGO is not one of the words I can translate
Enter English word to be translated into Spanish, Enter to end? YELLOW
YELLOW in Spanish is AMARILLO
Enter English word to be translated into Spanish, Enter to end?
Break in 180
Ok
```

PROGRAM 10.5   **A sequential search to translate English words into Spanish.**

would actually do is open the book where you think the name might be. If you found that you had overshot the name, you would look closer to the front of the book; if you found that you had undershot the name, you would look closer to the back of the book. The reason this logic works is that the telephone book is arranged in alphabetical order. Similarly, a **binary search** will work only if the elements of the array being searched are arranged in alphabetical or numerical order.

Since the elements of ENGLISH$ are in order, we can replace the sequential search in Program 10.5 with a binary search. To perform a binary search of ENGLISH$ for GREEN, for example, you compare GREEN with a particular element. If you overshoot—that is, if the element is greater than GREEN— you can eliminate all higher elements and look closer to the beginning of ENGLISH$. If you undershoot—that is, if the element is less than GREEN—you can eliminate all lower elements and look closer to the end of ENGLISH$.

Because each comparison eliminates part of the array, we introduce two new variables, LOW and HIGH, to help us keep track of what part of the array is still in the search. LOW is the subscript of the lowest element of ENGLISH$ that is still in the search, and HIGH is the subscript of the highest element that is still in the search. At the start, LOW = 1 and HIGH = 12, since the whole array has to be searched. As in the sequential search, J is the subscript of the element compared to GREEN.

At each step we compare GREEN with the element in the middle of the remaining array. You can calculate the subscript of the middle element of the remaining array using the equation

$$J = (LOW + HIGH) \setminus 2$$

If LOW + HIGH is an odd number, this equation makes J the lower of the two "middle" numbers.

With LOW = 1 and HIGH = 12, the equation makes J = 6. Figure 10.7 shows the pattern of elimination. In the first comparison (Figure 10.7a), we see that GREEN is "less than" element J, ORANGE. Therefore, GREEN must be in the lower half of ENGLISH$. With one comparison, we have eliminated half of ENGLISH$!

Since we know that GREEN must be below J (if it is anywhere in the array), we move the upper limit, HIGH, down to J − 1, or 5, as shown in Figure 10.7(b). With LOW = 1 and HIGH = 5, our equation gives the new J = 3. Comparing the third element of ENGLISH$ (BROWN) to GREEN, we find that GREEN is "larger." Thus, GREEN must be between J + 1 and HIGH.

To search this section of ENGLISH$, we move the lower limit, LOW, up to J + 1, or 4, as shown in Figure 10.7(c). With LOW = 4 and HIGH = 5, the equation gives J = 4. We compare GREEN to the fourth element of ENGLISH$ and find a match. The search is over.

You may be wondering what would have happened if GREEN had not been in the array ENGLISH$. Suppose the fourth element of ENGLISH$ were FUCHSIA instead of GREEN. When we got to the third comparison, we would have found GREEN "greater than" FUCHSIA. We then would have increased LOW to J + 1, or 5. With HIGH also at 5, the new J would have been 5, and the new comparison—to GREY—would show GREEN "less than" GREY. But if we then decrease HIGH to J − 1, or 4, HIGH would be less than LOW! This "crossing" of the upper and lower limits tells us that we have searched the complete array and that the word we were searching for is not in the array.

So the binary search ends either when we find a match, which means the search was successful, or when the upper and lower limits cross, which means that the search was unsuccessful.

Perhaps you think the binary search quite complicated and only a little faster than the sequential search. Certainly, in the example we have dis-

Binary search
A method of searching a sorted array in which half of the remaining array is eliminated from the search by each comparison.

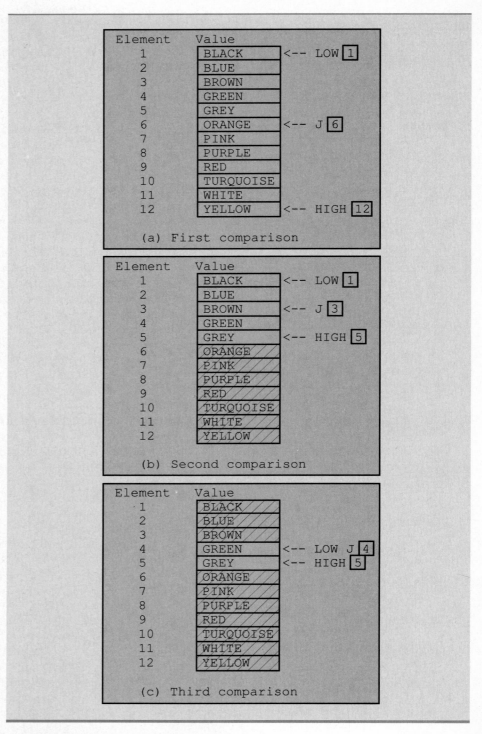

FIGURE 10.7   **Successful binary search for GREEN.**

cussed you would be right. But if you were searching an array of 100, 1000, or 10,000 elements, you would find a binary search much faster. A sequential search of a 1000-element array would require on the average 500 comparisons; a binary search would require at most 10 comparisons!

Clearly a binary search has advantages. However, it can be used only if your data are in order. If they are not, the binary search will likely report that the item you are searching for is not in the table, when in fact the item *is* in the table, but not in its correct position. Also, when you search an array, you don't always look for an equality; sometimes you look for a greater than or less than condition. Under those conditions, a binary search cannot be used and a sequential search must be performed.

PROGRAM

Program 10.6 shows a version of the translator program that uses a binary search. The only difference between this program and Program 10.5 which

```
100 REM *** TRANSLATING ENGLISH INTO SPANISH - BINARY SEARCH ***
110 DIM ENGLISH$(12), SPANISH$(12)
120 GOSUB 200                    'Initialize ENGLISH$ and SPANISH$
130 INPUT "Enter English word to be translated into Spanish, Enter to end";
        WORD$
140   IF WORD$ = ""
        THEN GOTO 180            'Test for trailer data
150   GOSUB 400                  'Search for WORD$ in ENGLISH$
160   IF FOUND$ = "YES"
        THEN PRINT WORD$; " in Spanish is "; SPANISH$(J)
        ELSE PRINT "Sorry, "; WORD$; " is not one of the words I can translate"
170 GOTO 130
180 STOP
190 '
200 REM *** Initialization routine
210   FOR J = 1 TO 12
220     READ ENGLISH$(J), SPANISH$(J)
230   NEXT J
240   DATA BLACK, NEGRO
250   DATA BLUE, AZUL
260   DATA BROWN, PARDO
270   DATA GREEN, VERDE
280   DATA GREY, GRIS
290   DATA ORANGE, NARANJA
300   DATA PINK, ROSADO
310   DATA PURPLE, MORADO
320   DATA RED, ROJO
330   DATA TURQUOISE, TURQUESA
340   DATA WHITE, BLANCO
350   DATA YELLOW, AMARILLO
360 RETURN
370 REM ***End of initialization routine
380 '
400 REM *** Binary search routine
410   LOW = 1
420   HIGH = 12
430   FOUND$ = "NO"
440   WHILE LOW <= HIGH
450     J = (LOW + HIGH) \ 2
460     IF ENGLISH$(J) = WORD$
          THEN FOUND$ = "YES": GOTO 490
470     IF ENGLISH$(J) > WORD$
          THEN HIGH = J - 1
          ELSE LOW = J + 1
480   WEND
490 RETURN
500 REM *** End of binary search routine
510 END
```

PROGRAM 10.6   **A binary search to translate English words into Spanish.**

uses a sequential search, is the subroutine that starts at line 400. This is a dramatic illustration of the advantages of using subroutines. To change the search method used in the program, we had only to replace the sequential search subroutine by the binary subroutine. The main program remains the same; the GOSUB 400 statement now executes a binary search instead of a sequential search.

EXERCISES

10.17 The words in ENGLISH$ in Program 10.5 are in alphabetical order. Would the sequential search work properly if the words were not in alphabetical order?

10.18 Trace the binary search algorithm and show the values taken by LOW, HIGH, and J, using WHITE and ROSE as the search words.

*10.19 Since the words in ENGLISH$ in Program 10.5 are in alphabetical order, we can improve the sequential search a little. If during the search we arrive at an element of ENGLISH$ that is greater than WORD$, the search has ended unsuccessfully, since WORD$ cannot be any further back in the ENGLISH$ array. Modify the program to include this improvement.

PROGRAMMING ASSIGNMENTS

*10.17 Re-solve Programming Assignment 5.14, but this time use arrays to hold the names of the planets and the weight factors. When a user enters the name of a planet, search the planet array to find the position of the planet and then extract the weight factor from the corresponding element of the weight factor array.

10.18 Write a program like the one in Program 9.1, but this time you pick the number and have the computer try to guess it using a binary search. Each time a guess is displayed, you must respond with an H if the guess is high, an L if it is low, and an E if it is equal to the number you picked.

10.19 A10-19.DAT contains the following data for all fifty states:

> DATA AB, State Name

where AB is a two-letter state abbreviation and State Name is the corresponding state name. The data are in order by abbreviation.

a) Write a program that accepts a two-letter state abbreviation and does a sequential search to find the state name.
b) Modify the program you wrote for (a) to perform a binary search.

10.20 In one school, letter grades are assigned as follows:

Grade >=	but <	Letter grade
95	—	A
90	95	A−
87	90	B+
84	87	B
80	84	B−
77	80	C+
74	77	C
70	74	C−
67	70	D+
64	67	D
60	64	D−
0	60	F

Write a program that accepts a grade and prints the corresponding letter grade. (Hint: This problem shows that when you search an array you don't always look for an equality. Set up a GRADE.BRACKET array containing the values 95, 90, 87, 84, ..., 0 and the parallel array LETTER.GRADE$ containing A, A-, B+, ..., F. Next, perform a sequential search to find the first J that makes GRADE >= GRADE.BRACKET(J). The letter grade is the corresponding element of LETTER.GRADE$. Notice that because of the 0 in the twelfth element of GRADE.BRACKET, the search must always be successful.)

TWO-DIMENSIONAL ARRAYS

Two-dimensional array
An array that requires two subscripts to specify an element.

One-dimensional array
An array that requires one subscript to specify an element.

Many problems require arrays that have two subscripts. For example, a bowling team might want to keep track of the scores of each of its members for each game that he or she bowls. If we let SCORES be the array of scores, then SCORES(3,2) could be the score of player number 3 for game number 2. Arrays that have two subscripts are called **two-dimensional arrays**, while arrays that have only one subscript, like those we have studied so far in this chapter, are called **one-dimensional arrays**. Arrays can have up to 255 dimensions, but arrays with more than three dimensions are not used very often.

Like one-dimensional arrays, two-dimensional arrays must be declared in a DIM statement. If our bowling team had four members and we wanted to keep track of the scores for a five-game tournament, SCORES would be declared in the following DIM statement:

```
DIM SCORES(4,5)
```

Notice the comma that is required between 4 and 5. Once a variable has been dimensioned as a two-dimensional array, then whenever we use that variable we must code two subscripts.

We refer to the elements of a two-dimensional array by row and column number, with the first subscript representing the row and the second representing the column. With the above DIM statement, the first subscript represents the players and the second subscript represents the games. Given the following statements:

```
DATA 186, 174, 163, 191, 206 :REM Scores for player 1
DATA 158, 193, 168, 177, 181 :REM Scores for player 2
DATA 202, 226, 214, 258, 197 :REM Scores for player 3
DATA 136, 141, 157, 132, 154 :REM Scores for player 4
```

we could draw a table like that shown in Figure 10.8. As you can see, BASIC stores the score for the first player in the first game (186) in location box 1,1, the score for the third player in the fifth game (197) in box 3,5, and so on.

Just as FOR-NEXT loops are the natural way to process one-dimensional arrays, so nested FOR-NEXT loops are the natural way to process two-dimensional arrays. Thus, we could enter the above data into the SCORES array by using the following nested FOR-NEXT loops:

```
210 FOR PLAYER = 1 TO 4
220    FOR GAME = 1 TO 5
230       READ SCORES(PLAYER, GAME)
240    NEXT GAME
250 NEXT PLAYER
```

The Bowling Tournament Problem

To illustrate the use of two-dimensional arrays, let's develop a program to calculate the average score of each player and the average score for each game in a bowling tournament.

Game

	1	2	1	4	5
1	1,1 186	1,2 174	1,3 163	1,4 191	1,5 206
2	2,1 158	2,2 193	2,3 168	2,4 177	2,5 181
3	3,1 202	3,2 226	3,3 214	3,4 258	3,5 197
4	4,1 136	4,2 141	4,3 157	4,4 132	4,5 154

Player

FIGURE 10.8   **The elements of the SCORES array, showing the player's scores.**

VARIABLE NAMES AND ALGORITHM

Following our structured procedure, we begin by choosing variable names:

Input variable	Score array	SCORES
Internal variables	Accumulator	TOTAL.SCORE
	Player subscript	PLAYER
	Game subscript	GAME
Output variable	Average	AVERAGE

Our second step, developing the algorithm, results in the following:

1. Read the scores into the SCORES array.
2. Calculate and print the AVERAGE for each player.
3. Calculate and print the AVERAGE for each game.
4. Stop execution.

Hierarchy diagram
A chart that shows the relationships between subroutines in a program.

We can use this problem as an opportunity to discuss a new design tool called a hierarchy diagram. A **hierarchy diagram** is a drawing that shows the relationships between subroutines in a program. Figure 10.9 shows a hierarchy diagram for the bowling tournament problem. The main function of the program is shown in a single box at the top of the diagram. This box corresponds to the main routine. The subroutines that are called from the main routine are shown in boxes at the second level. In this case, there are only two levels, but if any of the subroutines at the second level called another subroutine, it would be shown in a third level.

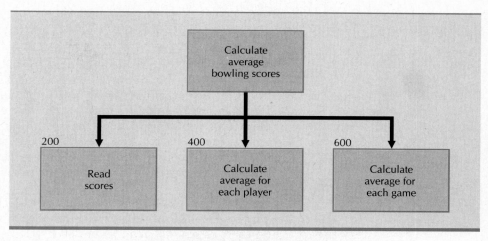

FIGURE 10.9   **A hierarchy diagram for the bowling tournament problem.**

Notice that, unlike a flowchart, a hierarchy diagram does not show the logic of a program—it does not show the conditions under which a subroutine is executed, nor does it show how many times a subroutine is executed. A hierarchy diagram shows what has to be done, not how it will be done. When you draw a hierarchy diagram, you just think about the subroutines that the program will contain. You can decide later how the subroutines will carry out their processing, using flowcharts if necessary. Hierarchy diagrams are most useful in complicated programs, as you will see in later chapters.

The logic of this program is relatively simple, so instead of drawing a flowchart, let's use pseudocode.

```
Calculate Average Bowling Scores
Input routine
FOR each player
  FOR each game
    READ SCORE
  NEXT game
NEXT player
Calculate player average routine
FOR each player
  Initialize TOTAL.SCORE to 0
  FOR each game
    Accumulate SCORE into TOTAL.SCORE
  NEXT game
  Calculate and print player average
NEXT player
Calculate game average routine
FOR each game
  Initialize TOTAL.SCORE to 0
  FOR each player
    Accumulate SCORE into TOTAL.SCORE
  NEXT player
  Calculate and print game average
NEXT game
```

PROGRAM

Program 10.7, which is based on this algorithm and pseudocode, consists of a main program and three subroutines. The first two subroutines consist of a GAME FOR-NEXT loop nested inside a PLAYER FOR-NEXT loop. The first subroutine, which starts at line 200, reads the data into SCORES. The second subroutine, which starts at line 400, has the same structure as the first. The differences are line 420, which initializes the accumulator, TOTAL.SCORE, to 0, and lines 460 and 470, which calculate and print AVERAGE. Inside the inner loop, in line 440, the SCORES array is accumulated one row at a time, instead of being read one row at a time, as it is in line 230 in the first subroutine. When we complete the inner loop, we calculate and print the average for a player.

You could easily incorporate the calculation and printing of the players' averages into the first subroutine and eliminate this second subroutine altogether, as we did in Program 10.1. But because two-dimensional arrays are more complicated than one-dimensional arrays, it is better to use two separate subroutines—one to read the data and the other to calculate the averages—to make the program easier to understand.

The third subroutine is entirely different. To calculate the average score for each game, we must process the SCORES array by game rather than by player. To do so, we must interchange the PLAYER and GAME loops, making the GAME loop the outer loop and the PLAYER loop the inner loop. Notice, however, that we do not interchange the subscripts on SCORES. PLAYER is still the first subscript, and GAME is still the second subscript.

Syntax Summary	DIM Statement	
	Form:	`DIM variable(subscript [,subscript]),...`
	Example:	`DIM EMPLOYEES$(150), CALLS(150,150)`
	Interpretation:	Allocates area for array variables and specifies the maximum value that the subscripts may have. In two-dimensional arrays, a variable has two subscripts, and the subscripts are separated by commas.

EXERCISES

*10.20 In Figure 10.8, what score did player 4 get in game 1? What score did player 1 get in game 4?

10.21 Assume A is dimensioned by the statement `DIM A(10,20)`. Write the statements to subtract 5 from every element of A.

*10.22 In Program 10.7, interchange lines 620 and 630. What value would be printed for the average score for the first game? What value would be printed for the average score for the second game?

10.23 Suppose in the bowling team problem the data were given by game rather than by player. In that case, the DATA statements would be

```
DATA 186, 158, 202, 136
DATA 174, 193, 226, 141
DATA 163, 168, 214, 157
DATA 191, 177, 258, 132
DATA 206, 181, 197, 154
```

How would you modify Program 10.7 to accept the data in this form?

```
100 REM *** AVERAGE BOWLING SCORES ***
110 DIM SCORES(4,5)
120 GOSUB 200          'Fill SCORES array
130 GOSUB 400          'Calculate and print average for each player
140 GOSUB 600          'Calculate and print average for each game
150 STOP
160 '
200 REM *** Routine to read scores
210   FOR PLAYER = 1 TO 4
220     FOR GAME = 1 TO 5
230       READ SCORES(PLAYER,GAME)
240     NEXT GAME
250   NEXT PLAYER
260 RETURN
270 REM *** End of input routine
280 '
400 REM *** Routine to calculate and print average for each player
410   FOR PLAYER = 1 TO 4
420     TOTAL.SCORE = 0
430     FOR GAME = 1 TO 5
440       TOTAL.SCORE = TOTAL.SCORE + SCORES(PLAYER,GAME)
450     NEXT GAME
460     AVERAGE = TOTAL.SCORE / 5
470     PRINT USING "Average score for player # is ###.#"; PLAYER, AVERAGE
480   NEXT PLAYER
490   PRINT
500 RETURN
510 REM *** End of player routine
520 '
600 REM *** Routine to calculate and print average for each game
610   FOR GAME = 1 TO 5
620     TOTAL.SCORE = 0
630     FOR PLAYER = 1 TO 4
640       TOTAL.SCORE = TOTAL.SCORE + SCORES(PLAYER,GAME)
650     NEXT PLAYER
660     AVERAGE = TOTAL.SCORE / 4
670     PRINT USING "Average score for game # is ###.#"; GAME, AVERAGE
680   NEXT GAME
690 RETURN
700 REM *** End of game routine
710 '
800 REM *** Data used by program
810 DATA 186,174,163,191,206              :REM Scores for player 1
820 DATA 158,193,168,177,181              :REM Scores for player 2
830 DATA 202,226,214,258,197              :REM Scores for player 3
840 DATA 136,141,157,132,154              :REM Scores for player 4
850 END

RUN
Average score for player 1 is 184.0
Average score for player 2 is 175.4
Average score for player 3 is 219.4
Average score for player 4 is 144.0

Average score for game 1 is 170.5
Average score for game 2 is 183.5
Average score for game 3 is 175.5
Average score for game 4 is 189.5
Average score for game 5 is 184.5
Break in 150
Ok
```

PROGRAM 10.7   **A program to calculate average bowling score.**

PROGRAMMING ASSIGNMENTS

*10.21 Investors are planning to build a ski resort in Schussboom. They have three possible sites under study. Naturally, they are interested in the snowfall at these sites. They have collected data on the snowfall, in inches, for the three sites for each of the last five years. The data are

		Year No.			
Site No.	*1*	*2*	*3*	*4*	*5*
1	106	147	139	153	126
2	143	151	117	134	139
3	136	143	130	142	145

Write a program that will calculate and print the average snowfall over the past five years for each site. Also calculate and print the grand average snowfall for all three sites.

10.22 The Megaplex movie theater sells soda, candy, and popcorn. During one week, the sales were

Day	Soda	Candy	Popcorn
Sunday	234	112	93
Monday	187	94	98
Tuesday	170	101	43
Wednesday	194	92	71
Thursday	158	73	52
Friday	381	153	149
Saturday	423	189	172

Write a program that will calculate and print the total sales for each day; the total sales for the week

for soda, candy, and popcorn; and the total sales for the week for all items.

10.23 a) Write a program that will assign the following values to the two-dimensional array A:

$$
\begin{array}{cccc}
1 & 2 & 3 & 4 \\
5 & 6 & 7 & 8 \\
9 & 10 & 11 & 12 \\
13 & 14 & 15 & 16
\end{array}
$$

(Hint: The equation

```
COLUMN + 4 * (ROW - 1)
```

calculates these values.)

b) Write a program that will assign the rows of the two-dimensional array A of part (a) to the columns of the two-dimensional array B. B should have the following values:

$$
\begin{array}{cccc}
1 & 5 & 9 & 13 \\
2 & 6 & 10 & 14 \\
3 & 7 & 11 & 15 \\
4 & 8 & 12 & 16
\end{array}
$$

10.24 The first six rows of a set of numbers known as Pascal's triangle are shown below:

$$
\begin{array}{ccccccccccc}
 & & & & & 1 & & & & & \\
 & & & & 1 & & 1 & & & & \\
 & & & 1 & & 2 & & 1 & & & \\
 & & 1 & & 3 & & 3 & & 1 & & \\
 & 1 & & 4 & & 6 & & 4 & & 1 & \\
1 & & 5 & & 10 & & 10 & & 5 & & 1
\end{array}
$$

Notice that the first and last numbers in each row are 1's, that the *j*th row contains *j* numbers, and that each interior number is the sum of the two numbers above it. Write a program that prints the first 12 rows of the triangle. (Hint: Create a two-dimensional array P and assign the value 1 to the elements that correspond to the exterior numbers. Then calculate the interior numbers.)

SIMULATION USING ARRAYS

▪ *Chocolate Chip Cookies*

As an example of a still more complex use of arrays, let's calculate the distribution of chocolate chips in chocolate chip cookies. Every day, Chip Bloch bakes 1000 cookies, using 3000 chocolate chips. Although the average cookie obviously contains 3 chips (3000 chips/1000 cookies), Chip wants to know the percent of cookies that have 0 chips, 1 chip, 2 chips, and so on.

Following the first step of our structured procedure, we choose the following variable names:

Internal variables	Array to represent the cookies	COOKIE
	Counter for chips	CHIP
	Number specifying a particular cookie	COOKIE.NUM
Output variable	Array used to count the number of cookies with 0, 1, . . . chips	COUNTER

The algorithm is simple:

---

1. Initialize COOKIE and COUNTER arrays to 0.
2. Distribute 3000 chips randomly among 1000 cookies.
3. Count and print the number of cookies that contain 0, 1, 2, etc., chips.
4. Stop execution.

Once again we do not need a flowchart; we can go right to Program 10.8. The COOKIE array represents the 1000 cookies. When the program is done, the value of COOKIE(J) will be the number of chips in cookie J. To reflect the fact that, when we start, the cookies contain 0 chips, we initialize the COOKIE array to 0. Since the COUNTER array is used as a counter, it too is initialized to 0. When the program is done, the value of COUNTER(J) will be the number of cookies with J chips. Since there will be some cookies with 0 chips, in line 240 we use a starting value of 0 so that the FOR-NEXT loop initializes the 0th through 11th elements of COUNTER.*

In the FOR-NEXT loop in lines 310 through 340, we simulate distributing 3000 chips in 1000 cookies. In line 320, BASIC generates a random number between 1 and 1000 and assigns it to COOKIE.NUM, where COOKIE.NUM is the number of the cookie that gets this chip. In line 330, the COOKIE.NUM element of COOKIE is incremented to simulate adding a chip to that cookie. Line 330 functions like line 230 in Program 10.2. The program repeats this procedure for all 3000 chips.

In the FOR-NEXT loop in lines 410 through 430, BASIC counts the number of cookies that have 0, 1, 2, . . . chips. Line 420 bears some study. The subscripted variable COOKIE is used as a subscript for COUNTER, showing that a subscripted variable may be used as a subscript. But what does this complicated statement *mean*? Let's trace it. When COOKIE.NUM is 1, the statement is interpreted as

```
COUNTER(COOKIE(1)) = COUNTER(COOKIE(1)) + 1
```

COOKIE(1) is the number of chips in the first cookie, but we don't know its value. Let's arbitrarily assume the first cookie has 5 chips, so that COOKIE(1) is 5. Then line 420 is interpreted as

```
COUNTER(5) = COUNTER(5) + 1
```

---

*We dimensioned COUNTER with a maximum subscript of 11 on the assumption that a cookie is unlikely to contain four times the average number of chips. If that assumption is wrong, we will get a Subscript out of bounds error, and we will have to increase the size of COUNTER.

```
100 REM *** COOKIE PROGRAM ***
110 DIM COOKIE(1000), COUNTER(11)
120 RANDOMIZE TIMER
130 GOSUB 200                         'Initialize COOKIE and COUNTER arrays
140 GOSUB 300                         'Distribute chips into cookies
150 GOSUB 400                         'Count chips in cookies
160 GOSUB 500                         'Print results
170 STOP
180 '
200 REM *** Initialization routine
210   FOR J = 1 TO 1000
220     COOKIE(J) = 0                 'Initially, cookies contain no chips
230   NEXT J
240   FOR J = 0 TO 11
250     COUNTER(J) = 0
260   NEXT J
270 RETURN
280 REM *** End of initialization routine
290 '
300 REM *** Distribute the chips into the cookies
310 FOR CHIP = 1 TO 3000                          'For each chip, find out
320    COOKIE.NUM = 1 + INT(1000 * RND)           'which cookie it went into,
330    COOKIE(COOKIE.NUM) = COOKIE(COOKIE.NUM) + 1 'and add it to that cookie.
340 NEXT CHIP
350 RETURN
360 REM *** End of routine to distribute chips
370 '
400 REM *** Count the number of cookies that have 0, 1, 2, ... chips
410 FOR COOKIE.NUM = 1 TO 1000
420    COUNTER(COOKIE(COOKIE.NUM)) = COUNTER(COOKIE(COOKIE.NUM)) + 1
430 NEXT COOKIE.NUM
440 RETURN
450 REM *** End of routine to count cookies
460 '
500 REM *** Routine to print results
510    PRINT "Chips     0    1    2    3    4    5    6    7    8    9   10   11"
520    PRINT "Percent";
530    FOR J = 0 TO 11
540      PRINT USING "##.# "; COUNTER(J) * 100 / 1000;
550    NEXT J
560 RETURN
570 REM *** End of routine to print results
580 END

RUN
Chips     0    1    2    3    4    5    6    7    8    9   10   11
Percent 3.8 13.2 24.6 23.7 18.4  9.0  4.9  1.4  0.6  0.2  0.1  0.1
Break in 170
Ok
```

PROGRAM 10.8   **A program to calculate the distribution of chocolate chips in cookies.**

So the fifth element of COOKIE is incremented. Since the fifth element of
COUNTER is supposed to contain the number of cookies with 5 chips, and since
we just counted a cookie with 5 chips, the statement does what we want.

After all 1000 cookies have been inspected, we are ready to print the
results, which is done in the subroutine that starts in line 500. In that rou-

tine, line 540 converts COUNTER(J) into a percent by dividing by 1000, because there are 1000 cookies, and multiplying by 100 to convert the fraction into a percent.

EXERCISES

10.24 If we wanted to use 4000 chips instead of 3000, what changes would have to be made to Program 10.8? What changes would have to be made if we baked 500 cookies instead of 1000?

*10.25 Suppose COOKIE.NUM = 2 and COOKIE(COOKIE.NUM) = 4. What does that mean?

10.26 Program 10.9 reads 12 monthly rainfalls and calculates and prints the yearly total and each month's percentage of the total. As you can see, the program contains an error. Find and correct the error.

```
100 REM *** RAINFALL PERCENTAGES ***
110 DIM RAIN(12)
120 TOTAL = 0
130 FOR J = 1 TO 12
140   READ RAIN(J)
150   TOTAL = TOTAL + RAIN(J)
160 NEXT J
170 DATA 2.3, 4.8, 3.3, 4.0, 5.2, 5.9, 5.3, 6.4, 4.7, 3.9, 2.1, 2.4
180 PRINT USING "The total rainfall is ###.# inches"; TOTAL
190 PRINT "Month     Rain     Percent"
200 FMT$ = "  ##       ##.#       ##.#"
210 FOR K = 1 TO 12
220   PERCENT = 100 * RAIN(J) / TOTAL
230   PRINT USING FMT$; J, RAIN(J), PERCENT
240 NEXT K
250 END

RUN
The total rainfall is  50.3 inches
Month     Rain     Percent
Subscript out of range in 220
Ok
```

PROGRAM 10.9   **An incorrect program that calculates rainfall percentages.**

PROGRAMMING ASSIGNMENTS

10.25 Write a program that will determine the expected sex distribution in four-children families. The program should simulate 500 four-children families and print the number of families with 0 boys and 4 girls; 1 boy and 3 girls; 2 boys and 2 girls; and so on. Assume that half the babies are boys and half are girls. (Hint: You do not need an array FAMILIES with 500 elements.)

*10.26 Jack Cracker is collecting cards that come in a cereal box. There are five different cards, and you can assume they are randomly distributed in

the cereal boxes. Write a program that will determine how many boxes on the average Jack has to buy to get a complete set. (Hint: Set up an array CARD$ with five elements and initialize the elements to NO. Generate a random integer between 1 and 5 to simulate getting a card and set the corresponding element of CARD$ to YES. Jack has a complete set when all the elements of CARD$ are YES.) To get a reliable average, simulate 50 trials.

10.27 It is hard to believe, but mathematicians tell us it is true, that in a group of 23 people, the probability that two or more people have the same birthday is greater than 50 percent. (You might like to take a survey of your class to test this assertion.) Write a program that will accept the size of a group and determine the probability that two people in it have the same birthday. Assume that all days are equally likely to be a birthday and ignore leap years. (Hint: Set up an array DAY with 365 elements and initialize the elements to 0. Simulate birthdays by generating a random integer between 1 and 365 and set the corresponding element of DAY to 1. When you generate an integer and find that the corresponding element of DAY already contains a 1, you have found a match.) To get a reliable estimate, simulate 50 trials.

10.28 Write a program that simulates an epidemic. Start with N people and assume person number 1 has a cold. He sneezes on a randomly selected member of the group, which could even be himself. If the person he sneezes on is already sick, the epidemic stops spreading. If the person is not sick, that person catches the cold, and then it is his or her turn to sneeze on a randomly selected member of the group. This continues until the epidemic stops spreading. Simulate 50 such epidemics and calculate the percentage of the group that catches cold.

SUMMARY

In this chapter you have learned that

☐ An array is a collection of storage locations with the same name. The individual parts of the array are called elements.

☐ The DIM statement is used to define the number of elements in an array.

☐ FOR-NEXT loops are used to process arrays.

☐ Common errors in using arrays include (1) using a subscript for an array that is greater than the value specified when that array was dimensioned and (2) using an array without specifying a subscript.

☐ The bubble sort may be used to arrange the elements of an array in numerical, alphabetical, or inverse numerical or alphabetical order.

☐ A flag is a variable that indicates the presence or absence of a condition.

☐ The SWAP statement interchanges the values of two variables.

☐ To sort parallel arrays, SWAP the same elements of all the parallel arrays whenever you SWAP the elements of the array being sorted.

☐ Arrays may be searched using a sequential search or a binary search. A binary search requires that an array first be sorted, but it is faster than a sequential search for large arrays.

☐ Two subscripts are required to reference a particular element of a two-dimensional array. Nested FOR-NEXT loops are used to process two-dimensional arrays.

KEY TERMS IN THIS CHAPTER

QUESTIONS FOR REVIEW

10.1 A binary search ends when either a match has been found or _____ .

10.2 Is the following DIM statement correct?

DIM A, B, C$

10.3 True or false: The bubble sort may be used only to sort in ascending order.

10.4 Which statement is used to specify the size of an array?

10.5 To specify a particular element of an array, you use a _____ .

10.6 A search technique that requires the array to be sorted is the _____ search.

10.7 In a LET statement, can subscripted variables be used on the left side only, the right side only, or either side of the equal sign?

10.8 For large arrays, is the sequential search faster or slower than the binary search?

10.9 A variable that indicates the presence or absence of a condition is called a _____ .

10.10 Can the SWAP statement be used to swap numeric variables only, string variables only, or both numeric and string variables?

10.11 How would you fix the error if during execution BASIC displays the error message Type mismatch in line 60 and line 60 contains a SWAP statement?

ADDITIONAL PROGRAMMING ASSIGNMENTS

10.29 a) Write a program that accepts 10 numbers entered in numerical order and stores them in an array. Then allow the user to enter an eleventh number and store it in the array in its correct numerical position.

b) Accept 10 numbers and store them as in (a), but now let the eleventh number entered be the number that is to be deleted. Search the array to find that element and delete it. Move the elements with higher values to close the hole.

*10.30 A number is a palindrome if it reads the same forward as backward. For example, 74347 is a palindrome. Write a program that accepts a number with up to 50 digits and determines whether it is a palindrome.

*10.31 The following table gives the mileage between some American cities:

Write a program that accepts two cities' names and prints the mileage between them. The distances should be included in DATA statements. However, since the distance, for example, from Atlanta to Boston is the same as the distance from Boston to Atlanta, your program should contain only half the numbers in this table and should generate the other half. To solve this problem, you must search the array of city names for the starting city and then search the same array of city names for the destination city. You can do that with just one search routine.

10.32 Write a program that prints the words to "Old MacDonald Had a Farm." In case you have forgotten, MacDonald's farm had chicks, ducks, turkeys, pigs, cows, and horses, and their sounds

| From | To | | | | | |
---	Atlanta	Boston	Chicago	Dallas	Los Angeles	New York
Atlanta	—	1068	730	805	2197	855
Boston	1068	—	975	1819	3052	216
Chicago	730	975	—	936	2095	840
Dallas	805	1819	936	—	1403	1607
Los Angeles	2197	3052	2095	1403	—	2915
New York	855	216	840	1607	2915	—

were cluck, quack, gobble, oink, moo, and neigh. Recall that each time a new animal is introduced, the sounds of the previous animals are repeated. If you exploit the repetitive nature of the song and use a nested FOR-NEXT loop, you will find that your program is less than 30 lines long. (Hint: Store the animal names in one array and their sounds in a second array.)

10.33   a)   Write a program that converts an ENGLISH$ message into MORSE$ code. The Morse code is

A	· —	N	— ·
B	— · · ·	O	— — —
C	— · — ·	P	· — — ·
D	— · ·	Q	— — · —
E	·	R	· — ·
F	· · — ·	S	· · ·
G	— — ·	T	—
H	· · · ·	U	· · —
I	· ·	V	· · · —
J	· — — —	W	· — —
K	— · —	X	— · · —
L	· — · ·	Y	— · — —
M	— —	Z	— — · ·

You can use a period for a dot and a hyphen for a dash. In your output, separate the code for adjacent letters by a space.

   b)   Write a program that converts Morse code into English. In your input, separate the code for adjacent letters by a space, and separate adjacent words by two spaces.

10.34   A prime number is an integer greater than 1 that is exactly divisible by only 1 and itself. For example, 2, 3, 5, and 7 are primes, but 9, which is equal to 3 times 3, is not a prime. One way of finding prime numbers is the Sieve of Eratosthenes. In terms of BASIC, it works like this: An array N is initialized so that N(J) = J for J from 2 to MAX, where MAX is the highest number you are interested in. Starting from 2, examine the elements of N. If the element is 0, nothing is done. If the element is not 0, then all the elements that are multiples of that element are set to 0. Continue in this way until you have examined all the elements up to and including the first element whose square is greater than or equal to MAX. Those elements of N that are not 0 are prime. For example, the first element examined is 2. It is not 0 (it was just initialized to 2), so elements 4, 6, 8, etc., are made 0. The next element examined is 3. It, too, is not 0, so elements 6, 9, 12, etc., are made 0. (We set element 6 to 0 twice, but that doesn't hurt anything.) We next examine element 4, but since it

is 0 we do not do anything. Write a program to find the prime numbers less than 1000. (Hint: See Exercise 10.9.)

10.35   Define an array A. Allow a user to enter a number N and to input N numbers and store them in A. Copy into a second array, B, only one of each of the numbers that occur in A. For example, if A is 7, 3, 2, 5, 3, 9, 3, 5, then B should contain 2, 3, 5, 7, 9.

10.36   Given the following data on the world's longest rivers

River	Length
Amazon	4,000
Amur	2,744
Chang	3,964
Congo	2,900
Huang	2,903
Lena	2,734
Nile	4,145
Ob-Irtysh	3,362

Write a program that will read these data and print a list in order by length, with the longest first.

10.37   Write a program that will read a tic-tac-toe board marked with Xs, Os, and blank spaces and determine if there is a win or not.

10.38   The Home Sweet Home Building Company offers houses at the following prices:

One bedroom	84,000
Two bedrooms	103,000
Three bedrooms	119,000

At extra cost, they also offer the following options:

Central air conditioning	3,400
Stone fireplace	2,700
Two-car garage	950
Finished basement	2,600
Deck	1,100
Pool	8,500

Write a program that will allow a customer to select a house and any options. The program should print a bill itemizing the cost of the house and the selected options and the total cost of the house including options.

10.39   One state lottery selects 6 numbers from the numbers 1 through 48. Write a program that randomly selects the 6 numbers and then examines them to determine if they contain two (or more)

consecutive numbers. For example, the set 4, 16, 23, 24, 38, 40 contains the pair 23–24. Simulate 100 such random selections to determine what percent of the sets contain a sequential pair.

*10.40 Flip a coin 10 times and keep track of how many heads come up. Repeat the operation 500 times to get an accurate estimate of the number of times 0, 1, 2, ..., 10 heads come up. (Hint: You will find a counter array like the one used in line 230 in Program 10.2 useful. And like Program 10.8, this is one of those rare cases where the zero element of the array is useful.)

BEYOND THE BASICS

10.1 Write a program that accepts an integer up to 1000 and finds its prime divisors.

10.2 Write a program that accepts an integer between 1 and 9999 and prints the number in words.

10.3 Write a program that will accept two dates in the twentieth century in the form month, day, year and that will determine the number of days between the two dates. Use the program to determine how many days old you are.

10.4 Re-solve Beyond the BASICs Problem 9.4, but this time print the big numbers on the printer instead of on the screen.

10.5 Write a program that will multiply exactly two integers with up to 20 digits each to produce an answer that could have up to 40 digits.

10.6 Write a program that will read names and addresses and print mailing labels three across.

Mr. John Smith	Ms. Mary Jones	Mr. Harry Brown
146 Heights Road	13-21 7th Drive	34 Maple Avenue
Kansas City, KS 66122	New York, NY 11034	Dallas, TX 75268

Of course, you should not assume that the number of names to be printed is an exact multiple of three, so the last set you print may contain only one or two labels.

10.7 Write a program that plays the game of Concentration. This version of the game uses a deck of 40 cards that contains two 1s, two 2s, and so on, up to two 20s. Shuffle the deck and lay the cards face down in a table that contains 5 rows and 8 columns. Represent the cards by 40 asterisks. Two players take turns selecting a pair of cards by entering their row and column numbers. Display the selected cards, and if they match, give the player a point and keep the cards displayed. If the cards do not match, the player does not get a point, and the cards are replaced by asterisks. The game continues until all the cards are displayed, and the player with the highest score wins. Hint: You can calculate a subscript based on the values the players enter for ROW and COLUMN using the formula

$$SUB = COLUMN + 8 * (ROW - 1)$$

10.8 For large arrays a sorting technique known as the Shell sort is many times faster than the bubble sort. Like the bubble sort, the shell sort compares elements and swaps those that are in the wrong order. Unlike the bubble sort, which compares only adjacent elements, the Shell sort changes the distance between the elements that are compared. An example will make its operation clear. Suppose we want to sort an array A, which contains 10 elements. Call the distance between the elements that are compared GAP. We start by making GAP = 10 \ 2 = 5, and we compare A(1) and A(6), A(2) and A(7), etc., finally comparing A(5) and A(10). If any pair of elements is in the wrong order, they are swapped. When all the pairs that are 5 elements apart are sorted, we calculate a new value for GAP, using the statement GAP = GAP \ 2, and we sort the elements that are this distance apart. We continue this way as long as GAP is greater than or equal to 1. When the calculation of a new value of GAP gives a value less than 1, the whole array is sorted. Write a program that implements the Shell sort.

10.9 Re-solve Program 7.2, but now allow for the possibility that two or more salespeople may have the same highest sales. Your program must use only one loop to find the highest sale and the names of the best salespeople.

11

Sequential Files

··

In previous chapters, we used READ and DATA statements to supply programs with "constant" data. For example, in Program 10.2 we used DATA statements for costs of the different orders at No Bum Steer, and in Program 6.1 we used DATA statements for Bat-O's employees' names and pay rates. But using DATA statements is not always suitable. For example, if Bat-O had thousands of employees, the number of DATA statements needed would make the program too big to fit in the computer's memory. Also, we sometimes might need to use the identical data in several different programs. To do so, in each case we would have to type in all the DATA statements again, a time-consuming process in which errors can arise. Not only that, but whenever the data changed, we'd have to correct it separately in each program that used it.

To solve these problems, programs often use *files* instead of DATA statements as the source for their data. The files serve as central supply sources for any program that might need the data they contain. Furthermore, programs can modify the data stored in files, which makes files the ideal way to store relatively stable data (such as employee pay rates) that still must be changed from time to time.

Files can also be used to store the results of a program execution. For example, teachers who use a program to calculate students' grade point averages will normally want the results they calculated at the end of one semester to be available for use at the end of the next semester. Writing the results to a file provides this storage.

In this chapter, we will discuss how to create and read files. In addition, you will learn how to add and delete records from a file and how to change the data in a file.

WHAT IS A SEQUENTIAL FILE?

About Files In General

In Chapter 2, we defined a file as a stored program. When you saved your programs, you were creating *program* files. In this chapter, you will learn how to create and use *data* files. Before you do so, however, you need to understand the parts of a data file.

Let's start with some definitions. A **field** is a storage area containing some distinct item of data. A person's name, for example, would be stored in a field reserved for that information. Similarly, a social security number, a selling price, and a pay rate would each be stored in a field reserved for that item of data.

A **record** is a group of related fields considered as a unit. In Bat-O's payroll system, for example, a record might consist of three fields: one for the social security number, one for the employee's name, and one for the pay rate. Each record would contain data for one employee. Figure 11.1 indicates how BASIC stores data records on a disk.

Now that you know what a record is, we can redefine a **file** as a collection of related records. In Bat-O's payroll system, the collection of all the employee records could be called the payroll file.

To use data from a file, you must be able to identify the record you want. You can do so by singling out one of the fields to be the **key field**, or, more simply, the **key**. Then, when you want to refer to a particular record, you specify the key.

Field
An area reserved in a record to store an item of data.

Record
A group of related fields treated as a unit.

File
A group of related records.

Key (key field)
A field in a record used as the identifying field.

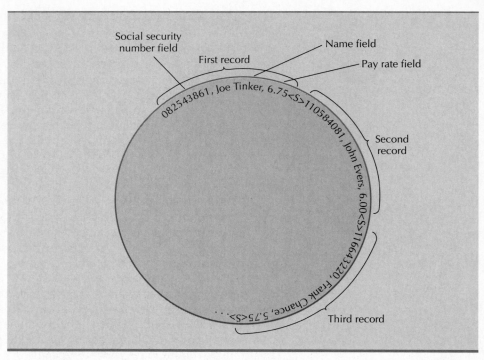

FIGURE 11.1   **An indication of how a payroll file is stored on a diskette. ⟨S⟩ represents the carriage return and line feed that are used to separate records.**

Since you want the key to find one and only one record, the information in the key field must be different for each record. Thus, for Bat-O, the social security number is a logical choice for the key field, because no two employees have the same social security number. The employee's name field would not be a good choice for the key field because the firm might employ two John Smiths.

■ *Creating a Sequential File*

Sequential file

A file in which records are stored, read, and processed in order from the first record to the last.

Keys play a special role in sequential data files because in a **sequential file** the records are stored, read, and written in sequential order based on the value of the key. (Another type of data file—random files—is discussed in Chapter 12.) When BASIC reads a sequential file, it must read the first record, then the second record, then the third, and so on, until it has read the last record. To give you a better idea of how a sequential file works, let's create a file for Mr. Croesus, who wants to keep track of his stock holdings. Each record will contain the stock name (which is the key field), the number of shares held, and the price.

As always, we start by choosing names for the variables. In this case we can use:

Stock name	STOCK.NAME$
Number held	NO.HELD
Price	PRICE

We do not classify the variables as input or output because, as you will see shortly, all of them are used for both input and output. We will name the file we create STOCKS.SEQ.

The algorithm is quite simple:

1. Open STOCKS.SEQ.
2. Read STOCK.NAME$, NO.HELD, and PRICE.
3. Write STOCK.NAME$, NO.HELD, and PRICE to STOCKS.SEQ.
4. Close STOCKS.SEQ.
5. Stop execution.

Program 11.1, based on this algorithm, creates the stock file. The program simply reads the data and writes them to the disk in the form of a file. The records that this program will use to create the file are given in the DATA statements.

THE OPEN STATEMENT

Program 11.1 contains several new BASIC statements. Line 110 shows an OPEN statement. An OPEN statement *must* be executed for a file before any data may be read from or written to a file.

The syntax of the OPEN statement for sequential files is

```
OPEN "filename" FOR mode AS #filenum
```

An OPEN statement associates a filename with a filenum (file number) that you assign and specifies the processing mode. The OPEN statement also as-

```
100 REM *** CREATING THE STOCK FILE ***
110 OPEN "STOCKS.SEQ" FOR OUTPUT AS #1
120 READ STOCK.NAME$, NO.HELD, PRICE
130    IF STOCK.NAME$ = "EOF"
          THEN GOTO 160
140    WRITE #1, STOCK.NAME$, NO.HELD, PRICE
150 GOTO 120
160 CLOSE #1
170 PRINT "The Stock file has been created"
180 '
190 REM *** Data to create file
200 DATA Amer T&T, 300, 21.375
210 DATA Bank Amer, 100, 19.25
220 DATA DuPont, 200, 55
230 DATA IBM, 125, 127
240 DATA K mart, 400, 33.25
250 DATA Litton, 30, 66.25
260 DATA Mobil, 100, 30
270 DATA NCR, 350, 28.25
280 DATA Pfizer, 250, 42.50
290 DATA Texaco, 150, 36.125
300 REM *** Trailer data follow
310 DATA EOF, 0, 0
320 END

RUN
The Stock file has been created
Ok
```

PROGRAM 11.1   **Creating the stock file.**

Buffer
A part of the computer's memory where data are temporarily stored when they are being read from or written to a disk.

signs a buffer to the file. A **buffer** is a part of the computer's memory where data are temporarily stored while they are being read from or written to a disk. In line 110 `filenum` is 1, `filename` is `STOCKS.SEQ`, and `mode` is `OUTPUT`.

Notice that `filename` must be enclosed in quotation marks. The rules for data filenames are the same as the rules for program filenames. It's a good idea to use a filename extension like `SEQ`, since this will help you distinguish between sequential data files and program files (which have the filename extension `BAS`) when you use the `FILES` command to list the names of the files on a disk. However, you may use a string variable instead of a string to specify the filename. And if you don't want to use the default drive, you may include the device name as part of the filename, for example, `"B:STOCKS.SEQ"`.

In an `OPEN` statement for a sequential file, `mode` must be one of three choices: `OUTPUT`, `INPUT`, or `APPEND`. If you select `OUTPUT`, the file will be written from the program to a disk. That is, BASIC will create a file with the specified name, which in line 110 is `STOCKS.SEQ`. Warning: If a file with that name already exists on the disk, the existing data will be *erased* and *replaced* by the new data.

`INPUT` is the mode you use to access a file that has already been stored on your disk. It means the file will be read. If a file with the name you specify in the `OPEN` statement does not exist on your disk, a `File not found` error occurs, and the program stops. `APPEND` is used when you want to add records to the end of a file that is stored on your disk. For example, if Mr. Croesus bought a new stock, you could open the file using `APPEND` and add his most recent acquisitions to the end of the file. If a file that is opened with `APPEND` does not exist, BASIC creates it.

As noted above, `filenum` specifies the file number to be associated with the filename. You use the filename only in the `OPEN` statement; in all other statements that refer to that file, you must use the file number. Notice that a number sign precedes the file number. The number sign is optional in the `OPEN` statement, but it helps make programs easier to read. Program 11.1 uses a `filenum` of 1. In programs that use more than one file, every file must have a separate `OPEN` statement, and each file must have a different file number. Normally, BASIC allows you to have only three files open at a time, that is, `filenum` must be 1, 2, or 3. If you want to have more than three files opened simultaneously, you have to use the `/F:` switch when you start BASIC. For example,

```
A>BASICA /F:4
```

tells BASIC you want to have four files opened simultaneously. The maximum number you may specify with the `/F:` switch is 15.

Before proceeding, make sure you understand how each of the following `OPEN` statements works.

OPEN Statement

```
OPEN "PAYROLL.SEQ" FOR INPUT AS #1
```

Effect

Opens the existing file `PAYROLL.SEQ` so it can be read and assigns file number 1 to it.

OPEN Statement

```
OPEN "INVENTRY.SEQ" FOR APPEND AS #3
```

Effect

Opens the file INVENTRY.SEQ and assigns file number 3 to it. If the file exists, new records will be added to the end of it. If the file does not exist, BASIC will create it.

OPEN Statement

OPEN FILENAME$ FOR OUTPUT AS #2

Effect

Opens and creates the file whose name has been previously assigned to the variable FILENAME$ and assigns it file number 2.

THE WRITE # AND CLOSE STATEMENTS

While an OPEN statement creates a file or allows you to add to an existing one, a WRITE # statement, like the one in line 140, is the instruction that actually puts the data in the file. The syntax of the WRITE # statement is

WRITE #filenum, variable [,variable] . . .

where filenum is the filenumber specified in a previous OPEN statement and variable contains the data we want to write to the file. The WRITE # statement in line 140 of Program 11.1 writes STOCK.NAME$, NO.HELD, and PRICE to filenum #1, which the OPEN statement specified is STOCKS.SEQ.

Other examples of the WRITE statement include the following statements:

WRITE Statement

WRITE #1, STUDENT$, CLASS$, GRADE

Effect

Writes the values of the variables STUDENT$, CLASS$, and GRADE to the file that was previously opened as file number 1.

WRITE Statement

WRITE #3, SSNO$, EMPLOYEE$, PAY

Effect

Writes the values of the variables SSNO$, EMPLOYEE$, and PAY to the file that was previously opened as file number 3.

Like the OPEN statement, the WRITE # statement uses the number sign. And like the PRINT statement, the WRITE # statement lets you list as many variables as you like, as long as the variables are separated by commas. The WRITE # statement automatically adds commas between fields when it writes the data on the disk and adds a carriage return and line feed as a separator between records.

The purpose of the CLOSE statement in line 160 is to tell BASIC that you are finished with the file. Executing a CLOSE statement for a file opened for OUTPUT also causes the final contents of the data buffer to be written to the file.*

The syntax of the CLOSE statement is

CLOSE [#filenum] [,#filenum] . . .

---

*Executing a RUN, NEW, END, or SYSTEM command also closes all open files, but it is good programming practice to close your files with a CLOSE statement and not depend on these other commands to do it for you.

As you can see, you may close several files with one CLOSE statement. For example,

CLOSE #1, #3

closes files associated with file numbers 1 and 3. If you type

CLOSE

omitting any file number, BASIC closes *all* open files.

Finally, notice the sequence of operations in Program 11.1:

1. Open the file.
2. Process the file.
3. Close the file.

All our file-processing programs will follow this sequence. In Program 11.1, the processing consisted of writing to the file. In other programs, we might read the file. But no matter what the processing, we always open, process, and close.

TRAILER DATA AND EXECUTION NOTICE

Before proceeding to use this data file, two other aspects of Program 11.1 deserve mention. First, notice that there is a test for trailer data (line 130) and that the test is placed before the WRITE # statement. This placement prevents the trailer data from being written to the file. Later in this chapter, we will discuss file processing problems where it is convenient if the files contain a trailer record. In that case, the test for trailer data will appear after the WRITE # statement.

Also, notice that while Program 11.1 is reading data from the DATA statements and writing to the file, it does not produce any output that can be seen on the screen or printer. Thus, we include the PRINT statement in line 170 to check that the program executed and created the file.

Printing a File

Even with the assurance of line 170, you may still want to see whether the program ran successfully. To do so, you can use the DOS command PRINT or TYPE. Save the BASIC program and then use the BASIC command SYSTEM to return to DOS. Now, if you use the command

PRINT STOCKS.SEQ

your printer will print out the contents of the file. (In other words, the DOS command PRINT performs like the BASIC command LLIST.) Notice that the filename is not enclosed in quotation marks. If the file is not in the default drive, you must include the drive specification:

PRINT B:STOCKS.SEQ

If you do not want to make a hard copy of the file, but just want to see it displayed on the screen, then from DOS you can use the TYPE command:

TYPE B:STOCKS.SEQ

Note that you do not have to leave BASIC to execute a DOS command. Instead, you can use the BASIC statement SHELL to execute DOS commands from within BASIC.

The syntax of the SHELL statement is

```
SHELL "DOS command"
```

So, for example, to get a printout of the STOCKS.SEQ file from within BASIC, you could type

```
SHELL "PRINT STOCKS.SEQ"
```

Reading a Sequential File

While PRINT and TYPE are fine for viewing a file, they would certainly not impress Mr. Croesus with your professionalism. So after the STOCKS.SEQ file has been created, we should write a program that will read and print the file with headings and in an attractive format.

We can use the same variable names as in Program 11.1, and our algorithm is almost as simple:

1. Open STOCKS.SEQ.
2. As long as records remain in the file, repeat steps 3 and 4.
3. Read a record from the file.
4. Print the record.
5. Close STOCKS.SEQ.
6. Stop execution.

In Program 11.2, which is based on this algorithm, BASIC reads this file. Note that the OPEN and CLOSE statements in Program 11.2 perform the same functions as in Program 11.1. However, this program uses 2 as the file number instead of 1, which was used in Program 11.1. The change was deliberate—to show that when you read a file you don't have to use the same file number as was used when the file was created. (You don't even need to know what that number was.) Also, although Program 11.2 uses the same data names as were used when the file was created, that was not necessary, either. Any data names, X and Y, for example, would do. The only name that must be the same is the filename, STOCKS.SEQ. And, of course, we must use file numbers and data names consistently *within this program*.

THE INPUT # STATEMENT

The INPUT # statement in line 180 tells BASIC to read the data from the file and to assign the next three values in filenum #2 (STOCKS.SEQ) to STOCK.NAME$, NO.HELD, and PRICE. The syntax of the INPUT # statement is

```
INPUT #filenum, variable [,variable]...
```

Like the WRITE # statement, the INPUT # statement uses a # sign before filenum. And as in the ordinary INPUT statement, the variables are separated by commas, and you may list as many variables as you like. Before proceeding, be sure you understand how each of the following INPUT # statements works:

INPUT# Statement

```
INPUT #1, STUDENT$, CLASS$, GRADE
```

```
100 REM *** READING AND PRINTING THE STOCK FILE ***
110 OPEN "STOCKS.SEQ" FOR INPUT AS #2
120 FMT$ = "\          \   ####      ###.##"
130 LPRINT "    STOCK HOLDINGS"
140 LPRINT
150 LPRINT "Stock        Number      Closing"
160 LPRINT "Name          Held        Price"
170 WHILE EOF(2) = 0
180    INPUT #2, STOCK.NAME$, NO.HELD, PRICE
190    LPRINT USING FMT$; STOCK.NAME$, NO.HELD, PRICE
200 WEND
210 CLOSE #2
220 LPRINT "End of the Stock file"
230 END

RUN
```

```
     STOCK HOLDINGS

Stock        Number      Closing
Name          Held        Price
Amer T&T      300        21.38
Bank Amer     100        19.25
DuPont        200        55.00
IBM           125       127.00
K mart        400        33.25
Litton         30        66.25
Mobil         100        30.00
NCR           350        28.25
Pfizer        250        42.50
Texaco        150        36.13
End of the Stock file
```

PROGRAM 11.2   **Reading the stock file.**

Effect

Reads the file that was previously opened as file number 1, and assigns the next three values from the disk to STUDENT$, CLASS$, and GRADE.

INPUT# Statement

INPUT #3, SSNO$, EMPLOYEE$

Effect

Reads the file that was previously opened as file number 3, and assigns the next two values from the disk to SSNO$ and EMPLOYEE$.

THE EOF FUNCTION

The main loop in Program 11.2 is a WHILE loop in lines 170 through 200. It continues executing as long as EOF(2) equals 0. The letters EOF stand for End Of File, and the EOF function determines when BASIC has read all the data in the file (in this case, file number 2). When a file is created, BASIC writes a special character, CHR$(26), after the last record in the file, to indicate the end of file. The EOF function returns a value of -1 if the end of file has been reached, and it returns a value of 0 if the end of file has not been reached.

Notice that the # symbol is not used before filenum in the parentheses following EOF, line 170.

The WHILE loop will keep executing as long as more data remain in the file. When the INPUT # statement in line 180 reads the last record, the EOF(2) function returns a value of -1, so the next time it is tested the condition in the WHILE statement will be false. Therefore, BASIC exits from the WHILE loop, closes the file, and executes the LPRINT statement in line 220.

Updating the Stocks File

Now let's assume that a week has ended and Mr. Croesus wants to update the stock file. He wants to enter the current prices and then calculate the percent change since last week and the current value.

Following the first step of our structured procedure, we select the following variable names:

Input and output variables	Stock name array	STOCK.NAME$
	Number held array	NO.HELD
	Price array	PRICE
Output variables	Price last week	LAST.WEEK.PRICE
	Percent change in price	PERCENT.CHANGE
	Current value of a stock	CURRENT.VALUE
	Total value of all stocks	TOTAL.VALUE

As you can see, the variables that are classified as both input and output are the same variables we used earlier, but now we have made them arrays.

The next step is to develop an algorithm. We can use the following:

1. Open STOCKS.SEQ for input.
2. Read STOCKS.SEQ into the STOCK.NAME$, NO.HELD, and PRICE arrays.
3. Close STOCKS.SEQ.
4. For each stock execute steps 5 and 6.
5. Set LAST.WEEK.PRICE equal to PRICE.
6. Enter new PRICE for stock, calculate and print PERCENT.CHANGE and CURRENT.VALUE, and accumulate CURRENT.VALUE into TOTAL.VALUE.
7. Print TOTAL.VALUE.
8. Open STOCKS.SEQ for output.
9. Write the STOCK.NAME$, NO.HELD, and PRICE arrays to STOCK.SEQ.
10. Close STOCKS.SEQ.
11. Stop execution.

Notice that in one program we will open a file for input, read it, close it, and then later open the same file for output and write to it.

In step 2 of the algorithm, we read the file into three parallel arrays because we have to hold the whole file in memory. After updating the PRICE array, in step 9 we write the three arrays back to the file.

This logic is shown in Program 11.3. The subroutine that starts at line 200 reads the STOCKS.SEQ file, the subroutine that starts at line 400 accepts new prices, and finally the subroutine that starts at line 700 rewrites the file.

Notice that there was a file named STOCKS.SEQ on the disk before Program 11.3 was run, and there is a file with the same name after the program is run, *but these are two different files*. When STOCKS.SEQ is opened for OUTPUT in line 710, the original STOCKS.SEQ is erased and the new STOCKS.SEQ takes its place. This new file is convenient, since it provides the proper starting point to figure stock price changes a week from now.

```
100 REM *** STOCK SYSTEM - ENTERING NEW WEEKLY PRICES ***
110 DIM STOCK.NAME$(25), NO.HELD(25), PRICE(25)
120 GOSUB 200                'Read the file
130 GOSUB 400                'Accept new prices and calculate results
140 GOSUB 700                'Rewrite file
150 STOP
160 '
200 REM *** Read stock file routine
210   OPEN "STOCKS.SEQ" FOR INPUT AS #1
220   J = 0
230   WHILE EOF(1) = 0
240     J = J + 1
250     INPUT #1, STOCK.NAME$(J), NO.HELD(J), PRICE(J)
260   WEND
270   NO.STOCKS = J
280   CLOSE #1
290 RETURN
300 REM *** End of routine to read stock file
310 '
400 REM *** Routine to accept new closing prices and calculate changes
410   TOTAL.VALUE = 0
420   FMT1$ = "\          \   ####      ###.##       ###.##       ###.#     ##,###.##"
430   FMT2$ = "TOTAL VALUE                                                ###,###.##"
440   LPRINT   "                     STOCK PERFORMANCE"
450   LPRINT
460   LPRINT "Stock      Number         Price            Percent    Current"
470   LPRINT "Name        Held    Last Week   This Week   Change     Value"
480   FOR J = 1 TO NO.STOCKS
490     LAST.WEEK.PRICE = PRICE(J)
500     PRINT "Enter the closing price of "; STOCK.NAME$(J);
510     INPUT PRICE(J)
520     PERCENT.CHANGE = (PRICE(J) - LAST.WEEK.PRICE) * 100 / LAST.WEEK.PRICE
530     CURRENT.VALUE = NO.HELD(J) * PRICE(J)
540     TOTAL.VALUE = TOTAL.VALUE + CURRENT.VALUE
550     LPRINT USING FMT1$; STOCK.NAME$(J), NO.HELD(J), LAST.WEEK.PRICE,
                         PRICE(J), PERCENT.CHANGE, CURRENT.VALUE
560   NEXT
570   LPRINT USING FMT2$; TOTAL.VALUE
580 RETURN
590 REM *** End of routine to accept new closing prices and calculate changes
600 '
```

PROGRAM 11.3   **Updating the stock file.**

```
700 REM *** Routine to rewrite file
710   OPEN "STOCKS.SEQ" FOR OUTPUT AS #1
720   FOR J = 1 TO NO.STOCKS
730     WRITE #1, STOCK.NAME$(J), NO.HELD(J), PRICE(J)
740   NEXT J
750   CLOSE #1
760 RETURN
770 REM *** End of rewrite file routine
780 END

RUN
Enter the closing price of Amer T&T? 23.50
Enter the closing price of Bank Amer? 19.00
Enter the closing price of DuPont? 56.875
Enter the closing price of IBM? 129.25
Enter the closing price of K mart? 33.75
Enter the closing price of Litton? 64.375
Enter the closing price of Mobil? 29.25
Enter the closing price of NCR? 29.50
Enter the closing price of Pfizer? 41.00
Enter the closing price of Texaco? 36.50
Break in 150
Ok
```

STOCK PERFORMANCE

Stock Name	Number Held	Price Last Week	This Week	Percent Change	Current Value
Amer T&T	300	21.38	23.50	9.9	7,050.00
Bank Amer	100	19.25	19.00	-1.3	1,900.00
DuPont	200	55.00	56.88	3.4	11,375.00
IBM	125	127.00	129.25	1.8	16,156.25
K mart	400	33.25	33.75	1.5	13,500.00
Litton	30	66.25	64.38	-2.8	1,931.25
Mobil	100	30.00	29.25	-2.5	2,925.00
NCR	350	28.25	29.50	4.4	10,325.00
Pfizer	250	42.50	41.00	-3.5	10,250.00
Texaco	150	36.13	36.50	1.0	5,475.00
TOTAL VALUE					80,887.50

PROGRAM 11.3   (Continued).

Syntax Summary

OPEN Statement
Form: OPEN "filename" FOR mode AS #filenum
Example: OPEN "STUDENTS.SEQ" FOR INPUT AS #2
Interpretation: Opens a file so it may be processed and associates it with file number filenum. mode must be one of the following: OUTPUT, which means the file will be created and written to, INPUT, which means the file exists and will be read, or APPEND, which means the file exists and new records will be added to the end of it.

WRITE # Statement
Form: `WRITE #filenum, variable [,variable] ...`
Example: `WRITE #1, CARD.NO$, PRICE`
Interpretation: Writes the values of the variables to the
                file that was previously opened as file
                number `filenum`.

CLOSE Statement
Form: `CLOSE [#filenum] [,#filenum] ...`
Example: `CLOSE #2`
Interpretation: Closes the file associated with file number
                `filenum`. If no file number is specified, all
                the open files are closed.

SHELL Statement
Form: `SHELL "DOS Command"`
Example: `SHELL "TYPE STUDENTS.SEQ"`
Interpretation: Exits to DOS, executes the given command, and
                then returns to BASIC.

INPUT # Statement
Form: `INPUT #filenum, variable [,variable] ...`
Example: `INPUT #1, CASE.NO$, FEE`
Interpretation: Reads the file that was opened with file
                number `filenum` and assigns values to the
                variables.

Getting the Bugs Out

Problem: During execution, BASIC displays the error message

                             `Bad file number in nn`

Reason: If `nn` is the line number of an OPEN statement, the file number
               you specified is too large. If `nn` is the line number of an INPUT #,
               WRITE #, or CLOSE statement or of an EOF function, a file with
               the specified file number was not opened.

Solution: If the error occurred on an OPEN statement, then use the /F:
               switch to increase the maximum file number. If the error oc-
               curred on an INPUT #, WRITE #, CLOSE, or EOF, make sure the file
               number specified in the statement is the same as the file num-
               ber specified when the file was opened.

Problem: During execution, BASIC displays the error message

                             `File not found`

Reason: You opened a file that does not exist for input.
Solution: You probably misspelled the filename.

Problem: During execution, BASIC displays the error message

                             `File already opened`

Reason: You tried to open a file twice, you used the same file number
               in two OPEN statements, or you tried to KILL a file that was
               open.
Solution: Delete the extra OPEN statement. Make sure that all the OPEN
               statements that are active at the same time use different file
               numbers. Close a file before you KILL it.

Problem:	During execution, BASIC displays the error message	

Input past end

Reason:	You tried to read past the end of a file.
Solution:	Make sure your program follows the logic shown in Program 11.2, using the EOF function to test for the end of the file.

EXERCISES

11.1 Write an OPEN statement that could be used in a program that creates a file named EMPLOYEE.SEQ.

*11.2 The records in the EMPLOYEE.SEQ file contain five fields: employee number, name, sex, year employed, and salary. Write a statement to put these data in the file.

11.3 Assume the EMPLOYEE.SEQ file has been created; write an OPEN statement that could be used in a program to print the contents of the file.

*11.4 Write a statement to read the data in the EMPLOYEE.SEQ file.

11.5 Given the statement

OPEN "INVENTRY.DAT" FOR INPUT AS #1

write the WHILE statement that could be used in a loop that executes until the end of INVENTRY.DAT is reached.

11.6 Modify Program 11.2 to print only those stocks whose current value, defined as the number of shares held times the price, is greater than $10,000.

PROGRAMMING ASSIGNMENTS

11.1 Write a program that allows Mr. Croesus to change the number of shares he owns of any stock by entering the name of the stock he wants to change.

11.2 The Molasses Delivery Service, Inc., has eight vans. The company keeps track of the total miles driven and gas used for each van so that it can calculate the miles per gallon (MPG). Write a program that creates a file in which each record contains the cumulative miles driven and gas used for a van. Then write a second program that accepts the current miles driven and gas used for each van. The program should update the file and print the current MPG and the cumulative MPG for each van, as well as the average values for all the vans.

11.3 Write two programs to create a home expenses system. The records in the file used by the system contain the name of an expense category and the year-to-date expenses in that category. Use the following categories: Auto, Clothing, Entertainment, Food, Insurance, Home, Savings, and Vacation. The first program should create this file, using zero for the year-to-date expenses. The second program should allow the user to enter category and expense data. The category should be indicated by a one-letter abbreviation (A, C, E, and so on). There may be several expenses in each category, and the user should be permitted to enter the data in any order. When the user indicates that all the data have been entered, the program should print the current and year-to-date expenses for each category and update the file.

*11.4 Write three programs to create a student grades system. The first program should create a file that stores the students' names and leaves room for three test marks. The second program should allow the instructor to enter test marks for a particular test. The third program, which should be executed only after marks for all three tests have been entered, should calculate average grades and then print each student's name, marks, and average. Assume that there are never more than 40 students in a class. (Hint: In the first program, accept students' names from the user and fill the students' names array. Create the file by writing the students' names array and a grades array, which is initially filled with zeros, to the file. In the second program, allow the user to enter the test number (1, 2, or 3) for which marks are to be entered. Display each student's name and allow the user to enter that student's mark. After all the marks have been entered, rewrite the file.)

11.5 Write a file version of Programming Assignment 10.10. Write one program to create a SEATS.SEQ file to store the orchestra and balcony seats arrays. Then write a second program that reads SEATS.SEQ to initialize the orchestra and balcony seats arrays. This program should make the seat reservations as described in Programming Assignment 10.10. When the user indicates a session is finished, save the two seat arrays back in SEATS.SEQ.

ADVANCED FILE PROCESSING

The logic of Program 11.3 depends on the fact that the STOCKS.SEQ file was so small that the whole file could be read into memory at one time. But in real applications, files often contain thousands or even tens of thousands of records, and the whole file cannot be read into memory at one time. As you will see, when a large file is processed, only one record at a time is read into the computer's memory. That record is processed, and then the next record is read. Large files take longer to process than small files, but they do not require more RAM.

Most file processing problems involve two files. The **master file** contains data that show the current status of a business or activity, just as Mr. Croesus' STOCKS.SEQ file showed his current stock portfolio. The **transaction file** contains data that reflect the changes that have occurred since the last time the master file was updated. (We did not use a transaction file for Mr. Croesus, but the new prices entered in Program 11.3 are transaction data and served the same purpose.)

Master file
A file that indicates the current status of a business or activity.

Transaction file
A file that indicates the changes that must be made to a master file.

◼ Sorting a File

Although the data in STOCKS.SEQ are in order by stock name, Programs 11.1, 11.2, and 11.3 would work even if the data were not in order. However, the sequential file processing programs that we will study next won't work unless the master and transaction files are in sequential order by key. The master file is automatically in sequential order, since it is created that way, and the processing never disturbs that order. The transaction file, however, is another story. Transaction files are likely to be created by a validation program that accepts data, checks them, and writes only correct data to the transaction file. Unless we sort the transaction data before we enter them into the validation program, the transaction file will not be in sequential order. Of course, we could sort the data by hand, but that would be tedious indeed! We should be able to get the computer to do this chore—and we can.

In Chapter 10, you learned how to use the bubble sort to sort an array. Sorting a file is more complicated. Fortunately, we can use the DOS file-sorting command SORT.

The syntax of the SORT command is

```
SORT <input-file >output-file
```

The < symbol tells the sort that the filename that follows is the name of the input file, and the > symbol tells the sort that the filename that follows is the name of the output file. For example, consider the file FLOWERS.1

```
ROSE      6.95
VIOLET    9.45
DAISY     7.25
```

where the flower name starts in column 1 and the price starts in column 10. We can sort this file in a number of ways:

SORT statement	Output
SORT <FLOWERS.1 >FLOWERS.2	FLOWERS.2 is in alphabetical order by name

DAISY	7.25
ROSE	6.95
VIOLET	9.45

SORT statement	Output
SORT /+10 <FLOWERS.1 >FLOWERS.3	/+10 means to start sorting on the 10th character, so that FLOWERS.3 is

ROSE	6.95
DAISY	7.25
VIOLET	9.45

SORT statement	Output
SORT /R/+10 <FLOWERS.1 >FLOWERS.4	/R means to sort in descending order, so that FLOWERS.4 is

VIOLET	9.45
DAISY	7.25
ROSE	6.95

Listing Selected Records

To see how a master file and a transaction file are processed together, consider the case of Cuff's department store, which has an extensive charge account system. Let's assume that the charge account file has already been created. In a real system, the records in the charge account file would contain lots of information, such as the customer's name and address, credit limit, and so on. However, to keep the problem simple, we will say that the records in the charge account file contain just the charge account number, which is the key, and the amount of money the customer owes.

To begin, let's assume that Cuff's owners have made a list of the account numbers of customers who have not recently made any purchases. They want you to write a program to list the balances of those accounts. The keys—that is, the charge account numbers—of the records they want listed have been stored in the transaction file. The records in the transaction file contain only this one field.

Figure 11.2 shows a system flowchart outlining the necessary processing. Just as a program flowchart shows the logic of a program, so a **system flowchart** shows the files used in a system.

The symbol

System flowchart
A flowchart that shows the relationships between the files and the programs used by a system.

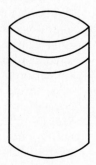

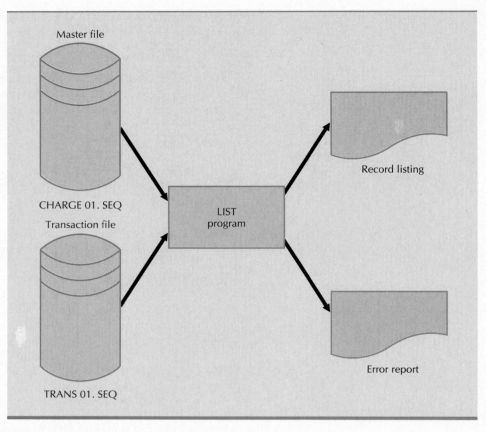

FIGURE 11.2   **System flowchart to list selected records.**

represents a file stored on a diskette or fixed disk. The symbol

represents the computer, and the symbol

represents a printed report.

Figure 11.2 shows two input files—the master file (CHARGE01.SEQ) and the transaction file (TRANS01.SEQ)—and two output files—the listing of selected records and an error report. (We will discuss the need for an error report later.) You may be surprised that we consider a report as a file, but it is convenient to do so. Each line on the report is a sort of record, and the collection of all the records (lines) is the file.

Transaction data need not be contained in a file. You could enter the transaction data using an INPUT statement, as we did in Program 11.3, or READ-DATA statements. However, when there are lots of data, obtaining transaction data from a file is often most convenient. A separate validation program would be written to create the transaction file. The transaction data could be entered in random order, and the program would create the raw transaction file. Then, as explained earlier, you could use the DOS SORT command to sort the raw transaction file.

Figure 11.3 shows the contents of two files. The records in the master file, CHARGE01.SEQ, contain the account number, which is the key, and the balance. The records in the transaction file, TRANS01.SEQ, contain just the account number. Notice that both files contain a trailer record, whose account number is 9999. As you will see shortly, the logic of the program is simplified if every file contains a trailer record with a key greater than the key of any real record in the file.

To understand exactly what we want the program to do, consider the first four master records and transaction records in parts (a) and (b) of Figure 11.3.

Comparing the keys of the two files, we see that master records 146, 175, and 334 have matching transaction records and therefore are to be listed.* Master record 212 has no matching transaction record and therefore is not to be listed. Finally, consider transaction record 152. The program is supposed to list the master records whose keys appear in the transaction file, but master record 152 does not exist! Clearly an error has been made, and it is most likely that transaction record 152 represents a typing error. To correct such errors, we will list transaction records that do not match any master record on an error report.

Even if we use a validation program to create this transaction file, it could not detect this kind of error. Such a program can verify that the data are in the correct range (for example, having three digits) and of the correct type (numeric). But short of reading the master file, a validation program cannot know that there is no master record 152.

146,45.46	146
175,33.07	152
212,9.219999	175
334,108.42	334
348,26.17	384
397,56.84	397
406,15.67	403
438,25.37	474
474,52.36	498
498,8.59	562
537,47.51	583
562,76.25	614
583,125	626
604,16.37	659
626,42.85	694
659,23.61	699
694,54.4	753
709,19.26	763
753,15.87	877
786,25.71	896
849,13.85	941
877,45.91	982
(a) 9999,0	(b) 9999

FIGURE 11.3   **(a) The master file: CHARGE01.SEQ. (b) The transaction file: TRANS01.SEQ.**

*Although I say "master records 146, 175, and 334," for complete accuracy I should say "master records with keys 146, 175, and 334," but my meaning should be clear and I will generally use the simpler expression.

VARIABLE NAMES AND ALGORITHM

As always, we begin by choosing variable names:

Input variables	Master record key	ACCT.NO.MSTR
	Master record balance	BALANCE
	Transaction record key	ACCT.NO.TRANS
Output variables	Master record key	ACCT.NO.MSTR
	Master record balance	BALANCE

The algorithm we will use is

1. Open all the files.
2. Repeat step 3 as long as transaction records remain.
3. Compare the keys from the master and transaction records.
   a) List master records that have matching transaction records.
   b) Do not list master records that do not have matching transaction records.
   c) Write on the error report transaction records that do not have matching master records.
   d) Read the next record(s).
4. Close the files.
5. Stop execution.

This program contains so many subroutines, you may find that the hierarchy diagram shown in Figure 11.4 helps you understand the program's structure. Notice that the upper left corner of some modules is shaded. The shading means that those modules are called from more than one place in the program.

FLOWCHART

The overall structure of this algorithm breaks down into three subroutines: initialization, listing, and termination. The termination subroutine simply closes the files and tells you the program run is finished, so it is not shown here. The initialization and listing subroutines are more complex, however, as Figure 11.5 shows.

The initialization subroutine (Figure 11.5a) opens the files, assigns initial values to some variables, and reads the first master and first transaction records. The files are read in subroutines so that any time a file must be read, you need only execute a simple GOSUB statement.

The listing subroutine (Figure 11.5b) consists of a WHILE loop that will keep repeating as long as the transaction file has not reached its end—that is, as long as EOF(2) equals 0. To make the flowchart (and program) clearer, we introduce a variable named FALSE, assign it the value 0, and code the condition on the WHILE statement as EOF(2) = FALSE.

The WHILE loop uses a case structure to determine if the master key is equal to, greater than, or less than the transaction key. BASIC then executes the keys equal, master greater, or master less subroutine (Figure 11.5c) to carry out the necessary processing.

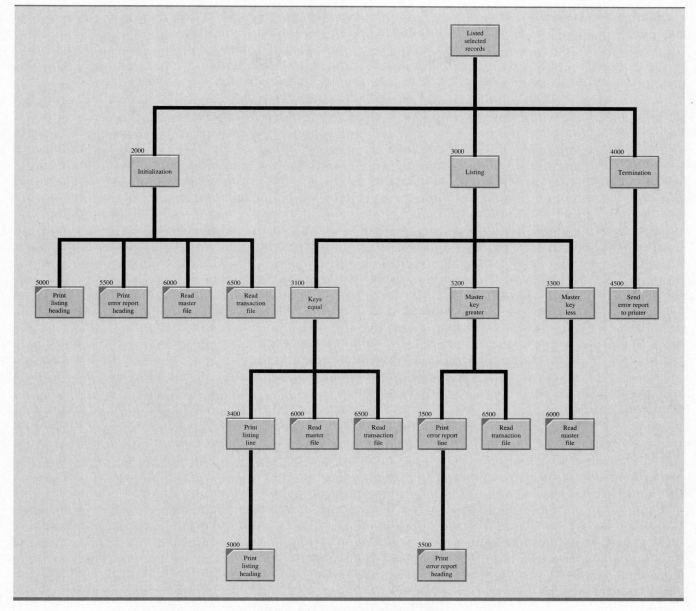

FIGURE 11.4 **Hierarchy diagram to list selected records.**

Let's see what the necessary processing is by tracing the listing subroutine, assuming the keys are as given in Figure 11.3. The key of the first record of both files is 146. BASIC therefore executes the keys equal subroutine. If the keys are equal we have found a master record that should be listed. So we list the record, read the next master and next transaction records, and return.

The next master record is 175; the next transaction record is 152. This time BASIC executes the master greater subroutine. What does this choice mean? We have just read master record 175. Clearly there is no master record 152; if there were such a master record, we would have read it before we got to master record 175. Thus, transaction record 152 has no matching master record. This transaction record must be an error, so we list it on the error report. We then read the next transaction record and return. We do

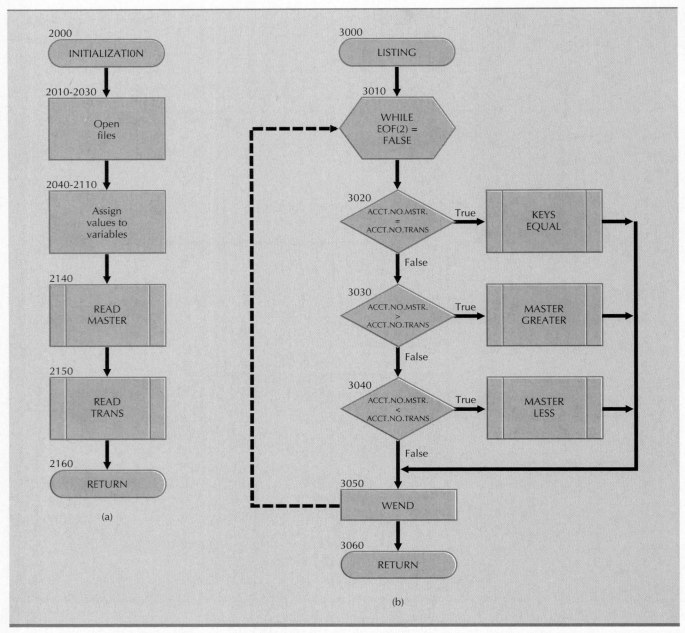

FIGURE 11.5   **Flowchart to list selected records. (a) Initialization subroutine. (b) Listing subroutine. (c) Keys equal, master greater and master subroutines.**

not read the next master record since we have a perfectly good master record, number 175, and must still see whether it should be listed or not.

In our example, the next transaction record is 175, so when the keys are compared we find they are equal. BASIC therefore again executes the keys equal subroutine.

The next master is 212 and the next transaction is 334. Once again the keys are not equal, but this time BASIC executes the master less subroutine. What does this choice mean? Applying the same logic we used before, we know there is no transaction record 212, because if there were we would have read it before we read transaction record 334. Since master record 212 has no matching transaction record, it should not be listed. We therefore read

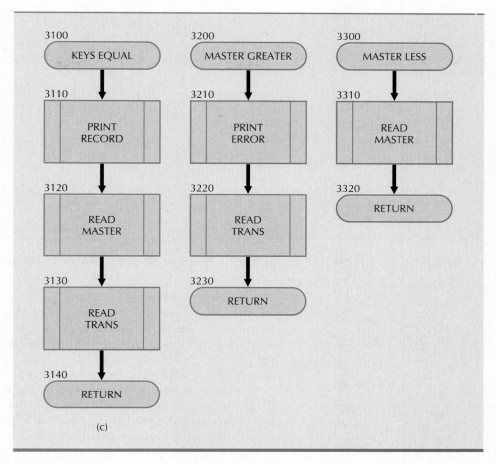

FIGURE 11.5   **(Continued).**

the next master record and return. We do not read the next transaction record because we have not yet processed the current transaction record, number 334. The program continues in this way until the transaction file reaches its end.

END-OF-FILE PROCESSING

To check this flowchart, let's examine what happens when the end of the file is reached.

The type of end-of-file processing required will depend on which file reaches its end first. Suppose the last few master records and transaction records have the keys shown in Figure 11.6(a). The EOF in this figure represents the end of file, and the 9999 is the key of the trailer record.

In this case, the transaction file will reach its end first. Why? Because after master record 786 has been listed, master record 849 will be read, but the next reading of the transaction file will retrieve the trailer record and encounter the end of file. The end of file will cause EOF(2) to be set to -1. With EOF(2) equal to -1, the WHILE loop will stop executing. BASIC will then return to the main program. This processing is correct because when the transaction file reaches its end the program is finished.

You may wonder what would happen if the master file reached its end first. Assume the last few master and transaction records have the keys shown in Figure 11.6(b). These keys show that after master record 877 is listed, the next reading of the master file will retrieve the trailer record,

File		Keys			
Master	786	849	877	9999 EOF	
Transaction	786	9999	EOF		

(a)

File		Keys			
Master	877	9999	EOF		
Transaction	877	896	941	982	9999 EOF

(b)

FIGURE 11.6   **(a) and (b) Keys of final master and transaction records.**

which sets the master key to 9999. The remaining transaction keys, 896, 941, and 982, are all errors. When they are compared, the master key will always be greater than the transaction key, so the master greater subroutine will write these transaction records on the error report. When the end of file is encountered, EOF(2) is set to -1, causing the WHILE loop to stop executing and returning BASIC to the main program.

As long as you create both master and transaction files with the key of the trailer record greater than the key of any actual record, the correct end-of-file processing takes place no matter which file reaches its end first.

Program 11.4 implements the logic of our algorithm and flowchart, but it also introduces new programming techniques that warrant explanation.

PROGRAM ORGANIZATION

First, notice that this is a large program; it contains 94 lines. When programs get that large, their organization becomes important. Thus, the four main routines begin at consecutive thousand-line numbers: the main program at line 1000, the initialization subroutine at line 2000, the listing subroutine at line 3000, and the termination subroutine at line 4000. Subroutines called only from within one routine are given numbers in the same thousand range. For example, the listing routine, which starts at line 3000, calls the keys equal, master greater, and master less subroutines, and these are given line numbers in the 3000 range. The only exceptions to this convention are the subroutines that are called from more than one routine. They are given line numbers higher than the other sections of the program. For example, the read master subroutine is called from both the initialization and listing routines, so it is started at line 6000.

PRINTING MORE THAN ONE REPORT

Another feature is the way this program prints two separate reports even though there is only one printer connected to the computer. (The vertical line that separates the two reports is meant to indicate that the reports are printed separately.) The record listing is printed using the usual LPRINT statements. In contrast, the error report is written to a file. Line 2030 opens ERROR.RPT as file number 3. Then a PRINT #3 USING statement (see line 3530) or a PRINT #3 statement (see line 5540) will write a line on the error report.

```
1000 REM *** LISTING SELECTED RECORDS ***
1010 GOSUB 2000          'Initialization routine
1020 GOSUB 3000          'Listing routine
1030 GOSUB 4000          'Termination routine
1040 STOP
1050 '
2000 REM *** Initialization routine =========================================
2010   OPEN "CHARGE01.SEQ" FOR INPUT AS #1
2020   OPEN "TRANS01.SEQ" FOR INPUT AS #2
2030   OPEN "ERROR.RPT" FOR OUTPUT AS #3
2040   PAGE.NO.LIST = 1
2050   PAGE.NO.ERROR = 1
2060   PAGE.SIZE = 54
2070   LIST.HEAD.FMT$ = " LISTING OF SELECTED RECORDS    ##"
2080   LIST.LINE.FMT$ = "         ###         #,###.##"
2090   ERROR.HEAD.FMT$ = " LISTING OF ERROR RECORDS    ##"
2100   ERROR.LINE.FMT$ = "         ###"
2110   FALSE = 0
2120   GOSUB 5000         'Print Listing heading
2130   GOSUB 5500         'Print Error Report heading
2140   GOSUB 6000         'Read first master record
2150   GOSUB 6500         'Read first transaction record
2160 RETURN
2170 REM *** End of initialization routine
2180 '
3000 REM *** Listing routine =================================================
3010   WHILE EOF(2) = FALSE
3020     IF ACCT.NO.MSTR = ACCT.NO.TRANS
           THEN GOSUB 3100: GOTO 3050
3030     IF ACCT.NO.MSTR > ACCT.NO.TRANS
           THEN GOSUB 3200: GOTO 3050
3040     IF ACCT.NO.MSTR < ACCT.NO.TRANS
           THEN GOSUB 3300: GOTO 3050
3050   WEND
3060 RETURN
3070 REM *** End of listing routine
3080 '
3100 REM *** Keys equal routine
3110   GOSUB 3400         'Print record
3120   GOSUB 6000         'Read next master record
3130   GOSUB 6500         'Read next transaction record
3140 RETURN
3150 REM *** End of keys equal routine
3160 '
3200 REM *** Master key greater routine
3210   GOSUB 3500            'Print transaction on Error Report
3220   GOSUB 6500            'Read next transaction record
3230 RETURN
3240 REM *** End of master key greater routine
3250 '
3300 REM *** Master key less routine
3310   GOSUB 6000            'Read next master record
3320 RETURN
3330 REM *** End of master key less routine
3340 '
```

PROGRAM 11.4   **Program to list selected records.**

```
3400 REM *** Print Listing routine
3410    LINE.COUNT.LIST = LINE.COUNT.LIST + 1
3420    IF LINE.COUNT.LIST >= PAGE.SIZE
           THEN GOSUB 5000
3430    LPRINT USING LIST.LINE.FMT$; ACCT.NO.MSTR, BALANCE
3440 RETURN
3450 REM *** End of print Listing routine
3460 REM
3500 REM *** Print Error Report routine
3510    LINE.COUNT.ERROR = LINE.COUNT.ERROR + 1
3520    IF LINE.COUNT.ERROR >= PAGE.SIZE
           THEN GOSUB 5500
3530    PRINT #3, USING ERROR.LINE.FMT$; ACCT.NO.TRANS
3540 RETURN
3550 REM *** End of print Error Report routine
3560 '
4000 REM *** Termination routine ================================================
4010    LPRINT
4020    LPRINT "     End of Listing"
4030    PRINT #3,
4040    PRINT #3, "End of Error Report"
4050    CLOSE
4060    GOSUB 4500            'Print Error Report
4070    PRINT "Normal end of program"
4080 RETURN
4090 REM *** End of termination routine
4100 '
4500 REM *** Send Error Report to printer routine
4510    OPEN "ERROR.RPT" FOR INPUT AS #3
4520    WHILE EOF(3) = FALSE
4530       LINE INPUT #3, ERROR.LINE$
4540       LPRINT ERROR.LINE$
4550    WEND
4560    CLOSE
4570 RETURN
4580 REM *** End of send Error Report to printer routine
4590 '
5000 REM *** Listing heading routine ============================================
5010    LPRINT CHR$(12);      'Send form feed signal to printer
5020    LPRINT USING LIST.HEAD.FMT$; PAGE.NO.LIST
5030    LPRINT
5040    LPRINT "   Account Number     Balance"
5050    LPRINT
5060    PAGE.NO.LIST = PAGE.NO.LIST + 1
5070    LINE.COUNT.LIST = 4
5080 RETURN
5090 REM *** End of Listing heading routine
5100 '
5500 REM *** Error Report heading routine
5510    PRINT #3,CHR$(12);
5520    PRINT #3, USING ERROR.HEAD.FMT$; PAGE.NO.ERROR
5530    PRINT #3,
5540    PRINT #3, "   Account Number
5550    PRINT #3,
5560    PAGE.NO.ERROR = PAGE.NO.ERROR + 1
5570    LINE.COUNT.ERROR = 4
5580 RETURN
5590 REM *** End of Error Report heading routine
5600 '
```

PROGRAM 11.4   (Continued).

```
6000 REM *** Read master file routine ==========================================
6010   INPUT #1, ACCT.NO.MSTR, BALANCE
6020 RETURN
6030 REM *** End of read master file routine
6040 REM
6500 REM *** Read transaction file routine
6510   INPUT #2, ACCT.NO.TRANS
6520 RETURN
6530 REM *** End of read transaction file routine
6540 END
RUN
Normal end of program
Break in 1040
```

LISTING OF SELECTED RECORDS 1		LISTING OF ERROR RECORDS 1
Account Number	Balance	Account Number
146	45.46	152
175	33.07	384
334	108.42	403
397	56.84	614
474	52.36	699
498	8.59	763
562	76.25	896
583	125.00	941
626	42.85	982
659	23.61	
694	54.40	End of Error Report
753	15.87	
877	45.91	
End of Listing		

PROGRAM 11.4   **(Continued).**

The syntaxes of the PRINT # and PRINT # USING statements are

> PRINT #filenum, expression,...

and

> PRINT #filenum, USING format string; expression,...

The PRINT # USING and PRINT # statements work just like the PRINT USING and PRINT statements, except that they write to a file instead of to the screen.*

Lines 5530 and 5550 in Program 11.4 show that to print a blank line you code

> 5530 PRINT #3,

The comma with nothing following looks strange, but the syntax shows that the comma after the file number is required.

When the listing routine is finished, the termination routine then prints the error report (see lines 4500 through 4570). ERROR.RPT is opened for

---

*WRITE # and PRINT # both write data to a file. The difference is that WRITE # writes the data in a form that can be read by an INPUT # statement.

output in the initialization routine and closed in line 4050. Then line 4510 reopens it, this time for input. The WHILE loop in lines 4520 through 4550 reads each line from the disk file and sends it to the printer.

The LINE INPUT # statement (line 4530) reads the lines from the disk file. The syntax of the LINE INPUT # statement is

`LINE INPUT # filenum, string variable`

Like the LINE INPUT statement (see Chapter 9), the LINE INPUT# statement ignores commas and quotation marks and reads a whole line. Thus, lines in the error report may contain any characters you like, and the LINE INPUT # statement will read them. After the LINE INPUT # statement reads a line into the variable ERROR.LINE$, the LPRINT statement in line 4540 prints that line. This reading and writing process continues until ERROR.RPT reaches its end and the WHILE loop ends.

PRINTING MULTIPAGE REPORTS

In earlier chapters, we printed headings only once, because we assumed that the report occupied only one page. But now that we are writing more professional programs, we should consider the possibility that the report could extend over several pages. In that case, we want the heading printed at the top of each page.

The first task of the heading subroutines in lines 5010 and 5510 is to send the printer a "form feed" character, CHR$(12), to advance to a new page. Even though the error report is being written to the disk, when the error report is printed, the form feed character will cause the printer to advance to the next page. Lines 5020 and 5520 then print the report titles and the page number, which is determined by the appropriate counter, PAGE.NO.LIST or PAGE.NO.ERROR. These counters are initialized at 1 in lines 2040 and 2050 and are incremented in lines 5060 and 5560.

One problem remains: How do you know that a page is full and a new page should be started? The answer is simple: you keep a running count of the lines that have been used on the page. Each report has its own line counter variable. For the record listing, it is LINE.COUNT.LIST; for the error report, it is LINE.COUNT.ERROR. These variables are given their initial values in the heading subroutines. Because the headings use four lines, the line counter variables are given initial values of 4 in lines 5070 and 5570.

As shown in lines 3410 and 3510, each time a line is written on a report, 1 is added to the line counter variable for that report. Then the line counter variable is tested to see whether it is time to start a new page. These tests are shown in lines 3420 and 3520. If the line counter variable is greater than or equal to PAGE.SIZE, the heading subroutine is executed. (PAGE.SIZE is a variable that is assigned the value 54 in line 2060. Standard printer paper is 11 inches long, and standard printing is 6 lines per inch, so there is room on a page for 66 lines. Leaving a one-inch margin at the top and bottom means that the report can run 9 inches, or 54 lines.)

The PAGE.SIZE variable provides a convenient way to make sure the heading routines will properly print reports that are more than one page long. With the data used for testing, the reports fit on one 54-line page. By temporarily setting PAGE.SIZE equal to 10, for example, you can quickly verify that the heading subroutines are working properly. You can then reset PAGE.SIZE to its standard value of 54.

Debugging

File processing programs produce so little output that the debugging techniques you have used in earlier chapters need to be supplemented. One of the simplest and most effective things you can do to aid your debugging is to print the records as you read them. For Program 11.4, the two statements

```
6015 PRINT "Current master record"; ACCT.NO.MAST, BALANCE
```

and

```
6515 PRINT "Current trans record"; ACCT.NO.TRANS
```

would be satisfactory. If you use this technique and the TRON command, you will see the data you are working with and the lines you executed. You will be able to figure out the lines you should have executed. If there is a discrepancy between what your program did and what it should have done, the output will help you to find logic errors.

Printing to the Screen or Printer

In previous chapters, you were advised to debug your programs using PRINT statements. After the programs were debugged, if you wanted hard copy output, you had to change the PRINT and PRINT USING statements to LPRINT and LPRINT USING statements. The PRINT # and PRINT # USING statements offer another way of directing output to either the screen or the printer that you may find more convenient.

The PRINT # and PRINT # USING statements can be used to direct output to either the screen or the printer because both the screen and the printer may be opened as files. The filename of the screen is SCRN:, and the filename of the printer is LPT1: (don't overlook the final :). For example, we can open the file named LPT1: for output as file number 1:

```
OPEN "LPT1:" FOR OUTPUT AS #1
```

This statement directs output from PRINT #1 and PRINT #1 USING statements to the printer. Similarly, opening the file named SCRN: for output as #1 directs output from PRINT #1 and PRINT #1 USING statements to the screen.

Building on these ideas, the following statements show how we print on the screen or the printer, depending on the user's wishes:

```
120 INPUT "Do you want output to printer "; RESPONSE$
130 IF RESPONSE$ = "Y"
        THEN DEVICE$ = "LPT1:"
        ELSE DEVICE$ = "SCRN:"
140 OPEN DEVICE$ FOR OUTPUT AS #1
```

Syntax Summary

PRINT # Statement
Form: PRINT #filenum, expression, ...
Example: PRINT #2, FILM$, DIRECTOR$, RECEIPTS
Interpretation: Writes the values of the expressions to the file previously opened as filenum.

PRINT # USING Statement
Form: PRINT #filenum, USING format string; expression, ...
Example: PRINT #2, USING "\   \ $##.##"; FLOWER$, PRICE
Interpretation: Writes the values of the expressions to the file previously opened as filenum, using the format specified in format string.

LINE INPUT # Statement
Form: LINE INPUT #filenum, string variable
Example: LINE INPUT #1, WHOLE.LINE$
Interpretation: Reads a whole line from the file that was opened with the file number filenum and assigns its value to string variable.

EXERCISES

*11.7 Suppose the keys of the master and transaction files were as follows:

File	Keys				
Master	24	53	9999	EOF	
Transaction	37	53	86	9999	EOF

Trace Program 11.4 using these keys. Make a list, in order, of the names of the subroutines that will be executed. To help you get started, the first names are: INITIALIZATION, LIST HEADING, ERROR REPORT HEADING, READ MASTER, READ TRANS.

11.8 Determine what would happen if Program 11.4 were executed using the following data:

File	Keys			
Master	32	74	9999	EOF
Transaction	32	32	9999	EOF

Notice that two transaction records have a key equal to 32.

11.9 Write the statement that could be used to print the variables AUTHOR$, TITLE$, and SALES to file number 2, using the format string named REPORT.LINE.FMT$.

11.10 What value would you assign to PAGE.SIZE if you wanted a 1½-inch margin at the top of the page and a 2-inch margin at the bottom?

*11.11 In a heading routine, what do you do to the line counter variable? What do you do to the page counter variable?

11.12 Write the SORT command to sort a file named BOOKS on the name field, which is the first field in the record, and create the file BOOKS.SRT.

PROGRAMMING ASSIGNMENTS

11.6 a) Write a program to create an inventory file named ICECREAM.SEQ for the Frozen Stiff Ice Cream company, which manufactures 31 different flavors. Each record should contain a three-digit flavor number, which is the key, the flavor name, and the number of gallons on hand. Use your imagination to invent delicious data. Don't forget to include a trailer record.

b) Write another program to read and print the file. Include headings and the total inventory on the report.

11.7 File A11-07.SEQ contains student numbers, names, credits completed, grade point averages, and a final trailer record. Write a program to list those students whose GPA is greater than 3.00. Include headings and a count of the number of students listed.

In the following programming assignments, you may either write a program to create the transaction file or supply the transaction data using an INPUT statement or READ-DATA statements. Whichever method you use, remember that the transactions must be in sequential order and the file must contain a trailer record. Be sure to include erroneous transactions.

11.8 Write a program to list selected records from the ICECREAM.SEQ file created in Programming Assignment 11.6.

11.9 Write a program to list selected records from file A11-07.SEQ mentioned in Programming Assignment 11.7. Use the following transactions: 185, 194, 285, 287, 749, and 825.

DELETING, ADDING, AND UPDATING RECORDS

Files are generally meant to change. Customers come and go; they buy new goods and pay off accounts. In this section, we will consider various ways to change files.

■ *Deleting Records*

Cuff's needs to be able to delete records from its master file when some customers close their accounts. To do so, Cuff's has created a transaction file that contains the keys of the records it wants to delete.

SYSTEM FLOWCHART

Figure 11.7 shows a system flowchart for this problem. To delete records from the master file, we must create a new version of the master file, one that contains all the records from the original master file except those we want to delete. Thus, we need two master files: the original (old) master file to use as an input file and a new master file to retain the records from the old master file that were not deleted.

The new master file is used as an output file. Other output includes an error report and a delete report. As before, the error report will list transactions that do not have a matching master record. The delete report will contain both the account numbers and the balances of the records that were deleted, providing a permanent log of deleted records.

We will use the same variable names we used in the listing program. We will use CHARGE01.SEQ as the old master file. TRANS02.SEQ (shown in Figure 11.8) will serve as the transaction file. A new file will serve as the new master file CHARGE02.SEQ.

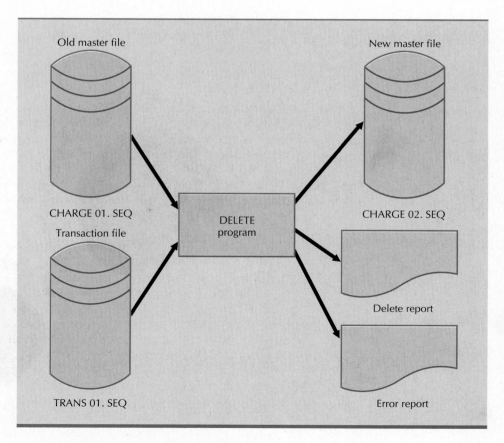

FIGURE 11.7   **System flowchart to delete records.**

■ *Deleting Records*

Cuff's needs to be able to delete records from its master file when some customers close their accounts. To do so, Cuff's has created a transaction file that contains the keys of the records it wants to delete.

SYSTEM FLOWCHART

Figure 11.7 shows a system flowchart for this problem. To delete records from the master file, we must create a new version of the master file, one that contains all the records from the original master file except those we want to delete. Thus, we need two master files: the original (old) master file to use as an input file and a new master file to retain the records from the old master file that were not deleted.

The new master file is used as an output file. Other output includes an error report and a delete report. As before, the error report will list transactions that do not have a matching master record. The delete report will contain both the account numbers and the balances of the records that were deleted, providing a permanent log of deleted records.

We will use the same variable names we used in the listing program. We will use CHARGE01.SEQ as the old master file. TRANS02.SEQ (shown in Figure 11.8) will serve as the transaction file. A new file will serve as the new master file CHARGE02.SEQ.

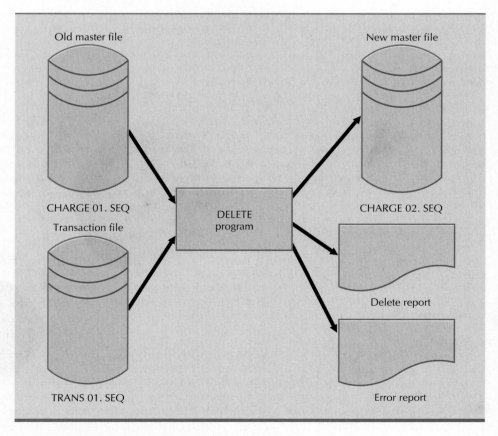

Old master file
New master file
CHARGE 01. SEQ
CHARGE 02. SEQ
Transaction file
DELETE program
Delete report
TRANS 01. SEQ
Error report

FIGURE 11.7 **System flowchart to delete records.**

```
                    200
                    334
                    474
                    720
                    9999
```

FIGURE 11.8   **The transaction file: TRANS02.SEQ.**

ALGORITHM

As the second step of our structured procedure, we can develop an algorithm for this problem as follows:

1. Open all files.
2. Repeat step 3 as long as either transaction or master records remain.
3. Compare the keys from the old master and transaction records.
   a) Delete old master records that have matching transaction records and list them on the delete report.
   b) Write to the new master file any old master records that do not have matching transaction records.
   c) List on the error report any transaction records that do not have matching old master records.
   d) Read the next record(s).
4. Close the files.
5. Stop execution.

PROGRAM

The logical structure of Program 11.5 is so similar to the logical structure of Program 11.4 that we do not need a separate flowchart. Program 11.5 opens four, not three, files (see lines 2010 through 2035). But the only major differences are what we do in the keys equal and master less subroutines.

If the keys are equal, the current old master record must be deleted. We do so by simply not writing that old master record to the new master file. Instead, we list that old master record on the delete report and read the next old master and transaction records.

If the master key is less than the transaction key, the current old master record has no matching transaction record. In this case, the old master record must *not* be deleted. So we write the old master record to the new master file and read the next old master record.

The greatest differences between Programs 11.4 and 11.5 occur in the end-of-file processing. In both programs if the old master file reaches its end before the transaction file, then all remaining transaction records must be errors, and BASIC continues processing until all the remaining transaction records are listed on the error report. But if the transaction file reaches its end first, then there are no more master records to be deleted. Yet in Program 11.5, we must continue processing until all the remaining old master records are written to the new master file. In other words, processing must continue until both the old master and the transaction files reach their ends. Line 3010 in Program 11.5 shows how this is done. BASIC executes the WHILE loop as long as either EOF(1) or EOF(2) is equal to FALSE.

```
1000 REM *** DELETING RECORDS ***
1010 GOSUB 2000          'Initialization routine
1020 GOSUB 3000          'Deleting routine
1030 GOSUB 4000          'Termination routine
1040 STOP
1050 REM
2000 REM *** Initialization routine =========================================
2010   OPEN "CHARGE01.SEQ" FOR INPUT AS #1
2020   OPEN "TRANS02.SEQ" FOR INPUT AS #2
2030   OPEN "ERROR.RPT" FOR OUTPUT AS #3
2035   OPEN "CHARGE02.SEQ" FOR OUTPUT AS #4
2040   PAGE.NO.DELETE = 1
2050   PAGE.NO.ERROR = 1
2060   PAGE.SIZE = 54
2070   DELETE.HEAD.FMT$ = " LISTING OF DELETED RECORDS    ##"
2080   DELETE.LINE.FMT$ = "          ###        #,###.##"
2090   ERROR.HEAD.FMT$ = "  LISTING OF ERROR RECORDS     ##"
2100   ERROR.LINE.FMT$ = "         ###"
2110   FALSE = 0
2120   GOSUB 5000          'Print Delete Report heading
2130   GOSUB 5500          'Print Error Report heading
2140   GOSUB 6000          'Read first master record
2150   GOSUB 6500          'Read first transaction record
2160 RETURN
2170 REM *** End of initialization routine
2180 '
3000 REM *** Deleting routine =============================================
3010   WHILE EOF(1) = FALSE OR EOF(2) = FALSE
3020     IF ACCT.NO.MSTR = ACCT.NO.TRANS
            THEN GOSUB 3100: GOTO 3050
3030     IF ACCT.NO.MSTR > ACCT.NO.TRANS
            THEN GOSUB 3200: GOTO 3050
3040     IF ACCT.NO.MSTR < ACCT.NO.TRANS
            THEN GOSUB 3300: GOTO 3050
3050   WEND
3060 RETURN
3070 REM *** End of listing routine
3080 '
3100 REM *** Keys equal routine
3110   GOSUB 3400          'Print master record on Delete Report
3120   GOSUB 6000          'Read next master record
3130   GOSUB 6500          'Read next transaction record
3140 RETURN
3150 REM *** End of keys equal routine
3160 '
3200 REM *** Master key greater routine
3210   GOSUB 3500          'Print transaction on Error Report
3220   GOSUB 6500          'Read next transaction record
3230 RETURN
3240 REM *** End of master key greater routine
3250 '
3300 REM *** Master key less routine
3310   GOSUB 3600          'Write master record on new master file
3320   GOSUB 6000          'Read next master record
3330 RETURN
3340 REM *** End of master key less routine
3350 '
```

PROGRAM 11.5   **Program to delete records.**

```
3400 REM *** Print Delete Report routine
3410    LINE.COUNT.DELETE = LINE.COUNT.DELETE + 1
3420    IF LINE.COUNT.DELETE >= PAGE.SIZE
           THEN GOSUB 5000
3430    LPRINT USING DELETE.LINE.FMT$; ACCT.NO.MSTR, BALANCE
3440 RETURN
3450 REM *** End of print Delete Report routine
3460 '
3500 REM *** Print Error Report routine
3510    LINE.COUNT.ERROR = LINE.COUNT.ERROR + 1
3520    IF LINE.COUNT.ERROR >= PAGE.SIZE
           THEN GOSUB 5500
3530    PRINT #3, USING ERROR.LINE.FMT$; ACCT.NO.TRANS
3540 RETURN
3550 REM *** End of print Error Report routine
3560 '
3600 REM *** Writing new master file routine
3610    WRITE #4, ACCT.NO.MSTR, BALANCE
3620 RETURN
3630 REM *** End of writing new master file routine
3640 '
4000 REM *** Termination routine ===============================================
4010    WRITE #4, 9999,0     'Write trailer record on new master file
4020    LPRINT
4030    LPRINT "     End of Delete Report"
4040    PRINT #3,
4050    PRINT #3, "End of Error Report"
4060    CLOSE
4070    GOSUB 4500           'Print Error Report
4080    PRINT "Normal end of program"
4090 RETURN
4100 REM *** End of termination routine
4110 '
4500 REM *** Send Error Report to printer routine
4510    OPEN "ERROR.RPT" FOR INPUT AS #1
4520    WHILE EOF(1) = FALSE
4530       LINE INPUT #1, ERROR.LINE$
4540       LPRINT ERROR.LINE$
4550    WEND
4560    CLOSE
4570 RETURN
4580 REM *** End of send Error Report to printer routine
4590 '
5000 REM *** Delete Report heading routine =======================================
5010    LPRINT CHR$(12);      'Send form feed signal to printer
5020    LPRINT USING DELETE.HEAD.FMT$; PAGE.NO.DELETE
5030    LPRINT
5040    LPRINT "   Account Number    Balance"
5050    LPRINT
5060    PAGE.NO.DELETE = PAGE.NO.DELETE + 1
5070    LINE.COUNT.DELETE = 4
5080 RETURN
5090 REM *** End of Delete Report heading routine
5100 '
```

PROGRAM 11.5   (Continued).

```
5500 REM *** Error Report heading routine
5510   PRINT #3,CHR$(12);
5520   PRINT #3, USING ERROR.HEAD.FMT$; PAGE.NO.ERROR
5530   PRINT #3,
5540   PRINT #3, "   Account Number"
5550   PRINT #3,
5560   PAGE.NO.ERROR = PAGE.NO.ERROR + 1
5570   LINE.COUNT.ERROR = 4
5580 RETURN
5590 REM *** End of Error Report heading routine
5600 '
6000 REM *** Read master file routine ============================================
6010   INPUT #1, ACCT.NO.MSTR, BALANCE
6020 RETURN
6030 REM *** End of read master file routine
6040 '
6500 REM *** Read transaction file routine
6510   INPUT #2, ACCT.NO.TRANS
6520 RETURN
6530 REM *** End of read transaction file routine
6540 END
RUN
Normal end of program
Break in 1040
```

LISTING OF DELETED RECORDS 1	LISTING OF ERROR RECORDS 1
Account Number Balance	Account Number
334 108.42	200
474 52.36	720
End of Delete Report	End of Error Report

PROGRAM 11.5   **(Continued).**

Another feature of Program 11.5 that is not found in Program 11.4 is the statements that write to the new master file. Line 3610, which is an ordinary WRITE # statement, writes the old master record to the new master file. And line 4010 in the termination subroutine writes the trailer record to the new master file. Figure 11.9 shows the resulting new master file.

Adding Records

Because Cuff's is a rapidly growing business, it needs to be able to add records to its master file. The system flowchart for this problem would be the same as the system flowchart for the delete problem (Figure 11.7) but without a delete report.

To add records to the master file, we must create a new master file that contains both the records from the old master file and the new records we are adding. The added records must, of course, be inserted in their proper sequential position.

```
                        146,45.46
                        175,33.07
                        212,9.219999
                        348,26.17
                        397,56.84
                        406,15.67
                        438,25.37
                        498,8.59
                        537,47.51
                        562,76.25
                        583,125
                        604,16.37
                        626,42.85
                        659,23.61
                        694,54.4
                        709,19.26
                        753,15.87
                        786,25.71
                        849,13.85
                        877,45.91
                        9999,0
```

FIGURE 11.9   **The new master file: CHARGE02.SEQ.**

We can use the same variable we used for deleting records, except that since we now have two balances we will call the balance read from the master file BALANCE.MSTR and the balance read from the transaction file BALANCE.TRANS. We will use CHARGE02.SEQ (Figure 11.9) as the old master file, and TRANS03.SEQ (Figure 11.10) as the transaction file. As shown in Figure 11.10, each transaction record must contain both the charge account number and the balance.

ALGORITHM

Again, step 2 of our structured procedure, to develop an algorithm, is simple.

1. Open all files.
2. Repeat step 3 as long as either transaction or master records remain.
3. Compare the keys from the old master and transaction records.
   a) List on the error report any transaction records that have matching master records.
   b) If the keys are not equal, write on the new master file the record with the lower key.
   c) Read the next record(s).
4. Close the files.
5. Stop execution.

You may have noticed a significant change from the previous problems. Earlier, transaction records with no matching master record were in error; now it is transaction records *with* matching master records that are in error.

```
107,41.75
178,90
215,23.62
348,55
377,21.63
709,15.85
9999,0
```

FIGURE 11.10   **The transaction file: TRANS03.SEQ.**

Why? Because we must add to the master file only records with keys different from those of existing master records. Thus, if a transaction record key equals a master record key, the transaction record must be an error.

If the keys are not equal, the algorithm says that the record with the lower key should be written on the new master file. This process ensures that the new master file will be in sequential order.

PROGRAM

Program 11.6, which adds records using this algorithm, is similar to Program 11.5. In the keys equal subroutine, BASIC lists the transaction record on the error report and reads the next transaction record. In the master greater subroutine, BASIC writes the transaction record to the new master file and reads the next transaction record. In the master less subroutine, BASIC writes the old master record to the new master file and reads the next old master record.

The only new subroutine in Program 11.6 is the one shown in lines 3600 through 3630. It writes the transaction records to the new master file. As you can see, this subroutine uses an ordinary WRITE # statement. Figure 11.11 shows the resulting new master file.

Updating Records

Finally, let's consider the case where customers charge new purchases against their accounts or make payments to their accounts. Cuff's wants to update the master file so that it reflects all the charges and payments made since the master file was created or last updated. The system flowchart for this problem is the same as that for the delete problem (Figure 11.7) but without a delete report.

We will use CHARGE03.SEQ (Figure 11.11) as the old master file. Each charge or payment becomes a record in the transaction file, TRANS04.SEQ. As shown in Figure 11.12, the transaction records contain the charge account number (which is the key), the amount of the transaction (AMOUNT), and a new variable, CODE, which indicates whether the transaction is a charge or a payment. If CODE is 1, the transaction is a charge, and if CODE is 2, it is a payment.

We update the balance on the old master record by adding the charges and subtracting the payments from the initial balance. An important feature of this problem is that we must allow for the possibility that some customers may have made more than one charge or payment to their accounts since the master file was last updated. Thus, we may have to apply more than one transaction record against a given old master record. Only after all relevant transactions have been applied to a particular old master can we write it to the new master file.

```
1000 REM *** ADDING RECORDS ***
1010 GOSUB 2000              'Initialization routine
1020 GOSUB 3000              'Adding routine
1030 GOSUB 4000              'Termination routine
1040 STOP
1050 '
2000 REM *** Initialization routine ===========================================
2010   OPEN "CHARGE02.SEQ" FOR INPUT AS #1
2020   OPEN "TRANS03.SEQ" FOR INPUT AS #2
2030   OPEN "CHARGE03.SEQ" FOR OUTPUT AS #3
2050   PAGE.NO.ERROR = 1
2060   PAGE.SIZE = 54
2090   ERROR.HEAD.FMT$ = " LISTING OF ERROR RECORDS  ##"
2100   ERROR.LINE.FMT$ = "           ###           #,###.##"
2110   FALSE = 0: TRUE = -1
2130   GOSUB 5500           'Print Error Report heading
2140   GOSUB 6000           'Read first master record
2150   GOSUB 6500           'Read first transaction record
2160 RETURN
2170 REM *** End of initialization routine
2180 '
3000 REM *** Adding routine =====================================================
3010   WHILE EOF(1) = FALSE   OR EOF(2) = FALSE
3020     IF ACCT.NO.MSTR = ACCT.NO.TRANS
           THEN GOSUB 3100: GOTO 3050
3030     IF ACCT.NO.MSTR > ACCT.NO.TRANS
           THEN GOSUB 3200: GOTO 3050
3040     IF ACCT.NO.MSTR < ACCT.NO.TRANS
           THEN GOSUB 3300: GOTO 3050
3050   WEND
3060 RETURN
3070 REM *** End of listing routine
3080 '
3100 REM *** Keys equal routine
3110   GOSUB 3500            'Print transaction on Error Report
3120   GOSUB 6500            'Read next transaction record
3130 RETURN
3140 REM *** End of keys equal routine
3150 '
3200 REM *** Master key greater routine
3210   GOSUB 3600            'Write new master from transaction
3220   GOSUB 6500            'Read next transaction record
3230 RETURN
3240 REM *** End of master key greater routine
3250 '
3300 REM *** Master key less routine
3310   GOSUB 3700            'Write new master from old master
3320   GOSUB 6000            'Read next master record
3330 RETURN
3340 REM *** End of master key less routine
3350 '
```

PROGRAM 11.6   Program to add records.

```
3500 REM *** Print Error Report routine
3510    LINE.COUNT.ERROR = LINE.COUNT.ERROR + 1
3520    IF LINE.COUNT.ERROR >= PAGE.SIZE
           THEN GOSUB 5500
3530    LPRINT USING ERROR.LINE.FMT$; ACCT.NO.TRANS, BALANCE.TRANS
3540 RETURN
3550 REM *** End of print Error Report routine
3560 '
3600 REM *** Writing new master file from transaction file routine
3610    WRITE #3, ACCT.NO.TRANS, BALANCE.TRANS
3620 RETURN
3630 REM *** End of new master from transaction file routine
3640 '
3700 REM *** Writing new master file from old master file routine
3710    WRITE #3, ACCT.NO.MSTR, BALANCE.MSTR
3720 RETURN
3730 REM *** End of writing new master from old master file routine
3740 '
4000 REM *** Termination routine ================================================
4010 WRITE #3, 9999,0    'Write trailer data on new master file
4020    LPRINT
4030    LPRINT "End of Error Report"
4040    CLOSE
4050    PRINT "Normal end of program"
4060 RETURN
4070 REM *** End of termination routine
4080 '
5500 REM *** Error Report heading routine ========================================
5510    LPRINT CHR$(12);           'Send form feed signal to printer
5520    LPRINT USING ERROR.HEAD.FMT$; PAGE.NO.ERROR
5530    LPRINT
5540    LPRINT "   Account Number    Balance"
5550    LPRINT
5560    PAGE.NO.ERROR = PAGE.NO.ERROR + 1
5570    LINE.COUNT.ERROR = 4
5580 RETURN
5590 REM *** End of Error Report heading routine
5600 '
6000 REM *** Read master file routine ===========================================
6010    INPUT #1, ACCT.NO.MSTR, BALANCE.MSTR
6020 RETURN
6030 REM *** End of read master file routine
6040 '
6500 REM *** Read transaction file routine
6510    INPUT #2, ACCT.NO.TRANS, BALANCE.TRANS
6520 RETURN
6530 REM *** End of read transaction file routine
6540 END
RUN
Normal end of program
Break in 1040
```

```
 LISTING OF ERROR RECORDS     1

   Account Number     Balance

        348             55.00
        709             15.85

End of Error Report
```

PROGRAM 11.6   **(Continued).**

```
107,41.75
146,45.46
175,33.07
178,90
212,9.219999
215,23.62
348,26.17
377,21.63
397,56.84
406,15.67
438,25.37
498,8.59
537,47.51
562,76.25
583,125
604,16.37
626,42.85
659,23.61
694,54.4
709,19.26
753,15.87
786,25.71
849,13.85
877,45.91
9999,0
```

FIGURE 11.11   **The new master file: CHARGE03.SEQ.**

ALGORITHM

In this case, we can use the following simplified algorithm:

1. Open all files.
2. Repeat step 3 as long as either transaction or master records remain.
3. Compare the keys from the old master and transaction records.
   a) Update master records that have matching transaction records.
   b) Copy to the new master file any master records that do not have matching transaction records.
   c) List on the error report any transaction records that do not have matching master records.
   d) Read the next record(s).
4. Close the files.
5. Stop execution.

PROGRAM

Program 11.7, which updates records using this algorithm, is similar to previous programs in this chapter. For example, the master greater subroutine writes a transaction record on the error report, just as it did in Program 11.5.

But Program 11.7 also contains two new features. First, the keys equal subroutine executes an update master subroutine, which checks to see whether CODE is 1. If it is, we add AMOUNT to BALANCE. If it is not, then CODE must be 2, and we subtract AMOUNT from BALANCE.* The update master sub-

*This program assumes that a previous program verified that CODE is either 1 or 2.

```
146,15,1
146,10,1
146,5,2
150,20,1
406,20,2
438,15,1
439,10,2
626,5,2
626,7.5,2
626,10,1
899,5,1
9999,0,0
```

FIGURE 11.12   **The transaction file: TRANS04.SEQ.**

routine then returns to the keys equal subroutine, which reads the next transaction record. It does not read the next old master record, since there may be additional transaction records to be applied against the current old master record.

If, on the next pass (or on any pass), the master key is less than the transaction key, no more transactions will apply against the current old master. The current old master is then written to the new master file. Notice that it does not matter whether the current old master record was updated by an earlier transaction, or whether it never had a matching transaction. In either case, the current old master record should be written to the new master file. Accordingly, the master less subroutine writes the current old master record to the new master file and reads the next old master record. Figure 11.13 shows the updated master file.

```
107,41.75
146,65.46
175,33.07
178,90
212,9.219999
215,23.62
348,26.17
377,21.63
397,56.84
406,-4.33
438,40.37
498,8.59
537,47.51
562,76.25
583,125
604,16.37
626,40.35
659,23.61
694,54.4
709,19.26
753,15.87
786,25.71
849,13.85
877,45.91
9999,0
```

FIGURE 11.13   **The new master file: CHARGE04.SEQ.**

```
1000 REM *** UPDATING RECORDS ***
1010 GOSUB 2000          'Initialization routine
1020 GOSUB 3000          'Updating routine
1030 GOSUB 4000          'Termination routine
1040 STOP
1050 '
2000 REM *** Initialization routine ============================================
2010    OPEN "CHARGE03.SEQ" FOR INPUT AS #1
2020    OPEN "TRANS04.SEQ" FOR INPUT AS #2
2030    OPEN "CHARGE04.SEQ" FOR OUTPUT AS #3
2050    PAGE.NO.ERROR = 1
2060    PAGE.SIZE = 54
2090    ERROR.HEAD.FMT$ = " LISTING OF ERROR RECORDS    ##"
2100    ERROR.LINE.FMT$ = "            ###         #,###.##    #"
2110    FALSE = 0
2130    GOSUB 5500          'Print Error Report heading
2140    GOSUB 6000          'Read first master record
2150    GOSUB 6500          'Read first transaction record
2160 RETURN
2170 REM *** End of initialization routine
2180 '
3000 REM *** Updating routine ==================================================
3010    WHILE EOF(1) = FALSE OR EOF(2) = FALSE
3020       IF ACCT.NO.MSTR = ACCT.NO.TRANS
             THEN GOSUB 3100: GOTO 3050
3030       IF ACCT.NO.MSTR > ACCT.NO.TRANS
             THEN GOSUB 3200: GOTO 3050
3040       IF ACCT.NO.MSTR < ACCT.NO.TRANS
             THEN GOSUB 3300: GOTO 3050
3050    WEND
3060 RETURN
3070 REM *** End of listing routine
3080 '
3100 REM *** Keys equal routine
3110    GOSUB 3400          'Update master record
3120    GOSUB 6500          'Read next transaction record
3130 RETURN
3140 REM *** End of keys equal routine
3150 '
3200 REM *** Master key greater routine
3210    GOSUB 3500          'Print transaction on Error Report
3220    GOSUB 6500          'Read next transaction record
3230 RETURN
3240 REM *** End of master key greater routine
3250 '
3300 REM *** Master key less routine
3310    GOSUB 3600          'Write master record on new master file
3320    GOSUB 6000          'Read next master record
3330 RETURN
3340 REM *** End of master key less routine
3350 '
3400 REM *** Update master record routine
3410    IF CODE = 1
          THEN BALANCE = BALANCE + AMOUNT
          ELSE BALANCE = BALANCE - AMOUNT
3420 RETURN
3430 REM *** End of update master record routine
3440 '
```

PROGRAM 11.7   **Program to update records.**

```
3500 REM *** Print Error Report routine
3510    LINE.COUNT.ERROR = LINE.COUNT.ERROR + 1
3520    IF LINE.COUNT.ERROR >= PAGE.SIZE
           THEN GOSUB 5500
3530    LPRINT USING ERROR.LINE.FMT$; ACCT.NO.TRANS, AMOUNT, CODE
3540 RETURN
3550 REM *** End of print Error Report routine
3560 '
3600 REM *** Writing new master file routine
3610    WRITE #3, ACCT.NO.MSTR, BALANCE
3620 RETURN
3630 REM *** End of writing new master file routine
3640 '
4000 REM *** Termination routine ================================================
4010    WRITE #3, 9999,0    'Write trailer record on new master file
4020    LPRINT
4030    LPRINT "End of Error Report"
4040    CLOSE
4050    PRINT "Normal end of program"
4060 RETURN
4070 REM *** End of termination routine
4080 '
5500 REM *** Error Report heading routine ======================================
5510    LPRINT CHR$(12);
5520    LPRINT USING ERROR.HEAD.FMT$; PAGE.NO.ERROR
5530    LPRINT
5540    LPRINT "   Account Number    Amount   Code"
5550    LPRINT
5560    PAGE.NO.ERROR = PAGE.NO.ERROR + 1
5570    LINE.COUNT.ERROR = 4
5580 RETURN
5590 REM *** End of Error Report heading routine
5600 '
6000 REM *** Read master file routine ==========================================
6010    INPUT #1, ACCT.NO.MSTR, BALANCE
6020 RETURN
6030 REM *** End of read master file routine
6040 '
6500 REM *** Read transaction file routine
6510    INPUT #2, ACCT.NO.TRANS, AMOUNT, CODE
6520 RETURN
6530 REM *** End of read transaction file routine
6540 END
RUN
Normal end of program
Break in 1040
```

```
  LISTING OF ERROR RECORDS       1
  _____

   Account Number    Amount  Code

        150           20.00   1
        439           10.00   2
        899            5.00   1

End of Error Report
```

PROGRAM 11.7   (Continued).

EXERCISES

11.13 What does it mean if, in a program to delete records, the master file reaches its end before the transaction file does? What does it mean if that happens in a program to add records?

11.14 In a program to add records to a master file, if the transaction key is less than the master key, which record is written to the new master file?

11.15 What changes have to be made to Program 11.7 to allow for the possibility that there may be more than one transaction to be applied against a particular old master?

11.16 What conclusion can we draw and what action do we take if, in a program to update records, we find that the master key is greater than the transaction key?

*11.17 Explain why the records in TRANS02.SEQ, which is used to delete records, contain only the key field (see Figure 11.8), but the records in TRANS03.SEQ, which is used to add records, contain both a key and a balance field (see Figure 11.10).

11.18 Program 11.8 shows the execution of a program that is supposed to print the contents of the CARS.SEQ file. As you can see, it didn't. Find and correct the error.

```
100 REM *** READING AND PRINTING THE CARS FILE ***
110 OPEN "CARS.SEQ" FOR INPUT AS #1
120 FMT$ = "\          \       ####"
130 LPRINT "        CARS SOLD"
140 LPRINT
150 LPRINT   "Stock        Number     Closing"
160 LPRINT   "Type             Sold"
170 WHILE EOF(2) = 0
180    INPUT #2, CAR.NAME$, NO.SOLD
190    LPRINT USING FMT$; CAR.NAME$, NO.SOLD
200 WEND
210 CLOSE #2
220 LPRINT "End of the Car file"
230 END

RUN
Bad file number in 170
Ok
```

PROGRAM 11.8   **A program that is supposed to print the CARS.SEQ file.**

PROGRAMMING ASSIGNMENTS

In the following programming assignments, you may either write a program to create the transaction file or supply the transaction data using an INPUT statement or READ-DATA statements. Whatever method you use, remember that transactions must be in sequential order and that files must contain a trailer record. Be sure to include erroneous transactions.

11.10 Write a program to delete records from the ICECREAM.SEQ file created in Programming Assignment 11.6.

11.11 Write a program to add records to the ICECREAM.SEQ file created in Programming Assignment 11.6.

11.12 Write a program to update the ICECREAM.SEQ file created in Programming Assignment 11.6. Your program should account for both receipts of ice cream from the manufacturing plant and shipments to customers.

11.13 Write a program to delete records from file A11-07.SEQ in Programming Assignment 11.7. Use the following transaction data: 218, 496, 515, 816.

11.14 Write a program to add records to file A11-07.SEQ mentioned in Programming Assignment 11.7. Use the following transactions:

Student Number	Name	Credits Completed	GPA
106	Queen	108	2.13
285	Poirot	37	2.73
607	Alleyn	92	1.95
857	Thatcher	54	2.47

11.15 Write a program to update file A11-07.SEQ mentioned in Programming Assignment 11.7. The transaction file should contain the student number, the number of credits completed this semester, and the GPA achieved this semester. The program should update the credits completed and calculate a new GPA using the equation

$$\text{GPA.NEW} = \frac{\text{GPA.OLD} * \text{CREDITS.OLD} + \text{GPA.TRANS} * \text{CREDITS.TRANS}}{\text{CREDITS.OLD} + \text{CREDITS.NEW}}$$

Use the following data:

Student Number	Credits Completed	GPA
134	9	3.06
285	15	3.24
381	10	4.00
749	16	2.74
876	9	1.00

SUMMARY

In this chapter you have learned that

☐ An OPEN statement must be executed before a file may be read or written to.

☐ The /F: switch must be used when BASIC is started if you want to have more than three files opened simultaneously.

☐ The WRITE # statement writes to a sequential file.

☐ After a program is finished with a file, the CLOSE statement closes it.

☐ The INPUT # statement reads a sequential file.

☐ The DOS commands PRINT and TYPE are used to view a sequential file.

☐ The SHELL statement permits DOS commands to be executed from within BASIC.

☐ The DOS command SORT sorts a disk file.

☐ System flowcharts show the files used by a program.

☐ The EOF function tests for the end of a sequential file.

☐ The PRINT # and PRINT # USING statements write a report to a disk file or direct output to the screen or the printer, depending on what the user wants.

☐ The LINE INPUT # statement reads a line from a file.

☐ A line counter variable and a page counter variable are needed to print multipage reports.

☐ Many file problems involve processing a master and a transaction file together. Records may be listed, deleted, added, and updated. To delete, add, or update records, a new master file must be created.

KEY TERMS IN THIS CHAPTER

buffer 316	**key** 313	**sequential file** 314
field 313	**master file** 326	**system flowchart** 327
file 313	**record** 313	**transaction file** 326

QUESTIONS FOR REVIEW

11.1 When the end of a file has been reached, the EOF function returns the value _____ .

11.2 The _____ statement is used to read data from a sequential file.

11.3 The _____ statement must be executed before a file may be read or written.

11.4 The _____ DOS command is used to sort a disk file.

11.5 Explain the difference between the LINE INPUT # statement and the LINE INPUT statement.

11.6 What is the difference between the statements CLOSE #1 and CLOSE?

11.7 A file consists of a group of related _____ .

11.8 A sequential file may be printed using the DOS command _____ .

11.9 Which BASIC statements are used to print to a file?

11.10 A sequential file may be displayed on the screen using the DOS command _____ .

11.11 The OPEN statement for sequential files specifies three things. What are they?

11.12 The _____ statement is used to write data to a sequential file.

11.13 What must you do to the line counter when you print a line?

11.14 If, during execution, BASIC displays the error message: File not found, what is the most likely cause of the error?

ADDITIONAL PROGRAMMING ASSIGNMENTS

11.16
a) Wreck-A-Mended Used Cars maintains a file of its customers' cars, named AUTO1.SEQ which contains four fields: the serial number (1-9999), the make, the year, and the mileage when the car was last serviced. Write a program to create this file with about a dozen records.

b) Write a program to read the AUTO1.SEQ file and print a report of the cars with more than 25,000 miles. Print a heading on the report.

In the following programming assignments, you may either write a program to create the transaction file or supply the transaction data using an INPUT statement or READ-DATA statements. Whichever method you use, remember that transactions must be in sequential order. Be sure to include erroneous transactions.

11.17 Write a program to list selected records from the AUTO1.SEQ file.

11.18 Write a program to delete records from the AUTO1.SEQ file. Create a new file named AUTO2.SEQ.

11.19 Write a program to add records to the AUTO1.SEQ file. Create a new file named AUTO3.SEQ.

11.20 Write a program to update records in the AUTO1.SEQ file. When a car is serviced, a transaction is created that contains the serial number and the current mileage. The mileage from the transaction is used to replace the mileage from the master file. Create a new file named AUTO4.SEQ.

BEYOND THE BASICS

11.1 Write a program that allows Mr. Croesus to add or delete stocks from his list of holdings. If he wants to delete a stock, the program should ask him the name of the stock, and after deleting it, the program should close up the gap in the arrays by moving the higher elements down. If he wants to add a stock, the program should request the name, number held, and price and insert the stock in its alphabetical position.

11.2 Write a program that merges three files—`FILE1.SEQ`, `FILE2.SEQ`, and `FILE3.SEQ`—to produce a new file, `FILE4.SEQ`. You will have to write a file creation program to create the three input files. The records in the files can consist of just the key fields. To simplify the problem, create your files so that there are no duplicate keys, thus avoiding any need for an error report.

11.3 The Cavalier Country Club maintains a master file of the annual dues for each member. Each record in this file contains the member's identification number (which is the key), the member's name, and the amount of that member's annual dues. Every January, the treasurer of the club prepares a transaction record for each dues check received. These transaction records contain the member identification number and the amount of the check.

Since you are a member of the club and also a BASIC expert, the treasurer has asked you to write a program that will read the master and transaction files and print a report listing the identification numbers and names of all members who have not paid their dues in full and the amount they still owe.

As usual, a transaction record without a matching master record is an error, but this problem involves a new condition: A master record without a matching transaction record indicates a member who has paid no dues at all. These cases, too, should be listed, together with members who have made only a partial payment.

12

Random Files

As you discovered in Chapter 11, sequential files are easiest to work with when they are small enough to be read into an array. However, to change one record in a sequential file you must read and write every record. Having to process every record in a large file is no problem if, as in a payroll system, you will need to process every record (that is, pay every employee) anyway. But processing every record is often impractical. In such situations, random files are much more useful.

For example, if you want to know whether there are seats available for a particular airline flight, the airline must be able to display the record for that particular flight without searching through the whole file. If you buy a ticket, the airline must be able to update the record for that flight without creating a completely new file. Systems that permit the user to display and update a particular record are called **on-line systems**. In BASIC, random files must be used in on-line systems.

On-line system
A system that permits individual records to be displayed and updated.

As you will see, in some applications you can use the record number as the record key. But in many real world situations, you may not use the record number as the record key, and you must create an index. We will discuss both kinds of applications in this chapter.

CREATING AND READING A RANDOM FILE

To simplify your introduction to random files, let's create a random version of the Cuff's Department Store charge account file, including the customer's name as a field in the record this time. We will assume that the charge account numbers range from 1 to 999. You can think of this file as a collection of pigeonholes numbered from 1 to 999. The balance and the name for each account are kept in the pigeonhole with the same number as the account, that is, the balance and the name for account 1 are kept in pigeonhole 1, for account 2 in pigeonhole 2, and so on.

◼ *Variable Names and Algorithm*

In line with the first step of our structured procedure, we select the following variable names:

Input variables	Account number	ACCT.NO
	Customer's name	NAME.IN$
	Balance in the account	BALANCE
Output variables	Customer's name	NAME.FLD$
	Balance in the account	BALANCE.FLD$

The reason we use separate input and output variables for the name and the balance will be explained shortly. The name of the file we will create is CHARGE.RND, where the extension RND is a reminder that this is a random file.

As step 2 of our procedure, we can use the following algorithm:

> 1. Open CHARGE.RND.
> 2. Initialize the file by marking every record as inactive.
> 3. Load the data into the file.
> 4. Close CHARGE.RND.
> 5. Stop execution.

The Program

Although the logic of Program 12.1, which is based on this algorithm, is so simple that you don't need a flowchart to understand it, it does introduce several new concepts and statements.

THE OPEN STATEMENT

The OPEN statement for random files differs somewhat from that for sequential files. Its syntax is

```
OPEN "filename" AS #filenum [LEN=reclength]
```

Here filename and filenum have the same meaning as they have with sequential files. But the OPEN statement for random files differs from that for sequential files in two ways. First, the mode is not specified, because random files are opened for both input and output at the same time. Second, the length, in bytes, of each record is specified by using the LEN parameter. In the OPEN statement in line 110 of Program 12.1, reclength is 24. We will discuss how to determine the record length shortly. For now, you should know that the maximum permitted value for reclength is 32,767 and that omitting the LEN parameter causes BASIC to use the default length of 128 bytes.* For example,

OPEN Statement

```
OPEN "PAYROLL.RND" AS #3 LEN = 74
```

Effect

Opens the file PAYROLL.RND for random processing, assigns it file number 3, and specifies a record length of 74.

OPEN Statement

```
OPEN RANDOM.FILE$ AS #1 LEN = 36
```

Effect

Opens the file whose name previously has been assigned to the variable RANDOM.FILE$, assigns it file number 1, and specifies a record length of 36.

---

*If you wish to use a record length greater than 128 bytes, you must use the /S: switch when you start BASIC. For example,

```
BASICA /S:175
```

allows record lengths up to 175 bytes.

```
100 REM *** CREATING THE RANDOM CHARGE ACCOUNT FILE ***
110 OPEN "CHARGE.RND" AS #1 LEN = 24
120 FIELD #1, 20 AS NAME.FLD$, 4 AS BALANCE.FLD$
130 GOSUB 200      'Initialize the file
140 GOSUB 300      'Load data into file
150 CLOSE #1
160 PRINT "The Charge Account file has been created"
170 STOP
180 '
200 REM *** Initialize file routine
210   LSET NAME.FLD$ = SPACE$(20)
220   LSET BALANCE.FLD$ = MKS$(0)
230   FOR J = 1 TO 999
240     PUT #1, J
250   NEXT J
260 RETURN
270 REM *** End of initialize file routine
280 '
300 REM *** Load data into file routine
310   READ ACCT.NO, NAME.IN$, BALANCE
320     IF ACCT.NO = 9999
          THEN GOTO 370
330     LSET NAME.FLD$ = NAME.IN$
340     LSET BALANCE.FLD$ = MKS$(BALANCE)
350     PUT #1, ACCT.NO
360   GOTO 310
370 RETURN
380 REM *** End of routine to load data into file
390 '
400 REM *** Data to create file
410 DATA 498, "English, Reynolds", 8.59
420 DATA 786, "Lee, Bohyon", 25.71
430 DATA 537, "Thompson, Stanley", 47.51
440 DATA 849, "Valdez, Fabio", 13.85
450 DATA 175, "Mato, Robert", 33.07
460 DATA 562, "Rizzuto, James", 76.25
470 DATA 877, "Schwartz, Michael", 45.91
480 DATA 212, "Rufino, Carlos", 9.22
490 DATA 583, "Morley, John", 125.00
500 DATA 334, "Brevil, James", 108.42
510 DATA 604, "Martin, Kathleen", 16.37
520 DATA 146, "Falconer, Edward", 45.46
530 DATA 348, "Yeung, Suk", 26.17
540 DATA 626, "Paul, Marina", 42.85
550 DATA 397, "Fradin, Shirley", 56.84
560 DATA 659, "Burns, Jeffrey", 23.61
570 DATA 406, "Katz, Hal", 15.67
580 DATA 694, "Wright, Donna", 54.40
590 DATA 438, "Cuomo, Maria", 25.37
600 DATA 709, "Lopez, Anna", 19.26
610 DATA 474, "Alexander, Lisa", 52.36
620 DATA 753, "Goldberg, Lori", 15.87
630 REM Trailer data follow
640 DATA 9999,"XXX", 0
650 END

RUN
The Charge Account file has been created
Break in 170
Ok
```

PROGRAM 12.1   **Creating the random charge account file.**

Record length is an important concept for random files. In a random file, every record must have the same length. That is how BASIC is able to retrieve a particular record. Suppose, for example, we ask BASIC to retrieve record number 57. BASIC uses the record length we specify in the OPEN statement to calculate how far the desired record is from the beginning of the file. It can then go directly to that record and retrieve it.

THE FIELD STATEMENT

Line 120 of Program 12.1 shows a FIELD statement, which is used only with random files. A FIELD statement specifies the name, size, and position of each field in a record. The syntax of the FIELD statement is

    FIELD #filenum, width AS stringvar [,width AS stringvar]...

where filenum, as usual, is the file number assigned to the file in the OPEN statement, width specifies the number of bytes in the field, and stringvar specifies the name of the field, which must be a string. (We will discuss how numbers are converted to string values shortly.) Variables defined in a FIELD statement are called **field variables**. Field variable names do not have to end in FLD$, but using distinctive names for them helps in complex programs. You must repeat width AS stringvar for each field in the record.

In line 120 of Program 12.1, the record consists of just two fields: NAME.FLD$, with a width of 20 bytes, and BALANCE.FLD$, with a width of 4 bytes.* Other examples of FIELD statements include

Field variable
A variable defined in a FIELD statement.

FIELD Statement

FIELD #2, 20 AS STUDENT.FLD$, 4 AS GPA.FLD$

Effect

Specifies that the record for file number 2 contains 20 bytes for STUDENT.FLD$ and 4 bytes for GPA.FLD$.

FIELD Statement

FIELD #1, 9 AS SSNO.FLD$, 25 AS EMPLOYEE.FLD$, 4 AS PAY.FLD$

Effect

Specifies that the record for file number 1 contains 9 bytes for SSNO.FLD$, 25 bytes for EMPLOYEE.FLD$, and 4 for PAY.FLD$.

The sum of all the widths specified in the FIELD statement must not be greater than the reclength specified in the OPEN statement. Usually, the sum of the widths will exactly equal reclength, as here (20 + 4 = 24).

The width parameter of a field variable is set in one of two ways, depending on whether the variable contains string or numeric data. For field variables that contain string data, you simply select a width that you believe is large enough to hold the longest string that will be assigned to that variable. For example, in Program 12.1 we chose 20 as the width for NAME.FLD$ because we think that no name will be longer than 20 characters. If any data string is longer than the width you have specified, BASIC will ignore the extra characters. For field variables that contain numeric data, the width is determined by certain rules that will be explained when we discuss the conversion of numeric to string values. For now, you should be aware that an

*Notice that the account number is not part of the record, because in this file, unlike the sequential file used in Chapter 11, the record number is the account number. The name and balance for account number 498 is stored in pigeonhole 498, so when we read the name and balance from pigeonhole 498 we know they are for account number 498.

OPEN statement must be executed before a FIELD statement for a file, and a FIELD statement must be executed before a value is assigned to a field variable. Thus, FIELD statements are usually coded near the beginning of a program or in an initialization routine.

THE LSET AND RSET STATEMENTS

The subroutine that starts in line 200 of Program 12.1 initializes the file. To understand why random files must be initialized (recall that we did not have to initialize sequential files), you must know something about how BASIC allocates disk space for random files. If we do not initialize the file, the first record BASIC will write will be record number 498, as specified in the DATA statement in line 410. Before BASIC writes that record, it will allocate space on the disk for records 1 through 497, but it will not write anything in the space. So, if the space allocated was at one time occupied by a file that has since been deleted, the space will still contain left-over data from the old file. (When you delete a file DOS does not erase the file's data—it simply erases the file's name from the disk's directory.) Later, when BASIC reads the new file, it may find left-over data mingled with new data. To avoid that problem, we must initialize the file. In this case, we do it by writing blank spaces in the name field and zero in the balance field of every record in the file. These values are assigned by means of the LSET statements in lines 210 and 220.

It would be incorrect to use a LET statement in line 210 or 220. Field variables *must* be assigned values by either the LSET or RSET statements. The syntaxes of the LSET and RSET statements are

```
LSET string variable = string expression
```

and

```
RSET string variable = string expression
```

LSET stands for left set. It gets its name because, if the value assigned to a variable contains fewer bytes than were allocated to the variable in the FIELD statement, LSET left-justifies the value and fills the extra positions with spaces. For example, if a variable named MONTH.FLD$ were allocated 9 bytes in a FIELD statement, the LSET statement

```
LSET MONTH.FLD$ = "May"
```

would assign the following data to MONTH.FLD$:

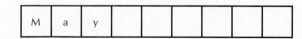

The only difference between LSET and RSET is that RSET right-justifies. So if the above example were

```
RESET MONTH.FLD$ = "May"
```

MONTH.FLD$ would contain the data

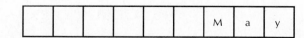

If the value assigned contains more characters than were allocated to the variable in the FIELD statement, both LSET and RSET drop characters from the right end of the string.

THE MKS\$, MKI\$, AND MKD\$ FUNCTIONS

Lines 220 and 340 in Program 12.1 use the MKS\$ function to assign numeric values to BALANCE.FLD\$. This example illustrates a general rule: All numeric values that are assigned to field variables must be converted to strings using one of the three "make" functions, MKS\$, MKI\$, or MKD\$. (Although the STR\$ function also converts a numeric value to a string, it may *not* be used with field variables; only the "make" functions may be used.) To understand why three different functions are needed, we have to explore the different types of numeric data used by BASIC.

Although we have disregarded it until now, BASIC has three different kinds of numeric variables: single-precision, integer, and double-precision. These are the types specified by the S, the I, and the D in the three MK functions. The difference between the three types is in the number of bytes used to store their values, the range of values and the accuracy to which they can be represented, and the speed with which calculations can be done. The different types of variables are defined by adding a special character to the end of the variable name, much as a string variable is defined by adding a \$ to the end of its name.

If a variable has no special character at the end of its name, it is a **single-precision variable**. All the numeric variables we have used so far are single-precision variables. Single-precision variables are stored in four bytes. The MKS\$ function converts a single-precision value to a four-byte string. For example, consider lines 220 and 340 in Program 12.1, where the MKS\$ function converts 0 and BALANCE to strings and assigns them to BALANCE.FLD\$ in LSET statements. Now you can see why we allocated four bytes to BALANCE.FLD\$ in the FIELD statement—because MKS\$ converts a single-precision value to a four-byte string.

If you know that the values a variable will have are whole numbers between −32,768 and 32,767, you can use an **integer variable**. Integer variables are defined by adding a % to the end of their names, as in NO.STUDENTS%, and are stored in two bytes. The computer is fastest when it performs arithmetic on integer variables. But the time difference is so small that we do not, in this book, feel a need to use integer variables. The MKI\$ function converts an integer value to a two-byte string.

It is important to understand that the MKI\$ function operates on an integer *value*; its argument does not have to have been defined as an integer *variable*. If the single-precision variable A has the value 454, the expression MKI\$(A) will return a two-byte string representation of 454, while the expression MKS\$(A) will return a four-byte string representation of 454.

In problems where round-off error is significant, **double-precision variables** may be preferable. Whereas single-precision variables store seven digits, double-precision variables store sixteen digits. The price you pay for the extra accuracy is that double-precision variables take twice as much storage space as single-precision variables, and the computer performs arithmetic on them more slowly. Double-precision variables are defined by adding a # to the end of their names, as in NATIONAL.DEBT#. In this book, we will not use double-precision variables. The MKD\$ function converts a double-precision value to an eight-byte string.

THE PUT STATEMENT

Another new feature in Program 12.1 is the use of PUT statements:

```
240 PUT #1, J
```

and

```
350 PUT #1, ACCT.NO
```

Single-precision variable
A variable that holds values with up to seven digits of accuracy and is stored in four bytes.

Integer variable
A variable that holds whole numbers in the range −32,768 to 32,767 and is stored in two bytes.

Double-precision variable
A variable that holds values with up to sixteen digits and is stored in eight bytes.

PUT statements are used to write both initializing data and real data to random files. The PUT statement in line 240, which lies in the middle of a FOR-NEXT loop, initializes the file by writing blank spaces and zeros to the file. The PUT statement in line 350 writes the real data to the file. Both these statements show that in a PUT statement you do not list the names of the variables that should be written to the file; the PUT statement writes the whole record, as defined in the FIELD statement, to the file.

The syntax of the PUT statement is

```
PUT #filenum, recordnum
```

where filenum, as usual, is the number assigned to the file in the OPEN statement, and recordnum is the record number that is to be written. In other words, recordnum is the number of the pigeonhole where the record is to be put. In line 240, when J is 1, the PUT statement writes record number 1, when J is 2, it writes record number 2, and so on, until J is 999, when it writes the 999th record.

The PUT statement in line 240 writes the records in sequential order because that is the most convenient way to initialize a file. However, the PUT statement also allows us to write records in random order. This is fortunate because in on-line systems the data may arrive in arbitrary order. To imitate an on-line system, the data in the DATA statements in lines 410 through 620 are not in order by ACCT.NO. The records written by the PUT statement in line 350 depend on the value of ACCT.NO. In the first DATA statement, in line 410, ACCT.NO is 498. Therefore, the first name, "English, Reynolds", and the first balance, 8.59, are written to record number (pigeonhole) 498. The second record is written to record number 786, and so on. Additional examples of PUT statements are

PUT Statement

PUT #1, REC.NO

Effect

Writes the data described in the FIELD #1 statement to record number REC.NO in the file opened as file number 1.

PUT Statement

PUT #3, 381

Effect

Writes the data described in the FIELD #3 statement to record number 381 in the file opened as file number 3.

The test for trailer data in line 320 ends the loop. With random files, the trailer data are not written to the file. After reading the trailer data, the program branches to the RETURN statement and returns to the main program, where it closes the file. The CLOSE statement for random files is the same as the CLOSE statement for sequential files.

Reading All the Records in a Random File

The WRITE statement, which is used to write records to a sequential file, adds a carriage return and line feed to the end of each record, thus separating records. But its alter-ego in random files, the PUT statement, does not add any separator between records. Thus, the DOS commands PRINT and TYPE cannot be used to list the random file CHARGE.RND. Instead, we need a separate BASIC program. We can use the same variable names as we used in Program 12.1 and compose a simple algorithm:

1. Open `CHARGE.RND`.
2. Read every record in the file.
3. If the record is active, print it; otherwise, do nothing.
4. Close `CHARGE.RND`.
5. Stop execution.

The logic of Program 12.2 is so simple you do not need a flowchart to understand it. The OPEN and FIELD statements are the same as they were when the file was created in Program 12.1.

```
100 REM *** READING THE RANDOM CHARGE ACCOUNT FILE ***
110 OPEN "CHARGE.RND" AS #1 LEN = 24
120 FIELD #1, 20 AS NAME.FLD$, 4 AS BALANCE.FLD$
130 LPRINT "Account Number        Name                Balance"
140 FMT$ = "       ###          \                \      #,###.##"
150 FOR ACCT.NO = 1 TO 999
160   GET #1, ACCT.NO
170   IF NAME.FLD$ <> SPACE$(20)
         THEN BALANCE = CVS(BALANCE.FLD$):
               LPRINT USING FMT$; ACCT.NO, NAME.FLD$, BALANCE
180 NEXT ACCT.NO
190 LPRINT "All the records have been read"
200 CLOSE
210 END

RUN
```

Account Number	Name	Balance
146	Falconer, Edward	45.46
175	Mato, Robert	33.07
212	Rufino, Carlos	9.22
334	Brevil, James	108.42
348	Yeung, Suk	26.17
397	Fradin, Shirley	56.84
406	Katz, Hal	15.67
438	Cuomo, Maria	25.37
474	Alexander, Lisa	52.36
498	English, Reynolds	8.59
537	Thompson, Stanley	47.51
562	Rizzuto, James	76.25
583	Morley, John	125.00
604	Martin, Kathleen	16.37
626	Paul, Marina	42.85
659	Burns, Jeffrey	23.61
694	Wright, Donna	54.40
709	Lopez, Anna	19.26
753	Goldberg, Lori	15.87
786	Lee, Bohyon	25.71
849	Valdez, Fabio	13.85
877	Schwartz, Michael	45.91

All the records have been read

PROGRAM 12.2   **Reading the random charge account file.**

THE GET STATEMENT

The FOR-NEXT loop in lines 150 through 180 reads the file. The GET statement in line 160 actually reads the data from the disk. The syntax of the GET statement is

```
GET #filenum, recordnum
```

Notice that just as with the PUT statement, you do not list the variables that are to be read with a GET statement. Each time a GET statement is executed, a whole record is read.

In Program 12.2, every record from record number 1 through record number 999 is read. After each record is read, the IF statement in line 170 tests NAME.FLD$ to determine whether it contains only spaces. If it does not, the record is active and is printed. Before proceeding, be sure you understand how the following GET statements work:

GET Statement

GET #2, STUDENT.NO

Effect

Reads the record whose number is STUDENT.NO from the file opened as file number 2 into the variables listed in the FIELD #2 statement.

GET Statement

GET #1, 174

Effect

Reads record number 174 from the file opened as file number 1 into the variables listed in the FIELD #1 statement.

THE CVI, CVS, AND CVD FUNCTIONS

Before they can be used in a program, field variables whose numeric values were converted by one of the MK functions must be restored to numeric form using one of the CV functions. CVD converts an eight-byte string created by the MKD$ function to a double-precision value. CVS converts a four-byte string created by the MKS$ function to a single-precision value, as in line 170, where the CVS function is used to convert the field variable BALANCE.FLD$ into the single-precision variable BALANCE. Similarly, CVI converts a two-byte string created by the MKI$ function to an integer.

Note that the result of a CVI function does not have to be assigned to an integer variable. The statement

```
A = CVI(A.FLD$)
```

assigns an integer value to the single-precision variable A.

Syntax Summary

OPEN Statement
Form: OPEN "filename" AS #filenum [LEN=reclength]
Example: OPEN "BOOKS.RND" AS #2 LEN = 64
Function: Opens a file so it can be processed and associates it
          with file number filenum. LEN specifies the number of
          bytes in each record; its default value is 128 bytes.

FIELD Statement
Form: FIELD #filenum, width AS stringvar [,width AS stringvar]
Example: FIELD #1, 30 AS TITLE.FLD$, 30 AS AUTHOR.FLD$, 4 AS SOLD.FLD$
Function: Specifies the name, size, and position of each field in a random
          file record.

LSET Statement
Form: LSET string variable = string expression
Example: LSET TITLE.FLD$ = TITLE.IN$
Function: Moves data into a field variable in preparation for
            a PUT statement. The data are left-justified.

RSET Statement
Form: RSET string variable = string expression
Example: RESET AUTHOR.FLD$ = AUTHOR.IN$
Function: Moves data into a field variable in preparation for
            a PUT statement. The data are right-justified.

PUT Statement
Form: PUT #filenum, recordnum
Example: PUT #2, BOOK.NUM
Function: Writes the variables listed in the FIELD #filenum
            statement to the recordnum record of the random file
            opened with file number filenum.

GET Statement
Form: GET #filenum, recordnum]
Example: GET #1, ACCT.NO
Function: Reads record number recordnum from the file that was
            opened with file number filenum into the variables listed
            in the FIELD #filenum statement.

Getting the
Bugs Out

Problem: During execution, BASIC displays the error message

Field overflow

Reason: The total of the widths specified in a FIELD statement is
               greater than the record length specified in the OPEN statement.

Solution: Change either the record length in the OPEN statement or the
               widths in the FIELD statement, whichever is wrong.

Problem: During execution, BASIC displays the error message

Bad file mode in nn

where nn is the line number of a GET or PUT statement.

Reason: You tried to execute a GET or a PUT using a file number that
               was not opened or that was opened as a sequential file.

Solution: Either change the file number in the GET or PUT or correct the
               OPEN statement for a random file.

Problem: During execution, BASIC displays the error message

Bad file number in nn

where nn is the line number of a FIELD statement.

Reason: You tried to execute a FIELD statement using a file number
               that was not opened.

Solution: Correct the file number in either the OPEN or FIELD statement.

Problem: During execution, BASIC displays the error message

Bad record number in nn

where nn is the line number of a GET or PUT statement.

Reason:	The record number specified in a GET or PUT statement was either 0 or greater than the maximum allowed, 16,777,215.
Solution:	Correct the record number.

EXERCISES

....

12.1 The first data listed in Program 12.1 are for account number 498 for "English, Reynolds", but the first record listed in Program 12.2 is for account number 146 for "Falconer, Edward". Why?

*12.2 Why must every record in a random file have the same length?

12.3 A record contains only two fields: A.FLD$ and B.FLD$. They are assigned values using the statements

```
LSET A.FLD$ = MKI$(A)
LSET B.FLD$ = MKS$(B)
```

Write the FIELD statement for this file.

*12.4 In a program that reads the file described in Exercise 12.3, write the statements that could be used to convert A.FLD$ and B.FLD$ to numeric variables.

*12.5 The records in GPA.RND consists of the following fields:

Name	Length
STUDENT.NAME.FLD$	25
CREDITS.FLD$	2
GPA.FLD$	4

CREDITS.FLD$ is a string version of an integer value, and GPA.FLD$ is a string version of a single-precision number.

a) Write the OPEN statement that could be used in a program that creates GPA.RND. Open the file as file number 1.

b) Write the OPEN statement that could be used in a program that reads GPA.RND. Open the file as file number 1.

c) Write the FIELD statement for GPA.RND.

d) Write the statements to assign values from the ordinary variables to the field variables.

e) Write the statement to write a record to the file. STUDENT.NO specifies the record to be written.

f) Write the statement to read a record from the file. STUDENT.NO specifies the record to be read.

12.6 The records in ADDRESS.RND consist of the following fields:

Name	Length
NAME.FLD$	20
STREET.FLD$	25
CITY.FLD$	20
STATE.FLD$	2
ZIP.FLD$	4

ZIP.FLD$ is a string version of a single-precision variable.

a) Write the OPEN statement that could be used in a program that creates ADDRESS.RND. Open the file as file number 1.

b) Write the OPEN statement that could be used in a program that reads ADDRESS.RND. Open the file as file number 1.

c) Write the FIELD statement for ADDRESS.RND.

d) Write the statements to assign values from the ordinary variables to the field variables.

e) Write the statement to write a record to the file. RECORD.NO specifies the record to be written.

f) Write the statement to read a record from the file. RECORD.NO specifies the record to be read.

12.7 The records in PAYROLL.RND consist of the following fields:

Name	Length
EMP.NAME.FLD$	25
PAY.RATE.FLD$	4
NO.DEPENDENTS.FLD$	2
YTD.GROSS.FLD$	4

Both PAY.RATE.FLD$ and YTD.GROSS.FLD$ are string versions of single-precision values, and NO.DEPENDENTS.FLD$ is a string version of an integer value.

a) Write the OPEN statement that could be used in a program that creates PAYROLL.RND. Open the file as file number 2.

b) Write the OPEN statement that could be used in a program that reads PAYROLL.RND. Open the file as file number 2.

c) Write the FIELD statement for PAYROLL.RND.

d) Write the statements to assign values from the ordinary variables to the field variables.

e) Write the statement to write a record to the file. EMP.NO specifies the record to be written.

f) Write the statement to read a record from the file. EMP.NO specifies the record to be read.

PROGRAMMING ASSIGNMENTS

....

In the following programming assignments, if your program to create the file fails, you should use the BASIC KILL command to delete the random file before you rerun the program.

*12.1 The file A12-01.RND contains the three fields described in Exercise 12.5. The student number is in the range 1 to 999. Write a program to list those students whose GPA is greater than 3.00. Include headings.

12.2 a) Write a program to create the ADDRESS.RND file described in Exercise 12.6. Assume that RECORD.NO will be in the range 1 to 99.

   b) Write a second program to list the active records in ADDRESS.RND. Include headings in the report.

MAINTAINING A RANDOM FILE

....

You may be thinking that random files don't offer any advantages over sequential files, since we had to read every record in the file, which we would have had to do with a sequential file. In addition, we had to test NAME.FLD$ to see if the record was active and should be printed, while in sequential files there are no inactive records. You have gotten a misleading impression of random files, because thus far we have listed every active record. But random files allow us to display only the record the user wants to see, which is not practical to do with sequential files. For example, let's write a program that adds, deletes, updates, and displays records in Cuff's charge account file.

■ *Variable Names and Algorithm*

To solve this problem, we can use the same variables as in Program 12.1 and 12.2, with the following additions:

Input variables	Code specifying operation to perform, string	CODE$
	Code specifying operation to perform, number	CODE
	Code specifying whether amount entered is a payment or charge	PAYMENT.CODE$

In keeping with step 2 of our structured procedure, we can use this algorithm:

> 1. Open CHARGE.RND.
> 2. Ask users whether they want to add, delete, update, or display a record or to exit.
> 3. To add a record, accept the data for the new record, field the record, and write the record.

4. To delete a record, accept the account number of the record to be deleted and delete that record by assigning spaces to the name and zero to the balance. Then rewrite the record.
5. To update a record, accept the account number of the record to be updated. Display the balance, then ask the user to enter an amount and to indicate whether the amount is a payment or a charge. Update the balance and rewrite the record.
6. To display a record, accept the account number and display the record.
7. To exit, close the file and stop execution.

Just as with sequential files, we must be aware that a request may be in error; we cannot add a record with the same account number as a record already in the file, nor can we delete, update, or display a record that does not exist.

The Program

Although Program 12.3 is long, it consists of several subroutines, none of which is complicated, so you shouldn't need a flowchart to understand it. The OPEN and FIELD statements in the initialization subroutine that begins on line 1500 are identical to the ones we used earlier. Notice that the name used in the OPEN statement is CHARGE.RND. You may recall that in sequential processing of the charge account file we used the names CHARGE01.SEQ, CHARGE02.SEQ, etc. The difference is significant. With sequential files, when a record is added, deleted, or updated, we must create a new master file. But with random files there is only one master file, so we do not need the designation 01, 02, etc.

After line 1540 displays the program name, the program executes the subroutine that starts at line 8100. This subroutine merely causes a short pause before the INPUT subroutine is executed. It uses the TIMER function to cause a two-second pause, as explained in Chapter 9. After two seconds, BASIC will exit from the WHILE loop, execute the CLS statement in line 8140 to clear the screen, and return to the initialization subroutine.

The important part of the main routine is the WHILE loop in lines 1020 through 1050. In this loop, the program first executes the display menu subroutine that starts at line 2000. This routine presents users with a menu, listing the functions they may request and asking them to make a selection. In line 2070, the INPUT$ function assigns the number of the request to CODE$, and in line 2080 the VAL function converts CODE$ to CODE.

THE ADD RECORDS ROUTINE

If the user enters a 1, the GOSUB statement in line 1040 executes the add records subroutine that starts at line 3000. This routine begins by executing the subroutine at line 8000, which asks the user to enter the account number of the record to be added. In line 8020, the INPUT$ function again obtains the string data, and in line 8030 the VAL function converts the string to a number, which is assigned to ACCT.NO. The GET statement in line 8050 reads the record pointed to by ACCT.NO. This is the first time we have used the ability of the GET statement to read a specific record, so it is important that

```
1000 REM *** MAINTAINING THE RANDOM CHARGE ACCOUNT FILE ***
1010 GOSUB 1500                               'Initialization routine
1020 WHILE FINISHED$ = "NO"
1030   GOSUB 2000                             'Display menu
1040   ON CODE GOSUB 3000, 4000, 5000, 6000, 7000
1050 WEND
1060 LOCATE 10,20:PRINT "Normal end of program"
1070 STOP
1080 '
1500 REM *** Initialization routine ========================================
1510   OPEN "CHARGE.RND" AS #1 LEN = 24
1520   FIELD #1, 20 AS NAME.FLD$, 4 AS BALANCE.FLD$
1530   CLS: KEY OFF
1540   LOCATE 5,23: PRINT "CHARGE ACCOUNT MAINTENANCE PROGRAM"
1550   GOSUB 8100                             'Pause and clear screen
1560   FINISHED$ = "NO"
1570 RETURN
1580 REM *** End of initialization routine
1590 '
2000 REM *** Display menu routine ===========================================
2010   LOCATE 2,20: PRINT "Enter 1 to Add a record"
2020   LOCATE 3,20: PRINT "      2 to Delete a record"
2030   LOCATE 4,20: PRINT "      3 to Update a record"
2040   LOCATE 5,20: PRINT "      4 to Display a record"
2050   LOCATE 6,20: PRINT "      5 to Exit program"
2060   LOCATE 7,20: PRINT "Function ? ";
2070   CODE$ = INPUT$(1)
2080   CODE = VAL(CODE$)
2090   PRINT CODE
2100 RETURN
2110 REM *** End of display menu routine
2120 '
3000 REM *** Add records routine =============================================
3010   GOSUB 8000                             'Get the record
3020   IF NAME.FLD$ <> SPACE$(20)
          THEN GOSUB 3200: GOTO 3100          'Account number is assigned; no add
3030   LOCATE 10,20: LINE INPUT "Enter name "; NAME.IN$
3040   LOCATE 11,20: INPUT "Enter starting balance";BALANCE
3050   LSET NAME.FLD$ = NAME.IN$              'Set name
3060   LSET BALANCE.FLD$ = MKS$(BALANCE) 'Convert balance
3070   PUT #1, ACCT.NO                        'Write record
3080   LOCATE 12,20:PRINT "Record number "; ACCT.NO; "has been added"
3090   GOSUB 8100                             'Pause and clear screen
3100 RETURN
3110 REM *** End of add records routine
3120 '
3200 REM *** Bad add routine
3210 BEEP
3220   LOCATE 15,20: PRINT "Account number "; ACCT.NO; "is currently assigned"
3230   GOSUB 8100
3240 RETURN
3250 REM *** End of bad add routine
3260 '
```

PROGRAM 12.3   **Maintaining the random charge account file.**

```
4000 REM *** Delete records routine ===============================================
4010    GOSUB 8000                               'Get the record
4020    IF NAME.FLD$ = SPACE$(20)
           THEN GOSUB 8200: GOTO 4080    'Account number not assigned; no delete
4030    LSET NAME.FLD$ = SPACE$(20)          'Set name for inactive
4040    LSET BALANCE.FLD$ = MKS$(0)          'Set balance to 0
4050    PUT #1, ACCT.NO                      'Write record
4060    LOCATE 11,20:PRINT "Record number "; ACCT.NO; "has been deleted"
4070    GOSUB 8100                               'Pause and clear screen
4080 RETURN
4090 REM ** End of delete records routine
4100 '
5000 REM *** Update records routine ===============================================
5010    GOSUB 8000                               'Get the record
5020    IF NAME.FLD$ = SPACE$(20)
           THEN GOSUB 8200: GOTO 5150      'Account number not assigned; no update
5030    LOCATE 9,20: PRINT USING "Current balance #,###.## "; BALANCE
5040    LOCATE 10,20: INPUT "Enter amount"; AMOUNT
5050    LOCATE 11,20
5060    PRINT "Enter 1 if amount is a charge, or 2 if it is a payment ";
5070    PAYMENT.CODE$ = INPUT$(1)
5080    PRINT PAYMENT.CODE$
5090    IF PAYMENT.CODE$ = "1"
           THEN BALANCE = BALANCE + AMOUNT
           ELSE BALANCE = BALANCE - AMOUNT
5100    LOCATE 12,20: PRINT USING "New balance #,###.## "; BALANCE
5110    LSET BALANCE.FLD$ = MKS$(BALANCE)   'Convert balance
5120    PUT #1, ACCT.NO                      'Write record
5130    LOCATE 13,20: PRINT "Record number ";ACCT.NO; "has been updated"
5140    GOSUB 8100                               'Pause and clear screen
5150 RETURN
5160 REM *** End of update records routine
5170 '
6000 REM *** Display records routine ==============================================
6010    GOSUB 8000                               'Get the record
6020    IF NAME.FLD$ = SPACE$(20)
           THEN GOSUB 8200: GOTO 6080      'Account number not assigned; no display
6030    LOCATE 9,20: PRINT "Account number "; ACCT.NO
6040    LOCATE 10,20: PRINT "Name "; NAME.FLD$
6050    LOCATE 11,20: PRINT USING "Current balance #,###.## "; BALANCE
6060    LOCATE 12,20: INPUT "Press Enter to continue", A$
6070    CLS
6080 RETURN
6090 REM *** End of display record routine
6100 '
7000 REM *** Exit program routine =================================================
7010    CLOSE
7020    FINISHED$ = "YES"
7030 RETURN
7040 REM *** End of exit program routine
7050 '
```

PROGRAM 12.3   **(Continued).**

```
7999 REM  =======================Utility Routines ============================
8000 REM *** Get record and convert balance routine
8010    LOCATE 8,20: PRINT "Enter the three-digit account number ";
8020    ACCT.NO$ = INPUT$(3)
8030    ACCT.NO = VAL(ACCT.NO$)
8040    PRINT ACCT.NO
8050    GET #1, ACCT.NO
8060    BALANCE = CVS(BALANCE.FLD$)
8070 RETURN
8080 REM *** End of get record and convert balance routine
8090 '
8100 REM *** Pause and clear screen routine
8110    LATER = TIMER + 2
8120    WHILE TIMER < LATER
8130    WEND
8140    CLS
8150 RETURN
8160 REM *** End of pause and clear screen routine
8170 '
8200 REM *** Bad delete, update and display routine
8210    BEEP
8220    LOCATE 15,20: PRINT "Account number "; ACCT.NO; "is currently inactive"
8230    GOSUB 8100
8240 RETURN
8250 REM *** End of bad delete, update, and display routine
8260 END
```

PROGRAM 12.3   (Continued).

you understand how it works. For example, if the user enters 582 as the account number, this GET statement will read the record in pigeonhole 582.

In line 8060, the CVS function converts BALANCE.FLD$ to BALANCE, and then the RETURN statement returns to the add records subroutine, where it tests NAME.FLD$ in line 3020. If it does not contain only spaces, the account number is already assigned, so a new record with that account number may not be added. In that case, an error message is printed, and BASIC returns to the main routine.

If NAME.FLD$ does contain spaces, the account number is not already assigned. In that case, lines 3030 and 3040 ask the user to enter the name and starting balance, and in lines 3050 and 3060 the LSET statement assigns values to the two field variables. Then the PUT statement in line 3070 writes the record in the pigeonhole specified by ACCT.NO, the PRINT statement in line 3080 displays a successful message, and line 3090 executes the subroutine to cause a pause and clear the screen. Finally, the RETURN statement in line 3100 returns control to the main loop.

THE DELETE RECORDS ROUTINE

The delete records subroutine begins at line 4000. It starts by executing the subroutine that reads the record. In line 4020, it determines whether NAME.FLD$ consists of spaces. If it does, the record is inactive and cannot be deleted. If it does not, the record is deleted by setting NAME.FLD$ to spaces in line 4030 and BALANCE.FLD$ to 0 in line 4040. The PUT statement in line 4050 rewrites the record, and the PRINT statement in line 4060 displays a message.

The routines to update and to display records are similar to the add records subroutine. You should trace them to be sure you understand how they work. The exit program subroutine closes the file and assigns YES to

FINISHED$, which causes BASIC to exit from the WHILE loop in lines 1020 through 1050. In lines 1060 and 1070, BASIC prints the Normal end of program message and executes a STOP statement.

■ *The DOS Copy Command*

Every time you run a BASIC random file maintenance program, you change the random file you are working with. During program development, this can present problems. For example, suppose your test data call for deleting a record. You run the program, delete the record, and then discover that in some other routine the program contains an error. So you correct the error and run the program again. However, when you run the program the second time, you cannot delete the same record, since it has already been deleted.

Backup file
A copy of a file that can be used to recreate the original.

You will not have this problem if you have a backup file. A **backup file** is a copy of a file that can be used to recreate the original. After you create the file, you can use the DOS command COPY to create a backup of the file, for example,

```
COPY CHARGE.RND CHARGE.BAK
```

You now have two versions of the charge account file: the original, named CHARGE.RND, and the backup, named CHARGE.BAK. After the maintenance program has been run and has changed CHARGE.RND, you can execute the command

```
COPY CHARGE.BAK CHARGE.RND
```

to create a fresh copy of CHARGE.RND that can be used by the maintenance program. Since CHARGE.BAK has not been changed, you can copy it as many times as you like. You can use the BASIC SHELL statement to execute these DOS commands without exiting BASIC.

EXERCISES

....

12.8 In Program 12.3, how would you change the subroutine at line 8100 if you wanted to pause for three seconds?

12.9 Write the DOS command that can be used to make a backup copy of RENTAL.RND.

PROGRAMMING ASSIGNMENTS

....

12.3 Write a program to add, delete, update, and display records from the file A12-01.RND. Update GPA as explained in Programming Assignment 11.15.

12.4 Write a program to add, delete, update, and display records from the ADDRESS.RND file created in Programming Assignment 12.2.

USING INDEXES WITH RANDOM FILES

....

At this point, you may be thinking that random files are much simpler to use than sequential files. Unfortunately, there is a serpent in our Garden of Eden. Thus far, we have used only a particularly simple example of a random file.

In the charge account example, we used the charge account number as the record number, assuming that all charge account numbers were three-digit numbers in the range 1 to 999. When we created the file in Program 12.1, we created a file with 999 records, one for each of the possible charge account numbers. It didn't matter that many of the records did not contain data, since the wasted space was not large.

But in real life, the key field often cannot be used as the record number. For example, in a payroll file a social security number is the most logical choice for key field. However, if we were to follow the example of our charge account program we would have to create a file with 999,999,999 records, because social security numbers contain 9 digits. The result would be a very large file—too large to be stored on a disk. Moreover, even if a firm had ten million employees, 99 percent of the file would be empty. To use random files when the key field cannot be used as the record number, we need indexes.

Index
An array used to locate records in a random file.

An **index** consists of an array that is used to locate records in a random file. The array contains the keys and is constructed so that if we are given the value of the key field, we can retrieve the record. The index array is stored as a separate sequential disk file.

Creating a File

To see how indexes are created and used, consider the membership file of the Bon Vivant Club. The fields in Bon Vivant's membership records are a five-digit membership number, last name, first name, title (Mr., Mrs., Ms., etc.), street address, town, state, zip code, annual dues, and amount paid. The membership number will be the key.

VARIABLES AND ALGORITHM

As usual, we begin by choosing names for the variables.

Input variables	Membership number	MEM.NO
	Last name	LNAME$
	First (given) name	GNAME$
	Title	TITLE$
	Street address	STREET$
	Town	TOWN$
	State	STATE$
	Zip code	ZIP
	Annual dues	DUES
	Amount paid	PAID
Internal variables	Record number	REC.NO
	Membership number array	MEM.NO.INDEX
Output (field) variables	Membership number	MEM.NO.FLD$
	Last name	LNAME.FLD$
	First (given) name	GNAME.FLD$
	Title	TITLE.FLD$

Street address	STREET.FLD$
Town	TOWN.FLD$
State	STATE.FLD$
Zip code	ZIP.FLD$
Annual dues	DUES.FLD$
Amount paid	PAID.FLD$

Note that GNAME$ (given name) is used for the variable name for the first name because FNAME$ is a reserved word.

The name of the membership file we will create is MEMBER.RND, and the name of the index file is MEMBER.IDX.

We can use the following algorithm:

1. Open MEMBER.RND.
2. Read the input variables.
3. If these are trailer data, go to step 8.
4. Assign values to the field variables.
5. Write a record to MEMBER.RND.
6. Store the membership number in the index array.
7. Repeat steps 2 through 6 for all members.
8. Close MEMBER.RND.
9. Open MEMBER.IDX.
10. Write the index array to disk.
11. Close MEMBER.IDX.
12. Stop execution.

THE PROGRAM

The logic of Program 12.4 is so simple you do not need a flowchart to understand it. The index consists of the array MEM.NO.INDEX. This array is dimensioned with 1000 elements, because the exclusive Bon Vivant Club would never have more than 1000 members. In line 2010 in the initialization subroutine, the MEMBER.RND file is opened with a length of 98 bytes. The record layout is given in the FIELD statement in line 2020. Notice that although the membership number and the zip code are five-digit numbers, when they are converted by the MKS$ function they will occupy only four bytes.

The READ DATA subroutine, which starts at line 3000, reads the data and increments REC.NO. It then executes the subroutine at line 3200, which assigns values to the field variables and writes the record. Notice that the records are written in the order that they are read from the DATA statements. Thus, the data in the first DATA statement are written as record number 1, the data in the second DATA statement are written as record number 2, and so on. Since there is no meaning to the order in which the records are listed in the DATA statements, there is no meaning to the order in which the records are stored in the file.

We have just written the record whose membership number is MEM.NO as record number REC.NO. Therefore, line 3050 sets MEM.NO.INDEX (REC.NO) equal to MEM.NO. For example, if the record whose membership number is 32167 is stored as record number 7, then the seventh element of MEM.NO.INDEX is set equal to 32167. In later programs, we will be able to search MEM.NO.INDEX

```
1000 REM *** CREATING THE MEMBERSHIP FILE - WITH INDEX ***
1010 DIM MEM.NO.INDEX(1000)
1020 GOSUB 2000            'Initialization routine
1030 GOSUB 3000            'Read data and create files and indexes
1040 GOSUB 4000            'Write index to disk
1050 PRINT "Normal end of program"
1060 STOP
1070 '
1080 '
2000 REM *** Initialization routine ============================================
2010   OPEN "MEMBER.RND" AS #1 LEN = 98
2020   FIELD #1, 4 AS MEM.NO.FLD$, 15 AS LNAME.FLD$, 10 AS GNAME.FLD$,
               10 AS TITLE.FLD$, 25 AS STREET.FLD$, 20 AS TOWN.FLD$,
               2 AS STATE.FLD$, 4 AS ZIP.FLD$, 4 AS DUES.FLD$, 4 AS PAID.FLD$
2030   REC.NO = 0
2040 RETURN
2050 REM *** End of initialization routine
2060 '
3000 REM *** Read data and create file and index routine =====================
3010   READ MEM.NO, LNAME$, GNAME$, TITLE$, STREET$, TOWN$, STATE$, ZIP, DUES,
          PAID
3020     IF MEM.NO = 999999!
           THEN GOTO 3070
3030     REC.NO = REC.NO + 1                      'Increment record number
3040     GOSUB 3200                               'Field variables and write record
3050     MEM.NO.INDEX(REC.NO) = MEM.NO            'Add data to index array
3060   GOTO 3010
3070   CLOSE
3080 RETURN
3090 REM *** End of read data and create indexes routine
3100 '
3200 REM *** Field variables and write record routine
3210   LSET MEM.NO.FLD$ = MKS$(MEM.NO)
3220   LSET LNAME.FLD$ = LNAME$
3230   LSET GNAME.FLD$ = GNAME$
3240   LSET TITLE.FLD$ = TITLE$
3250   LSET STREET.FLD$ = STREET$
3260   LSET TOWN.FLD$ = TOWN$
3270   LSET STATE.FLD$ = STATE$
3280   LSET ZIP.FLD$ = MKS$(ZIP)
3290   LSET DUES.FLD$ = MKS$(DUES)
3300   LSET PAID.FLD$ = MKS$(PAID)
3310   PUT #1, REC.NO
3320 RETURN
3330 REM *** End of field variables and write record routine
3340 '
4000 REM *** Write index to disk routine =======================================
4010   OPEN "MEMBER.IDX" FOR OUTPUT AS #1
4020   FOR J = 1 TO REC.NO
4030     WRITE #1, MEM.NO.INDEX(J)
4040   NEXT J
4050   CLOSE
4060 RETURN
4070 REM *** End of write index to disk routine
4080 '
```

PROGRAM 12.4   Creating the membership file with an index.

```
5000 REM Data to create file ========================================================
5010 DATA 60573, Ripps, David, Dr. & Mrs., 705 East 55 Street, New York, NY, 100
28, 25, 25
5020 DATA 31684, Padilla, Rudy, Mr. & Mrs., 4944 18 Place, Garrison, NY, 10524,
20, 10
5030 DATA 35675, Carnes, Cecil, Mr., 2394 Welby Way, Los Alamos, NM, 87544, 35,
35
5040 DATA 42516, Lindauer, George, Dr. & Mrs., 2978 Ambleglen Court, Corydon, ID
, 47122, 25, 20
5050 DATA 42329, Wardak, Henry, Mr. & Mrs., 130 Rover Road, Conoga Park, CA, 900
47, 50, 50
5060 DATA 97514, Sanzeri, Philip, Mr. & Mrs., 39 Beechwood, Clearwater, FL, 3351
9, 35, 25
5070 DATA 32167, Mezquita, Fred, Mr., 8 Danbury Court, El Segundo, CA, 90245, 25
, 15
5080 DATA 72577, Schoenwald, Richard, Dr. & Mrs., 709 Lincoln Ave, Pittsburg, PA
, 15206, 35, 20
5090 DATA 27923, Switzer, Steven, Mr. & Mrs., 8 Lequer Road, Port Washington, NY
, 11050, 50, 50
5100 DATA 73492, Donner, Rachel, Ms., 147-16 92 Street, Forest Hills, NY, 11375,
 20, 10
5110 REM Trailer data follows
5120 DATA 999999,0,0,0,0,0,0,0,0,0
5130 END

RUN
Normal end of program
Break in 1060
Ok
```

PROGRAM 12.4   **(Continued).**

to determine the record number of a record with a specified membership number.

The READ loop repeats until the trailer data are read, when the IF statement in line 3020 sends control to line 3070, which closes the file. Notice that the trailer data are not written to the file.

At this point, MEMBER.RND has been created, and the index array is filled with data. The routine that starts at line 4000 writes the array to a disk as MEMBER.IDX, which is an ordinary sequential file. Figure 12.1 shows the file. As you probably expected, the membership numbers are in the same order in the file as they are in the DATA statements in Program 12.4. Remember that this is the same order that the records occur in the file.

Querying the Membership File

Now that Bon Vivant's membership file has been created, its treasurer wants to be able to check on a member's standing at any time. She needs a program that will allow her to enter a membership number and see the corresponding record.

```
                              60573
                              31684
                              35675
                              42516
                              42329
                              97514
                              32167
                              72577
                              27923
                              73492
```

FIGURE 12.1   **The index file MEMBER.IDX.**

We can use the same variables we used when the file was created. In addition, we need

Membership number entered by user, string	MEM.NO.IN$
Membership number entered by user, numeric	MEM.NO.IN
Flag used in search routine	FOUND$
Record number found by search	REC.NO
Number of active elements in MEM.NO.INDEX	NO.ELEMENTS

As step 2 of our structured procedure, we can use the following algorithm:

1. Open MEMBER.RND and MEMBER.IDX.
2. Read the MEMBER.IDX file and fill MEM.NO.INDEX.
3. Close MEMBER.IDX.
4. While the user wants to continue, repeat steps 5 through 8.
5. Accept MEM.NO.IN$ and convert it to MEM.NO.IN.
6. Perform a sequential search of MEM.NO.INDEX for MEM.NO.IN.
7. If MEM.NO.IN was found as the Jth element of MEM.NO.INDEX, read the Jth record from the file and display it.
8. If the search was unsuccessful, display an error message.
9. Close MEMBER.RND.
10. Stop execution.

THE PROGRAM

The logic of Program 12.5 is so simple that again you do not need a flow-chart to understand it. The main routine presents nothing new. The OPEN and FIELD statements in the initialization subroutine are identical to those in Program 12.4. Line 2030 opens the membership number index file, and line 2040 initializes J to 0. The index file is read in a WHILE loop that continues until the end of file is reached. In the WHILE loop, J serves as a subscript; it is incremented so that it always points to the next available element in the array. When BASIC exits from the WHILE loop, J equals the number of elements in the array, so line 2100 sets NO.ELEMENTS equal to J.

```
1000 REM *** QUERYING THE MEMBERSHIP FILE ***
1010 CLS: KEY OFF
1020 FALSE = 0
1030 DIM MEM.NO.INDEX(1000)
1040 LOCATE 2,20: PRINT "QUERY THE MEMBERSHIP FILE"
1050 GOSUB 2000          'Initialization routine
1060 GOSUB 3000          'Query routine
1070 CLOSE
1080 LOCATE 8,20:PRINT "Normal end of program"
1090 STOP
1100 '
2000 REM *** Initialization routine =========================================
2010   OPEN "MEMBER.RND" AS #1 LEN = 98
2020   FIELD #1, 4 AS MEM.NO.FLD$, 15 AS LNAME.FLD$, 10 AS GNAME.FLD$,
                10 AS TITLE.FLD$, 25 AS STREET.FLD$, 20 AS TOWN.FLD$,
                2 AS STATE.FLD$, 4 AS ZIP.FLD$, 4 AS DUES.FLD$, 4 AS PAID.FLD$
2030   OPEN "MEMBER.IDX" FOR INPUT AS #2
2040   J = 0
2050   WHILE EOF(2) = FALSE
2060     J = J + 1
2070     INPUT #2, MEM.NO.INDEX(J)
2080   WEND
2090   CLOSE #2
2100   NO.ELEMENTS = J                        'Set value of NO.ELEMENTS
2110 RETURN
2120 REM *** End of initialization routine
2130 '
3000 REM *** Query routine ===================================================
3010   LOCATE 8,12: PRINT "Enter 5 digit membership number (00000 to quit) ";
3020     MEM.NO.IN$ = INPUT$(5): PRINT MEM.NO.IN$
3030     MEM.NO.IN = VAL(MEM.NO.IN$)
3040     IF MEM.NO.IN = 0
             THEN LOCATE 8,12: PRINT SPC(53): GOTO 3070
             ELSE GOSUB 3100
3050     IF FOUND$ = "YES"
             THEN GOSUB 3300:LOCATE 24,30:INPUT; "Press Enter to continue",A$:CLS
             ELSE GOSUB 3500
3060   GOTO 3010
3070 RETURN
3080 REM *** End of query routine
3090 '
3100 REM *** Search of index array routine
3110   FOUND$ = "NO"
3120   FOR J = 1 TO NO.ELEMENTS
3130     IF MEM.NO.INDEX(J) = MEM.NO.IN
           THEN FOUND$ = "YES": REC.NO = J: GOTO 3150
3140   NEXT J
3150 RETURN
3160 REM *** End of search of index array routine
3170 '
```

PROGRAM 12.5   **Querying the membership file.**

The query routine, which starts at line 3000, asks users to enter the membership number of the record to be displayed. The VAL function converts the value entered and assigns it to the variable MEM.NO.IN. If a user enters 00000, the IF statement in line 3040 erases the instructions from the

```
3300 REM *** Read and display the record routine
3310    GET #1, REC.NO                              'Read record
3320    MEM.NO = CVS(MEM.NO.FLD$)                    'Convert
3330    ZIP = CVS(ZIP.FLD$)                          'numeric
3340    DUES = CVS(DUES.FLD$)                        'fields for
3350    PAID = CVS(PAID.FLD$)                        'printing
3360    LOCATE 10,5: PRINT MEM.NO
3370    LOCATE 10,20: PRINT LNAME.FLD$
3380    LOCATE 10,40: PRINT GNAME.FLD$
3390    LOCATE 10,60: PRINT TITLE.FLD$
3400    LOCATE 15,5: PRINT STREET.FLD$
3410    LOCATE 15,38: PRINT TOWN.FLD$
3420    LOCATE 15,60: PRINT STATE.FLD$
3430    LOCATE 15,64: PRINT ZIP
3440    LOCATE 20,20: PRINT USING "##.##"; DUES
3450    LOCATE 20,40: PRINT USING "##.##"; PAID
3460 RETURN
3470 REM *** End of read and display the record routine
3480 '
3500 REM *** Display error message routine
3510    BEEP: LOCATE 25,20
3520    PRINT "Membership number"; MEM.NO.IN; "is not in file";
3530    GOSUB 3600
3540 RETURN
3550 REM *** End of display error message routine
3560 '
3600 REM *** Pause and clear screen routine
3610    LATER = TIMER + 2
3620    WHILE TIMER < LATER
3630    WEND
3640    CLS
3650 RETURN
3660 REM *** End of pause and clear screen routine
3670 END
```

PROGRAM 12.5   **(Continued).**

screen and branches to the RETURN statement in line 3070. Otherwise, BASIC executes the subroutine that starts at line 3100, performing a sequential search of the MEM.NO.INDEX array. If the search finds that element J of this array is equal to MEM.NO.IN, then it sets FOUND$ equal to YES and REC.NO equal to J.

The logic here is vital, so let's make sure you understand it. Suppose the user enters the membership number 42516. Figure 12.1 shows that the fourth element of MEM.NO.INDEX is equal to 42516, which means that the record number for record 42516 is 4. When the condition in the IF statement in line 3130 is true, J will be 4, and we therefore set REC.NO equal to J.

When BASIC returns from the search, line 3050 tests FOUND$. If FOUND$ equals YES, BASIC executes the subroutine that starts at line 3300. The GET statement in line 3310 reads the record specified by REC.NO. The CVS function converts the numeric variables, and the PRINT statements display the record. If FOUND$ is not equal to YES, it means the search for the membership number was unsuccessful. In that case, the ELSE clause executes the subroutine starting at line 3500, which displays an error message.

■ *Maintaining a File*

Of course, Bon Vivant also needs a program to add, delete, and update records in its membership file.

VARIABLES AND ALGORITHM

We can use the same variables we used earlier, with the following additions:

Flag to indicate user is finished	FINISHED$
Number of records in file	NO.REC
Value entered to select from menu, string	CODE$
Value entered to select from menu, number	CODE
Record number of record to be updated	UPDATE.REC.NO
Number of field to be updated	UPDATE.FLD
New value entered for field being updated	NEW.VALUE$
Flag to indicate that updating of a record is finished	UPDATE.FINISHED$

The algorithm is

1. Open MEMBER.RND and MEMBER.IDX.
2. Read the MEMBER.IDX file and fill MEM.NO.INDEX.
3. Ask the users whether they want to add, delete, or update a record or to exit.
4. To add a record, accept the data for the new record, field the record, write the record to the end of the file, and update MEM.NO.INDEX.
5. To delete a record, accept the membership number of the record to be deleted. Delete the record by replacing that record's membership number with 0 in MEM.NO.INDEX.
6. To update a record, accept the membership number of the record to be updated. Display the record and allow users to change any field. When all the changes have been made, rewrite the record.
7. To exit, close the files, open MEMBER.IDX for output, and write MEM.NO.INDEX to MEMBER.IDX. Then close MEMBER.IDX.
8. Stop execution.

Program 12.6, which is based on this algorithm, involves many subroutines. The hierarchy diagram shown in Figure 12.2 may help you understand the program's structure.

THE LOF FUNCTION

The program begins by executing the initialization subroutine that starts at line 2000. Notice the use of the LOF function in line 2030. The LOF function returns the number of bytes allocated to a file. When we divide that number by the record length, we get the number of records in the file—something

```
1000 REM *** MAINTAINING THE MEMBERSHIP FILE ***
1010 CLS: KEY OFF
1020 FALSE = 0
1030 DIM MEM.NO.INDEX(1000)
1040 LOCATE 5,20: PRINT "MEMBERSHIP MAINTENANCE PROGRAM"
1050 GOSUB 2000                          'Initialization routine
1060 FINISHED$ = "NO"
1070 WHILE FINISHED$ = "NO"
1080   GOSUB 3000                        'Display menu
1090   IF CODE < 4
         THEN GOSUB 1200: GOSUB 1300     'Get membership number and search index
1100   ON CODE GOSUB 4000, 5000, 6000, 7000     'Perform requested function
1110 WEND
1120 LOCATE 14,1: PRINT SPACE$(79);
1130 LOCATE 14,20:PRINT "Normal end of program"
1140 STOP
1150 '
1200 REM *** Get membership number routine
1210   LOCATE 14,20: PRINT "Enter 5-digit membership number ";
1220   MEM.NO.IN$ = INPUT$(5)
1230   MEM.NO.IN = VAL(MEM.NO.IN$)
1240   PRINT MEM.NO.IN
1250 RETURN
1260 REM *** End of get membership number routine
1270 '
1300 REM *** Search of index array routine
1310   FOUND$ = "NO"
1320   FOR J = 1 TO NO.ELEMENTS
1330     IF MEM.NO.INDEX(J) = MEM.NO.IN
           THEN FOUND$ = "YES": REC.NO = J: GOTO 1350
1340   NEXT J
1350 RETURN
1360 REM *** End of search of index array routine
1370 '
2000 REM *** Initialization routine ==========================================
2010   OPEN "MEMBER.RND" AS #1 LEN = 98
2020   FIELD #1, 4 AS MEM.NO.FLD$, 15 AS LNAME.FLD$, 10 AS GNAME.FLD$,
              10 AS TITLE.FLD$, 25 AS STREET.FLD$, 20 AS TOWN.FLD$,
              2 AS STATE.FLD$, 4 AS ZIP.FLD$, 4 AS DUES.FLD$, 4 AS PAID.FLD$
2030   NO.REC = LOF(1) / 98            'Calculate number of records
2040   OPEN "MEMBER.IDX" FOR INPUT AS #2
2050   J = 0
2060   WHILE EOF(2) = FALSE
2070     J = J + 1
2080     INPUT #2, MEM.NO.INDEX(J)
2090   WEND
2100   CLOSE #2
2110   NO.ELEMENTS = J
2120 RETURN
2130 REM *** End of initialization routine
2140 '
```

PROGRAM 12.6   **Maintaining the membership file.**

```
3000 REM *** Display menu routine =================================================
3010    LOCATE 8,20:  PRINT "Enter 1 to Add a record"
3020    LOCATE 9,20:  PRINT "      2 to Delete a record"
3030    LOCATE 10,20: PRINT "      3 to Update a record"
3040    LOCATE 11,20: PRINT "      4 to Exit program"
3050    LOCATE 12,20: PRINT "Function ? ";
3060    CODE$ = INPUT$(1)
3070    CODE = VAL(CODE$)
3080    PRINT CODE
3090 RETURN
3100 REM *** End of display menu routine
3110 '
4000 REM *** Add record routine ===================================================
4010    IF FOUND$ = "YES"
           THEN GOSUB 8000: GOTO 4090
           ELSE LSET MEM.NO.FLD$ = MKS$(MEM.NO.IN)
4020    GOSUB 4200                          'Good add, get rest of data
4030    NO.REC = NO.REC + 1                 'Update number of records
4040    PUT #1, NO.REC                      'Write record
4050    NO.ELEMENTS = NO.ELEMENTS + 1       'Update number of elements
4060    MEM.NO.INDEX(NO.ELEMENTS) = MEM.NO.IN     'Update index array
4070    LOCATE 25,20: PRINT "Record"; MEM.NO.IN; "added";
4080    GOSUB 8100                          'Pause and clear screen
4090 RETURN
4100 REM *** End of add record routine
4110 '
4200 REM *** Get rest of data and field data for add record routine
4210    LOCATE 15,10: INPUT "Enter last name";LNAME$
4220    LSET LNAME.FLD$ = LNAME$
4230    LOCATE 16,10: INPUT "Enter first name"; GNAME$
4240    LSET GNAME.FLD$ = GNAME$
4250    LOCATE 17,10: INPUT "Enter title"; TITLE$
4260    LSET TITLE.FLD$ = TITLE$
4270    LOCATE 18,10: INPUT "Enter street"; STREET$
4280    LSET STREET.FLD$ = STREET$
4290    LOCATE 19,10: INPUT "Enter town"; TOWN$
4300    LSET TOWN.FLD$ = TOWN$
4310    LOCATE 20,10: INPUT "Enter state"; STATE$
4320    LSET STATE.FLD$ = STATE$
4330    LOCATE 21,10: INPUT "Enter zip code"; ZIP
4340    LSET ZIP.FLD$ = MKS$(ZIP)
4350    LOCATE 22,10: INPUT "Enter dues"; DUES
4360    LSET DUES.FLD$ = MKS$(DUES)
4370    LOCATE 23,10: INPUT "Enter paid"; PAID
4380    LSET PAID.FLD$ = MKS$(PAID)
4390 RETURN
4400 REM *** End of get rest of data and field data for add record routine
4410 '
5000 REM *** Delete record routine ================================================
5010    IF FOUND$ = "NO"
           THEN GOSUB 8000: GOTO 5040
           ELSE MEM.NO.INDEX(REC.NO) = 0              'Update index array
5020    LOCATE 25,20: PRINT "Record"; MEM.NO.IN; "deleted";
5030    GOSUB 8100                                    'Pause and clear screen
5040 RETURN
5050 REM *** End of delete record routine
5060 '
```

PROGRAM 12.6   (Continued).

```
6000 REM *** Update record routine ==============================================
6010    IF FOUND$ = "NO"
           THEN GOSUB 8000: GOTO 6080
           ELSE UPDATE.REC.NO = REC.NO
6020    GOSUB 6200                                    'Get record and convert numbers
6030    GOSUB 6300                                    'Display record
6040    GOSUB 6600                                    'Update fields
6050    PUT #1, UPDATE.REC.NO                         'Rewrite record
6060    LOCATE 25,20: PRINT "Record"; MEM.NO.IN; "updated";
6070    GOSUB 8100                                    'Pause and clear screen
6080 RETURN
6090 REM *** End of update record routine
6100 '
6200 REM *** Get record and convert numbers routine
6210    GET #1, UPDATE.REC.NO
6220    ZIP = CVS(ZIP.FLD$)
6230    DUES = CVS(DUES.FLD$)
6240    PAID = CVS(PAID.FLD$)
6250    DUES = CVS(DUES.FLD$)
6260 RETURN
6270 REM *** End of get record and convert numbers routine
6280 '
6300 REM *** Display record routine
6310    LOCATE 14,1:  PRINT SPACE$(79)
6320    LOCATE 14,10: PRINT " 1. Membership number"
6330    LOCATE 14,32: PRINT USING "#####"; MEM.NO.IN
6340    LOCATE 15,10: PRINT " 2. Last name"
6350    LOCATE 15,32: PRINT LNAME.FLD$
6360    LOCATE 16,10: PRINT " 3. First name"
6370    LOCATE 16,32: PRINT GNAME.FLD$
6380    LOCATE 17,10: PRINT " 4. Title"
6390    LOCATE 17,32: PRINT TITLE.FLD$
6400    LOCATE 18,10: PRINT " 5. Street"
6410    LOCATE 18,32: PRINT STREET.FLD$
6420    LOCATE 19,10: PRINT " 6. Town"
6430    LOCATE 19,32: PRINT TOWN.FLD$
6440    LOCATE 20,10: PRINT " 7. State"
6450    LOCATE 20,32: PRINT STATE.FLD$
6460    LOCATE 21,10: PRINT " 8. Zip code"
6470    LOCATE 21,32: PRINT USING "#####"; ZIP
6480    LOCATE 22,10: PRINT " 9. Dues"
6490    LOCATE 22,32: PRINT USING "##.##"; DUES
6500    LOCATE 23,10: PRINT "10. Paid"
6510    LOCATE 23,32: PRINT USING "##.##"; PAID
6520 RETURN
6530 REM *** End of display record routine
6540 '
6600 REM *** Update fields routine
6610    UPDATE.FINISHED$ = "NO"
6620    WHILE UPDATE.FINISHED$ = "NO"
6630      LOCATE 25,1: PRINT SPACE$(79);
6640      LOCATE 25,5,1
6650      INPUT; "Enter 2 to 10 to update field, or 0 to end"; UPDATE.FLD
6660      IF UPDATE.FLD = 0
             THEN LOCATE 25,1,0:PRINT SPACE$(79);: UPDATE.FINISHED$ = "YES"
6670      IF UPDATE.FLD > 1 AND UPDATE.FLD < 11
             THEN GOSUB 6800: LOCATE 25,1: PRINT SPACE$(79);
6680    WEND
6690 RETURN
6700 REM *** End of update fields routine
6710 '
```

```
6800 REM *** Get new data routine
6810   LOCATE 13 + UPDATE.FLD,32: PRINT SPACE$(25): LOCATE 13 + UPDATE.FLD,32
6820   INPUT NEW.VALUE$                        'Accept new data
6830   GOSUB 6900                              'Assign data to variables
6840 RETURN
6850 REM *** End of get new data routine
6860 '
6900 REM *** Assign value to field routine
6905   IF UPDATE.FLD = 2
         THEN LSET LNAME.FLD$ = NEW.VALUE$: GOTO 6950
6910   IF UPDATE.FLD = 3
         THEN LSET GNAME.FLD$ = NEW.VALUE$: GOTO 6950
6915   IF UPDATE.FLD = 4
         THEN LSET TITLE.FLD$ = NEW.VALUE$: GOTO 6950
6920   IF UPDATE.FLD = 5
         THEN LSET STREET.FLD$ = NEW.VALUE$: GOTO 6950
6925  IF UPDATE.FLD = 6
         THEN LSET TOWN.FLD$ = NEW.VALUE$: GOTO 6950
6930   IF UPDATE.FLD = 7
         THEN LSET STATE.FLD$ = NEW.VALUE$: GOTO 6950
6935   IF UPDATE.FLD = 8
         THEN LSET ZIP.FLD$ = MKS$(VAL(NEW.VALUE$)): GOTO 6950
6940   IF UPDATE.FLD = 9
         THEN LSET DUES.FLD$ = MKS$(VAL(NEW.VALUE$)): GOTO 6950
6945   IF UPDATE.FLD = 10
         THEN LSET PAID.FLD$ = MKS$(VAL(NEW.VALUE$)): GOTO 6950
6950 RETURN
6955 REM *** End of assign value to field routine
6960 '
7000 REM *** Exit program routine ==================================================
7010   CLOSE
7020   OPEN "MEMBER.IDX" FOR OUTPUT AS #1
7030   FOR J = 1 TO NO.ELEMENTS
7040     WRITE #1, MEM.NO.INDEX(J)
7050   NEXT J
7060   CLOSE
7070   FINISHED$ = "YES"
7080 RETURN
7090 REM *** End of exit program routine
7100 '
7999 REM ==================== Utility Routines ============================
8000 REM *** Display error message routine
8010   BEEP: LOCATE 25,20
8020   IF CODE$ = "1"
         THEN PRINT "Membership number "; MEM.NO.IN; " is in file, no add";
8030   IF CODE$ = "2"
         THEN PRINT "Membership number";MEM.NO.IN;" is not in file, no delete";
8040   IF CODE$ = "3"
         THEN PRINT "Membership number";MEM.NO.IN;" is not in file, no update";
8050   GOSUB 8100                                'Pause and clear screen
8060 RETURN
8070 REM *** End of display error message routine
8080 '
8100 REM *** Pause and clear screen routine
8110   LATER = TIMER + 2
8120   WHILE TIMER < LATER
8130   WEND
8140   CLS
8150 RETURN
8160 REM *** End of pause and clear screen routine
8170 END
```

PROGRAM 12.6   (Continued).

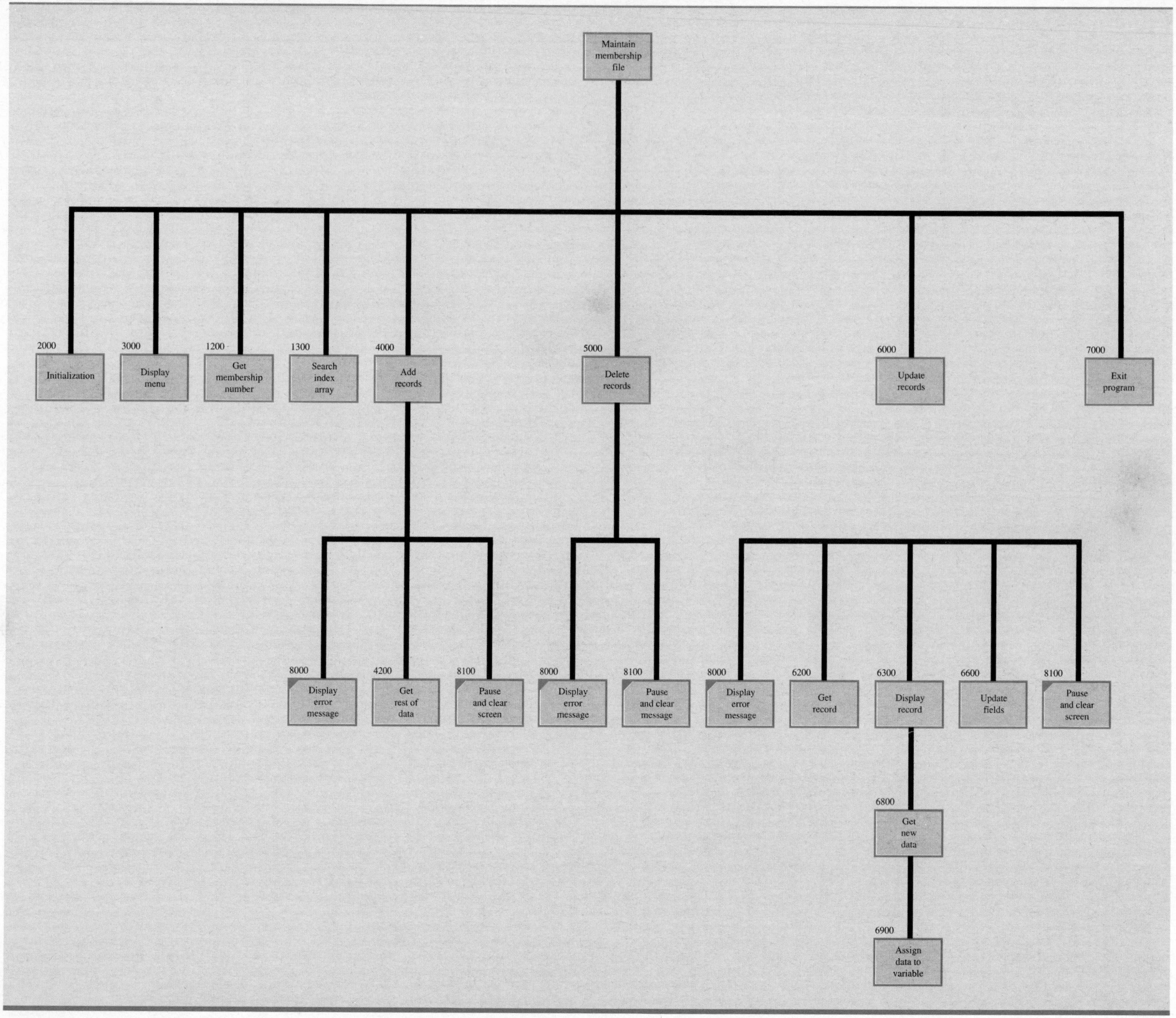

FIGURE 12.2   A hierarchy diagram for Program 12.6.

we must know when we want to add records to the end of the file. In line 2030 we divide LOF(1) by the record length of 98 and assign the result to the variable NO.REC.

The program next executes a WHILE loop (lines 1070 to 1110) until the user is finished. In the loop, line 1080 executes the DISPLAY MENU subroutine, which displays a menu from which the user makes a selection. If the user asks to add, delete, or update a record (CODE equal to 1, 2, or 3), the IF statement in line 1090 executes two subroutines. The first subroutine, which starts at line 1200, gets the membership number from the user. The second subroutine, which starts at line 1300, searches the MEM.NO.INDEX to determine whether that membership number is in use. If it is, FOUND$ is set to YES and REC.NO is set to J; if it is not, FOUND$ is set to NO, and REC.NO is not assigned a value. Upon returning from these subroutines, line 1100 executes the appropriate routine, depending on the user's request.

ADDING RECORDS

The add records subroutine starts by testing FOUND$ on line 4010. Since we cannot add a record if the membership number is in use, if FOUND$ equals YES the subroutine at line 8000 (see page 387) prints an error message. Otherwise, the subroutine at line 4200 obtains the rest of the data and assigns them to the field variables. Since we are adding a record, line 4030 increments NO.REC, and line 4040 writes the record. Finally, the index array must be updated. Since we will add an element to the array, line 4050 increments NO.ELEMENTS.* Line 4060 assigns the membership number of the added record to the NO.ELEMENTS element of the index array.

DELETING RECORDS

The delete records subroutine also begins by testing FOUND$. We cannot delete a record that isn't there, so if FOUND$ equals NO, the subroutine at line 8000 (see page 387) displays an error message. Otherwise, the ELSE branch deletes the record by replacing the record's membership number in MEM.NO.INDEX with 0. To understand this statement, recall that if FOUND$ is YES, then REC.NO points to the element of MEM.NO.INDEX that contains the record's membership number. Notice that the record on the disk is not erased, but since the membership number has been removed from the index array, neither this program nor Program 12.5 can retrieve this record. We can consider the record logically deleted, even though it is not physically deleted.

UPDATING RECORDS

Finally, let's consider the update records subroutine. Because we don't have to update the index array, this subroutine is even easier than the others.

As usual, the subroutine begins by testing FOUND$. We cannot update a record that isn't there, so if FOUND$ equals NO, the subroutine at line 8000 displays an error message. Otherwise, the record is read and the numeric variables are converted by the subroutine that starts at line 6200. Then the record is displayed by the subroutine that starts at line 6300. Finally, the fields are updated by the subroutine that starts at line 6600. Figure 12.3 shows the screen with a displayed record, ready for updating.

---

*NO.REC and NO.ELEMENTS are always equal, but it is clearer to use separate variables to refer to the number of records in the file and the number of elements in the index array.

```
                    MEMBERSHIP MAINTENANCE PROGRAM


                    Enter 1 to Add a record
                          2 to Delete a record
                          3 to Update a record
                          4 to Exit program
                    Function ?  3

             1. Membership number 32167
             2. Last name         Mezquita
             3. First name        Fred
             4. Title             Mr.
             5. Street            ?
             6. Town              El Segundo
             7. State             CA
             8. Zip code          90245
             9. Dues              25.00
            10. Paid              15.00

      Enter 2 to 10 to update field, or 0 to end? 5
```

FIGURE 12.3   **A displayed record ready for updating.**

The subroutine that starts at line 6600 uses a WHILE loop to update fields. It starts by displaying a message on line 25 on the screen that asks the user to enter the number of the field to be updated. In line 6650, this value is assigned to UPDATE.FLD. The semicolon immediately after the word INPUT in line 6650 prevents the screen from scrolling when the user presses the Enter key. The user is not allowed to update the membership number since this field is the key, but all the other fields may be updated. If the user enters a valid value for UPDATED.FLD, the subroutine that starts at line 6800 is executed. This subroutine moves the cursor to the start of the field that is to be updated. In Figure 12.3, the user has entered a 5, and you can see the question mark positioned at the start of field 5.

Getting the cursor to the start of the field that is to be updated is not difficult. As you can see in the subroutine that displays the record, which starts in line 6300, when the record is displayed the first field is displayed on line 14, the second field is displayed on line 15, and so on. This means that the field to be updated is displayed on line 13 + UPDATE.FLD. All the fields are displayed starting at column 32. So the first LOCATE statement in line 6810 positions the cursor at row 13 + UPDATE.FLD, column 32. The PRINT statement in that line prints 25 spaces to erase the current data, and the second LOCATE statement repositions the cursor to the start of the field.

The INPUT statement in line 6820 assigns the entered data to NEW.VALUE$, and the subroutine that starts at line 6900 uses a case structure to assign NEW.VALUE$ to the field that was being updated.

Back in line 6650, a 0 is entered to indicate that updating this record is finished. BASIC exits from the WHILE loop and returns to line 6050, which rewrites the updated record. Figure 12.4 shows the index file after deleting records 35675 and 97514 and adding record 51734. Notice that record 51734 was added as record number 11, at the end of the file.

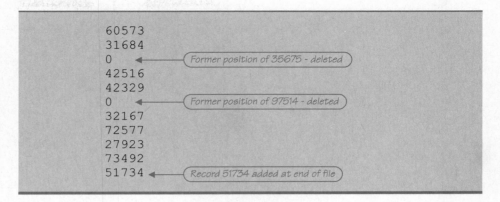

```
                    60573
                    31684
                    0        ←  Former position of 35675 - deleted
                    42516
                    42329
                    0        ←  Former position of 97514 - deleted
                    32167
                    72577
                    27923
                    73492
                    51734    ←  Record 51734 added at end of file
```

FIGURE 12.4   The index file after updating.

EXERCISES

*12.10   If the record length of a file is 40, the file contains 20 records, and the file is opened as file number 1, what value is returned by LOF(1)?

12.11   If the record length of a file is 53, and the file is opened as file number 2, what is the statement to calculate the number of records in the file?

12.12   Why is it necessary in Program 12.1 to initialize the charge account file, but not necessary in Program 12.4 to initialize the membership file?

*12.13   In Program 12.5, why isn't a binary search used to search MEM.NO.INDEX?

12.14   In Program 12.6, the update records subroutine does not update MEM.NO.INDEX, but both the add records and delete records subroutines do. Why?

12.15   In Program 12.6, the add records subroutine increases NO.REC, but the delete records subroutine does not decrease it. Why?

*12.16   In a program to list the membership file, would the following coding retrieve the deleted records?

```
40 FOR J = 1 TO NO.REC
50     GET #1, J
60 NEXT J
```

12.17   In Program 12.6, the user is not permitted to change the membership number. How would you correct the error if a record were stored with the wrong membership number?

12.18   Program 12.7 shows the execution of a program that was supposed to create A12-01.RND. As you can see, it didn't. Find and correct the error.

PROGRAMMING ASSIGNMENTS

12.5   Write a program that could be used to print all the active records in the membership file.

12.6   a)   Write a program to create a file that could be used in an inventory system. The fields in the records are the item number (key), which is a five-digit number; the item description, which is a 20-character string; the cost per unit; the price per unit; the reorder point; and the quantity on hand.
   b)   Write a query program for the file created in (a).
   c)   Write a program that adds, deletes, and updates the records in the file created in (a).

12.7   The file A12-07.RND contains a five-digit STUDENT.NO, which is the key, followed by the three fields described in Exercise 12.5. The index for the file is in A12-07.IDX.
   a)   Write a query program for this file.
   b)   Write a program that adds, deletes, and updates the file described above. Update the GPA field as described in Programming Assignment 11.15.

```
100 REM *** PROGRAMMING ASSIGNMENT 12.1 - CREATE A12-07.RND ***
110 OPEN "A12-01.RND" AS #1 LEN = 31
120 FIELD #1, 25 AS STUDENT.NAME.FLD$, 2 AS CREDITS.FLD$, 4 AS GPA.FLD$
130 GOSUB 200      'Initialize the file
140 GOSUB 300      'Load data into file
150 CLOSE #1
160 PRINT "The Grade Point Average file has been created"
170 STOP
180 '
200 REM *** Initialize file routine
210   LSET STUDENT.NAME.FLD$ = SPACE$(25)
220   LSET CREDITS.FLD$ = MKI$(0)
230   LSET GPA.FLD$ = MKS$(0)
240   FOR J = 0 TO 999
250     PUT #1, J
260   NEXT J
270 RETURN
280 REM *** End of initialize file routine
290 '
300 REM *** Load data into file routine
310   READ STUDENT.NO, NAME.IN$, CREDITS, GPA
320     IF STUDENT.NO = 9999
            THEN GOTO 380
330     LSET STUDENT.NAME.FLD$ = NAME.IN$
340     LSET CREDITS.FLD$ = MKI$(CREDITS)
350     LSET GPA.FLD$ = MKS$(GPA)
360     PUT #1, STUDENT.NO
370   GOTO 310
380 RETURN
390 REM *** End of routine to load data into file
400 '
500 REM *** Data to create file

RUN
Bad record number in 250
Ok
```

PROGRAM 12.7   **An incorrect program to create** A12-01.RND.

SUMMARY

In this chapter you have learned that

☐ The OPEN statement for a random file specifies the filename, the file number, and the record length.

☐ The FIELD statement specifies the record layout for a random file.

☐ The LSET and RSET statements must be used to assign values to field variables.

☐ The MKI$, MKS$, and MKD$ functions must be used to assign numeric values to field variables.

☐ The PUT statement writes a record to a random file.

☐ The GET statement reads a record from a random file.

☐ The CVI, CVS, and CVD functions convert field variables to numeric variables.

□ The DOS command COPY makes a copy of a file.

□ An index for a random file consists of an array that contains the keys. The order of the keys in the array is the same as the order of the records in the file.

□ The LOF function returns the number of bytes allocated to a file.

KEY TERMS IN THIS CHAPTER

....

backup file 375   **index** 376   **on-line system** 359
double-precision variable 364   **integer variable** 364   **single-precision variable** 364
field variable 362

QUESTIONS FOR REVIEW

....

12.1 Which statements must be used to assign values to field variables?

12.2 The _____ statement is used to read data from a random file.

12.3 Which DOS command allows you to make a backup copy of a file?

12.4 Which functions are used to assign a numeric value to a field variable?

12.5 Name two ways in which an OPEN statement for a random file differs from the OPEN statement for a sequential file.

12.6 The _____ statement is used to write data to a random file.

12.7 True or false: The LOF function returns the number of records in a file.

12.8 Choose the correct ending: The variables named in a FIELD statement must be (a) string only; (b) numeric only; or (c) string or numeric, it doesn't matter.

12.9 Choose the correct ending: The FIELD statement is used with (a) random files only; (b) sequential files only; or (c) both random and sequential files.

12.10 Name the three types of numeric variables available in BASIC.

12.11 When numeric variables are read from a random file, which functions are used to convert them from strings to numbers?

12.12 The OPEN statement for random files specifies three things. What are they?

12.13 The FIELD statement is used to specify the _____, _____, and _____ of each field in the record.

12.14 Is the index array for a random file stored as a sequential or a random file?

12.15 What is the cause of the error if, during execution, BASIC displays the error message Bad file number in nn, where nn is the line number of a FIELD statement?

12.16 What is the cause of the error if, during execution, BASIC displays the error message Field overflow?

ADDITIONAL PROGRAMMING ASSIGNMENTS

....

12.8 a) Write a program to create the PAYROLL.RND file described in Exercise 12.7. Assume that there will be no more than 99 employees.

b) Write a program to list the active records in PAYROLL.RND. Include headings in the report.

c) Write a program to add, delete, update, and display records from the file.

12.9 a) Write a program to create the PAYROLL.RND file described in Exercise 12.7, but add the social

security number to the record, use it as the key, and name the file PAYROLL1.RND.

b) Write a query program for this file.

c) Write a maintenance program for this file.

12.10 a) Write a program to create a file to store information about a stamp collection. The fields in the records are a four-digit catalog number, which is the key; the name of the stamp; the number owned; the total cost; and the current price.

b) Write a query program for this file. The program should display the fields in the records and calculate the total value, which is the product of the number owned and the current price. It should also calculate the profit (or loss), which is the difference between the total value and the total cost.

c) Write a maintenance program for this file.

BEYOND THE BASICS

. . . .

12.1 The membership file can be used to print mailing labels. The format of the label should be

```
TITLE$ GNAME$ LNAME$
STREET$
TOWN$, STATE$ ZIP
```

To make the label attractive, you should strip off trailing spaces. For example, in the file the width of TITLE$ is 10 characters. If a member's title is Ms., TITLE$ will contain 7 trailing spaces. Printing those 7 extra spaces between the title and the first name would make the label look funny. Similar considerations apply to GNAME$ and TOWN$.

12.2 Write a program to list the records in the membership file in order by membership number. (Hint: Sort MEM.NO.INDEX and remember the original order.)

13

Drawing Points, Lines, and Circles

BASIC OBJECTIVES OF THIS CHAPTER

☐ To consider the hardware required to execute graphics programs

☐ To put the screen into a graphics mode

☐ To draw and color points, lines, and circles

☐ To use the BASIC statements SCREEN, COLOR, PSET, PRESET, WIDTH, LINE, PAINT, and CIRCLE

☐ To use the DOS command GRAPHICS

In earlier chapters, you learned how to use the computational capabilities of a personal computer, but in these final chapters you will learn how to use its extensive graphics capabilities. In this chapter, you will learn how to draw and color points, lines, boxes, and circles. In Chapter 14, you will learn how to draw graphs and charts and how to move figures around the screen.

INTRODUCTION TO GRAPHICS

To use the graphics features of your personal computer, your machine must have a color/graphics monitor adapter. If your computer has only the monochrome display adapter, you will not be able to execute the programs in this chapter or in Chapter 14. You do not need a color monitor, but if you have one, your graphics will be more interesting.

■ *The Graphics Modes*

In all our programs thus far, we have used BASIC in the text mode. But BASIC also works in two graphics modes: medium-resolution graphics and high-resolution graphics. Whenever you start BASIC, it automatically begins in text mode. To change to a graphics mode, you must use the SCREEN statement.

Recall from Chapter 6 that the syntax of the SCREEN statement is

```
SCREEN [mode] [,burst]
```

and that a value of 0 for mode specifies text mode; a value of 1, medium-resolution graphics mode; and a value of 2, high-resolution graphics mode. Pressing the F10 function key executes a SCREEN 0 statement and returns BASIC to text mode.

The burst parameter is supposed to turn color on and off, but on most monitors, including the IBM color displays, color is always on. On those few monitors for which burst has an effect, its workings are confusing. In text mode (mode = 0), a burst value of 0 turns color off and a value of 1 turns color on. In medium-resolution graphics mode, the values have opposite meaning: a value of 0 turns color on and a value of 1 turns color off. Thus to change to medium-resolution graphics mode with color on, you would use the statement

```
SCREEN 1,0
```

High-resolution graphics mode has no color, so burst has no effect in that mode. To change to high-resolution graphics mode, you would use the statement

```
SCREEN 2
```

■ *The Coordinate Systems*

Now that you know how to switch to the graphics modes, you no doubt are wondering what they are and why there are two of them: medium resolution and high resolution. In the graphics modes, you can draw a point anywhere

All points addressable
Allowing the user to draw a point anywhere on the screen by means of a graphics instruction.

Coordinates
A pair of numbers that locate a point on the screen.

Physical coordinates
The coordinate system that refers to specific points on the screen.

Pixel
A dot, or picture element, on the screen.

on the screen. Thus we say that in the graphics modes the screen is **all points addressable**. To address any point on the screen, we must have a method of specifying that particular point. The method used is to give the point's **coordinates**, which are simply two numbers that permit BASIC to locate that point on the screen. Because the coordinates refer to specific physical points on the screen, we call them **physical coordinates**. One important way in which the two graphics modes differ is in the physical coordinate systems they use.

In medium-resolution graphics mode, the screen is divided into 320 dots horizontally and 200 dots vertically. These dots are called **pixels** (from *picture ele*ments). Pixels are numbered from 0 through 319 going from left to right, and from 0 through 199 going from top to bottom. The horizontal coordinate of each pixel is called the X coordinate, and the vertical coordinate is called the Y coordinate because the top edge of the screen is the X axis and the left edge is the Y axis.

As Figure 13.1 shows, the pixel in the upper left corner has an X coordinate of 0 and a Y coordinate of 0. The pixel in the lower right corner has an X coordinate of 319 and a Y coordinate of 199. For convenience, the coordinates of a point are given in the form (x coordinate, y coordinate). For example, the coordinates of the pixel in the lower right corner are written as (319,199). The coordinates of the pixel in the center of the screen are written as (160,100).

For high-resolution graphics, the physical coordinate system is similar, except that the X coordinates go from 0 through 639. In other words, there are twice as many pixels in the horizontal direction. As in medium-resolution graphics, the Y coordinate goes from 0 through 199. The high-resolution coordinate system is shown in Figure 13.2.

Because there are more pixels in high-resolution mode, you can draw figures with more detail. However, you must pay a price—you cannot use color. Medium-resolution mode allows you to use up to four colors at a time; in high resolution, you can use only black and white.

The WIDTH Statement

The characters displayed in text mode are somewhat clearer than the characters displayed in either graphics mode, so when you are entering or correcting programs you will probably find it more convenient to work in text mode.

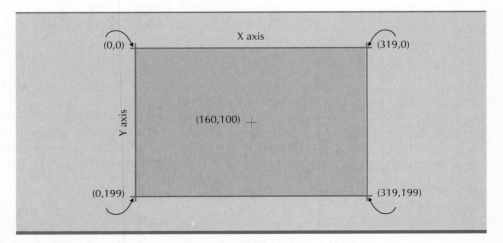

FIGURE 13.1   **Medium-resolution coordinate system.**

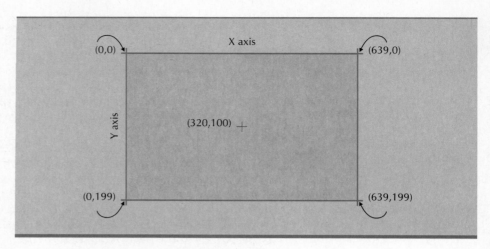

FIGURE 13.2   **High-resolution coordinate system.**

If you go from medium resolution to text mode by executing a SCREEN 0 statement, the screen will display only 40 characters on a line.* You can change to 80 characters on a line by using the WIDTH statement,

WIDTH 80

which sets the screen width.

The syntax of the WIDTH statement is simply

WIDTH size

where size must be either 40 or 80.

■ *COLOR*

You studied the COLOR statement used in text mode in Chapter 6, but the COLOR statement in medium-resolution graphics mode is entirely different.† The syntax of the COLOR statement in graphics mode is

COLOR [background] [,palette]

where background is a number or numeric expression with a value between 0 and 15, which specifies the background color. As you can see from Table 13.1, background colors and numbers in graphics mode are the same as foreground colors and numbers in text mode. When you execute a COLOR statement, the screen changes to the background color, but the background color can be used like any other color; it is not restricted to the background portions of the screen. In the graphics modes, the border is the same color as the background.

To complete the COLOR statement, you also code a palette parameter, a number or numeric expression with a value of either 0 or 1, which specifies one of two **palettes**, or sets of colors, that you may use. The colors in the two palettes are given in Table 13.2. (For your convenience, Tables 13.1 and 13.2 are reproduced in Appendix C.)

Palette
A set of four colors that may be
used to color figures.

---

*If you change from high resolution to text mode, the screen will display 80 characters on a line.
†Since high-resolution mode does not support color, it is illegal to execute a COLOR statement in high resolution.

TABLE 13.1   **Colors available as background in medium-resolution mode**

Number	Color	Number	Color
0	Black	8	Grey
1	Blue	9	Light Blue
2	Green	10	Light Green
3	Cyan	11	Light Cyan
4	Red	12	Light Red
5	Magenta	13	Light Magenta
6	Brown	14	Yellow
7	White	15	High-intensity White

TABLE 13.2   **Colors in the medium-resolution palettes**

Color	Palette 0	Palette 1
0	Background	Background
1	Green	Cyan
2	Red	Magenta
3	Brown	White

If a COLOR statement is not executed, the default is

COLOR 0,1

This statement specifies a background color of black with palette 1.

We will discuss how you select particular colors from a palette in a moment. For now, it should be clear that in medium-resolution graphics mode you can have a maximum of four colors on the screen at one time. This situation is in marked contrast to text mode, where you can have 16 different colors on the screen at one time. In addition, there are limitations on the combinations you can have. Suppose, for example, you wanted to color a flag yellow, green, and red. Although yellow is not in either palette, you could get yellow by making it the background color, which Table 13.1 shows is color 14. Then to get green and red, you could specify palette 0. Thus, the color statement you would use is

COLOR 14,0

However, you could not use a similar procedure to color an American flag. Since red is in palette 0, white is in palette 1, and blue is in neither palette, there is no way to get the colors red, white, and blue on the screen at the same time.

Drawing Points

Now that you know how to select colors, you are ready to learn how to draw figures. Let's start by drawing points.

PSET AND PRESET

The simplest graphics statements are PSET and PRESET, which draw points.
Their syntaxes are

```
PSET(x,y)[,color]
PRESET(x,y)[,color]
```

where x and y are the coordinates of the pixel at which the point is to be
drawn and may be a number or numeric expression. If the coordinates of a
point off the screen are coded—for example, (1000,75)—no point is drawn,
and no error message is printed. In medium-resolution mode, you code color
as a number between 0 and 3 (see Table 13.2) to specify which color from the
current palette will be used to draw the point. In high-resolution mode,
which offers only black and white, a color of 0 or 2 always produces black
points and a color of 1 or 3 always produces white points.

Take a moment here to be sure you understand how the following PSET
and PRESET statements work.

PSET and PRESET Statement

PSET(0,199),3

Effect

Draws a point in the lower left corner of the screen in color 3
selected from the current palette.

PSET and PRESET Statement

PSET(160,100),2

Effect

Draws a point in the center of the screen in color 2 selected from the
current palette.

PSET and PRESET Statement

PRESET(0,0)

Effect

Draws a point in the background color in the upper left corner of the
screen.

Notice that color is optional. If you omit it, PSET uses color 3 (brown or
white, depending on which palette is active) in medium-resolution mode
and color 1 (white) in high-resolution mode, while PRESET uses color 0, the
background color, in both modes. Drawing points in the background color
makes then blend into the background—in effect, they disappear. Loosely
speaking, then, we can say that when you use them without coding color,
PSET draws points and PRESET erases them.

When you do code color, PSET and PRESET are identical in their effects.
For example, assuming that a previously executed COLOR statement selected
palette 0, the statements

```
PSET(319,0),2
```

and

```
PRESET(319,0),2
```

both draw a red point in the upper right corner of the screen.

The method of specifying colors does involve a complication. Consider the statement

PRESET(160,100),2

What color will be used when this statement executes? The answer is that we can't tell without also seeing the previously executed COLOR statement that specified the palette from which color number 2 is to come. Table 13.2 shows that color number 2 is red if a previously executed COLOR statement selected palette 0, and it is magenta if a previously executed COLOR statement selected palette 1.

▪ *Program to Plot Points*

Program 13.1 illustrates the PSET and PRESET statements.* Because it may be difficult to see individual points, let alone determine their color, Program 13.1 plots a cluster of four points at the center of the screen.

In line 110, the SCREEN statement sets the screen to medium resolution with color on, the CLS statement clears the screen, and the KEY OFF statement erases the function key display on line 25. Since this program does not contain a COLOR statement, the default values—black background and palette 1— are used. Line 120 asks you to enter a value, 1, 2, or 3, to be used for the color of the points. (If you enter 0 by mistake, the points will be drawn in the background color, and you will not be able to see them.) Lines 140 through 170 draw four points in the center of the screen.

Line 180 illustrates a technique that is useful when you are trying to understand or debug a graphics program. When BASIC executes line 180, the program will pause, without disturbing the screen with a prompt or a question mark, and wait for you to enter a value to be assigned to A$. When you

```
100 REM *** DEMONSTRATING PSET AND PRESET ***
110 SCREEN 1,0: CLS: KEY OFF
120 INPUT "Enter color, 1 to 3, (-1 to stop)"; CLR
130 IF CLR = -1
        THEN GOTO 240
140     PSET(160,100),CLR
150     PSET(161,100),CLR
160     PSET(160,101),CLR
170     PSET(161,101),CLR
180     A$ = INPUT$(1)
190     PRESET(160,100)
200     PRESET(161,100)
210     PRESET(160,101)
220     PRESET(161,101)
230 GOTO 120
240 END
```

PROGRAM 13.1   **Demonstrating the PSET and PRESET statements.**

*Because this and other simple graphics problems require no variable names and only the most simple logic, I have not used our systematic procedure in developing the programs in this chapter.

have examined the screen as long as you want, you can press any key and the program will continue. When you debug a complicated graphics program, you may find it helpful to use several such statements. You can type the statement once and then use the BASIC editor to change the line number, thus inserting the statement wherever you want it.

If you run this program, you will notice that the input prompt is printed in large white characters. Only 40 of these large characters fit on a line. All characters placed on the screen in medium resolution are printed in this larger size. They are also displayed in color 3 from the current palette, in this case white.

After you press a key to satisfy line 180, the four PRESET statements in lines 190 through 220 erase the four points that were just drawn. The program then loops back to the INPUT statement, so you can enter a new value for CLR. (CLR is used as a variable name because COLOR is a reserved word.)

After you have tried all the colors, you can stop execution and enter the following statement in direct mode:

```
COLOR 12,0
```

This statement changes the background color to light red and the palette to palette 0. You will notice that the screen changes immediately from black to light red and that the color of any text on the screen changes from white to brown. In graphics mode, a COLOR statement instantly changes all the colors on the screen. You can then run the program to see the colors in palette 0.

PLOTTING POINTS IN HIGH-RESOLUTION MODE

You can also run Program 13.1 in high-resolution mode by changing the SCREEN statement in line 110 to

```
SCREEN 2
```

When you run the program in high resolution, you will see two differences. First, entering 1 for CLR will give you white points, while entering 2 will give you black points—which, since they are the same color as the background, are invisible. Second, the points will appear one-quarter of the way across the screen, not in the center as they were before. As you may recall, in high resolution there are 640 pixels in the X direction. Therefore, the pixels with X coordinates of 160 and 161 are only one-quarter of the way across the screen. The points are still halfway *down* the screen, however, since both medium resolution and high resolution have 200 pixels in the Y direction.

When you run the program in high resolution, you will also notice that the input prompt is printed in white, standard 80-characters-per-line size. That is true of all characters placed on the screen in high resolution.

Relative Coordinates

Absolute form
The expression of a pixel's location in terms of its X and Y coordinates.

Relative form
The expression of a pixel's location in terms of the X and Y distances from a point mentioned earlier in the program.

Last point referenced
The point from which a relative coordinate is measured.

So far, we have specified the position of a pixel by giving its X and Y coordinates. This way of specifying position is called **absolute form**. There is a second way of specifying position called the relative form. In the **relative form**, the position of a pixel is specified by giving its distance from a point mentioned earlier in the program. This point, called the **last point referenced**, differs according to the graphics statement executed. For PSET and PRESET, the last point referenced is the last point drawn. When the screen is first set to one of the graphics modes, before any graphics statements have been executed, the last point referenced is the center of the screen.

To use the relative form you must include the word STEP in a graphics statement. STEP is used as follows:

STEP(x offset,y offset)

where x offset and y offset are the distances in the *X* and *Y* directions from the last point referenced. For example,

PSET STEP(20,4)

means that the next point shoud be drawn 20 pixels to the right and 4 pixels down from the last point referenced. The *x* and *y* offsets may be positive or negative. Referring to Figures 13.1 and 13.2, you see that a positive value for x offset means move to the right, while a negative value means move to the left. A positive value for y offset means move down, while a negative value means move up.

PROGRAM

Program 13.2 illustrates the relative form of specifying coordinates. Like Program 13.1, it draws a cluster of four points. The PRESET statement in line 120 uses the absolute form to draw a point in the background color at the pixel whose coordinates are (50,50). Since the screen and the point are in the background color, the point is not visible; the purpose of the statement is to set the last point referenced to (50,50). The PSET statements that follow use the relative form. Line 130 draws a point, in color 3, that is 10 pixels to the right and 5 pixels up from the last point referenced, that is, at (60,45). This point then becomes the last point referenced. The PSET statement in line 140 draws a point 1 pixel to the right at the same vertical coordinate as (60,45), which is (61,45). Before you read further, figure out the coordinates of the points drawn by the statements in lines 150 and 160 and by the following statements.

PSET and PRESET Statement

PSET STEP(30,-10),2

Effect

Draws a point in color 2 from the current palette, 30 pixels to the right and 10 pixels up from the last point referenced.

PSET and PRESET Statement

PRESET STEP(-5,15)

Effect

Draws a point in the background color, 5 pixels to the left and 15 pixels down from the last point referenced.

```
100 REM *** DEMONSTRATING RELATIVE COORDINATES ***
110 SCREEN 1,0: CLS: KEY OFF: COLOR 1,1
120 PRESET(50,50)
130 PSET STEP(10,-5)
140 PSET STEP(1,0)
150 PSET STEP(-1,1)
160 PSET STEP(1,0)
170 END
```

PROGRAM 13.2   **Demonstrating relative coordinates.**

As Program 13.2 shows, you may use both the absolute and the relative forms of specifying coordinates in the same program. This flexibility lets you use the form that is most convenient for a particular statement.

Syntax Summary

SCREEN Statement
Form: SCREEN [mode][,burst]
Example: SCREEN 1, 1
Function: Sets the screen mode. When mode is 0, the screen is set to text mode; when mode is 1, the screen is set to low-resolution graphics mode; and when mode is 2, the screen is set to high-resolution graphics mode. For most systems, burst has no effect.

WIDTH Statement
Form: WIDTH size
Example: WIDTH 80
Function: Sets the number of characters that can be displayed on one line on the screen. size must be either 40 or 80.

COLOR Statement
Form: COLOR [background][,palette]
Example: COLOR 10,0
Function: Sets colors in graphics mode. background, which must be in the range 0 through 15, selects the background color, and palette, which must be 0 or 1, selects the palette.

PSET Statement
Form: PSET(x,y)[,color]
Example: PSET(125,175),2
Function: Plots a point at the given coordinates using color from the current palette. In medium-resolution mode, if color is not coded, color 3, brown or white, is used. In high-resolution, if color is not coded, white is used.

PRESET Statement
Form: PRESET(x,y)[,color]
Example: PRESET(150,25),1
Function: Plots a point at the given coordinates using color from the current palette. If color is not coded, in medium-resolution mode color 0, the background color, is used; in high-resolution, black is used.

Getting the Bugs Out

Problem: During execution, BASIC displays the error message

                    Illegal function call in nn

Reason: If nn is the line number of a graphics statement, you are trying to execute a graphics statement in text mode. If nn is the line number of a COLOR statement, you are in high-resolution mode (SCREEN 2).

Solution: Include a SCREEN 1 statement in your program before the line that caused the error.

EXERCISES

13.1 Draw a rectangle that represents the medium-resolution screen and locate the following points on it:

a) (175,50)
b) (50,175)
c) (300,100)
d) (100,160)

13.2 What is the color of the dots drawn by the PRESET statements in Program 13.1?

*13.3 Write the SCREEN statement that you would use to switch to medium-resolution mode with color on.

13.4 Write the COLOR statement that you would use to select a blue background color and palette 0.

*13.5 Write a COLOR statement that could be used in a program that draws a design colored red, magenta, and white.

13.6 Write a PSET statement to draw a point in color 1 that is 50 pixels to the left and 70 pixels up from the last point drawn.

PROGRAMMING ASSIGNMENTS

*13.1 Write a program that will draw a cluster of four magenta points in the upper right corner of the medium-resolution screen. Use both the absolute and the relative forms to specify the coordinates.

13.2 Write a program that draws a cluster of four points in the lower left corner of the high-resolution screen. Use both the absolute and the relative forms to specify the coordinates.

13.3 Use the fact that a COLOR statement changes all the colors on the screen in a program that tests reflexes. The program should present instructions in white characters on a red background. The instructions should explain that a short time after the test starts, the screen will turn blue, after which the user should press the space bar as quickly as possible. Allow the user to indicate that she is ready to start the test by pressing the Enter key. (Hint: Use the RND function to generate a random delay before turning the screen red; use the TIMER function to measure the interval between the time the screen turns red and the user presses the space bar. The RND and TIMER functions are explained in Chapter 9. You can use the INKEY$ function, described in Chapter 6, to capture and discard any key that is pressed too soon.)

DRAWING LINES

The LINE statement is used to draw lines and boxes. The full syntax of the LINE statement is

```
LINE[(x1,y1)]-(x2,y2)[,color][,B[F]]
```

This syntax is rather formidable, so let's begin with a simpler form. The simplest form of the LINE statement is

```
LINE(x1,y1)-(x2,y2)
```

This statement draws a line from the pixel at the first set of *X* and *Y* coordinates listed (x1,y1) to the pixel at the second set (x2,y2). For example, in medium resolution the statement

```
LINE(319,0)-(0,199)
```

draws a line from the upper right corner of the screen to the lower left corner. The pixel (0,199) then becomes the last point referenced.

Line clipping
Cutting a figure at the edge of the screen.

If by mistake your program specifies coordinates of a pixel that are off the screen, the line is drawn and "clipped" at the edge of the screen, a process known as **line clipping**. Thus

```
LINE(160,100)-(400,300)
```

draws a line that starts from the center of the screen and goes off the bottom of the screen. Line clipping is used by all the graphics statements.

You can examine the effect of any graphics statements by entering them in direct mode. First, make sure that the screen is in a graphics mode (SCREEN 1 or SCREEN 2) and that the function key display is erased. Then you can enter a graphics statement, like the LINE statement given above, and watch what happens. You can even use the editor to modify the statement and see the effects of the modifications. When the screen becomes too cluttered, you can clear it using the Ctrl + Home keys and start over again.

Another form of the LINE statement omits the first pair of coordinates:

```
LINE -(x2,y2)
```

This statement draws a line from the last point referenced to the point whose coordinates are (x2,y2). Consider the statements

```
LINE(10,100)-(200,100)
LINE -(120,20)
```

The first statement draws a horizontal line from near the left edge to about the center of the screen. The second statement draws a line from pixel (200,100), which became the last point referenced when the first statement executed, to the pixel (120,20).

Since each line starts where the previous line ended, this method of specifying coordinates automatically draws connected lines. To draw a closed figure, all you have to do is make the coordinates of the last statement the same as the first set of coordinates of the first statement. For example, the following statements draw a triangle:

```
LINE(90,25)-(190,80)
LINE -(120,150)
LINE -(90,25)
```

Don't confuse this method of specifying coordinates with relative coordinates. The coordinates given in the second LINE statement are the *absolute* coordinates of the pixel to which the line will be drawn. Relative coordinates can be used only when the word STEP is coded.

Either or both of the coordinates in a LINE statement may be given in relative form, however. The statement

```
LINE STEP(10,-5)-(20,0)
```

will draw a line starting 10 pixels to the right and 5 pixels up from the last point referenced, to the pixel (20,0). The statement

```
LINE(100,100)-STEP(50,10)
```

will draw a line from pixel (100,100) to pixel (150,110). Notice that when the relative form is used for the second pair of coordinates, they are relative to the first pair of coordinates. You can also use relative coordinates when the first pair of coordinates is omitted. For example,

```
LINE -STEP(50,10)
```

will drawn a line from the last point referenced to the pixel 50 pixels to the right and 10 pixels down.

Finally, relative form may be used for both coordinates. Thus

```
LINE STEP(100,50)-STEP(30,40)
```

will draw a line that starts 100 pixels to the right and 50 pixels down from the last point referenced. The end point of the line is 30 pixels to the right and 40 pixels down from the starting point.

■ *Color*

Now that you understand the first half of the LINE syntax statement, let's look at the other parameters.

All the lines we have drawn thus far have been in the default color. As we said when discussing points, in high resolution the default color is color 1, white. And in medium resolution, the default color is color 3, which is brown for palette 0 and white for palette 1. If we wish to draw lines in other colors, we can do so by including the color number after the second pair of coordinates, as shown in the syntax of the LINE statement. In medium resolution, we can use colors 0 through 3. For example, the statement

```
LINE(10,10)-(300,190),2
```

draws a line in color 2. In high resolution, we can use color 0, which is black, or 1, which is white.

■ *Drawing Boxes*

If you look again at the syntax of the LINE statement, you'll see that we can include the letter B or the letters BF after the color parameter. The letter B means that a box (a rectangle) should be drawn, and the letters BF (box fill) mean that the box should be filled with the specified color. The statement

```
LINE(40,180)-(100,80),1,B
```

draws a box in color 1, with one corner at pixel (40,180) and the opposite corner at pixel (100,80). This box is shown in Figure 13.3(a), but not in the colors you will see on the screen.

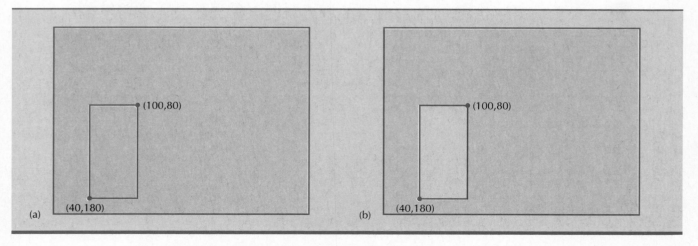

FIGURE 13.3   **(a) Drawing a box with the LINE statement, using the B parameter. (b) Drawing a box with the LINE statement, using the BF parameter.**

You can draw the same box by specifying the two other opposite corners, as in the statement

LINE(40,80)-(100,180),1,B

You draw the same box no matter which set of coordinates you specify first. So the statement

LINE(100,180)-(40,80),1,B

draws the same box as the two previous statements.

If the last parameter in the above statements were BF instead of B, the box would be filled with color 1, as shown in Figure 13.3(b). When the B or BF parameter is used, the box drawn always has its sides parallel to the sides of the screen.

Program 13.3 uses many of the graphics features you have learned. The PRESET statement in line 130 uses the x and y values entered in response to line 120 to set the last point referenced, which becomes the upper left corner of the shaft of the arrow. Line 140 draws a rectangle, which is the

```
100 REM *** DEMONSTRATING THE LINE STATEMENT ***
110 SCREEN 1,0: CLS: KEY OFF: COLOR 1,1
120 INPUT "Enter x,y coordinates, 0 to end ",X,Y
125    IF X = 0
          THEN GOTO 210
130    PRESET(X,Y)
140    LINE -STEP(30,10),,B
150    LINE -STEP(0,10)
160    LINE -STEP(12,-15)
170    LINE -STEP(-12,-15)
180    LINE -STEP(0,10)
190    LINE -STEP(0,10),0
200 GOTO 120
210 END

RUN

Enter x,y coordinates, 0 to end 50,50
Enter x,y coordinates, 0 to end 100,100
Enter x,y coordinates, 0 to end 150,150
Enter x,y coordinates, 0 to end 200,200
Enter x,y coordinates, 0 to end 0,0
Ok
```

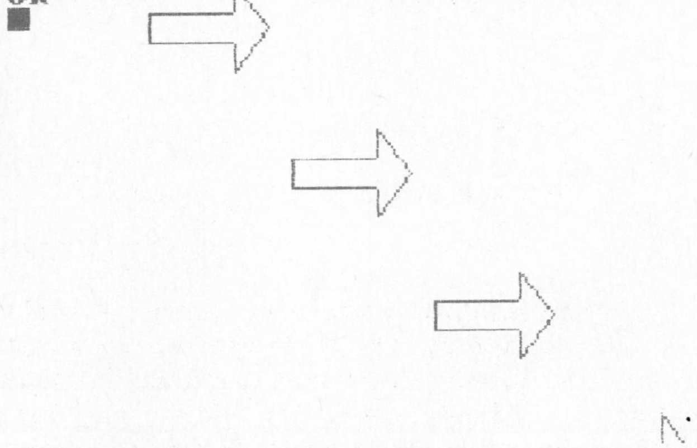

PROGRAM 13.3   **Demonstrating the LINE statement.**

shaft of the arrow, and lines 150 through 180 draw the triangle, which is the point of the arrow. Line 190 draws a line in color 0, erasing a line we don't want. Notice in Program 13.3 that only part of the last arrow that lies within the screen is drawn. This is an example of line clipping, which was mentioned earlier.

Before proceeding, be sure you understand how the following LINE statements work:

LINE Statement

`LINE(0,0)-(319,199),2`

Effect

Draws a line from the upper left corner of the screen (0,0) to the lower right corner (319,199), in color 2 from the current palette.

LINE Statement

`LINE -(160,100),1`

Effect

Draws a line from the last point referenced to the center of the screen (160,100), in color 1 from the current palette.

LINE Statement

`LINE STEP(20,-5)-STEP(-30,10)`

Effect

Draws a line that starts 20 pixels to the right and 5 pixels up (20,-5) from the last point referenced. The end point of the line is 30 pixels to the left and 10 pixels down (-30,10) from the starting point. The line is drawn in the default color.

LINE Statement

`LINE(190,20)-(240,140),2,BF`

Effect

Draws and fills a box in color 2 from the current palette. The upper left corner of the box is at (190,20), and the lower right corner is at (240,140).

■ *Aspect Ratio*

You would expect that the statement

`LINE(120,60)-STEP(80,80),,B`

would draw a square 80 pixels high and 80 pixels wide. But if you enter it, you will see that it draws a rectangle that is taller than it is wide. To understand why this happens, you need to understand **aspect ratio**.

Most screens are wider than they are tall. Usually, the vertical dimension is three-quarters of the horizontal dimension. Suppose a screen is 12 inches wide. If it is a standard screen, it will be 9 inches tall (the actual dimensions do not matter: only the ratio is important). Recall that in

Aspect ratio
The ratio of the horizontal distance between pixels to the vertical distance between pixels.

medium resolution there are 320 pixels horizontally and 200 pixels vertically. The distances between pixels are

$$\text{Horizontal distance} = 12 \text{ inches}/320 \text{ pixels} = 0.0375 \text{ inches}$$

$$\text{Vertical distance} = 9 \text{ inches}/200 \text{ pixels} = 0.045 \text{ inches}$$

Again, the absolute values of these distances are not important; what is important is their ratio, which is

$$\text{Aspect ratio} = \frac{\text{Horizontal distance}}{\text{Vertical distance}} = \frac{0.0375}{0.045} = 0.833$$

The aspect ratio of 0.833 is usually expressed as the fraction $5/6$. This calculation shows, then, that the horizontal distance between pixels is only $5/6$ as great as the vertical distance. In other words, the distance spanned by 6 pixels in the horizontal direction is equal to the distance spanned by 5 pixels in the vertical direction. Not all screens have an aspect ratio of exactly $5/6$, but for most screens the aspect ratio is close to $5/6$.

To draw a square on a standard screen, we must make the number of pixels in the horizontal (that is, the X) direction $6/5$ times the number of pixels in the vertical (that is, the Y) direction. If we want a square with a side that is 80 pixels in the Y direction, the side in the X direction must be

$$X \text{ pixels} = 6/5 * 80 = 96$$

Therefore, the statement

```
LINE(120,60)-STEP(96,80),,B
```

will draw the desired square.

Performing this calculation every time you wanted to draw a complicated figure would be quite tedious, so you may want to use a graphics layout form. In fact, in writing graphics programs, such a layout form often proves more useful than a flowchart. Figure 13.4 shows a form for medium-resolution graphics. On this form, the distances between pixels in the X and Y directions are in the same ratio as they are on a standard screen. You can reproduce this form (enlarged if possible), draw the figure you want to create, and read the coordinates of the pixels from the form. When you read the coordinates from the form, you can use the numbers along the axes, which mark the spaces that represent the pixel positions. However, you should realize that because of space constraints, only every fourth pixel is labeled.

In high resolution, there are twice as many pixels in the horizontal direction as there are in medium resolution, so the horizontal distance between pixels is half as great. There are the same number of pixels in the vertical direction, so the vertical distance between pixels is the same. This means that the aspect ratio in high resolution is half what it is in medium resolution, or $5/12$. You can use the graphics layout form in Figure 13.5 to design figures to be drawn in high resolution. Because this figure is even more crowded then the medium-resolution one, in the horizontal position only every eighth pixel is labeled.

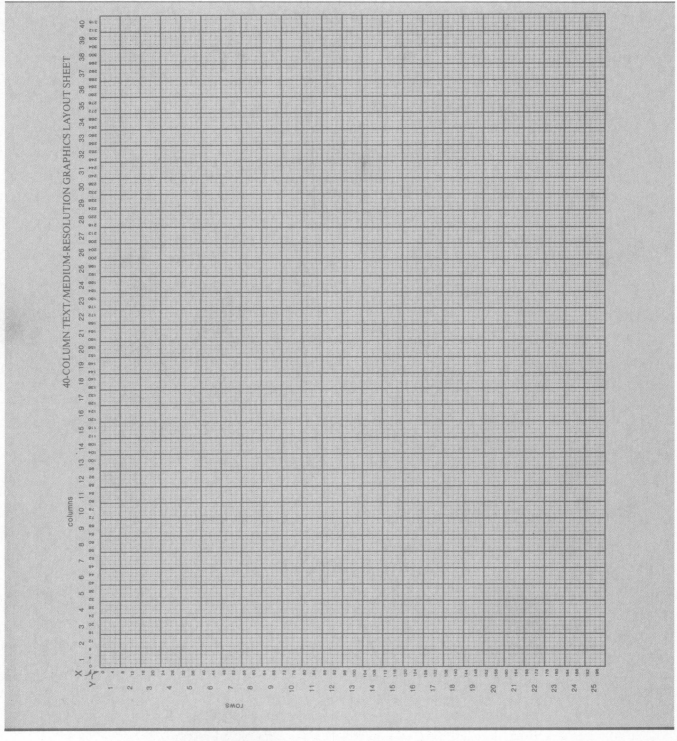

FIGURE 13.4   **Medium-resolution graphics layout form. The aspect ratio is included in the form's design. To program a figure, simply draw it exactly as you want it to appear and use the resulting coordinates. Note that each box represents 2 pixels in both the *X* and *Y* directions.**

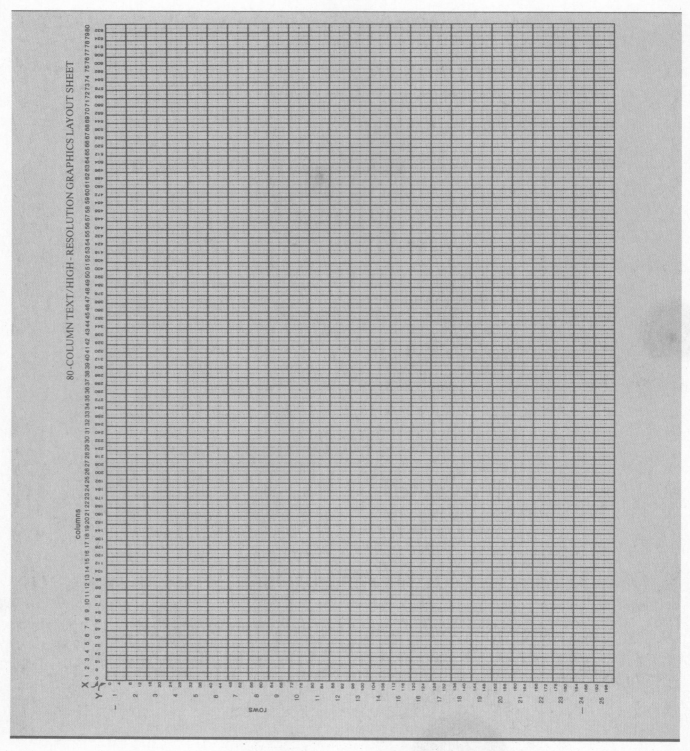

FIGURE 13.5   **High-resolution graphics layout form. The aspect ratio is included in the form's design. To program a figure, simply draw it exactly as you want it to appear and use the resulting coordinates. Note that each box represents 4 pixels in both the *X* and *Y* directions.**

Whether it is enlarged or not, you may find reading the graphics layout form difficult. If so, you may prefer to use the following equations for any row or column in both medium- and high-resolution graphics.

$$\begin{array}{l}\text{Coordinate of first pixel} \\ \text{in column (or row)}\end{array} = 8 \times \text{column (or row) number} - 8$$

$$\begin{array}{l}\text{Coordinate of last pixel} \\ \text{in column (or row)}\end{array} = 8 \times \text{column (or row) number} - 1$$

$$\begin{array}{l}\text{Coordinate of middle pixel} \\ \text{in column (or row)}\end{array} = 8 \times \text{column (or row) number} - 4$$

For column 10, these equations give

$$\text{Coordinate of first pixel in column } 10 = 8 \times 10 - 8 = 72$$

$$\text{Coordinate of last pixel in column } 10 = 8 \times 10 - 1 = 79$$

$$\text{Coordinate of middle pixel in column } 10 = 8 \times 10 - 4 = 76$$

To calculate the row or column number when you know the coordinate, you need only one equation:

$$\text{Row or column number} = \text{Coordinate}\backslash 8 + 1$$

Notice that this equation uses integer division.

Printing a Graphics Screen

While it is great fun to produce images on the screen, you may sometimes need to print your output (when doing homework problems, for example). If you have the IBM graphics printer or other compatible printer, you can use the DOS GRAPHICS command. To use the GRAPHICS command, while you are still in DOS and before you start BASIC, type the command GRAPHICS. This command loads a screen-printing program into RAM. Then you can start BASIC and execute programs that create graphics screens. Whenever you want to print a screen, you simply use the Print Screen key just as you would if you were printing a screen in text mode.

If you don't have the IBM graphics printer or a compatible printer, you will have to get a screen printing program from your instructor.

Syntax Summary

LINE Statement
Form: `LINE[(x1,y1)]-[(x2,y2)][,color][,B[F]]`
Example: `LINE(25,100)-(280,15),3,BF`
Interpretation: Draws a line from the pixel whose coordinates are (x1,y1) to the pixel whose coordinates are (x2,y2), in the color number color, selected from the current palette. If B is coded, a box is drawn with the given coordinates as the opposite corners. If BF is coded, the box is filled with the color.

EXERCISES

*13.7   Write a LINE statement to draw a line from the center of the medium-resolution screen to the upper right corner. Would the statement be different for a high-resolution screen? If so, what would be the correct statement?

13.8   We developed the LINE statement that draws a square whose Y dimension is 80 pixels. Write the LINE statement that draws a square whose X dimension is 80 pixels and whose upper left corner is at (120,60).

*13.9   Note that the following statement uses absolute coordinates:

LINE(20,10)-(60,60)

Rewrite the statement, expressing the second set of coordinates in relative form.

13.10   Which point is the last point referenced by the following statement?

LINE(100,160)-(5,10)

13.11   In medium resolution, which is longer: a vertical line 100 pixels long or a horizontal line 115 pixels long?

PROGRAMMING ASSIGNMENTS

13.4   Write a program to draw an arrow like the one in Program 13.3, but facing left.

*13.5   Write a program to draw this flag:

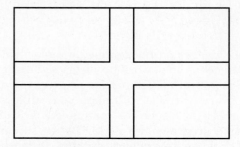

13.6   Write a program to draw a rocket:

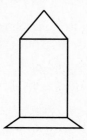

*13.7   Write a program to draw three nested boxes on a red background. The common center of all three boxes should be the center of the medium-resolution screen. The largest box should have sides of 120 pixels and be colored cyan, the next box should have sides of 60 pixels and be colored magenta, and the innermost box should have sides of 30 pixels and be colored white.

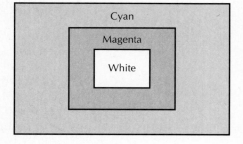

PAINTING

We have noted that using the BF parameter of the LINE statement fills a box with color. But the BF parameter cannot be used to color an irregular shape, such as the arrow in Program 13.3. In contrast, the PAINT statement may be used to color a figure of any shape.

■ *The PAINT Statement*

The syntax of the PAINT statement is

PAINT(x,y)[,paint][,boundary]

where x and y are the coordinates of any pixel inside the enclosed area that is to be painted, paint is the color used to paint that area, and boundary is the color of the edges of the area.

The PAINT statement will be easier to understand if we start with a simple example. Suppose we draw a box with the following statement:

LINE(100,160)-(220,80),1,B

If a previously executed COLOR statement selected palette 1, the outline of this box will be cyan. We could have filled the box with cyan by coding BF instead of B, but let's use the following PAINT statement to fill it with white instead:

PAINT(110,150),3,1

In this statement, x is 110, y is 150, paint is 3, and boundary is 1. This statement paints in color 3 (white), starting at pixel (110,150) and moving in all directions until pixels of color 1 (cyan) are encountered.

The PAINT statement is always used this way:

1. Outline an area in a particular color.
2. Select any point within the area.
3. Execute a PAINT statement in which you code the coordinates of that point as the starting point, any color you want as paint, and the color that was used to draw the outline as boundary.

PAINT Statement

PAINT(200,100),2,1

Effect

Paints color 2 starting from the pixel (200,100) going in all directions until a boundary of color 1 is encountered.

PAINT Statement

PAINT(X.INSIDE,Y.INSIDE),CLR,BDRY

Effect

Paints color CLR starting from pixel (X.INSIDE,Y.INSIDE) going in all directions until a boundary of color BDRY is encountered.

Warning: When you paint an area, be careful that the area is completely surrounded by an outline of boundary color. If you leave a gap, the paint will "leak out."

In medium resolution, paint and boundary may be 0 through 3. In high resolution, they may be either 0 or 1. Because there are only two colors in high resolution, it doesn't make sense for paint to be different from boundary. You can paint the screen white only until a white outline is reached, or black until a black outline is reached. (Think about painting the screen black until a white outline is reached. Since the outline is white, the area must have been black already!)

If paint is not coded, it defaults to color 3 in medium resolution and color 1 in high resolution. If boundary is not coded, it defaults to the value of paint. The coordinates of the starting point may be given in either absolute or relative form. When it finishes executing, PAINT sets the last point referenced to the starting point.

▪ *Painting a House*

Program 13.4 shows the easiest way to construct and paint a house.

Line 110 changes to medium resolution graphics mode, clears the screen, and selects a background color of blue with palette 0. Lines 130 through 170 draw the outline of the roof and the two attic windows in color 3 (brown). Line 180 paints the roof color 3. It was not necessary to code boundary in this statement, since the default for boundary is paint, but including it makes the statement easier to understand. In lines 190 and 200 BASIC paints the two attic windows color 1 (green). Note that you could not use the BF parameter in lines 160 and 170 to fill the windows with color 1, because these statements draw the windows in color 3 so that the PAINT statement in line 180 will not cover them.

The same procedure is used in lines 220 through 340 to draw and paint the body of the house. Notice that it is not necessary to paint these windows, since they are to be in the background color. Lines 360 and 370 draw and paint the grass and are straightforward.

The LOCATE and PRINT statements in lines 380 and 390 show that it is possible to have both text and graphics on the same screen. The graphics statements have no effect on where output produced by PRINT statements is placed on the screen. To put the output where we want it, we use the LOCATE statement, just as we do in text mode. The row and column indications on the graphics layout forms in Figures 13.4 and 13.5 are helpful in choosing the values of row and column for the LOCATE statement. In medium-resolution mode, the characters placed on the screen by a PRINT statement are the large, 40-character-per-line size, and are in color 3. In high-resolution mode, the characters are in standard, 80-character-per-line size, and are white.

Syntax Summary	PAINT Statement
	Form: PAINT(x,y),[paint][,boundary]
	Example: PAINT(160,100),1,3
	Interpretation: Paints color paint in all directions starting from pixel (x,y) until BASIC encounters an outline of color boundary.

EXERCISES

....

13.12 Suppose an area has been drawn with a white outline. Write the PAINT statement to paint the area magenta. (Assume the point (160,100) is inside the area.)

*13.13 Explain what the following PAINT statement does:

PAINT(40,70),3,2

```
100 REM *** DRAW AND PAINT A HOUSE ***
110 SCREEN 1,0: CLS: KEY OFF: COLOR 1,0
120 REM *** Draw and paint roof
130 LINE(100,80)-(160,30),3                'Draw
140 LINE -(220,80),3                       'the
150 LINE -(100,80),3                       'roof
160 LINE(140,70)-(150,55),3,B              'Draw two
170 LINE(170,70)-(180,55),3,B              'windows
180 PAINT(160,70),3,3                      'Paint roof
190 PAINT(145,60),1,3                      'Paint
200 PAINT(175,60),1,3                      'windows
210 REM *** Draw and paint body
220 LINE(100,160)-(220,80),2,B             'Draw body
230 LINE(120,110)-STEP(20,-25),2,B         'Draw three
240 LINE(150,110)-STEP(20,-25),2,B         'second-floor
250 LINE(180,110)-STEP(20,-25),2,B         'windows
260 LINE(120,155)-STEP(20,-25),2,B         'Draw two first-
270 LINE(180,155)-STEP(20,-25),2,B         'floor windows
280 LINE(150,160)-STEP(0,-30),2            'Draw
290 LINE -STEP(10,-10),2                   'the
300 LINE -STEP(10,10),2                    'door
310 LINE -STEP(0,30),2                     'with
320 LINE -STEP(-20,0),2                    'peak
330 PAINT(110,150),2,2                     'Paint body
340 PAINT(160,140),3,2                     'Paint the door
350 REM *** Draw and paint the grass
360 LINE(0,160)-(320,160),1
370 PAINT(10,170),1,1
380 LOCATE 23,14
390 PRINT "Home Sweet Home"
400 A$ = INPUT$(1)                         'Pause
410 END

RUN
```

PROGRAM 13.4   Drawing and painting a house.

PROGRAMMING ASSIGNMENTS

....

13.8 Modify the program you wrote for Programming Assignment 13.4 to paint the arrow cyan.

*13.9 Modify the program you wrote for Programming Assignment 13.5 to paint the flag. The background should be blue, the cross white, the upper left and lower right sections cyan, and the lower left and upper right sections magenta.

13.10 Add a red chimney to the house drawn in Program 13.4. The fire code requires that the chimney be higher than the peak of the roof. Since it is difficult to determine the exact coordinates where the chimney meets the roof, you may outline the chimney in brown and then paint it red.

DRAWING CIRCLES

....

The CIRCLE statement permits us to draw circles and parts of circles as easy as pi (pun intended). The syntax of the CIRCLE statement is

CIRCLE(x,y), radius[,color][,start][,end][,aspect]

Like the LINE statement, the full syntax of the CIRCLE statement is rather intimidating, so let's start with a simpler form,

CIRCLE(x,y),radius[,color]

where x and y are the coordinates of the center of the circle and may be given in either absolute or relative form, radius is the radius (plural, radii) of the circle, and color is the color in which the circle should be drawn. The color parameter in the CIRCLE statement works the same way as it works in the LINE statement, except that there is no way to fill the inside of the circle with color, the way the BF parameter does with the LINE statement. The statement

CIRCLE(100,50),20,1

draws a circle of radius 20 pixels in color 1, centered at pixel (100,50). The center of the circle then becomes the last point referenced.

Make sure you understand how the following CIRCLE statements work before proceeding:

CIRCLE Statement

CIRCLE STEP(50,90),30,2

Effect

Draws a circle with a radius of 30 pixels, in color 2, centered at the pixel that is 50 pixels to the right and 90 pixels down from the last point referenced.

CIRCLE Statement

CIRCLE(200,150),40,3

Effect

Draws a circle with a radius of 40 pixels, in color 3, that is centered at pixel (200,150).

```
100  REM *** DEMONSTRATING THE CIRCLE STATEMENT ***
110  SCREEN 1,0: CLS: KEY OFF: COLOR 0,1
120  CIRCLE(160,100),50,3
130  PAINT STEP(0,0),1,3
140  CIRCLE STEP(0,0),75,3
150  PAINT STEP(60,0),2,3
160  A$ = INPUT$(1)
170  END

RUN
```

PROGRAM 13.5 **Demonstrating the CIRCLE statement.**

Program 13.5 draws and paints two circles. Line 120 draws the inner circle with its center at (160,100), its radius 50 pixels, and its outline white. The PAINT statement in line 130 paints the inner circle cyan. This statement uses the relative form to specify the starting point for painting. Since the last point referenced by the CIRCLE statement is the center of the circle, line 130 uses 0 for both the *x* offset and the *y* offset to start painting at the center of the circle. Line 140 draws the outer circle with the same center, (160,100), its radius 75 pixels, and its outline white. This statement also uses the relative form to specify the center of the circle and 0 for both the *x* and *y* offsets. The 0 value is based on the fact that the last point referenced by the PAINT statement is the starting pixel. The PAINT statement in line 150 starts painting in magenta at (220,100), which is inside the outer circle.

Drawing Parts of Circles

The CIRCLE statement also allows us to draw an arc—that is, just some part of a circle. When we draw part of a circle, we must tell BASIC where to start drawing and where to stop. The parameters start and end are used for this purpose. Before you can learn how to use start and end, though, you have to understand how BASIC measures angles.

DEGREES AND RADIANS

If you have a Ph.D. in mathematics, fine. If you hated every minute of high school algebra, don't despair. The following section is easier than it sounds.

A circle is divided into 360 degrees. As Figure 13.6 shows, 0 degrees is at "3 o'clock." Mathematicians find it useful to use radians instead of degrees to measure the size of angles. BASIC also measures the size of angles in radians. Most of us, however, find it is easier to think in terms of degrees. So we need an easy way to convert degrees to radians.

If you include in your programs the following two statements

```
PI = 3.14159
CF = (2 * PI) / 360
```

then whenever you need to use radians you can just multiply the number of degrees by CF (conversion factor). For example,

```
CF * 45
```

will convert 45 degrees into radians. If you use these equations, you don't need to know how many radians there are in 45 degrees. BASIC will do all the work for you.*

CODING THE START AND END PARAMETERS

Now that you understand about radians, coding start and end is easy. You use start to specify the angle where the drawing of the arc should begin and end to specify the angle where the drawing of the arc should end. For example, if CF has been defined in a program, then the statement

```
CIRCLE(200,75),25,1,CF*270,CF*90
```

will draw an arc from 270 degrees to 90 degrees in color 1, that is,

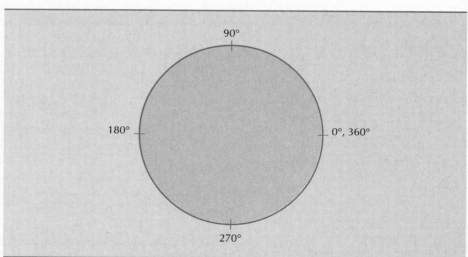

FIGURE 13.6   **Dividing a circle into 360 degrees.**

*I derived the conversion factor as follows. A circle contains either 360 degrees or $2 \times \pi$ radians, where π (pronounced "pi") is the famous numeric constant that equals 3.14159. Since 360 degrees = $2 \times \pi$ radians, it follows that 1 degree = $(2 \times \pi)/360$ radians.

Notice that it is legal for start to be greater than end. If start or end are omitted, as they were in all the examples before this section, BASIC uses default values of 0 degrees, for start and 360 degrees for end. You can also draw a line from the center of the circle to an arc, by preceding start or end with a minus sign. For example, the statement

```
CIRCLE(80,150),30,,-CF*90,-CF*180
```

draws the following wedge in the default color, color 3:

(As usual, if we omit a parameter, in this case color, and code a later parameter, we must code a comma to indicate the missing parameter.)

You might think that coding -CF*0 or -0 for start or end would cause BASIC to draw a line from the center of the circle to 0 degrees, but that doesn't work. Instead, to draw a wedge that begins or ends at 0 degrees, code some small angle in place of 0, for example, -CF*.01. That way, you'll get what you need and keep BASIC happy, too. Other examples of wedge drawing with the CIRCLE statement include

CIRCLE Statement

```
CIRCLE(240,130),50,1,-CF*90,-CF*270
```

Effect

Draws a wedge with a radius of 50 pixels, going from 90 degrees to 270 degrees, in color 1, centered at pixel (240,130). This example assumes that CF has been defined in the program as shown in the text.

CIRCLE Statement

```
CIRCLE(50,100),30,2,-CF*.01,-CF*45
```

Effect

Draws a wedge with a radius of 30 pixels, going from 0 degrees to 45 degrees, in color 2, centered at pixel (50,100). This example assumes that CF has been defined as shown in the text.

Program 13.6 draws a Pac-Man–like figure. Notice that the PAINT statement in line 170 does not cause painting to begin at the center of the circle. When only part of a circle is drawn, as it is in Program 13.6, the center of the circle is on the boundary of the figure. And painting must start *inside* the area that is to be painted. Any number of points could have served as the starting point; here we arbitrarily use a point 10 pixels to the left of the center of the circle.

When you want to write a program to draw a complex figure like this one, you should first draw the figure on the graphics layout form and then convert the drawing into graphics statements. Some adjustments will be required to get the figure exactly the way you want it. In making these adjustments, you will find the BASIC editor very helpful.

Good programming can also help in making adjustments. For example, it was necessary to try several sets of coordinates for the CIRCLE statements that draw the eyes (lines 180 to 210) to find the best ones: (140,74) and (160,65). If you use the relative form to specify the coordinates for the PAINT and PSET statements that follow CIRCLE statements, you will not have

```
100 REM *** DRAWING PAC-MAN ***
110 SCREEN 1,0: CLS: KEY OFF: COLOR 0,0
120 REM *** Initialization
130 PI = 3.14159
140 CF = (2 * PI) / 360
150 REM *** Draw and paint face
160 CIRCLE(160,100),60,3,-CF*45,-CF*335
170 PAINT(150,100),3,3
180 CIRCLE(140,74),5,0        'Draw
190 PAINT STEP(0,0),0,0       'and
200 PSET STEP(0,0)            'paint
210 CIRCLE(160,65),5,0        'both
220 PAINT STEP(0,0),0,0       'his
230 PSET STEP(0,0)            'eyes
240 A$ = INPUT$(1)            'Pause
250 END

RUN
```

PROGRAM 13.6   **Drawing Pac-Man.**

to change the PAINT and PSET statements with each change in the CIRCLE statements.

Coding Aspect

The final parameter of the CIRCLE statement is aspect, which is related, but not identical, to the aspect ratio we discussed earlier. Coding aspect in a CIRCLE statement lets you draw ellipses (ovals). To draw an ellipse we must specify two radii; the X radius, which is measured along the X axis, and the Y radius, which is measured along the Y axis. In the CIRCLE statement, aspect is the ratio of Y radius to X radius, where both radii are measured in pixels.

When a CIRCLE statement without aspect is coded, BASIC uses the default value of $5/6$ in medium resolution and $5/12$ in high resolution. These default values compensate for the aspect ratio of the medium- and high-resolution screens and ensure that when a CIRCLE statement without aspect is executed, a circle—a figure in which the physical lengths of the X radius and Y radius are equal—will be drawn. By coding aspect, we can create the "stretched circles" known as ellipses.

```
100 REM *** DEMONSTRATING ASPECT PARAMETER ***
110 SCREEN 1,0: CLS: KEY OFF: COLOR 0,1
120 CIRCLE(80,100),75,,,,1        'aspect
130 CIRCLE(80,100),75,,,,2        '1 and
140 CIRCLE(80,100),75,,,,3        'greater
150 REM ***
160 CIRCLE(240,100),75,,,,1       'aspect
170 CIRCLE(240,100),75,,,,.5      '1 and
180 CIRCLE(240,100),75,,,,.25     'smaller
190 A$ = INPUT$(1)                'Pause
200 END

RUN
```

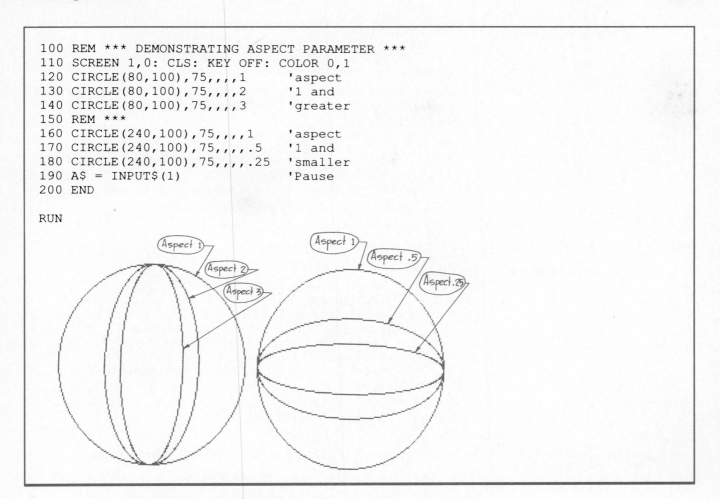

PROGRAM 13.7   **Demonstrating the aspect parameter.**

Program 13.7 draws ellipses with various values of aspect. Note that while all these circles have the same radius, 75, they have different shapes, because of the different values assigned to aspect. The circles on the left have values of 1 or more, and those on the right have values of 1 or less. If aspect is less than 1, BASIC uses the radius coded in the CIRCLE statement as the X radius and calculates the Y radius using the equation Y radius = X radius * aspect. In Program 13.7, the X radius of the three circles on the right is 75, but the Y radii are different. If aspect is greater than 1, BASIC uses the radius coded in the CIRCLE statement as the Y radius and calculates the X radius using the equation X radius = Y radius/aspect. In Program 13.7, the Y radius of the three circles on the left is 75, but the X radii are different.

Before proceeding, be sure you understand how the following CIRCLE statements produce oval shapes:

CIRCLE Statement

CIRCLE(100,100),50,2,,,.5

Effect

Draws an ellipse with an X radius of 50 pixels, in color 2 centered at pixel (100,100), with aspect ratio of .5.

CIRCLE Statement

```
CIRCLE(100,100),80,1,CF*180,CF*270,1.5
```

Effect

Draws an arc of an ellipse from 180 degrees to 270 degrees, with a *Y* radius of 80 pixels, in color 1, centered at pixel (100,100), with an aspect ratio of 1.5.

When you draw an ellipse on the graphics layout chart, you can determine the value of aspect to code in the CIRCLE statement by dividing the *Y* radius by the *X* radius, where both radii are measured in pixels. Then code the CIRCLE statement using the larger radius as radius.

Syntax Summary

CIRCLE Statement
Form: `CIRCLE(x,y),radius[,color,][,start][,end][,aspect]`
Example: `CIRCLE(175,90),50,3,CF*180,CF*270,1.5`
Interpretation: Draws a circle (or ellipse if aspect is coded) that is centered at (x,y), has a radius of radius pixels in color color. start and end specify the starting and ending angles of the curve, and aspect specifies the ratio of the *Y* radius to the *X* radius (both measured in pixels).

Getting the Bugs Out

Problem: During execution, BASIC displays the error message

```
Illegal function call in nn
```

Reason: If nn is a CIRCLE statement, you have specified a start and/or end outside the range of 0 to 360 degrees.

Solution: Correct the start and/or end parameter.

EXERCISES

13.14 Write the CIRCLE statement to draw a circle in cyan that is centered at pixel (100,80) and has a radius of 60 pixels. Write the PAINT statement to paint the circle white.

13.15 Write the CIRCLE statement to draw the following wedge, centered at (160,100) with a radius of 90 pixels:

PAINT the wedge green.

*13.16 Suppose a circle is drawn using the statement

```
CIRCLE(160,100),80,,,,2
```

What is the *X* radius of this circle? What is the *Y* radius?

13.17 Program 13.8 shows a program that is supposed to draw a half circle wedge. The only output the program produced was a single point. Find and correct the error.

```
10  REM *** DRAWING A HALF-CIRCLE WEDGE ***
20  SCREEN 1,0: CLS: KEY OFF: COLOR 12,0
30  CF = (2 * PI) / 360
40  CIRCLE(160,100),75,3,-CF*90,-CF*270
50  A$ = INPUT$(1)
60  END
```

PROGRAM 13.8   **A program that is supposed to draw a half circle wedge.**

PROGRAMMING ASSIGNMENTS

....

13.11 Write a program that draws a face like the one in Program 13.6, but have the face facing left.

*13.12 Write a program that draws a happy face like that pictured below. The face should be cyan, the mouth white, and the eyes black.

*13.14 Write a program that divides the screen into four quadrants. In the upper left quadrant, draw a cyan circle on a blue background. In the upper right quadrant, draw a magenta circle on a cyan background. In the lower right quadrant, draw a white circle on a magenta background, and in the lower left quadrant, draw a blue circle on a white background.

13.13 Write a program that draws the truck shown to the right:

SUMMARY

....

In this chapter you have learned that

☐ To execute graphics programs, your computer must be equipped with one of the many color/graphics monitor adapters available.

☐ You can use either medium-resolution or high-resolution graphics.

☐ The SCREEN statement puts the screen into a text, medium-resolution, or high-resolution graphics mode.

☐ In medium-resolution mode, the *X* coordinates run from 0 to 319; in high-resolution mode, they run from 0 to 639. In both modes, the *Y* coordinates run from 0 to 199.

☐ The WIDTH statement sets the number of characters displayed on a line to either 40 or 80.

☐ The COLOR statement specifies a background color and a palette.

☐ The PSET statement draws points, and the PRESET statement erases them.

☐ You can specify coordinates using either absolute or relative form. To use relative form, you must include the word STEP in a graphics statement.

☐ The LINE statement draws lines and boxes.

☐ In medium resolution, the aspect ratio is ⁵⁄₆; in high resolution, it is ⁵⁄₁₂.

☐ The DOS command GRAPHICS allows you to print a graphics screen.

☐ The PAINT statement colors a figure.

☐ The CIRCLE statement draws circles, ellipses, and parts of circles and ellipses.

KEY TERMS IN THIS CHAPTER

absolute form 402	**last point referenced** 402	**physical coordinates** 397
all points addressable 397	**line clipping** 406	**pixel** 397
aspect ratio 409	**palette** 398	**relative form** 402
coordinates 397		

QUESTIONS FOR REVIEW

13.1 If aspect is not coded with a CIRCLE statement, what value is used? Is the same value used in both medium resolution and high resolution?

13.2 What is the last point referenced after a CIRCLE statement is executed?

13.3 What are the coordinates of the four corner points in medium resolution and in high resolution?

13.4 What color number is used by the PRESET statement if color is not specified?

13.5 Explain the difference between coding B and coding BF with a LINE statement.

13.6 True or false: On a medium-resolution screen, the PRINT statement always produces white characters.

13.7 What colors are available with palette 0?

13.8 What are the differences between the medium- and the high-resolution graphics modes?

13.9 What color is used by the LINE statement if color is not specified?

13.10 What is the cause of the error if, during execution, BASIC displays the error message Illegal function call in nn, where nn is the line number of a LINE statement?

ADDITIONAL PROGRAMMING ASSIGNMENTS

13.15 Write a program to draw a crescent moon:

*13.16 Write a program to draw a pizza with a slice removed as shown to the right:

13.17 Write a program to draw 100 circles randomly on the screen. For each circle, the X coordinate of the center should be a random number between 0 and 319, the Y coordinate should be a random number between 0 and 199, and the radius should be a random number between 5 and 25. Paint the circle with a random color chosen from the four available colors.

13.18 Write a program to draw the church shown below:

13.19 Write a program to draw the football field shown below:

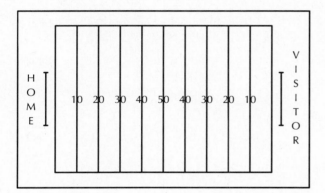

13.20 Write a program to draw the Star of David shown below:

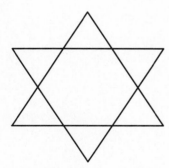

13.21 Write a program to draw the stop sign shown above to the right. The sign should be red and the letters white. Use any color other than red or white for the background.

13.22 Write a program to draw the valentine shown below:

13.23 Write a program to draw the pail shown below:

*13.24 Write a program to draw the design shown below. Paint the center portion in color 3 and the other portions as indicated.

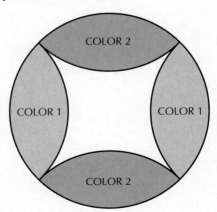

BEYOND THE BASICS

13.1 Write a program to draw the checkerboard shown below.

13.2 Write a graphics version of the random walk problem presented in Programming Assignment 9.24.

Make the bridge 100 pixels long and 60 pixels wide. Each time Sherry takes a step she walks 10 pixels along the length of the bridge and lurches 10 pixels to the side. Plot her progress. If she falls in, print SPLASH! near where she fell in. If she makes it safely, print SAFE! near her arrival point. Then ask whether the user wants to see another walk.

13.3 Write a graphics version of the hangman playing program presented in Beyond the BASICs 9.6. Begin by drawing a gallows, and every time the user enters a wrong letter, draw part of a figure. Also display the wrong letters in alphabetical order on row 25, leaving spaces for correct and not-yet-guessed letters. For example

D H JK N   R U   Y

Graphs, Charts, and Animation

In Chapter 13, you learned how to use graphics statements to draw pictures. In this chapter, you will learn how to use these statements to draw line and bar graphs and pie charts and how to make pictures move on the screen.

ESSENTIALS FOR DRAWING GRAPHS AND CHARTS

Two graphics statements, VIEW and WINDOW, are useful in programs that draw graphs and charts.

■ *The VIEW Statement*

Viewport
A section of the screen that functions like an independent screen.

The VIEW statement lets you define a separate portion of the screen as an independent screen. This separate portion of the screen is called a **viewport**. We will discuss how viewports work shortly.

The syntax of the VIEW statement is

        VIEW [(x1, y1)-(x2,y2)] [,color][,boundary]

where (x1, y1) are the coordinates of the upper left corner of the viewport and (x2, y2) are the coordinates of the lower right corner of the viewport. The color parameter specifies the color the viewport should be painted and works the same way as color works in the other graphics statements. If you do not code color, the viewport is not painted. The boundary parameter specifies the color to be used to draw a boundary line around the viewport. In medium resolution, boundary may be 0 through 3. In high resolution, boundary may be either 0 or 1. If you do not code boundary, no boundary is drawn.

Figure 14.1 shows a viewport that was established by the statement.*

        VIEW(50,25)-(250,175),,1

The coordinates of the upper left corner of the viewport are (50,25), and those of the lower right corner are (250,175). The result is that an *X* (verti-

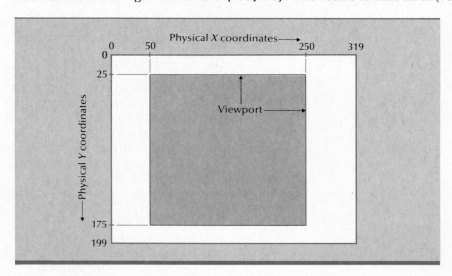

FIGURE 14.1   **A viewport (shown in grey) created by the statement VIEW(50,25)-
(250,175),,1.**

*Of course, the colors shown here are not those you will see on the screen.

cal) line at 50 forms the left boundary of the viewport and an X line at 250 the right boundary, while a Y (horizontal) line at 25 forms the upper boundary and a Y line at 175 the lower boundary. If you code a VIEW statement with no parameters, you reestablish the whole screen as one viewport.

Before proceeding, be sure you understand how each of the following VIEW statements work:

VIEW Statement

```
VIEW(70,30)-(270,130),3,1
```

Effect

Establishes a viewport painted in color 3 with a border of color 1 whose upper left corner is at (70,30) and lower right corner is at (270,130).

VIEW Statement

```
VIEW(150,90)-(170,110)
```

Effect

Establishes a viewport whose upper left corner is at (150,90) and lower right corner is at (170,110). The viewport is not painted, and the boundary is not drawn.

VIEW Statement

```
VIEW
```

Effect

Reestablishes the whole screen as one viewport.

Program 14.1 shows how the VIEW statement works. Note that in this program all three circles were drawn by the same CIRCLE statement—the statement in line 260. Let's see how that could happen.

BASIC draws the first circle when it executes the GOSUB 250 statement in line 140. This circle looks exactly as you would expect: Its center is at (45,40), and its radius is 30. Next, BASIC executes the VIEW statement in line 150. This statement defines the section of the screen between pixels (200,20) and (300,90) as a viewport. Now when the GOSUB 250 statement in line 180 executes, the CIRCLE statement in line 260 draws a circle in the viewport labeled VIEW 1.

How did the circle get in the viewport? After you create a viewport, BASIC adds the coordinates used to specify the upper left corner of the viewport, (x1,y1), to the coordinates specified in any graphics statements. In the VIEW statement in line 150, x1 equals 200 and y1 equals 20. When it executed the CIRCLE statement in line 260, BASIC added these values to the coordinates specified in the statement, so that the statement was effectively

```
CIRCLE(45+200,40+20),30 = CIRCLE (245,60),30
```

This is the statement that drew the circle labeled VIEW 1.

The second viewport, which is created in line 190, is similar to the first, except that it is too small to contain the circle. As you can see, only that portion of the circle that fits in the viewport is drawn. Once a viewport is created, it is as though the rest of the screen does not exist; figures are drawn relative to the viewport, and because of line clipping, parts of figures that would fall outside the viewport are not drawn.

If you have several viewports, you can treat them as independent screens. The CLS statement clears only the most recently created viewport, but Ctrl + Home clears the whole screen.

```
100 REM    DEMONSTRATING THE VIEW STATEMENT
110 SCREEN 1,0: CLS: KEY OFF: COLOR 0,1
120 LOCATE 1,3
130 PRINT "NO VIEW"
140 GOSUB 250                    'Circle with no viewport
150 VIEW(200,20)-(300,90),,1     'Viewport 1
160 LOCATE 4,29
170 PRINT "VIEW 1"
180 GOSUB 250                    'Circle in viewport 1
190 VIEW(200,100)-(250,170),,2   'Viewport 2
200 LOCATE 14,26
210 PRINT "VIEW 2"
220 GOSUB 250                    'Circle in viewport 2
230 A$ = INPUT$(1)               'Pause
240 STOP
250 REM *** Subroutine to draw circle
260 CIRCLE(45,40),30
270 RETURN
280 END

RUN
```

PROGRAM 14.1   **Demonstrating the VIEW statement.**

The WINDOW Statement

The WINDOW statement may be used alone, but it is often used with the VIEW statement to redefine the coordinates of a viewport. Redefining the coordinates of a viewport makes it much easier to draw graphs.

The syntax of the WINDOW statement is

```
WINDOW[SCREEN][(x1,y1)-(x2,y2)]
```

where (x1,y1) and (x2,y2) are the coordinates you want to use. Normally, (x1,y1) are the coordinates of the lower left corner, and (x2,y2) are the coordinates of the upper right corner. If you include the SCREEN parameter in the WINDOW statement, the coordinates will be reversed. That is, (x1,y1) will be the coordinates of the upper left corner and (x2,y2) will be the coordinates of the lower right corner.

If you execute a WINDOW statement without executing a VIEW statement, the coordinates apply to the whole screen. If you execute a WINDOW statement with no parameters, the coordinate system created by a previously executed WINDOW statement is abolished, and the screen returns to the usual physical coordinates.

World coordinates
A coordinate system established by the user to fit a given problem.

We call the coordinates specified by a WINDOW statement **world coordinates,** in contrast to our usual physical coordinates (see Chapter 13). Coding world coordinates lets you match the coordinates of the screen to the needs of your problem.

Check your understanding of the WINDOW statement against the following examples:

WINDOW Statement
```
WINDOW(0,0)-(10,100)
```

Effect
Assigns (0,0) as the coordinates of the lower left corner and (10,100) as the coordinates of the upper right corner of a previously defined viewport. If a viewport was not previously defined, the coordinates apply to the whole screen.

WINDOW Statement
```
WINDOW(-1,-1)-(1,1)
```

Effect
Assigns (-1,-1) as the coordinates of the lower left corner and (1,1) as the coordinates of the upper right corner of a previously defined viewport.

WINDOW Statement
```
WINDOW
```

Effect
Abolishes any previously established world coordinate system and returns the screen to the usual physical coordinates.

Figure 14.2 shows a viewport with world coordinates defined by the statements

```
120 VIEW(50,25)-(250,175)
130 WINDOW(0,1000)-(500,2000)
```

Program 14.2 uses these VIEW and WINDOW statements to create the output shown in Figure 14.3. The VIEW statement in line 120 defines a viewport in the center of the screen. The WINDOW statement in line 130 defines the world coordinate system for that viewport: (0,1000) is the coordinate of the lower left corner and (500,2000) is the coordinate of the upper right corner. Notice that in this coordinate system *Y* increases as we move toward the top of the screen. As you might expect, this orientation will make it much easier to draw graphs.

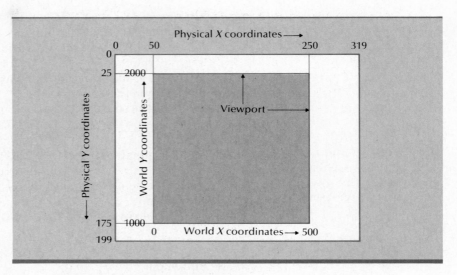

FIGURE 14.2   **A viewport with world coordinates.**

```
100 REM *** DEMONSTRATING THE WINDOW STATEMENT ***
110 SCREEN 1,0: CLS: KEY OFF: COLOR 0,1
120 VIEW(50,25)-(250,175),,1      'Create viewport
130 WINDOW(0,1000)-(500,2000)     'Establish coordinates
140 LOCATE 4,3: PRINT "2000"      'Print
150 LOCATE 13,5: PRINT "Y"        'the
160 LOCATE 22,3: PRINT "1000"     'Y
170 LOCATE 24,7: PRINT "0";       'and
180 LOCATE 24,20: PRINT "X";      'X
190 LOCATE 24,31: PRINT "500";    'coordinates
200 LINE(100,1000)-(500,1500)     'Draw line
210 A$ = INPUT$(1)                'Pause
220 END
```

PROGRAM 14.2   **Demonstrating the WINDOW statement.**

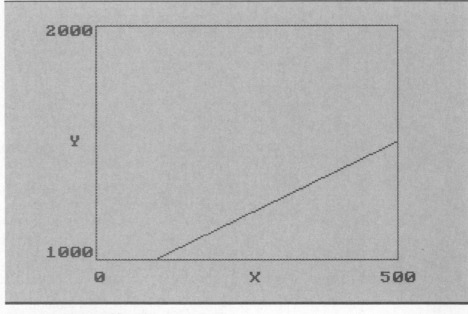

FIGURE 14.3   **Output produced by Program 14.2.**

The LOCATE and PRINT statements in lines 140 through 190 label the Y and X axes. The LINE statement in line 200 draws a line between pixels (100,1000) and (500,1500). Although there are no pixels with these physical coordinates, the WINDOW statement allows us to define the screen with the coordinates we want. BASIC translates our world coordinates into physical coordinates and draws the line where it should be.

We have to modify the definition of aspect ratio for a viewport with world coordinates. In such a viewport, the definition of aspect ratio is the physical length of a line one unit long in the X direction divided by the physical length of a line one unit long in the Y direction. If we let L_x be the length in pixels of the viewport in the X direction, L_y be the length in the Y direction, R_x be the range of coordinates in the X direction, and R_y be the range of coordinates in the Y direction, then in the medium resolution screen the aspect ratio of the viewport is given by

$$a = 0.833 * \frac{L_x/R_x}{L_y/R_y}$$

In the high resolution screen, the constant is 0.417. This aspect ratio is used by the CIRCLE statement as the default value for aspect to draw a circle in a viewport with world coordinates. Similarly, this is the definition you would have to use to draw a square in a viewport with world coordinates.

As an example of applying this equation, line 120 in Program 14.2 shows that $L_x = 250 - 50 = 200$ and $L_y = 175 - 25 = 150$. Line 130 shows that $R_x = 500 - 0 = 500$, and $R_y = 2000 - 1000 = 1000$. Substituting these values into the equation gives

$$a = 0.833 * \frac{200/500}{150/1000} = 2.22$$

as the aspect ratio of this viewport.

Syntax Summary

VIEW Statement
Form: VIEW[(x1,y1)-(x2,y2)][,color][,boundary]
Example: VIEW(60,50)-(260,150),2,1
Function: Defines a viewport that is painted color with a border of boundary. The upper left corner of the viewport has coordinates (x1,y1), and the lower right corner has coordinates (x2,y2).

WINDOW Statement
Form: WINDOW[SCREEN] [(x1,y1)-(x2,y2)]
Example: WINDOW(1980,0)-(2000,1000)
Function: Establishes world coordinates in a previously defined viewport. If SCREEN is omitted, (x1,y1) are the coordinates of the lower left corner of the viewport, and (x2,y2) are the coordinates of the upper right corner. If SCREEN is coded, these assignments are reversed, with (x1,y1) the coordinates of the upper left corner and (x2,y2) the coordinates of the lower right corner. If a viewport was not previously defined, the world coordinates apply to the whole screen.

Getting the
Bugs Out

Problem: During execution, BASIC displays the error message

```
Illegal  function call in nn
```

where nn is the line number of a VIEW statement

Reason: The coordinates were outside the limits of the screen.

Solution: Correct the coordinates so that in medium resolution X is between 0 and 319, and in high resolution X is between 0 and 639, and so that Y is between 0 and 199.

EXERCISES

14.1 Code the VIEW statement to establish a viewport whose left boundary is the line X = 120, whose right boundary is the line X = 200, whose upper boundary is the line Y = 100, and whose lower boundary is the line Y = 190.

14.2 Suppose a viewport has been established between (250,100) and (300,150). Describe the line drawn by the statement

```
LINE(0,0)-(50,50)
```

*14.3 Suppose a program contains the following statements:

```
VIEW(30,30)-(100,100)
WINDOW(0,0)-(10,10)
PSET(0,0)
```

What are the physical coordinates of the point drawn by the PSET statement?

14.4 A homework assignment required students to define a viewport whose lower left corner had world coordinates of (0,0) and whose upper right corner had coordinates of (100,100). One student used the statement

```
VIEW(0,0)-(100,75)
```

to define the viewport. Code the WINDOW statement for this student. A second student used the statement

```
VIEW(100,100)-(200,175)
```

to define the viewport. Code the WINDOW statement for this student.

PROGRAMMING ASSIGNMENTS

14.1 Write a program that creates a viewport whose upper left corner is at (100,60) and whose lower right corner is at (200,140). Paint the viewport color 1 and outline it in color 2. Use a WINDOW statement to assign coordinates of (0,0) to the lower left corner of this viewport and (10,10) to the upper right corner. Use a LINE statement to draw a box in color 3 two of whose corners are (1,1) and (9,9).

14.2 Write a program that plots a sine wave for angles between 0 and 360 degrees, in steps of 5 degrees. It will be helpful to establish a viewport with coordinates (0,-1) and (360,1). Use a LINE statement to draw a horizontal line through (0,0) to represent the X axis and a PSET statement to plot the points.

DRAWING DIFFERENT TYPES OF GRAPHS AND CHARTS

It is remarkably easy to draw graphs and charts using BASIC; as you will see, the hardest part is printing the labels and coordinates for them.

Drawing a Line Graph

The U.S. Department of Overexpenditures wants a graph of the inflation rate for the years 1975 through 1990. The layout of the graph we want to draw is shown in Figure 14.4.

Following our structured procedure, we must first choose variable names:

Input and output variables	A character	CHAR$
	Inflation rate	INFLATION.RATE
	Year	YEAR
Internal variable	Counter variable	J

The algorithm is

1. Set up the graph.
2. Plot the data.

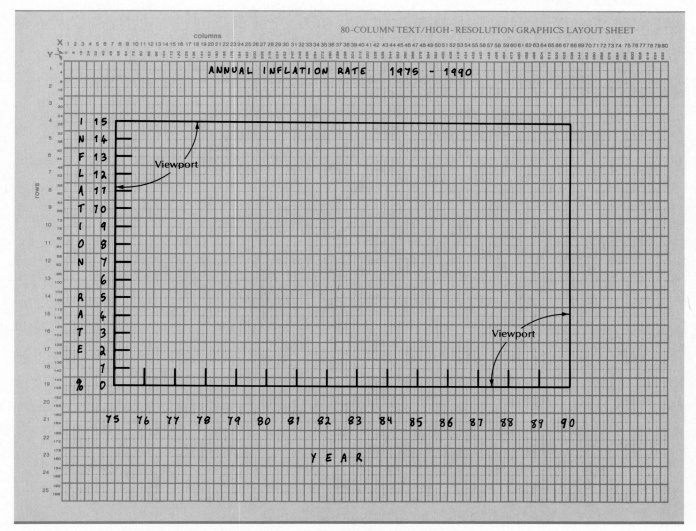

FIGURE 14.4   **Layout of a graph of inflation rates.**

There are no answers to calculate by hand, although after the graph is drawn, you should check it to make sure the points are plotted where they should be. The algorithm does not involve any complicated logic, so we will omit the flowchart here. Since this graph does not use color, we will use the high-resolution mode to take advantage of the extra detail available in high resolution. Program 14.3 draws the graph.

Let's consider first how the X (horizontal) coordinates are printed. Figure 14.4 shows that we want to print the years 75, 76, etc., in row 21, starting in column 7, with two blank columns between years. The FOR-NEXT loop in lines 310 through 330 does this. Line 320, which prints the years, uses the expression 4 * YEAR - 293 to specify the column number in the LOCATE statement. We will use these kinds of expressions frequently in this chapter, so it is important that you understand how to determine them.

The form for such expressions is always

$$\left. \begin{array}{c} \text{Column number} \\ \text{or} \\ \text{Row number} \end{array} \right\} = a \times J + b$$

where J represents the X or Y coordinate value, depending on whether you want to find the column (X) or the row (Y). In line 320, the expression is

$$\text{Column number} = 4 * \text{YEAR} - 293$$

In this equation, a is 4 and b is -293.

You may wonder where these values for a and b come from. Figure 14.4 shows that we want YEAR 75 to start in column 7 and YEAR 76 to start in column 11. We can calculate a by the equation

$$a = \frac{\text{Change in column or row number}}{\text{Change in coordinate value}}$$

In our example,

$$a = \frac{11 - 7}{76 - 75} = \frac{4}{1} = 4$$

The value of b is determined by calculating the value it must have to make any one YEAR come out in the correct column. Since we want to print 75 starting in column 7, we can calculate the column number as

$$7 = 4 * 75 + b$$

or

$$b = -293$$

That's all there is to it, but to be sure we didn't make an arithmetic error, we should check the formula to make sure it works with another value of YEAR. Figure 14.4 shows that 90 should be printed starting in column 67. Our formula gives

$$\text{Column number} = 4 * 90 - 293$$

$$\text{Column number} = 67$$

which is correct.

```
100 REM *** DRAWING A LINE GRAPH ***
110 SCREEN 2,0: CLS: KEY OFF
120 GOSUB 200                               'Set up graph
130 GOSUB 500                               'Plot data
140 A$ = INPUT$(1)                          'Pause
150 STOP
160 '
200 REM *** Set up graph routine
210    LOCATE 1,20: PRINT "ANNUAL INFLATION RATE   1975 - 1990"
220    FOR J = 1 TO 16                      'Print Y label
230      READ CHAR$
240      LOCATE J+3,3: PRINT CHAR$
250    NEXT J
260    REM Data for READ in 230
270    DATA I, N, F, L, A, T, I, O, N, " ", R, A, T, E, " ", %
280    FOR INFLATION.RATE = 0 TO 15               'Print Y coordinates
290      LOCATE -INFLATION.RATE+19,5: PRINT USING "##"; INFLATION.RATE
300    NEXT INFLATION.RATE
310    FOR YEAR = 75 TO 90                  'Print X coordinates
320      LOCATE 21,4*YEAR-293: PRINT USING "##"; YEAR
330    NEXT YEAR
340    LOCATE 23,34: PRINT "Y E A R"        'Print X label
350    VIEW(55,28)-(535,148),,1             'Define viewport
360    WINDOW(75,0)-(90,15)                 'Define coordinates
370    FOR YEAR = 75 TO 90                  'Draw
380      LINE(YEAR,1)-(YEAR,0)              'tick marks
390    NEXT YEAR                            'along X axis
400    FOR INFLATION.RATE = 0 TO 15                'Draw
410      LINE(70,INFLATION.RATE)-(70.5,INFLATION.RATE)    'tick marks
420   NEXT INFLATION.RATE                           'along Y axis
430 RETURN
440 REM *** End of set up graph routine
450 '
500 REM *** Plot data routine
510    READ INFLATION.RATE
520    PSET(75,INFLATION.RATE)              'Plot first point
530    FOR YEAR = 76 TO 90
540      READ INFLATION.RATE
550      LINE -(YEAR,INFLATION.RATE)        'Plot remaining points
560    NEXT YEAR
570    REM Inflation rate for READ in 510 and 540
580    DATA 9.1,5.8,6.5,7.7,11.3,13.5,10.4,6.1,3.2,4.2,4.4,2.3,4.4,5.3,4.7,3.5
590 RETURN
600 REM *** End of plot data routine
610 END
```

PROGRAM 14.3   **Drawing a line graph.**

The row numbers for the *Y* coordinates are calculated by a similar formula in line 290. Figure 14.4 shows that we want to print an INFLATION.RATE of 15 in row 4 and an INFLATION.RATE of 14 in row 5. The equation for *a* gives

$$a = \frac{4 - 5}{15 - 14} = \frac{-1}{1} = -1$$

Notice that because INFLATION.RATE increases when the row number decreases, *a* has a negative value. Once we know the value of *a*, it is easy to find *b*. When INFLATION.RATE is 0, we want to print 0 in row 19. Therefore, we can calculate the row number as

$$19 = -1 * 0 + b$$

so that *b* must be 19. You can check these values of *a* and *b* by noticing that when INFLATION.RATE is 15, they give a row number of 4, which Figure 14.4 shows is correct.

Line 240 uses a similar equation to print the *Y* label, INFLATION RATE %. Since we want the row number to increase by 1 when J increases by 1, we use a value of 1 for *a*. To get the first letter to print in row 4, we use a value of 3 for *b*.

DEFINING THE VIEWPORT AND COORDINATES

Now that we have printed the *X* and *Y* coordinates, we must make sure that when we plot the points their positions agree with the coordinates. We do that by defining a viewport and world coordinates to go with it. The VIEW statement is in line 350. You can determine the coordinate values for this statement from the graphics layout form as follows.

The year 75 is printed in columns 7 and 8. We want the viewport to start at the last line in column 7, which is line 55, so in the VIEW statement we make x1 = 55. Similarly, y1 must be 28, which is the middle of row 4. The second set of coordinates is determined in the same way.

Notice that the VIEW statement in line 350 includes a value of 1 for the boundary parameter. This causes the boundary of the viewport to be drawn in color 1, white. The boundary of the viewport serves as the *X* and *Y* axes of the graph.

Once the viewport has been created, you can use a WINDOW statement to define the coordinates to go with it. Specifying the parameters for the WINDOW statement is easy; we want *X* to go from 75 to 90 and *Y* to go from 0 to 15. These values give the WINDOW statement used in line 360. The FOR-NEXT loops in lines 370–390 and 400–420 draw horizontal and vertical tick marks on the axes.

PLOTTING THE DATA

With the viewport and its coordinates defined, BASIC executes the plot data subroutine and draws the graph. Line 510 reads the first inflation rate. Line 520 uses a PSET statement to plot a point with the coordinates (75, INFLATION.RATE).

The FOR-NEXT loop in lines 530 through 560 draws the graph. Line 540 reads the remaining inflation rates, and line 550 draws a line from the last point referenced to the point (YEAR, INFLATION.RATE). The first time this LINE statement executes, the last point referenced is the point plotted by the PSET statement. Every other time the LINE statement executes, the last point referenced is the last point drawn the previous time the LINE statement was executed. In this way, BASIC connects one point on the graph to the next.

Figure 14.5 shows the output produced by Program 14.3.

Drawing a Bar Graph

Sometimes bar graphs are more useful than line graphs. Hy Teck is analyzing sales in the computer industry, and wants a bar graph to show the sales of three major producers. Since a bar graph is most effective in color, we

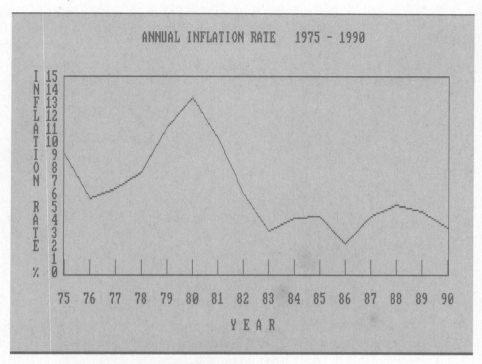

FIGURE 14.5   **Graph produced by Program 14.3.**

will need to use medium-resolution graphics. The graphics layout form is shown in Figure 14.6.*

Following the first step of our procedure, we will use the following variable names:

Input and output variables	A character	CHAR$
	IBM sales	IBM
	Apple sales	APPLE
	Tandy sales	TANDY
Internal variable	Counter variables	J,SALES,YEAR

The algorithm is simply to set up the graph and to draw the bars.

Program 14.4 draws the bar chart. Printing the title, the *X* and *Y* labels and coordinates, and drawing the axes involve techniques that we have already discussed. Line 300 uses hyphens to draw the tick marks on the *Y* axis. Lines 410, 430, and 450 use the LINE statement with the BF parameter to draw the legend as three small boxes, with three different colors.

In this program, the viewport should not coincide with the axes. The year 86 is printed in columns 9 and 10. In order to draw the bars, we need the coordinate of the first line in column 9 to be 86. Therefore, the VIEW and WINDOW statements in line 470 and 480 make the first line in column 9, line 64, the left vertical boundary of the viewport, and make the *X* coordinates start at 86.

Determining the right vertical boundary of the viewport is a little tricky. YEAR 90 is printed in columns 25 and 26, so that the first line in column 25, line 192, must have a coordinate of 90. However, we want to draw

*The data used in this chart were invented and should not be interpreted as giving past or future sales.

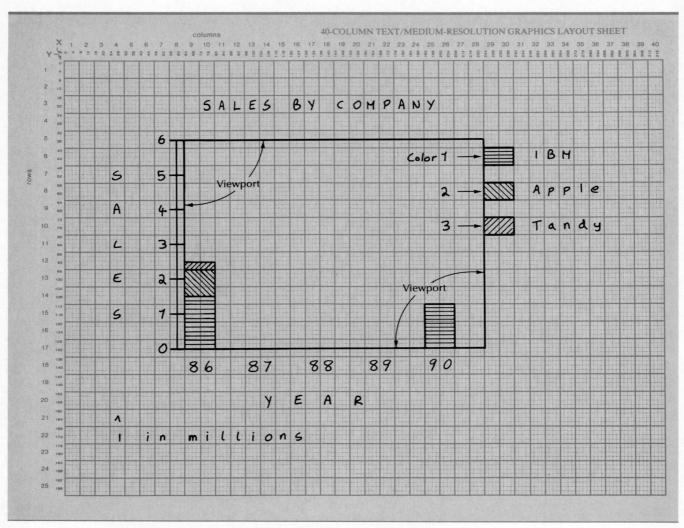

FIGURE 14.6   **Layout of a bar chart of sales.**

the bar for year 90 in columns 25 and 26, that is between lines 192 and 207. If we make the right vertical boundary of the viewport line 192, we won't be able to draw anything beyond line 192. So we have to make the right vertical boundary of the viewport somewhere beyond line 192. How far should we extend it? The easiest thing is to extend it to some line whose coordinates we know. We are using four columns (that is, 32 lines) for each year. The coordinate of line 192 is 90, so the coordinate of line 192 + 32 = 224 is 91. So even though we won't be drawing anything beyond line 207, it is convenient to make the right vertical boundary of the viewport line 224. Then, in the WINDOW statement, we make the maximum *X* coordinate 91.

The bars are drawn in the subroutine that starts in line 600. In a FOR-NEXT loop, the program reads the data for one year and uses three LINE statements with the BF parameter to draw three boxes. The first box, which is drawn by line 630, starts at the point (YEAR, 0) and extends up to the point (YEAR + .5, IBM). Since we are using four columns per year, year 86 occupies columns 9, 10, 11, and 12, using a coordinate of YEAR + .5 draws a box that is two columns wide. The height of the box is determined by the size of IBM's sales. The other two boxes are drawn by lines 640 and 650, starting from

```
100 REM *** DRAWING A BAR CHART ***
110 SCREEN 1,0: CLS: KEY OFF: COLOR 0,1
120 GOSUB 200                       'Set up graph
130 GOSUB 600                       'Plot data
140 A$ = INPUT$(1)                  'Pause
150 STOP
160 '
200 REM *** Set up graph routine
210   LOCATE 3,10: PRINT "SALES BY COMPANY"            'Print title
220   FOR J = 1 TO 5                                   'Print Y label
230     READ CHAR$
240     LOCATE 2*J+5,4: PRINT CHAR$
250   NEXT J
260   REM Data for READ in 230
270   DATA S, A, L, E, S
280   FOR SALES = 0 TO 6                               'Print Y coordinates
290     ROW = -2 * SALES + 17
300     LOCATE ROW,6: PRINT USING "##!"; SALES, "-"
310   NEXT SALES
320   LOCATE 21,4: PRINT "^"
330   LOCATE 22,4: PRINT "| in millions"
340   FOR YEAR = 86 TO 90                              'Print X coordinates
350     COL = 4 * YEAR - 335
360     LOCATE 18,COL: PRINT USING "##"; YEAR
370   NEXT YEAR
380   LOCATE 20,14: PRINT "Y E A R"                    'Print X label
390   LINE(60,30)-(60,132)                             'Draw Y axis
400   LINE(60,132)-(208,132)                           'Draw X axis
410   LINE(223,39)-(239,47),1,BF                       'Draw legend
420   LOCATE 6,32: PRINT "IBM"
430   LINE(223,55)-(239,63),2,BF
440   LOCATE 8,32: PRINT "Apple"
450   LINE(223,71)-(239,79),3,BF
460   LOCATE 10,32: PRINT "Tandy"
470   VIEW(64,36)-(224,132)                            'Define viewport
480   WINDOW(86,0)-(91,6)                              'Define coordinates
490 RETURN
500 REM *** End of set up graph routine
510 '
600 REM *** Plot data routine
610   FOR YEAR = 86 TO 90
620     READ IBM, APPLE, TANDY
630     LINE(YEAR,0)-(YEAR+.5,IBM),1,BF
640     LINE(YEAR,IBM)-(YEAR+.5,IBM+APPLE),2,BF
650     LINE(YEAR,IBM+APPLE)-(YEAR+.5,IBM+APPLE+TANDY),3,BF
660   NEXT YEAR
670   REM Data for READ in 620
680   DATA .2, .3, .28                 :'1986 Sales
690   DATA .58, .70, .38               :'1987 Sales
700   DATA 1.16, 1.05, .55             :'1988 Sales
710   DATA 1.73, 1.38, .81             :'1989 Sales
720   DATA 2.50, 1.79, 1.19            :'1990 Sales
730 RETURN
740 REM *** End of plot data routine
750 END
```

PROGRAM 14.4   **Drawing a bar graph.**

where the previous box ended. The program then repeats the loop until the bars for all the years are drawn.

Figure 14.7 shows the output from Program 14.4.

Drawing a Pie Chart

Finally, let's develop a program to draw a pie chart. The graphic layout form is shown in Figure 14.8. The first segment of the pie chart starts at 3 o'clock, and the segments are plotted counterclockwise, to agree with the way degrees are measured, as we showed in Figure 13.6.

Following the first step of our structured approach to programming, we will use the following variable names:

Input variables	Amount array	AMT
	Name array	LABEL$
	Number of categories	NUMBER
Internal variables	Angular size of wedge	ANGLE
	Color to paint wedge	CLR
	Coordinates for painting	X.PAINT and Y.PAINT
	Ending angle of wedge	END.ANGLE
	Middle angle of wedge	MID.ANGLE
	Percentage array	PERCENT
	Starting angle of wedge	START.ANGLE
	Subscript	J
	Total of amounts	TOTAL

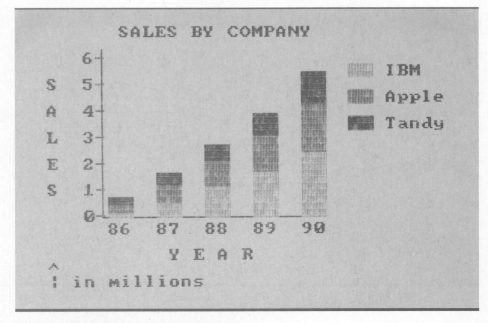

FIGURE 14.7   **Bar chart produced by Program 14.4.**

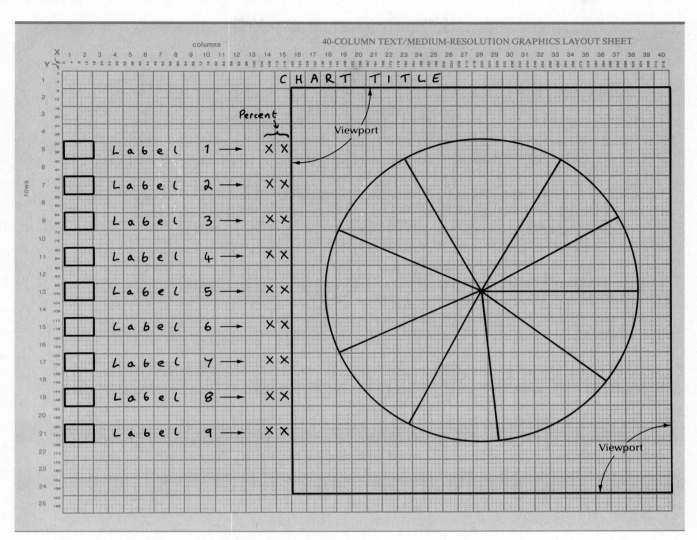

FIGURE 14.8   **Layout of a pie chart.**

The algorithm is

1. Accept data on the number of categories and the size and name of each.
2. Calculate the percentage of the total for each category.
3. Draw the legend.
4. Draw the pie chart.

The logic of this program is simple enough that you do not need a flowchart to understand it.

To make Program 14.5 general, the title, the number of categories, and the amount and name of each category are obtained using INPUT statements in lines 320, 330, and 350. The FOR-NEXT loop in lines 380 through 400 calculates the percentage of the total for each category and stores the answers in the PERCENT array. The routine that starts at line 500 prints the title and the legend. In the legend each category is identified by a box with its color, its name, and its percentage.

```
100 REM *** DRAWING A PIE CHART ***
110 DIM AMT(9), LABEL$(9), PERCENT(9)        'Maximum number of categories is 9
120 SCREEN 0,1: WIDTH 80: CLS                'Text mode to accept data
130 GOSUB 300                                'Accept data and calculate percentage
140 SCREEN 1,0: CLS: COLOR 0,1              'Graphics mode to draw chart
150 GOSUB 500                                'Print title and draw legend
160 GOSUB 700                                'Define viewport and coordinates
170 GOSUB 800                                'Draw pie chart
180 A$ = INPUT$(1)                           'Pause
190 STOP
200 '
300 REM *** Read data and calculate percentages routine
310   TOTAL = 0
320   INPUT "Enter the name of the chart"; CHART.NAME$
330   INPUT "Enter number of categories (< 10)"; NUMBER
340   FOR J = 1 TO NUMBER
350     INPUT "Enter name and value"; LABEL$(J), AMT(J)
360     TOTAL = TOTAL + AMT(J)
370   NEXT J
380   FOR J = 1 TO NUMBER
390     PERCENT(J) = AMT(J) / TOTAL
400   NEXT J
410 RETURN
420 REM *** End of read data and calculate percentages routine
430 '
500 REM *** Print title and draw legend routine
510  LOCATE 1,1: PRINT SPC((40-LEN(CHART.NAME$)) \2);CHART.NAME$ 'Print title
520   FOR J = 1 TO NUMBER                    'Draw legend for each category
540     LINE(0,16*J+15) -STEP(16,8),3,B      'Draw box,
550     CLR = J MOD 4                        'calculate color, and
560     PAINT (8,16*J+19),CLR,3              'paint it
570     LOCATE 2*J+3,4:PRINT USING "\       \ ##"; LABEL$(J), 100 * PERCENT(J)
580   NEXT J
590 RETURN
600 REM *** End of print title and draw legend routine
610 '
700 REM *** Create viewport and establish coordinates routine
710   VIEW(119,8)-(319,191)
720   WINDOW(-1.1,-1.1)-(1.1,1.1)
730 RETURN
740 REM *** End of create viewport and establish coordinates routine
750 '
```

PROGRAM 14.5   **Drawing a pie chart.**

DRAWING THE WEDGES

The routine that defines the viewport and coordinates starts in line 700.
The VIEW statement in line 710 makes that part of the screen that is not
used for the legend or title one large viewport. The WINDOW statement in line
720 establishes a coordinate system in which both *X* and *Y* run from -1.1 to
1.1. These coordinates were chosen so that a circle whose radius is 1 would
fill the viewport. Notice that this choice makes the coordinates of the center
of the viewport $(0, 0)$.

The subroutine starting in line 800 consists primarily of a FOR-NEXT loop
that draws the wedge for each category. In this program, since we don't have
to specify the size of angles directly, it is convenient to work with radians.

```
800 REM *** Draw pie chart routine
810    START.ANGLE = 0                                   'Initialize start angle
820    PI = 3.14159                                      'Constant
830    FOR J = 1 TO NUMBER                               'Draw wedge for each category
840      ANGLE = PERCENT(J) * 2 * PI                     'Size of wedge as % of circle
850      END.ANGLE = ANGLE + START.ANGLE                 'End of wedge
860      MID.ANGLE = (START.ANGLE + END.ANGLE) /2 'Mid is average of start & end
870      CIRCLE(0,0),1,3,-START.ANGLE-.001,-END.ANGLE 'Draw wedge
880      X.PAINT = .5 * COS(MID.ANGLE)                   'Calculate X and
890      Y.PAINT = .901* .5 * SIN(MID.ANGLE)             'Y coordinates for paint
900      CLR = J MOD 4                                   'Calculate color
910      PAINT(X.PAINT,Y.PAINT),CLR,3                    'Paint wedge
920      START.ANGLE = END.ANGLE                         'Start of next wedge
930    NEXT J
940 RETURN
950 REM *** End of routine to draw pie chart
960 END


RUN
Enter the name of the chart? SQUIRREL NUT CO.
Enter number of categories (< 10)? 6
Enter name and value? PEANUTS,47
Enter name and value? WALNUTS,38
Enter name and value? CASHEWS,35
Enter name and value? ALMONDS,26
Enter name and value? PECANS,20
Enter name and value? FILBERTS,16
```

PROGRAM 14.5   **(Continued)**

A circle contains 2 * PI radians, where PI = 3.14159. Therefore, in line 840 we calculate the ANGLE of the wedge for the Jth category by multiplying PERCENT(J) by 2 * PI. For example, if a category accounts for 25 percent of the total, its wedge will be 25 percent of the circle.

Now we know how big the wedge is to be, but to draw it we need to tell BASIC where to start and end the wedge. Wedge 1 will, of course, start at 0 degrees, which is why START.ANGLE is initialized at 0 in line 810. In line 850, we add the ANGLE from line 840 to START.ANGLE to find END.ANGLE. Line 860 calculates the middle angle of the wedge as the average of the starting and ending angles. We will discuss the need for the middle angle shortly.

The CIRCLE statement in line 870 actually draws the wedge. The trigonometric equations we will derive shortly require that the center of the circle be at (0,0). Therefore, in line 870 the center of the circle is coded as (0,0). The wedge goes from START.ANGLE to END.ANGLE, and we outline it by including minus signs in front of both of these angles.*

FINDING A POINT INSIDE THE WEDGE

Next we must paint the wedge, which requires that we start at a point inside the wedge. To find the coordinates of a point inside the wedge, we must use a little trigonometry. If you wish to skip the next paragraph, just use lines 880 and 890 to calculate the coordinates of a point inside a wedge in any pie chart you draw. If you're feeling brave, come along.

---

*Because coding –0 as an angle does not draw a line from the center to the arc, we subtract the small constant, .001, from START.ANGLE.

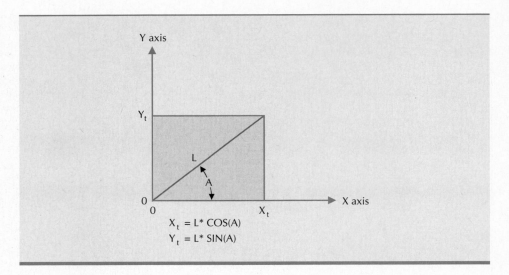

FIGURE 14.9   **Finding the coordinates of the endpoint of a line.**

Figure 14.9 shows that if the coordinates of one end of a line are at $(0,0)$, and if the line is L units long and makes an angle A with the X axis, then the X and Y coordinates of the endpoint of the line are given by the two equations

$$X_t = L \times \cos(A)$$
$$Y_t = L \times \sin(A)$$

These values are called X_t and Y_t because they represent the values calculated by trigonometric equations. Before we can use them in our program, they must be corrected for the aspect ratio of the viewport. The equation we derived earlier in this Chapter gives an aspect ratio of .910 for this viewport. We calculate X.PAINT and Y.PAINT in lines 880 and 890. In these lines, L is set equal to 0.5 and A is set equal to MID.ANGLE. If you recall that the radius of the pie chart is 1, you will realize that these values represent a point in the center of the wedge. X.PAINT is simply set equal to the trigonometric value, but Y.PAINT is calculated by multiplying the trigonometric value by the aspect ratio of the viewport, 0.910. If the aspect ratio were greater than 1, Y.PAINT would be set equal to the trigonometric value, and X.PAINT would be calculated by dividing the trigonometric value by the aspect ratio.

Line 900 calculates the color to paint the wedge. This statement generates colors 1, 2, 3, 0 and then repeats. The PAINT statement in line 910 paints the wedge.

Figure 14.10 shows the output produced by Program 14.5.

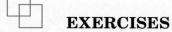

EXERCISES

*14.5 Code the single statement, including its line number, that could be added to Program 14.3 to print tick marks along the right Y axis.

14.6 Suppose we want to draw a graph in which the Y coordinates run from 0 to 9 and are printed in column 16. The Y coordinate of 0 should be printed in

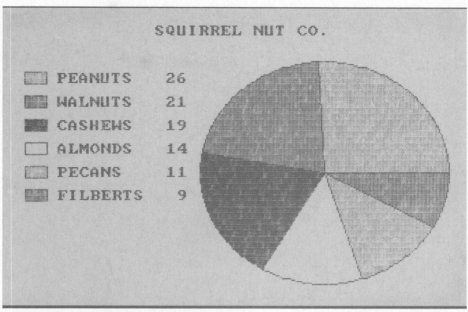

FIGURE 14.10   **Pie chart produced by Program 14.5.**

row 21, the coordinate of 1 in row 19, and so on. Write the statements to print the Y coordinates.

14.7 Suppose we want to draw a graph in which the X axis represents the twelve months. We will print the X coordinates in row 23 and print a J (for January) in column 4, an F in column 7, and so on. Write the statements to print the X coordinates.

14.8 Program 14.3 draws a graph starting in 1975, but the starting value of the FOR statement in line 530 is 76. Explain why.

*14.9 Figure 14.7 would be easier to read if the Y axis tick marks were continued across the graph as a series of dotted horizontal lines. Write the code to draw these dotted lines. (Hint: The PSET statement can be used to draw a dotted line.)

14.10 In Program 14.5, if the number of categories is 5 or 9, then the last category is painted the same color as the first, making it difficult to read the graph. Show how you would change the program to avoid   problem.

PROGRAMMING ASSIGNMENTS

*14.3 Write a program to draw a line graph of the following average monthly precipitation data for Miami:

Month	Jan	Feb	Mar	Apr	May	Jun	Jul	Aug	Sep	Oct	Nov	Dec
Inches	2.2	2.0	2.1	3.6	6.1	9.0	6.9	6.7	8.7	8.2	2.7	1.6

14.4 Modify Program 14.4 to draw the bars next to each other, instead of on top of each other. Make the bars one column wide.

14.5 The data in the table to the right show the profit, in millions of dollars, that Monolith Inc. made from three geographical areas over five years. Write a program to draw a bar graph to display these data.

		Year		
Source of profit	1986	1987	1988	1989	1990
USA	16	18	22	23	26
Europe	6	8	9	10	11
Japan	2	3	6	11	14

14.6 Write a program that draws a pie chart in which, for emphasis, the last wedge is displaced from the center of the chart, as shown in the following figure.

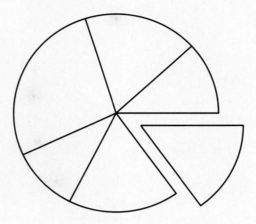

SCREEN ANIMATION

Now that you have learned how to draw figures on the screen, let's discuss how you can move them. To move a figure on the screen, five steps are necessary:

1. Draw the figure.
2. Save the figure.
3. Display the figure.
4. Erase the figure.
5. Display the figure at a new location.

For the first step, you can use any of the graphics commands we have studied, LINE or CIRCLE, for example. For the remaining steps, you must use the GET and PUT statements we will study now. These GET and PUT statements are completely different from the GET and PUT statements used with random files, which were discussed in Chapter 12.

The GET Statement

The GET statement reads the colors of the pixels in a rectangular section of the screen and saves them in a numeric array. The syntax of the GET statement for graphics is

        GET(x1,y1)-(x2,y2),arrayname

where (x1,y1) are the coordinates of one corner of the rectangle and (x2,y2) are the coordinates of the opposite corner. Note that (x1,y1) and (x2,y2) define the same rectangle in the GET statement that they do in the LINE statement with the B parameter. The colors of the pixels inside this rectangle are saved in the array named arrayname. The GET and PUT statements refer to the whole array and are the only statements in which it is legal to code the name of an array without including a subscript.

```
100 REM *** DEMONSTRATING THE GET AND PUT STATEMENTS ***
110 SCREEN 1,0: CLS: KEY OFF: COLOR 0,1
120 DIM SAVE.CIRCLE(33)
130 DELAY = .2                              'Length of pause
140 CIRCLE(10,10),10,2                      'Draw circle
150 PAINT(10,10),1,2                        'Paint it
160 GET(0,0)-(20,20),SAVE.CIRCLE            'Save it
170 A$ = INPUT$(1)                          'Pause
180 PUT(0,0),SAVE.CIRCLE                    'Erase it
190 A$ = INPUT$(1)                          'Pause
200 FOR X = 0 TO 290 STEP 10                'Step across the screen
210   PUT(X,100),SAVE.CIRCLE                'Display circle
220   NOW = TIMER: WHILE TIMER < NOW + DELAY: WEND        'Pause
230   PUT(X,100),SAVE.CIRCLE                'Erase circle
240 NEXT X
250 END
```

PROGRAM 14.6   **Demonstrating the GET and PUT statements.**

Program 14.6 illustrates both the GET and PUT statements. Line 140 draws a circle with a magenta outline. The center of the circle is at (10,10), and the radius of the circle is 10. Line 150 paints the circle cyan. The GET statement in line 160 saves the circle in the array SAVE.CIRCLE. Actually, the GET statement saves a rectangle that includes the circle. The upper left corner is at (0,0), and the lower right corner is at (20,20). Before proceeding, make sure you understand how each of the following GET statements works:

GET Statement

GET(225,10)-(250,20),FIGURE

Effect

Stores the colors of the pixels in the rectangle whose upper left corner is at (225,10) and whose lower right corner is at (250,20) in the array FIGURE.

GET Statement

GET(0,0)-(319,199),SAVE.SCREEN

Effect

Stores the whole screen in the array SAVE.SCREEN.

CALCULATING THE SIZE OF THE ARRAY

Now that you know a bit about the GET statement, let's back up to line 120, where we dimension the SAVE.CIRCLE array we will use in the GET statement. You might wonder how we decided to dimension SAVE.CIRCLE at 33. You can calculate the proper size for the array in a graphics program by using a two-step process. First, calculate the number of bytes needed, using the equation

$$\text{Number of bytes} = 4 + L_y \times \text{INT}((L_x \times B + 7)/8)$$

In this equation, L_x and L_y are the X and Y lengths of the rectangle, and B equals 2 in medium resolution and 1 in high resolution. In the example, L_x

and L_y are both 21 (the rectangle goes from 0 to 20—which is a length of 21, not 20), and B is 2. The equation gives

$$\text{Number of bytes} = 4 + 21 \times \text{INT}((21 * 2 + 7)/8)$$
$$= 4 + 21 \times \text{INT}(49/8)$$
$$= 4 + 21 \times \text{INT}(6.125)$$
$$= 4 + 21 \times 6 = 4 + 126 = 130$$

So 130 bytes are required to store the figure.

Next, find the number of elements required, using the equation

$$\text{Number of elements} = \text{Number of bytes}/F$$

where F equals 2 for integer arrays, 4 for single-precision arrays, and 8 for double-precision arrays. Since SAVE.CIRCLE is a single-precision array, the number of elements required is

$$\text{Number of elements} = 130/4 = 32.5$$

which we rounded up to 33.

The PUT Statement

The INPUT$ statement in line 170 halts execution until you press a key, to give you time to study the screen. When you press a key, BASIC executes the PUT statement in line 180, which erases the circle.

The syntax of the PUT statement is

```
PUT(x,y),arrayname
```

where (x,y) are the coordinates at which the top left corner of the rectangle is to be placed and arrayname is the name of the array that contains the figure. Thus, line 180 of Program 14.6 puts the image stored in SAVE.CIRCLE on the screen with its upper left corner at (0,0). Because this coordinate is the same as the upper left corner of the GET statement that saved the image, the circle is erased. In general, when a figure is PUT on itself, the figure is erased. Line 190 causes another pause so you can see the erasure. Other examples of PUT statements include

PUT Statement
PUT(30,50),STORE

Effect
Puts the image stored in array STORE on the screen with its upper left corner at (30,50).

PUT Statement
PUT(0,0),SAVE.SCREEN

Effect
Puts the image stored in array SAVE.SCREEN on the screen with its upper left corner at (0,0).

After you press a key to satisfy line 190, lines 200–240 will cause the circle to move across the screen. The FOR-NEXT loop displays the circle in line 210 and erases it in line 230. On each pass through the loop, a larger value of X is used in these two PUT statements, so that the circle moves from left to right across the screen. To make the animation realistic, each image must be displayed just long enough for its position to register with the user. Therefore, line 220 causes a pause of DELAY seconds. The best value to use for the duration of the pause depends on the size of the image and the characteristics of the monitor, but it is always small. Notice that in line 130 DELAY is set to only .2, meaning two tenths of a second. There are no rules for calculating the duration of the pause; the best value is found by trial and error. Using a larger step size in line 200 makes the circle move faster; using a smaller step size makes the circle move slower.

Since the rectangle saved by the GET statement in line 160 measures 21 pixels in both the X and Y directions, when we PUT the rectangle, the X coordinate must not be greater than 298, and the Y coordinate must not be greater than 178.

Syntax Summary   GET Statement (for graphics)

Form: `GET(x1,y1)-(x2,y2),arrayname`

Example: `GET(20,20)-(100,30),SAVE.PIC`

Interpretation: Saves the rectangular portion of the screen defined by (x1,y1) and (x2,y2) in the array arrayname.

PUT Statement (for graphics)

Form: `PUT(x,y),arrayname`

Example: `PUT(160,100),SAVE.ARRAY`

Interpretation: Puts the image stored in the array arrayname on the screen, with its top left corner at (x,y).

 Getting the Bugs Out

Problem: During execution, BASIC displays the error message

`Illegal function call in nn`

where nn is the line number of a GET statement.

Reason: Either the array designated to hold the image is too small or the coordinates refer to a point outside the screen.

Solution: Verify that the coordinates are valid. If they are, recalculate the size of the array using the equations in the text. Note: An array that is too large does not cause any difficulty.

Problem: During execution, BASIC displays the error message

`Illegal function call in nn`

where nn is the line number of a PUT statement.

Reason: Part of the figure to be PUT does not fit on the screen.

Solution: Change the coordinates of the PUT statement so that the whole figure fits on the screen.

EXERCISES

*14.11 Modify Program 14.6 to make the circle move down the screen.

14.12 What would happen if the final value in the FOR statement in line 200 in Program 14.6 were changed from 290 to 300?

14.13 Explain why the GET statement requires two sets of coordinates, but the PUT statement requires only one.

14.14 A medium-resolution graphics program contains the statement

GET(0,0)-(40,50),SAVE.FIG

Calculate the number of elements SAVE.FIG needs.

*14.15 Write the GET statement to save a circle, whose center is at (100,100) and whose radius is 50, in the array BIG.CIRCLE. Assuming the program uses medium-resolution graphics, calculate the number of elements BIG.CIRCLE needs.

14.16 Write the PUT statement to display the circle saved in BIG.CIRCLE (see Exercise 14.15) so that the center of the circle is at the center of the screen.

14.17 Program 14.7 shows the execution of a program that is supposed to draw a circle inside a viewport in the center of the screen. Only the viewport was drawn, with no sign of the circle. No error message was displayed. Find and correct the error.

```
100 REM *** DRAWING A CIRCLE IN A VIEWPORT
110 SCREEN 1, 0: CLS : KEY OFF: COLOR 0, 1
120 VIEW (120, 60)-(200, 140), , 1       'Establish viewport
130 WINDOW (-1, -1)-(1, 1)               'Establish coordinates
140 CIRCLE (160, 100), 1, 2              'Draw circle
150 A$ = INPUT$(1)                       'Pause
160 END
```

PROGRAM 14.7   **A program that is supposed to draw a circle inside a viewport.**

PROGRAMMING ASSIGNMENTS

14.7 Write a program to move the arrow drawn in Program 13.3 across the screen.

*14.8 Write a program to move the sailboat shown to the right across the screen. Draw a horizontal line to represent the water surface, and sail the boat on the surface. Instead of using a FOR-NEXT loop, like the one in Program 14.6, sail the boat using a GO-TO loop, but code an INKEY$ statement to allow the player to reverse the direction of sail by pressing an R.

14.9 Write a program to move Tom's delivery truck, which is drawn in Programming Assignment 13.13,

across the screen. Draw a horizontal line to represent a highway and drive the truck on the highway.

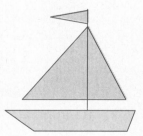

SUMMARY

In this chapter you have learned that
- The VIEW statement defines a viewport.
- The WINDOW statement creates a coordinate system chosen by the user.

- Animation requires that a figure be displayed, that it be erased, and that it then be displayed at a new location.
- The GET statement saves a figure on the screen in an array.
- The PUT statement displays a previously saved figure.

KEY TERMS IN THIS CHAPTER

viewport 430   world coordinates 423

QUESTIONS FOR REVIEW

14.1 True or false: If the array named in a GET statement is too small for the specified rectangle, only part of the rectangle is saved.

14.2 The WINDOW statement establishes the (physical/world) coordinate system.

14.3 Describe the viewport created by the statement

    VIEW(160,100)-(319,199)

14.4 How can a user abolish a coordinate system established by a WINDOW statement?

14.5 True or false: If a figure is PUT upon itself, it is erased.

14.6 True or false: If a VIEW statement is coded without the boundary parameter, the boundary is drawn in the foreground color.

14.7 What is the most likely cause of the error if, during execution, BASIC displays the error message Illegal function call for a line that contains a PUT statement? What is the most likely cause of the error if the message refers to a line that contains a GET statement?

ADDITIONAL PROGRAMMING PROBLEMS

14.10 Cheap Skates Inc. had the following annual sales (in millions of dollars). Write a program to draw a line graph of these data.

Year	1981	1982	1983	1984	1985
Sales	6.9	6.3	5.8	4.9	4.2

Year	1986	1987	1988	1989	1990
Sales	5.3	7.4	7.7	8.3	8.6

*14.11 The following data show the percent of families in the Kingdom of Serendip with incomes in the specified ranges for the years 1970, 1980, and 1990.

Family income	1970	1980	1990
Above $25,000	18.9	37.5	39.3
$15,000–$25,000	33.4	31.0	27.7
$0–$15,000	47.7	31.4	33.1

Write a program that will draw a bar graph to display these data.

14.12 Modify Program 9.2 to perform 5 trials of 30 coin tosses each and plot a bar graph of the number of heads and the number of tails in each trial. (Hint: Store the number of heads and tails in each trial in an array.)

14.13 Write a program to "pass" a football from one goal post to the other on the football field you drew in Programming Assignment 13.19. You can draw an acceptable football using a CIRCLE statement with a radius of 16 and an aspect ratio of 0.4. Your program will be more impressive if the ball follows a long arc rather than a straight line. A reasonable arc is a semicircle with an aspect ratio of 0.4. To calculate X and Y coordinates, you can adapt the technique used in Program 14.5 to calculate X.PAINT and Y.PAINT.

14.14 Bézier curves are widely used in computer graphics. A Bézier curve is described by four points, the coordinates of which we can write as (x_1, y_1),

(x_2, y_2), (x_3, y_3), and (x_4, y_4). The points on the Bézier curve are calculated using the following equations:

$$x(t) = (1 - t)^3 x_1 + 3t(1 - t)^2 x_2$$
$$+ 3t^2(1 - t)x_3 + t^3 x_4$$
$$y(t) = (1 - t)^3 y_1 + 3t(1 - t)^2 y_2$$
$$+ 3t^2(1 - t)y_3 + t^3 y_4$$

In these equations, t is a parameter that goes from 0 to 1. As these equations show, the Bézier curve goes through only the first (x_1, y_1) and last (x_4, y_4) points. The figure will be more interesting if, in addition to the Bézier curve, you draw straight lines between (x_1, y_1) and (x_2, y_2) and between (x_3, y_3) and (x_4, y_4). Write a program that allows a user to enter the coordinates of four points and draws the Beizer curve described by them. Since you cannot know what values the user will enter for the coordinates of the four points, your program will have to determine the minimum and maximum values of x and y and establish a coordinate system for a viewport that accommodates these values. One set of data that gives an interesting figure is $(0,0)$, $(4,2)$, $(-2,-2)$, and $(2,0)$.

14.15 The following is a common problem: Given a set of data points (x_i, y_i), $i = 1, 2, \ldots, n$, find the equa- tion of the straight line that best represents these data. The equation of the straight line is

$$y = mx + b$$

where m and b are calculated by the equations

$$m = \frac{\sum y_i x_i - \left(\sum y_i\right)\left(\sum x_i\right) \Big/ n}{\sum x_i^2 - \left(\sum x_i\right)^2 \Big/ n}$$

and

$$b = \frac{\left(\sum y_i - m \sum x_i\right)}{n}$$

Write a program that accepts n followed by n data points and calculates m and b. Plot the data points and the line. Since you cannot know the range of values of the data, your program will have to determine the minimum and maximum values of x and y and establish a coordinate system for a viewport that accommodates these values. It is not necessary to label the graph with the X and Y coordinates.

BEYOND THE BASICS

14.1 Write a program that draws two Pac-Man–like faces, one with its mouth open, like the one in Program 13.6, and one with its mouth closed. Move these two faces across the screen, displaying first one and then the other face, so that the face looks as though it is eating as it moves. (Hint: The anima- tion will be more effective if the faces are about half the size of the face in Program 13.6.)

14.2 When characters are displayed by a PRINT statement, they may be placed only at a specified row and column. However, if characters are displayed by a PRINT statement and then saved by a GET statement, a subsequent PUT statement can place them any- where on the screen. To save a character with a GET statement, you should know that characters are dis- played in a square that is 8 pixels on each side. Use this technique to draw and label the pitcher shown to the right on a medium-resolution screen. The pitcher should be 41 pixels wide by 69 pixels high.

14.3 Write a program to draw the birthday cake shown to the right. You should ask the user's age and dis- play the appropriate number of candles. You should then ask the user to blow out the candles, and after a short delay the program should erase the flames.

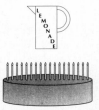

14.4 Write a program that accepts a time, in hours and minutes, and then draws a clock face, like the one shown below, displaying that time. To get the num- bers displayed correctly, you will have to use a PUT statement, as explained in Beyond the Basics 14.2.

14.5 Demonstrate your mastery of BASIC by creating the design shown below. (Hint: Display the message and GET it. Then reverse the direction of the Y coor- dinate and PUT the message.)

I AM A BASIC EXPERT
I AM A BASIC EXPERT

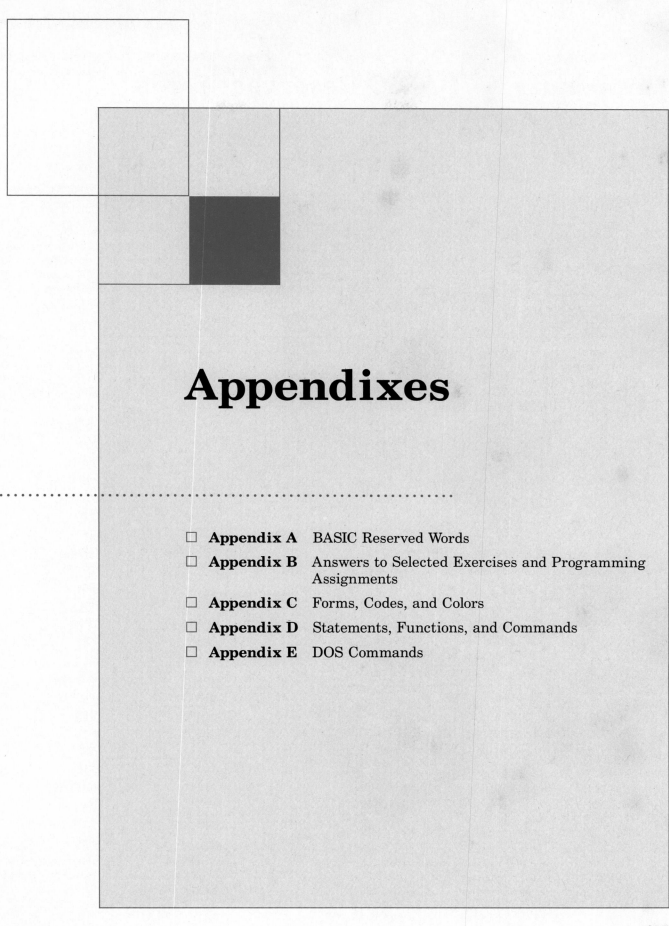

Appendixes

Appendix A   BASIC Reserved Words

Certain words have special meaning to BASIC. These words are called *reserved words*. Reserved words include all BASIC commands, statements, function names, and operator names. Reserved words cannot be used as variable names. You should always separate reserved words from data or other parts of a BASIC statement by using spaces or other special characters as allowed by the syntax. The following table lists all of the reserved words in BASIC.

ABS	DEF	GOSUB	LPOS	POS	STICK
AND	DEFDBL	GOTO	LPRINT	PRESET	STOP
ASC	DEFINT	HEX$	LSET	PRINT	STR$
ATN	DEFSNG	IF	MERGE	PRINT#	STRIG
AUTO	DEFSTR	IMP	MID$	PSET	STRING$
BEEP	DELETE	INKEY$	MKDIR	PUT	SWAP
BLOAD	DIM	INP	MKD$	RANDOMIZE	SYSTEM
BSAVE	DRAW	INPUT	MKI$	READ	TAB(
CALL	EDIT	INPUT#	MKS$	REM	TAN
CDBL	ELSE	INPUT$	MOD	RENUM	THEN
CHAIN	END	INSTR	MOTOR	RESET	TIME$
CHDIR	ENVIRON	INT	NAME	RESTORE	TIMER
CHR$	ENVIRON$	INTER$	NEW	RESUME	TO
CINT	EOF	IOCTL	NEXT	RETURN	TROFF
CIRCLE	EQV	IOCTL$	NOT	RIGHT$	TRON
CLEAR	ERASE	KEY	OCT$	RMDIR	USING
CLOSE	ERDEV	KEY$	OFF	RND	USR
CLS	ERDEV$	KILL	ON	RSET	VAL
COLOR	ERL	LEFT$	OPEN	RUN	VARPTR
COM	ERR	LEN	OPTION	SAVE	VARPTR$
COMMON	ERROR	LET	OR	SCREEN	VIEW
CONT	EXP	LINE	OUT	SGN	WAIT
COS	FIELD	LIST	PAINT	SHELL	WEND
CSNG	FILES	LLIST	PEEK	SIN	WHILE
CSRLIN	FIX	LOAD	PEN	SOUND	WIDTH
CVD	FNxxxxxxxx	LOC	PLAY	SPACE	WINDOW
CVI	FOR	LOCATE	PMAP	SPC(	WRITE
CVS	FRE	LOF	POINT	SQR	WRITE#
DATA	GET	LOG	POKE	STEP	XOR
DATE$					

Appendix B   Answers to Selected Exercises and Programming Assignments

CHAPTER 2 EXERCISES

2.1 d) Illegal; a name may not contain a hyphen.

    e) Illegal; AUTO is a reserved word.

2.2 a) Illegal; a numeric constant may not contain a $.

    b) Legal.

2.3 a) Incorrect; remove comma: B = 6500.

    c) Correct.

2.4 c) B will be 9.

2.7 The program is incorrect. To correct it, interchange lines 30 and 40.

2.12 The output will be the same: 156.25.

2.14 The output will be: 6 8 14 -2

2.17 A syntax error can be corrected by retyping the line. The cause of a logic error can be discovered by tracing the program. The logic error can then be corrected by retyping the line.

CHAPTER 2 PROGRAMMING ASSIGNMENTS

```
10 REM *** PROGRAMMING ASSIGNMENT 2.2 ***
20 USUAL.PRICE = 19.98
30 DISCOUNT = .2 * USUAL.PRICE
40 SALE.PRICE = USUAL.PRICE - DISCOUNT
50 PRINT SALE.PRICE
60 END
```

```
10 REM *** PROGRAMMING ASSIGNMENT 2.5 ***
20 PRICE.YEN = 30000
30 PRICE.DOLLARS = PRICE.YEN / 131.46
40 PRINT PRICE.DOLLARS
50 END
```

```
10 REM *** PROGRAMMING ASSIGNMENT 2.8 ***
20 REM WIDTH is a BASIC reserved word, so we use WDTH instead
30 WDTH = 4
40 LENGTH = 5.3
50 AREA = WDTH * LENGTH
60 COST = 18 * AREA
70 PRINT COST
80 END
```

```
10 REM *** PROGRAMMING ASSIGNMENT 2.10 ***
20 OATMEAL.PER.HOUR = .25
30 BRAIN = 1456
40 HOURS.WATCHED = 250
50 TOTAL.OATMEAL = OATMEAL.PER.HOUR * HOURS.WATCHED
60 PERCENTAGE.OATMEAL = TOTAL.OATMEAL / BRAIN * 100
70 PRINT PERCENTAGE.OATMEAL
80 END
```

CHAPTER 3 EXERCISES

3.2 INPUT "Enter three test scores"; TEST1, TEST2, TEST3

3.3 a) No output is produced.

    c) Only the first line of output will be produced.

    e) The first line of output will be repeated forever.

3.7 b) Legal.

    e) Illegal; COLOR is a reserved word.

3.8 SIGNER$ = "Button Gwinnett"

3.9 b) Add a dollar sign at the end of the data name: ZIP.CODE$ = "10050", or remove the quotation marks.
  d) Add quotation marks around ROSE.
3.13 AUTO 100, 20

CHAPTER 3 PROGRAMMING ASSIGNMENTS

```
10 REM *** PROGRAMMING ASSIGNMENT 3.1 ***
20 INPUT "Enter usual price"; USUAL.PRICE
30    DISCOUNT = .2 * USUAL.PRICE
40    SALE.PRICE = USUAL.PRICE - DISCOUNT
50    PRINT USUAL.PRICE, SALE.PRICE
60 GOTO 20
70 END
```

```
10 REM *** PROGRAMMING ASSIGNMENT 3.5 ***
20 INPUT "Enter the hours watched"; HOURS.WATCHED
30    OATMEAL.HOUR = .25
40    BRAIN = 1456
50    TOTAL.OATMEAL = OATMEAL.HOUR * HOURS.WATCHED
60    PERCENTAGE.OATMEAL = TOTAL.OATMEAL / BRAIN * 100
70    PRINT PERCENTAGE.OATMEAL
80 GOTO 20
90 END
```

```
10 REM *** PROGRAMMING ASSIGNMENT 3.6 ***
20 INPUT "Enter usual price, 0 to stop"; USUAL.PRICE
30    IF USUAL.PRICE = 0
         THEN GOTO 80
40    DISCOUNT = .2 * USUAL.PRICE
50    SALE.PRICE = USUAL.PRICE - DISCOUNT
60    PRINT USUAL.PRICE, SALE.PRICE
70 GOTO 20
80 END
```

```
10 REM *** PROGRAMMING ASSIGNMENT 3.10 ***
20 INPUT "Enter the hours watched, 0 to stop"; HOURS.WATCHED
30    IF HOURS.WATCHED = 0
         THEN GOTO 100
40    OATMEAL.HOUR = .25
50    BRAIN = 1456
60    TOTAL.OATMEAL = OATMEAL.HOUR * HOURS.WATCHED
70    PERCENTAGE.OATMEAL = TOTAL.OATMEAL / BRAIN * 100
80    PRINT PERCENTAGE.OATMEAL
90 GOTO 20
100 END
```

```
10 REM *** PROGRAMMING ASSIGNMENT 3.11 ***
20 INPUT "Enter name and usual price, XXX to stop"; ITEM.NAME$, USUAL.PRICE
30    IF ITEM.NAME$ = "XXX"
         THEN GOTO 80
40    DISCOUNT = .2 * USUAL.PRICE
50    SALE.PRICE = USUAL.PRICE - DISCOUNT
60    PRINT ITEM.NAME$, USUAL.PRICE, SALE.PRICE
70 GOTO 20
80 END
```

```
10 REM *** PROGRAMMING ASSIGNMENT 3.13 ***
20 INPUT "Enter name and price, 0 to stop"; ITEM.NAME$, PRICE.YEN
30    IF PRICE.YEN = 0
         THEN GOTO 70
40    PRICE.DOLLARS = PRICE.YEN / 131.46
50    PRINT ITEM.NAME$, PRICE.YEN, PRICE.DOLLARS
60 GOTO 20
70 END
```

```
10 REM *** PROGRAMMING ASSIGNMENT 3.17 ***
20 INPUT "Enter name, years smoking and packs per day, XXX to stop";
         SMOKERS.NAME$, YEARS, PACKS.PER.DAY
30    IF SMOKERS.NAME$ = "XXX"
         THEN GOTO 100
40    CIG.SMOKED = PACKS.PER.DAY * 20 * 365 * YEARS
50    MINUTES.LOST = 14 * CIG.SMOKED
60    MINUTES.IN.A.DAY =  60 * 24
70    DAYS.LOST = MINUTES.LOST / MINUTES.IN.A.DAY
80    PRINT SMOKERS.NAME$, YEARS, PACKS.PER.DAY, DAYS.LOST
90 GOTO 20
100 END
```

CHAPTER 4 EXERCISES

4.1 c) An asterisk is missing between the 5 and the (.

d) The expression contains one too many left parentheses. A right parenthesis must be added, but where it should be added cannot be determined.

4.2 c) A = 14 / 4 = 3.5

d) A = 2 + 36 / 9 + 1 = 7

4.3 a) A = 3

c) A = 4

4.4 c) $T = D * ((1 + R)^{\wedge} N - 1)/R$

4.8 PRINT "   BOOKS BORROWED"
PRINT "Author", "Title"

4.12 It will delete all the lines from 70 to the end of the program.

CHAPTER 4 PROGRAMMING ASSIGNMENTS

```
10 REM *** PROGRAMMING ASSIGNMENT 4.2 ***
20 INPUT "Enter year, 0 to stop"; YEAR
30    IF YEAR = 0
         THEN GOTO 70
40    TEMP = 72 + .08 * (YEAR - 1990)
50    LPRINT YEAR, TEMP
60 GOTO 20
70 END

10 REM  *** PROGRAMMING ASSIGNMENT 4.6 ***
20 INPUT "Enter last year's and current prices, 0 to stop"; LAST.YEAR, CURRENT
30    IF LAST.YEAR = 0
         THEN GOTO 80
40    PERCENT.CHANGE = (CURRENT - LAST.YEAR) / LAST.YEAR * 100
50    NEXT.YEAR = CURRENT * (1 + PERCENT.CHANGE / 100)
60    LPRINT LAST.YEAR, CURRENT, PERCENT.CHANGE, NEXT.YEAR
70 GOTO 20
80 END

10 REM *** PROGRAMMING ASSIGNMENT 4.9 ***
20 INPUT "Enter number of feet, 0 to end"; FEET
30    IF FEET = 0
         THEN GOTO 90
40    CASSETTES = FEET \ 275
50    LEFT.OVER = FEET MOD 275
70    PRINT FEET, CASSETTES, LEFT.OVER
80 GOTO 20
90 END
```

```
10 REM *** PROGRAMMING ASSIGNMENT 4.11 ***
20 INPUT "Enter first name, XXX to stop "; FIRST.NAME$
30    IF FIRST.NAME$ = "XXX"
         THEN GOTO 70
40    PRINT "Good Morning, "; FIRST.NAME$
50    PRINT "Have a good day"
60 GOTO 20
70 END
```

```
10 REM  *** PROGRAMMING ASSIGNMENT 4.12 ***
20 LPRINT,,"PAYROLL REPORT"
30 LPRINT "Name   "; "Pay Rate "; "Hours "; "Gross Pay "; "Withholding ";
          "Soc. Sec "; "Net Pay"
40 INPUT "Enter employee name, pay rate, hours worked, XXX to stop";
          EMPLOYEE.NAME$, PAY.RATE, HOURS.WORKED
50    IF EMPLOYEE.NAME$ = "XXX"
         THEN GOTO 130
60    GROSS.PAY = PAY.RATE * HOURS.WORKED
70    WITHHOLDING = .18 * GROSS.PAY
80    SOCIAL.SECURITY = .08 * GROSS.PAY
90    MEDICAL = 15
100   NET.PAY = GROSS.PAY - (WITHHOLDING + SOCIAL.SECURITY + MEDICAL)
110   LPRINT EMPLOYEE.NAME$; PAY.RATE; HOURS.WORKED; GROSS.PAY; WITHHOLDING;
             SOCIAL.SECURITY; NET.PAY
120 GOTO 40
130 END
```

```
10 REM  *** PROGRAMMING ASSIGNMENT 4.16 ***
20 PRINT "Face", "Coupon", "No. Years", "Yield", "Price"
30 INPUT "Enter face value, coupon, years to maturity, and yield, 0 to stop ";
          FACE, COUPON, NO.YEARS, YIELD
40    IF FACE = 0
         THEN GOTO 100
50    V = (1 + YIELD) ^ (-NO.YEARS)
60    A = (1 - V) / YIELD
70    PRICE = FACE * V + COUPON * A
80    PRINT FACE, COUPON, NO.YEARS, YIELD, PRICE
90 GOTO 30
100 END
```

```
10 REM  *** PROGRAMMING ASSIGNMENT 4.18 ***
20 PRINT "Side 1", "Side 2", "Side 3", "Area"
30 INPUT "Enter three sides of a triangle, 0 to stop "; A, B, C
40    IF A = 0
         THEN GOTO 90
50    S = (A + B + C) / 2
60    AREA = (S * (S - A) * (S - B) * (S - C)) ^ .5
70    PRINT A, B, C, AREA
80 GOTO 30
90 END
```

```
10 REM *** PROGRAMMING ASSIGNMENT 4.21 A ***
20 LPRINT "First Term", "Difference", "No. of Terms", "Sum"
30 INPUT "Enter first term, difference, and number of terms, 0 to stop";
          A, D, N
40    IF A = 0
         THEN GOTO 80
50    SUM = N * (2 * A + (N - 1) * D) / 2
60    LPRINT A, D, N, SUM
70 GOTO 30
80 END
```

```
10 REM *** PROGRAMMING ASSIGNMENT 4.21 B ***
20 LPRINT "First Term", "Ratio", "No. of Terms", "Sum"
30 INPUT "Enter first term, ratio, and number of terms, 0 to stop"; A, R, N
40   IF A = 0
        THEN GOTO 80
50   SUM = A * (R ^ N - 1) / (R - 1)
60   LPRINT A, R, N, SUM
70 GOTO 30
80 END
```

CHAPTER 5 EXERCISES

5.1 b) False

5.2 IF A > B
        THEN PRINT "A is greater"
        ELSE PRINT "A is not greater"

5.5 IF YEAR MOD 4 = 0
        THEN PRINT "Election Year"

5.6 a) False.
    d) True.

5.7 30 REM Start of case structure
    40 IF WPM > 60
        THEN PRINT "Excellent": GOTO 70
    50 IF WPM >= 40 AND WPM <= 60
        THEN PRINT "Good": GOTO 70
    60 IF WPM < 40
        THEN PRINT "Weak": GOTO 70
    70 REM End of case structure

5.15 130 REM Start of case structure
    140 If DAY$ = "SUN"
        THEN PRINT "SUNDAY": GOTO 220
    150 IF DAY$ = "MON"
        THEN PRINT "MONDAY": GOTO 220
    160 IF DAY$ = "TUE"
        THEN PRINT "TUESDAY": GOTO 220
    170 IF DAY$ = "WED"
        THEN PRINT "WEDNESDAY": GOTO 220
    180 IF DAY$ = "THU"
        THEN PRINT "THURSDAY": GOTO 220
    190 IF DAY$ = "FRI"
        THEN PRINT "FRIDAY": GOTO 220
    200 IF DAY$ = "SAT"
        THEN PRINT "SATURDAY": GOTO 220
    210 BEEP: PRINT "You entered an incorrect abbreviation": GOTO 120
    220 REM End of case structure

5.19 No. The GOSUB statement requires a line number, not a name.

5.21 520 RETURN

CHAPTER 5 PROGRAMMING ASSIGNMENTS

```
10 REM  *** PROGRAMMING ASSIGNMENT 5.3 ***
20 LPRINT "Name", "Test 1", "Test 2", "Test 3", "Average", "Status"
30 INPUT "Enter student name and three test marks, XXX to stop ";
         STUDENT$,TEST1,TEST2,TEST3
40   IF STUDENT$ = "XXX"
        THEN GOTO 90
50   AVERAGE = (TEST1 + TEST2 + TEST3) / 3
60   IF AVERAGE < 60
        THEN STATUS$ = "failing"
        ELSE STATUS$ = "passing"
70   LPRINT STUDENT$, TEST1, TEST2, TEST3, AVERAGE, STATUS$
80 GOTO 30
90 END
```

```
10 REM   *** PROGRAMMING ASSIGNMENT 5.5 ***
20 LPRINT "Membership", "Bill"
30 INPUT "Enter length of membership in months, 0 to stop "; MEMBERSHIP
40   IF MEMBERSHIP = 0
        THEN GOTO 80
50   IF MEMBERSHIP <= 12
        THEN BILL = MEMBERSHIP * 20
        ELSE BILL = MEMBERSHIP * 15
60   LPRINT MEMBERSHIP, BILL
70 GOTO 30
80 END

10 REM   *** PROGRAMMING ASSIGNMENT 5.8 ***
20 LPRINT "        SKI BILLS"
30 LPRINT "No. Days", "Bill"
40 INPUT "Enter Number of Days Skis Rented, 0 to stop "; NO.DAYS
50   IF NO.DAYS = 0
        THEN GOTO 90
60   IF NO.DAYS <= 2
        THEN BILL = NO.DAYS * 15
        ELSE BILL = .8 * NO.DAYS * 15
70   LPRINT NO.DAYS, BILL
80 GOTO 40
90 END


10 REM *** PROGRAMMING ASSIGNMENT 5.10 ***
20 LPRINT "    ELECTRIC BILLS"
30 LPRINT "KW Used", "Bill"
40 INPUT "Enter kilowatts of electricity used, 0 to stop"; KW
50   IF KW = 0
        THEN GOTO 130
60   REM Start of case structure
70   IF KW <= 12
        THEN BILL = 2.8: GOTO 100
80   IF KW > 12 AND KW <= 90
        THEN BILL = 2.8 + .08 * (KW - 12): GOTO 100
90   IF KW > 90
        THEN BILL = 2.8 + .08 * 78 + .1 * (KW - 90): GOTO 100
100    REM End of case structure
110    LPRINT KW, BILL
120 GOTO 40
130 END

100 REM   *** PROGRAMMING ASSIGNMENT 5.15 ***
110 LPRINT "Area", "Duration", "Bill"
120 INPUT "Enter area (A, B, C, or D) and duration, Q to quit"; AREA$, MINUTES
130    IF AREA$ = "Q"
          THEN GOTO 240
140    REM Start of case structure
150    IF AREA$ = "A"
          THEN  COST.FIRST =.087: COST.OVER = 0: GOTO 200
160    IF AREA$ = "B"
          THEN  COST.FIRST = .106: COST.OVER = .029: GOTO 200
170    IF AREA$ = "C"
          THEN  COST.FIRST = .144: COST.OVER = .048: GOTO 200
180    IF AREA$ = "D"
          THEN  COST.FIRST = .183: COST.OVER = .058: GOTO 200
190    BEEP: PRINT "Incorrect zone": GOTO 110
200    REM End of case structure
210    BILL = COST.FIRST +  COST.OVER * (MINUTES - 1)
220    LPRINT AREA$, MINUTES, BILL
230 GOTO 120
240 END
```

```
100 REM *** PROGRAMMING ASSIGNMENT 5.17 ***
110 INPUT "Enter year, 0 to stop "; YEAR
120    IF YEAR = 0
          THEN GOTO 150
130    IF YEAR MOD 100 = 0
          THEN GOSUB 200
          ELSE GOSUB 300
140 GOTO 110
150 STOP
160 '
200 REM *** Check century year subroutine
210    IF YEAR MOD 400 = 0
          THEN PRINT YEAR "is a leap year"
          ELSE PRINT YEAR "is not a leap year"
220    RETURN
230 REM *** End check century year subroutine
240 '
300 REM *** Check regular year subroutine
310    IF YEAR MOD 4 = 0
          THEN PRINT YEAR "is a leap year"
          ELSE PRINT YEAR "is not a leap year"
320    RETURN
330 REM *** End check regular year subroutine
340 END



10 REM *** PROGRAMMING ASSIGNMENT 5.22 ***
20 LPRINT "Name", "Rate ", " Hours", "Gross Pay", "Withholding", "Net Pay"
30 INPUT "Enter employee name, pay rate, and hours worked, Stop to end";
          EMP.NAME$, PAY.RATE, HOURS.WORKED
40    IF EMP.NAME$ = "Stop"
         THEN GOTO 100
50    GROSS.PAY = PAY.RATE * HOURS.WORKED
60    IF GROSS.PAY < 200
         THEN WITHHOLDING = GROSS.PAY * .1
         ELSE WITHHOLDING = GROSS.PAY * .2
70    NET.PAY = GROSS.PAY - WITHHOLDING
80    LPRINT EMP.NAME$, PAY.RATE, HOURS.WORKED, GROSS.PAY, WITHHOLDING, NET.PAY
90 GOTO 30
100 END



100 REM *** PROGRAMMING ASSIGNMENT 5.24 ***
110 LPRINT "  MPG", "Tax"
120 INPUT "Input miles per gallon, 0 to stop "; MILEAGE
130    IF MILEAGE = 0
          THEN GOTO 220
140 REM *** Determine tax routine
150    IF MILEAGE >= 21
          THEN TAX = 0: GOTO 190
160    IF MILEAGE >= 14
          THEN TAX = 500: GOTO 190
170    IF MILEAGE >= 10
          THEN TAX = 1000: GOTO 190
180    IF MILEAGE < 10
          THEN TAX = 2500: GOTO 190
190 REM End of case structure
200    LPRINT MILEAGE, TAX
210 GOTO 120
220 END
```

```
100 REM *** PROGRAMMING ASSIGNMENT 5.29 ***
110 INPUT "Enter channel number, 0 to stop"; CHANNEL
120    IF CHANNEL = 0
          THEN GOTO 250
130    REM Start of case structure
140    IF CHANNEL = 2
          THEN STATION$ = "WCBS": GOTO 220
150    IF CHANNEL = 4
          THEN STATION$ = "WNBC": GOTO 220
160    IF CHANNEL = 5
          THEN STATION$ = "WNYW": GOTO 220
170    IF CHANNEL = 7
          THEN STATION$ = "WABC": GOTO 220
180    IF CHANNEL = 9
          THEN STATION$ = "WWOR": GOTO 220
190    IF CHANNEL = 11
          THEN STATION$ = "WPIX": GOTO 220
200    IF CHANNEL = 13
          THEN STATION$ = "WNET": GOTO 220
210    BEEP: PRINT "Valid channels are 2, 4, 5, 7, 9, 11, and 13": GOTO 110
220    REM End of case structure
230    PRINT "Channel"; CHANNEL; "is station "; STATION$
240 GOTO 110
250 END
```

CHAPTER 6 EXERCISES

6.1 a) READ RUNNER$, DASH.TIME
     b) DATA Huey, 9.8
        DATA Louie, 9.2
        DATA Dewey, 9.7

6.7 Peachsbbbbbbb$b1.35 (b = blank space)

6.10 PRICE.FMT$ = "Sticker price ......$##,###.##"

6.13 LOCATE 20, 10
      PRINT "How many tickets please"

6.15 SCREEN 0, 1
      COLOR 1, 14

6.17 GO$ = INKEY$

CHAPTER 6 PROGRAMMING ASSIGNMENTS

```
100 REM *** PROGRAMMING ASSIGNMENT 6.2 ***
110 LPRINT "Student Name", "Test 1", "Test 2", "Test 3", "Average", "Status"
120 GOSUB 200                                        'Input subroutine
130    AVERAGE = (TEST1 + TEST2 + TEST3) / 3
140    IF AVERAGE < 60
          THEN STATUS$ = "Failing"
          ELSE STATUS$ = "Passing"
150    LPRINT STUDENT$, TEST1, TEST2, TEST3, AVERAGE, STATUS$
160 GOTO 120
170 PRINT "Normal end of program"
180 STOP
190 '
200 REM *** Input subroutine
210    READ STUDENT$
220    IF STUDENT$ = "XXX"
          THEN RETURN 170
230    PRINT "Enter three test grades for "; STUDENT$;
240    INPUT TEST1, TEST2, TEST3
250    RETURN
260 REM *** End of input subroutine
270 '
300 REM *** Data for input subroutine
310    DATA Mary Contrary
320    DATA Willie Winkie
330    DATA Jack Sprat
340    DATA XXX                          :REM Trailer data
350 REM *** End of data for input subroutine
360 END
```

```
10 REM   *** PROGRAMMING ASSIGNMENT 6.3 ***
20 PRINT "Membership", "Bill"
30 READ MEMBERSHIP
40   IF MEMBERSHIP = 0
       THEN GOTO 100
50   IF MEMBERSHIP <= 12
       THEN BILL = MEMBERSHIP * 20
       ELSE BILL = MEMBERSHIP * 15
60   PRINT MEMBERSHIP, BILL
70 GOTO 30
80 DATA 10, 20
90 DATA 0                              :REM Trailer data
100 END


10 REM *** PROGRAMMING ASSIGNMENT 6.7 ***
20 PRINT TAB(10); "*********"
30 PRINT TAB(10); "*"; SPC(7);"*"
40 PRINT TAB(10); "*"; SPC(7);"*"
50 PRINT TAB(10); "*"; SPC(7);"*"
60 PRINT TAB(10); "*"; SPC(7);"*"
70 PRINT TAB(10); "*********"
80 END


100 REM   *** PROGRAMMING ASSIGNMENT 6.10 ***
110 LPRINT "Area     Duration     Bill"
120 FMT$ = "   !          ##         #.##"
130 SCREEN 0,1: COLOR 7,1: CLS: KEY OFF
140 LOCATE 8,29
150 PRINT "TELEPHONE BILLS PROGRAM"
160 LOCATE 9,29
170 PRINT "========================="
180 GOSUB 300                                   'Input, verify zone
190   GOSUB 700                                 'Determine rates
200   BILL = COST.FIRST +  COST.OVER * (MINUTES - 1)
210   LPRINT USING FMT$; AREA$, MINUTES, BILL
220 GOTO 180
230 STOP
240 '
300 REM *** Input Routines =====================================================
310   LOCATE 12,26
320   PRINT "Enter call area (A, B, C, or D, Q to quit) ";
330   AREA$ = INPUT$(1)
340   IF AREA$ = "Q"
        THEN RETURN 230
350   IF AREA$ = "A" OR AREA$ = "B" OR AREA$ = "C" OR AREA$ = "D"
        THEN PRINT AREA$: GOSUB 600
        ELSE GOSUB 500: GOTO 310
360   LOCATE 13,26
370   INPUT "Enter the call's duration"; MINUTES
380   LOCATE 12,1
390   PRINT SPACE$(160)
400 RETURN
410 REM *** End input zone subroutine
420 '
500 REM *** Error message subroutine
510   BEEP
520   LOCATE 25,25
530   COLOR 16,7
540   PRINT "Inapplicable zone code: retry";
550   COLOR 7,1
560 RETURN
570 REM *** End error message subroutine
580 '
600 REM *** Routine to erase error message
610   LOCATE 25,25
620   PRINT SPACE$(30);
```

```
630 RETURN
640 REM *** End of routine to erase error message
650 '
700 REM *** Routine to determine rates ========================================
710    IF AREA$ = "A"
          THEN  COST.FIRST = .087: COST.OVER = 0: GOTO 750
720    IF AREA$ = "B"
          THEN  COST.FIRST = .106: COST.OVER = .029: GOTO 750
730    IF AREA$ = "C"
          THEN  COST.FIRST = .144: COST.OVER = .048: GOTO 750
740    IF AREA$ = "D"
          THEN  COST.FIRST = .183: COST.OVER = .058: GOTO 750
750    RETURN
760 REM *** End determine rates routine
770 END
```

CHAPTER 7 EXERCISES

7.3 TOTAL.AREA = TOTAL.AREA + AREA

7.5 The salespersons' names contain commas, and therefore must be enclosed in quotation marks. Since FINISHED does not contain a comma, it does not have to be enclosed in quotation marks.

7.8 HELLO will not be printed by this program. To print it once, change line 20 to
```
   20 WHILE A = 10
```
or
```
   20 WHILE A < 11
```

7.10 The output will be: 4 8 16 32 64

7.12 The subtotal for department 57 would not be printed.

7.13 a) Line number 80 will be executed.
      b) Line number 30 will be executed.
      c) The next line will be executed.

7.17 This statement prints a heart.

7.20 Simple Simon is wrong, because CHR$ is enclosed in quotation marks and BASIC considers it part of the string, rather than an execution of the CHR$ function.

CHAPTER 7 PROGRAMMING ASSIGNMENTS

```
100 REM *** PROGRAMMING ASSIGNMENT 7.2 ***
102 TOTAL.REGULAR.PAY = 0
104 TOTAL.OVERTIME.PAY = 0
106 TOTAL.GROSS.PAY = 0
110 LPRINT "Name", "Rate", "Hours", "Regular Pay", "Overtime Pay", "Gross Pay"
120 GOSUB 300                          'Obtain input
130    IF HOURS > 40
          THEN GOSUB 500
          ELSE GOSUB 600
140    GROSS.PAY = REGULAR.PAY + OVERTIME.PAY
142    TOTAL.REGULAR.PAY = TOTAL.REGULAR.PAY + REGULAR.PAY
144    TOTAL.OVERTIME.PAY = TOTAL.OVERTIME.PAY + OVERTIME.PAY
146    TOTAL.GROSS.PAY = TOTAL.GROSS.PAY + GROSS.PAY
150    LPRINT EMP.NAME$, PAY.RATE, HOURS, REGULAR.PAY, OVERTIME.PAY, GROSS.PAY
160 GOTO 120
170 LPRINT "Totals",,,TOTAL.REGULAR.PAY, TOTAL.OVERTIME.PAY, TOTAL.GROSS.PAY
175 PRINT "Normal end of program"
180 STOP
190 '
300 REM *** Input Routine
310    READ EMP.NAME$, PAY.RATE
320    IF EMP.NAME$ = "Stop"
          THEN RETURN 170
330    PRINT "Enter hours for employee "; EMP.NAME$;
340    INPUT HOURS
350 RETURN
360 REM *** End of input routine
370 '
```

```
500 REM *** Overtime pay routine
510    REGULAR.PAY = PAY.RATE * 40
520    OVERTIME.PAY = 1.5 * PAY.RATE * (HOURS - 40)
530 RETURN
540 REM *** End of overtime pay routine
550 '
600 REM *** Regular pay routine
610    REGULAR.PAY = PAY.RATE * HOURS
620    OVERTIME.PAY = 0
630 RETURN
640 REM *** End of regular pay routine
650 '
700 REM *** Data used by input routine
710 DATA Joe Tinker, 6.75
720 DATA John Evers, 6.00
730 DATA Frank Chance, 5.75          : REM Trailer data
740 DATA Stop, 0
750 END


100 REM *** PROGRAMMING ASSIGNMENT 7.7 ***
110 HIGHEST.SALES = 0
115 LOWEST.SALES = 100000!
120 READ SALES.NAME$, SALES
130    IF SALES.NAME$ = "FINISHED"
          THEN GOTO 170                    'Check for trailer data
140    IF SALES > HIGHEST.SALES
          THEN HIGHEST.SALES = SALES       'Search for highest sales
150    IF SALES < LOWEST.SALES
          THEN LOWEST.SALES = SALES        'Search for lowest sales
160 GOTO 120
170 PRINT "Highest Sales", HIGHEST.SALES, "Lowest Sales", LOWEST.SALES
180 REM *** DATA
190    DATA "Hart, M", 300
200    DATA "Lee, G.R.", 700
210    DATA "Rand, S.", 200
220    DATA FINISHED, 0
230 REM *** END DATA
240 END


100 REM *** PROGRAMMING ASSIGNMENT 7.11 ***
110 TOTAL = 100000!
120 COUNTER = 0
130    WHILE TOTAL > 0
140       TOTAL = TOTAL + (TOTAL * .08) - 15000
150       COUNTER = COUNTER + 1
160    WEND
170 PRINT COUNTER, TOTAL
180 END


100 REM *** PROGRAMMING ASSIGNMENT 7.13 ***
110 PRINT "Earnings of -1 ends computation"     'Trailer data warning
120 GOSUB 300                                   'Perform initiation
130 WHILE EARNINGS >= 0                          'Execute loop until trailer
140    GOSUB 600                                'Process data
150    INPUT "Enter client name and earnings "; CLIENT$, EARNINGS
160 WEND
170 GOSUB 700                                   'Print subtotal for last client
180 LPRINT USING CLIENT.TOTAL.FORMAT$; GRAND.TOTAL, OVERALL.AVERAGE
190 STOP
200 '
300 REM *** Initialization Procedures ==========================================
310 '
320 REM *** Initialize accumulators
330    CLIENT.TOTAL = 0
340    GRAND.TOTAL = 0
350    COUNTER = 0
360    COUNTER.TOTAL = 0
```

```
370     GOSUB 500                                           'Print headings
380     INPUT "Enter client name and earnings "; CLIENT$, EARNINGS
390     PREVIOUS.CLIENT$ = CLIENT$                          'Initialize PREVIOUS.CLIENT
400 RETURN
410 REM *** End of accumulator initialization
420 '
500 REM *** Headings and formats subroutine
510     LPRINT TAB(32); "EARNINGS BY CLIENT"
520     LPRINT
530     LPRINT
540     LPRINT TAB(3); "Client Name"; TAB(30); "Earnings"; TAB(64); "Average"
545     LPRINT
550     DETAIL.LINE.FORMAT$ = "  \                    \              #,###
560     CLIENT.TOTAL.FORMAT$ = "              Total Earnings    #,###
Average Earnings  #,###.## "
570 RETURN
580 REM *** End headings and formats
585 '
600 REM *** Data Processing Routines ===========================================
610 '
620 REM *** Process 1 set data
630     IF CLIENT$ = PREVIOUS.CLIENT$
            THEN GOTO 640
            ELSE GOSUB 700                                  'Control break
640     CLIENT.TOTAL = CLIENT.TOTAL + EARNINGS
650     COUNTER = COUNTER + 1
660     LPRINT USING DETAIL.LINE.FORMAT$; CLIENT$, EARNINGS
670 RETURN
680 REM *** End 1 set of data processing
690 '
700 REM *** Control break routine
710     CLIENT.AVERAGE = CLIENT.TOTAL/COUNTER
720     COUNTER.TOTAL = COUNTER.TOTAL + COUNTER
730     GRAND.TOTAL = GRAND.TOTAL + CLIENT.TOTAL
735     OVERALL.AVERAGE = GRAND.TOTAL/COUNTER.TOTAL
740     LPRINT
750     LPRINT USING CLIENT.TOTAL.FORMAT$; CLIENT.TOTAL, CLIENT.AVERAGE
760     LPRINT
770     REM *** Get ready for new client
780         CLIENT.TOTAL = 0
790         PREVIOUS.CLIENT$ = CLIENT$
800         COUNTER = 0
810 RETURN
820 REM *** End control break
830 END

100 REM *** PROGRAMMING ASSIGNMENT 7.15 ***
110 CLS : KEY OFF
120 GOSUB 400                      'Display menu
125 TOTAL.BILL = 0                 'Initialize TOTAL.BILL for first customer
130 LOCATE 17, 16, 1
140 PRINT "Enter Code Number of Customer's Bill ";
150     CODE$ = INPUT$(1)
160     PRINT CODE$
170     CODE = VAL(CODE$)
180     ON CODE GOTO 210, 230, 250, 270, 290, 310, 330, 352, 360
190     GOSUB 700                              'Error routine
200     GOTO 130
210     BILL = 1.25
220     GOTO 340
230     BILL = .9
240     GOTO 340
250     BILL = 1
260     GOTO 340
270     BILL = 2
280     GOTO 340
290     BILL = 2.15
```

```
300     GOTO 340
310     BILL = 1.75
320     GOTO 340
330     BILL = 2.95
340     LPRINT USING " Code  #    Bill   ##.##"; CODE; BILL
342     TOTAL.BILL = TOTAL.BILL + BILL
350 GOTO 130
352     REM Print total bill for a customer
354     LPRINT USING " Total bill is  $###.##"; TOTAL.BILL
355     LPRINT                           'Print a blank line between bills
356     TOTAL.BILL = 0                   'Initialize TOTAL.BILL for next customer
358 GOTO 130
360 STOP
370 '
400 REM  *** Start of subroutine to display menu
410     LOCATE 2, 25
420     PRINT "WELCOME TO NO BUM STEER"
430     LOCATE 4, 16
440     PRINT "Enter the number that corresponds to order"
450     LOCATE 6, 17
460     PRINT "Code    Order                         Price"
470     LOCATE 7, 17
480     PRINT "  1      Hamburger                    1.25"
490     LOCATE 8, 17
500     PRINT "  2      Fries                         .90"
510     LOCATE 9, 17
520     PRINT "  3      Shake                        1.00"
530     LOCATE 10, 17
540     PRINT "  4      Hamburger and Fries          2.00"
550     LOCATE 11, 17
560     PRINT "  5      Hamburger and Shake          2.15"
570     LOCATE 12, 17
580     PRINT "  6      Fries and Shake              1.75"
590     LOCATE 13, 17
600     PRINT "  7      Hamburger, Fries, and Shake  2.95"
610     LOCATE 14, 17
620     PRINT "  8      To print total bill for customer"
622     LOCATE 15, 17
624     PRINT "  9         To quit"
630 RETURN
640 REM *** End of routine to display menu
650 '
700 REM *** Start of error routine
710     BEEP
720     LOCATE 17, 16
730     PRINT "Enter a value between 1 and 8 please"
740 RETURN
750 REM *** End of Error Routine
760 END


100 REM  *** PROGRAMMING ASSIGNMENT 7.21 ***
110 INPUT "Enter growth rate, 0 to stop "; RATE
120    IF RATE = 0
          THEN GOTO 220
130    POP = 3.5E+09
140    YEAR = 0
150    WHILE POP < 6E+09
160       YEAR = YEAR + 1
170       GROWTH  = RATE * POP
180       POP = POP + GROWTH
190    WEND
200    PRINT "When the growth rate is "; RATE; "it takes ";YEAR;
             "years for the population to grow to "; POP
210 GOTO 110
220 END
```

CHAPTER 8 EXERCISES

8.1 The output would not be changed if lines 120 and 130 were interchanged. The output would be changed if lines 160 and 170 were interchanged.

8.5 a) NEXT I
b) 2 5 8
c) 3 5 7 9

8.8 The program shown does not work. To fix it, delete line 30.

8.9 The program is incorrect as written. To correct it, interchange lines 50 and 60. The corrected program prints 4 5 6 5 6 7 6 7 8

CHAPTER 8 PROGRAMMING ASSIGNMENTS

```
100 REM *** PROGRAMMING ASSIGNMENT 8.3 ***
110 INPUT "Enter initial population and growth rate, 0 to end";
          INITIAL.POPULATION, INITIAL.RATE
120    IF INITIAL.POPULATION = 0
          THEN GOTO 240
130    POPULATION = INITIAL.POPULATION
140    RATE = INITIAL.RATE
150    PRINT       "Year        Growth         Population"
160    FORMAT$ = "  ##         #,###          ###,###"
170    FOR YEAR = 1 TO 5
180      GROWTH = RATE * POPULATION
190      POPULATION = POPULATION + GROWTH
200      RATE = 1.05 * RATE
210      PRINT USING FORMAT$; YEAR, GROWTH, POPULATION
220    NEXT YEAR
230 GOTO 110
240 END


100 REM *** PROGRAMMING ASSIGNMENT 8.10 ***
110 INPUT "Enter a number between 1 and 30, 0 to stop"; NUMBER
120    IF NUMBER = 0
          THEN GOTO 190
130    FACTORIAL = 1
140    FOR K = 1 TO NUMBER
150      FACTORIAL = FACTORIAL * K
160    NEXT K
170    PRINT NUMBER; "factorial is"; FACTORIAL
180 GOTO 110
190 END


100 REM *** PROGRAMMING ASSIGNMENT 8.14 ***
110 PRINT "                    EARTHQUAKE DAMAGE"
120 PRINT "                 Intensity on Richter Scale"
130 PRINT "Distance      4        5        6        7        8"
140 FOR DISTANCE = 5 TO 20 STEP 5
150   PRINT USING "   ##        "; DISTANCE;
160   FOR RICHTER = 4 TO 8
170     DAMAGE = .8 * RICHTER ^ 3 / DISTANCE ^ 2
180     PRINT USING "##.##    "; DAMAGE;
190   NEXT RICHTER
200   PRINT
210 NEXT DISTANCE
220 END


100 REM *** PROGRAMMING ASSIGNMENT 8.16 ***
110 FOR FEET = 1 TO 300
120    IF FEET MOD 5 = 4 AND FEET MOD 6 = 5 AND FEET MOD 7 = 6
          THEN PRINT "The number of feet to walk is "; FEET: GOTO 140
130 NEXT FEET
140 END
```

```
100 REM *** PROGRAMMING ASSIGNMENT 8.19 ***
110 FOR COCONUTS = 1 TO 100
120    PILE = COCONUTS
130    FOR SAILOR = 1 TO 3
140      ' Calculate the number left after the pile is divided in thirds
150      LEFT = PILE MOD 3
160      ' If the number left is not 1, go on to the next number of coconuts
170      ' If the number left is 1, calculate the size of the pile after the
180      ' sailor takes his share and gives one to the monkey.
190      IF LEFT <> 1
             THEN GOTO 250
             ELSE PILE = PILE - PILE \ 3 - 1
200    NEXT SAILOR
210    ' Calculate the number left in the morning, when pile is again divided
220    LEFT = PILE MOD 3
230    ' If number left is again 1, we have found a solution
240    IF LEFT = 1
          THEN PRINT USING "The original number of coconuts was ####"; COCONUTS:
               GOTO 260
250 NEXT COCONUTS
260 END
```

```
100 REM *** PROGRAMMING ASSIGNMENT 8.22 ***
110 INPUT "Enter an integer, 0 to stop"; N
120    IF N = 0
          THEN GOTO 200
130    SUM = 0
140    IF N MOD 2 = 0
             THEN START = 2
             ELSE START = 1
150    FOR J = START TO N STEP 2
160      SUM = SUM + J
170    NEXT J
180    PRINT SUM
190 GOTO 110
200 END
```

CHAPTER 9 EXERCISES

9.1   c) 17
      e) 17
      g) 6

9.4   b) N = 1 + INT(7 * RND)

9.7   Add line 195:
      195 IF ABS(GUESS – NUMBER) <= 5
            THEN PRINT "You are getting close"

9.9   The average value printed is 50.

9.14 Change line 50 to read
      50 FOR J = L TO 1 STEP -1

9.16 b) SI
      e) FORMATION
      h) ON

9.17 c) TED

9.18 b) 8
      e) 5

9.20 b) OUTLOOK

9.24 In line 320, POSITION will be set to 0, since purple does not occur in TEXT$,
      the WHILE loop will not be executed, and in line 390 all of TEXT$ will be
      assigned to NEW.TEXT$.

9.26 Two different letters in ENGLISH$ would be translated into the same letter
      in CODE$. If that happened CODE$ could not be decoded.

9.28 Just extend ALPHA$ and TRANS$ to include the lower case letters.

9.29 The value printed is .8888889

CHAPTER 9 PROGRAMMING ASSIGNMENTS

```
100 REM *** PROGRAMMING ASSIGNMENT 9.1 A ***
110 CLS: KEY OFF
120 RANDOMIZE TIMER
130 COUNTER = 0
140 FOR PROBLEM = 1 TO 10
150    NUMBER1 = 1 + INT(10 * RND)
160    NUMBER2 = 1 + INT(10 * RND)
170    ANSWER = NUMBER1 + NUMBER2
180    PRINT "WHAT IS THE SUM OF"; NUMBER1; "and"; NUMBER2;
190    INPUT GUESS
200    IF GUESS = ANSWER
          THEN PRINT "THAT'S RIGHT": COUNTER = COUNTER + 1
          ELSE PRINT "SORRY, THE CORRECT ANSWER IS"; ANSWER
210 NEXT PROBLEM
220 PRINT "OUT OF 10 PROBLEMS, YOU GOT"; COUNTER; "RIGHT"
230 END
```

```
100 REM *** PROGRAMMING ASSIGNMENT 9.1 B ***
110 CLS: KEY OFF
120 RANDOMIZE TIMER
130 COUNTER = 0
140 FOR PROBLEM = 1 TO 10
150    NUMBER1 = 1 + INT(10 * RND)
160    NUMBER2 = 1 + INT(10 * RND)
170    ANSWER = NUMBER1 + NUMBER2
180    TIME1 = TIMER
190    PRINT "WHAT IS THE SUM OF"; NUMBER1; "and"; NUMBER2;
200    INPUT GUESS
210    TIME2 = TIMER
220    IF GUESS = ANSWER
          THEN GOSUB 300
          ELSE PRINT "SORRY, THE CORRECT ANSWER IS"; ANSWER
230 NEXT PROBLEM
240 PRINT "OUT OF 10 PROBLEMS, YOU GOT"; COUNTER; "RIGHT"
250 STOP
260 '
300 REM *** Correct answer was given, calculate elapsed time routine
310    ELAPSED.TIME = TIME2 - TIME1
320    PRINT USING "THAT'S RIGHT IN ## SECONDS"; ELAPSED.TIME
330    COUNTER = COUNTER + 1
340 RETURN
350 REM *** End of correct answer was given routine
360 END
```

```
100 REM *** PROGRAMMING ASSIGNMENT 9.7 ***
110 RANDOMIZE TIMER
120 TOTAL.TRAVEL = 0
130 PREVIOUS.POSITION = 1 + INT(40 * RND)
140 FOR CASE = 1 TO 100
150    POSITION = 1 + INT(40 * RND)
160    TRAVEL = ABS(POSITION - PREVIOUS.POSITION)
170    TOTAL.TRAVEL = TOTAL.TRAVEL + TRAVEL
180    PREVIOUS.POSITION = POSITION
190 NEXT CASE
200 PRINT USING "Average arm motion is ##.# tracks"; TOTAL.TRAVEL / 100
210 END
```

```
100 REM *** PROGRAMMING ASSIGNMENT 9.10 ***
110 KEY OFF: CLS
120 RANDOMIZE TIMER
130 MONEY = 10000
140 GOSUB 300                             'Get initial investment
150 WHILE MONEY > 0 AND INVEST <> 0
160   X = RND
170   IF X < .5
         THEN MONEY = MONEY - INVEST:
              PRINT "You lost your investment": GOTO 210
180   IF X < .9
         THEN MONEY = (MONEY - INVEST) + 2 * INVEST:
              PRINT "Good work, you just doubled your investment": GOTO 210
190   MONEY = (MONEY - INVEST) + 10 * INVEST
200   PRINT "Congratulations, your investment multiplied by 10"
210   IF MONEY <> 0
         THEN GOSUB 300                   'If any money is left, get next investment
220 WEND
230 REM Find out why we left loop, and print appropriate message
240 IF INVEST = 0
       THEN PRINT USING "You finished with $#,###,### "; MONEY
       ELSE PRINT "Sorry, you are bankrupt.  Better luck next time."
250 STOP
300 REM *** Input subroutine
310   PRINT USING "You have $#,###,###. How much do you want to invest ";MONEY
320   PRINT "(Enter 0 to stop the game)";
330   INPUT INVEST
340   IF INVEST > MONEY
         THEN PRINT "That's more than you have.  I'll invest all your money":
              INVEST = MONEY
350 RETURN
360 END
```

```
100 REM *** PROGRAMMING ASSIGNMENT 9.14 ***
110 INPUT "Enter a word with up to 11 letters"; WORD$
120 CLS: KEY OFF
130 FOR J = 1 TO LEN(WORD$)
140   LETTER$ = MID$(WORD$,J,1)
150   LOCATE 2 * J - 1, 40
160   PRINT LETTER$
170 NEXT J
180 END
```

```
100 REM *** PROGRAMMING ASSIGNMENT 9.17 ***
110 INPUT "Enter a stock price (0 to end)"; PRICE$
120   IF PRICE$ = "0"
         THEN GOTO 170
130   SLASH.POSITION = INSTR(PRICE$,"/")
140   IF SLASH.POSITION = 0
         THEN PRICE = VAL(PRICE$)
         ELSE GOSUB 200
150   PRINT USING "The price & is equal to ###.##"; PRICE$, PRICE
160 GOTO 110
170 STOP
180 '
200 REM *** Routine to extract fractional part of price
210   NUMERATOR$ = MID$(PRICE$,SLASH.POSITION-1,1)
220   DENOMINATOR$ = MID$(PRICE$,SLASH.POSITION+1,1)
230   DOLLAR.PRICE$ = LEFT$(PRICE$,SLASH.POSITION-2)
240   NUMERATOR = VAL(NUMERATOR$)
250   DENOMINATOR = VAL(DENOMINATOR$)
260   DOLLAR.PRICE = VAL(DOLLAR.PRICE$)
270   PRICE = DOLLAR.PRICE + NUMERATOR / DENOMINATOR
280 RETURN
290 REM *** End of routine to extract fractional part of price
300 END
```

```
100 REM *** PROGRAMMING ASSIGNMENT 9.19 ***
110 INPUT "Enter a string (press Enter to end)"; TEXT$
120    IF TEXT$ = ""
          THEN GOTO 240
130    BACKWARD$ = ""
140    TEXT$ = TEXT$ + " "                    'Add a blank at the end for last word
150    LENGTH = LEN(TEXT$)
160    START = 1                              'Start at first character
170    WHILE START < LENGTH                   'Examine whole string
180      J = INSTR(START,TEXT$," ")           'Find end of word
190      GOSUB 300                            'Reverse word
200      START = J + 1                        'Point to start of next word
210    WEND
220    PRINT "Backward string "; BACKWARD$
230 GOTO 110
240 STOP
250 '
300 REM *** Routine to reverse a word
310    BACKWARD.WORD$ = ""
320    FOR K = J - 1 TO START STEP -1
330      BACKWARD.WORD$ = BACKWARD.WORD$ + MID$(TEXT$,K,1)
340    NEXT K
350    BACKWARD$ = BACKWARD$ + BACKWARD.WORD$ + " "
360 RETURN
370 REM *** End of routine to reverse word
380 END

100 REM *** PROGRAMMING ASSIGNMENT 9.21 ***
110 READ TEXT$
120    IF TEXT$ = "XXX"
          THEN GOTO 160
130    GOSUB 200
140    PRINT TEXT$
150 GOTO 110
160 STOP
200 REM *** Routine to replace asterisks
210    POSITION = INSTR(TEXT$,"*")
220    WHILE POSITION <> 0
230      MID$(TEXT$,POSITION,1) = " "
240      POSITION = INSTR(TEXT$,"*")
250    WEND
260 RETURN
270 REM *** End of routine to replace asterisks
300 REM *** Data used in program
310 DATA "Of*all*the*gin*joints*in*all*the*towns*in*the*world,"
320 DATA "she*has*to*walk*into*mine."
330 DATA "XXX"
340 END

100 REM *** PROGRAMMING ASSIGNMENT 9.23 ***
110 INPUT "Enter the number to be checked (0 to end)"; NUMBER$
120    IF NUMBER$ = "0"
          THEN GOTO 260
130    CHECK.DIGIT.IN = VAL(RIGHT$(NUMBER$,1))
140    TOTAL.PRODUCT = 0
150    FOR J = 1 TO 5
160      IF J MOD 2 = 0
            THEN WEIGHT = 1
            ELSE WEIGHT = 2
170      DIGIT$ = MID$(NUMBER$,J,1)
180      DIGIT = VAL(DIGIT$)
190      PRODUCT = WEIGHT * DIGIT
200      TOTAL.PRODUCT = TOTAL.PRODUCT + PRODUCT
210    NEXT J
220    REMAINDER = TOTAL.PRODUCT MOD 10
230    IF REMAINDER = 0
          THEN CHECK.DIGIT = 0
          ELSE CHECK.DIGIT = 10 - REMAINDER
```

```
240    IF CHECK.DIGIT = CHECK.DIGIT.IN
           THEN PRINT NUMBER$; " is a valid number"
           ELSE PRINT NUMBER$; " is not a valid number"
250 GOTO 110
260 END
```

```
100 REM *** PROGRAMMING ASSIGNMENT 9.24 ***
110 RANDOMIZE TIMER
120 LENGTH = 10
130 DEPTH = 3
140 SPLASH = 0: SAFE = 0
150 FOR ATTEMPT = 1 TO 100
160    IF ATTEMPT MOD 10 = 0
           THEN PRINT USING "We are on the ###th attempt"; ATTEMPT
170    POSITION = 0: SIDEWAYS = 0
180    REM We exit from WHILE loop either when she makes it across or falls in
190    WHILE POSITION < LENGTH AND ABS(SIDEWAYS) <= DEPTH
200       POSITION = POSITION + 1
210       X = RND
220       IF X < .5
              THEN SIDEWAYS = SIDEWAYS + 1
              ELSE SIDEWAYS = SIDEWAYS - 1
230    WEND
240    REM Find out why we exited from the WHILE LOOP
250    IF POSITION = LENGTH
           THEN SAFE = SAFE + 1
           ELSE SPLASH = SPLASH + 1
260 NEXT ATTEMPT
270 PRINT USING "She fell into the water ### times and was safe ### times";
                 SPLASH, SAFE
280 END
```

```
100 REM *** PROGRAMMING ASSIGNMENT 9.28 ***
110 INPUT "Enter a number (0 to end)"; NUMBER$
120    IF NUMBER$ = "0"
           THEN GOTO 280
130    NUMBER$ = " " + NUMBER$          'Add a leading blank to make input
                                         number compatible with numbers
                                         derived from STR$ function in line 240
140    SOS = 0                          'SOS is sum of squares
150    WHILE NOT (SOS = 4 OR SOS = 1)
160       SOS = 0
170       LENGTH = LEN(NUMBER$)
180       FOR J = 2 TO LENGTH
190          DIGIT$ = MID$(NUMBER$,J,1)
200          DIGIT = VAL(DIGIT$)
210          SOS = SOS + DIGIT ^ 2
220       NEXT J
230       PRINT SOS;
240       NUMBER$ = STR$(SOS)
250    WEND
260    PRINT
270 GOTO 110
280 END
```

```
100 REM *** PROGRAMMING ASSIGNMENT 9.31 B ***
110 INPUT "Enter English message, press Enter to stop"; ENGLISH$
120    IF ENGLISH$ = ""
           THEN GOTO 210
130    CODE$ = ""
140    LENGTH = LEN(ENGLISH$)
150    HALF = LENGTH \ 2 + LENGTH MOD 2
160    FOR J = 1 TO HALF
170       CODE$ = CODE$ + MID$(ENGLISH$,J,1) + MID$(ENGLISH$,J+HALF,1)
180    NEXT J
190    PRINT "Encoded message: "CODE$
200 GOTO 110
210 END
```

CHAPTER 10 EXERCISES

10.5 a) −6

b) 18

c) This statement generates a negative subscript, and will cause an Illegal function call error.

10.7 The output produced is 5 9 2 4 6

10.10 Simple Simon is wrong because the input value is used as a subscript (in line 220, for example), and subscripts must be numeric variables.

10.14 a) The numbers would be printed in the order that they were entered.

b) The program would execute an endless loop.

c) The program would correctly sort the input numbers.

10.16 The following statement swap A(K) and A(K + 1)

```
TEMP = A(K)
A(K) = A(K+1)
A(K+1) = TEMP
```

10.19 Add the following statement

```
435  IF ENGLISH$(J) > WORD$
        THEN GOTO 450
```

10.20 In game 1 player 4 scored 136, and in game 4 player 1 scored 191.

10.22 The average score for the first game would be 34.0, and for the second game it would be 35.3.

10.25 Cookie number 2 contains 4 chips.

CHAPTER 10 PROGRAMMING ASSIGNMENTS

```
100 REM *** PROGRAMMING ASSIGNMENT 10.3 ***
110 DIM VALUE(100)
120 INPUT "Enter the number of numbers you will enter"; N
130 FOR J = 1 TO N                              'Input loop
140    INPUT "Enter a number"; VALUE(J)
150 NEXT J
160 FOR J = N TO 1 STEP -1                      'Output loop
170    PRINT VALUE(J);
180 NEXT J
190 END


100 REM *** PROGRAMMING ASSIGNMENT 10.8 ***
110 DIM COUNTER(26)
120 GOSUB 300                                   'Initialize COUNTER
130 ALPHA$ = "ABCDEFGHIJKLMNOPQRSTUVWXYZ"
140 READ TEXT$                                  'Read a line of text
150    IF TEXT$ = "XXX"
          THEN GOTO 230                         'If finished, print results
160    L = LEN(TEXT$)
170    FOR J = 1 TO L                           'For every character in text
180       CHAR$ = MID$(TEXT$,J,1)               'Extract the character
190       N = INSTR(ALPHA$,CHAR$)               'See if it is a letter
200       IF N <> 0
             THEN COUNTER(N) = COUNTER(N) + 1   'If it is, count it
210    NEXT J
220 GOTO 140
230 ' PRINT RESULTS
240 FOR J = 1 TO 26
250    L$ = MID$(ALPHA$,J,1)
260    LPRINT USING "  ! ### "; L$, COUNTER(J)
270 NEXT J
280 STOP
290 '
300 REM *** Initialization routine
310    FOR J = 1 TO 26
320       COUNTER(J) = 0
330    NEXT J
340 RETURN
350 REM *** End of initialization routine
360 '
```

```
1010 DATA "FOURSCORE AND SEVEN YEARS AGO OUR FATHERS BROUGHT
1020 DATA "FORTH ON THIS CONTINENT A NEW NATION, CONCEIVED IN LIBERTY,
1030 DATA "AND DEDICATED TO THE PROPOSITION THAT ALL MEN ARE CREATED
1040 DATA "EQUAL.  NOW WE ARE ENGAGED IN A GREAT CIVIL WAR, TESTING
1050 DATA "WHETHER THAT NATION, OR ANY NATION SO CONCEIVED AND SO
1060 DATA "DEDICATED, CAN LONG ENDURE.  WE ARE MET ON A GREAT BATTLE-
1070 DATA "FIELD OF THAT WAR.  WE HAVE COME TO DEDICATE A PORTION OF
1080 DATA "THAT FIELD, AS A FINAL RESTING PLACE FOR THOSE WHO HERE GAVE
1090 DATA "THEIR LIVES THAT THAT NATION MIGHT LIVE.  IT IS ALTOGETHER
1100 DATA "FITTING AND PROPER THAT WE SHOULD DO THIS.  BUT, IN A LARGER
1110 DATA "SENSE, WE CANNOT DEDICATE - WE CANNOT CONSECRATE - WE
1120 DATA "CANNOT HALLOW - THIS GROUND.  THE BRAVE MEN, LIVING AND
1130 DATA "DEAD, WHO STRUGGLED HERE, HAVE CONSECRATED IT, FAR ABOVE
1140 DATA "OUR POOR POWER TO ADD OR DETRACT.  THE WORLD WILL LITTLE
1150 DATA "NOTE, NOR LONG REMEMBER, WHAT WE SAY HERE, BUT IT CAN
1160 DATA "NEVER FORGET WHAT THEY DID HERE.  IT IS FOR US THE LIVING,
1170 DATA "RATHER, TO BE DEDICATED HERE TO THE UNFINISHED WORK WHICH
1180 DATA "THEY WHO FOUGHT HERE HAVE THUS FAR SO NOBLY ADVANCED.
1190 DATA "IT IS RATHER FOR US TO BE HERE DEDICATED TO THE GREAT TASK
1200 DATA "REMAINING BEFORE US, - THAT FROM THESE HONORED DEAD WE
1210 DATA "TAKE INCREASED DEVOTION TO THAT CAUSE FOR WHICH THEY GAVE
1220 DATA "THE LAST FULL MEASURE OF DEVOTION - THAT WE HERE HIGHLY
1230 DATA "RESOLVE THAT THESE DEAD SHALL NOT HAVE DIED IN VAIN - THAT
1240 DATA "THIS NATION, UNDER GOD, SHALL HAVE A NEW BIRTH OF FREEDOM -
1250 DATA "AND THAT GOVERNMENT OF THE PEOPLE, BY THE PEOPLE, FOR THE
1260 DATA "PEOPLE, SHALL NOT PERISH FROM THE EARTH.
1270 DATA "XXX"

100 REM *** PROGRAMMING ASSIGNMENT 10.11 ***
110 DIM SET(100)
120 INPUT "Enter the number of numbers"; NUMBER
130 PRINT "Enter the numbers one at a time"
140 FOR J = 1 TO NUMBER
150    INPUT "Number"; SET(J)
160 NEXT J
170 GOSUB 300                          'Sort SET
180 MID.POINT = NUMBER \ 2 + NUMBER MOD 2
190 IF NUMBER MOD 2 = 0
       THEN MEDIAN = (SET(MID.POINT) + SET(MID.POINT + 1)) / 2
       ELSE MEDIAN = SET(MID.POINT)
200 PRINT "The median is "; MEDIAN
210 STOP
220 '
300 REM *** Sorting routine
310    SORTED.FLAG$ = "NO"
320    WHILE SORTED.FLAG$ = "NO"
330      SORTED.FLAG$ = "YES"
340      FOR J = 1 TO NUMBER - 1
350        IF SET(J) > SET(J + 1)
             THEN SWAP SET(J),SET(J + 1): SORTED.FLAG$ = "NO"
360      NEXT J
370    WEND
380 RETURN
390 REM *** End of sorting routine
400 END

100 REM    *** PROGRAMMING ASSIGNMENT 10.14 ***
110 DIM MEN$(10), WOMENS$(10)
120 RANDOMIZE TIMER
130 GOSUB 200                      'Input routine
140 GOSUB 300                      'Shuffle routines
150 GOSUB 500                      'Print pairs
160 STOP
170 '
200 REM *** Input routine
210    FOR J = 1 TO 10             'Read men's names
220      READ MEN$(J)
```

```
230    NEXT J
240    FOR J = 1 TO 10              'Read women's names
250      READ WOMEN$(J)
260    NEXT J
270 RETURN
280 REM *** End of input routine
290 '
300 REM *** Shuffle routines
310    FOR J = 1 TO 10              'Shuffle men's names
320      K = 1 + INT(10*RND)        'K is between 1 and 10
330      SWAP MEN$(J),MEN$(K)
340    NEXT J
350    FOR J = 1 TO 10              'Shuffle women's names
360      K = 1 + INT(10*RND)        'K is between 1 and 10
370      SWAP WOMEN$(J),WOMEN$(K)
380    NEXT J
390 RETURN
400 REM *** End of shuffle routines
410 '
500 REM *** Print pairs routine
510  PRINT " PAIR  MEN          WOMEN"
520    FOR J = 1 TO 10
530      PRINT USING " ##    \      \ \        \"; J, MEN$(J), WOMEN$(J)
540    NEXT J
550 RETURN
560 REM *** End of print pairs routine
570 '
600 REM *** Data used in program
610 DATA Steve, Phil, Hank, Nick, Gary, Dave, Dick, Edgar, Bob, Ed
620 DATA Ruth, Carole, Bette, Alex, Louise, Faye, Audrey, Roberta, Maria,Kathy
630 END

100 REM *** PROGRAMMING ASSIGNMENT 10.15 ***
110 DIM BABY.NAME$(10)
120 RANDOMIZE TIMER
130 INPUT "How many names do you want to enter"; N
140 FOR J = 1 TO N
150    INPUT "Enter a name"; BABY.NAME$(J)
160 NEXT J
170 SELECT = 1 + INT(N * RND)
180 PRINT "Name the baby "; BABY.NAME$(SELECT)
190 END

100 REM *** PROGRAMMING ASSIGNMENT 10.17 ***
110 DIM PLANET$(8), FACTOR(8)
120 GOSUB 300                      'Initialize PLANET and FACTOR
130 PRINT "Enter planet names in CAPITAL LETTERS (and weight of 0 to stop)"
140 INPUT "Enter your weight and the name of a planet"; WEIGHT, PLANET.NAME$
150    IF WEIGHT = 0
         THEN GOTO 190             'Test for trailer data
160    GOSUB 500                   'Search PLANET for PLANET.NAME
170    IF FOUND$ = "YES"
         THEN PRINT "On "; PLANET.NAME$; " you weigh "; WEIGHT * FACTOR(J);"lbs"
         ELSE PRINT "There is no planet named "; PLANET.NAME$; " try again"
180 GOTO 140
190 STOP
200 '
300 REM *** Initialize PLANET and FACTOR arrays
310    FOR J = 1 TO 8
320      READ PLANET$(J), FACTOR(J)
330    NEXT J
340    DATA MERCURY, .37
350    DATA VENUS, .88
360    DATA MARS, .38
370    DATA JUPITER, 2.64
380    DATA SATURN,1.15
390    DATA URANUS, 1.15
```

```
400     DATA NEPTUNE, 1.12
410     DATA PLUTO, .04
420 RETURN
430 REM *** End of initialization routine
440 '
500 REM *** Sequential search routine
510   FOUND$ = "NO"
520   FOR J = 1 TO 8
530     IF PLANET$(J) = PLANET.NAME$
          THEN FOUND$ = "YES": GOTO 550
540   NEXT J
550 RETURN
560 REM *** End of sequential search routine
570 END

100 REM *** PROGRAMMING ASSIGNMENT 10.21 ***
110 DIM SNOWFALL(3,5)
120 GRAND.TOTAL = 0
130 GOSUB 200                                    'fill snowfall array
140 GOSUB 300                                    'calc & print averages
150 STOP
160 '
200 REM *** Read Snowfall
210   FOR SITE = 1 TO 3
220     FOR FALL = 1 TO 5
230       READ SNOWFALL(SITE, FALL)
240     NEXT FALL
250   NEXT SITE
260   RETURN
270 REM *** End Read
280 '
300 REM *** Calculate and Print Averages
310   FOR SITE = 1 TO 3
320     TOTAL.FALL = 0
330     FOR FALL = 1 TO 5
340       TOTAL.FALL = TOTAL.FALL + SNOWFALL(SITE, FALL)
350     NEXT FALL
360     AVERAGE = TOTAL.FALL/5
370     PRINT USING "Average snowfall for site # is ###.## inches."; SITE,
          AVERAGE
380     GRAND.TOTAL = GRAND.TOTAL + TOTAL.FALL
390   NEXT SITE
400   GRAND.AVERAGE = GRAND.TOTAL / (3 * 5)
410   PRINT USING "The average snowfall for all sites is ###.## inches.";
                   GRAND.AVERAGE
420   RETURN
430 REM *** End Calculate and Print
440 '
500 REM *** Data Used
510   DATA 106, 147, 139, 153, 126
520   DATA 143, 151, 117, 134, 139
530   DATA 136, 143, 130, 142, 145
540 REM *** End Data
550 END

100 REM *** PROGRAMMING ASSIGNMENT 10.26 ***
105 RANDOMIZE TIMER
110 DIM CARD$(5)
120 TOTAL = 0
125 NUM.TRIALS = 50
130 FOR TRIAL = 1 TO NUM.TRIALS
140   GOSUB 500                          'Initialize CARD$ array to NO
150   COMPLETE.SET$ = "NO"               'We don't have a full set yet
160   NUM = 0                            'We have tried 0 times
170   WHILE COMPLETE.SET$ = "NO"
180     CARD.NUM = 1 + INT(5 * RND)      'Select next card,
190     NUM = NUM + 1                    'Count it, and
```

```
200     CARD$(CARD.NUM) = "YES"              'Record it
210     IF NUM >= 5
          THEN GOSUB 600                     'See if set is complete
220   WEND
230   TOTAL = TOTAL + NUM
240 NEXT TRIAL
250 AVERAGE = TOTAL / NUM.TRIALS
260 PRINT "Average number of cards to make a complete set is "; AVERAGE
270 STOP
280 '
500 REM *** Initialization routine
510   FOR J = 1 TO 5
520     CARD$(J) = "NO"
530   NEXT J
540 RETURN
550 REM *** End of initialization routine
560 '
600 REM *** Routine to see if set is complete
620   FOR J = 1 TO 5
630     IF CARD$(J) = "NO"
          THEN GOTO 660
640   NEXT J
650   COMPLETE.SET$ = "YES"
660 RETURN
670 REM End of routine to see if set is complete
680 END


100 REM *** PROGRAMMING ASSIGNMENT 10.30 ***
110 DIM A(50)                     'Allow up to 50 digit numbers
120 INPUT "Enter a number you want to check (0 to end)"; N$
130   IF N$ = "0"
        THEN GOTO 180
140   GOSUB 200                   'Take N$ apart and put digits in A
150   GOSUB 300                   'Test for palindrome
160   IF PAL$ = "NO"
        THEN PRINT N$; " is not a palindrome"
        ELSE PRINT N$; " is a palindrome"
170 GOTO 120
180 STOP
190 '
200 REM *** Routine to take N$ apart and store digits in A
210   L = LEN(N$)
220   FOR J = 1 TO L
230     S = L - J + 1
240     A(S) = VAL(MID$(N$,J,1))   'Convert input number to elements of A array
250   NEXT
260 RETURN
270 REM *** End of routine to take N$ apart
280 '
300 REM *** Routine to test for palindrome
310   PAL$ = "YES"
320   HALF = L \ 2
330   FOR J = 1 TO HALF
340     K = L - J + 1
350     IF A(J) = A(K)
          THEN GOTO 360
          ELSE PAL$ = "NO": GOTO 370
360   NEXT J
370 RETURN
380 REM *** End of routine to test for palindrome
390 END


100 REM *** PROGRAMMING ASSIGNMENT 10.31 ***
110 DIM DISTANCE(6,6), CITY.NAME$(6)
120 GOSUB 300                             'Initialize arrays
130 INPUT "Enter the name of the starting city, Enter to stop"; START.CITY$
```

```
135    IF START.CITY$ = ""
          THEN GOTO 230
140    SEARCH.NAME$ = START.CITY$
150    GOSUB 600                              'Search for city name
160    IF FOUND$ = "NO"
          THEN PRINT "Sorry, no data available on ";START.CITY$: GOTO 130
          ELSE SUBSCRIPT1 = K
170    INPUT "Enter the name of the destination city"; DESTINATION.CITY$
180    SEARCH.NAME$ = DESTINATION.CITY$
190    GOSUB 600                              'Search for city name
200    IF FOUND$ = "NO"
          THEN PRINT "Sorry, no data available on ";DESTINATION.CITY$: GOTO 170
          ELSE SUBSCRIPT2 = K
210    PRINT USING "The distance between & and & is #,### miles";
             START.CITY$, DESTINATION.CITY$, DISTANCE(SUBSCRIPT1,SUBSCRIPT2)
220 GOTO 130
230 STOP
240 '
300 REM *** Initialization routine
310    FOR J = 1 TO 6
320      READ CITY.NAME$(J)
330    NEXT J
340    DATA ATLANTA, BOSTON, CHICAGO, DALLAS, LOS ANGELES, NEW YORK
350    FOR COL = 1 TO 6
360      FOR ROW = COL TO 6
370        READ DISTANCE(ROW,COL)
380      NEXT ROW
390    NEXT COL
400    DATA 0, 1068, 730,  805, 2197,  855
410    DATA        0, 975, 1819, 3052,  216
420    DATA           0,  936, 2095,  840
430    DATA              0, 1403, 1607
440    DATA                 0, 2915
450    DATA                    0
460    FOR ROW = 1 TO 6
470      FOR COL = ROW + 1 TO 6
480        DISTANCE(ROW,COL) = DISTANCE(COL,ROW)
490      NEXT COL
500    NEXT ROW
510 RETURN
520 REM *** end of Initialization routine
530 '
600 REM *** Routine to search CITY.NAME$ array
610    FOUND$ = "NO"
620      FOR K = 1 TO 6
630        IF CITY.NAME$(K) = SEARCH.NAME$
              THEN FOUND$ = "YES": GOTO 650
640      NEXT K
650 RETURN
660 REM *** End of search routine
670 END


100 REM *** PROGRAMMING ASSIGNMENT 10.40 ***
110 DIM COUNTER(10)
115 CLS : KEY OFF
120 RANDOMIZE TIMER
122 FOR J = 0 TO 10
124   COUNTER(J) = 0
126 NEXT J
130 FOR TRIAL = 1 TO 500
140    HEADS = 0
150    FOR TOSS = 1 TO 10
160      X = RND
170      IF X < .5 THEN HEADS = HEADS + 1
```

```
180    NEXT TOSS
190    COUNTER(HEADS) = COUNTER(HEADS) + 1
200 NEXT TRIAL
210 PRINT "Heads   0    1    2    3    4    5    6    7    8    9   10"
220 PRINT "Number";
230 FOR J = 0 TO 10
240   PRINT USING "###  "; COUNTER(J);
250 NEXT J
260 END
```

CHAPTER 11 EXERCISES

11.2 WRITE #1, EMP.NO, EMP.NAME$, SEX$, YEAR, SALARY

11.4 INPUT #1, EMP.NO, EMP.NAME$, SEX$, YEAR, SALARY

11.7 INITIALIZATION, LIST HEADING, ERROR REPORT HEADING, READ MASTER, READ TRANS, MASTER KEY LESS, READ MASTER, MASTER KEY GREATER, PRINT ERROR REPORT, READ TRANS, KEYS EQUAL, PRINT LISTING, READ MASTER, READ TRANS, MASTER KEY GREATER, PRINT ERROR REPORT, READ TRANS, TERMINATION.

11.11 In a heading routine, you initialize the line counter variable and increment the page counter variable.

11.17 When we delete a record we need to know only the key of the record to be deleted, but when we add a record we need to know all the fields in the record.

CHAPTER 11 PROGRAMMING ASSIGNMENTS

```
100 REM *** PROGRAMMING ASSIGNMENT 11.4 - PART 1 - CREATE GRADES.SEQ FILE ***
110 DIM STUDENT.NAMES$(40), GRADES(40,3)          'Allow 40 students and 3 tests
120 GOSUB 200                                     'Get student names
130 GOSUB 300                                     'Create file
140 PRINT "The GRADES.SEQ file has been created"
150 STOP
160 '
200 REM *** Accept names routine
210   PRINT "Enter student names, one at a time.  Enter End to stop"
220   FOR J = 1 TO 41
230     INPUT STUDENT.NAMES$(J)
240     IF STUDENT.NAMES$(J) = "End"
          THEN NO.STUDENTS = J - 1: GOTO 260
250   NEXT J
260   RETURN
270 REM *** End of accept names routine
280 '
300 REM *** Create file routine
310   OPEN "GRADES.SEQ" FOR OUTPUT AS #1
320   FOR J = 1 TO NO.STUDENTS
330     WRITE #1, STUDENT.NAMES$(J), GRADES(J,1), GRADES(J,2), GRADES(J,3)
340   NEXT J
350   CLOSE #1
360 RETURN
370 REM *** End of create file routine
380 END


100 REM *** PROGRAMMING ASSIGNMENT 11.4 - PART 2 - ENTER GRADES ***
110 DIM STUDENT.NAME$(40), GRADES(40,3)           'Allow 40 students and 3 tests
120 GOSUB 200                                     'Read the file
130 GOSUB 400                                     'Accept grades
140 GOSUB 500                                     'Rewrite file
150 STOP
160 '
200 REM *** Read grades file routine
210   OPEN "GRADES.SEQ" FOR INPUT AS #1
```

```
220    J = 0
230    WHILE EOF(1) = 0
240      J = J + 1
250      INPUT #1, STUDENT.NAMES$(J), GRADES(J,1), GRADES(J,2), GRADES(J,3)
260    WEND
270    NO.STUDENTS = J
280    CLOSE #1
290 RETURN
300 REM *** End of read grades file routine
310 '
400 REM *** Accept grades routine
410    INPUT "For which test are grades being entered (1, 2, or 3)"; TEST.NO
420    FOR J = 1 TO NO.STUDENTS
430      PRINT "Enter grade for "; STUDENT.NAMES$(J);
440      INPUT GRADES(J,TEST.NO)
450    NEXT J
460 RETURN
470 REM *** End of accept grades routine
480 '
500 REM *** Rewrite file routine
510    OPEN "GRADES.SEQ" FOR OUTPUT AS #1
520    FOR J = 1 TO NO.STUDENTS
530      WRITE #1, STUDENT.NAMES$(J), GRADES(J,1), GRADES(J,2), GRADES(J,3)
540    NEXT J
550    CLOSE #1
560 RETURN
570 REM *** End of rewrite file routine
580 END


100 REM *** PROGRAMMING ASSIGNMENT 11.4 - PART 3 - PRINT GRADES ***
110 DIM STUDENT.NAME$(40), GRADES(40,3)          'Allow 40 students and 3 tests
120 GOSUB 200                                    'Read the file
130 GOSUB 400                                    'Print grades
140 STOP
150 '
200 REM *** Read grades file routine
210    OPEN "GRADES.SEQ" FOR INPUT AS #1
220    J = 0
230    WHILE EOF(1) = 0
240      J = J + 1
250      INPUT #1, STUDENT.NAMES$(J), GRADES(J,1), GRADES(J,2), GRADES(J,3)
260    WEND
270    NO.STUDENTS = J
280    CLOSE #1
290 RETURN
300 REM *** End of read grades file routine
310 '
400 REM *** Print grades routine
410    PRINT "                        Test Number"
420    PRINT "Student Name             1    2    3    Avg"
430    FOR J = 1 TO NO.STUDENTS
440      PRINT USING "\                    \"; STUDENT.NAMES$(J);
450      TOTAL.GRADE = 0
460      FOR K = 1 TO 3
470        PRINT USING "  ###"; GRADES(J,K);
480        TOTAL.GRADE = TOTAL.GRADE + GRADES(J,K)
490      NEXT K
500      AVERAGE = TOTAL.GRADE / 3
510      PRINT USING "    ###"; AVERAGE
520    NEXT J
530 RETURN
540 REM *** End of print grades routine
550 END
```

CHAPTER 12 EXERCISES

12.2 When BASIC retrieves a specific record, it uses the constant record length to determine the location of the record on the disk.

12.4 A = CVI(A.FLD$)
B = CVS(B.FLD$)

12.5 a) OPEN "GPA.RND" AS #1 LEN = 31
b) Same as a)
c) FIELD #1, 25 AS STUDENT.NAME.FLD$, 2 AS CREDITS.FLD$, 4 AS GPA.FLD$
d) LSET STUDENT.NAME.FLD$ = STUDENT.NAME$
LSET CREDITS.FLD$ = MKI$(CREDITS)
LSET GPA.FLD$ = MKS$(GPA)
e) PUT #1, STUDENT.NO
f) GET #1, STUDENT.NO

12.10 LOF(1) returns 800.

12.13 The data in MEM.NO.INDEX are not in sequential order, so a binary search cannot be used.

12.16 The coding would retrieve all the records, including the deleted records, because deleted records are still in the file, and the coding reads every record.

CHAPTER 12 PROGRAMMING ASSIGNMENTS

```
100 REM *** PROGRAMMING ASSIGNMENT 12.1  ***
110 OPEN "A12-01.RND" AS #1 LEN = 31
120 FIELD #1, 25 AS STUDENT.NAME.FLD$, 2 AS CREDITS.FLD$, 4 AS GPA.FLD$
130 LPRINT "Student Number     Name                        Credits    GPA"
140 FMT$ = "      ###        \                 \     ###     #.##"
150 FOR STUDENT.NO = 1 TO 999
160   GET #1, STUDENT.NO
170   GPA = CVS(GPA.FLD$)
180   IF GPA > 3
         THEN CREDITS = CVI(CREDITS.FLD$):
              LPRINT USING FMT$; STUDENT.NO, STUDENT.NAME.FLD$, CREDITS, GPA
190 NEXT STUDENT.NO
200 LPRINT "All the students whose GPA is greater than 3 have been listed"
210 CLOSE
220 END


1000 REM *** PROGRAMMING ASSIGNMENT 12-3 ***
1010 GOSUB 1500                              'Initialization routine
1020 WHILE FINISHED$ = "NO"
1030   GOSUB 2000                           'Display menu
1040   ON CODE GOSUB 3000, 4000, 5000, 6000, 7000
1050 WEND
1060 LOCATE 10,20:PRINT "Normal end of program"
1070 STOP
1080 '
1500 REM *** Initialization routine =============================================
1510   OPEN "A12-01.RND" AS #1 LEN = 31
1520   FIELD #1, 25 AS STUDENT.NAME.FLD$, 2 AS CREDITS.FLD$, 4 AS GPA.FLD$
1530   CLS: KEY OFF
1540   LOCATE 5,23: PRINT "GRADE POINT AVERAGE MAINTENANCE PROGRAM"
1550   GOSUB 8100                           'Pause and clear screen
1560   FINISHED$ = "NO"
1570 RETURN
1580 REM *** End of initialization routine
1590 '
2000 REM *** Display menu routine ===============================================
2010   LOCATE 2,20: PRINT "Enter 1 to Add a record"
2020   LOCATE 3,20: PRINT "      2 to Delete a record"
2030   LOCATE 4,20: PRINT "      3 to Update a record"
2040   LOCATE 5,20: PRINT "      4 to Display a record"
2050   LOCATE 6,20: PRINT "      5 to Exit program"
2060   LOCATE 7,20: PRINT "Function ? ";
2070   CODE$ = INPUT$(1)
```

```
2080    CODE = VAL(CODE$)
2090    PRINT CODE
2100 RETURN
2110 REM *** End of display menu routine
2120 '
3000 REM *** Add records routine =============================================
3010    GOSUB 8000                          'Get the record
3020    IF STUDENT.NAME.FLD$ <> SPACE$(25)
            THEN GOSUB 3200: GOTO 3100      'Student number is assigned; no add
3030    LOCATE 10,20: LINE INPUT "Enter name "; NAME.IN$
3040    LOCATE 11,20: INPUT "Enter number of credits completed"; CREDITS
3045    LOCATE 12,20: INPUT "Enter grade point average"; GPA
3050    LSET STUDENT.NAME.FLD$ = NAME.IN$            'Set name
3060    LSET CREDITS.FLD$ = MKI$(CREDITS) 'Convert credits
3065    LSET GPA.FLD$ = MKS$(GPA)              'Convert gpa
3070    PUT #1, STUDENT.NO                    'Write record
3080    LOCATE 13,20:PRINT "Record number "; STUDENT.NO; "has been added"
3090    GOSUB 8100                            'Pause and clear screen
3100 RETURN
3110 REM *** End of add records routine
3200 REM *** Bad add routine
3210 BEEP
3220    LOCATE 15,20:PRINT "Student number ";STUDENT.NO;"is currently assigned"
3230    GOSUB 8100
3240 RETURN
3250 REM *** End of bad add routine
3260 '
4000 REM *** Delete records routine ==========================================
4010    GOSUB 8000                          'Get the record
4020    IF STUDENT.NAME.FLD$ = SPACE$(25)
            THEN GOSUB 8200: GOTO 4080    'Student number not assigned; no delete
4030    LSET STUDENT.NAME.FLD$ = SPACE$(25)         'Set name for inactive
4040    LSET CREDITS.FLD$ = MKI$(0)       'Set credits to 0
4045    LSET GPA.FLD$ = MKS$(0)           'Set gpa to 0
4050    PUT #1, STUDENT.NO                'Write record
4060    LOCATE 11,20:PRINT "Record number "; STUDENT.NO; "has been deleted"
4070    GOSUB 8100                           'Pause and clear screen
4080 RETURN
4090 REM ** End of delete records routine
4100 '
5000 REM *** Update records routine ==========================================
5010    GOSUB 8000                          'Get the record
5020    IF STUDENT.NAME.FLD$ = SPACE$(25)
            THEN GOSUB 8200: GOTO 5150    'Student number not assigned; no update
5030    LOCATE 9,20: PRINT USING "Current credits ### GPA #.##"; CREDITS, GPA
5040    LOCATE 10,20: INPUT "Enter credits completed this semester"; CREDITS.IN
5050    LOCATE 11,20: INPUT "Enter GPA for this semester";GPA.IN
5060    TOTAL.CREDITS = CREDITS + CREDITS.IN
5070    NEW.GPA = (GPA * CREDITS + GPA.IN * CREDITS.IN) / TOTAL.CREDITS
5100    LOCATE 12,20
5105    PRINT USING "New credits ###, new GPA #.##"; TOTAL.CREDITS, NEW.GPA
5110    LSET CREDITS.FLD$ = MKI$(TOTAL.CREDITS)
5115    LSET GPA.FLD$ = MKS$(NEW.GPA)
5120    PUT #1, STUDENT.NO                    'Write record
5130    LOCATE 13,20: PRINT "Record number ";STUDENT.NO; "has been updated"
5140    GOSUB 8100                           'Pause and clear screen
5150 RETURN
5160 REM *** End of update records routine
5170 '
6000 REM *** Display records routine =========================================
6010    GOSUB 8000                          'Get the record
6020    IF STUDENT.NAME.FLD$ = SPACE$(25)
            THEN GOSUB 8200: GOTO 6080    'Student number not assigned; no display
6030    LOCATE 9,20: PRINT "Student number "; STUDENT.NO
6040    LOCATE 10,20: PRINT "Name "; STUDENT.NAME.FLD$
6050    LOCATE 11,20: PRINT USING "Current credits completed ###"; CREDITS
6055    LOCATE 12,20: PRINT USING "Current GPA #.##"; GPA
```

```
6060    LOCATE 13,20: INPUT "Press Enter to continue", A$
6070    CLS
6080 RETURN
6090 REM *** End of display record routine
6100 '
7000 REM *** Exit program routine ============================================
7010    CLOSE
7020    FINISHED$ = "YES"
7030 RETURN
7040 REM *** End of exit program routine
7050 '
7999 REM    =========================Utility Routines ===========================
8000 REM *** Get record and convert credits and GPA routine
8010    LOCATE 8,20: PRINT "Enter the three-digit student number ";
8020    STUDENT.NO$ = INPUT$(3)
8030    STUDENT.NO = VAL(STUDENT.NO$)
8040    PRINT STUDENT.NO
8050    GET #1, STUDENT.NO
8060    CREDITS = CVI(CREDITS.FLD$)
8065    GPA = CVS(GPA.FLD$)
8070 RETURN
8080 REM *** End of get record and convert balance routine
8090 '
8100 REM *** Pause and clear screen routine
8110    LATER = TIMER + 2
8120    WHILE TIMER < LATER
8130    WEND
8140    CLS
8150 RETURN
8160 REM *** End of pause and clear screen routine
8170 '
8200 REM *** Bad delete, update and display routine
8210    BEEP
8220    LOCATE 15,20:PRINT "Student number ";STUDENT.NO;"is currently inactive"
8230    GOSUB 8100
8240 RETURN
8250 REM *** End of bad delete, update, and display routine
8260 END
```

CHAPTER 13 EXERCISES

13.3 SCREEN 1, 0

13.5 COLOR 4, 1

13.7 In medium resolution LINE(160,100)-(319,0)
In high resolution LINE(320,100)-(639,0)

13.9 LINE(20,10)-STEP(40,50)

13.13 It paints an area outlined in color 2 with color 3, starting at pixel (40,70).

13.16 The Y radius is 80, and the X radius is 40.

CHAPTER 13 PROGRAMMING ASSIGNMENTS

```
100 REM *** PROGRAMMING ASSIGNMENT 13.1 ***
110 SCREEN 1,0: CLS: KEY OFF: COLOR 0,1
120 PSET(319,0),2
130 PSET STEP(0,1),2
140 PSET STEP(-1,0),2
150 PSET STEP(0,-1),2
160 END
```

```
100 REM *** PROGRAMMING ASSIGNMENT 13.5 ***
110 SCREEN 1,0: CLS: KEY OFF: COLOR 1,1
120 LINE(75,50)-(225,150),,B              'Draw outline of flag
130 LINE(75,50)-STEP(65,42),,B            'Upper left section
140 LINE(160,50)-STEP(65,42),,B           'Upper right section
150 LINE(75,108)-STEP(65,42),,B           'Lower left section
160 LINE(160,108)-STEP(65,42),,B          'Lower right section
170 A$ = INPUT$(1)                        'Pause
180 END

100 REM *** PROGRAMMING ASSIGNMENT 13.7 ***
110 SCREEN 1,0: CLS: KEY OFF: COLOR 4,1
120 LINE(100,40) - STEP(120,120),1,BF             'Draw outer box
130 LINE(130,70) - STEP(60,60),2,BF               'Draw middle box
140 LINE(145,85) - STEP(30,30),3,BF               'Draw inner box
150 A$ = INPUT$(1)                                'Pause
160 END

100 REM *** PROGRAMMING ASSIGNMENT 13.9 ***
110 SCREEN 1,0: CLS: KEY OFF: COLOR 1,1
120 LINE(75,50)-(225,150),,B              'Draw outline of flag
130 LINE(75,50)-STEP(65,42),,B            'Upper left section
140 LINE(160,50)-STEP(65,42),,B           'Upper right section
150 LINE(75,108)-STEP(65,42),,B           'Lower left section
160 LINE(160,108)-STEP(65,42),,B          'Lower right section
170 PAINT(160,100),3,3                    'Paint cross
180 PAINT(100,70),1,3                     'Paint upper left
190 PAINT(200,70),2,3                     'Paint upper right
200 PAINT(100,130),2,3                    'Paint lower left
210 PAINT(200,130),1,3                    'Paint lower right
220 A$ = INPUT$(1)                        'Pause
230 END

100 REM *** PROGRAMMING ASSIGNMENT 13.12 ***
110 SCREEN 1,0: CLS: KEY OFF: COLOR 0,1
120 REM   Initialization
130 PI = 3.14159
140 CF = (2 * PI) / 360
150 CIRCLE(160,100),60,1                  'Draw and
160 PAINT(160,100),1,1                    'paint face
170 CIRCLE(160,100),40,3,CF*210,CF*330    'Draw
180 LINE(120,118) - STEP(10,-6)           'the
190 LINE(200,118) - STEP(-10,-6)          'mouth
200 CIRCLE(145,93),10,0,,,2               'Draw
210 PAINT STEP(0,0),0,0                    'and
220 CIRCLE(175,93),10,0,,,2               'paint
230 PAINT STEP(0,0),0,0                    'eyes
240 A$ = INPUT$(1)                        'Pause
250 END

100 REM *** PROGRAMMING ASSIGNMENT 13.14 ***
110 SCREEN 1,0: CLS: KEY OFF: COLOR 1,1
120 LINE(160,0)-STEP(0,200)               'Divide screen into
130 LINE(0,100)-STEP(320,0)               'four quadrants
140 CIRCLE(80,50),40,1                    'Draw circle in first quadrant
150 PAINT STEP(0,0),1,1                   'and paint it
160 PAINT(240,50),1,3                     'Paint second quadrant
170 CIRCLE(240,50),40,2                   'Draw circle in second quadrant
180 PAINT STEP(0,0),2,2                   'and paint it
190 PAINT(240,150),2,3                    'Paint third quadrant
200 CIRCLE(240,150),40,3                  'Draw circle in third quadrant
210 PAINT STEP(0,0),3,3                   'and paint it
220 PAINT(80,150),3,3                     'Paint fourth quadrant
230 CIRCLE(80,150),40,0                   'Draw circle in fourth quadrant
240 PAINT STEP(0,0),0,0                   'and paint it
250 A$ = INPUT$(1)                        'Pause
260 END
```

```
100 REM *** PROGRAMMING ASSIGNMENT 13.16 ***
110 PI = 3.14159
120 CF = (2 * PI) / 360
130 SCREEN 1,0: CLS: KEY OFF: COLOR 0,0
140 CIRCLE(160,100),80,2,-CF*45,-CF*360          'Draw pizza
150 CIRCLE(160,100),70,2,CF*45,CF*360            'Draw crust
160 PAINT(150,100),2,2                           'Paint it
170 CIRCLE STEP(35,-10),80,2,-CF*.1,-CF*45       'Draw slice
180 CIRCLE STEP(0,0),70,2,CF*.1,CF*45            'Draw crust on slice
190 PAINT STEP(5,-3),2,2                         'Paint it
200 A$ = INPUT$(1)
210 END
```

```
100 REM *** PROGRAMMING ASSIGNMENT 13.24 ***
110 SCREEN 1,0: CLS: KEY OFF: COLOR 1,1
120 PI = 3.14159
130 CF = (2 * PI) / 360
140 CIRCLE(160,100),80,3                         'Draw center circle
150 CIRCLE(47,100),80,3,CF*315,CF*45             'Draw left segment
160 PAINT(90,100),1,3                            'Paint left segment
170 CIRCLE(160,194),80,3,CF*45,CF*135            'Draw bottom segment
180 PAINT(160,150),2,3                           'Paint bottom segment
190 CIRCLE(273,100),80,3,CF*135,CF*225           'Draw right segment
200 PAINT(230,100),1,3                           'Paint right segment
210 CIRCLE(160,6),80,3,CF*225,CF*315             'Draw top segment
220 PAINT(160,40),2,3                            'Paint top segment
230 PAINT(160,100),3,3                           'Paint center segment
240 A$ = INPUT$(1)                               'Pause
250 END
```

CHAPTER 14 EXERCISES

14.3 The coordinates are (30,100).

14.5 `415 LINE(89.5,INFLATION.RATE)-(90,INFLATION.RATE)`

14.9
```
482 FOR SALES = 1 TO 6
483   FOR YEAR = 86 TO 90.5 STEP .1
484     PSET(YEAR,SALES)
485   NEXT YEAR
486 NEXT SALES
```

14.11 Change the following statements
```
200 FOR Y = 0 TO 170 STEP 10
210   PUT(160,Y),SAVE.CIRCLE
230   PUT(160,Y),SAVE.CIRCLE
240 NEXT Y
```

14.15 An acceptable answer is
```
    GET(50,50)-(150,150),BIG.CIRCLE
```
where BIG.CIRCLE has 658 elements. Alternately, if the default aspect of 5/6 is considered, the statement can be written as
```
    GET(50,58)-(150,142),BIG.CIRCLE
```
where BIG.CIRCLE has only 554 elements.

CHAPTER 14 PROGRAMMING ASSIGNMENTS

```
100 REM *** PROGRAMMING ASSIGNMENT 14.11 ***
110 SCREEN 1,0: CLS: KEY OFF: COLOR 0,1
120 GOSUB 200                       'Set up graph
130 GOSUB 600                       'Plot data
140 A$ = INPUT$(1)                  'Pause
150 STOP
160 '
200 REM *** Set up graph routine
210   LOCATE 1,12: PRINT "FAMILY INCOME"         'Print title
220   FOR J = 1 TO 7                             'Print Y label
230     READ CHAR$
```

```
240       LOCATE 2*J+5,4: PRINT CHAR$
250     NEXT J
260     REM Data for READ in 230
270     DATA P, E, R, C, E, N, T
280     FOR PERCENT = 0 TO 100 STEP 10                  'Print Y coordinates
290       ROW = -.2 * PERCENT + 22
300       LOCATE ROW,7: PRINT USING "###!"; PERCENT,"-"
310     NEXT PERCENT
340     FOR YEAR = 70 TO 90 STEP 10                     'Print X coordinates
350       COL = .6 * YEAR - 30
360       LOCATE 23,COL: PRINT USING "##"; YEAR
370     NEXT YEAR
380     LOCATE 24,14: PRINT "Y E A R";                  'Print X label
390     LINE(76,12)-(76,172)                            'Draw Y axis
400     LINE(76,172)-(208,172)                          'Draw X axis
410     LINE(208,39)-(224,47),1,BF                      'Draw legend
420     LOCATE 6,30: PRINT "< $15,000"
430     LINE(208,55)-(224,63),2,BF
440     LOCATE 8,30: PRINT "<= $25,000"
450     LINE(208,71)-(224,79),3,BF
460     LOCATE 10,30: PRINT "> $25,000"
470     VIEW(80,12)-(224,172)                           'Define viewport
480     WINDOW(70,0)-(100,100)                          'Define coordinates
490   RETURN
500   REM *** End of set up graph routine
510   '
600   REM *** Plot data routine
610     FOR YEAR = 70 TO 90 STEP 10
620       READ HIGH, MIDDLE, LOW
630       LINE(YEAR,0)-(YEAR+6,LOW),1,BF
640       LINE(YEAR,LOW)-(YEAR+6,LOW+MIDDLE),2,BF
650       LINE(YEAR,LOW+MIDDLE)-(YEAR+6,LOW+MIDDLE+HIGH),3,BF
660     NEXT YEAR
670     REM Data for READ in 620
680     DATA 18.9, 33.4, 47.7              :'1970 Data
690     DATA 37.5, 31.0, 31.4              :'1980 Data
700     DATA 39.3, 27.7, 33.1              :'1990 Data
710   RETURN
720   REM *** End of plot data routine
730   END


100   REM *** PROGRAMMING ASSIGNMENT 14.8 ***
110   SCREEN 1,0: CLS: KEY OFF: COLOR 1,1
120   DIM BOAT(210)                        'Array to save boat
130   DELAY = .1                           'Delay for animation
140   LINE(0,40)-STEP(64,0)                'Draw
150   LINE -(60,48)                        'and
160   LINE -(14,48)                        'paint
170   LINE -(0,40)                         'the
180   PAINT(40,44),1,3                     'hull
190   LINE(40,40)-(40,0)                   'Mast
200   LINE(8,36)-(40,6)                    'Draw
210   LINE -(60,36)                        'the
220   LINE -(8,36)                         'sails
230   LINE(40,1)-(24,3)                    'Draw
240   LINE -(40,5)                         'pennant
250   GET(0,0)-(64,48),BOAT                'Save boat
260   PUT(0,0),BOAT                        'Erase boat
270   LINE(0,160)-(319,160)                'Draw water surface
280   PAINT(160,100),3,3                   'Paint sky white
290   DIRECTION = 1                        'Direction is initially positive
300   X = 0                                'Start at X = 0
310   REM Top of loop                      'Sail boat in a loop
320     KEYSTROKE$ = INKEY$                'Did player press key?
```

```
330  IF KEYSTROKE$ = "R"
        THEN DIRECTION = DIRECTION * -1   'If R pressed, reverse direction
340    PUT(X,112),BOAT                    'Put boat in new location
350    NOW = TIMER: WHILE TIMER < NOW + DELAY: WEND  'Delay
360    PUT(X,112),BOAT                    'After delay, erase boat
370    X = X + DIRECTION * 10             'New X position
380 GOTO 310
390 A$ = INPUT$(1)                        'Pause
400 END

100 REM *** PROGRAMMING ASSIGNMENT 14.3 ***
110 SCREEN 2,0: CLS: KEY OFF
120 GOSUB 200                             'Set up graph
130 GOSUB 500                             'Plot data
140 A$ = INPUT$(1)                        'Pause
150 STOP
160 '
200 REM *** Set up graph routine
210    LOCATE 1,25: PRINT "AVERAGE MONTHLY PRECIPITATION"
220    FOR J = 1 TO 20                    'Print Y label
230      READ CHAR$
240      LOCATE J+1,3: PRINT CHAR$
250    NEXT J
260    REM Data for READ in 230
270    DATA P, R, E, C, I, P, I, T, A, T, I, O, N, " ", I, N, C, H, E, S
280    FOR INCHES = 0 TO 10               'Print Y coordinates
290      LOCATE -2 * INCHES+22,5: PRINT USING "##"; INCHES
300    NEXT INCHES
310    FOR MONTH = 1 TO 12                'Print X coordinates
315      READ MONTH$
320      LOCATE 23,6*MONTH+1: PRINT MONTH$
330    NEXT MONTH
334    REM Data for READ in 315
335    DATA J, F, M, A, M, J, J, A, S, O, N, D
340    LOCATE 24,36: PRINT "M O N T H";   'Print X label
350    VIEW(52,12)-(580,172),,1           'Define viewport
360    WINDOW(1,0)-(12,10)                'Define coordinates
370    FOR MONTH = 1 TO 12                'Draw
380      LINE(MONTH,.5)-(MONTH,0)         'tick marks
390    NEXT MONTH                         'along X axis
400    FOR INCHES = 0 TO 10               'Draw
410      LINE(1,INCHES)-(1.2,INCHES)      'tick marks
420    NEXT INCHES                        'along Y axis
430 RETURN
440 REM *** End of set up graph routine
450 '
500 REM *** Plot data routine
510    READ INCHES
520    PSET(1,INCHES)                     'Plot first point
530    FOR MONTH = 2 TO 12
540      READ INCHES
550      LINE -(MONTH,INCHES)             'Plot remaining points
560    NEXT MONTH
570    REM Precipitation data for READ in 510 and 540
580    DATA 2.2, 2.0, 2.1, 3.6, 6.1, 9.0, 6.9, 6.7, 8.7, 8.2, 2.7, 1.6
590 RETURN
600 REM *** End of plot data routine
610 END
```

Appendix C Forms, Codes, and Colors

BASIC keywords can be typed by holding down the Alt key and pressing one of the alphabetic keys. The keyword associated with each letter is given in the table. Letters not having reserved words are marked "(no word)."

A	AUTO	N	NEXT
B	BSAVE	O	OPEN
C	COLOR	P	PRINT
D	DELETE	Q	(no word)
E	ELSE	R	RUN
F	FOR	S	SCREEN
G	GOTO	T	THEN
H	HEX$	U	USING
I	INPUT	V	VAL
J	(no word)	W	WIDTH
K	KEY	X	XOR
L	LOCATE	Y	(no word)
M	MOTOR	Z	(no word)

Colors available as foreground in text mode and as background in medium-resolution mode with a color/graphics adaptor.

Number	Color	Number	Color
0	Black	8	Grey
1	Blue	9	Light Blue
2	Green	10	Light Green
3	Cyan	11	Light Cyan
4	Red	12	Light Red
5	Magenta	13	Light Magenta
6	Brown	14	Yellow
7	White	15	High-intensity White

Note: In text mode, colors 0 through 7 may be used as background.

Colors in the medium-resolution palettes.

Color	Palette 0	Palette 1
0	Background	Background
1	Green	Cyan
2	Red	Magenta
3	Brown	White

Colors allowed for foreground in text mode with the monochrome adapter.

0	Black
1	Underlined white characters
7	White
9	Underlined high-intensity white characters
15	High-intensity white

ASCII Codes

ASCII value	Character	Control character	ASCII value	Character	ASCII value	Character
000	(null)	NUL	044	′	087	W
001	☺	SOH	045	-	088	X
002	●	STX	046	·	089	Y
003	♥	ETX	047	/	090	Z
004	♦	EOT	048	0	091	[
005	♣	ENQ	049	1	092	\
006	♠	ACK	050	2	093	]
007	(beep)	BEL	051	3	094	∧
008	(backspace)	BS	052	4	095	—
009	(tab)	HT	053	5	096	`
010	(line feed)	LF	054	6	097	a
011	(home)	VT	055	7	098	b
012	(form feed)	FF	056	8	099	c
013	(carriage return)	CR	057	9	100	d
014	♪	SO	058	:	101	e
015	☼	SI	059	;	102	f
016	▶	DLE	060	<	103	g
017	◀	DC1	061	=	104	h
018	↕	DC2	062	>	105	i
019	‼	DC3	063	?	106	j
020	¶	DC4	064	@	107	k
021	§	NAK	065	A	108	l
022	▬	SYN	066	B	109	m
023	↨	ETB	067	C	110	n
024	↑	CAN	068	D	111	o
025	↓	EM	069	E	112	p
026	→	SUB	070	F	113	q
027	←	ESC	071	G	114	r
028	(cursor right)	FS	072	H	115	s
029	(cursor left)	GS	073	I	116	t
030	(cursor up)	RS	074	J	117	u
031	(cursor down)	US	075	K	118	v
032	(space)		076	L	119	w
033	!		077	M	120	x
034	"		078	N	121	y
035	#		079	O	122	z
036	$		080	P	123	{
037	%		081	Q	124	¦
038	&		082	R	125	}
039	′		083	S	126	~
040	(		084	T	127	⌂
041	)		085	U	128	Ç
042	*		086	V	129	ü
043	+					

ASCII Codes

ASCII value	Character	ASCII value	Character	ASCII value	Character
130	é	172	¼	214	╓
131	â	173	¡	215	╫
132	ä	174	≪	216	╪
133	à	175	≫	217	┘
134	å	176	▒	218	┌
135	ç	177	▓	219	■
136	ê	178	▓	220	▬
137	ë	179	│	221	▌
138	è	180	┤	222	▐
139	ï	181	╡	223	▀
140	î	182	╢	224	α
141	ì	183	╖	225	β
142	Ä	184	╕	226	Γ
143	Å	185	╣	227	π
144	É	186	║	228	Σ
145	æ	187	╗	229	σ
146	Æ	188	╝	230	μ
147	ô	189	╜	231	τ
148	ö	190	╛	232	ϕ
149	ò	191	┐	233	θ
150	û	192	└	234	Ω
151	ù	193	┴	235	δ
152	ÿ	194	┬	236	$\propto$
153	Ö	195	├	237	$\varnothing$
154	Ü	196	─	238	ϵ
155	¢	197	┼	239	$\cap$
156	£	198	╞	240	$\equiv$
157	¥	199	╟	241	$\pm$
158	Pt	200	╚	242	$\geq$
159	ƒ	201	╔	243	$\leq$
160	á	202	╩	244	⌠
161	í	203	╦	245	⌡
162	ó	204	╠	246	$\div$
163	ú	205	═	247	$\approx$
164	ñ	206	╬	248	°
165	Ñ	207	╧	249	•
166	ª	208	╨	250	·
167	º	209	╤	251	$\sqrt{}$
168	¿	210	╥	252	n
169	⌐	211	╙	253	^{2}
170	¬	212	╘	254	■
171	½	213	╒	255	(blank 'FF']

Appendix D   Summary of Statements, Functions, and Commands

Statements	Purpose
BEEP	Sounds the speaker.
CIRCLE(x,y),radius[,color] [,start] [,end] [,aspect]	Draws a circle.
CLOSE [#filenum] [,#filenum] ...	Closes open files.
CLS	Clears the screen.
COLOR [background] [,palette] (Graphics mode)	Selects colors.
COLOR [foreground] [,background] [,border] (Text mode)	Selects colors.
DATA value, ...	Provides data for READ statements.
DEF FName[(arg, ...)] = expression	Defines a user-created function.
DIM variable (n[,m]), ...	Specifies the size of an array.
END	Stops execution of a program.
FIELD #filenum, width AS string variable [,width AS string variable] ...	Describes a record in a random file.
FOR counter variable = starting value TO final value [STEP step size]	Marks the top of a counter-controlled loop.
GET #filenum [,recordnum]	Reads a record from a random file.
GET (x1,y1)-(x2,y2), arrayname (Graphics mode)	Saves the colors of the pixels in an area of a graphics screen.
GOSUB line number	Executes a subroutine.
GOTO line number	Branches to the specified line.
IF condition THEN clause [ELSE clause]	Tests a condition. The THEN clause is executed when the condition is true, and the ELSE clause is executed when the condition is false.
INPUT #filenum, variable [,variable] ...	Reads data from a sequential file.
INPUT [;] ["prompt";] variable, ...	Accepts data entered at the keyboard.
KEY n,string	Establishes the meaning of a function key.
KEY LIST, or KEY ON, or KEY OFF	Lists the meanings of the function keys, turns the function key display on line 25 on and off.
[LET] variable = expression	Assigns a value to a variable.
LINE INPUT [;] ["prompt";] string variable	Reads a line of data entered at the keyboard.
LINE INPUT #filenum, string variable	Reads a line of data from a file.
LINE [(x1,y1)]-(x2,y2) [,color] [,B[F]]	Draws a line.
LOCATE [row] [,column] [,cursor]	Positions the cursor.
LPRINT expression, ...	Prints values on the printer.
LPRINT USING format string; expression, ...	Prints values on the printer using the specified format.

Statements	Purpose
LSET string variable = string expression	Assigns values to field variables.
MID$ (string variable,n,m) = string expression	Replaces characters in a string variable.
NEXT [counter variable]	Marks the end of a counter-controlled loop.
ON n GOSUB line [,line] . . .	Executes one of several subroutines depending on the value of *n*.
ON n GOTO line [,line] . . .	Branches to one of several lines depending on the value of *n*.
OPEN "filename" AS #filenum [LEN = reclength] (Random files)	Opens a random file.
OPEN "filename" FOR mode AS #filenum (Sequential files)	Opens a sequential file.
PAINT(x,y) [,paint] [,boundary]	Colors an area of the screen.
PRESET (x,y) [,color]	Draws a point of the specified color.
PRINT USING format string; expression,. . .	Prints values on the screen using the specified format.
PRINT expression,. . .	Prints values on the screen.
PRINT #filenum, expression,. . .	Writes data to a sequential file.
PRINT #filenum USING format string; expression,. . .	Writes data to a file using the specified format.
PSET(x,y) [,color]	Draws a point of the specified color.
PUT #filenum [,recordum]	Writes a record to a random file.
PUT (x,y),arrayname (Graphics mode)	Writes colors onto an area of a graphics screen.
RANDOMIZE [n] or RANDOMIZE TIMER	Reseeds the random number generator.
READ variable,. . .	Assigns variable values read from a DATA statement.
REM any comment you like	Allows documentation in a program.
RETURN [line number]	Returns from a subroutine.
RSET string variable = string expression	Assigns values to a field variable.
SCREEN [mode] [,burst]	Sets the screen mode.
SHELL "DOS command"	Permits DOS commands to be executed from within BASIC.
STOP	Stops program execution.
SWAP variable1, variable2	Exchanges the values of two variables.
VIEW [(x1,y1)-(x2,y2)] [,color] [,boundary]	Establishes a viewport.
WEND	Marks the end of a WHILE loop.
WHILE condition	Marks the top of a WHILE loop.
WIDTH size	Sets the number of characters in a line on the screen.
WINDOW [SCREEN] [x1,y1)-(x2,y2)]	Establishes world coordinates.
WRITE #filenum, variable [,variable] . . .	Writes data to a sequential file in a form that can be read by an INPUT # statement.

Functions	Purpose
ABS(x)	Returns the absolute value of x.
ASC(X$)	Returns the ASCII code of the first character of x$.
ATN(x)	Returns the arctangent (in radians) of x.
CHR$(n)	Returns the character whose ASCII code is n.
COS(x)	Returns the cosine of angle x, where x is in radians.
CVD(x$)	Converts the eight-byte string x$ into a double-precision number.
CVI(x$)	Converts the two-byte string x$ into an integer.
CVS(x$)	Converts the four-byte string x$ into a single-precision number.
DATE$	Returns the date, in the form mm-dd-yyyy.
EOF(n)	Returns −1 if the end of file n has been reached, and 0 if the end of file n has not been reached.
EXP(x)	Raises e (2.71828..) to the x power.
FIX(x)	Truncates x to an integer.
INPUT$(n)	Returns a string of n characters read from the keyboard.
INSTR(n,x$,y$)	Returns the position of y$ in x$. n specifies the position in x$ where the search is to begin.
INT(x)	Returns the largest integer less than or equal to x.
LEFT$(x$,n)	Returns the n leftmost characters of x$.
LEN(x$)	Returns the length of x$.
LOF(n)	Returns the length of file n in bytes.
LOG(x)	Returns the natural logorithm of x.
MID$(x$,n,m)	Returns m characters of x$ starting with the nth character.
MKD$(x)	Converts the double-precision expression x into a string.
MKI$(x)	Converts the integer expression x into a string.
MKS$(x)	Converts the single-precision expression x into a string.
RIGHT$(x$,n)	Returns the n rightmost characters of x$.
RND	Returns a random number.
SGN(x)	Returns −1 if x is negative, 0 if x is 0, and +1 if x is positive.
SIN(x)	Returns the sine of angle x, where x is in radians.
SPACE$(n)	Returns a string of n spaces.
SPC(n)	Skips n spaces in a PRINT statement.
SQR(x)	Returns the square root of x; x must be >= 0.
STR$(n)	Converts n to a string.
STRING$(n,m)	Returns a string of n characters, all consisting of the character whose ASCII codes is m.
STRING$(n,x$)	Returns a string of n characters, all consisting of the first character of x$.
TAB(n)	Tabs to column n in a PRINT statement.
TAN(x)	Returns the tangent of angle x, where x is in radians.
TIME$	Returns the time of day, in the form hh:mm:ss.
TIMER	Returns the time, in seconds, from the PC's clock.
VAL(x$)	Returns the numeric value of x$.

Commands	Purpose
AUTO [number] [,increment]	Generates line numbers automatically, starting at *number* using *increment* as the increment.
CONT	Continues execution after STOP, END, or Ctrl + Break.
DELETE [line1] [-line2]	Deletes lines from *line1* to *line2*.
EDIT line	Displays line number *line* for editing.
FILES [partial filename]	Displays the names of the files on a diskette that match *partial filename*. If *partial filename* is omitted, all the files on the default drive are listed.
KILL filename	Deletes the specified file from a disk.
LIST [[line1] [-line2]	Lists lines from *line1* to *line2* on the screen.
LLIST [line1] [-line2]	Lists lines from *line1* to *line2* on the printer.
LOAD filename	Loads the specified program from a disk.
MERGE filename	Merges the specified file with the program currently in memory.
NAME filename1 AS filename2	Renames *filename1* to *filename2*.
NEW	Erases the program in memory.
RENUM [newnum] [,oldnum] [,increment]	Renumbers a program, where *newnum* is the first number to be used, *old-num* is the old number where renumbering is to begin, and *increment* is the increment to be used.
RUN	Executes a program.
SAVE filename	Saves a program on disk.
SYSTEM	Exits BASIC and returns to DOS.
TROFF	Stops the display of line numbers started by TRON.
TRON	Displays on the screen the number of each line as it is executed.

Appendix E   Introduction to DOS

DOS, which stands for Disk Operating System, is a collection of programs some of which control the computer and others of which, called "utility" programs, make it easier for you to use the computer. DOS programs that control the computer include IBMDOS.COM, IBMBIO.COM (on non-IBM computers, these are named MSDOS.SYS and IO.SYS), and COMMAND.COM. A diskette that contains these control programs is called a DOS or system diskette and may be used to start the computer.

When you turn on the computer or perform a system reset, the program in ROM reads IBMDOS.COM and IBMBIO.COM (or their non-IBM counterparts) from the diskette in drive A into RAM. That is why, if you are using a diskette system, you must insert your DOS/BASIC diskette into drive A before you turn on the computer. With a hard-disk system, if there is no diskette in drive A, the ROM program will read IBMDOS.COM and IBMBIO.COM from the hard disk into RAM. They in turn read COMMAND.COM into RAM. After COMMAND.COM is loaded, it displays the date and time prompts.

In addition to programs that control the computer, DOS includes 20 to 40 "utility" programs that make it easier to use the computer. You get these programs—usually called "commands"—and a manual that explains them when you buy DOS from the computer's manufacturer. In this appendix, we will explain only a few of the more useful DOS commands.

USING UTILITY COMMANDS

The DOS utility commands can be divided into two groups: internal and external. Internal commands, such as COPY, DEL, and DIR, are part of COMMAND.COM and are always available once DOS has been loaded. In a diskette system, external commands such as DISKCOPY and FORMAT are stored on the DOS diskette, and the diskette must be in a disk drive for these commands to be executed. In a hard-disk computer, all the DOS commands are usually copied to the hard disk; therefore, both the internal and external commands are always available. Both internal and external DOS commands may be entered in either uppercase or lowercase.

THE FORMAT COMMAND

Before a new diskette can be used to store files, you must format it using the FORMAT command. A diskette needs to be formatted only once, before its first use. Formatting a diskette erases all the data stored on it, so be careful that you don't accidentally format a diskette that contains files you want to keep. Since FORMAT is an external command, in a diskette system you would usually have a diskette that contains the FORMAT program in drive A and the diskette to be formatted in drive B. To format the diskette in drive B, use the command FORMAT B:. On a hard-disk system, you usually format new diskettes in drive A, so the appropriate command is FORMAT A:. In either case, the FORMAT program is loaded into RAM, and you are told to insert a new diskette into the appropriate drive and then to press the Enter key.

This kind of formatting is fine if your intention is to prepare a diskette to store program files, but not if you want to create a DOS diskette that can be used to start the computer. To format a diskette so that it can be used as a DOS diskette, use the command FORMAT B:/S in a diskette system and FORMAT A:/S in a hard-disk system. Each command formats the diskette and then copies the DOS control programs to it.

THE DIR COMMAND

The DIR command, which lists the names of the files on a disk, is similar to BASIC's FILES command (see Chapter 3). To display the names of the files on the default drive, simply type DIR and press the Enter key. When the DIR command is used with the DOS/BASIC diskette used at Queensborough Community College, it produces the following output:

```
          Volume in drive A has no name
          Directory of A:\

          COMMAND    COM    37637  06-17-88    12:00p
          BASICA     COM    36285  06-17-88    12:00p
          PRINT      COM    14163  06-17-88    12:00p
          SORT       EXE     5914  06-17-88    12:00p
          GRAPHICS   COM    16733  06-17-88    12:00p
          AUTOEXEC   BAT      354  11-17-89    10:59p
                 6 File(s)       616448 bytes free
```

The columns in this listing show the filename and extension, the size of the file in bytes, and the date and time the file was created or last changed. The last line shows the number of files on the diskette and the number of unused bytes available on the diskette. The filenames and numbers you will see when you use the DIR command will be different, depending on the version of DOS and the type of diskette you are using.

Notice that IBMDOS.COM and IBMBIO.COM are not included in the above listing. These two files are on the diskette, but they are "hidden," which means that their names do not appear when the DIR command is used.

To obtain a listing the names of files on a diskette that is not in the DOS default drive, simply include the name of the drive in the DIR command. For example, the command DIR B: produces a listing of the filenames on the diskette in drive B.

If a disk contains many files, they cannot all be displayed on the screen at the same time. You can use the /P parameter with the DIR command to cause the screen to pause when it is full, for example, DIR B:/P. A full screen of filenames will be displayed, with the prompt Press any key to continue on the last line.

You can also use the asterisk to stand for part of a filename, as explained in Chapter 3. So to see the names of only your BASIC programs, you would use the command DIR *.BAS.

THE COPY COMMAND

The COPY command is used to copy files from one disk to another. Assuming that drive A is the default drive, to copy the file named PA3-4.BAS from the diskette in drive A to the diskette in drive B, you would use the command COPY PA3-4.BAS B:.

You can also use the asterisk to represent part of the filename, as explained in Chapter 3. So to copy all the BASIC programs from the diskette in default drive A to the diskette in drive B, you would use the command COPY *.BAS B:. This is an easy way to create backup copies of your BASIC programs, which is good insurance against losing or damaging your working diskette.

To copy all the files from the diskette in default drive A to the diskette in drive B, use the command COPY *.* B:. Note, though, that since the files IBMDOS.COM and IBMBIO.COM are hidden, they are not copied. Therefore, you cannot use the COPY command to create a DOS diskette.

THE DISKCOPY COMMAND

The DISKCOPY command allows you to make an exact copy of a diskette to a diskette of the same storage capacity. To make a copy of a diskette, type the command DISKCOPY A: B:. The DISKCOPY program is loaded into RAM, and then you are prompted to insert the source diskette into drive A and the target diskette into drive B. Follow these instructions and press any key when you are ready. On a computer that contains only one diskette drive (as in most hard-disk systems), you will be prompted to insert alternately the source and the target diskettes.

The contents of the target diskette will be destroyed, so make sure it does not contain any files you wish to keep. If the target diskette is not formatted, DISKCOPY will format it as it makes the copy.

DISKCOPY makes an exact copy of the source diskette, including the hidden files IBMDOS.COM and IBMBIO.COM. Therefore, if the source diskette is a DOS diskette, the target diskette will also be a DOS diskette.

THE DEL AND ERASE COMMANDS

The DEL command and its identical twin, the ERASE command, allow you to delete files from a disk. They are equivalent to the BASIC KILL command (see Chapter 3). The command DEL PA3-5.BAS deletes the file PA3-5.BAS from the diskette in the default drive.

You can use asterisks to delete a family of files with one command. For example, the command DEL *.BAS would delete all the BASIC files from the diskette in the default drive. The command DEL *.* would delete all the files from the diskette in the default drive. Since that is such a drastic step, DOS asks, Are you sure (Y/N), before it executes the command. If you type Y and press the Enter key, DOS erases all the files.

Glossary

absolute form The expression of a pixel's location in terms of its X and Y coordinates.

accumulator A variable used to accumulate the values of another variable.

algorithm A series of steps that can be followed by a computer to solve a problem.

all points addressable Allowing the user to draw a point anywhere on the screen by means of a graphics instruction.

argument A constant, variable, or expression supplied to a function and used by the function to determine a result.

arithmetic step A step in which a value is assigned to a variable.

array A collection of storage locations that have the same name.

ASCII code American Standard Code for Information Interchange. The code used to store data in a computer.

aspect ratio The ratio of the horizontal distance between pixels to the vertical distance between pixels.

background color The color of the background against which text is displayed.

backup file A copy of a file that can be used to recreate the original.

binary search A method of searching a sorted array in which half of the remaining elements are eliminated from the search by each comparison.

branching statement A statement that causes a change in the normal sequence of execution, so that the computer acts on some line other than the line with the next-higher line number.

bubble sort A method of sorting an array in which adjacent elements are compared and in which elements move slowly toward their final positions.

buffer A part of the computer's memory where data are temporarily stored while they are being read from or written to a disk.

bugs Errors in a program.

byte A unit of storage that can hold one character.

case structure A structure that tests data against a series of conditions, only one of which can be true.

command An order to the computer to perform some function immediately.

compound condition A set of two or more simple conditions joined by the reserved words AND or OR.

computer An electronic device that can accept data, process the data according to your instructions, and display results.

concatenation Adding together strings or string variables.

condition A statement by means of which a variable is compared with another variable or with a constant. A condition is either true or false.

conditional branching statement A statement that causes one branch to be taken if a condition is true and a different branch if it is false.

control break A change in the value of a control variable, which means that some special processing, such as printing subtotals, should be performed.

coordinates A pair of numbers that locate a point on the screen.

counter A variable used to keep track of some number, such as the number of sets of data entered.

counter-controlled loop A loop containing a counter that controls the number of times it is executed.

CPU (central processing unit) The computer component in which arithmetic and logical operations are performed.

cursor A flashing line that indicates where the next character you type will appear on the screen.

data Values in the form of numbers or words that are to be processed by a computer.

debugging Eliminating errors (bugs) in a program.

decision symbol A flowchart symbol in the shape of a diamond, used to show a decision.

default drive The drive that is used when you read from and write to a disk, unless you specify otherwise.

default value A value assigned automatically. This value is used if you don't specify a value.

device name The name of the device that is to be used with a command. The name always ends in a colon (:).

direct mode The operating style in which a statement is entered without a line number.

diskette drive A secondary storage device that can read and write data on diskettes.

diskette *or* **floppy disk** A magnetic-coated plastic disk that is used to store programs and data.

documenting Adding comments to a program to explain what the program does and how it does it.

DOS (Disk Operating System) A collection of programs that control the computer and make it easier for you to use it.

double-precision variable A variable that holds values with up to 16 digits and is stored in 8 bytes.

dummy variable A variable that has meaning only within the function in which it is defined.

elements The individual components of an array.

endless loop A loop that executes continuously.

exponentiation Raising to a power.

expression A combination of variables, numbers, and arithmetic operation symbols that can be evaluated to produce a number.

field An area reserved in a record to store an item of data.

field variable A variable defined in a FIELD statement.

file A program (or other data) stored on a diskette or a fixed disk; a group of related records.

filename The name of a file.

filename extension Up to three characters that may be added to the end of a filename. BASIC automatically uses BAS as the filename extension.

flag A variable whose purpose is to control the execution of a program by indicating whether some condition has or has not occurred.

floppy disk *See* diskette.

flowchart A picture of an algorithm that shows the logical structure of the algorithm clearly.

flowline A line on a flowchart that connects boxes.

foreground color The color used to display text.

full-screen editing The technique of changing any line on the screen by simply moving the cursor to the line and making the change.

function A part of BASIC that operates on one or more arguments and returns a value.

function keys Any of the 10 keys labeled F1 through F10 on the left side of the keyboard, or the 12 keys labeled F1 through F12 across the top of the enhanced keyboard.

hanging punctuation A comma or a semicolon that appears after the last variable in a print list.

hard copy output Printed output.

hard disk A high-capacity, fast-access secondary storage device.

header data Data that specify the number of cases to be processed and that are entered before the rest of the data.

independent loops FOR-NEXT loops that do not intersect.

index An array used to locate records in a random file.

indirect mode The operating style in which a statement is entered with a line number.

initialize To assign an initial value to a variable.

input unit The component of a computer system that allows you to enter data and instructions into the computer.

input/output symbol A flowchart symbol in the shape of a parallelogram that is used to show both input and output.

integer division Division that yields as its answer only the integer part of the quotient. Specified by the backslash, \.

integer variable A variable that holds whole numbers in the range $-32,768$ to $32,767$ and is stored in two bytes.

internal variable A variable that is not input into a program or output from it.

interpreter A program that translates a program written in BASIC into machine language.

K 1024 bytes.

key A field in a record that is used as the identifying field.

last point referenced The point from which a relative coordinate is measured.

left-justified Printed as far to the left in a field as possible.

line clipping Cutting a figure at the edge of the screen.

loading Reading a program from secondary storage into RAM.

logic error An error in a program that causes the program to calculate the wrong answer.

logical operator In this book, one of the reserved words AND, OR, or NOT.

loop A series of instructions that are executed repeatedly.

M Approximately 1 million bytes (exactly 1,048,576 bytes).

machine language The only language that does not have to be translated for the computer to understand it.

master file A file that indicates the current status of a business or activity.

menu A list of values from which the user may choose.

modulo arithmetic Arithmetic in which the answer is the integer that is the remainder of an integer division. Specified by the operator MOD.

monitor A television-like display device.

Monte Carlo simulation A simulation that involves random elements.

nested loops FOR-NEXT loops in which an inner loop is completely enclosed in an outer loop.

null string The string that contains no characters.

numeric variable A variable whose value is a number.

on-line system A system that permits individual records to be displayed and updated.

one-dimensional array An array that requires one subscript to specify an element.

output unit The component of a computer system that displays the computer's results.

palette A set of four colors that may be used to paint figures.

parallel arrays Two or more arrays in which data stored in a particular element of one array correspond to data stored in the other(s).

PC Personal computer.

physical coordinates The coordinate system that refers to specific points on the screen.

pixel A dot, or picture element, on the screen.

primary storage unit The computer component in which data and instructions that are being processed are stored.

process symbol A flowchart symbol in the shape of a rectangle that is used to show an arithmetic step.

program A set of instructions to be followed by a computer to solve a problem.

prompt A message indicating that the computer is waiting for you to enter instructions or data.

pseudocode A language somewhere between English and BASIC used in developing the algorithm for a program.

RAM (random access memory) The part of primary storage whose contents can be changed by a program.

random number A number that cannot be predicted.

random number generator The mathematical function used to generate random numbers.

random number seed The number used to start generating a sequence of random numbers.

record A group of related fields treated as a unit.

relational operator One of the six symbols =, <, >, <=, >=, and <>.

relative form The expression of a pixel's location in terms of the X and Y distances from a point mentioned earlier in the program.

reserved word A word that has a special meaning to BASIC.

reverse image A display in which black characters appear against a white background.

right-justified Printed as far to the right in a field as possible.

ROM (read only memory) The part of primary storage whose contents cannot be changed by a program.

round-off error A small numerical error that occurs in a computer-calculated answer because of the way computers store numbers.

rules of precedence The order in which the computer evaluates expressions. The order is (0) expressions inside parentheses, (1) exponentiation, (2) multiplication and division, (3) addition and subtraction.

scientific notation A method of printing very small and very large values in the form a.bcdefgE+hi. The actual value is obtained by moving the decimal point to the right if h i is positive and to the left if h i is negative.

scrolling The process in which lines move off the top of the screen as new lines are displayed on the bottom of the screen.

secondary storage device A component, built into or connected to the computer, that enables you to store data and programs for as long as you want them.

sequential file A file in which records are stored, read, and processed in order from the first record to the last.

sequential search A method of searching an array in which the elements of the array are examined in sequence.

simulation Modeling the behavior of a system.

single-precision variable A variable that holds values with up to seven digits of accuracy and is stored in four bytes.

soft copy output Output displayed on the monitor's screen.

spacing chart A chart used to design printed reports and screens.

statement An instruction the computer is to follow.

stepwise refinement *See* top-down design.

string A group of letters, numbers, or special characters.

string expression A combination of string variables, constants, and functions and the concatenation operator that evaluates to a string.

string variable A variable whose value is one or more letters or a combination of letters and numbers.

subroutine A group of statements that together perform some calculation or function.

subscript A numeric constant, variable, or expression that specifies a particular element of an array.

substring Part of a string.

syntax error A violation of the rules for writing BASIC statements.

syntax statement A model that shows the correct way of writing a particular BASIC statement.

system flowchart A flowchart that shows the relationships between the files and programs used by a system.

system reset An action equivalent to turning the computer off and then on. Accomplished by pressing the Ctrl + Alt + Del keys.

terminal symbol A flowchart symbol in the shape of an oval that is used to show the start and the end of a flowchart.

toggle A key that is turned on or off with the same keystroke.

top-down design *or* **stepwise refinement** A method of developing an algorithm by breaking a complex problem into a set of less complex problems.

tracing Executing a program by hand, line by line, and keeping track of the changing values of the variables.

trailer data Extra data entered after all the real data to indicate that all the real data have been entered.

transaction file A file that indicates the changes that must be made to a master file.

two-dimensional array An array that requires two subscripts to specify an element.

unconditional branching statement A statement that causes a branch to be taken every time the statement is encountered.

uninitialized variable A variable to which a value has not been assigned.

variable A quantity whose value may change when a program is executed.

viewpoint A section of the screen that functions like an independent screen.

WHILE loop A loop, defined by a `WHILE` and a `WEND` statement, that is executed while the condition in the `WHILE` statement is true.

word processing Using a computer to simplify the creation and revision of written material.

world coordinates A coordinate system established by the user to fit a given problem.

SYMBOL INDEX